Lecture Notes in Computer Science

Edited by G. Goos, J. Hartmanis and J. van L

Springer
Berlin
Heidelberg
New York
Barcelona
Hong Kong
London
Milan
Paris
Singapore
Tokyo

Larry Carter   Jeanne Ferrante (Eds.)

Languages
and Compilers
for Parallel Computing

12th International Workshop, LCPC'99
La Jolla, CA, USA, August 4-6, 1999
Proceedings

Springer

Series Editors

Gerhard Goos, Karlsruhe University, Germany
Juris Hartmanis, Cornell University, NY, USA
Jan van Leeuwen, Utrecht University, The Netherlands

Volume Editors

Larry Carter
Jeanne Ferrante
University of California, San Diego
Department of Computer Science
9500 Gilman Drive, La Jolla, CA 92093-0114, USA
E-mail: {carter, ferrante}@cs.ucsd.edu

Cataloging-in-Publication Data applied for

Die Deutsche Bibliothek - CIP-Einheitsaufnahme

Languages and compilers for parallel computing : 12th international
workshop ; proceedings / LCPC '99, La Jolla, CA, USA, August 4 - 6,
1999. Larry Carter ; Jeanne Ferrante (ed.). - Berlin ; Heidelberg ;
New York ; Barcelona ; Hong Kong ; London ; Milan ; Paris ; Singapore ;
Tokyo : Springer, 2000
    (Lecture notes in computer science ; Vol. 1863)
    ISBN 3-540-67858-1

CR Subject Classification (1998): D.3, D.1.3, F.1.2, B.2.1, C.2

ISSN 0302-9743
ISBN 3-540-67858-1 Springer-Verlag Berlin Heidelberg New York

Springer-Verlag Berlin Heidelberg New York
a member of BertelsmannSpringer Science+Business Media GmbH
© Springer-Verlag Berlin Heidelberg 2000
Printed in Germany

Typesetting: Camera-ready by author, data conversion by PTP-Berlin, Stefan Sossna
Printed on acid-free paper   SPIN: 10722248   06/3142   5 4 3 2 1 0

Preface

In August 1999, the Twelfth Workshop on Languages and Compilers for Parallel Computing (LCPC) was hosted by the Hierarchical Tiling Research group from the Computer Science and Engineering Department at the University of California San Diego (UCSD). The workshop is an annual international forum for leading research groups to present their current research activities and the latest results. It has also been a place for researchers and practitioners to interact closely and exchange ideas about future directions. Among the topics of interest to the workshop are language features, code generation, debugging, optimization, communication and distributed shared memory libraries, distributed object systems, resource management systems, integration of compiler and runtime systems, irregular and dynamic applications, and performance evaluation. In 1999, the workshop was held at the International Relations/Pacific Studies Auditorium and the San Diego Supercomputer Center at UCSD. Seventy-seven researchers from Australia, England, France, Germany, Korea, Spain, and the United States attended the workshop, an increase of over 50% from 1998.

The program committee of LCPC '99 along with external reviewers as needed, were responsible for evaluating the submitted papers. Forty-eight papers were submitted, and of those, twenty-seven were selected to be presented as full papers at the workshop. In addition, thirteen submissions were presented as posters in a special poster session. Using feedback provided both before and after the presentations, all authors were given the opportunity to improve their papers before submitting the final versions contained in this volume. Short abstracts of the poster presentations are also included.

In addition to the paper and poster sessions, LCPC '99 also featured an invited talk by Burton Smith, Chief Scientist at Tera Computer (now renamed Cray) on "Optimization for the Tera MTA". This talk gave an overview of the MTA architecture and the program transformations in the MTA compiler that allow it to take advantage of the MTA's unique architectural characteristics. The home of the first Tera MTA is the San Diego Supercomputer Center, and a tour of SDSC, including the Tera MTA, was offered to all participants. We gratefully thank Burton Smith for his excellent presentation and for his full participation in the workshop.

A final feature of this year's workshop was a panel session on Benchmarking organized by Keshav Pingali. This session grew out of a seminar on Tiling for Optimal Resource Allocation (hosted by the International Conference and Research Center for Computer Science at Schloss Dagstuhl in 1998) in which setting up a suite of benchmarks for locality that could be used by the general community was proposed. The panel, whose members also included Rudi Eigenmann, David Padua, and Sanjay Rajopadhye, presented a lively and diverse discussion on the merits of such a suite.

The organizers wish to acknowledge the San Diego Supercomputer Center and UCSD for their help. In particular, the conference was organized by Joann Pagan of UCSD Conference Services, with help from Nancy Jensen at SDSC. We especially wish to thank the software support staff, particularly Cindy Paloma, and graduate students Kang Su Gatlin, Karin Hogstedt, Beth Simon, and Michelle Mills Strout, all of the Computer Science and Engineering Department, for their excellent help. We also wish to acknowledge the great help of Chanathip Namprempre in editing and putting together this volume.

We would like to give special thanks to the LCPC'99 program committee and the nameless external reviewers for their efforts in reviewing the submissions. Both the steering committee and the program committee helped with advice and suggestions on the organization of the workshop. Finally, we wish to thank all of the participants who helped to create a lively and constructive atmosphere of discussion, and the authors for sharing their significant research with us at LCPC '99.

May 2000   Larry Carter, Jeanne Ferrante
                                                        Program Chair
                                                            LCPC'99

Organization

Program Committee

Program Chair:	Larry Carter (University of California, San Diego, USA)
	Jeanne Ferrante (University of California, San Diego, USA)
General Chair:	Larry Carter (University of California, San Diego, USA)
	Jeanne Ferrante (University of California, San Diego, USA)
Program Committee:	Larry Carter (University of California, San Diego, USA)
	Jeanne Ferrante (University of California, San Diego, USA)
	Manish Gupta (IBM Research, USA)
	Zhiyuan Li (Purdue University, USA)
	Sam Midkiff (IBM Research, USA)
	Jose Moreira (IBM Research, USA)
	Jan Prins (University of North Carolina at Chapel Hill, USA)
	Pen-Chung Yew (University Minnesota, USA)

Panel

Keshav Pingali (Cornell University, USA) (organizer)
Rudi Eigenmann (Purdue University, USA)
David Padua (University of Illinois at Urbana Champaign, USA)
Sanjay Rajopadhy (IRISA, France)

Steering Committee

Utpal Banerjee (Intel Corporation, USA)
Alex Nicolau (University of California, Irvine, USA)
David Gelernter (Yale University, USA)
David Padua (University of Illinois at Urbana Champaign, USA)

Sponsoring Institutions

San Diego Supercomputer Center, La Jolla, CA USA
University of California, San Diego, La Jolla, CA USA

Table of Contents

Low-Level Transformation B

Posters

High Performance Numerical Computing in Java: Language and Compiler Issues

Pedro V. Artigas, Manish Gupta, Samuel P. Midkiff, and José E. Moreira

IBM Thomas J. Watson Research Center
Yorktown Heights NY 10598-0218
{artigas,mgupta,smidkiff,jmoreira}@us.ibm.com

Abstract. Poor performance on numerical codes has slowed the adoption of Java within the technical computing community. In this paper we describe a prototype array library and a research prototype compiler that support standard Java and deliver near-Fortran performance on numerically intensive codes. We discuss in detail our implementation of: (i) an efficient Java package for true multidimensional arrays; (ii) compiler techniques to generate efficient access to these arrays; and (iii) compiler optimizations that create safe, exception free regions of code that can be aggressively optimized. These techniques work together synergistically to make Java an efficient language for technical computing. In a set of four benchmarks, we achieve between 50 and 90% of the performance of highly optimized Fortran code. This represents a several-fold improvement compared to what can be achieved by the next best Java environment.

1 Introduction

Despite the advantages of Java[TM][1] as a simple, object oriented programming language, it has not been widely adopted within the technical computing community. The primary reason for this is that the performance of technical computing programs written in Java, and executed with currently available commercial Java environments, trails far behind the equivalent Fortran programs. In this paper we discuss a prototype array library and a prototype research compiler developed by the Numerically Intensive Java group at IBM Research that allows standard Java programs to achieve Fortran-like performance. These techniques deliver several-fold speedups on uniprocessor codes. They make Java a practical language for numerical computing.

There are several Java language features which together degrade Java performance in the domain of technical computing. Three very useful Java features – (i) array reference and null-pointer checks; (ii) using objects to represent all but the most widely used numeric types; and (iii) the structure of Java arrays – are extremely detrimental to performance in the domain of numerical computing [1]. Most compiler research on Java has focused on optimizations for more general applications, leading to naive (from the point of view of technical computing) implementations of the features mentioned above. These naive implementations lead to poor performance, reinforcing the perception that Java is not appropriate for technical computing and reducing the emphasis on improving Java performance for numerical applications.

---

[1] Java is a trademark of Sun Microsystems Inc.

L. Carter and J. Ferrante (Eds.): LCPC'99, LNCS 1863, pp. 1–17, 2000.

We will now give an overview of the detrimental effects of these language features. The rest of the paper will discuss in detail our library and compiler approach and how it overcomes these detrimental effects. Our approach is an example of language and compiler codesign. Although we make absolutely no modifications to the Java language *per se*, we introduce a class library (a package) for multidimensional arrays and advocate its use in developing technical codes. (An implementation of the Array package can be downloaded for free from http://www.alphaworks.ibm.com. More information on our research can be found at http://www.research.ibm.com/ninja.) In effect, we *grow* the language without having to modify any part of it. The Array package has been designed to enable powerful compiler optimization techniques that significantly improve the performance of technical computing.

Array references and null-*pointer checks:* The Java language specification requires that references through a pointer first check that the pointer is not null. Java also requires that each array access be checked to ensure that the element being referenced is within the declared bounds of the array. Both features help enforce security and reliability of Java programs. On many architectures, the direct cost of the checks is quite low for valid references. The real problem arises from the combined effects of the required checks and Java's precise exception model [22]. Because Java strictly specifies the order of evaluation of expressions – including accesses of expression operands – an exception must appear to have been thrown exactly after previous accesses and operations have been performed in strict program order. This prohibits the reordering of accesses and operations that are the foundation of the aggressive optimizations that make Fortran a high performance language [27]. Our general solution is to create different static instances of the loop body, with and without bounds and null-pointer exceptions. The proper static instance is dynamically selected to execute the iteration space of the loop. The static instance of the loop body which has no exceptions can be aggressively optimized.

Efficient array structures: Java native arrays (which will be referred to as *Java arrays*, with a lower case first *a*) allow the construction of very general random access data structures. Unfortunately, this same generality makes the the array reference checking optimizations described above more expensive, and dataflow analysis necessary for aggressive optimization nearly impossible. Consider the example in Figure 1, which illustrates several problems with Java arrays. First, general optimization of bounds checking requires finding out the extent of all rows of a Java two-dimensional array. This is an $O(n)$ operation, where n is the number of rows. If the array was known to be rectangular, it would be an $O(1)$ operation. Second, different rows of the array can be aliased (*e.g.*, rows 2 and $n - 2$ of A) even though their indices have different values. This is an example of intra-array aliasing. It is also possible to have inter-array aliasing as shown in Figure 1 for rows 0 of B and A. Thus, pointer alias analysis, not the cheaper dependence analysis, is necessary for optimization. Because of the dynamic nature of Java arrays, the alias analysis is very difficult. Our solution to the problem with Java arrays is the creation of an Array package for Java. This Array package implements multidimensional rectangular *Arrays* (with a capital first *A*) which are necessary for technical computing. The Array package, combined with appropriate compiler optimizations, overcomes both the dataflow analysis problems and the array reference bounds checking problems.

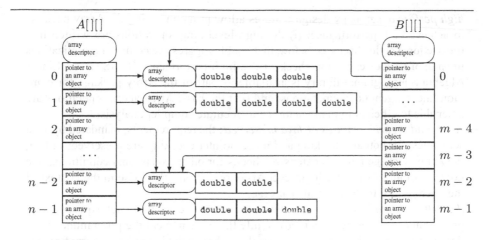

Fig. 1. Structure of two-dimensional Java arrays.

The Array package for Java and its associate compiler optimizations create an environment that delivers both the functionality and performance of Fortran 90 programming in Java. (This approach is similar to other successful object-oriented numerical computing environments such as POOMA and A++/P++ [25,23,29].) We show in this paper that we can raise the performance of 100% pure Java from a mere 1-2% to 65-90% of highly optimized Fortran. Even when compared to the highest performing Java environment (JDK 1.1.8 with the IBM JIT) currently available for our platform, which already incorporates advanced optimizations such as bounds checking elimination, we still show a several-fold improvement in performance. We note that the Fortran codes we compare Java against are representative of truly optimized computations, that achieve between 35-90% of the hardware peak performance.

The rest of this paper is organized as follows. Section 2 describes our Array package for Java, discussing its main components and presenting an example of its usage. Section 3 describes the compiler optimizations that we implemented in conjunction with the Array package. Section 4 reports our experimental results from using the Array package with four numerical benchmarks. Finally, Section 5 discusses related work and Section 6 presents our conclusions.

2 The Array Package for Java

A major design goal for the Array package was to overcome the limitations inherent in Java arrays in terms of performance and ease of use, without losing any key benefits of Java arrays or requiring any changes to the language semantics. The Array package provides the following benefits:

- *more expressivity*: the package allows programmers to use high-level Array operations (like Array addition, transpose), which are similar to those provided by languages like Fortran 90.

- *high performance*: many design features allow programs using the Array package to achieve high performance: (i) the high-level array operations are written in a transactional style, discussed below, that enables aggressive compiler optimizations in spite of various exception checks; (ii) a high-performance BLAS (Basic Linear Algebra Subprograms) library is available as part of the Array package for common linear algebraic computations; and (iii) the basic Array access operations are amenable to efficient implementation and accurate compiler analysis.
- *safety and security features of Java preserved*: the requirements, mandated by Java semantics, for bounds checking and null-pointer checking are preserved; in fact, the Array package requires extensive checks for other exceptional conditions, like nonconforming Arrays for high-level Array operations, that arise in the context of the operations introduced in the package.
- *flexibility of data layout*: the actual data layout for the Arrays is not exposed to the programmer (as it is not specified). While this may prevent the programmer from doing certain optimizations, we believe this is beneficial in the longer term because it facilitates data layout optimizations for Arrays [9,16,18,19,26]. The compiler has fewer constraints on ensuring the correctness of the program in the presence of data layout transformations, and can avoid copy operations otherwise needed to restore the data layout to a fixed format.

The class hierarchy of the Array package is shown in Figure 2. It has been defined to enable aggressive compiler optimizations. There is a separate class for each Array *elemental data type* and *rank* (currently, we support ranks 0 through 3). There are also separate classes for Arrays of complex numbers and Arrays of Objects. This approach enables easy static type checking of Arrays defined by the Array package. We make extensive use of *final* classes, since most Java compilers (and, in particular, *javac*) are able to apply method inlining to methods of final classes. Since the type and rank of an Array are defined by a final class, the semantics of any Array operation (and in particular element access) are defined statically. This is a key feature exploited in our optimization techniques. Obviously, by making the Array classes final we prevent application programmers from extending those classes directly. A *decorator* design pattern [13] can be used if programmers want to "extend" Array classes.

In contrast to Java arrays discussed in the previous section, an Array defined by the Array package has a nonragged rectangular shape and constant bounds over its lifetime. An axis of this Array can be indexed by either an integer (specifying a single element), a Range (specifying a triplet), or an Index (specifying an enumerated list). Indexing operations are used in *accessor methods* that read/write data from/to an Array, and in *sectioning methods* that create views of an Array. A valid index for an Array axis must be greater than or equal to zero and less than the extent of that axis.

All operations (methods and constructors) of the Array package have, in the absence of JVM failure, transactional behavior. That is, there are only two possible outcomes of an Array operation: (i) the operation completes without an exception being thrown, or (ii) an exception is thrown before any data is changed. This allows aggressive program transformations in the main computational part of the method, while honoring the Java exception semantics.

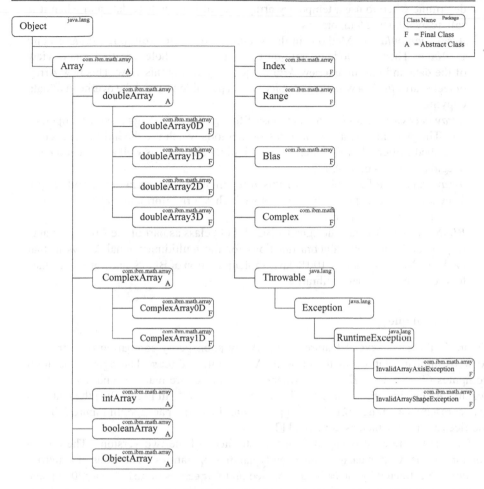

Fig. 2. Simplified class hierarchy chart.

2.1 Package Methods

The Array package defines the following groups of methods:

- *Array operations*: These are scalar operations applied element-wise to a whole Array. The methods in this category include assignment, arithmetic and arithmetic-assign operations (analogous, for example, to += and *= operators in Java), comparison operations, and logic operations (where appropriate for the elemental data type). These operations implement *array semantics*: In evaluating an expression (*e.g.*, $A += C$), all data is first fetched (*i.e.*, A and C are read from memory), the computation is performed (*i.e.*, $A + C$ is evaluated), and only then the result is stored (*i.e.*, A is modified). The Array package uses a form of dynamic dependence analysis [3] to determine when to use a temporary array to hold intermediate data and when it is safe to avoid using temporaries.

- *Array manipulation*: Methods in this group include section, permuteAxes and reshape. These methods operate on the Array as a whole, creating a new view of the data and returning a new Array object expressing this view. This new Array object shares its data with the old object when possible to avoid the overhead of data copying.
- *Array accessor methods*: The methods of this group include get and set operations. The get and set are basic accessor methods which use the indexing schemes described earlier. They can operate on individual elements as well as on regular and irregular sections of an Array.
- *Array inquiry methods*: Methods in this group include last, size, rank and shape. They are fast, descriptor-only operations which return information about the (invariant) properties of an Array.
- *BLAS routines*: We have designed a BLAS [11] class as part of the Array package, to provide basic linear algebra functions for the multidimensional Arrays in that package. Note that this is a 100% Java implementation of BLAS, and not an interface to already existing native libraries.

2.2 An Example

Figure 3 illustrates several features of the Array package by comparing two straightforward implementations of the basic BLAS operation dgemm. The dgemm operation computes $C = \alpha A^* \times B^* + \beta C$, where A, B, and C are matrices and α and β are scalars. A^* can be either A or A^T. The same holds for B^*. In Figure 3(a) the matrices are represented as doubleArray2D objects from the Array package. In Figure 3(b) the matrices are represented as double[][].

The first difference is apparent in the interfaces of the two versions. The dgemm version for the Array package transparently handles operations on sections of a matrix. Section are extracted by the caller and passed on to dgemm as doubleArray2D objects. Section descriptors have to be explicitly passed to the Java arrays version, using the m, n, p, i0, j0, and k0 parameters.

Next, we note that the computational code in the Array package version is independent of the orientation of A or B. We just perform a (very cheap) transposition if necessary, by creating a new descriptor for the data using the permuteAxes method. In comparison, the code in the Java arrays version has to be specialized for each combination of orientation of A and B. (We only show the two cases in which A is not transposed.)

Finally, in the Array package version we can easily perform some shape consistency verifications before entering the computational loop. If we pass that verification, we know we will execute the entire loop iteration space without exceptions. Such verifications would be more expensive for the Java arrays, as we would have to traverse each row of the array to make sure they are all of the appropriate length. Furthermore, at least the row-pointer part of each array would have to be privatized inside the method, to guarantee that no other thread changes the shape of the array [22].

```
public static void dgemm(int transa,
                         int transb,
                         double alpha,
                         doubleArray2D a,
                         doubleArray2D b,
                         double beta,
                         doubleArray2D c)
    throws NonconformingArrayException {

    if (transa == Transpose)
        a = a.permuteAxes(1,0);
    if (transb == Transpose)
        b = b.permuteAxes(1,0);

    int m = a.size(0);
    int n = a.size(1);
    int p = b.size(1);

    if (n != b.size(0))
        throw new NonconformingArrayException();
    if (p != c.size(1))
        throw new NonconformingArrayException();
    if (m != c.size(0))
        throw new NonconformingArrayException();

    for (int i=0; i<m; i++) {
        for (int j=0; j<p; j++) {
            double s = 0;
            for (int k=0; k<n; k++) {
                s += a.get(i,k)*b.get(k,j);
            }
            c.set(i,j,alpha*s+beta*c.get(i,j));
        }
    }
}
```

(a)

```
public static void dgemm(int transa,
                         int transb,
                         int m,
                         int n,
                         int p,
                         int i0, j0, k0,
                         double alpha,
                         double[][] a,
                         double[][] b,
                         double beta,
                         double[][] c) {

    if (transa != Transpose) {
        if (transb != Transpose) {
            for (int i=i0; i<i0+m; i++) {
                for (int j=j0; j<j0+p; j++) {
                    double s = 0;
                    for (int k=k0; k<k0+n; k++) {
                        s += a[i][k]*b[k][j];
                    }
                    c[i][j] = alpha*s+beta*c[i][j];
                }
            }
        } else {
            for (int i=i0; i<i0+m; i++) {
                for (int j=j0; j<j0+p; j++) {
                    double s = 0;
                    for (int k=k0; k<k0+n; k++) {
                        s += a[i][k]*b[j][k];
                    }
                    c[i][j] = alpha*s+beta*c[i][j];
                }
            }
        }
    } else {
        .
        .
        .
    }
}
```

(b)

Fig. 3. An implementation of dgemm using (a) the Array package and (b) Java arrays.

3 Compiler Optimizations

In this section we discuss the compiler support required to extract high performance of numerically intensive Java code written with the Array package. First we present an overview of our compiler infrastructure. Then we discuss the two major compiler optimizations that we implemented: semantic expansion [30] and bounds checking optimization [20].

3.1 The IBM XL Family of Compilers

Our compiler infrastructure is based on the IBM XL family of compilers. Figure 4 shows the high-level architecture of these compilers. The compilers from the XL family are able to compile source code from various source languages and generate code for various target architectures. The compilation process consists of three major steps:

1. The language-specific front-end translates the source code into an intermediate representation called W-Code. For Java, this step is implemented by a combination of *javac*, which translates Java into bytecode, and the High Performance Compiler for Java (HPCJ), which translates bytecode into W-Code.
2. The portable optimizer implements language and architecture independent optimizations. It consumes and produces intermediate representations in W-Code. The portable optimizer step is implemented by TPO (Toronto Portable Optimizer).
3. The back-end implements architecture and implementation specific optimizations and generates the actual executable code. It translates W-Code to machine code. In our case, the back-end step is implemented by TOBEY, which generates executable code for the POWER and PowerPC families.

Our optimizations were implemented in two of the modules described above. Semantic expansion was implemented in HPCJ, because it is a language-dependent optimization. The bounds checking optimization was implemented in TPO because it is, in principle, independent of language and architecture (even though it is particularly useful for Java). We note that semantic expansion must, in any case, precede the bounds checking optimization to allow effective analysis of code using the Array package, which is necessary for applying bounds checking optimization on that code.

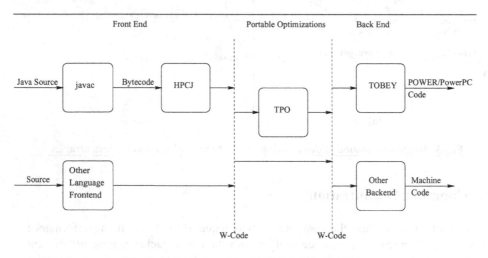

Fig. 4. Architecture of the XL family of compilers.

3.2 Semantic Expansion of Array References

To avoid changing the Java language itself, we added support for true multidimensional arrays in the form of a set of classes comprising the Array package. All data access in the Array package is through accessor methods. In the absence of aggressive compiler optimizations, these method invocations are expensive, both in terms of their overhead and in making analysis for the containing program regions very conservative. In order to obtain high performance, we must perform the array accesses in a more transparent, compiler-optimizable, way. We use the semantic expansion technique [30] to achieve this.

Our Java front-end (HPCJ) implements semantic expansion of the get and set accessor methods for Arrays. A call to a get or set method that accesses a single array element is replaced by inline code that performs the same array access, including the checks for null-pointer exception and out-of-bounds array exception that might be thrown due to that access. The compiler exploits information about the dense layout of Array data to generate code using the multidimensional array indexing operations in the W-Code intermediate representation. We note that this information could not have been exposed to the later compilation phases by applying regular method inlining instead of semantic expansion, since there is no Java bytecode for expressing references to true multidimensional arrays. The resulting code can be optimized by the W-Code based optimizer (TPO) using standard techniques (in conjunction with the bounds checking optimization). Thus, the Java Array package, combined with semantic expansion in the compiler, effectively provides the advantages of true multidimensional arrays in Java without any changes to the JVM or to the language itself and without violating the safety benefits provided by the Java language.

3.3 Bounds Checking Optimization

The Java requirement that every array access be checked for null-pointer and out-of-bounds exceptions, coupled with its precise exceptions model, provides the benefits of safety and security, and also helps in the debugging of programs. On the other hand, it has a severe impact on the performance of numerical codes. The goal of the bounds checking optimization is to enable the generation of high performance machine code without eliminating the benefits provided by the exception checks (we use the term *bounds checking* loosely to cover null-pointer checks as well).

Our approach is to create *safe regions* by program transformation so that all array accesses in the safe regions are guaranteed not to generate a null-pointer or out-of-bounds exception [22]. This has both direct and indirect benefits. First, the exception checks on all array references inside the safe regions can be removed, reducing their direct overhead. Second, the safe region code can now be freely transformed (for example, using loop transformations like tiling) without violating the precise exceptions model of Java. In this work, we use the *versioning* technique to create safe and unsafe regions, with a run-time test to check whether the safe or the unsafe region should be executed [22]. The optimization is done in two phases: the *array range analysis phase* and the *safe region creation phase*. We note that this optimization can be applied to arrays in any language (including the Arrays from the Array package).

Array range analysis: In the analysis phase, the compiler obtains summary access information for each array with respect to the *intervals* (*i.e.*, the loops and the overall procedure) in a method. This information is represented using a bounded *regular section descriptor* (RSD) [7,17], which provides information about the lower bound and the upper bound on (read and write) accesses in each array axis. The procedure for computing the bounded RSDs uses a combination of standard array analysis techniques and sophisticated symbolic analysis, described further in [15]. However, an important difference in the context of applying this analysis for the bounds checking optimization is that we can ignore certain aliasing information while identifying the section of an array that is read or written. For example, in Figure 5, we can summarize the access information for the array A accurately (for the purpose of the bounds checking optimization), even if A may potentially overlap any part of the array C. The bounds checks for A can be safely eliminated based only on the summary of accesses for A. Of course, a different transformation, such as loop reordering or parallelization, would have to consider the aliasing between A and C.

For cases where the compiler is unable to obtain, even symbolically, information about the range of array accesses, the corresponding range information is set to $\bot$, indicating an unknown value. For example, if the base address of an array A changes inside a loop in an unknown manner, the lower and upper bounds information for each axis of A is set to $\bot$.

Safe region creation: In this phase, the information from array range analysis is used to drive the versioning transformation which creates safe and unsafe regions. Our current implementation processes all loops in the method, and then selects each outermost loop for which complete array range information is symbolically available for every array reference (*i.e.*, there are no $\bot$ expressions in the array range information, although there may be symbolic variables appearing in the expressions which are invariant with respect to that loop). A duplicate code copy is created for each selected loop. From the copy which is to be made the safe region, all null-pointer checks and out-of-bounds checks for the arrays are eliminated. An expression for the run-time test, to check whether the safe or the unsafe region should be executed, is created in two parts: The first part verifies that none of the arrays is null. The second part verifies for each axis of every array that the lower and upper bounds of accesses are within the actual bounds of the array. This expression is simplified by expression-folding techniques.

An example of Array range analysis and safe region creation: As an example of our bounds checking optimization technique, Figure 5 shows what happens with a simple code for matrix multiplication. For the purpose of clarity in this example, we use the notation A[i,j] to represent either A.get(i,j) or A.set(i,j,x). The original code, provided as input to the compiler, is shown in Figure 5(a). The $\text{CHK}_b()$ operation denotes explicit bounds checks for each index, while $\text{CHK}_n()$ denote the null-pointer checks. The code optimized through versioning is shown in Figure 5(b). The safe region contains no explicit checks and can be aggressively optimized.

The original code in Figure 5(a) contains three potential safe regions, one for each loop. For the innermost (k) region/loop we can prove that the range of accesses for the three Arrays are:

$$C[i:i, j:j]$$
$$A[i:i, 0:n-1] \tag{1}$$
$$B[0:n-1, j:j]$$

```
for (i=0;i<m;i++)
  for (j=0;j<p;j++)
    for (k=0;k<n;k++)
      CHKₙ(C)[CHK_b(i),CHK_b(j)] =
        CHKₙ(C)[CHK_b(i),CHK_b(j)] +
        CHKₙ(A)[CHK_b(i),CHK_b(k)] *
        CHKₙ(B)[CHK_b(k),CHK_b(j)];
```

```
if (A!=null)&&(B!=null)&&(C!=null)&&
   (m-1 < A.size(0))&&(n-1 < A.size(1))&&
   (n-1 < B.size(0))&&(p-1 < B.size(1))&&
   (m-1 < C.size(0))&&(p-1 < C.size(1)) {

  for (i=0;i<m;i++)
    for (j=0;j<p;j++)
      for (k=0;k<n;k++)
        C[i,j] = C[i,j] + A[i,k]*B[k,j];

} else {

  for (i=0;i<m;i++)
    for (j=0;j<p;j++)
      for (k=0;k<n;k++)
        CHKₙ(C)[CHK_b(i),CHK_b(j)] =
          CHKₙ(C)[CHK_b(i),CHK_b(j)] +
          CHKₙ(A)[CHK_b(i),CHK_b(k)] *
          CHKₙ(B)[CHK_h(k),CHK_b(j)];

}
```

(a)   (b)

Fig. 5. An example of safe region creation through range analysis and versioning: (a) the original code, (b) optimized code.

For the middle (j) loop we compute the following range information:

$$C[i:i, 0:p-1]$$
$$A[i:i, 0:n-1] \tag{2}$$
$$B[0:n-1, 0:p-1]$$

And finally, for the outermost (i) loop we compute:

$$C[0:m-1, 0:p-1]$$
$$A[0:m-1, 0:n-1] \tag{3}$$
$$B[0:n-1, 0:p-1]$$

Since complete information is available for the outermost loop, the compiler generates the versioning code of Figure 5(b). Note that the tests to verify in-bounds access with respect to the lower bounds of the arrays are folded away, as they evaluate to *true* at compile time.

3.4 Array Package Advantages for Bounds Checking Optimization

We now discuss the advantages of using Arrays from the Array package over Java arrays, in terms of the complexity of the bounds checking optimization. First, since Java multi-dimensional Arrays are actually arrays of arrays, eliminating bounds checks completely on those arrays requires a limited form of pointer chasing analysis, to correlate references to different rows of the same base multidimensional array, while summarizing accesses to that array. Alternatively, an implementation could view two different rows of a multidimensional array as separate arrays, in which case, the optimization would only be effective for the last axis of the array. Second, in a multithreaded environment, we need an array privatization scheme to prevent other threads from asynchronously changing the shape of the multidimensional array being subjected to the optimization [22]. For an $(n_1 \times n_2 \times \ldots \times n_d)$ d-dimensional array, this is an $O(n_1 \times n_2 \times \ldots \times n_{d-1})$ operation, which can be potentially expensive. These costs can be avoided for Array package Arrays, as the shapes of these Arrays are invariant during their lifetime.

4   Experimental Results

We performed a series of experiments to measure the impact of the Array package and our compiler optimizations on the performance of Java numerical codes. In this section we present a summary of results for four benchmarks. We performed all our experiments on an IBM RS/6000 model 590 workstation. This machine has a 67 MHz POWER2 processor with a 256 kB single-level data cache and 512 MB of main memory. Its peak computational speed is 266 Mflops.

We compare the performance of three different versions of each benchmark. The first version is implemented in Fortran and serves as a performance reference. The second version is implemented in Java using only Java arrays. The third version is also implemented in Java, but using the Array package. Fortran programs are compiled using version 6.1 of the IBM XLF compiler with the highest level of optimization (-O3 -qhot, which performs high-order loop transformations [27]). For the Java arrays version, we report performance obtained using JDK 1.1.8 with the IBM JIT, which delivers the best performance for this version from all the Java environments available for our platform, including HPCJ. (The IBM JIT incorporates many advanced optimizations such as bounds checking and null-pointer checking optimization.) For the Array package version, we report the performance using our HPCJ-based compiler.

The benchmarks: The four benchmarks used are: MATMUL, BSOM, MICRO DC, and TOMCATV. MATMUL computes $C = C + A \times B$, where C, A, and B are matrices of size 500×500. We use a dot-product version of matrix multiplication, with an This benchmark *does not* use the BLAS routines in the Array package. BSOM (Batch Self-Organizing Map) benchmark is a data-mining kernel. We time the execution of the *training* phase of this algorithm, which consists of 25 *epochs*. Each epoch updates a neural network with 16 nodes using 256 records of 256 fields each. MICRO DC solves the equation $\nabla^2 \Phi = -\frac{\rho}{\epsilon}$ on a discretized domain using Jacobi relaxation [24]. For this benchmark, we use the problem configuration described in [21], with a 1000×1000 grid and four parallel microstrips of cross section 100×10 each. TOMCATV is part of the SPECfp95 suite (www.spec.org). For our experiments, we use a problem size $n = 513$.

Results: Results for the four benchmarks are summarized in Table 1 and Figure 6. Table 1 summarizes the efficacy of our bounds checking optimization. For each benchmark, column "loops" lists the total number of loop constructs in the program. (The nest of Figure 5(a) counts as three loops.) Column "optimized" lists the number of loop constructs that can be optimized with our compiler. That is, the number of loops for which the compiler was able to compute complete array range information. Column "coverage" is the ratio, in percentage, of loops optimized to total loops. Finally, column "safe regions" list the actual number of safe regions created for the benchmark. Since safe regions are created per loop nest, the number of safe regions can be much less than the number of optimized loops. For example, the safe region of Figure 5(b) optimizes three loops.

Table 1. Summary of loops optimized in each benchmark.

benchmark	loops	optimized	coverage	safe regions
MATMUL	17	14	82.4%	6
BSOM	25	21	84.0%	13
MICRO DC	12	11	91.7%	5
TOMCATV	20	20	100.0%	5

In the plots of Figure 6, the height of each bar is normalized with respect to the performance of the Fortran version. The numbers on the top of the bars indicate actual Mflops achieved for that version. The JDK118 bar shows the result for the Java array version, with JDK 1.1.8 + JIT. The HPCJ bar shows the result for the Array package version, as compiled by plain HPCJ (i.e., with neither the semantic expansion nor bounds checking optimization). The HPCJ+SE bar shows the result for the Array package version with semantic expansion. The BOUNDS bar shows the best result that can be accomplished with 100% pure Java: it uses the Array package with semantic expansion and bounds checking optimization. The FMA bar shows the extra boost in performance that we can get by allowing Java to use the fused-multiply add (fma) instruction of the POWER architecture. Finally, the FORTRAN bar shows the result for the Fortran version of the benchmark. The Fortran version uses the fma instruction. (For the purpose of completeness, we report here that JDK 1.1.6 + JIT achieves 3.2, 1.7, 1.3, and 1.4 Mflops, or approximately the same as HPCJ, for the Array package versions of MATMUL, BSOM, MICRO DC, and TOMCATV, respectively.)

Discussion: The performance of numerical codes using Java arrays (the JDK116 bars) is clearly unsatisfactory. It is typically between 10% (MATMUL,MICRO DC) and 25% (BSOM) of Fortran performance. The performance of Array package code is terrible with standard Java environments (the HPCJ bars). The execution cost in this case is dominated by the overhead of method invocation. Even when semantic expansion is used (the HPCJ+SE bars), the performance of the Array package versions are almost always worse than the performance with Java arrays. Although semantic expansion eliminates the method overhead, the explicit bounds and null-pointer checks are expensive and prevent optimizations. It is only when bounds checking (and null-pointer checking) optimization is performed (the BOUNDS bars) that we start to see Java performance that is much better than with Java arrays and comparable with Fortran. Speedups over Java arrays vary from 2.5 (BSOM) to 6.3 (MICRO DC). Performance with semantic expansion and bounds optimization is between 50% (MATMUL) and 80% (MICRO DC) of Fortran. When fmas are allowed, the performance can be as high as 90% (MATMUL)

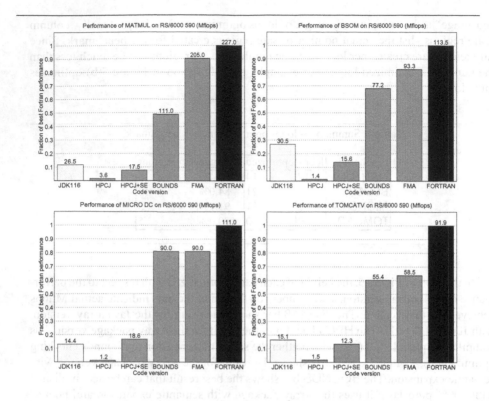

Fig. 6. Experimental results for all benchmarks.

of Fortran. We note that for three benchmarks (MATMUL, BSOM, and TOMCATV), fmas were generated by the compiler when enabled. The benefits of fmas are substantial for MATMUL and BSOM, less so for TOMCATV. For MICRO DC, no fmas were generated by the compilers (not even by the Fortran compiler).

5 Related Work

The importance of having high-performance libraries for numerical computing in Java has been recognized by many authors. In particular, [5,6,28] describe projects to develop such libraries entirely in Java. In addition, there are approaches in which access to existing numerical libraries (typically coded in C and Fortran) is provided to Java applications [4, 8,14]. All of these approaches shift the burden of delivering high performance entirely to the libraries. It is well know that programming with libraries has its limitations. For this reason, the Array package is more than just a library: It is a mechanism to represent array operations in a manner that can be highly optimized by compilers.

In [10], Cierniak and Li describe a global analysis technique for determining that the shape of a Java array of arrays (*e.g.*, double [] []) is indeed rectangular and not modified. The array representation is then transformed to a dense storage and element access is performed through index arithmetic. This approach can lead to results that are as good as from using multidimensional Arrays in the Array package. We differ in that we do not need global analysis: Arrays from the Array package are intrinsically rectangular and can always be stored in a dense form.

The technique of semantic expansion we use is similar to the approach taken by Fortran compilers in implementing some *intrinsic* procedures [2]. Intrinsic procedures can be treated by the Fortran compiler as language primitives, just as we treated the get and set methods in various classes of the Array package. Semantic expansion differs from the handling of intrinsics in Fortran in that both new data types and operations on the new data types are treated as language primitives.

Marmot [12] is an optimizing static Java compiler being developed at Microsoft Research. It implements both standard scalar (Fortran and C style) optimizations and basic object oriented optimizations. It also performs bounds checking optimization by determining, through a form of range analysis, which checks are redundant. There is no discussion of versioning in [12]. Marmot shows significant speedups relative to other Java environments in several benchmarks, but its performance is only average for the numerical benchmarks listed in [12].

6 Conclusion

We have demonstrated that high-performance numerical codes can be developed in Java. The benefits of Java from a productivity and demographics point of view have been known for a while. Many people have advocated the development of large, computationally intensive applications in Java based on those benefits. However, Java performance has consistently been considered an impediment to its applicability to numerical codes. This paper has presented a set of techniques that lead to Java performance that is comparable with the best Fortran implementations available today.

Adopting a language and compiler codesign approach, we have used a class library to introduce in Java features of Fortran 90 that are of great importance to numerical computing. These features include complex numbers, multidimensional arrays, and libraries for linear algebra. These features have a strong synergy with the compiler optimizations that we are developing, particularly bounds checking optimization and semantic expansion. All components of the Array package, including the BLAS library, are implemented entirely in Java. This guarantees portability of code and reproducibility of results in various platforms.

We demonstrated that we can deliver Java performance in the 65-90% range of the best Fortran performance for a variety of benchmarks. This is a very important step in making Java the preferred environment for developing large-scale computationally intensive applications. However, there is more than just performance to our approach. The Array package and associated libraries create a Java environment with many of the features that experienced Fortran programmers have grown accustomed to. This combination of delivering Fortran array manipulation features and performance, while maintaining the safety and elegance of Java, is the core of our approach to making Java the environment of choice for new numerical computing.

Acknowledgements. The authors wish to thank Rick Lawrence and Marc Snir for fruitful technical discussions, and for strongly supporting our research. We also wish to thank the members of the HPCJ and TPO teams at the IBM Toronto Lab for their work on the compiler infrastructure.

References

1. Java Grande Forum report: Making Java work for high-end computing. Java Grande Forum Panel, SC98, Orlando, FL, November 1998. URL: http://www.javagrande.org/reports.htm.
2. J. C. Adams, W. S. Brainerd, J. T. Martin, B. T. Smith, and J. L. Wagener. *Fortran 90 Handbook: Complete ANSI/ISO Reference.* McGraw-Hill, 1992.
3. Utpal Banerjee. *Dependence Analysis.* Loop Transformations for Restructuring Compilers. Kluwer Academic Publishers, Boston, MA, 1997.
4. A. Bik and D. B. Gannon. A note on level 1 BLAS in Java. In *Proceedings of the Workshop on Java for Computational Science and Engineering - Simulation and Modeling II,* June 1997. URL http://www.npac.syr.edu/users/gcf/03/javaforcse/acmspecissue/latestpapers.html.
5. B. Blount and S. Chatterjee. An evaluation of Java for numerical computing. In *Proceedings of ISCOPE'98,* volume 1505 of *Lecture Notes in Computer Science,* pages 35–46. Springer Verlag, 1998.
6. R. F. Boisvert, J. J. Dongarra, R. Pozo, K. A. Remington, and G. W. Stewart. Developing numerical libraries in Java. In *ACM 1998 Workshop on Java for High-Performance Network Computing.* ACM SIGPLAN, 1998. URL: http://www.cs.ucsb.edu/conferences/java98.
7. D. Callahan and K. Kennedy. Analysis of interprocedural side effects in a parallel programming environment. *Journal of Parallel and Distributed Computing,* 5:517–550, 1988.
8. H. Casanova, J. Dongarra, and D. M. Doolin. Java access to numerical libraries. *Concurrency, Pract. Exp. (UK),* 9(11):1279–91, November 1997. Java for Computational Science and Engineering - Simulation and Modeling II Las Vegas, NV, USA 21 June 1997.
9. M. Cierniak and W. Li. Unifying data and control transformations for distributed shared memory machines. In *Proc. ACM SIGPLAN '95 Conference on Programming Language Design and Implementation,* La Jolla, CA, June 1995.
10. M. Cierniak and W. Li. Just-in-time optimization for high-performance Java programs. *Concurrency, Pract. Exp. (UK),* 9(11):1063–73, November 1997. Java for Computational Science and Engineering - Simulation and Modeling II, Las Vegas, NV, June 21, 1997.
11. J. J. Dongarra, I. S. Duff, D. C. Sorensen, and H. A. van der Vorst. *Solving Linear Systems on Vector and Shared Memory Computers.* Society for Industrial and Applied Mathematics, 1991.
12. R. Fitzgerald, T. B. Knoblock, E. Ruf, Bjarne Steensgaard, and D. Tarditi. Marmot: an optimizing compiler for Java. Technical report, Microsoft Research, October 1998. URL: http://research.microsoft.com/apl/default.htm.
13. E. Gamma, R. Helm, R. Johnson, and J. Vlissides. *Design Patterns: Elements of Reusable Object-Oriented Software.* Addison-Wesley Publishing Company, 1995.
14. V. Getov, S. Flynn-Hummel, and S. Mintchev. High-performance parallel programming in Java: Exploiting native libraries. In *ACM 1998 Workshop on Java for High-Performance Network Computing.* ACM SIGPLAN, 1998. URL: http://www.cs.ucsb.edu/conferences/java98.
15. M. Gupta, S. Mukhopadhyay, and N. Sinha. Automatic parallelization of recursive procedures. Technical Report RC 21333(96110)4NOV1998, IBM Research, November 1998.

16. F. G. Gustavson. Recursion leads to automatic variable blocking for dense linear algebra algorithms. *IBM Journal of Research and Development*, 41(6):737–755, November 1997.
17. P. Havlak and K. Kennedy. An implementation of interprocedural bounded regular section analysis. *IEEE Transactions on Parallel and Distributed Systems*, 2(3):350–360, July 1991.
18. M. Kandemir, A. Choudhary, J. Ramanujam, and P. Banerjee. A matrix-based approach to the global locality optimization problem. In *Proceedings of International Conference on Parallel Architectures and Compilation Techniques (PACT'98), Paris, France*, October 1998.
19. M. Kandemir, A. Choudhary, J. Ramanujam, N. Shenoy, and P. Banerjee. Enhancing spatial locality via data layout optimizations. In *Proceedings of Euro-Par'98, Southampton, UK*, volume 1470 of *Lecture Notes in Computer Science*, pages 422–434. Springer Verlag, September 1998.
20. S.P. Midkiff, J.E. Moreira, and M. Snir. Optimizing array reference checking in Java programs. *IBM Systems Journal*, 37(3):409–453, August 1998.
21. J. E. Moreira and S. P. Midkiff. Fortran 90 in CSE: A case study *IEEE Computational Science & Engineering*, 5(2):39–49, April-June 1998.
22. J. E. Moreira, S. P. Midkiff, and M. Gupta. From flop to Megaflops: Java for technical computing. In *Proceedings of the 11th International Workshop on Languages and Compilers for Parallel Computing, LCPC'98*, 1998. IBM Research Report 21166.
23. R. Parsons and D. Quinlan. Run time recognition of task parallelism within the P++ parallel array class library. In *Proceedings of the Scalable Parallel Libraries Conference*, pages 77–86. IEEE Comput. Soc. Press, October 1993.
24. W. H. Press, S. A. Teukolsky, W. T. Vetterling, and B. P. Flannery. *Numerical Recipes in FORTRAN: The Art of Scientific Computing*. Cambridge University Press, 1992.
25. J. V. W. Reynders, J. C. Cummings, M. Tholburn, P. J. Hinker, S. R. Atlas, S. Banerjee, M. Srikant, W. F. Humphrey, S. R. Karmesin, and K. Keahey. POOMA: A framework for scientific simulation on parallel architectures. In *Proceedings of First International Workshop on High Level Programming Models and Supportive Environments, Honolulu, HI*, pages 41–49, April 16 1996. URL: http://www.acl.lanl.gov/PoomaFramework/papers/papers.html.
26. G. Rivera and C.-W. Tseng. Data transformations for eliminating conflict misses. In *Proceedings of the ACM SIGPLAN'98 Conference on Programming Language Design and Implementation*, pages 38–49, Montreal, Canada, June 1998. ACM Press.
27. V. Sarkar. Automatic selection of high-order transformations in the IBM XL Fortran compilers. *IBM Journal of Research and Development*, 41(3):233–264, May 1997.
28. M. Schwab and J. Schroeder. Algebraic Java classes for numerical optimization. In *ACM 1998 Workshop on Java for High-Performance Network Computing*. ACM SIGPLAN, 1998. URL: http://www.cs.ucsb.edu/conferences/java98.
29. G. V. Wilson and P. Lu, editors. *Parallel Programming using C++*. MIT Press, 1996.
30. P. Wu, S. P. Midkiff, J. E. Moreira, and M. Gupta. Efficient support for complex numbers in Java. In *Proceedings of the 1999 ACM Java Grande Conference*, 1999. IBM Research Division report RC21393.

Instruction Scheduling in the Presence of Java's Runtime Exceptions

Matthew Arnold[1], Michael Hsiao[2], Ulrich Kremer[1], and Barbara Ryder[1]

[1] Department of Computer Science, Rutgers University, Piscataway NJ 08855, USA
{marnold,uli,ryder}@cs.rutgers.edu,
http://www.prolangs.rutgers.edu
[2] Department of Electrical and Computer Engineering, Rutgers University,
Piscataway NJ 08855, USA
mhsiao@ece.rutgers.edu

Abstract. One of the challenges present to a Java compiler is Java's frequent use of runtime exceptions. These exceptions affect performance directly by requiring explicit checks, as well as indirectly by restricting code movement in order to satisfy Java's precise exception model. Instruction scheduling is one transformation which is restricted by runtime exceptions since it relies heavily on reordering instructions to exploit maximum hardware performance. The goal of this study was to investigate the degree to which Java's runtime exceptions hinder instruction scheduling, and to find new techniques for allowing more efficient execution of Java programs containing runtime exceptions.

1 Introduction

Java programs were originally executed by compiling Java source into bytecodes and interpreting these bytecodes on a Java Virtual Machine. Today, interpretation is being replaced by *Just In Time* (JIT) and dynamic compilers. As Java is becoming more popular as a general purpose programming language, the demand for a high performance native code Java compiler is increasing as well.

One of the challenges present to any Java compiler is Java's frequent use of exceptions. Several Java statements implicitly throw exceptions, including array accesses, pointer uses, casts, and integer division. These implicit exceptions, or *runtime exceptions*, directly affect performance by requiring the insertion of explicit runtime checks. Performance is also affected indirectly by Java's precise exception model which restricts code movement, making many optimizations and transformations more difficult.

Instruction scheduling is one example of a compiler transformation which is affected by Java's runtime exceptions since it relies heavily on reordering instructions to exploit maximum hardware performance, particularly on advanced architectures such as superscaler and VLIW. The instruction reordering restrictions imposed by runtime exceptions can hinder the effectiveness of the instruction scheduler, and as a result, substantially reduce the amount of instruction level parallelism.

L. Carter and J. Ferrante (Eds.): LCPC'99, LNCS 1863, pp. 18–34, 2000.

One approach to reduce the overhead introduced by runtime exceptions is to use static analysis to identify instructions which are known never to throw exceptions, allowing the runtime checks for these instructions to be safely removed. While this technique important, it may not be sufficient if many of the checks cannot be eliminated.

The goal of this study was to investigate the degree to which Java's runtime exceptions hinder instruction scheduling, and to find new techniques for allowing more efficient execution of Java programs containing runtime exceptions.

The contributions of this paper are as follows:

- We discuss the issues related to instruction scheduling in the presence of Java's runtime exceptions.
- We discuss existing techniques which can be used to improve performance without violating the Java exception model semantics.
- We offer experimental results showing the degree to which runtime exceptions hinder performance on both modern and future architectures. We also show results confirming that techniques such as superblock scheduling can be used to substantially reduce this penalty.

1.1 Exceptions in Java

Java's precise exception model imposes restrictions on optimizations in the presence of exceptions. The exception model is defined in [8], section 11.3.1, as follows

> *Exceptions in Java are precise: when the transfer of control takes place, all effects of the statements executed and expressions evaluated before the point from which the exception is thrown must appear to have taken place. No expressions, statements, or parts thereof that occur after the point from which the exception is thrown may appear to have been evaluated. If optimized code has speculatively executed some of the expressions or statements which follow the point at which the exception occurs, such code must be prepared to hide this speculative execution from the user-visible state of the Java program.*

Section 6 contains further discussion regarding interpreting the Java specification. For now, we will assume that meeting the following three restrictions is sufficient to satisfy the exception model described above, and we will show that our transformations satisfy these restrictions.

1. Exceptions occur in the same order in the optimized and unoptimized code, regardless of what optimizations are performed.
2. An exception is thrown if and only if it is thrown in the unoptimized program.
3. When an exception occurs, program execution following the point of the exception will observe the user visible state to be identical to what it would have been if no optimization had taken place.

The most obvious solution to maintain exception order is to add the explicit exception checks *before* any optimizations take place. As long as the compiler does not re-order the checks themselves, the exceptions will occur in the original order. The compiler must then speculate code in such a way that state is guaranteed to be correct if an exception occurs. The addition of runtime checks increases the number of jumps and reduces the size of the basic blocks, greatly hindering traditional instruction schedulers.

2   Advanced Instruction Scheduling

The following is a review of existing instruction scheduling techniques which were designed for programs written in C. One of the primary goals of these techniques is to allow speculation of instructions while ensuring that hardware exceptions occur correctly. At this point we must make it clear that this work deals with hardware exceptions, not Java's runtime exceptions. To avoid confusion, for the rest of this paper exceptions will always be referred to as either *hardware exceptions* or *Java exceptions*. There are also two types of hardware exceptions – those which terminate the program execution, such as segmentation fault and bus errors, and those which do not, such as page faults, cache misses and TLB misses. These non-terminating exceptions will be referred to as *transparent exceptions*.

In later sections we will discuss how the techniques described below can be used to improve instruction scheduling for Java programs.

2.1   Superblock Scheduling

Superblock scheduling [10] is an extension of trace scheduling [7]. The goal of superblock scheduling is to combine sets of basic blocks which are likely to execute in sequence, thus allowing more effective instruction scheduling. Flow of control may exit the superblock early along branches which are unlikely to be taken. Side entrances into the superblock are eliminated by using tail duplication.

To ensure proper program execution, two restrictions must be enforced when moving instructions within the superblock. An instruction, J, may be moved before a branch, BR if (1) the destination of J is not used before it is redefined when BR is taken, and (2) J will not cause a hardware exception which alters the execution result of the program when BR is taken.

Restricted Percolation The scheduler enforces both restrictions (1) and (2) when using the restricted percolation model. Only those instructions which are guaranteed not to cause a hardware exception can be speculatively executed; otherwise an incorrect, or *spurious exception* could occur.

General Percolation The scheduler completely ignores restriction (2) when using the general percolation model. This can be accomplished if the architecture supports non-excepting, or silent, instructions. When a terminating hardware exception occurs for a silent instruction, the exception is simply ignored and a garbage value is written into the destination register. This ensures that spurious exceptions will not affect program execution. If the exception is not spurious (i.e., it would have appeared in the original program) it will be ignored by general percolation and program execution will continue. This may lead to incorrect results, or a later exception being raised.

The obvious drawback of general percolation is the inability to detect hardware exceptions properly, making debugging and error detection very difficult. Failure to accurately detect hardware exceptions is unacceptable in many cases, and thus general percolation is used mostly as a best case scenario for other speculation models.

2.2   Sentinel Scheduling

Sentinel scheduling [13] attempts to provide the scheduling freedom of general percolation while always detecting hardware exceptions and identifying the excepting instructions. The basic idea behind sentinel scheduling is that each *potentially excepting instruction* (PEI) has a *sentinel* which reports any exception that was caused by the PEI. The sentinel resides in the PEI's original basic block, or *home block*. If the home block is never reached then the exception is not raised, thus eliminating spurious exceptions.

If a sentinel for an excepting instruction is reached, the process of *recovery* is begins. Program execution jumps back to the speculatively executed instruction and it is re-executed non-speculatively, thus causing the exception to occur. If the exception is non-terminating then the exception is processed and program execution continues. The sequence of instructions between the PEI and the sentinel are re-executed thus the compiler must ensure that this sequence of instruction is always re-executable.

Sentinel scheduling requires architectural support, including an extra bit on all registers to record whether a speculative instruction caused an exception, as well an extra bit in the opcode to distinguish speculative and non-speculative instructions. It is worth noting that the IA-64 architecture [11] will provide this hardware support for speculative loads, making sentinel scheduling and general percolation possible.

One of the problems associated with sentinel scheduling is that maintaining this sequence of re-executable instructions significantly increases register pressure. Techniques such as [4][3] were presented in an attempt to solve this problem and thus decrease the performance difference between sentinel scheduling and general percolation.

3   Combining Advanced Scheduling and Java

Superblock scheduling is very effective for code consisting of small basic blocks in combination with predictable branches; this is exactly the type of code that is created when runtime exception checks are added to a Java program. We propose that the following algorithm is effective for reducing the performance penalty of Java's runtime exceptions.

Algorithm 1

1. **Remove unnecessary checks.** If it can be determined at compile time that an exception can not occur, that exception check can be removed. Removing as many checks as possible eliminates the overhead of the checks and relaxes restrictions on code movement.
2. **Make all remaining exception checks explicit.**[1] For example, the code:
   `x = A[i];` becomes:
   `if (A == null) throw new NullPointerException();`
   `if (OUT_OF_BOUND(A,i))throw new ArrayIndexOutOfBoundException();`
   `x = A[i];`
3. **Form superblocks.** Form superblocks and schedule using general percolation as the speculation model.

Notice that general percolation is used as the speculation model in step 3, therefore requiring the architectural support discussed in Section 2. By using general percolation, instructions may be speculated without concern for hardware exceptions. The result is that hardware exceptions may go undetected, but as long as these exceptions would not have occurred in the original code, the program is guaranteed to execute properly (as if no speculation had occurred). For now it should be assumed that the original program does not raise terminating hardware exceptions and thus the use of general percolation is acceptable. This issue is discussed in detail in section 5.1.

Superblock scheduling is particularly effective for code containing exceptions because it takes advantage of the fact that exceptions rarely occur. Each exception check becomes a branch exiting the superblock. By using general percolation, the compiler is given more leeway to speculate instructions within the superblock.

As for any Java transformation, the compiler must ensure that the Java exception model is not violated. As discussed in section 1.1, the following 3 properties are satisfied.

1. **Java exception order is preserved.** The key to maintaining exception order is the fact that each potentially excepting instruction is guarded by an explicit exception check. Instructions such as array accesses may be speculated; however, since the bounds checks are executed in the original order, Java exceptions are guaranteed to occur in the same order.
2. **Java exceptions occur if and only if they occur in the original program.** Again, the Java exception checks were made explicit, so assuming that the superblock scheduler maintains the semantics of the original program, Java exceptions will occur as they did in the original program.

---

[1] Some exceptions can be checked implicitly by looking for the hardware exception that occurs when the instruction is executed. This technique can be used, but requires a more intelligent scheduler. This issue is discussed in Section 5.3 in detail.

3. **State is maintained when a Java exception occurs.** Recall restriction
   (1) from section 2. Even in general percolation, an instruction, J, is not
   speculated above a branch if J's destination register is used before defined
   when the branch is taken. Thus when a Java exception occurs, all variables
   and registers which are used during and after the handling of the exception
   will be the same as if superblock scheduling had not taken place.

4 Experimental Results

To measure the performance impact of Java's runtime exceptions we modified
Toba [15], a Java to C converter, so that the insertion of runtime exception
checks could be turned on and off. Since the Java exceptions will not be detected
when the checks are not inserted, this experimental technique works only for
programs which do not throw runtime exceptions. The resulting C programs
were then compiled using the Trimaran [1] system, a framework designed for
research in instruction level parallelism. The Trimaran compiler performs many
optimizations and transformations, including superblock scheduling, and allows
the code to be simulated on a parameterized processor architecture called HPL-
PD.

The C programs produced by Toba were compiled with and without superblock scheduling, and simulated on two of the sample machines provided in
the Trimaran release. Both machines were specified using MDES, Trimaran's
machine description language. The first machine, a VLIW machine capable of
issuing 9 instructions per cycle, contains 4 integer units, 2 floating point units,
2 memory units, and 1 branch unit. The second machine, which will be referred
to as the *single-issue* machine, is capable of issuing only one instruction per cycle and has one of each functional unit mentioned above. Each machine has 64
general purpose registers.

This framework allowed us to measure the effectiveness of Algorithm 1 by
comparing the cost of Java's runtime exception checks on different architectures
as well as with different scheduling techniques. The only drawback to this framework is that Toba does not perform any optimizations, including elimination
of unnecessary exception checks. Trimaran does perform heavy optimization of
the C program, but once the Java has been converted to C, some optimizations
may become too difficult for the Trimaran compiler to perform since much of the
high level information is lost. If we can obtain a more advanced Java compilation
framework, we plan to investigate the impact that object-oriented optimizations
may have on the relative cost of runtime exceptions.

The programs included in the results are described in Table 1, and were
chosen for their extensive use of runtime exceptions. We expect to have results
for larger programs in the future, but we currently constrained by a bug in our
experimental framework.

Results Figure 1 compares the performance impact of exceptions on different
combinations of scheduling techniques and architectures. From left to right, the

Table 1. Program Characteristics

Programs	LOC (Java/C)	Description
matrix	106/1532	Matrix multiply
euler	250/1524	Calculate Eulerian circuits in randomized graph
graycodes	121/1560	Computes all graycodes for a list of bit strings
binary	31/427	Performs 10,000 binary searches on a list of 200,000 elements
mergesort	55/766	Sorts a list of 10,000 elements using the recursive mergesort

bars represent the following scheduling/architecture pairs: no superblock/single-issue, superblock/single-issue, no superblock/VLIW, superblock/VLIW, where "No superblock" means that superblock scheduling was not performed, and "Superblock" means that superblock scheduling was performed using general percolation as the speculation model.

With the scheduling technique and architecture fixed, the exception checks were inserted and removed. The y-axis represents the slowdown that occured when all checks were inserted. All measurements are normalized to 1, where 1 unit represents the execution time of the program with no checks on the particular scheduling/architecture pair. Note that this graph does *not* show the overall performance gained by superblock scheduling. The programs ran faster with superblock scheduling regardless of whether the checks were on or off.

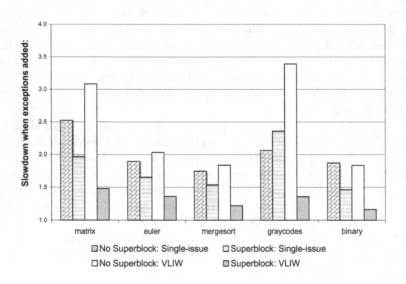

Fig. 1. A comparison of the cost of Java's runtime exceptions across different scheduling techniques and architectures.

There are two interesting things to notice in this graph. First, it compares the slowdown on both machines which occurs when superblock scheduling is not used (the first and third bars). For two programs, *matrix* and *graycodes*, the exceptions checks hurt performance significantly more on the VLIW machine than on the single-issue machine. This was our expectation since the insertion of exception checks breaks up existing instruction level parallelism. However, to our surprise, the performance impact of exceptions for the remaining programs was similar on both machines.

Secondly, this graph shows the slowdown which occurs on the VLIW machine, without and with superblock scheduling (third and fourth bars). The performance penalty of exceptions is drastically reduced when superblock scheduling is used. When used on single-issue machines, superblock scheduling helps reduce the penalty of exceptions, but not to the degree which it does on the VLIW machine. The code movement enabled by the superblock scheduler cannot be taken advantage of on the single-issue machine, since there is no room in the original schedule in which the checks can be hidden. When used on a VLIW architecture, superblock scheduling allows the runtime checks to be moved into words which were not fully used, thus increasing the machine utilization and reducing the overall cost of the exception checks.

Figure 2 is similar to Figure 1 except it is used to compare the effect of restricted and general percolation as well as the impact of eliminating all null pointer checks. The graph shows the slowdown caused by runtime exceptions checks on the VLIW machine only. The bars represent, from left to right, no superblock scheduling, superblock scheduling with restricted percolation, and superblock scheduling with general percolation. The numbers are normalized to 1, where 1 unit represents the execution time of the program with no runtime exception checks using the particular scheduling method on the VLIW machine. The full height of the bar represents the slowdown which occurs when all checks are on, while the height of the line within each bar represents the slowdown which occurs when only null pointer checks are turned off (all others are on), thus representing the potential savings of implicit null pointer checks.

This graph shows that superblock scheduling in combination with general percolation is clearly most useful for reducing the cost of exceptions. Superblock scheduling with restricted percolation still reduces the penalty of the checks, but not as substantially as general percolation. For the program *matrix*, the smallest slowdown was obtained when using restricted rather than general percolation. (Again, this does not mean that *matrix* ran most quickly with restricted percolation, but rather that inserting exception checks had the smallest impact when restricted percolation was used.) A possible explanation is that the superblock scheduler creates a particularly tight schedule with general percolation, thus leaving no room to squeeze in the exception checks. Restricted percolation, on the other hand, produced a worse schedule and therefore had more room to hide the checks. This result demonstrates that better instruction scheduling can potentially *increase* the cost of exceptions by creating a tight schedule which has no room to hide extra instructions.

Figure 3 shows the overall speedup obtained by using superblock scheduling on the VLIW machine. The first bar shows the speedup of superblock scheduling

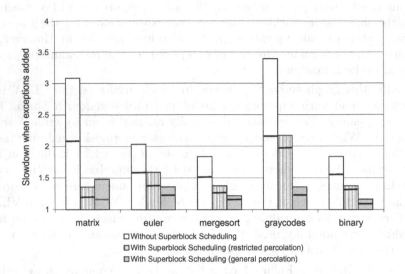

Fig. 2. The cost of exceptions: with and without superblock scheduling on VLIW machine. The height of the full bar represents all exception checks turned on. The height of the line within each bar represents null pointer checks turned off, all others on.

when the program contains no checks. The second bar shows the speedup when the program contains all checks. Running times are normalized to 1, where 1 unit represents the running time without superblock scheduling for that particular exception scenario (checks or no checks). The height of each bar shows the speedup gained when general percolation is used as the speculation model, while the line within each bar represents the speedup obtained using restricted percolation.

The speedups obtained by superblock scheduling are substantially larger for programs containing runtime exceptions, demonstrating that superblock scheduling is even more important for Java programs than for languages without runtime exception checks. Superblock scheduling with restricted percolation also offers reasonable speedups, however they are significantly less than general percolation.

5   Specific Issues

5.1   Is General Percolation Sufficient?

The previous experiments were performed using general percolation, so proper execution is guaranteed assuming that no terminating hardware exceptions occur

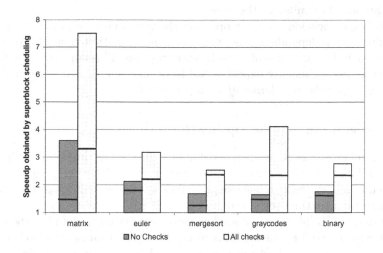

Fig. 3. Speedups gained by using superblock scheduling on VLIW machine. The height of the full bar is with general percolation. The height of the line within each bar is restricted percolation.

in the original program. However, if terminating hardware exceptions *do* occur in the original program, they may go undetected in the optimized program allowing execution to continue with unpredictable behavior, making debugging very difficult. Before we conclude that general percolation is unacceptable for Java programs, the following question must be answered: "When *do* terminating hardware exceptions occur in Java programs?"

In fact, the Java language definition ensures that most common hardware exceptions *don't* occur. For example, consider the following:

- **Divide by zero** - Prevented by runtime check
- **Dereference null** - Prevented by runtime check
- **Dereference memory location out of segment** - Prevented by a combination of factors.
  1. Pointer use is restricted.
  2. Array bounds are explicitly checked.
  3. Memory storage management is left up to the compiler, most commonly via garbage collection.
  4. Casting is checked, preventing invalid casts.

  Using these facts it can be shown (via structural induction on program syntax) that the Java language specification prevents reference variables from referring to anything except valid objects or null. Thus, dereferencing a reference variable cannot cause a segmentation violation.

Hardware exceptions are architecture specific, so to prove that they *never* occur, every exception for the particular architecture would need to be considered, applying arguments similar to the above.

The Java specification does not preclude the use of general percolation since it is architecture independent, and thus does not mention how the program should behave in the presence of a hardware exception. This supports the notion that hardware exceptions are expected *not* to occur, *making general percolation a viable option for the scheduling of Java programs.*

5.2 Is General Percolation Optimal?

General percolation has been proposed for use with Java, thus eliminating the need for sentinel scheduling and its associated overhead. However, care must be taken when using general percolation, as it does not necessarily guarantee better performance than sentinel scheduling.

Previous work [13][4][3] has treated general percolation as defining the upper limit on performance for sentinel scheduling. It is true that sentinel scheduling has several performance disadvantages compared to general percolation. First, sentinel scheduling requires the sequence of instructions between the speculated instruction and the sentinel to be re-executable. This eliminates speculation across irreversible instructions as well as increases register pressure by extending the live ranges of the registers used in the sequence. Sentinel scheduling also potentially reduces performance by inserting extra instructions when no existing instruction can be used as a sentinel.

However, the assumption that general percolation *always* outperforms sentinel scheduling is not correct if the effects of transparent exceptions (cache misses, TLB misses, page fault, etc) are considered, because sentinel scheduling does have one potential performance *advantage* over general percolation. For speculated instructions, sentinel scheduling has the ability to delay the handling of transparent exceptions until the sentinel is reached, whereas general percolation must process all transparent exceptions immediately, even though the home block of the instruction may never be reached. The result is that general percolation may increase the number of transparent exceptions which occur; sentinel scheduling will not.

For example, consider the follow scenarios which are possible when an instruction is being speculated. A page fault is used as a sample transparent exception.

1. The instruction will cause a page fault regardless of whether it is speculated.
2. The instruction will *not* cause a page fault regardless of whether it is speculated.
3. The instruction will cause a page fault *only* if it is speculated.

General percolation wins in cases 1 and 2 since no spurious exceptions are introduced in either case. Sentinel scheduling is particularly poor in case 1 since it would delay the exception until the home block is reached, start recovery, then re-execute all needed instructions. However, sentinel scheduling wins in case 3, since it prevents the spurious page fault from being processed. If case 3 occurs frequently enough and the spurious exceptions are expensive to process, sentinel scheduling could outperform general percolation, leaving us with the question, "Is general percolation really optimal?"

A study combining sentinel scheduling with predicated execution for C programs [2] reported that for their benchmarks, 31% of cache misses and 13% TLB misses and page faults were spurious and thus could potentially be avoided by delaying their handling until the sentinel was reached. The study did not provide numbers showing the performance impact of avoiding these spurious exceptions nor mention any performance comparisons to general percolation.

Possible Solutions One strategy to reduce the number of spurious transparent exceptions introduced by general percolation would be to use profiling to identify the instructions which are likely to be in case 3, and prevent these instructions from being speculated. Since it is not uncommon for a small number of instructions to cause a substantial number of the page faults [9], it may be possible to reduce the number of spurious transparent exceptions without overly restricting speculation.

Another possibility would be to encode a bit in the opcode representing whether or not a transparent exception should be processed immediately or delayed. Instructions which fit into case 2 should handle the transparent exception immediately, while those in case 3 could delay the handling. This would allow the best possible performance for all scenarios which were compile time predictable, although it is not clear whether the potential performance gains warrant such extreme measures as hardware modification.

5.3   How to Handle Implicit Exception Checks?

Algorithm 1 from Section 3 tests explicitly for all Java exceptions; however, some exceptions, such as divide by zero and null pointer exceptions, can be detected without explicit checks by looking for the hardware exception that occurs when the instruction is executed. The process of detecting Java exceptions without explicit checks will be referred to as checking *implicitly*.

There are two reasons why Algorithm 1 cannot check for exceptions implicitly. First, the algorithm relies on the explicit checks to ensure state is maintained and that the exceptions occur in the correct order. Secondly, Algorithm 1 uses general percolation which ignores terminating hardware exceptions on all speculative instructions, and thus cannot use these hardware exceptions to detect Java exceptions.

Checking for exceptions implicitly also has challenges independent of Algorithm 1. When implicit checks are used, code movement is restricted since moving an instruction implies moving the exception check as well. Figure 4 shows the two types of code movement which are possible when the checks are explicit, but not not possible when they are implicit. Intelligent use of implicit exceptions requires balancing the tradeoff between saving cycles at the cost of decreased code movement.

Original Program

```
if (p==null) throw ...
p.f = 1;
```

Scenario 1   Scenario 2

```
if (p==null) throw ...              p.f = 1;
// Code ''X'' inserted here         // Code ''X'' inserted here
p.f = 1;                            if (p==null) throw ...
```

Fig. 4. Two scenarios for code movement which are possible when the exception checks are explicit, but not possible when the checks are implicit. In Scenario 1, the excepting instruction is moved downward from the check. In Scenario 2 it speculated before the check. Code "X" represents any instructions moved from above or below the code shown in the the original program.

Possible Solution The experimental results in Section 4 suggest that limiting code movement can substantially reduce performance, particularly on the wide issue machine. Thus a reasonable approach may be to give priority to code motion, but to use implicit exceptions whenever it does not restrict code movement. This approach is taken in [5], however their scheduler does not allow speculative execution, as shown in Figure 4, Scenario 2.

The following algorithm is one possible way of allowing speculation with full code movement while taking advantage of implicit exceptions when possible.

Algorithm 2

1. **Perform algorithm 1.**
2. **Try to make each explicit exception check implicit.**
   Making a check implicit essentially moves the check to the PEI. For example, in figure 4, making the check implicit moves the check across the code labeled "X" (since the Java exception would be detected implicitly and raised by the assignment statement). Thus, a check can be made implicit only if this movement of the check does not violate the exception model, i.e., it does not modify exception order and does not corrupt the visible state.
3. **For those checks which cannot be made implicit**
   Leave the explicit check, under the assumption that the code motion made possible is worth the cost of the check. If in Scenario 2 of Figure 4, it may still be possible to avoid the explicit check, if hardware support is available for delayed detection of hardware exceptions (as discussed in section 2.2). The exception check could be replaced by a hardware exception check instruction, which, depending on the hardware, could potentially be "piggy-backed" on top of an existing instruction.

6   Interpreting the Java Specification

We have argued that the transformations presented in this paper do not violate Java's precise exception model by showing that they meet the three restrictions presented in section 1.1. This section carefully considers the wording of these restrictions and discusses some of the fine points of complying with the specification.

The third restriction of section 1.1 states:

When an exception occurs, program execution following the point of the exception will observe the user visible state to be identical to what it would have been if no optimization had taken place.

The wording for this restriction was chosen very carefully. Notice that it does not require the entire user visible state to be correct when an exception occurs. It requires correctness only for *state which may be observed during the remaining program execution*. State which is never observed, (for example, registers which are dead), may be different from what it would have been in an unoptimized execution.[2] If a source level debugger is being used on the Java code, all variables could potentially be viewed at all program points. We are presuming that this is not the case in these examples.

Program 1

```
foo() {
  int x=0; int y=0;

  try {
    x = 1;     // STMT 1
    x = A[i];  // STMT 2
    y = 3;     // STMT 3
    System.out.print(x + y);
  }
  catch(Throwable e) {
    // x and y not used
    return;
}}
```

Program 2

```
foo() {
  int a=0; int b=0;

  try{
    a = p.f;  // STMT 4
    b = q.f;  // STMT 5

    System.out.print(a + b);
  }
  catch (Throwable e) {
    // a and b not used
    return;
}}
```

Fig. 5. Programs demonstrating interpretation of the Java specification

Consider Program 1 in figure 5 and assume that STMT 2 throws an exception. The values of x and y are not used within the catch clause and they are locals so they cannot be used after foo() returns. Since the remaining program execution does not access x and y, there is no possible way for the user to observe their values and therefore there is no need to ensure that they contain the correct values when the exception occurs. STMT 1 could then be removed since it is dead code, and STMT 3 could be speculated before STMT 2.

These transformations are in compliance with the Java Specification. As quoted in section 1.1, the specification states that if speculation has occured, "...

---

[2] Algorithm 1 from section 3 takes advantage of the wording of this restriction. When an exception branch is taken, only registers which are used before defined are guaranteed to contain the correct value.

such code must be prepared to hide this speculative execution from the user visible state ...". However, if it can be proved that no code ever observes a particular state, then there does not exist a scenario where the speculation must be hidden.

Similar arguments can be used to relax the restrictions on exception order as well. Both Algorithm 1 and Algorithm 2 guarantee that if a statement, S, throws an exception in the unoptimized code, then S will throw the exception in the optimized code. However, nothing in the specification requires the exception to be thrown by S. As long as *some* statement throws the same exception, and the state is correct at the point of the exception, then the specification is still satisfied.

For example, consider Program 2 in Figure 5. The order in which STMT 4 and STMT 5 are executed has no effect on program execution, and is therefore irrelevant. Say one, or both, of p and q are null. Once execution jumps to the catch clause, the only way to know which statement threw the exception is to examine the values of a and b. Since neither a nor b is referenced in (or after) the catch clause, there is no way for the user to detect that STMT 4 and STMT 5 were interchanged.

These transformations allow additional code movement without affecting the behavior of the program as detectable by the user, and therefore may be used by optimizing Java compilers to produce more efficient code.

7　Related Work

Le [12] presents a runtime binary translator which allows speculation of potentially excepting instructions. The translator produces native code on demand at runtime, processing basic blocks as they are reached and combining them into superblocks when appropriate. It takes advantage of the fact that the translator can intercept all exceptions reported by the native OS, and decides which exceptions should be made visible to the application. When an exception is raised by a speculated instruction, a recovery algorithm reverts flow of control back to a pre-computed *checkpoint* in the unspeculated code. The remainder of the basic block is then interpreted, raising any exceptions which may occur.

The main advantage of Le's work is that it does not require any hardware support, such as non-faulting loads. The disadvantage is that when an exception occurs, recovery must be used to determine whether the exception should actually be raised, or whether it is a *false exception*. In sentinel scheduling, recovery begins only if an exception is raised *and* the sentinel in the home block is reached, thus never processing false exceptions.

To avoid wasting time repeatedly recovering from false exceptions, any superblock in Le's work which raises a false exception is permanently rescheduled with no speculation. This could substantially reduce the amount of speculation possible using this technique.

Ebcioglu and Altman proposed an out-of-order translation technique called DAISY [6] to run RISC programs on VLIW processors. DAISY assumes the architecture modifications used by sentinel scheduling to allow speculation of potentially excepting instructions. The emphasis of the paper is how to produce VLIW code with significant levels of ILP while keeping compilation overhead to a minimum.

In [14], Moreira et. al. evaluate the performance impact of Java's runtime exceptions for numerically intensive programs. Their work partitions the iteration space of a loop-nest into regions with the goal of finding *safe regions* which are free of exceptions. Exception checks are not needed in safe regions, and instruction reordering transformations can be applied, thus allowing numerical applications written in Java to approach the performance obtainable by other languages such as C++.

8 Conclusions

We have proposed using superblock scheduling in combination with general percolation to reduce the cost of Java's runtime exception checks (Algorithm 1), and have shown that doing so does not violate the the the Java's precise exception model.

Our experimental results show that runtime exceptions hinder performance considerably on both single issue and VLIW machines. Superblock scheduling and general percolation significantly reduce this penalty on the VLIW machine by taking advantage of words which are not fully utilized to partially hide the cost of the exception checks. Superblock scheduling helped only moderately on the single-issue machine.

We have presented a modification to Algorithm 1 which allows for exceptions to be detected implicitly. The algorithm gives priority to code movement and takes advantage of implicit checks when possible.

Acknowledgments. We would like to thank Ben Goldberg, Rodric Rabbah, and Hansoo Kim of New York University for their help facilitating the use of the Trimaran infrastructure.

References

1. Trimaran: An infrastructure for research in instruction-level parallelism. Produced by a colaboration between Hewlet Packard, University of Illinois, and New York University. URL: http://www.trimaran.org.
2. D. August, D. Connors, S. Mahlke, J. Sias, K. Crozier, B. Cheng, P. Eaton, Q. Olaniran, and W. Hwu. Integrated predicated and speculative execution in the IMPACT EPIC architecture. In *Proceedings of the 25th Annual International Symposium on Computer Architecture (ISCA-98)*, volume 26,3 of *ACM Computer Architecture News*, pages 227–237, New York, June 27–July 1 1998. ACM Press.
3. D. August, B. Deitrich, and S. Mahlke. Sentinel scheduling with recovery blocks. Computer Science Technical Report CRHC-95-05, University of Illinoiss, Urbana, IL, February 1995.

4. R. A. Bringmann, S. A. Mahlke, R. E. Hank, J. C. Gyllenhaal, and W.-M. W. Hwu. Speculative execution exception recovery using write-back suppression. In *Proceedings of the 26th Annual International Symposium on Microarchitecture (MICRO'93)*, volume 24 of *SIGMICRO Newsletter*, pages 214–224, Los Alamitos, CA, USA, December 1993. IEEE Computer Society Press.

5. C. Chambers, I. Pechtchanski, V. Sarkar, M. J. Serrano, and H. Srinivasan. Dependence analysis for Java. In *Proceedings of the 12th International Workshop on Languages and Compilers for Parallel Computing, LCPC'99*, August 1999.

6. K. Ebcioglu and E. R. Altman. DAISY: Dynamic compilation for 100In *Proceedings of the 24th Annual International Symposium on Computer Architecture (ISCA-97)*, volume 25,2 of *Computer Architecture News*, pages 26–37, New YOrk, June 2–4 1997. ACM Press.

7. J. A. Fisher. Trace scheduling : A technique for global microcode compaction. *IEEE Trans. Comput.*, C-30(7):478–490, 1981.

8. J. Gosling, B. Joy, and G. L. Steele. *The Java^{TM} Language Specification*. The Java Series. Addison-Wesley, Reading, MA, USA, 1996.

9. J. L. Hennessy and D. A. Patterson. *Computer Archetecture A Quantitative Approach*. Morgan Kaufmann Publishers Inc., Santo Mateo, California, 1990. 3rd Printing.

10. W. W. Hwu, S. A. Mahlke, W. Y. Chen, P. P. Chang, N. J. Warter, R. A. Bringmann, R. G. Ouellette, R E. Hank, T. Kiyohara, G. E. Haab, J. G. Holm, and D. M. Lavery. The superblock: An effective technique for VLIW and superscalar compilation. *The Journal of Supercomputing*, 7:229–248, 1993.

11. Intel.   Ia-64 application developer's architecture guide.   URL: http://developer.intel.com/design/ia64, 1999.

12. B. C. Le. An out-of-order execution technique for runtime binary translators. In *Proceedings of the 8th International Conference on Architectural Support for Programming Languages and Operating System (ASPLOS)*, volume 33, pages 151–158, November 1998.

13. S. A. Mahlke, W. Y. Chen, R. A. Bringmann, R. E. Hank, W. W. Hwu, B. R. Rau, and M. S. Schlansker. Sentinel scheduling: A model for compiler-controlled speculative execution. *ACM Transactions on Computer Systems*, 11(4):376–408, November 1993.

14. J. E. Moreira, S. P. Midkiff, and M. Gupta. From flop to Megaflops: Java for technical computing. In *Proceedings of the 11th International Workshop on Languages and Compilers for Parallel Computing, LCPC'98*, 1998. IBM Research Report 21166.

15. T. A. Proebsting, G. Townsend, P. Bridges, J. H. Hartman, T. Newsham, and S. A. Watterson. Toba: Java for applications: A way ahead of time (WAT) compiler. In *Proceedings of the 3rd Conference on Object-Oriented Technologies and Systems*, pages 41–54, Berkeley, June 16–20 1997. Usenix Association.

Dependence Analysis for Java

Craig Chambers*, Igor Pechtchanski, Vivek Sarkar, Mauricio J. Serrano, and
Harini Srinivasan

IBM Thomas J. Watson Research Center
P. O. Box 704, Yorktown Heights, NY 10598, USA
{chambers, igor, vivek, mserrano, harini}@watson.ibm.com

Abstract. We describe a novel approach to performing data dependence
analysis for Java in the presence of Java's "non-traditional" language
features such as exceptions, synchronization, and memory consistency.
We introduce new classes of edges in a dependence graph to model code
motion constraints arising from these language features. We present a
linear-time algorithm for constructing this augmented dependence graph
for an extended basic block.

1 Introduction

Data dependence analysis is a fundamental program analysis technique used by
optimizing and parallelizing compilers to identify constraints on data flow, code
motion, and instruction reordering [11]. It is desirable for dependence analysis to
be as precise as possible so as to minimize code motion constraints and maximize
opportunities for program transformations and optimizations such as instruction
scheduling. Precise dependence analysis for scalar variables is well understood;
e.g., an effective solution is to use SSA form [6]. In addition, much previous
work has studied dependence analysis for memory accesses, typically focusing on
references to array variables with affine subscripts (*e.g.,* [15]) and on dereferences
of pointer variables (*e.g.,* [14]). In this paper, we address the problem of data
dependence analysis for Java [2], focusing on Java's "non-traditional" language
features such as exceptions and synchronization.

As in past work , we represent the result of data dependence analysis as
a data dependence graph. We unify all dependences (due to scalars, memory
locations, exceptions, synchronization, and the memory model) as dependences
on *abstract locations*. Each register or scalar temporary is its own abstract
location, and abstract locations for memory are derived from the results of an
earlier alias analysis, such as type-based alias analysis [8]. We handle Java's
plethora of instructions that may potentially raise exceptions by (a) constructing the dependence graph over extended basic blocks, unbroken by *potentially
excepting instructions* (PEIs), (b) introducing a new kind of dependence (on an

---

* On sabbatical from the Dept. of Computer Science and Engineering,
University of Washington, Box 352350, Seattle, WA 98195-2350, USA;
chambers@cs.washington.edu.

L. Carter and J. Ferrante (Eds.): LCPC'99, LNCS 1863, pp. 35–52, 2000.
© Springer-Verlag Berlin Heidelberg 2000

"exception state" abstract location) to sequence PEIs, and (c) treating each PEI as reading all scalar/memory locations live in the exception handler for the PEI. Instructions that do not read or write any abstract locations live in the exception handler of a PEI will end up being unrelated to the PEI in the dependence graph, and thus can be moved across the PEI during scheduling. (Previous Java implementations have routinely considered PEIs as barriers to code motion for all instructions.) We also separate the tests for exception conditions (such as null-pointer and array-bounds checks) from the instructions doing the work (such as field and array load and store operations), keeping only a special "validated" dependence edge from the test instruction to the work instruction, so that they can be optimized independently and scheduled more flexibly. To ensure proper memory consistency at synchronization points, we treat each acquire-lock Java instruction (`monitorenter`) as a write of all memory abstract locations, and each release-lock Java instruction (`monitorexit`) as a read of all memory abstract locations. Overall, these dependence constraints preserve the correct semantics of Java programs, but still allow significant scheduling and code motion flexibility. We present a linear-time algorithm for constructing this dependence graph for for a single extended basic block. This algorithm has been implemented in the Jalapeño optimizing compiler, where it is used for performing instruction selection and instruction scheduling [3].

The rest of the paper is organized as follows. Section 2 provides an overview of our design decisions for modeling basic blocks and control flow due to Java exceptions. Section 3 describes the main algorithm used for data dependence analysis. Section 4 presents an example illustrating our approach to dependence analysis. Section 5 discusses related work, and section 6 contains our conclusions.

2   Modeling Basic Blocks and Control Flow due to Java Exceptions

In this section, we provide an overview of our design decisions for modeling basic blocks and control flow due to Java exceptions. A detailed description of this approach is given in [4], which describes how the Jalapeño optimizing compiler builds extended basic blocks and performs global analysis in the presence of exceptions. The focus of the work in [4] was program analysis; it did not address the problem of code motion (dependence analysis) in the presence of exceptions.

Exceptions in Java are *precise*. When an exception is thrown at a program point, (a) all effects of statements and expressions before the exception point must appear to have taken place; and (b) any effects of speculative execution of statements and expressions after the exception point should not be present in the user-visible state of the program. Our goal is to efficiently compute the most precise (least constrained) set of dependences that we can, while obeying Java's exception semantics. For checked exceptions and runtime exceptions, the Java language specification identifies all statements/operations that can potentially throw an exception. In the remainder of this paper, we use the term *PEI* (*P*otentially *E*xception-throwing *I*nstruction) to denote these state-ments/operations.

Traditionally, a basic block consists of a set of instructions that is sequen-tially executed: if the first instruction of the basic block is executed, then each subsequent instruction in the basic block will be executed in turn [11]. Thus, in the standard model of a basic block as a single-entry, single-exit region of the control flow graph, any PEI will signify the end of its basic block. Since PEIs are quite frequent in Java, the approach taken by the Jalapeño optimizing compiler is that PEIs do not force the end of a basic block. Therefore, a basic block can be a single-entry multiple-exit sequence of instructions (similar to an extended basic block [11] or a superblock), and can be significantly larger than basic blocks that must be terminated by PEIs.

Another key decision in the design of the Jalapeño optimizing compiler is to separate out the checking performed in a PEI from its actual work. For exam-ple, a `getfield` (or `putfield`) instruction is split into an explicit `null_check` instruction followed by a `load` (or `store`) instruction. `null_check` instructions are also used to guard against accessing null arrays and invoking virtual methods on null objects. Explicit instructions are generated for array-bounds and zero-divide checks, in a similar manner. The ordering relationship between the test and worker instructions is captured by having the test instruction contain a pseudo-assignment of a scalar temporary, and having the later worker instruction contain a pseudo-read of this temporary. (Strictly speaking, the temporary does not hold a boolean condition, but instead a "validated" signal. The value in the temporary is immaterial to the worker instruction; all that matters is that the test has been successfully performed.) The advantage of creating explicit test instructions is that they are eligible for redundancy elimination via global analysis, just like other instructions in the IR (Intermediate Representation).

Even if some of the tests can be performed implicitly by hardware, such as implicit null pointer tests in the Jalapeño JVM [1], there is value in modeling the tests explicitly in the IR because doing so can enable more flexibility in code motion and instruction scheduling. Additionally, virtual method invocations can be optimized (such as through static binding and inlining) without worry that a required `null_check` might be lost. To reclaim the efficiency of implicit hardware-performed checks, we include a post-pass that merges each remaining `null_check` instruction with the first following load or store instruction (when legal). After this merging, the `null_check` becomes implicit in the load or store instruction, and is accomplished by an underlying hardware mechanism.

3   Dependence Analysis

Traditionally, data dependence graphs represent dependences among register reads and writes, and memory reads and writes. A data dependence can be classified as a *true* dependence (a write to a location followed by a read of the same location), an *anti* dependence (a read of a location followed by a write of the same location), or an *output* dependence (a write of a location followed by another write of the same location) [15]. Data dependences can be easily computed for (virtual or physical) registers, because registers are explicitly named as operands of instructions. Computing data dependences for memory locations (*e.g.,* object fields and array elements) is a harder problem, and exact solutions are undecidable in general. The difficulty arises from the *aliasing* problem, where syntactically different expressions may nevertheless refer to the same memory location. In addition to pointer-induced aliases, certain reads and writes of locations must be ordered so as to obey the semantics of *exceptions*, *synchronization*, and the *memory model* in Java. Finally, exceptions themselves must be properly ordered in order to ensure that the view of program state as needed by the corresponding exception handlers is preserved.

Our approach integrates all these new kinds of dependence constraints into a single framework, based on true, anti, and output dependences. We model registers, memory locations, and even exception and synchronization states as *abstract locations*. We present a simple two-pass algorithm, given in Figure 2, that iterates over the instructions in each (extended) basic block to construct the dependence graph. The execution time and space for the algorithm is linear in the size of the basic block, *i.e.,* linear in the number of defs and uses of abstract locations across all instructions in the basic block.

The rest of this section is organized as follows. Section 3.1 summarizes the abstract locations used in our approach. Section 3.2 contains a brief description of the dependence analysis algorithm in figure 2. Sections 3.3 to 3.7 outline how the scheduling constraints of ALU instructions, memory instructions, exception-generating instructions, call instructions, and synchronization instructions are modeled using abstract locations. Section 3.8 outlines the impact of Java's memory coherence assumption on dependence analysis. Section 3.9 discusses some extensions to our basic algorithm.

3.1   Abstract Locations

As illustrated in Figure 1, we use type information to partition concrete memory locations into *abstract locations* (location types). Each abstract location represents a "may-aliased" equivalence class of concrete locations, *i.e.,* any two references to the same abstract location can potentially interfere, but two references to distinct abstract locations cannot interfere.

The following abstract locations represent different cases of global or heap-allocated data:

Fields: Each field declaration has a corresponding abstract location; all loads of that field *use* its abstract location, and stores of that field *define* its abstract location. Distinct fields have distinct abstract locations.

Array Elements: Each primitive array type (*i.e.,* `bool[]`, `short[]`, `int[]`, `long[]`, `float[]`, `double[]`, and `char[]`) has a unique abstract location modeling the concrete locations of its elements, accessed by `aload` and `astore` instructions for an array of the corresponding type. An additional

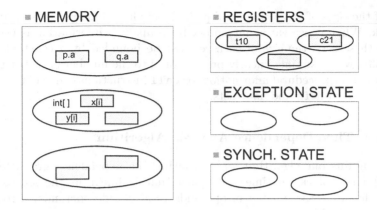

Fig. 1. Examples of abstract locations

abstract location, `Object[]`, is used to represent the locations of elements of all arrays of objects, including arrays of arrays.

This refinement of array element abstract locations based on the type of the elements of the arrays reflect a simple kind of type-based alias analysis [8]. Results of more extensive alias analysis can be incorporated as further refinements of these abstract locations, so long as the resulting abstract locations partition the underlying concrete locations.

Statics: Each static data element (including static fields) has a distinct abstract location.

In addition, there is a distinct abstract location associated with each of the following that represent method-local data:

– A symbolic register.
– A spill location, based on its constant offset in the stack frame. (This abstract location is only used when performing dependence analysis after register allocation.)
– `exception_type`, that is used to model all exception dependences. A PEI contains a pseudo-assignment of this abstract location, assigning it the class of the raised exception.

Each operand of an IR instruction accesses an underlying abstract location, as described above. In some cases, this requires creating pseudo-operands that specify defs/uses of abstract locations, even though these defs/uses are not part of the concrete semantics of the instruction. For example, a load instruction has an explicit operand that is a use of the symbolic register that contains the load address, and a pseudo-operand that represents the abstract location being accessed in global memory.

In this paper, `p.uses` will be used to denote the set of abstract locations used (*i.e.*, read) by instruction p, and `p.defs` will be used to denote the set of abstract locations defined (*i.e.*, written) by p. It is important to note that the execution time of the dependence analysis algorithm presented in section 3.2 is linear in the sum of the sizes of the p.uses and p.defs sets for all instructions, p, in the basic block. When conservative intraprocedural analysis information is used to determine these sets, the size of each set will be bounded by a constant, and the algorithm will take time linearly proportional to the number of instructions. More precise interprocedural information for call instructions can lead to larger, non-constant-sized defs and uses sets.

3.2   Linear-Time Dependence Analysis Algorithm

Figure 2 contains our algorithm for computing the dependence graph for an (extended) basic block, in time and space that is linear in the size of the block, *i.e.,* linear in the number of operands (and pseudo-operands) across all instructions in the block.

The first pass of the algorithm traverses the instructions in the block in forward order. The key idea is to associate a "last definition" value, last_def, with each abstract location used in the block. For a given abstract location, loc, loc.last_def is initialized to NULL. As this pass proceeds, loc.last_def is set to the most recent definition operand that performs a write on abstract location loc. In general, when a use u is encountered with loc = u.location such that loc.last_def ≠ NULL, a flow dependence edge is created from loc.last_def .instruction to u.instruction. As with all dependence edges created by this algorithm, this edge may represent a register, memory, or exception dependence, depending on the underlying abstract location. Similarly, when a def d is encountered with loc = d.location such that loc.last_def ≠ NULL, an output dependence edge is created from loc.last_def.instruction to d.instruction. In addition, loc.last_def is updated to d.

The second pass of the algorithm traverses the instructions in the reverse order. All last_def values are reinitialized to NULL. As this pass proceeds, loc.last_def is set to the most recent definition operand (in a backwards traversal) that performs a write on abstract location loc. When a use u is encountered such that u.location.last_def ≠ NULL, an anti dependence edge is created from u.instruction to u.location.last_def.instruction.

The use of a single last_def value for each abstract location guarantees the linear-sized time and space complexity for this algorithm. Consider the following IR fragment as an example:

```
s1:     putfield a.x := t1
s2:     putfield b.x := t2
s3:     t3 := getfield c.x
```

All three instructions access the same abstract location (field x). Therefore, our algorithm will only insert an output dependence edge from s1 to s2 and a flow dependence edge from s2 to s3.

In contrast, traditional dependence analysis algorithms (*e.g.,* [15]) will also insert a flow dependence edge from s1 to s3 (assuming that object references a, b, c can potentially be aliased). In general, there can be quadratic number

```
Dependence_Graph_Construction(BasicBlock bb) {

    foreach abstract location loc in bb.locations do
        loc.last_def := NULL      // clear last defs
    end for

    for each instruction p in bb.instructions in forward order do
        let pnode := dependence graph node corresponding to instruction p

        // Abstract location determines if register/memory/exception dependence
        for each use operand u in p.uses do
            let loc := u.location
            if loc.last_def != NULL then
                create TRUE dependence edge from loc.last_def.instruction to pnode
            endif
        end for

        for each def operand d in p.defs do
            let loc := d.location
            if loc.last_def != NULL then
                create OUTPUT dependence edge from loc.last_def.instruction to pnode
            endif
            loc.last_def := d  // record last def
        end
    end

    foreach loc in bb.locations do
        loc.last_def := NULL  // clear last defs
    end

    for each instruction p in bb.instructions in backward order do
        let pnode := dependence graph node corresponding to instruction p
        // record last def
        foreach def operand d in p.defs do
            let loc := d.location
            loc.last_def := d
        end

        // create anti dependence edges
        foreach use operand u in p.uses do
            let loc := u.location
            if loc.last_def != NULL then
                create ANTI dependence edge from pnode to loc.last_def.instruction
            endif
        end
    end
}
```

Fig. 2. Algorithm to compute dependence graph of an extended basic block

of extra edges created by using traditional dependence analysis algorithms. Our algorithm avoids creating such transitively implied edges by ensuring that each use or def is the target of at most one edge in the dependence graph.

3.3   ALU Instructions

Simple arithmetic instructions have some number of register operands and some number (typically one) of register destinations. Each register is modeled in our system by a unique abstract location, distinct from any other abstract location, representing the fact that a register is not aliased with any other register or memory location. Given this definition of abstract locations, our algorithm will construct data dependence edges for registers.

3.4   Memory Instructions

Memory instructions have abstract locations that represent the global data being accessed. A load instruction has a use pseudo-operand that reads the abstract location representing the area of memory possibly read by the load, while a store instruction has a def pseudo-operand that writes to the abstract location representing the area of memory possibly written by the store.

The appropriate abstract locations for memory pseudo-operands are determined by an alias analysis preceding dependence graph construction. Alias analysis is a rich research area, but fortunately it is separable from the dependence graph construction problem. Our dependence graph construction algorithm only assumes that the results of alias analysis can be expressed as a partitioning of concrete locations, as discussed in section 3.1.

3.5   Exception Instructions

A conservative approach to dependence analysis of exception instructions would simply prevent any write operation (including updates to scalar local variables) from moving above or below a PEI. However, this would greatly limit opportunities for scheduling, and largely defeat the purpose of scheduling across PEIs.

Given a PEI p, our approach is to include in p.uses abstract locations for all variables and memory locations live at the entry of the exception handler to which the exception would be routed. Then, write operations that do not modify an abstract location in p.uses can be free to move across the PEI p. Live variable analysis can compute the set of local variables that are live on entry to each handler (all global and heap-allocated data would normally be considered to be live, by default).

In addition, we include in p.defs the exception_type abstract location. This ensures that PEIs are contrained to be executed in order via the output dependences between them generated by the defs of exception_type.

3.6   Call Instructions

The explicit operands of a call instruction identify the call's arguments and result. In addition, pseudo-operands are introduced to represent abstract memory locations possibly read and/or written by the callee(s). In the absence of interprocedural analysis information, a `call` instruction is assumed to define all abstract locations that represent memory locations (*i.e.,* all fields, arrays, and static data). More precise sets of abstract locations could result from interprocedural use and side-effect analysis.

In addition, for calls that can raise exceptions, the rules for PEIs described in section 3.5 should be followed.

3.7   Synchronization Instructions

The `monitorenter` and `monitorexit` synchronization instructions define a critical section. Java's memory model defines the effect of these instructions on memory locations from the point of view of a particular thread as follows: at a `monitorenter` instruction, the thread updates its local view of memory based on the "true" or global view, and at a `monitorexit` instruction, the thread flushes its local view of memory back to the global view.

To construct a safe dependence graph, we expand a `monitorenter` instruction into a `lock` operation and an `update` operation, and a `monitorexit` instruction into a `publish` operation and an `unlock` operation, as shown in the example in Figure 3. A single abstract location S (representing the global synchronization state) is used to serialize all `lock`/`unlock` instuctions within a thread (by treating each of them as a def of S). The memory model semantics is captured by treating the `update` operation as a write of all abstract locations (more precisely, all locations that can be written by another thread), and the `publish` operation as a read of all abstract locations (more precisely, all locations that can be read by another thread). Finally, an abstract location for the synchronized object (*lock1* in Figure 3) is used to ensure that all memory read/write operations remain within their original critical section (by treating `lock` and `unlock` as defs of *lock1*, and memory operations in the critical section as uses of *lock1*).

Note that instructions that access only scalars can be moved freely across synchronization instructions *e.g.,* see the defs of scalars a and b in Figure 3. A memory read operation (*e.g.,* the read of r.z in Figure 3) can be moved above a `monitorexit` if so desired (but not above a `monitorenter`); further, because of the presence of the *lock1* abstract location, the code motion can be reversed by moving the memory read back below the `monitorenter` without exhibiting the anomaly described in [13]. Finally, the expansion of the `monitorenter` and `monitorexit` instructions enables synchronization elimination to be performed by removing the `lock`/`unlock` operations, while still retaining the memory model requirements that are captured by the `update` and `publish` operations.

```
        a = ...
    S, lock1 = monitorenter
        ... = p.x <lock1>
        q.y = ... <lock1>
          b =
    S, lock1 = monitorexit
        ... = r.z
```

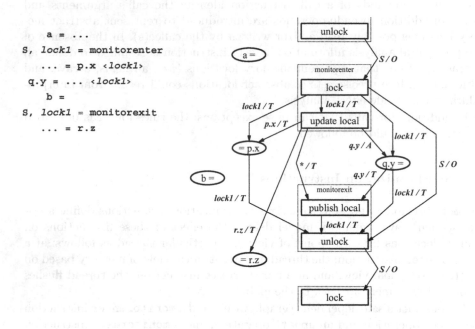

Fig. 3. Example of modeling dependences due to monitorenter and monitorexit

3.8   Memory Coherence

The Java memory model enforces a strict memory coherence semantics for all accesses to the same (concrete) location, even when not guarded by synchronization instructions. It has been observed that reordering of potentially aliased load instructions can be an illegal transformation for multithreaded programs written for a memory model that includes the strict memory coherence assumption [10, 13]. For example, consider the following code fragment:

```
getfield p.x
getfield q.x
```

Suppose p and q may be aliased. While one thread (T1) executes the above code fragment, another thread (T2) can execute multiple putfield p.x instructions. The Java memory model requires that, if p and q point to the same object in memory, then thread T1 should not see the values written by thread T2 out of order. Since the compiler must conservatively assume the possible existence of a thread like T2, it would be illegal for the compiler to reorder the above getfield instructions. Therefore, under this strict memory coherence model, the dependence graph must contain an edge from the first getfield instruction to the next, so as to prevent this reordering.

Unfortunately, adding read dependences between all possibly aliased loads can significantly constrain opportunities for instruction reordering. As an alternative to the default, strict memory coherence model, the Jalapeño optimizing compiler allows users to select a *weak consistency model* that does not require memory coherence *e.g.,* Location Consistency (LC) [9]. This memory model guarantees that properly synchronized programs will have the same execution semantics as in the default model, without imposing additional constraints on the dependence graph. Recently, there has been a proposal for a new memory model for Java [12] that is based on the LC model.

3.9   Extensions

The dependence analysis algorithm described in this section takes linear time because of the use of a single `last_def` value for each abstract location. This algorithmic property relies on the fact that abstract locations do not overlap. Requiring abstract locations to be disjoint can limit the precision and expressiveness of more sophisticated alias analyses. Our algorithm can be extended to handle abstract locations that form a lattice of possibly overlapping regions, but the worst-case time complexity of the algorithm may degrade to quadratic time (although a factored representation of the resulting dependence graph can still require only a linear amount of space).

PEIs, calls, and synchronization instructions may all be considered to read and/or write all global memory abstract locations. Representing all these abstract memory locations explicitly would greatly increase the size of the basic block and the resulting dependence graph. To reduce the number of such abstract memory locations, only those abstract memory locations referenced explicitly by some load or store instruction in the same (extended) basic block need to be included explicitly; all other abstract memory locations can be summarized by a single "rest of memory" abstract location (this extra abstract location is only needed in basic blocks that contain no explicit loads or stores, but do contain synchronization instructions and/or calls). The resulting abstract locations still form a partition of the set of concrete locations accessed by that block.

Currently, PEIs are considered to write to the special `exception_type` abstract location, ensuring that PEIs are serialized. However, two PEIs with the same exception handler can be *indistinguishable* from the perspective of the exception handler, if (a) both PEIs raise the same kind of exception (*e.g.,* both are null-pointer tests or both are array-bounds checks) or if the handler always handles whatever exceptions both PEIs raise and the handler otherwise ignores the exception object it is passed, (b) both report the exception at the same place in the program as determined by the resolution of the Java implementation's `getStackTrace` debugging native method, and (c) both have the same dependence constraints on the set of abstract locations live in the handler. Indistinguishable PEI instructions can be freely reordered, up to any other dependence constraints on their operands. This reordering ability can be implemented by extending our algorithm to track the *value* assigned to the special `exception_type` abstract location, where this value reflects the kind of exception raised by the PEI (if the handler cares) and the debugging location information for the PEI. Then a PEI's assignment to the exception_type abstract location leads to an output dependence with the location's last_def PEI only if they assign different values to the location. Otherwise the new PEI is inserted in the dependence graph "in parallel" with the previous PEI, forming a kind of equivalence class in the dependence graph of PEIs that are indistinguishable. A straightforward implementation of this idea would lead to a quadratic-time and - space algorithm, but a more sophisticated algorithm exists, based on maintaining a factored representation of the dependence graph, that has only linear time and space complexity.

4   Example

Java source program:

```
public class LCPC {
    int f1, f2;
    static void foo(int[] x, int i, LCPC b, int q) {
        if (q != 0)
            x[i] = ((b.f1 = x[i]) + b.f2 + i/q);
    }
}
```

Fig. 4. An example Java program

In this section, we use a simple example to illustrate the key aspects of our approach to computing data dependences in a Java program, and how this algorithm fits into the rest of the compiler framework. Consider method foo() in the Java program shown in Figure 4. In the remainder of this section, we will focus our attention on the main basic block for the q != 0 case in method foo(). Figure 5 shows the (unoptimized) HIR (high-level IR) for this basic block[1]. The "PEI" annotation is used to identify exception-generating instructions.

Note that all exception tests are explicit in Figure 5. For example, the load of x[i] in Figure 4 is translated into three HIR instructions — null_check, bounds_check, and int_aload. If an exception test fails, then control is transferred from the exception test instruction to a runtime routine in JVM; this runtime routine examines the exception table (not shown in the IR figures) to determine how the exception should be handled (either by transferring to a handler block or exiting from the method). If an exception test succeeds, the instruction(s) dependent on the exception test can be enabled for execution.

---

[1] As described in [3], the HIR is actually generated from the bytecodes for method foo(), and not from the Java source code.

```
Bytecode
Offset       Operator          Operands
------       --------          --------
  4          LABEL1            B1@4
  9    PEI   null_check        c21 = a0
  9    PEI   bounds_check      c22 = a0, a1, c21
  9          int_aload         t4 = @{ a0, a1 }, [c21,c22]
 11    PEI   null_check        c23 = a2
 11          putfield          a2, t4, <LCPC.f1>, c23
 15    PEI   null_check        c24 = a2          . .        (*)
 15          getfield          t5 = a2, <LCPC.f2>, c24   . . --> c23
 18          int_add           t6 = t4, t5
 21    PEI   int_zero_check    c25 = a3          . .        (*)
 21          int_div           t7 = a1, a3, c25  . . --> none
 22          int_add           t8 = t6, t7
 23    PEI   null_check        c26 = a0          . .        (*)
 23    PEI   bounds_check      c27 = a0, a1, c26 . .        (*)
 23          int_astore        t8, @{ a0, a1 }, [c26,c27] . . --> [c21,c22]
             END_BBLOCK        B1@4
```

Fig. 5. HIR generated from bytecode for basic block 1 (bytecodes 4 ... 23) in method foo(). a0 ... a3 are the method arguments. t4 ...t7 are temporaries. c21 ... c27 are condition registers. Lines marked with (*) are removed by subsequent optimizations, and condition codes are replaced by the ones following the arrows.

```
Bytecode                                             Issue   Dependence
Offset       Operator      Operands                  Time    Graph Node
------       --------      --------                   -----   ----------
  4          LABEL1        B1@4
  9    PEI   null_check    c21 = a0                     0        (1)
  9          ppc_lwz       t10 = @{ -4, a0 }, c21       0        (2)
  9    PEI   ppc_tw        c22 = ppc_trap <=U, t10, a1  2        (3)
  9          ppc_slwi      t11 = a1, 2                  2        (4)
  9          ppc_lwzx      t4 = @{ a0, t11 }, [c21,c22] 3        (5)
 11    PEI   null_check    c23 = a2                     5        (6)
 11          ppc_stw       t4, @{ -16, a2 }, c23        5        (7)
 15          ppc_lwz       t5 = @{ -20, a2 }, c23       6        (8)
 18          ppc_add       t6 = t4, t5                  8        (9)
 21          ppc_divw      t7 = a1, a3                  9        (10)
 22          ppc_add       t8 = t6, t7                 29        (11)
 23          ppc_stwx      t8, @{ a0, t11 }, [c21,c22] 30        (12)
             END_BBLOCK    B1@4
--------------------------------------------------------------------------
Completion time:                                              34 cycles
```

Fig. 6. MIR generated for basic block 1 in method foo(). c21 ... c23 are condition registers. Issue times assume no out-of-order execution.

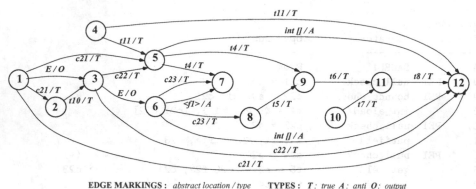

EDGE MARKINGS : *abstract location / type*   **TYPES :** *T : true A : anti O : output*

ABSTRACT LOCATIONS :
   scalars :   *t4, t5, t6, t7, t8, t10, t11*
   exceptions :   *E*
   fields :   *<f1>*
   arrays :   *int []*

Fig. 7. Dependence graph of basic block 1 in method `foo()`

To make explicit the connection between an exception test and the instructions that it guards in our IR, an exception test is assumed to compute a "condition register" temporary as a result. Each instruction that depends on the success of the exception test takes the condition register as an extra input operand. These condition registers do not appear in the final machine code, but their presence in the IR ensures that IR optimizations will not cause a guarded instruction to be executed prior to its exception test. For example, condition register `c23` in figure 5 captures the result of a null-pointer check for argument `a2` (*viz.*, object reference `b`). `c23` is then used as an input operand by the `putfield` instruction. For future work, we are exploring the possibility of allowing a guard instruction for an arithmetic exception (*e.g.*, the `zero_check` guard for a divide-by-zero exception) to be performed after its corresponding compute instruction. These possibilities are processor-specific and can be expressed in the IR by removing the condition register from the IR instructions when the test instruction need not precede the compute instructions.

Redundant check elimination is performed during global optimizations on the HIR [3]. All exception test instructions in figure 5 that are marked (*) are redundant and can be removed. The instructions marked `-->` are then modified to use condition registers from equivalent exception tests. Note that the number of PEIs has been reduced from seven to three in figure 5 after optimization. This is one of the key benefits of making exception tests explicit in our IR. After elimination of redundant tests, we are left with one `null_check` for each of `x` and `b`, and one `bounds_check` for `x`. Note that the `zero_check` instruction for the divide instruction was eliminated because of the `q != 0` test in method `foo()`. Further optimization of the remaining tests might be possible with knowledge of interprocedural calling context information for method `foo()`.

As described in [3], the optimized HIR in figure 5 is next converted to LIR (lower-level IR). High-level operations such as `aload`, `astore`, `getfield`, `putfield` are expanded into multiple low-level operations that are closer to machine code. After LIR optimizations are performed, the LIR is translated to MIR (machine-level IR) by performing instruction selection; the resulting MIR is shown in figure 6. MIR instructions belong to the target instruction set architecture (in this case, the PowerPC) with two minor extensions. First, `null_check` instructions are allowed to be present in the MIR because their presence gives greater flexibility for instruction scheduling. (After scheduling, the `null_check` instructions will be merged with load/store instructions when possible, so as to be performed implicitly[2].) Second, the condition register operands are included in the MIR instructions so as to enable precise dependence analysis for instruction scheduling. (The condition registers will be discarded prior to generation of machine code.)

Next, our dependence graph algorithm is applied to construct the dependence graph over MIR instructions. Figure 7 shows the resulting data dependence graph for the extended basic block from figure 6.

Bytecode Offset		Operator	Operands	Issue Time
4		LABEL1	B1@4	
9	PEI	null_check	c21 = a0	0
9		ppc_lwz	t10 = @{ -4, a0 }, c21	0
9		ppc_slwi	t11 = a1, 2	0
21		ppc_divw	t7 = a1, a3	0
9	PEI	ppc_tw	c22 = ppc_trap <=U, t10, a1	2
11	PEI	null_check	c23 = a2	2
15		ppc_lwz	t5 = @{ -20, a2 }, c23	2
9		ppc_lwzx	t4 = @{ a0, t11 }, [c21,c22]	3
11		ppc_stw	t4, @{ -16, a2 }, c23	5
18		ppc_add	t6 = t4, t5	5
22		ppc_add	t8 = t6, t7	20
23		ppc_stwx	t8, @{ a0, t11 }, [c21,c22]	21
		END_BBLOCK	B1@4	

Completion time:	25 cycles

Fig. 8. MIR generated after instruction scheduling for basic block 1 in method `foo()`. This schedule assumes that the order of exception-generating instructions must be preserved. Issue times assume no out-of-order execution.

---

[2] Jalapeño uses a layout where an object's fields and an array's length are stored at negative offsets from the object's reference [1], to support hardware null checking on the PowerPC architecture where low memory (including address 0) is not page-protected but high memory is.

```
Bytecode
Offset        Operator           Operands
------        --------           --------
  6           LABEL1             B1@4
  9     PEI   ppc_lwz            t10 = @{ -4, a0 }
  9           ppc_slwi           t11 = a1, 2
 21           ppc_divw           t7 = a1, a3
  9     PEI   ppc_tw             ppc_trap <=U, t10, a1
 15     PEI   ppc_lwz            t5 = @{ -20, a2 }
  9           ppc_lwzx           t4 = @{ a0, t11 }
 11           ppc_stw            t4, @{ -16, a2 }
 18           ppc_add            t6 = t4, t5
 22           ppc_add            t8 = t6, t7
 23           ppc_stwx           t8, @{ a0, t11 }
              END_BBLOCK         B1@4
```

Fig. 9. Final MIR after merging null_check instructions in figure 8.

Next, instruction scheduling is applied to the dependence graph over MIR instructions. Figure 8 shows the new sequence of target instructions obtained when applying a simple list scheduling algorithm to the dependence graph from figure 7. The use of explicit exception tests enables more reordering to be performed than would otherwise have been possible. For example, since b.f2 is used as an input to a (time-consuming) divide operation, it is beneficial to move the load of this field as early as possible. As shown in figure 8, the divide instruction and the load of b.f2 (at stack offset -20) are both moved prior to the load of x[i] and the store of b.f1. This reordering would not have been possible if exception tests were not modeled explicitly in the IR. To appreciate the impact of instruction scheduling for this example, note that the completion time for the basic block was reduced from 34 cycles (when using the instruction ordering in figure 6) to 25 cycles (when using the new ordering in figure 8). (Completion times were estimated assuming that the processor does not perform any out-of-order execution of instructions.)

Finally, figure 9 contains the MIR obtained after merging each null_check instruction with the first following load or store instruction that uses its condition register result. In this example, the two null_check instructions have been successfully merged with load instructions. Note that the load instructions (ppc_lwz) are now marked as PEIs. No update is required to the exception handler tables when this merging is performed because the handler blocks are identical for all PEIs that belong to the same basic block.

5   Related Work

Dependence analysis for scalar variables has been well understood for a long time; for example, def-use chaining [11] was an early technique for identifying true dependences within and across basic blocks. The same principle has also been used to compute anti and output dependences for scalar variables. Scalar

renaming [5] is an effective technique for eliminating anti and output dependences, and SSA form is a popular approach to obtain a canonical renaming of
scalars [6].

The bulk of past research on dependence analysis for memory accesses has
focused on array variables with affine subscripts and on pointer dereferences. The
advent of vectorizing and parallelizing compilers led to several data dependence
analysis techniques being developed for array accesses with affine subscript
expressions (e.g., [15]); this is a special case that is important for optimization
of scientific programs written in Fortran and C. A lot of attention has also been
paid to "points-to" alias analysis of pointer variables, with the goal of improving
the effectiveness of compiler optimizations of pointer-intensive programs written
in C and C++. Points-to analysis of general C and C++ programs is a hard
problem and the experience thus far has been that most algorithms for points-to
analysis consume excessive amounts of time and space (the algorithm in [14] is a
notable exception). More recently, it has been observed [8] that type-based alias
information can be used to obtain simple and effective dependence analysis of
object references in statically-typed OO languages such as Modula-3 and Java.
Finally, [13] has identified restrictions due to Java's memory model that must
be imposed on compiler optimizations for multithreaded Java programs.

This paper addresses the problem of data dependence analysis for Java in
the presence of Java's "non-traditional" language features such as exceptions,
synchronization, and memory consistency. The "abstract locations" introduced
in section 3 can be viewed as an generalization of type-based alias analysis to also
deal with exceptions. Most previous compilers for object-oriented languages (e.g.,
[7]) modeled exceptions as branch instructions that terminate basic blocks, and
hence did not have to deal with dependence analysis for exceptions. In contrast,
our compiler builds extended basic blocks that can include multiple PEIs within
the same basic block.

6   Conclusions and Future Work

In this paper, we addressed the problem of data dependence analysis for Java
in the presence of features such as exceptions, synchronization, and memory
consistency. We introduced dependences on new classes of abstract locations
to model code motion constraints arising from these language features. We
presented a linear-time algorithm for constructing this augmented dependence
graph for an extended basic block (using type-based alias analysis for Java). As
motivation for dependence analysis, we discussed two phases of the Jalapeño
dynamic optimizing compiler, instruction selection and instruction scheduling,
that use the data dependence graph. An interesting direction for future work
is to use the dependence rules for abstract locations presented in this paper to
enable code motion transformaction across regions that are larger than a single
extended basic block.

References

1. B. Alpern, A. Cocchi, D. Lieber, M. Mergen, and V. Sarkar. Jalapeño — a Compiler-Supported Java Virtual Machine for Servers. In *ACM SIGPLAN 1999 Workshop on Compiler Support for System Software (WCSSS'99)*, May 1999. Also available as INRIA report No. 0228, March 1999.

2. K. Arnold and J. Gosling. *The Java Programming Language*. Addison-Wesley, 1996.

3. M. G. Burke, J.-D. Choi, S. Fink, D. Grove, M. Hind, V. Sarkar, M. J. Serrano, V. C. Sreedhar, H. Srinivasan, and J. Whaley. The Jalapeño Dynamic Optimizing Compiler for Java. In *ACM Java Grande Conference*, June 1999.

4. J.-D. Choi, D. Grove, M. Hind, and V. Sarkar. Efficient and precise modeling of exceptions for the analysis of Java programs. In *Proc. of the ACM SIGPLAN-SIGSOFT Workshop on Program Analysis for Software Tools and Engineering*, Toulouse, France, Sept. 1999.

5. R. Cytron and J. Ferrante. What's in a Name? Or the Value of Renaming for Parallelism Detection and Storage Allocation. *Proceedings of the 1987 International Conference on Parallel Processing*, pages 19–27, August 1987.

6. R. Cytron, J. Ferrante, B. K. Rosen, M. N. Wegman, and F. K. Zadeck. Efficiently Computing Static Single Assignment Form and the Control Dependence Graph. *ACM Transactions on Programming Languages and Systems*, 13(4):451–490, October 1991.

7. J. Dean, G. DeFouw, D. Grove, V. Litvinov, and C. Chambers. Vortex: An optimizing compiler for object-oriented languages. In *ACM SIGPLAN Conference on Object-Oriented Programming Systems, Languages and Applications (OOPSLA)*, San Jose, CA, Oct. 1996.

8. A. Diwan, K. S. McKinley, and J. E. B. Moss. Type-based alias analysis. In *SIGPLAN '98 Conference on Programming Language Design and Implementation*, pages 106–117, May 1998.

9. G. R. Gao and V. Sarkar. Location Consistency: Stepping Beyond the Memory Coherence Barrier. *International Conference on Parallel Processing*, August 1995.

10. G. R. Gao and V. Sarkar. On the Importance of an End-To-End View of Memory Consistency in Future Computer Systems. *Proceedings of the 1997 International Symposium on High Performance Computing, Fukuoka, Japan*, November 1997.

11. S. S. Muchnick. *Advanced Compiler Design & Implementation*. Morgan Kaufmann Publishers, Inc., San Francisco, California, 1997.

12. W. Pugh. A new memory model for Java. Note sent to the JavaMemoryModel mailing list, http://www.cs.umd.edu/ pugh/java/memoryModel, October 22, 1999.

13. W. Pugh. Fixing the Java Memory Model. In *ACM Java Grande Conference*, June 1999.

14. B. Steensgaard. Points-to analysis in almost linear time. In *23rd Annual ACM SIGACT-SIGPLAN Symposium on the Principles of Programming Languages*, pages 32–41, Jan. 1996.

15. M. J. Wolfe. *Optimizing Supercompilers for Supercomputers*. Pitman, London and The MIT Press, Cambridge, Massachusetts, 1989. In the series, Research Monographs in Parallel and Distributed Computing.

Comprehensive Redundant Load Elimination
for the IA-64 Architecture

Youngfeng Wu and Yong-fong Lee

Intel Corporation
2200 Mission College Blvd
Santa Clara, CA 95052-8119
(youfeng.wu@intel.com)
(you-fong.lee@intel.com)

Abstract. . For IA-64 architecture, a compiler can aggressively utilize control and data speculation to increase instruction-level parallelism. Aggressive speculation normally generates many speculative (control-speculative) and advanced (data-speculative) loads with the same addresses. Traditional redundant load elimination handles only regular loads. It cannot be straightforwardly applied to removing speculative and advanced loads. In this paper, we present a framework for comprehensive redundant load elimination, which correctly handles all six types of the following loads: regular loads, advanced loads, check loads, check advanced loads, speculative loads, and speculative advanced loads. Our preliminary experimental results demonstrate that it is important to perform comprehensive redundant load elimination in a compiler for architectures supporting control and data speculation.

1. Introduction

For IA-64 architecture, a compiler can aggressively utilize control and data speculation to increase instruction-level parallelism [1, 3, 4]. Control speculation allows instructions to be executed speculatively by ignoring control dependence. Data speculation allows loads to be executed speculatively before aliased stores (i.e., by ignoring data dependence). Hardware mechanisms are provided for program execution to "recover" from incorrect speculation.

Aggressive speculation normally generates many *speculative* (control-speculative) and *advanced* (data-speculative) loads with the same addresses. Traditional redundant load elimination handles only regular loads [2]. When a regular load is detected to be redundant, it can simply be removed (or replaced by a register move instruction if necessary). This is not the case when there are speculative loads and, in particular, advanced loads that are found to be redundant. If the traditional technique is straightforwardly applied to removing speculative and advanced loads, a program executable may become incorrect and/or less efficient.

In this paper, we present a framework for *comprehensive redundant load elimination* to remove redundant loads that mainly result from control and data speculation. Our approach is global and performed over the control flow graph of a function. Even

L. Carter and J. Ferrante (Eds.): LCPC'99, LNCS 1863, pp. 53–69, 2000.

when speculative and advanced loads do not lie on critical paths of program execution, their presence can make redundant regular loads that are on critical paths. In addition, removing redundant loads of any type can help reduce resource requirements and, potentially, memory traffic. All these are beneficial to improving program execution. Later in the paper, we give some preliminary experimental results to demonstrate the importance of performing comprehensive redundant load elimination in the presence of speculation.

The rest of the paper is organized as follows. In Section 2, we define various types of loads under consideration and give a redundant load example due to data speculation. Section 3 describes the framework for comprehensive redundant load elimination. Section 4 provides more details about three cases of comprehensive redundant load elimination. Section 5 presents preliminary experimental results, and Section 6 gives concluding remarks.

2. Preliminaries

In this section, we define control speculation, data speculation, and six types of loads handled by our framework. A real example from the SPEC95 integer benchmark *ijpeg* is shown to illustrate how speculation generates additional redundancy of load operations.

2.1 Control Speculation

When a load operation is guarded by a condition, it may be unsafe to execute it unconditionally. Control speculation converts the conditional load into a *speculative load* (spec_load) which defers exceptions that may be caused by the load and, in addition, places a speculative check (spec_check) operation to detect the deferred exceptions. The speculative load then can be executed unconditionally. When it generates an exception, the exception is deferred and is encoded in the destination register. (The destination register can be used in other exception deferring operations.) The speculative check operation stays at the original location, and when it detects the deferred exception, the exception will then be handled. The spec_check operation takes as the argument a register that may contain the deferred exception information, and a label representing the location of the exceptional handling code (the label is omitted for simplicity in the paper).

Example. In Figure 1, the conditional load is converted into a speculative load followed by a speculative check operation. The speculative load is executed unconditionally.

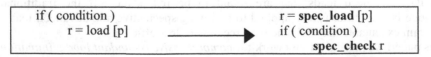

Figure 1. Control speculation example

2.2 Data Speculation

Data speculation allows for speculatively executing a load before aliased stores. The original load is replaced by both an *advanced load* (adv_load) and a *check load* (check_load). The advanced load can be moved before the potentially aliased stores. When the advanced load is executed, its load address is placed in a hardware structure called ALAT (Advanced Load Address Table, similar to the memory conflict buffer in [1]). Whenever a store is executed, its address is checked against the load addresses in ALAT. The matching entries in ALAT are invalidated. The check load stays at the original location of the load and acts like a conditional load. It checks weather the speculatively executed load is still valid. If not, the check load reloads the value.

The check load uses the destination register and the load address to match the corresponding advanced load. So the advanced load and the check load must have the same destination register name. In Figure 2, the transformation of data speculation moves a load before an aliased store.

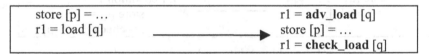

Figure 2. Data speculation example

Another flavor of check load operation is a *check advanced load* (check_adv_load). A check advanced load is the same as a check load except that its reloading of the value is performed as an advanced load (this is useful for speculating a load out of a loop).

A more aggressive data speculation allows for additionally moving the operations depending on the speculatively executed load before stores. In this case, a conditional load is not sufficient for program execution to recover from invalidated load speculation. Instead, an *advanced load check* (adv_load_check) is used, which by itself does not load any value. If the speculatively executed load is invalidated, the advanced load check operation transfers control to recovery code, and there the load and all the necessary dependent operations will be performed. Figure 3 shows an example of data speculating a load with its uses.

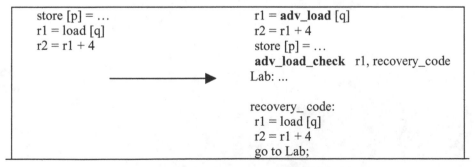

Figure 3. Data speculation of a load and its uses

2.3 Combined Control and Data Speculation

We can further speculate an advanced load by control speculation or speculate a speculative load by data speculation. The result is a *speculative advanced load* (spec_adv_load). A speculative advanced load is defined such that if the load generates a deferred exception, a special invalidation is passed to its corresponding check load. Thus a check load (or adv_load_check) operation is sufficient to detect both load invalidation and deferred exception. Note that the check load (or adv_load_check) can re-generate the exception by repeating the load so there is no need to defer the exception identity from the speculative advanced load to the check load (or adv_load_check).

In Figure 4, the conditional load is converted into a speculative advanced load followed by a check load operation. The speculative advanced load is executed unconditionally and before an aliased store.

if (condition)
    store [q] = ...
    r = load [p]
	r = **spec_adv_load** [p]
	if (condition)
	    store [q] = ...
	    r = **check_load** [p]

Figure 4. Combined data and control speculation

2.4 Six Types of Load Operations

Figure 5 summarizes load operations that are handled by our comprehensive redundant load elimination. Among them, four types of loads—regular loads, advanced loads, speculative loads, and speculative advanced loads—always access the memory. The other two types of loads—check loads and check advanced loads—may not access the memory when their corresponding advanced loads are still valid. When there is a choice, we attempt to remove the former types of loads before trying to remove the latter types of loads.

Names	Syntax	IA-64 mnemonic	Semantics
Regular load	r = load [address]	ld	Load the value at address to r.
Advanced load	r = adv_load [address]	ld.a	Load the value at address to r and enter anALAT entry.
Check load	r = check_load [address]	ld.c.clr	Check the ALAT entry.If the entry is invalidated, perform a regular load.
Check advanced load	r = check_adv_load [address]	ld.c.nc	Check the ALAT entry. If the entry is invalidated, perform an advanced load
Speculative load	r= spec_load [address]	ld.s	Load the value at address to r. If an Exception occurs, defer it by propagatingits identity in register r.
Speculative advanced load	r = spec_adv_load [address]	ld.sa	Same as advanced load, except that when an exception occurs, it will not allocate an ALAT entry.

Figure 5. Six types of loads under consideration

2.5 A Real Example

Figure 6 shows the innermost loop of a 5-level nested loop from function *compress_output* in the SPEC95 *ijpeg* benchmark.

```
for (xindex = 0; xindex < compptr->MCU_width; xindex++)
    coef->MCU_buffer[blkn++] = buffer_ptr++;
```

Figure 6. Example C code from ijpeg benchmark

Figure 7(a) shows its low-level code.   The loads for compptr->MCU_width and coef->MCU_buffer are potentially aliased to the store to coef->MCU_buffer[blkn++].   But the chance for them to access the same memory locations is very small. We want to speculatively move them out of the loop. Figure 7(b) is the code after speculative load motion. For simplicity, we assume that both MCU_width and MCU_buffer have offsets 0 into the structures where they are defined. Figure 7(c) shows the dependence graph of the loop body. Also assume a 3-cycle latency for loads and a 1-cycle latency for arithmetic operations. Then the critical path is r1->r2->store->cmp->jless, which has a total latency of 5 cycles. After the load of r1 is moved out of the loop, the path length becomes 2 (0 cycle for check_adv_load assumed), and the path r3->cmp->jless becomes the critical path (length 4). After the load of r3 is moved out of the loop, the critical path length of the loop body becomes 2. The speedup from the data speculation is 2.5 in this case.

After the data speculation, there are three loads before entering the loop and there is redundancy. Notice that there is a four-level outer loop enclosing the code segment, so removing the redundancy before the loop can significantly improve performance. We copy the code including the three loads into Figure 8 and add line numbers for ease of reference.

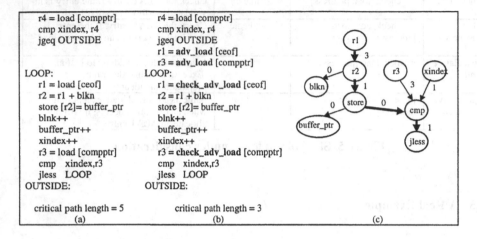

```
r4 = load [compptr]              r4 = load [compptr]
cmp xindex, r4                   cmp xindex, r4
jgeq OUTSIDE                     jgeq OUTSIDE
                                 r1 = adv_load [ceof]
                                 r3 = adv_load [compptr]

LOOP:                            LOOP:
   r1 = load [ceof]                 r1 = check_adv_load [ceof]
   r2 = r1 + blkn                   r2 = r1 + blkn
   store [r2]= buffer_ptr           store [r2]= buffer_ptr
   blnk++                           blnk++
   buffer_ptr++                     buffer_ptr++
   xindex++                         xindex++
   r3 = load [compptr]              r3 = check_adv_load [compptr]
   cmp  xindex,r3                   cmp  xindex,r3
   jless  LOOP                      jless  LOOP
OUTSIDE:                         OUTSIDE:

critical path length = 5         critical path length = 3
        (a)                              (b)                                   (c)
```

Figure 7. Low-level code for example

```
L1:      r4 = load [compptr]
L2:      cmp xindex, r4
L3:      jgeq OUTSIDE
L4:      r1 = adv_load [ceof]
L5:      r3 = adv_load [compptr]
```

Figure 8. Code sequence with redundant loads due to speculation

The first load (to r4) accesses the same memory location as the load at L5, and there is no store between them. Traditional redundant load elimination might suggest that we remove the load at L5. However, doing so could severely degrade program performance since the check advanced load corresponding to the advanced load is inside a loop. Without the advanced load, the check advanced load will miss the ALAT and redo a load, since there is no corresponding entry in the ALAT (for the advanced load is assumed invalidated in this case). Also, we must not attempt to resolve the performance problem by removing the check advanced load. Otherwise, the value loaded outside the loop may be invalidated by an aliased store, and there is no check advanced load to correct the value. Later we will show that for this example, the correct way to remove the redundancy is to remove the first load and move the adv_load earlier in its place.

The significance of removing redundant loads from speculation is also observed in the SPEC95 *go* benchmark. The frequently executed routine *addlist* contains a tree type control flow graph with many leaves. The global scheduler speculatively moves many loads from leaf blocks to two blocks near the function entry. Many of the loads in the two blocks are redundant. By removing these redundant loads, the performance of this function can be greatly improved.

3. Comprehensive Redundant Load Elimination

Comprehensive redundant load elimination could be performed either in a separate pass after all speculative optimizations are completed or on demand during speculative optimizations when speculative loads are created. For example, we could perform comprehensive redundant load elimination during instruction scheduling. However, the scheduler in an IA-64 compiler is normally very complex, and performing redundancy elimination at the same time will further increase its complexity. Moreover, comprehensive load redundancy often involves instructions in different scheduling regions, and individual scheduling scopes are not large enough to expose the redundancy. In this paper, we describe our approach as a separate pass, after global scheduling and before register allocation. It is performed globally over the entire function. This method first performs the Available Loads analysis to identify redundant loads and then applies program transformations to remove them. In the following, we will refer to two loads with the same address as "same-address loads".

Analysis. The Available Loads analysis tells us what loads are redundant in a function. We will use *ld[r]* to denote a generic type of load. We say a load expression ld[r] is available at some program point if and only if along every execution path to the program point, ld[r] is executed at least once, and after it is executed r is not redefined and there is no aliased store operation executed. Therefore, a load expression ld[r] at a program point is redundant if and only if its loaded value is already available at that program point.

Transformation. For each redundant load, our method performs appropriate program transformation according to its load type and the types of same-address loads that cause the load to be redundant. Given the six types of loads we consider, the transformation can be very complicated. This is a major reason why one cannot straightforwardly apply traditional redundant load elimination to the problem under consideration here.

3.1 The Available Loads Analysis

Our algorithm works on the control flow graph (CFG) of a function that has a unique START node from which every block is reachable. It performs a global data flow analysis called the "Available Loads" (AVLD) analysis to detect redundant loads in the function. We say a load L

$$L: \quad \ldots = ld[r1]$$

is redundant if there exists another same-address load L2

$$L2: \quad \ldots = ld[r1]$$

on every path from the START node of the control flow graph to L and r1 is not redefined/killed between L2 and L. It is likely that there are different L2's on different paths from START to L. The load L is redundant since the value loaded by L2 can be used correctly as the value loaded by L.

For each node n in the control flow graph, we define the set of Available Loads reaching the entry of n as follows:

$$AVLD(START) = \Phi$$

$$AVLD(n) = \bigcap_{\forall m \in pred(n)} ((AVLD(m) \cap PRES(m)) \cup GEN(m))$$

where pred(n) represents the set of immediate predecessors of n. A load ld[r1] is preserved in node m, denoted by PRES(m), if and only if there is no definition of r1 in m and there is no aliased store to address r1. A load ld[r1] is generated in node m, denoted by GEN(m), if and only if there is a downward exposed load ld[r1] in m. A load ld[r1] is downward exposed in node m if and only if there is no definition of r1 from the load to the exit of node m. For correctness, we also need to consider the size of a loaded value. But we leave out this detail to simplify our presentation.

The resulting AVLD information tells us what loads are available at the entry of each basic block. This information can then be propagated within individual basic blocks to obtain what loads are available when the program executes up to a particular instruction I. If I is a load instruction and the load is available right before I is executed, then I contains a redundant load.

Once a load L is identified to be redundant, we can then find a set of "covering" loads that together make L redundant. Both the set of covering loads and the redundant load are used in program transformation.

3.2 Code Transformation

The outline of the comprehensive redundant load elimination algorithm is shown in Figure 9. It first performs the Available Loads analysis. Then for each redundant load, it determines the set of covering loads and attempts to remove redundancy. If this covering set contains only one load, the program transformation is relatively simple. If this covering set consists of multiple loads, the program transformation is more complex, although similar, except for the cases where the redundant load is a regular load. We will describe only the simple case in this paper. More details can be found in [5].

```
Comprehensive_Redundant_Load_Elimination ( )
    Available_Loads_Analysis();
    For each load ld that is redundant with respect to a covering load cover_ld
        Do_Elimination (cover_ld, ld);
```

Figure 9. Outline of comprehensive redundant load elimination

The **Do_Elimination**(ld1, ld2) function in the code above is simple if both ld1 and ld2 are regular loads. For general speculative redundant load elimination, we have a matrix of cases to consider. The entry at (i, j) in the matrix is the name of the routine called by **Do_Elimination** when load_type(ld1) is i, and load_type(ld2) is j. We will refer to the matrix as *comprehensive load matrix* or CLM. The CLM matrix is defined in Figure 10. The routine **Do_Elimination** is listed in Figure 11.

Load Type	regular load	advanced load	check load	check advanced load	speculative load	speculative advanced load
regular load	R_R	R_A	R_C	R_CA	R_S	R_SA
advanced load	A_R	A_A	A_C	A_CA	A_S	A_SA
check load	C_R	C_A	C_C	C_CA	C_S	C_SA
check advanced load	CA_R	CA_A	CA_C	CA_CA	CA_S	CA_SA
speculative load	S_R	S_A	S_C	S_CA	S_S	S_SA
speculative advanced load	SA_R	SA_A	SA_C	SA_CA	SA_S	SA_SA

Figure 10. Comprehensive Load Matrix

```
Enum loadType = { regular load, advanced load, check load,
        check advanced load, speculative load, speculative
        advanced load };

Do_Elimination (ld1, ld2)
    routine_name = CLM(load_type(ld1), load_type(ld2));
    call routine_name(ld1, ld2);
```

Figure 11. Do_Elimination routine

For each load operation op: r = load [addr], the destination register r is denoted by dest(op). To eliminate one of the redundant load operations ld1 and ld2, we often need to consider the situation when dest(ld2) != dest(ld1) to decide whether to simply remove a load or change it to a copy. We define the utility routine Elim_A2_or_Copy_A1_to_A2(ld1, ld2) in Figure 12, which eliminates ld2 if dest(ld2) is equal to dest(ld1) or change ld2 to a copy "dest(ld2) = dest(ld1)" otherwise.

```
Elim_A2_or_Copy_A1_to_A2(ld1, ld2)
    if ( dest(ld2) == dest(ld1) )
        Eliminate (ld2)
    else
        change ld2 to "dest(ld2) = dest(ld1)"
```

Figure 12. The Elim_A2_or_Copy_A1_to_A2 utility routine

4. The CLM Routines

There are a total of 36 routines in the CLM matrix. We only describe a few most interesting ones here for space limit. More details can be found in [5]. We generate copy operations at liberty by assuming that copy propagation or register coalescing will remove them if desirable.

4.1 Regular Load and Advanced Load (the R_A Routine)

The code in Figure 8 has shown an example of an advanced load that is redundant because a regular load is available at its program point. The R_A routine cannot simply remove the advanced load because its corresponding check load needs the preparation made by the advanced load. However, it may remove the regular load. Alternatively, one can see this as removing the advanced load and converting the regular load into an advanced load. Notice that the destination register of the advanced load must not change. Register renaming can be performed to remove the use and definition of destination (ld2) between ld1 and ld2. The R_A routine is listed in Figure 13. The transformation of the code in Figure 8 is shown in Figure 14.

```
R_A (ld1, ld2)
    if any use/def of dest(ld2) between ld1 and ld2
        return
    move ld2 before ld1
    Elim_A2_or_Copy_A1_to_A2(ld2, ld1)
```

Figure 13. R_A routine

r4 = **load** [compptr]	r3 = **adv_load** [compptr]
cmp xindex, r4	r4 = r3
jgeq OUTSIDE ⟶	cmp xindex, r4
r1 = adv_load [ceof]	jgeq OUTSIDE
r3 = **adv_load** [compptr]	r1 = adv_load [ceof]

Figure 14. Example of A_R redundancy elimination

Notice that, if the covering load and the redundant load are not in control equivalent blocks, moving the advanced load to the covering load location may cause the advanced load to be executed more often than necessary. This may cause resource pressure for data speculation. So this optimization should take into consideration branch probabilities and the available data speculation resources.

4.2 Advanced Load and Advanced Load (the A_A Routine)

Figure 15 shows a scenario where redundant advanced loads may be created. The two regular loads are not redundant as they are separated by an aliased store. After both loads are speculated above the two aliased stores, the second advanced load becomes redundant.

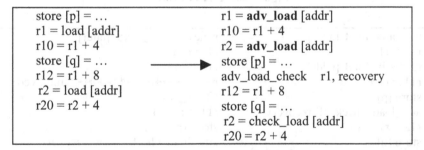

Figure 15. A_A redundancy

The two advanced loads can be replaced by a single advanced load. A complication lies in that an advanced load and its check load must have the same destination register. When one of the advanced loads is eliminated, we cannot simply change its corresponding check load to check the destination for the other advanced load, as the check load may modify its destination register whose original value may be used after the check load.
So if the destination registers of the two advanced loads are the same, either advanced load can be removed. Otherwise, we first perform the following transformation over the code such that the two advanced loads have the same destination register.

1. Create a new register r_new.
2. Change each advanced load "ri = adv_load [addr]" to "r_new = adv_load[addr]" and "ri = r_new",   and change each check load "ri = check_load [addr]" to "r_new = check_load[addr]" and "ri = r_new".

The A_A routine is shown in Figure 16, and a transformation example is shown in Figure 17.

```
A_A (ld1, ld2)
    if dest(ld1) != dest(ld2)
        r_new = new register;
        change ld1 to the following two instructions
            "r_new = adv_load[addr1]" and "dest(ld1) = r_new"
        change ld1's check load to the following two instructions
            "r_new = check_load[addr1]" and "dest(ld1) = r_new"
        change ld2 to the following two instructions
            "r_new = adv_load[addr2]" and "dest(ld2) = r_new"
        change ld2's check load to the following two instructions
            "r_new = check_load[addr2]" and "dest(ld2) = r_new"
    Eliminate (ld2)
```

Figure 16. A_A routine

```
r1 = adv_load [addr]                r_new = adv_load [addr]
r10 = r1 + 4                         r1 = r_new
r2 = adv_load [addr]                 r10 = r1 + 4
r11 = r1 + 4                         r_new = adv_load [addr] /* removed */
store [p] = ...                      r2 = r_new
adv_load_check  r1, recovery         r11 = r1 + 4
r12 = r1 + 8                         store [p] = ...
store [q] = ...                      adv_load_check r_new, recovery
 r2 = check_load   [addr]            r1 = r_new
r20 = r2 + 4                         r12 = r1 + 8
r13 = r1 + 12                        store [q] = ...
                                     r_new = check_load  [addr]
                                     r2 = r_new
                                     r20 = r2 + 4
                                     r13 = r1_new + 12
```

Figure 17. Example of A_A redundancy elimination

4.3 Check Load and Speculative Load (the C_S Routine)

Figure 18 shows a scenario where a check load and a speculative load may be brought together to expose redundancy. By advancing the first load to past the store and speculating the second load above the if-condition, a full redundancy is exposed between the check load and the speculative load.

```
                                  r1 = adv_load  [addr]
                                  store [p] = ...
   store [p] = ...                r1 = check_load   [addr]
   r1 = load   [addr]    ──────▶  r2 = spec_load    [addr]
   if (condition)                 if (condition)
      r2 = load   [addr]             spec_check r2
      r10 = r1 + r2                  r10 = r1 + r2
```

Figure 18. C_S redundancy

The check load can catch the exception that the speculative load is intended to defer. So the speculative load can be removed. When removing the speculative load, its speculative check should be removed when it is dominated by the speculative load (remember that a load may be moved to several target locations that collectively dominate their spec_check's). The C_S routine is shown in Figure 19 and the code was optimized as shown in Figure 20.

```
   C_S (ld1, ld2)
   Elim_A2_or_Copy_A1_to_A2(ld1, ld2);
      for each spec_check of ld2
         if (it is dominated by ld2)
            remove the spec_check
```

Figure 19. C_S routine

```
   r1 = adv_load  [addr]            r1 = adv_load   [addr]
   store [p] = ...                  store [p] = ...
   r1 = check_load [addr]  ──────▶  r1 = check_load   [addr]
   r2 = spec_load   [addr]          r2 = r1
   if (condition)                   if (condition)

      ....                             ....


   spec_check r2
      r10 = r1 + r2                     r10 = r1 + r2
```

Figure 20. Example of C_S redundancy elimination

4.4 Speculative Load and Speculative Load (the S_S Routine)

Multiple speculative loads may be brought together from different branches of an if-statement. Figure 21(a) shows an if-statement with loads on both branches. When the two loads are speculated above the branch, we have two speculative loads and one of them is redundant. We cannot simply remove one of the speculative loads together with its speculative check. For example, if we remove "r2 = spec_load [addr]" and "spec_check r2", as shown in Figure 21(c), the "r20 = r2 + 4" instruction may use a value that carries a deferred exception that should have been raised.

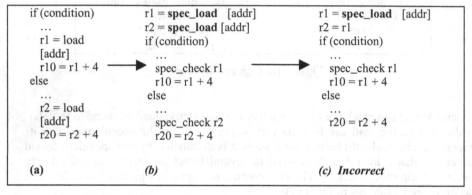

Figure 21. S_S redundancy and an incorrect elimination

We can remove the spec_check only if it is dominated by other spec_checks. The S_S routine is shown in Figure 22, and the optimized code is shown in Figure 23 (assuming that r1 is not defined in the else clause).

```
S_S (ld1, ld2)
    Elim_A2_or_Copy_A1_to_A2(ld1, ld2);
    If (ld2's spec_check is dominated by the spec_check of ld1)
        Remove ld2's spec_check
    Else
        Change ld2's spec_check to "spec_check dest(ld1)"
```

Figure 22. S_S routine

```
r1 = spec_load [addr]              r1 = spec_load [addr]
r2 = spec_load [addr]              r2 = r1
if (condition)                     if (condition)
   ...                                ...
   spec_check r1      ———————→        spec_check r1
   r10 = r1 + 4                       r10 = r1 + 4
else                               else
   ...                                ...
   spec_check r2                      spec_check r1
   r20 = r2 + 4                       r20 = r2 + 4
```

Figure 23. Example of S_S redundancy elimination

5. Preliminary Experimental Results

We have implemented the technique presented above in our IA-64 research compiler. Here we report on some preliminary results, in Table 1, collected from our experiment with SPEC95 integer benchmarks. Although the results are specific to a certain experiment configuration, they demonstrate that it is necessary to perform comprehensive redundant load elimination in a compiler for architectures supporting control and data speculation.

Table 1. Preliminary results for comprehensive redundant load elimination.

Benchmark	Static loads removed	Dynamic loads removed	Total dynamic instr
compress	12	725	272,460,901
gcc	1,750	1,722,569	598,391,405
go	221	2,538,400	552,959,062
ijpeg	153	1,844,735	1,375,429,729
li	28	1,741,222	506,142,623
m88ksim	186	943,612	453,089,914
perl	313	163,570	227,247,542
vortex	616	916,803	228,065,213

In this experiment, comprehensive redundant load elimination was performed, as a separate phase, after global scheduling and before global register allocation. Additionally, traditional redundant load elimination of regular loads was performed earlier in a high-level optimizer. Edge profile information was used to guide optimization and scheduling decisions. There was no data speculation, while control speculation was moderate. The inputs to the benchmarks were the "lite" inputs, used by us internally at Intel.

In Table 1, the first column lists the eight SPEC95 integer benchmarks. The second column reports the number of loads removed by our compiler for each benchmark. The numbers range from 12 (for *compress*) to as many as 1,750 (for *gcc*). The third column reports the number of loads removed by taking into account their execution frequencies (i.e., the frequencies of the basic blocks where they reside). A good way to measure the benefit of performing comprehensive redundant load elimination, is to compare this number with the total number of instructions executed for each benchmark, reported in the last column. Among all the benchmarks, we observed the best effect for *go*. The results for *gcc* and *li* were also good. By contrast, the result obtained for *compress* was not significant.

Note that different results may be obtained for different degrees of aggressiveness in speculation. Our aim here is not to evaluate the effectiveness of comprehensive redundant load elimination with respect to different experiment configurations. Instead, the preliminary results are intended to show the importance of our technique in a compiler when it performs control and/or data speculation.

6. Conclusion and Future Work

We have designed a framework for comprehensive redundant load elimination, which correctly handles redundant loads generated mainly through control and data speculation. Our technique addresses all six types of loads: regular loads, advanced loads, check loads, check advanced loads, speculative loads, and speculative advanced loads. We also presented some experimental results that demonstrate the importance of performing comprehensive redundant load elimination in a compiler for architectures supporting control and data speculation.

We have ignored one important issue in this paper, namely the cost-benefit consideration. Removing a redundant load may not always give performance improvement. For example, when removing a redundant advanced load, in the worst case we may need to insert four copies. If the advanced load is outside a loop while the copies must be inserted inside the loop body, it may be better not to remove the redundancy. We will incorporate cost-benefit analysis into our framework in the future.

Acknowledgments

We wish to thank our colleagues David Berson, Dong-Yuan Chen, and Perry Wang for their inputs to this work; Jesse Fang and Hans Mulder for their management support; and the anonymous reviewers for their comments that help improve our presentation.

References

1. D. M. Gallagher, W. Y. Chen, S. A. Mahlke, J. C. Gyllenhaal, W. W. Hwu, "Dynamic Memory Disambiguation Using the Memory Conflict Buffer," Proceedings of the 6th International Conference on Architecture Support for Programming Languages and Operating Systems, San Jose, California, October 1994, pp.183-195.

2. A. V. Aho, R. Sethi, J. D. Ullman, Compilers, Principles, Techniques, and Tools, Addison Wesley, 1987.

3. S. A. Mahlke, W. Y. Chen, R. A. Bringmann, R. E. Hank, W. W. Hwu, B. R. Rau, and M. S. Schlansker, "Sentinel Scheduling: A Model for Compiler-Controlled Speculative Execution," Transactions on Computer Systems, Vol. 11, No. 4, Nov. 1993.

4. Intel Corp, "IA-64 Application Developers Architecture Guide," May 1999.

5. Youfeng Wu and Yong-fong Lee, "Generalized Redundant Load Elimination for Architectures Supporting Control and Data Speculation," Intel Microcomputer Research Labs Technical Report TR_MRL_1997_23.0, October 1997.

Minimum Register Instruction Scheduling: A New Approach for Dynamic Instruction Issue Processors [*]

R. Govindarajan[1], Chihong Zhang[2], and Guang R. Gao[2]

[1] Supercomputer Edn. & Res. Centre
Dept. of Computer Science & Automation
Indian Institute of Science
Bangalore, 560 012, India
govind@{serc,csa}.iisc.ernet.in
[2] Dept. of Electrical & Computer Engg.
University of Delaware
Newark, DE 19716
U.S.A
{czhang,ggao}@capsl.udel.edu

Abstract. Modern superscalar architectures with dynamic scheduling and register renaming capabilities have introduced subtle but important changes into the tradeoffs between compile-time register allocation and instruction scheduling. In particular, it is perhaps not wise to increase the degree of parallelism of the static instruction schedule at the expense of excessive register pressure which may result in additional spill code. To the contrary, it may even be beneficial to reduce the register pressure at the expense of constraining the degree of parallelism of the static instruction schedule. This leads to the following interesting problem: given a data dependence graph (DDG) G, can we derive a schedule S for G that uses the least number of registers ?

In this paper, we present a heuristic approach to compute the near-optimal number of registers required for a DDG G (under all possible legal schedules). We propose an extended list-scheduling algorithm which uses the above number of required registers as a guide to derive a schedule for G that uses as few registers as possible. Based on such an algorithm, an integrated approach for register allocation and instruction scheduling for modern superscalar architectures can be developed.

1 Introduction

Efficient instruction scheduling [7,9,14,20] and register allocation [1,6,14] are essential to achieve high performance in modern superscalar processors. Instructions scheduling exposes the parallelism in the code, while register allocation assigns registers to frequently accessed variables. In many early compilers these two phases were performed separately, with each phase being ignorant of the requirements of the other, leading to degradation in performance. If register allocation precedes instruction scheduling, false dependences (anti and output dependences) may be introduced due to register

---

[*] This work was supported by research grants NSF CCR-9808522, NSF MIPS-970715, and NSF CISE-9726388.

L. Carter and J. Ferrante (Eds.): LCPC'99, LNCS 1863, pp. 70–84, 2000.
© Springer-Verlag Berlin Heidelberg 2000

reuse, which in turn limits the scheduler's reordering opportunities. On the other hand, instruction scheduling, due to the parallelism exposed, typically increases the register requirement of the constructed schedule.

Recently, a number of integrated techniques have been proposed in the literature [17, 4,3]. These integrated techniques increase the instruction-level parallelism without increasing the register requirements considerably. However, these works have concentrated only on VLIW and in-order issue superscalar processors. Many of the modern processors may issue instructions out of program order. Out-of-order (o-o-o) issue is supported by a runtime scheduling hardware (which determines which instructions can be issued in parallel in each cycle) and a register renaming mechanism (which detects and removes anti and output dependences between instructions by renaming the logical registers to hardware physical registers or to re-order buffer locations [18]). Typically the number of available physical registers is larger (roughly twice) than the number of logical registers visible to the register allocator.

The presence of such o-o-o issue hardware introduces a new dimension in the tradeoff between instruction scheduling and register allocation. For example, it is not always beneficial to statically reorder the instructions to maximally expose the parallelism if this increases the register pressure to cause extra spill code [2,3,11,13,19]. Such spill code may not be necessary if some of the "hidden" physical registers can be utilized at runtime through the hardware renaming mechanism. However, once the spill code is generated at compile time, they will have to be executed and incur extra cost! Such tradeoffs lead to the following observation (which seems somewhat counter-intuitive): for o-o-o issue processors, it may even be beneficial to reduce the register pressure and avoid spill code at the expense of constraining the degree of parallelism of the static instruction schedule[1]. In other words, it is perhaps more efficient to reuse some of the registers through reordering of instructions which, in turn, may decrease the parallelism exposed at compile time due to the anti and output dependences. Though it appears certain parallelism is lost at compile time, the renaming hardware ensures the obscured parallelism (due to false dependences) will be uncovered. Recent studies on o-o-o issue processors, which establish the above point, indicate that reducing the register pressure, and hence the register spill is more crucial to the performance than improving the parallelism [3,13,19]. This motivates the question:

> **Problem 1:** Given a data dependence graph (DDG) G, derive a schedule S that uses the minimum number of registers possible.

We refer to the above problem as the minimum register scheduling problem. To provide a feasible solution method to the problem, we propose a new approach which solves the problem in two steps as formulated by the following two subproblems (Problem 2 and 3).

> **Problem 2:** Given a data dependence graph (DDG) G, can we find a minimum register bound (MRB) such that no legal schedule S for G uses fewer registers than MRB?

---

[1] Because our focus in this paper is to reduce the register requirements rather than increasing the exposed parallelism, we do not consider (processor) resource constraints in our schedule.

Problem 3: Given a data dependence graph (DDG) G, and a register bound RB (*e.g.*, as defined in Problem 2), can we use RB as a guide to derive a schedule S that uses as few registers as possible.

Our solution to Problems 2 and 3 can be summarized as follows. We propose a new approach that uses the concept of *batons* which allows the reuse of a register for nodes in a *chain* or *path*. By identifying all the chains in the DDG, we develop an interference graph, called a *chain interference graph*, which represents which pairs of chains in the DDG must **definitely overlap** in all legal schedules. A heuristic graph coloring method can be used to find a near-optimal value for the minimum register bound (MRB).

We present a modified list scheduling method which uses the above register bound as a guide, and attempts to construct a schedule that uses no more than the register bound, even if the scheduling length may be compromised. However, it may not always be possible to construct such a schedule and the scheduler may encounter a deadlock in certain cases. We proposed a simple solution that overcomes the deadlock problem by gradually increasing the register bound. The heuristic proposed ensures that the scheduler finds a feasible solution which uses as few extra registers as possible (over and above the register bound).

The rest of the paper is organized as follows. In the following section we motivate minimum register scheduling problem and our approach to this. In Section 3, we discuss computing the minimum number of registers required for the given DDG. Section 4 deals with scheduling the code using the given number of minimum registers. Section 5 deals with an application of our minimum register scheduling approach in conventional prepass or postpass scheduling methods. In Section 5.3 we discuss some interesting extensions to our work. Related work and conclusions are presented in Sections 6 and 7.

2   Motivating Example

In this section we bring out the motivation for our work with a simple example.

2.1   Example

In this paper we consider basic blocks or, more generally, program regions not involving loops or conditionals represented by acyclic data dependence graphs (DDG). We start with the DDG for the basic block rather than its code. This is because, in the latter, there is an implicit ordering of instructions. As will be discussed subsequently, such implicit ordering may themselves cause unnecessary register spills even in a conventional postpass algorithm [1,14].

Consider the DDG shown in Figure 1(a). Nodes in the DDG represent instructions and arcs represent data dependency. Conceptually, at least, we will assume that each arc requires one register to hold the data produced by a node[2]. However, two arcs, for example, arcs (a, b) and (c, d) can share the same register if the live ranges of the two

---

[2] If any of the arcs contain a token indicating loop-carried dependency, then an additional register would be required for such loop carried dependences. We omit further discussion on this as it is beyond the scope of this paper.

data values do not overlap. In the case of simple (acyclic) instruction scheduling (but not software pipelining) the lives ranges of these two arcs do not overlap, no matter how we schedule the instructions corresponding to nodes a, b, c, and d. Hence the respective live ranges can share the same register. Similarly, it can be seen that the live ranges of variables corresponding to arcs (c, d) and (f, d) always overlap, no matter how we schedule the different instructions, and hence cannot share the same register.

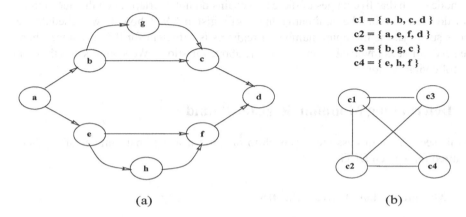

$$c1 = \{ a, b, c, d \}$$
$$c2 = \{ a, e, f, d \}$$
$$c3 = \{ b, g, c \}$$
$$c4 = \{ e, h, f \}$$

(a)   (b)

Fig. 1. Motivating Example

What about the live ranges corresponding to arcs (b, g) and (e, h)? They may or may not overlap depending on when the corresponding instructions are scheduled. Thus, a schedule where the live ranges (b, g) and (e, h) do not overlap is interesting from the point that it requires fewer registers. More generally, we want to find a schedule that requires minimum registers, allowing register sharing wherever possible. Notice that the schedule of different nodes can be so selected in order to reduce the number of overlapping live ranges, and hence the number of registers required for the schedule.

2.2   Register Sharing: Our Approach

Consider a path or a *chain* in the DDG. It can be seen that the live ranges corresponding to the various arcs of the path or the chain can share the same color. Notice that since we assume that each arc has an associated register[3], the live range of the variable corresponding to an arc ends as soon as the consumer is scheduled. Hence the same register can be used for result write. In other words, a node in a chain passes the register to its successor, which after consuming the value, passes the register, with the result written in the register, to a successor. This passing of registers, resembles passing the *baton* among the members of a relay team. Thus each chain or path gets a single register or baton which is passed among the nodes in the chain.

---

[3] The idea of associating a register with an arc is only conceptual, and can be removed easily in a subsequent pass through the code, as will be shown in Section 5.1.

It can be seen that path $a \rightarrow b \rightarrow c \rightarrow d$ and $a \rightarrow e \rightarrow f \rightarrow d$ are two paths in the given DDG. Of the remaining arcs not covered by the above paths, path $b \rightarrow g \rightarrow c$ and $e \rightarrow h \rightarrow f$ form two more paths. If we assign one register or baton for each path, then we can derive a schedule that uses 4 registers.

The next question is, can two different paths share the same baton? More specifically, can path $b \rightarrow g \rightarrow c$ and $e \rightarrow h \rightarrow f$ share the same baton? If so, then we can schedule the nodes such that only 3 registers are required. In this example it is possible to schedule the nodes such that live ranges of these two chains do not overlap. Then the question is, how do we determine the minimum number of registers? And, how do we schedule the nodes such that the minimum number of registers is sufficient for the schedule? There are several issues involved in answering the above questions. We shall discuss these in the following sections.

3   Determining Minimum Register Bound

In this section we discuss our approach to obtain a near-optimal number of registers required for a given DDG.

3.1   Minimum Chain Cover for a DDG

We begin with a number of definitions.

Definition 1. *A* **Data Dependence Graph (DDG)** *is a directed graph $G = (V, E, d, m)$, where V is the set of vertices representing the instructions in the (low-level) code and E, the set of arcs, representing* true *data dependence between the instructions. Associated with each vertex v, is the delay or execution time of the instruction, denoted by $d(v)$. The value $m(v1, v2)$ represents the dependence distance on edge $(v1, v2)$; that is, the value produced by $v1$ is consumed by $v2$ after $m(v1, v2)$ iterations.*

In this paper, we focus our attention to acyclic DDGs and DDGs where $m(v1, v2)$ on all arcs $(v1, v2)$ is 0. Each edge in a DDG represents a true data dependence between the producer and consumer instructions. As mentioned earlier, we will, initially associate a register with each arc for passing the produced value to the consuming node.

Definition 2. *A* **chain** *is a sequence of adjacent arcs $\{(v_1, v_2), (v_2, v_3), \cdots, (v_{k-2}, v_{k-1}), (v_{k-1}, v_k)\}$ in the DDG.*

Henceforth, for simplicity, we shall denote such a chain as $\{v_1, v_2, \cdots, v_k\}$. As mentioned in the earlier section, in our approach, we will assign a single register for a chain. In other words, the same register (or baton) is passed among the arcs $(v_1, v_2), (v_2, v_3), \cdots$ (v_{k-1}, v_k).

A first step to our minimum register scheduling problem is to identify a set of chains in the DDG such that the chains cover all the arcs in the DDG and there are no common arcs between any pair of chains. Further, we want to reduce the number of chains in the DDG. This problem is termed as *Minimum Chain Cover Problem.*

Notice that since our objective is to minimize the number of chains that covers the DDG, we require each chain to be as maximal a sequence (of edges) as possible. More specifically, if $c_i = \{v_1, v_2, \cdots, v_k\}$ is a chain in the minimum chain problem, and if there exists an edge (v_k, v_l) in the DDG, then we require (v_k, v_l) to be a part of some other chain c_j, and c_j doesn't start with the edge (v_k, v_l)[4].

We propose a simple depth-first search algorithm to find the minimum chain cover of a DDG. As edges are included in a chain, we mark them. For the purpose of this discussion, we define a **source node** in the DDG as a node with no incoming edges, or a node all of whose incoming edges are *marked*. Similarly, a **sink node** is one having no outgoing edges, or all the outgoing edges are already marked. The algorithm derives a path, starting with a source node in the DDG, following unmarked edges, and reaching a sink node. The edges in this path are marked and constitute a chain. This process is repeated until all edges in the DDG are included in some chain. A formal description of the algorithm is given below.

Minimum Chain Algorithm:

```
while (not all edges of the graph are marked)
do
   start with a source node u which has at least one
         unmarked  outgoing edge from it;
   increment the chain number;
   while (u is not a sink node)
   do
      add one of the unmarked edges (u,v) to the chain;
      mark edge (u,v);
      move to v, i.e., set u = v;
   end
end.
```

3.2   Overlapping of Live Ranges of Chains

In order to determine whether two chains can share a register, we need to identify whether the live ranges of these chains overlap. The live range of a chain is defined as follows.

Definition 3. *The **live range** of chain* $c = \{v_1, v_2, \cdots, v_k\}$ *starts at time* t_1 *in which vertex* v_1 *is scheduled for execution and ends at time* t_k *in which vertex* v_k *is scheduled for execution. In other words, the live range of chain c is* $[t_1, t_k]$ *(inclusive of both time steps* t_1 *and* t_k*).*

It should, however, be noted here that our approach is to find a schedule that minimizes the register requirements. And in this process, when we try to identify which chains have non-overlapping live ranges, the schedule for the different instructions are not yet fixed. In other words, the schedule time of instructions, and as a consequence, the live ranges of different chains are all *floating*. As a consequence, when we determine the overlap information of the live ranges of two chains, it can be one of the following: (i) definitely overlapping, (ii) definitely non-overlapping, and (iii) may be overlapping.

---

[4] It may be possible to do it otherwise, and still achieve the same number of chains, and eventually the same number of registers, but not lower, as is required in our approach. We do not consider such a possibility in this paper.

Definition 4. *The live ranges of two chains c_u and c_v are said to be* **definitely overlapping** *if, no matter how the operations/nodes in the DDG are scheduled, the dependences in the DDG ensure that the live ranges of these two chains always overlap.*

Definition 5. *The live ranges of two chains c_u and c_v are said to be* **definitely non-overlapping** *if, no matter how the operations/nodes in the DDG are scheduled, the dependences in the DDG ensure that the live ranges of these two chains never overlap.*

The concepts of definite overlap and definite non-overlap can be directly applied to the chain coloring problem. Similar to the what is done in conventional register allocation, two chains can share the same color/register if their live ranges definitely do not overlap. Further, if the live ranges of two chains definitely overlap, then they must use different colors or registers.

Theorem 1. *The live ranges of chains $c_u = \{u_1, u_2, \cdots, u_m\}$ and $c_v = \{v_1, v_2, \cdots, v_n\}$* **definitely overlap** *if the following condition holds.*

C1: *There exist directed paths from u_1 to v_n and v_1 to u_m.*

Due to space limitation, we omit the proof. Refer to [12] for proofs of theorems and lemmas presented in this paper.

Next, we derive the conditions for definite non-overlap as follows.

Theorem 2. *The live ranges of chains $c_u = \{u_1, u_2, \cdots, u_m\}$ and $c_v = \{v_1, v_2, \cdots, v_n\}$* **definitely do not overlap** *if the following condition holds.*

C2: *There exists a directed path from v_n to u_1* or *there exists a directed path from u_m to v_1*

3.3   Interference Graph for Live Ranges of Chains

The next step is to generate an interference graph for the live ranges of the various chains obtained from our minimum chain algorithm. The interference graph $\mathcal{I}$ consists of n nodes, where n is the number of chains in $\mathcal{C}$, each node representing the live range of a chain. Two nodes corresponding to chains c_i and c_j of the interference graph are connected by an (undirected) edge if and only if the live ranges of the respective chains definitely overlap. We refer to the interference graph for chains as chain interference graph. Well known heuristic methods can be used to color the chain interference graph to get a sub-optimal solution for the minimum register bound.

Once the interference graph is colored, it tells us which chains of the DDG must share the same register. Two questions that arise are: (i) Can we always construct a schedule for this register bound? and (ii) How tight is this register bound obtained? We shall address the first in the following section. The second question is deferred to Section 5.3.

4   Scheduling with Minimum Registers

This section deals with constructing a schedule for the DDG that uses no more than the minimum register bound computed from the chain interference graph.

4.1 Modified List Scheduling

Our modified list scheduling approach schedules nodes based on the availability of registers. Like in list scheduling we maintain a list of ready instructions that can be scheduled in the current schedule. In addition to checking the availability of function units, we also check for the availability of registers. In order to perform list scheduling, we maintain the following information.

Let G be the DDG under consideration and $C = \{c_1, c_2, \cdots, c_n\}$ be a minimum cover chain discovered by the minimum chain cover algorithm. We use $\mathcal{R}(c_i)$ to denote the coloring assigned to chain c_i by the graph coloring algorithm discussed in Section 3.3. If $\mathcal{R}(c_i) = \mathcal{R}(c_j)$ then the two chains c_i and c_j share the same color. Lastly, with each node v_i of the DDG, we associate two sets, $Start$ and $Release$ defined as follows.

Definition 6. *If x_s and x_e are the start and end nodes of some chain x, then $\mathcal{R}(x)$ is included in $Start(x_s)$. Similarly $\mathcal{R}(x_e)$ is included in $Release(x_e)$.*

Intuitively, $Start(x_s)$ defines the set of colors that would be required if instruction x_s is scheduled for execution. Similarly $Release(x_e)$ represents the colors that will be freed once the execution of x_e starts. For example, in Figure 1, $Start(a) = \{\mathcal{R}(c_1), \mathcal{R}(c_2)\}$ and $Release(f) = \{\mathcal{R}(c_4)\}$. Note that if node x_m is in the middle of some chain x, then $\mathcal{R}(x)$ is included neither in the $Start(x_m)$ nor in the $Release(x_m)$. It is interesting to note that our modified list scheduling approach need not check for the availability of color $\mathcal{R}(x)$ while scheduling the middle node x_m, even though the color (or register) is required for x_m. Our baton approach guarantees that color $\mathcal{R}(x)$ is available at the time of scheduling the start node of chain x and remains available until the schedule of the end node of x.

The list scheduler maintains the `Ready_List` of nodes at each step and the list of `Available_Colors` at each step. To start with, the source nodes of the DDG form the `Ready_List`. Likewise the (minimum) set of colors determined by the graph coloring algorithm forms the initial available colors. A node v in the `Ready_List` is scheduled if the colors in $Start(v)$ are all available. Note that $Start(v)$ can possibly be empty. A node v scheduled at time t completes its execution at time $t + d(v)$, where $d(v)$ corresponds to execution latency of node v. Thus the list scheduler can free the resource allocated used by v at time $t + d(v)$, and $Release(v)$, the registers corresponding to the set of live ranges that terminate at v can be added to the `Available_Colors`. For example, in Figure 1(a), when the execution of node f completes, it can release the color assigned to the path $e \rightarrow h \rightarrow f$. However, it cannot release the color assigned to the chain $a \rightarrow e \rightarrow f \rightarrow d$ as it is used by the arc (f, d). Lastly, the `Ready_List` is updated to indicate if any successor node w is ready to be scheduled. That is, a node w is added to the `Ready_List` at time t, if all its predecessors have completed their execution by time t. Formally,

$$t = \max_{v:(v,w)\in E} (\text{sched\_time}(v) + d(v))$$

The list scheduler proceeds to schedule nodes in the above manner. It can be seen that the schedule guarantees no more registers than determined by the graph coloring algorithm, when the scheduler is able to schedule all the nodes. Unfortunately, the scheduler may deadlock, unable to schedule all the nodes in the DDG. We illustrate this problem in the subsequent sections and present a simple solution.

4.2 Deadlocks in Scheduling

We shall illustrate the problem with the help of two examples. Consider the DDG shown in Figure 2(a). Assume unit execution latency for each node of the DDG. Let the $\mathcal{C} = \{c_1, c_2, c_3, c_4, c_5\}$, where

$$c_1 = \{a, b, c, d\}, \quad c_2 = \{a, e, f, d\}, \quad c_3 = \{b, g, c\}, \quad c_4 = \{b, f\}, \quad c_5 = \{e, h, f\},$$

be the chains discovered by the minimum cover algorithm. The interference graph for the chains are shown in Figure 2(b). From the interference graph it can be seen that 4 colors C_1, C_2, C_3, C_4 are required and chains c_3 and c_5 can share the same color C_3.

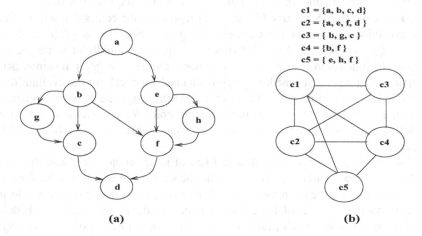

Fig. 2. Deadlock – Example 1

The initial `Ready_List= ` $\{a\}$ and the `Available_Colors= ` $\{C_1, C_2, C_3, C_4\}$. After node a is scheduled at time 0, the `Available_Colors` becomes $\{C_3, C_4\}$. Now at time 1, the nodes b and e are ready. If e is scheduled at time 1, then color C_3 from the `Available_Colors` is removed. Subsequently node h will also be scheduled. But, node b cannot be scheduled as color C_3 is not available and no further nodes can be scheduled. Notice that color C_3 can be released by node f, but node f is data dependent on node b. Hence no further nodes in the DDG can be scheduled and the scheduler is deadlocked.

It can be seen that if we had scheduled node b at time 1 instead of node e, then the scheduler would have appropriately scheduled all the nodes, using only 4 colors, without getting deadlocked. To illustrate why scheduling b instead of e does not cause a deadlock, consider the releaser of color C_3, namely node c. Since color C_3 is shared by chains c_3 and c_5, if we draw an imaginary precedence edge from the releaser, in this case c, to node e, it does not make the DDG cyclic. However, in the earlier case, when node e is scheduled first, the imaginary precedence edge from f to b results in a cycle (b, f, b). Thus, it may be necessary to check which ordering of scheduling nodes does not deadlock, by considering all orderings of start and end nodes of chains that share the same color. However, the complexity of such an approach is high as it involves considering the permutations of all chains that share the color, and running the all pairs shortest path algorithm with the imaginary edges included in the DDG for each of the permutations.

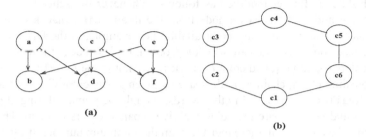

(a)

(b)

Fig. 3. Deadlock – Example 2

Another example is the DDG shown in Figure 3. In this case each edge is a chain by itself. Hence

$$c_1 = (a, b), \quad c_2 = (a, d), \quad c_3 = (c, d), \quad c_4 = (c, f), \quad c_5 = (e, f), \quad c_6 = (e, b)$$

The interference graph for the chains (using only the actual overlap relation as derived using condition C1) is shown in Figure 3(b). The graph coloring algorithm will find two colors C_1 and C_2 can be shared by the chains as:

$$C_1 = \{c_1, c_3, c_5\} \quad C_2 = \{c_2, c_4, c_6\}$$

It can be seen that the $Start$ sets for nodes a, c, and e are identical and equal to $\{C_1, C_2\}$. Similarly, the $Release$ sets for nodes b, d, and f includes the colors C_1 and C_2. Thus, no matter in what order we schedule the source nodes a, c, and e, the scheduler will deadlock unable to schedule any other node subsequently. That is, it is impossible to obtain a schedule for this DDG that uses at most 2 registers.

Next, we formalize the notion of avoidable and unavoidable deadlocks.

Definition 7. *We call a deadlock an* **avoidable deadlock** *if the occurrence of deadlock depends on the order in which the operations are scheduled; otherwise, we call it an* **unavoidable deadlock**.

The deadlock discussed for the DDG shown in Figure 2 is an avoidable deadlock and that for the DDG shown in Figure 3 is unavoidable. This is because, in this DDG, the bound computed is lower than what is required. In other words, the cause for an unavoidable deadlock is that there are not enough colors/registers for the list scheduler.

Thus the register bound RB obtained from coloring the chain interference graph may underestimate, as the chain interference graph only represents the definitely overlap relation. Second, unfortunately, it seems quite involved to determine whether a deadlock is an avoidable one or not. Our heuristic scheduling algorithm discussed in the following subsection, gradually increases the register requirements when it encounters a deadlock, and tries to obtain a schedule that uses as few extra registers as possible.

4.3   Heuristics to Avoid Deadlocks

The list scheduler is further modified as follows. Whenever the scheduler is unable to schedule any nodes, it chooses a node from the Ready_List that has the lowest number of colors that are currently not available. For example, in the DDG shown in Figure 2(a), once nodes a, e and h are scheduled, only node b will be in the Ready_List. It requires colors C_3 and C_4, and color C_3 is currently not in the Available_Colors. The corresponding chain, chain c_3 in this case, is given a new color C_5, and the color is added to Available_Colors. In other words, though the graph coloring algorithm found that c_3 and c_5 can share the color, we give separate colors to them. Thus, our simple solution has resulted in more registers than the minimum number. It can be seen that the scheduling algorithm with this modification is guaranteed not to deadlock.

5   Application of Minimum Register Scheduling Approach

In this section we will apply the minimum register scheduling method on our motivating example. Subsequently, we will illustrate the practical usefulness of our approach in the conventional postpass scheduling method.

5.1   Register Minimum Scheduling on Our Motivating Example

Consider the DDG shown in Figure 1(a). Let the code corresponding to this DDG, as generated by a code generator be as shown in Figure 4(a). The live range of each variable is shown by the side of the code in this figure. In a normal post-pass type scheduler, the register allocator first constructs the interference graph. The interference graph is shown in Figure 4(b). Four live ranges s2, s3, s4, and s5 overlap with each other and hence four registers are required for this code.

As illustrated by our minimum register scheduling method, it is possible to schedule the code using only 3 registers although this may obscure some instruction-level parallelism (at compile time) due to false dependences. Our minimum register scheduling method, as discussed earlier, suggests that chains $b \rightarrow g \rightarrow c$ and $e \rightarrow h \rightarrow f$ can share the same register. This forces the list scheduling method either to schedule node e after node c or to schedule b after node f. Suppose the scheduler arrives at the schedule shown in Figure 5(a). The live ranges of the variables are shown by the side of the code. From the live ranges it can be seen that three register are sufficient for this schedule.

There is one last issue. In our approach we have associated one register with each output arc. This implies that an instruction must potentially write its result in multiple registers, which is not supported in most modern architectures. However, we earlier

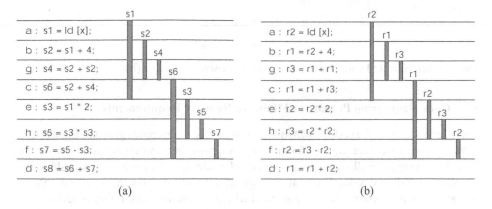

Fig. 4. Example Code, Live Ranges and Interference Graph

mentioned that this association is only conceptual. Now we see how this is achieved. In our example, suppose that registers r1 and r2 are associated with the output arcs of node a.

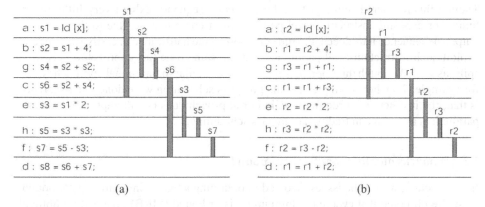

Fig. 5. (a) Reordered and (b) Register Allocated Code

Initially the instruction maintains both registers as destination registers. That is,

$$a : \mathtt{r1, \ r2 \ = \ ld \ [x]}$$

Thus nodes b and c will have, respectively, r1 and r2 as one of the source operands in them. Once the scheduling of nodes is complete, a subsequent pass can identify that among the consumer nodes for a, instruction e is scheduled later. That is, e will be the last use for a. Hence, using the register value r2, corresponding to the chain that contains e, as the destination for the ld instruction would ensure that instruction b can also read this register r2 without stretching its live range. Thus instructions a and b are adjusted as:

```
a : r2 = ld [x]
b : r1 = r2 + 4
```

The register allocated code for the example is shown in Figure 5(b).

5.2   Code Reordering Prepass to Minimize Register Requirements

Consider once again the code shown in Figure 4(a). The interference graph in Figure 4(b) shows that 4 registers are required for this code. Suppose the number of available registers is 3. Then the register allocator in a post-pass scheduler will spill one of the variables, by introducing spill and re-load code at appropriate places. Note that the situation will be aggravated in a pre-pass scheduling method where instruction scheduling is performed. Thus, in this case, while prepass and postpass scheduling methods would produce code with register spills, our approach obtains a schedule that uses only 3 registers and without any spills.

In order to achieve this, we need to introduce a re-ordering phase before the register allocator. This reordering phase concentrates only on reducing the number of overlapping live ranges, while obeying data dependency. In the above example, this phase tries to schedule the execution of e and h after c as in Figure 5(b). By doing so, it is possible to reduce the maximum number of live ranges that overlap with each other to 3. Though this reordered, and register allocated code sequence exhibit very little opportunity for exposing instruction-level parallelism at compile time, due to the anti- and output-dependence introduced, the runtime o-o-o issue hardware can easily uncover and exploit such instruction-level parallelism. At the same time this approach reduces the spills as well. Although this approach appears to be similar to traditional approaches (see for example [7]) where both prepass and postpass scheduling were done, the difference is that, the instruction reordering pass in our approach does not attempt to expose any parallelism as is done in traditional prepass scheduling.

5.3   Remarks on Minimum Register Bound

In this section, we list the issues involved in obtaining a tight minimum register bound. First, we observed that even the minimum register bound (MRB) obtained by optimal coloring of the chain interference graph is not tight and may lead to an unavoidable deadlock (refer to Figure 3). Second, using a heuristic approach to obtain the register bound (RB) may result in sub-optimal solution. Third, our chain interference graph relies on the notion of allocating a register for each arc rather than for each node. This may introduce certain additional interference, as registers get committed early in the chain, and hence increase the register bound.

6   Related Work

Several instruction scheduling [9,14,20] and register allocation methods [6,5,8,15] have been proposed in the past. The need for integrating the two techniques and proposals integrating them have also been reported [4,11,17,16,3]. However, all these studies have concentrated on Very Large Instruction Word (VLIW) architectures and in-order issue processors where it is important to expose the available instruction-level parallelism at compile time. Studies on out-of-order issue processors indicate that reducing the register pressure, and hence the register spill is more crucial to the performance than improving the parallelism [19,13]. In this paper, we focus on the problem of obtaining a minimum register schedule. The unified resource allocator (URSA) method deals with function unit and register allocation simultaneously [2]. The method uses a three-phase *measure-reduce-and-assign* approach, where resource requirements are measured and regions of excess requirements are identified in the first phase. The second phase reduces the requirements to what is available in the architecture, and final phase carries out resource assignment. More recently, they (Berson, Gupta and Soffa) have used *register reuse dags* for measuring the register pressure [3]. A register reuse dag is similar to a chain discussed in this paper. They have evaluated register spilling and register splitting methods for reducing the register requirements in the URSA method.

7   Conclusions

In this paper we motivate the need for obtaining schedules that use minimum registers. Such schedules reduce possible register spills, perhaps at the expense of some instruction-level parallelism. However, in out-of-order issue superscalar processors, the obscured parallelism is likely to be exposed by the runtime instruction scheduling and register renaming hardware. Thus reducing the register spills, or primarily, reducing the register requirements in these out-of-order issue processors is critical to the performance of the generated code.

We proposed the use of *chains* in the data dependence graph that can share a single register. We developed an interference graph representation where the nodes of the graph correspond to the chains in the DDG and edges represent which chains definitely overlap. We proposed the use of existing heuristic methods to obtain a sub-optimal solution for the minimum register bound. Lastly, we proposed a simple list scheduling algorithm that attempts to schedule the code using the register bound as a guide. However, due to certain heuristics used in the scheduling algorithm to avoid deadlocks, a few additional registers may be required by our scheduling method.

As future work, we plan to evaluate the proposed the approach to see how efficient it is in deriving minimum register schedules in an experimental framework. Our experimental work will also evaluate how often do we use additional registers to avoid deadlock. Lastly, using a simulator we plan to measure the dynamic performance improvements obtained by our scheduling method in an out-of-order issue processor.

References

1. A. V. Aho, R. Sethi, and J. D. Ullman. *Compilers — Principles, Techniques, and Tools.* Addison-Wesley Publishing Co., Reading, MA, corrected edition, 1988.
2. D. Berson, R. Gupta, and M. L. Soffa. URSA: A Unified ReSource Allocator for registers and functional units in VLIW architectures. In *Proc. of the Conf. on Parallel Architectures and Compilation Techniques, PACT '98*, Paris, France, June 1998.

3. D. Berson, R. Gupta, and M. L. Soffa. Integrated instruction scheduling and register allocation techniques. In *Proc. of the Eleventh International Workshop on Languages and Compilers for Parallel Computing, LNCS, Springer Verlag*, Chapel Hill, NC, Aug. 1998.
4. D. G. Bradlee, S. J. Eggers, and R. R. Henry. Integrating register allocation and instruction scheduling for RISCs. In *Proc. of the Fourth Intl. Conf. on Architectural Support for Programming Languages and Operating Systems*, pages 122–131, Santa Clara, CA, Apr. 1991.
5. P. Briggs, K. D. Cooper, and L. Torczon. Rematerialization. In *Proc. of the ACM SIGPLAN '92 Conf. on Programming Language Design and Implementation*, pages 311–321, San Francisco, CA, June 1992.
6. G. J. Chaitin. Register allocation and spilling via graph coloring. In *Proc. of the SIGPLAN '82 Symp. on Compiler Construction*, pages 98–105, Boston, MA, June 1982.
7. P. P. Chang, D. M. Lavery, S. A. Mahlke, W. Y. Chen, and W. W. Hwu The importance of prepass code scheduling for superscalar and superpipelined processors *IEEE Transactions on Computers*, 44(3):353–370, March 1995.
8. L. George and A. W. Appel. Iterated register coalescing. In *Conf. Record of the 23rd ACM SIGPLAN-SIGACT Symp. on Principles of Programming Languages*, pages 208–218, St. Petersburg, FL, Jan. 1996.
9. P. B. Gibbons and S. S. Muchnick. Efficient instruction scheduling for a pipelined architecture. In *Proc. of the SIGPLAN '86 Symp. on Compiler Construction*, pages 11–16, Palo Alto, CA, June 1986.
10. M.C. Golumbic. *Algorithmic Graph Theory and Perfect Graphs*. Academic Press, New York, 1980.
11. J. R. Goodman and W-C. Hsu. Code scheduling and register allocation in large basic blocks. In *Conf. Proc., 1988 Intl. Conf. on Supercomputing*, pages 442–452, St. Malo, France, July 1988.
12. R. Govindarajan, C. Zhang, and G. R. Gao. Minimum register instruction scheduling: A new approach for dynamic instruction issue processors. CAPSL Technical Memo, Dept. of Electrical and Computer Engg., University of Delaware, Newark, DE, July 1999.
13. Madhavi G. Valluri and R. Govindarajan. Evaluating register allocation and instruction scheduling techniques in out-of-order issue processors. in *Proc. of the Conf. on Parallel Architectures and Compilation Techniques, PACT '99*, Newport Beach, CA, Oct., 1999.
14. S.S. Muchnick. *Advanced Compiler Design and Implementation*. Morgan Kaufmann Publishers, Inc., San Francisco, CA, 1997.
15. C. Norris and L. L. Pollock. Register allocation over the Program Dependence Graph. In *Proc. of the ACM SIGPLAN '94 Conf. on Programming Language Design and Implementation*, pages 266–277, Orlando, FL, June 20–24, 1994.
16. C. Norris and L. L. Pollock. An experimental study of several cooperative register allocation and instruction scheduling strategies. In *Proc. of the 28th Ann. Intl. Symp. on Microarchitecture*, pages 169–179, Ann Arbor, MI, Nov. 1995.
17. S. S. Pinter. Register allocation with instruction scheduling: A new approach. In *Proc. of the ACM SIGPLAN '93 Conf. on Programming Language Design and Implementation*, pages 248–257, Albuquerque, NM, June 1993.
18. J.E. Smith and G. Sohi. The microarchitecture of superscalar processors. *Proc. of the IEEE*, 83(12):1609–1624, Dec. 1995.
19. Raúl Silvera, Jian Wang, Guang R. Gao, and R. Govindarajan. A register pressure sensitive instruction scheduler for dynamic issue processors. In *Proc. of the Conf. on Parallel Architectures and Compilation Techniques, PACT '97*, pages 78–89, San Francisco, CA, June 1997.
20. H. S. Warren, Jr. Instruction scheduling for the IBM RISC System/6000 processor. *IBM Jl. of Research and Development*, 34(1):85–92, Jan. 1990.

Unroll-Based Copy Elimination for Enhanced Pipeline Scheduling

Suhyun Kim, Soo-Mook Moon, Jinpyo Park, and HanSaem Yun

Seoul National University, #012 Kwanak P.O. BOX 34, Seoul, South Korea
{zelo, smoon, jp, slater}@altair.snu.ac.kr

Abstract. Enhanced pipeline scheduling (EPS) is a software pipelining technique which can achieve a *variable* initiation interval (II) for loops with control flows via its code motion pipelining. EPS, however, leaves behind many renaming copy instructions that cannot be coalesced due to interferences. These copies take resources, and more seriously, they may cause a stall if they rename a multi-latency instruction whose latency is longer than the II aimed for by EPS.

This paper describes how those renaming copies can be deleted through unrolling, which enables EPS to avoid a serious slowdown from latency handling and resource pressure while keeping its variable II and other advantages. In fact, EPS's renaming through copies, followed by unroll-based copy elimination, provides a more general and simpler solution to the cross-iteration register overwrite problem in software pipelining which works for loops with control flows as well as for straight-line loops. Our empirical study performed on a VLIW testbed with a two-cycle load latency shows that the unrolled version of the 16-ALU VLIW code includes fewer no-op VLIWs caused by stalls, improving the performance by a geometric mean of 18%, yet the peak improvement with a longer latency reaches as much as a geometric mean of 25%.

1 Introduction

Enhanced pipeline scheduling (EPS) is a software pipelining technique that is unique due to its code motion pipelining [1]. This feature allows EPS to pipeline any type of loop including those with arbitrary control flows and outer loops. EPS, however, leaves behind many renaming copies that cannot be coalesced due to interferences, suffering from problems caused by those copies.

For example, consider the loop in Fig. 1 (a) which searches for the first non-zero element of an array. Let us assume for the moment that each instruction takes a single cycle. After the loop is scheduled by EPS as in Fig. 1 (b) (we will show later how the loop is scheduled), no true data dependences exist among the three data instructions in the loop (cc=(y==0),y=load(x'),x"=x'+4). The loop can be executed at a rate of one cycle per iteration on a superscalar or a VLIW machine capable of executing two integer instructions, one load and one branch per cycle, assuming we can get rid of the two copies located at the beginning of the loop (we assume the branch executes in parallel with other instructions of

L. Carter and J. Ferrante (Eds.): LCPC'99, LNCS 1863, pp. 85–99, 2000.
© Springer-Verlag Berlin Heidelberg 2000

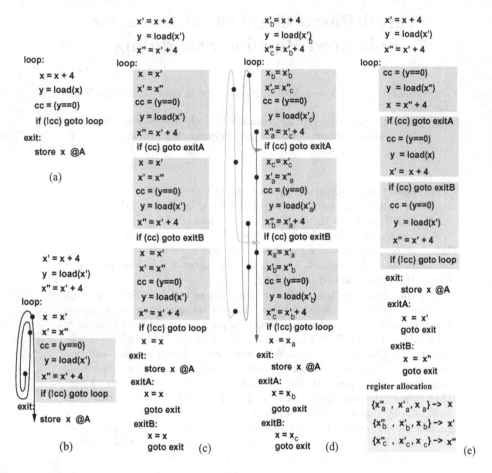

Fig. 1. An example of hard-to-delete copy instructions and the unroll-based copy elimination.

the next iteration). However, we cannot coalesce any of these two copies due to interferences; x' is live when x" is defined, so is x when x' is defined.

Both copies in Fig. 1 (b) can be removed if we transform the code as follows: first, unroll the loop twice (thus generating three copies of the original loop) and insert a dummy copy x=x at each loop exit for the variable x which was live at the original loop exit, as shown in Fig. 1 (c); then calculate live ranges as in Fig. 1 (d) and perform coalescing. The final result after coalescing is performed is shown in Fig. 1 (e) where all copies disappeared except for those dummy artifact copies at loop exits which have now become real copies. The loop will execute at a rate of three cycles per three iterations and give the correct result of x at the loop exit (exit:).

There are two independent issues involved in this example. The first issue is about the unrolling technique itself, i.e., how many times the loop should be unrolled and what dummy copies are inserted at the unrolled loop exits. The second issue is about the benefit of the technique, i.e., why copies are generated by EPS and what unroll-based copy elimination does for EPS.

The first issue has been addressed in detail in [2] where we have proposed a technique for determining the precise unroll amount by extending the definition of a live range by tracing the flow of values via copies. For example in Fig. 1 (b), the *extended live range* (ELR) of the target x" of the add instruction at the end of the loop, possibly going through copies (x'=x" and x=x'), crosses the iteration boundary and the original add instruction (its birth point) twice before it is finally used at the loop exit (see the execution trace in the left). The transformation performed in Fig. 1 (d) was to stretch the ELR over three loop bodies, removing previous interferences among x, x', and x" which were caused by "locking" them in a single loop body. For example, a duplicate of the ELR composed of x''_a, x'_a, and x_a in Fig. 1 (d) includes no interferences in it and can be assigned the same register. So does the duplicate starting from x''_b or x''_c (see the execution trace of each duplicate in the left). We also had to insert a dummy copy x=x at each of the unrolled loop exits for the register x that is live at the original loop exit. This is so that the resulting value of the register, which may reside in different registers due to the copy elimination, can be copied to the correct target register. This is also done automatically by coalescing.

The second issue will be addressed in this paper. In fact, it is closely related to the *cross-iteration register overwrite* problem in software pipelining [3], and we will show EPS's renaming through copies, followed by unroll-based copy elimination, provides a more general and simpler solution than previous ones, which works for loops with branches as well as for straight-line loops.

This paper will be structured as follows. Section 2 reviews EPS and shows how copies are indispensable for generating high-performance code. Section 3 describes why copy elimination is important, especially in the context of handling latencies by EPS. Section 4 includes the comparison with previous solutions used in other software pipelining techniques. Section 5 summarizes the unrolling technique itself. Section 6 shows our experimental results on the performance impact of unroll-based copy elimination for EPS. A summary follows in Sect. 7.

2   Copy Generation in Enhanced Pipeline Scheduling

In software pipelining, we often need to schedule a definition of a register of iteration $n+1$, at a point where the same register of iteration n is still live, which requires renaming. Renaming is simple in the context of *code motion* because it can be handled using copies on an as-needed basis when parallelism opportunities arise. For example, when x=x+4 cannot be moved due to its target register x (e.g., x is live at the other target of a branch when we want to move the instruction speculatively above the branch), its target is renamed to x' and a copy instruction copy x=x' is left at the original place of the instruction. This technique is called *partial renaming* [4].

Although partial renaming leaves behind copies, they do not impose any true data dependences during subsequent code scheduling, with the use of a technique called *forward substitution* [4]. For example, if y=load(x) passes through x=x' during its code motion, it becomes y=load(x') (both operations can also be grouped together for parallel execution after this transformation).

Partial renaming and forward substitution have been successfully employed in EPS [1], as have been noted in [5]. EPS achieves software pipelining by moving operations across the backedge of the loop (which has the effect of moving operations between loop iterations), rather than by operation placement in a *flat schedule* as in *modulo scheduling* (MS) [6]. Due to its code motion pipelining, EPS can easily pipeline loops with arbitrary control flows. A unique feature of EPS is that loops with control flows can be pipelined with a tight, *variable* initiation interval (II) so that a variable cycles/iteration rate can be achieved depending on which path is followed through the loop at execution time. This is in sharp contrast with MS where such loops are pipelined with a worst-case, *fixed* II across all paths after branches are eliminated through if-conversion[1].

It should be noted that EPS is not explicitly guided by any precomputed minimum II (MII) as in MS. Rather, EPS blindly "aims for" a tight II by repeated, greedy DAG scheduling (which will be described shortly). The exact II for each path is known only after the EPS process is over.

Figure 2 shows the EPS process for the example loop in Fig. 1. During the first stage of EPS, the first cycle of the first iteration is scheduled only with x=x+4 as shown in Fig. 2 (a). In the second stage, we schedule the second cycle of the first iteration. In order to generate increasingly compact groups as software pipelining proceeds, EPS is performed as follows: after a cycle is scheduled in a stage, all instructions scheduled in that cycle are available for code motion in the next stages. In fact, this is done by defining a DAG on the CFG of the loop, starting right after the previous cycle, extending across the backedge, and ending at the bottom of the previous cycle, and by performing DAG scheduling to create a parallel group at the root of the DAG (which comprises the current cycle). Figure 2 depicts the DAG defined in each stage with unshaded edges. EPS repeats the DAG scheduling until the backedge is encountered.

In Fig. 2 (b), it is acceptable to move x=x+4 from the second iteration across the backedge, to the second cycle of the first iteration. Moving the operation requires renaming since x is live at the exit. In addition, since there is an edge that enters the loop from outside, a copy of the moved instruction is made at the entry, so the instruction is still executed when the loop is entered.

In the third stage, after scheduling cc=(y==0) in Fig. 2 (c), the load and add instructions are moved across the backedge to fill the third cycle of the first iteration, from the second and third iterations, respectively. The target of the add is renamed to x" and its source operand is forward substituted when it passes through the copy x=x'. The three data instructions that were originally

---

[1]   Although there are MS-based techniques that can achieve a variable-II [7,8], their
      IIs are not as tight as in EPS because they penalize the IIs of the transition paths
      and there is no speculative code motion.

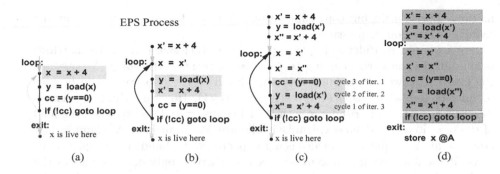

Fig. 2. Enhanced pipeline scheduling for the example in Fig. 1 and the DAG in each stage.

constrained by strict data dependences can now be executed in parallel. However, the parallel schedule requires two uncoalescible copies at the loop entry.

In the context of DAG scheduling, these copies are generated to avoid non-true data dependences for DAG code motion. In the context of software pipelining, they are actually generated for avoiding register-overwrites between iterations. That is, the loop can be initiated in every cycle (i.e., the II is one), yet the lifetime of register x is longer than the II so we need to "extend" its value by copying it (compared to y whose lifetime is the same as the II, thus having no need to be copied). Copies facilitated the code motion across the backedge that would have otherwise been constrained by this cross-iteration output dependence, thus leading to a tighter EPS schedule.

3   Impact of Copy Elimination

While copies are essential for obtaining a more parallel schedule as we have seen in Fig. 2, it might be questioned if eliminating those copies are indeed required. Since forward substitution allows copies to execute in parallel with any instructions that are data dependent on them, copies might be accommodated if there are enough resources. For example in Fig. 2 (c), after x's in y=load(x') and x"=x'+4 are forward substituted by x", there are no data dependences inside the loop as shown in Fig. 2 (d) (none of those two copies can be removed even after the forward substitution, though). The parallel group can be executed every cycle, achieving II=1. Consequently, copy elimination is less critical in this case unless there are insufficient resources.

Copy elimination becomes more crucial when we schedule multi-latency instructions. Latency scheduling in the context of EPS is straightforward: for a definition with a latency of n, EPS simply schedules the use n cycles after the definition is scheduled. To keep track of latencies beyond stages, EPS employs a *latency table* of registers (similar to reservation table) which is propagated from one stage to the next stage after advancing a cycle so as to delay the scheduling of non-elapsed register uses. Copies are generated as usual to facilitate code motion as previously, but copy elimination in this context means more than just reducing the resource pressure.

For example, consider a simple loop, L: x=load(); store(x); cjump L, which is simplified code corresponding to for (i=0;i<n;i++) A[i]=B[i]. We assume the load takes two cycles. Since this is a "do-all" style loop, we should be able to initiate a new iteration every cycle (i.e., II=1). However, there is a cross-iteration register overwrite for x with II=1 because x will be live when the load of the next iteration defines x. Unlike in the previous unit-latency example, this cross-iteration output dependence is not expected to be handled by copies alone (even if there are enough resources), because there is only one instance of the load which cannot be issued every cycle with the same target register. In order to obtain a schedule of II=1, it is evident that we must unroll the loop once, allocating different registers for x in alternating iterations.

Let us see how the problem is actually handled by EPS through our unroll-based coalescing. The EPS process for the loop is shown in Fig. 3 (a)-(c), where there is an additional scheduling stage (b) corresponding to the delay cycle of the load. As previously, two copies are generated to facilitate the code motion of the load, allowing it to be scheduled in every cycle (i.e., aiming for II=1). After the EPS process in Fig. 3 (c), forward substitution (after swapping store(x) and x'=x")[2] generates a parallel group [store(x'); x'=x"; x"=load()] (x=x' is deleted since x is dead now) where there are no data dependences inside. This parallel group cannot be executed every cycle, though, because x'=x" cannot be issued in the next cycle right after x"=load() is issued, due to unelapsed load latency. This requires a stall (hence a no-op VLIW) which leads to a schedule of two cycles per iteration (II=2) as shown in Fig. 3 (d). However, if we unroll the loop once to remove copies, we can obtain two parallel groups, leading to a schedule of two cycles per two iterations (II=1) while satisfying all latency requirements, as shown in Fig. 3 (e).

Copy elimination in this context is more important because it reduces stalls as well as resource pressure. The stall in Fig. 3 (d) is due to EPS's code motion pipelining on a *single* loop body, which makes the latency of the longest operation in the loop form an artificial lower bound of the II. If this lower bound is indeed longer than the II that has been aimed for during the EPS process, there must be stalls in the final schedule and we cannot achieve EPS's intended II.

It should be mentioned that in the VLIW context there is a moderately elaborate, local grouping phase after EPS[3] where latency constraints are rechecked to generate the final VLIW code [4]. A stall, if any, is detected in this phase when a copy generated for renaming a multi-latency instruction is located

---

[2] The swapping is for illustration purposes only because forward substitution without it would generate a group [x'=x"; store(x'); x"=load()] which is incorrect with sequential execution semantics; however, this is a valid parallel group with reads-first-then-writes parallel execution semantics [4].

[3] EPS for VLIW requires this phase anyway. Since EPS generates parallel groups on the CFG of the sequential code, resource constraints and data dependences may also need to be violated in the schedule as operations move through one group on its way to another group [9], requiring a final VLIW code generation phase.

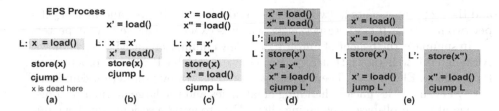

Fig. 3. An example of EPS with latencies; each box in (d) and (e) means a VLIW.

in a VLIW where the latency of the instruction has not yet elapsed. This latency violation can occur only at a copy that has been generated for code motion across the backedge from an already-scheduled cycle (e.g., both copies in Fig. 3), because it is generated without the control of the latency table during EPS unlike other instructions.

What unroll-based coalescing does is eliminate these latency-violating copies, thus obviating the need of stalls. That is, although EPS guarantees separation of a definition with a latency n and its "real" uses at least n cycles away, EPS may insert renaming copies in the intermediate cycles if EPS aims for II $< n$. These copies become "bogus" uses of the definition, causing stalls. By eliminating these bogus uses, we can restore the original II that EPS has aimed for.

It might be questioned what would happen if we do not rename a multi-latency instruction to avoid latency-violating copies. In Fig. 3, if we delay the code motion of the load later at stage 3, we can get a parallel group without any copy [store(x); x=load()]. This group also cannot be issued every cycle due to a stall, but with this schedule we cannot achieve II=1 even after unrolling. This is true because the II aimed for by EPS is already longer than 1.

It is somewhat interesting that copy elimination leads to stall elimination. However, the copy elimination problem itself is identical to and is solved in the same way as the unit-latency case. A more important point is that latency handling via EPS's renaming through copies, followed by unroll-based copy elimination, also works for loops with control flows.

Figure 4 shows a variable-II EPS example with latencies where unrolling removes copies causing a stall. Figure 4 (a) shows the EPS process for a loop which have two paths in it. We assume a load latency of two cycles. In this loop, there is a cyclic data dependence in the cc=T path while there is none in the cc=F path, so EPS should get an II=3 for the cc=T path and an II=1 for the cc=F path, respectively. The cc=F path can initiate every cycle and its EPS process stops at stage 4, while the EPS process for the cc=T path continues until stage 6. The schedule at the end of stage 6 includes many copies, some of which cause a stall if the VLIW code generator attempts to convert parallel groups into VLIWs (e.g., the cc=F path cannot be grouped into a single VLIW because the copy r4=r6 at the beginning of the loop causes a stall when grouped with r6=load(r1) at the end of the cc=F path). The loop is unrolled once as in Fig. (b) and the coalescing is performed. In Fig. 4 (c), there are no more copies left and the loop can execute in two cycles per two iterations if cc=F and in six cycles per two iterations if cc=T, respectively, which is exactly what we have expected.

In summary, the benefit of unroll-based copy elimination for EPS is as follows. Although it is well known that EPS can achieve a variable II and can pipeline any type of loop, EPS has not been as well accepted as MS by production compilers, partly because of its unclear handling of latencies and the large number of copies it generates. Unroll-based coalescing allows EPS to avoid a serious slowdown due to these problems while keeping its variable II and other advantages.

4   Comparison with Related Work

The cross-iteration register-overwrite problem is not new since any software pipelining technique must deal with it. In MS, there is a hardware solution called *rotating register files* [10] which support compiler-managed hardware renaming. If no hardware support is available, MS employs a technique called *modulo variable expansion* [3] which is also based on loop unrolling: the flat schedule is generated ignoring any cross-iteration register overwrites, yet if some live range in the schedule overlaps between iterations, it is unrolled so as to allocate separate registers.

For straight-line loops, our unroll-based coalescing after EPS, in essence, produces the same result as modulo variable expansion after MS. The real difference is that our approach is also applicable to loops with control flows. For such loops, we need to take care of cross-iteration register-overwrites for every combination of execution paths, which would make modulo variable expansion quite complex even if a flat schedule with a variable II were available. In EPS, partial renaming and forward substitution are applied in the context of DAG scheduling, so copies are generated without any distinction between straight-line loops and loops with control flows. Moreover, our unroll-based coalescing technique works even if there are control flows inside the loop (see Sect. 5). Copy generation at unrolled loop exits for obtaining correct values of live-out registers is also straightforward because it is handled simply by inserting dummy copies at unrolled exits and the coalescing automatically does the job (this is not that simple with modulo variable expansion even for straight-line loops if there are early exits). Consequently, our approach provides a simpler and more general solution than modulo variable expansion.

There is also an approach that unrolls the loop even before the scheduling starts [11]. In fact, it might be questioned why we do not unroll the loop and rename registers before EPS so as to avoid copies. Generally, it is difficult to decide the precise unroll amount before scheduling because we cannot determine where copies will be needed. For the stall problem, we might be able to estimate the unroll amount by dividing the latency of the longest operation in the loop by the MII, if we can compute the MII as in MS and let it guide the EPS [12]. However, this is plausible only for straight-line loops and we cannot compute the MII precisely for loops with control flows. In fact, even MS, which estimates the MII accurately, unrolls the loop after scheduling.

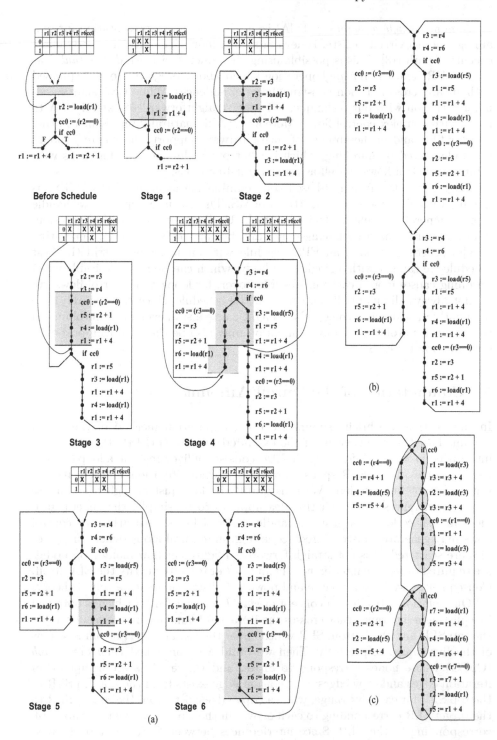

Fig. 4. A variable-II EPS example with latencies where unrolling obviates a stall.

Dynamic single assignment (DSA) is an intermediate representation for renaming where a virtual register is never assigned more than once on any dynamic execution path [13]. This is possible using the concept of *expanded virtual registers* (EVR) and the *remap()* operation which allows programs to be expressed without any cross-iteration non-true data dependences. While DSA shares a similar intuition with our technique, it is not straightforward to extend DSA to loops with complex control flows. Moreover, EVRs naturally represent rotating register files, and in the absence of such hardware support, the *remap()* should be implemented by unrolling, which is what our technique does for loops with arbitrary control flows as well as for straight-line loops.

One might classify unroll-based copy elimination as an artifact of EPS, as modulo variable expansion is an artifact of MS. This is true except that we handle a more general problem as does EPS itself. Unlike modulo variable expansion, however, unroll-based coalescing is not an absolute requirement for generating a valid schedule; in fact, an EPS schedule without unrolling is still the best schedule we can get with a single loop body, which can be more desirable when unrolling causes more I-cache misses. Moreover, for loops with control flows, we cannot always eliminate all the copies in the schedule, since there (rarely) are inherently uncoalescible copies which might cause a stall even after unrolling. In this respect, unroll-based copy elimination may also be classified as a post-pass optimization for EPS.

5   Computation of the Unroll Amount

In this section, we briefly summarize the computation method of the unroll amount based on the concept of the extended live range (ELR) that has been introduced in Sect. 1. Informally, an ELR consists of live ranges in a loop connected via copies. If an ELR spans more than a whole iteration, some of its live ranges cannot but interfere. We thus unroll the loop just enough to eliminate those interferences. Although the idea appears to be simple, the general problem in real code is not easy to handle. EPS of loops with arbitrary control flows may generate "unstructured" code (e.g., unnatural loops) where many copies are scattered. It is not straightforward to figure out how many loop bodies are required to remove interferences in an ELR or even to identify the ELR itself. Consequently, we need a precise and powerful abstraction with a sound theory.

Our solution introduces a concept of *split live range* (SLR) which is obtained by splitting a live range that crosses the iteration boundary into two subranges: the top SLR and the bottom SLR which cover the top and the bottom fractions of the live range, respectively. Then we build a graph called *copy flow graph* (CpFG) whose nodes correspond to SLRs, and whose edges are composed of iteration edges and copy edges; an iteration edge exists from the bottom SLR to the top SLR for each live range, while a copy edge exists from the source SLR to the target SLR corresponding to each copy. On the CpFG, we define a subgraph corresponding to the ELR. Since interferences between SLRs is more detailed than those between live ranges, and the iteration difference between SLRs in an ELR can be readily known (which is the number of iteration edges between them), we can easily decide the minimum unroll amount required to stretch the loop just enough to relocate all interfering SLRs in different loop bodies. If a loop is unrolled with this unroll amount, the ELR can be allocated to a single register which removes all copies in it. Our definitions of SLR, CpFG, and ELR work even when there are control flows inside the loop.

For a given loop, there can be more than one ELR in its CpFG. Finding a set of ELRs for a given loop corresponds to partitioning its CpFG into disjoint subgraphs of ELRs. Unfortunately, it is not always possible to make every copy in the loop belong to some ELR due to interferences. This raises the issue of finding an optimal set of ELRs that maximizes the number of coalescible copies while minimizing the unroll amount. We have developed a partitioning technique that is is simple, yet precise and powerful, such that we can precisely tell which copies will be coalescible and which will not after unrolling (in contrast to roughly coalescing some copies after unrolling some times). Moreover, the set of coalescible copies, in most cases, is maximal and requires the minimum unroll amount. All of these results have been confirmed via extensive experiments [2].

6   Experimental Results

In this section, we evaluate the performance impact of unroll-based copy elimination for EPS. We build the interference graph for the unrolled code, allocate the interference graph with a limited number of machine registers, and simulate the allocated code. Since not all of those coalescible copies after unrolling can be coalesced because of the increased register pressure caused by longer live ranges coalesced from smaller ones, we need a heuristic which coalesces as many copies as possible without causing any spill. We use the *iterated coalescing* technique by George and Appel [14] on top of an *optimistic register allocation* framework by Briggs et al [15].

6.1   SPARC-Based VLIW Testbed

The experiments have been performed on a SPARC-based VLIW testbed [16]. The input C code is compiled into optimized SPARC assembly code (without register windows) by the *gcc* compiler. The SPARC-based assembly code is scheduled into VLIW code by the EPS compiler [4], targeting a *tree* VLIW architecture which supports parallel execution of branches and data operations [17]. In the EPS compiler, our transformation is applied to parallelized code, producing better parallelized code having less copies. The parallelized code is transformed into VLIW code by converting parallel groups into VLIWs. The VLIW code is simulated, producing results and statistics. Our benchmarks consist of eight non-trivial integer programs (eqntott, espresso, li, compress, yacc, sed, gzip, wc) which include many loops with arbitrary control flows.

The resource constraint of the VLIW machine is based on parametric resource constraints of m ALUs and m-way branching, and we have evaluated four machines, with $m = 2$, 4, 8, and 16. All ALUs can perform arithmetic operations and memory operations, yet an ALU can perform either a memory operation or an arithmetic operation in one cycle. Branches are handled by a dedicated branch unit. All these machines have 64 general-purpose registers (32 SPARC + 32 scratch for renaming), 16 condition registers, and perfect D-caches. We have experimented with a load latency of one, two, three, and four cycles and with unit latencies for all other operations.

6.2   Performance Impact of Copy Elimination

We have found that many copies in innermost loops scheduled by EPS can be eliminated through unrolling. In 16-ALU VLIW with a two-cycle load latency, for example, 86% of otherwise uncoalescible copies in innermost loops become coalescible when unrolled 2.2 times on average. It has also been demonstrated that the unroll amount obtained is precise and the most efficient.

We examine how the reduction of copies due to unrolling affects the VLIW performance. As described in Sect. 3, copy elimination may improve performance (1) by reducing resource pressure, and (2) by obviating no-op VLIWs caused by latency-violating copies. The performance impact of (1) is that it reduces the resource usage in each parallel group, exposing the opportunity of merging two parallel groups into one. In fact, our VLIW code generator eagerly seeks further parallelism not exposed during the scheduling phase, by *peephole compaction* of adjacent VLIWs if the resource constraints, data dependences, and latencies are not violated. Therefore, unroll-based copy elimination may produce more opportunities for peephole compaction. In our experiments, the performance benefit comes only from this when the load latency is one cycle.

Figure 5 depicts the performance impact of copy elimination for each load latency in the four VLIW machines which are assumed to have perfect I-caches. For each configuration, the graph shows the *reduction ratio* of VLIW execution cycles for the unrolled code, compared to the non-unrolled code (which is also copy-coalesced). The corresponding useful IPC for the unrolled version of the 2-ALU, 4-ALU, 8-ALU, and 16-ALU VLIW code with a load latency of one is 1.90, 2.66, 3.16, and 3.92 respectively, which indicates that our EPS compiler is aggressive in exploiting ILP.

The graph shows that the unrolled version of the 16-ALU VLIW code with a load latency of one, two, three, and four cycles improves performance by a geometric mean of 4%, 18%, 22%, and 25%, respectively. Although the performance benefit is not uniformly distributed since it depends on the resource requirement of loops as well as resource constraints of the target machine, the graph clearly indicates that unroll-based copy elimination is critical to performance.

The graph also shows that when the load latency is one, the performance benefit is somewhat marginal ($\leq 4\%$ in geometric mean). This means that improved resource pressure due to copy elimination is less critical to performance[4], as discussed in Sect. 3. Most of the performance benefit thus comes from obviating

---

[4] However, our evaluation for all resource constraints (for m-ALUs where $2 \leq m \leq 16$) shows a peak improvement of a geometric mean of 7% at 13-ALU with occasional significant ($\geq 10\%$) improvements for some benchmarks [2].

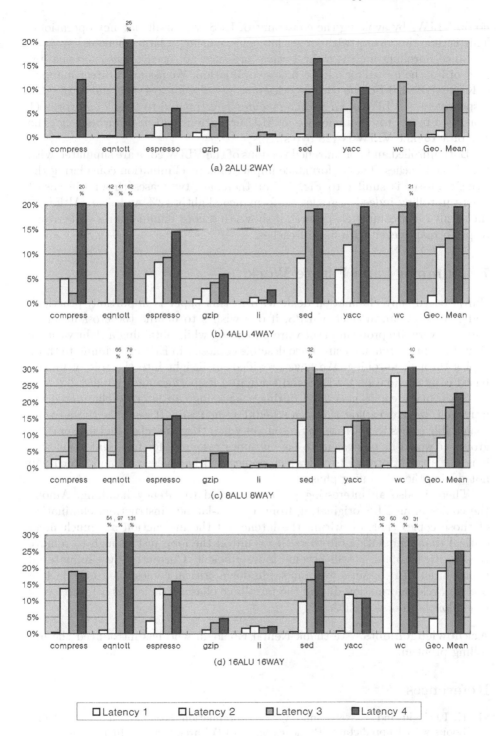

Fig. 5. Performance impact of copy elimination.

no-op VLIWs by avoiding the constraint of EPS with multi-latency operations. This is more important with longer latencies, causing a larger benefit.

Since unrolling increases the I-cache pressure, we need to measure the impact of I-cache misses for a more precise evaluation. We assumed direct-mapped 64KB and 128KB I-cache with 6-cycles miss penalty for 2/4-ALU and 8/16-ALU, respectively. A VLIW of an m-ALU machine is estimated to take $2 \cdot m$ words (1 word = 4 bytes) to accommodate m ALU operations and m branches (e.g., the size of a 16-ALU VLIW is 128 bytes).

Both unrolled and non-unrolled versions of the VLIW code are simulated with the above I-caches. The performance impact of copy elimination considering the I-cache misses is similar to Fig. 5, but there are two cases (from 128 cases) where unrolling indeed degrades performance slightly (2% and 6%). Although the result is not completely general, it shows that copy elimination is still critical to performance even with finite I-caches.

7   Summary and Future Work

Unroll-based copy elimination dealt with in this paper is important, practical, and is not just an artifact of EPS; if one wishes to handle the cross-iteration register overwrite problem in software pipelining while obtaining a tight variable II, it is simple to rename using uncoalescible copies as in EPS and eliminate those copies through unrolling. We have provided an insight into the role of unroll-based copy elimination for EPS and evaluated its performance impact.

Since many copies generated during scheduling can later be eliminated via unrolling, we may exploit this as a scheduling heuristic. If we make those to-be-coalescible copies to not take any resources when they are scheduled in a parallel group, it would be equivalent to having more resources for free. Unfortunately, it is not straightforward to tell which copies will be coalescible and which will not during the scheduling phase.

There is also an interesting problem related to latency handling. Among the copies in an ELR originating from a multi-latency instruction, elimination of those copies that are within the latency of the instruction are much more critical than elimination of others. If we unroll the loop just enough to remove these critical copies, it will become more efficient. Currently, we eliminate all copies in an ELR because we cannot pin down critical copies due to the lack of precise cycle information during the unrolling phase. It is left as a future work to exploit both opportunities.

Acknowledgements. We thank Kemal Ebcioğlu who has introduced the unrolling problem.

References

1. K. Ebcioğlu and T. Nakatani. A New Compilation Technique for Parallelizing Loops with Unpredictable Branches on a VLIW architecture. In *Languages and Compilers for Parallel Computing*, pages 213–229. MIT Press, 1989.

2. S.-M. Moon, S. Kim, and J. Park. Unroll-based Copy Coalescing. Technical report, Seoul National University, 1997.
3. M. Lam. Software Pipelining: An Effective Scheduling Technique for VLIW Machines. In *Proceedings of the SIGPLAN 1988 Conference on Programming Language Design and Implementation*, pages 318–328, 1988.
4. S.-M. Moon and K. Ebcioğlu. Parallelizing Nonnumerical Code with Selective Scheduling and Software Pipelining. *ACM Transactions on Programming Languages and Systems*, 19(6):853–898, Nov. 1997.
5. V. Allan, R. Jones, R. Lee, and S. Allan. Software Pipelining. *ACM Computing Surveys*, 27(3):367–432, Sep. 1995.
6. B. Rau and C. Glaeser. Some Scheduling Techniques and an Easily Schedulable Horizontal Architecture for High Performance Scientific Computing. In *Proceedings of the 14th Annual Workshop on Microprogramming (Micro-14)*, pages 183–198, 1981.
7. Nancy J. Warter-Perez and Noubar Partamian. Modulo Scheduling with Multiple Initiation Intervals. In *Proccedings of the 28th Annual ACM/IEEE International Symposium on Microarchitecture (Micro-28)*, pages 111–118, 1995.
8. Mark G. Stoodley and Corinna G. Lee. Software Pipelining Loops with Conditional Branches. In *Proceedings of the 29th Annual ACM/IEEE International Symposium on Microarchitecture (Micro-29)*, 1996.
9. A. Aiken, A. Nicolau, and S. Novack. Resource-Constrained Software Pipelining. *IEEE Transactions on Parallel and Distributed Systems*, 6(12):1248–1269, Dec 1995.
10. J. Dehnert, P. Hsu, and J. Bratt. Overlapped Loop Support in the Cydra 5. In *Proceedings of the 3rd International Conference on Architectural Support for Programming Languages and Operating Systems (ASPLOS-3)*, pages 26–38, 1989.
11. S. Jain. Circular Scheduling: A New Technique to Perform Software Pipelining. In *Proceedings of the SIGPLAN 1991 conference on Programming Language Design and Implementation*, pages 219–228, Jun 1991.
12. SangMin Shim and Soo-Mook Moon. Split-Path Enhnaced Pipeline Scheduling for Loops with Control Flows. In *Proceedings of the 31st Annual ACM/IEEE International Symposium on Microarchitecture (Micro-31)*, pages 93–102, 1998.
13. B. Rau. Data Flow and Dependence Analysis for Instruction Level Parallelism. In *Languages and Compilers for Parallel Computing*, pages 236–250. MIT Press, 1994.
14. L. George and A. Appel. Iterated Register Coalescing. *ACM Transactions on Programming Languages and Systems*, 18(3):300–324, May 1996.
15. P. Briggs, K. Cooper, and L. Torczon. Improvements to Graph Coloring Register Allocation. *ACM Transactions on Programming Languages and Systems*, 16(3):428–455, May 1994.
16. S. Park, S. Shim, and S.-M. Moon. Evaluation of Scheduling Techniques on a SPARC-based VLIW Testbed. In *Proceedings of the 30th Annual International Symposium on Microarchitecture*, Dec 1997.
17. S.-M. Moon and K. Ebcioğlu. Performance Analysis of Tree VLIW Architecture for Exploiting Branch ILP in Non-Numerical Code. In *Proceedings of the 1997 International Conference on Supercomputing*, pages 301–308, New York, July 1997.

A Linear Algebra Formulation for Optimising Replication in Data Parallel Programs

Olav Beckmann and Paul H.J. Kelly*

Department of Computing, Imperial College,
180 Queen's Gate, London SW7 2BZ, U.K.
{ob3,phjk}@doc.ic.ac.uk

Abstract. In this paper, we present an efficient technique for optimising data replication under the data parallel programming model. We propose a precise mathematical representation for data replication which allows handling replication as an explicit, separate stage in the parallel data placement problem. This representation takes the form of an invertible mapping. We argue that this property is key to making data replication amenable to good mathematical optimisation algorithms. We further outline an algorithm for optimising data replication, based on this representation, which performs interprocedural data placement optimisation over a sequence of loop nests. We have implemented the algorithm and show performance figures.

1 Introduction

Choosing parallel data placements which minimise communication is key to generating efficient data parallel programs. Under the data parallel programming model, parallel data placement is typically represented by a two-stage mapping. In the first stage, an affine alignment function maps array elements onto virtual processors. In the second stage, a distribution function then maps virtual processors onto physical ones. Examples for such a two-stage approach are listed in [5]. This decomposition fails to account properly for data replication: rather than using an explicit replication stage, replication is often handled implicitly as part of the alignment stage through *replicated alignments*. In this paper, we propose an efficient mathematical representation for data replication which expresses replication as an independent third stage of parallel data placement.

While a good range of optimisation techniques has been described for the alignment stage, distribution and replication have received less attention. We argue that the representation which we propose in this paper is a step towards making data replication amenable to the same type of mathematical optimisation algorithms which have previously been used for alignment optimisation. We demonstrate this assertion by describing and implementing an algorithm

---

* While this work was carried out, Paul Kelly was a visiting research scientist at the Department of Computer Science and Engineering, University of California at San Diego, USA.

L. Carter and J. Ferrante (Eds.): LCPC'99, LNCS 1863, pp. 100–116, 2000.
© Springer-Verlag Berlin Heidelberg 2000

which performs interprocedural data replication optimisation across a sequence of loop nests. The objective function which our optimisation algorithm attempts to minimise is communication volume.

The practical importance of maintaining multiple copies of certain data is evident:

- The programmer may specify a replicated placement, e.g. through **spread** operations [5], replicated alignments in HPF [8] or flooding operators in ZPL [12].
- If a read-only array is accessed by several processors in a particular subroutine or loop, it is more efficient to use a broadcast operation, generally $O(\log P)$, to replicate that array than to let processors access the array by remote reads, which would most likely be $\Theta(P)$, unless a special scheme, such as proxies [13] is used.
- Arrays may be replicated in order to facilitate parallelisation of a loop nest which would otherwise be blocked by anti- or output-dependencies on those arrays. This is a highly effective technique, known as *array privatisation* [11].
- In certain circumstances, runtime re-alignments of arrays can be avoided by replication. Specifically, mobile offset alignments can be realised through replication [4].

Default Strategies. Implementations have typically made the assumption that scalars are replicated everywhere (e.g. HPF [8]), or sometimes more generally, that when mapped onto a higher-dimensional processor grid, lower-dimensional arrays are replicated in those dimensions where their extent is 1 (e.g. our own work [2]). There are other possible default strategies for choosing which arrays and scalars to replicate. However, while such a uniform default layout might conceivably be optimal in some circumstances, it is commonly much more efficient (as we show in an example shortly) to choose whether and how to replicate each value according to context.

Motivation. The key performance benefits from optimising data replication arise from:

1. *Replacing All-Reduce Operations with Simple Reductions.*
   A reduction which leaves its result in replicated form on all participating processors is known as an all-reduce. On most platforms, all-reduce operations are significantly more expensive than simple reductions; their complexity generally is that of a simple reduction followed by a broadcast. This is illustrated in Figure 1. Kumar et al. [9] show that theoretically-better implementations do exist, but they require at least the connectivity of a hypercube with two-way communication links. We therefore frequently have the opportunity of a significant performance gain by making an optimal choice about whether the result of a reduction is replicated or not.

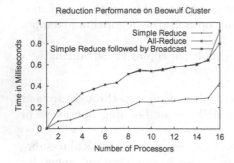 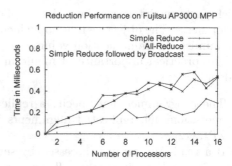

Fig. 1. Performance comparison of simple reduction and all-reduce (reduction over addition, 1 scalar per processor). *Left:* Cluster of 350MHz Pentium II workstations, running Linux 2.0.36 (TCP patched), connected by 100Mb/s ethernet and using `mpich-1.1.1`. *Right:* Fujitsu AP3000 MPP: Nodes are 300 MHz UltraSPARC, connected by 200 MB/s AP-Net. Averages of 100 runs; for both platforms, 5% of peak values were left out. In both cases, all-reduce takes roughly twice as long as reduce. Further, the figures illustrate that the performance of all-reduce is on these two platforms the same as that of a simple reduction followed by a broadcast.

2. *Reducing the Cost of Residual Affine Communications.*
   In many programs, it is not possible to find a set of affine alignments which eliminate all redistributions. However, the cost of these residual affine communications will be less if the data being communicated is not replicated.

Concrete instances of these two optimisations are illustrated in the working example introduced at the end of this section.

Background: DESO BLAS Library. Although this work is applicable to compile-time optimisation, it has been developed and implemented in the context of our delayed evaluation, self-optimising (DESO) library [2] of parallel numerical routines (mainly level 1 and 2 BLAS [10]). This library uses delayed evaluation — more details will be given in Section 3 — to capture the calling program's data flow and then performs runtime interprocedural data placement optimisation. Finding algorithms efficient enough for use at run-time is a key motivation for our work.

Contributions of This Paper. We propose a technique for optimising data replication:

- We describe a mathematical representation for replication which takes the form of an invertible mapping. We argue that this property is key to making data replication amenable to good mathematical optimisation algorithms.
- We describe an optimisation algorithm, based on this representation, which performs interprocedural data placement optimisation over a sequence of loop nests.
- We argue that our optimisation algorithm is efficient enough to be used in a runtime system.

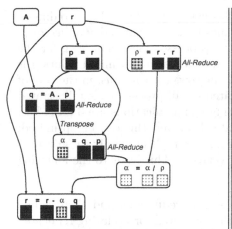
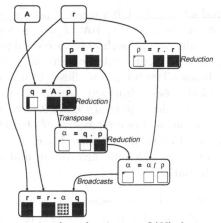

- 1 all-reduce on $O(N)$ data ($q = Ap$)
- 2 all-reduce operations on $O(P)$ data (vector dot products)
- 1 transpose on $O(PN)$ data

- 1 simple reduction on $O(N)$ data
- 2 simple reductions on $O(1)$ data
- 1 transpose on $O(N)$ data
- 2 broadcasts, of $O(1)$ and $O(N)$ data.

Fig. 2. Sequence of operations from the conjugate gradient iterative algorithm for solving linear systems $Ax = b$, showing data layout on a mesh of processors. Affine alignment has already been optimised in both examples.

Our optimisation algorithm works from aggregate loop nests which have been parallelised in isolation. We do not address any parallelism vs. replication trade-offs; we assume that decisions about which arrays have to be privatised for parallelisation have been taken separately.

The paper builds on related work in the field of optimising affine alignment, such as [5, 6]. Chatterjee et al. [4] provides a key point of reference for our work and we evaluate our work in comparison to their approach at the end of the paper in Section 5.

Overview of This Paper. After the final section of this introduction, which presents an example to illustrate the potential performance benefits of optimising replication, Section 2 describes our proposed representation for data replication. In Section 3, we describe an algorithm for interprocedural optimisation of data replication, which is based on the representation from the previous section. Section 4 discusses evaluation of our work using our DESO library of parallel numerical routines. Finally, Section 5 reviews related work and Section 6 concludes.

Example: Conjugate Gradient. Consider the sequence of operations from the first iteration of the conjugate gradient algorithm which is shown in Figure 2. By far the most compute-intensive part of this algorithm is the vector-matrix product $q = Ap$. On a mesh of processors, this can be parallelised in two dimensions as long as every row of the processor mesh has a private copy of vector p. It would not be profitable to reconfigure the processor mesh as a ring for the remaining vector-vector operations; rather, the easiest unoptimised solution is to block all vectors, in replicated form, over the rows (or columns, in the case of q) of the mesh. Similarly, scalars are replicated on all processors. As illustrated in the left-hand part of Figure 2, the resulting communications are 3 all-reduce operations and one transpose of $O(NP)$ data. However, this can be optimised: the solution in the right-hand part of Figure 2 keeps replicated only those scalars and vectors which are involved in updating vector p. This leads to the following optimisations:

- We replace all-reduce operations with simple reductions and then choose optimum points to broadcast data which is required for updating replicated vectors. On many platforms, this will save a broadcast operation.
- Further, the transpose operation which is necessary to align q and p for the dot-product $\alpha = q.p$ now only has to communicate $O(N)$ data and involves $2P - 1$ rather than $P^2 - P$ processors.

Our choice of unoptimised implementation is arguably somewhat arbitrary; the point is that unless replication is incorporated into the data placement optimisation process, optimisations like these will be missed. Note also that we can improve further still on the solution shown here by choosing a skewed affine placement for q. Detecting this automatically requires our optimiser to take account of both affine alignment and replication. We will address this issue again when we discuss future work in Section 6.

2   Representing Data Replication

In this section, we introduce our representation for data replication. Our objective has been to develop a representation which is both efficient to implement and which facilitates efficient optimisation.

2.1   Overview of Data Placement for Data Parallel Programs

Our starting point is the typical data parallel two-stage approach of a mapping onto virtual processors followed by a distribution of virtual processors onto physical ones. The notion of a virtual processor grid is equivalent to that of a template, as described by Chatterjee et al. [5].

We *augment* the dimensionality of all arrays in an optimisation problem to the highest number of dimensions occurring in that problem. This is a purely conceptual step which does not imply any data movement and it is equivalent to the concept that a template is a Cartesian grid of "sufficiently high dimension" into which all arrays can be mapped [5]. If we wish to map an N-vector over a two-dimensional processor grid, we conceptually treat this vector as a $(1, N)$

matrix[1]. Scalars are handled in the same way, so a scalar would be treated as a $(1,1)$-array when mapped onto the same grid. Following augmentation, our representation for data placement consists of three stages:

1. *Replication descriptors* allow us to represent the replication of arrays in any dimension where their extent is 1. We describe these descriptors in detail later in this section.
2. *Affine alignment functions* act on augmented, replicated array index vectors i and map them onto virtual processor indices. They take the form

$$f(i) = Ai + t .$$ (1)

   The alignment function for mapping a row vector over the rows of a processor mesh is $f(i) = \left(\begin{smallmatrix} 1 & 0 \\ 0 & 1 \end{smallmatrix}\right)i + \left(\begin{smallmatrix} 0 \\ 0 \end{smallmatrix}\right)$. Note that this representation allows us to capture axis, stride and offset alignment as defined in [5]. Some approaches [5, 8] limit the nature of the matrix A, such as to require exactly one non-zero entry per column and no more than one non-zero entry per row. The only restriction we impose on these alignment functions is that they be invertible. Thus, we can represent skewings, as well as simple permutations for axis alignments.
3. *Distribution* or *folding* functions map virtual processor index vectors onto pairs of physical processor and local indices. We currently use the well-known symbolic representations `block`, collapsed (*) and `cyclic(N)` as distribution functions. Notice that folding allows us to "serialise" some of the replication we may have introduced in step 1, leaving no more than one copy of each array per physical processor.

Properties of Affine Alignment Functions. The affine alignment functions we have described above have two properties which facilitate efficient implementation and optimisation: *invertibility* and *closure under composition*.

- Invertibility means that, given an affine alignment function, we can always calculate both which virtual processor holds a particular array element, and also, which array element is held by a particular virtual processor. This property facilitates sender-initiated communication, an important optimisation on distributed-memory architectures.
- Further, given the above properties and two affine alignment functions f and g for an array, we may always calculate a *redistribution* function $r = f^{-1} \circ g$, which is itself an affine function (invertibility gives us the existence of f^{-1} and closure under composition that r is affine). As we will discuss in more detail in Section 3, this property facilitates efficient optimisation. We define a weight function w, which returns an estimate of the amount of data movement generated by r. The optimisation problem we need to solve is then to minimise, over all edges in a DAG, the sum of weights $w(r)$ associated with the redistributions r along the edges, subject to placement constraints. Examples for this approach are [6, 2].

---

[1] We always add dimensions in initial positions. Thus, when augmenting an N-vector to 2 dimensions, we always treat it as a $(1, N)$ matrix, never as a $(N, 1)$ matrix.

2.2   Replication Descriptors

Our aim in designing descriptors for data replication has been to re-use as much previous work on optimising affine alignment as possible; we have therefore required that our descriptors have both the above-mentioned properties of invertibility and closure under composition. The advantages become apparent in Section 3 where we outline our optimisation algorithm.

Let d_v be the number of dimensions of an array after augmentation (i.e. the number of dimensions of the virtual processor grid). Let V be the index space of the array after augmentation and let V_n be the set of all possible index values in dimension n of V. Let i be an array index vector. We define (,) to be a constructor function which takes two $d_v \times d_v$ matrices D_1, D_2 and returns a function (D_1, D_2), where

$$(D_1, D_2)\, i = D_1 \cdot \mathrm{Solve}(D_2, i)\ . \tag{2}$$

$\mathrm{Solve}(M, v)$, where M is a matrix and v a vector, is the set of solutions to the equation $Mx = v$, i.e. $\mathrm{Solve}(M, v) \overset{\text{def}}{=} \{x M x = v\}$. This is also known as the pre-image of M.

Definition 1 (Copy Function). *We now define a replication or copy function c to be (D_1, D_2), where D_1, D_2 are $d_v \times d_v$ matrices, and we have*

$$\begin{aligned}
c\, i &\overset{\text{def}}{=} (D_1, D_2)\, i \\
&= D_1 \cdot Solve(D_2, i) \\
&= \{D_1 x D_2 x = i \text{ and } x \in V\}\ .
\end{aligned} \tag{3}$$

Matrix D_2 is used to generate sets of locations to copy data to; D_1 is used to collapse sets. We first give one preliminary example and then prove that this definition does indeed meet the properties which we require. Further examples and rationale follow.

Example 1. The copy function for replicating a vector down the columns of a processor mesh is $\left(\left(\begin{smallmatrix}1&0\\0&1\end{smallmatrix}\right), \left(\begin{smallmatrix}0&0\\0&1\end{smallmatrix}\right)\right)$. Note that the vector x is a row-vector, i.e. a $(1, n)$ array. Its first index value is therefore always 0. Thus, we have:

$$\begin{aligned}
\left(\begin{smallmatrix}1&0\\0&1\end{smallmatrix}\right) \cdot \mathrm{Solve}\left(\left(\begin{smallmatrix}0&0\\0&1\end{smallmatrix}\right), i\right) &= \{x \left(\begin{smallmatrix}0&0\\0&1\end{smallmatrix}\right) x = \left(\begin{smallmatrix}0\\i\end{smallmatrix}\right), x \in V\} \\
&\overset{H}{=} \{x \left(\begin{smallmatrix}0&0\\0&1\end{smallmatrix}\right) x = \mathbf{0}, x \in V\} + \left(\begin{smallmatrix}0\\j\end{smallmatrix}\right) \\
&= \{\left(\begin{smallmatrix}x_1\\0\end{smallmatrix}\right) x_1 \in V_1\} + \left(\begin{smallmatrix}0\\i\end{smallmatrix}\right) \\
&= \{\left(\begin{smallmatrix}x_1\\i\end{smallmatrix}\right) x_1 \in V_1\}\ .
\end{aligned}$$

The second equality, marked H, is due to the homomorphism theorem [7]. We will expand shortly. Each vector element i, which after augmentation corresponds to $\left(\begin{smallmatrix}0\\i\end{smallmatrix}\right)$, therefore gets mapped to all virtual processor indices in its column.

Remark 1. The only formal restriction which we have imposed on the matrices D_1 and D_2 in a replication descriptor is that their dimensions are $d_v \times d_v$. However, we do not lose any expressive power in practice by only using *diagonal* matrices: A skewed replication such as $\left(\left(\begin{smallmatrix} 1 & 0 \\ 0 & 1 \end{smallmatrix} \right), \left(\begin{smallmatrix} 1 & -1 \\ 0 & 0 \end{smallmatrix} \right) \right)$ can always be achieved by using a replication descriptor consisting of diagonal matrices $\left(\left(\begin{smallmatrix} 1 & 0 \\ 0 & 1 \end{smallmatrix} \right), \left(\begin{smallmatrix} 0 & 0 \\ 0 & 1 \end{smallmatrix} \right) \right)$ together with a skewed affine alignment function $f(i) = \left(\begin{smallmatrix} 1 & 0 \\ 1 & 1 \end{smallmatrix} \right) i + \left(\begin{smallmatrix} 0 \\ 0 \end{smallmatrix} \right)$.

Proposition 1. *The composition of two copy functions* $c_1 = (D_1, D_2)$, $c_2 = (E_1, E_2)$ *is*

$$c_1 \circ c_2 = (D_1 \cdot E_1, \ E_2 \cdot D_2) . \tag{4}$$

Proof. We have

$$
\begin{aligned}
(c_1 \circ c_2)(i) &= c_1 \left(\ \{ E_1 x E_2 x = i, x \in V \} \ \right) \\
&= \{ D_1 y D_2 y = E_1 x, \ E_2 x = i, \ y, x \in V \} \\
&= \{ D_1 E_1 y D_2 y = x, \ E_2 x = i, \ y, x \in V \} \\
&= \{ D_1 E_1 y E_2 D_2 y = i, \ y \in V \} .
\end{aligned}
$$

$\square$

Proposition 2. *The composition of two copy functions is again a copy function.*

Proof. Follows from the fact that the product of two $d_v \times d_v$ matrices is a $d_v \times d_v$ matrix.

Proposition 3. *If the matrices* D_1 *and* D_2 *contain identical entries in corresponding locations, we may "cancel" those entries by replacing them with 1 in both matrices.*

Proof. We examine the one-dimensional case. Let d_1, d_2 be arbitrary scalars. Thus, we have $(d_1, d_2) \, i = d_1 \cdot \text{Solve}(d_2, i)$. If we now assume that $d_1 = d_2$, we have

$$
\begin{aligned}
(d_1, d_2) \, i &= d_1 \cdot \text{Solve}(d_1, i) \\
&= \{ d_1 x d_1 x = i \} \\
&= \{ i \} \\
&= (1, 1) \, i .
\end{aligned} \tag{5}
$$

The multidimensional case easily follows. Note that this type of "cancellation" even applies if the identical corresponding entries are zeros. $\square$

Proposition 4. *The inverse of a copy function* $c = (D_1, D_2)$ *is*

$$c^{-1} = (D_2, D_1) . \tag{6}$$

Proof. $c \circ c^{-1} = (D_1 D_2, D_1 D_2)$. Therefore, the two matrices in $c \circ c^{-1}$ are identical, which means that according to Proposition 3, we can replace all entries with 1, so we have $c \circ c^{-1} = (I, I)$. $\square$

Rationale. The first problem that had to be addressed when trying to represent replication is that a one-to-many "mapping" is not a function. The first idea in trying to work around this problem was to represent the "inverse replication" function instead, i.e., a many-to-one mapping. Given such an inverse function f, we have to solve equations of the form $f(x) = i$ in order to establish which virtual processors the data element with index vector i is replicated on.

Since we wish to optimise at runtime, the second challenge was to ensure that these equations can be solved very efficiently; in particular, their solution complexity should not depend on either array data size or processor numbers. We make use of the homomorphism theorem [7]: Formally, an equation is a pair (f, y) of a function $f : D \longrightarrow R$ and an element y of R. The *solution* of (f, y) is the set $\{x \in Df(x) = y\}$. The *kernel* of f is the solution to $(f, 0_R)$: $= \{x \in Df(x) = 0_R\}$. If a function f is a homomorphism, it may not be invertible, but, we can make a very useful statement about the nature of the solution to all equations of the form (f, y) with $y \in R$: the homomorphism theorem states that for all $y \in R$,

$$\text{Solve}(f, y) = \{x \in Df(x) = y\} = +y \ . \tag{7}$$

This means that although we may not be able to formulate an inverse for such a function, we need only solve *one* equation, the kernel, in order to be able to state the solutions to *all* possible equations involving this function: they may then be calculated by simple addition. The requirement that the inverse copy function be a homomorphism meant choosing a vector-matrix product, i.e. multiplication by the matrix D_2 in our replication descriptor.

Finally, since the inverse copying homomorphisms D_2 are not invertible, we cannot use them to represent collapsing, i.e. a change from replicated to non-replicated placement. We therefore use a pair (D_1, D_2) of matrices. Multiplying the solutions to the equation $D_2 x = i$ by D_1 allows us to represent collapsing.

Intuition. Our construction of an invertible representation for data replication is in many aspects analogous to the construction of rational numbers from integers, which is prompted by the lack multiplicative inverses in $\mathbb{Z}$. In both cases, the answer is to use a pair (fraction) of elements. Note also the parallel nature of the definitions for composition (multiplication) and inverse, and the notion of 'cancel and replace with 1'. One important difference, though, is that since we are dealing with finite sets of numbers (index vector spaces), having zeros in the right hand component ('denominator') does not cause problems.

2.3   Examples

1. The copy function for replicating a scalar on column 0 of a processor mesh is $\left(\left(\begin{smallmatrix} 1 & 0 \\ 0 & 1 \end{smallmatrix}\right), \left(\begin{smallmatrix} 0 & 0 \\ 0 & 1 \end{smallmatrix}\right)\right)$ (see Example 1).
2. The copy function for replicating a scalar on row 0 of a mesh of processors is $\left(\left(\begin{smallmatrix} 1 & 0 \\ 0 & 1 \end{smallmatrix}\right), \left(\begin{smallmatrix} 1 & 0 \\ 0 & 0 \end{smallmatrix}\right)\right)$.

3. The *redistribution* function for changing the placement of a scalar from replicated on column 0 to replicated on row 0 is $\left(\left(\begin{smallmatrix}0&0\\0&1\end{smallmatrix}\right),\left(\begin{smallmatrix}1&0\\0&0\end{smallmatrix}\right)\right)$.

4. We conclude with a more complicated example: Suppose we have an $n \times n$ matrix distributed (block, block) over a $p \times p$ processor mesh, and that we wish to replicate an m-element vector on every processor, i.e., 'align' the entire vector with every $\frac{n}{p} \times \frac{n}{p}$ block of the matrix. We can represent such a placement. We augment the virtual processor space dimensions to 3, treating the matrix as $1 \times n \times n$, and then choose the following placement descriptors:

<table>
<tr><td>Matrix:</td><td>Vector:</td></tr>
<tr>
<td>Replication: $\left(\left(\begin{smallmatrix}1&0&0\\0&1&0\\0&0&1\end{smallmatrix}\right),\left(\begin{smallmatrix}1&0&0\\0&1&0\\0&0&1\end{smallmatrix}\right)\right)$</td>
<td>Replication: $\left(\left(\begin{smallmatrix}1&0&0\\0&1&0\\0&0&1\end{smallmatrix}\right),\left(\begin{smallmatrix}1&0&0\\0&0&0\\0&0&0\end{smallmatrix}\right)\right)$</td>
</tr>
<tr>
<td>Affine: $f(i) = \left(\begin{smallmatrix}1&0&0\\0&1&0\\0&0&1\end{smallmatrix}\right)i + \left(\begin{smallmatrix}0\\0\\0\end{smallmatrix}\right)$</td>
<td>Affine: $f(i) = \left(\begin{smallmatrix}0&1&0\\0&0&1\\1&0&0\end{smallmatrix}\right)i + \left(\begin{smallmatrix}0\\0\\0\end{smallmatrix}\right)$</td>
</tr>
<tr>
<td>Folding: (*, block, block)</td>
<td>Folding: (*, *, *)</td>
</tr>
</table>

The point here is that although we cannot replicate the vector along a dimension where its data extent is more than 1, we can use a combination of augmentation, affine permutation of axes, replication along those axes which after permutation have an extent of 1 and collapsed distribution to represent the same effect.

Summary. We have presented a powerful and efficient, invertible mathematical representation for data replication in data parallel programs. We have illustrated that we can represent a wide range of replicated data placements. We will discuss related work, in particular by Chatterjee et al. [4] in Section 5.

3   Optimisation

We have developed the techniques described in this paper in the context of a delayed evaluation, self-optimising (DESO) library of parallel numerical routines. The library uses delayed evaluation of library operators to capture the control flow of a user program at runtime. This is achieved through wrappers round the actual parallel numerical routines. When we encounter a *force point* (a point in the user program where evaluation of our library calls can be delayed no longer, such as when output is required), we call our interprocedural data placement optimiser on the DAG of library calls that has been accumulated.

We have previously described [2] and implemented an affine alignment optimisation algorithm, loosely based on that of Feautrier [6]. In this following section, we outline an algorithm for optimising replication. We make use of the invertibility and closure properties of our replication descriptors so that this algorithm follows a very similar pattern to our affine alignment optimisation algorithm.

It is not possible within the confines of this paper to give an exhaustive description of our optimisation algorithm; we will therefore focus on describing key enabling techniques for our algorithm which rely on the replication representation described in Section 2: metadata for operators, redistributions and redistribution cost.

3.1 Library Operator Placement Constraints

Our library operators have one or more parallel implementations. Each of these implementations is characterised by a set of placement constraints (metadata) that constrain our search during optimisation. In our case, these have been provided by the library implementor; however, they could also have been computed by a compiler. Note that each call to a library operator forms a node in the DAG we are optimising. Our library operators therefore precisely correspond to single statements in the compile-time alignment optimisation approach of Chatterjee [5], where nodes in the graph represent array operations. In this paper, we will concentrate on those placement constraints which describe replication.

- The replication placement constraints for library operators describe the *placement relationship* between the result and the operands. For a library operator which defines an array y, reading array x, we denote the replication descriptor for the result y by c_y and the descriptor for the operand x by c_{yx}. For example, for the daxpy loop $y \leftarrow \alpha x + y$, we have

$$c_{yx} = ((\begin{smallmatrix} 1 & 0 \\ 0 & 1 \end{smallmatrix}), (\begin{smallmatrix} 1 & 0 \\ 0 & 1 \end{smallmatrix})) \circ c_y \qquad c_{y\alpha} = ((\begin{smallmatrix} 1 & 0 \\ 0 & 1 \end{smallmatrix}), (\begin{smallmatrix} 1 & 0 \\ 0 & 0 \end{smallmatrix})) \circ c_y . \qquad (8)$$

   This means that the input vector x always has the same degree of replication as the result y, while α has replication along dimension 1 added to the placement of y.
- Thus, when doing a vector update the result of which is required in non-replicated form, the chosen replication placements will be that the input vector x is not replicated, while α is replicated along row 0 of a processor mesh.

   However, when the required placement for the result is replicated on all rows of a processor mesh, i.e., $c_y = ((\begin{smallmatrix} 1 & 0 \\ 0 & 1 \end{smallmatrix}), (\begin{smallmatrix} 0 & 0 \\ 0 & 1 \end{smallmatrix}))$, then we can work out the resulting placements for the operands x and α as follows:

$$c_{yx} = ((\begin{smallmatrix} 1 & 0 \\ 0 & 1 \end{smallmatrix}), (\begin{smallmatrix} 1 & 0 \\ 0 & 1 \end{smallmatrix})) \circ ((\begin{smallmatrix} 1 & 0 \\ 0 & 1 \end{smallmatrix}), (\begin{smallmatrix} 0 & 0 \\ 0 & 1 \end{smallmatrix})) \qquad c_{y\alpha} = ((\begin{smallmatrix} 1 & 0 \\ 0 & 1 \end{smallmatrix}), (\begin{smallmatrix} 1 & 0 \\ 0 & 0 \end{smallmatrix})) \circ ((\begin{smallmatrix} 1 & 0 \\ 0 & 1 \end{smallmatrix}), (\begin{smallmatrix} 0 & 0 \\ 0 & 1 \end{smallmatrix}))$$
$$= ((\begin{smallmatrix} 1 & 0 \\ 0 & 1 \end{smallmatrix}), (\begin{smallmatrix} 0 & 0 \\ 0 & 1 \end{smallmatrix})) \qquad\qquad\qquad = ((\begin{smallmatrix} 1 & 0 \\ 0 & 1 \end{smallmatrix}), (\begin{smallmatrix} 0 & 0 \\ 0 & 0 \end{smallmatrix})) .$$

   Thus, x will now be replicated on every row of the processor grid, while α is replicated on every processor.
- When our optimiser changes the placement of one of the operands or of the result of any node in a DAG, it can use these placement constraints to recalculate the placements for the other arrays involved in the computation. Library operators also have to adapt dynamically their behaviour so as to always comply with their placement constraints.

3.2   Calculating Required Redistributions

While accumulating a DAG, our library assigns placements to library operands according to the default scheme mentioned in Section 1: when aligned with higher-dimensional arrays, lower-dimensional arrays are replicated in dimensions where, after augmentation, their extent is 1. In particular, this means that scalars are by default replicated on all processors.

Once a DAG has been accumulated and is available for optimisation, our algorithm begins by calculating the required *replication redistributions* between the placements of arrays at the source and sink of all edges in the DAG. We denote *nodes* in a DAG by the values they calculate. For an edge $a \longrightarrow b$, we denote the replication descriptor (copy function) of a at the source by c_a and the copy function at the sink by c_{a_b}. The replication redistribution function $r_{a \to b}$ for this edge is defined by $c_a = r_{a \to b} \circ c_{a_b}$ and may be calculated as $r_{a \to b} = c_a \circ c_{a_b}^{-1}$.

3.3   Cost Model for Redistributions

We define the *size vector* N_a of an array a to be the vector consisting of the array's data size in all dimensions, so for an $n \times m$ matrix M, we have $N_M = \binom{n}{m}$. We define the data volume V_a of a as $V_a = \prod_{0 \leqslant i \leqslant d_v} N_a[i]$, in other words, V_a is the total data size of a. Let P be the vector consisting of the physical processor grid's size in all dimensions. Given these definitions, we may build a reasonably accurate model of communication cost for a *replication redistribution* function $r_{a \to b} = (D_1, D_2)$ as follows: We first calculate which dimensions i, $0 \leqslant i \leqslant d_v$ are replicated by $r_{a \to b}$. We then define the cost, or weight, of the edge $a \longrightarrow b$ as

$$W_{a \to b} = \sum_{\substack{0 \leqslant i \leqslant d_v \\ \text{dimension } i \text{ replicated}}} C_{\text{bcast}}(P_i, V_a) , \qquad (9)$$

where $C_{\text{bcast}}(p, m)$ is the cost of broadcasting an array of size m over p processors. On typical platforms, we have $C_{\text{bcast}}(p, m) \approx (t_s + t_w m) \log p$, with t_s being the message startup time and t_w per-word transfer time.

The key aspect of this cost model is that it takes account of both the data size and the number of processors involved in broadcast operations that may result from replication redistributions.

3.4   The Algorithm

Given that our replication descriptors now have the same essential properties as our affine alignment descriptors, the same algorithm which we have previously described for affine alignment optimisation [2] applies. It is originally based on the algorithm proposed by Feautrier in [6].

1. We select the edge with the highest weight. Suppose this is an edge $a \to b$.

2. We change the distribution at the *sink* of the edge such that the redistribution $r_{a \to b}$ is avoided, i.e., we substitute $c_{a_b} \leftarrow c_a$. We then use the constraint equations at node b for calculating the resulting placement of b and any other operands and *forward-propagate* this change through the DAG.
3. We check the weight of the DAG following the change. If the weight has gone up, we abandon the change and proceed to step 4. If the weight has gone down, we jump to step 6.
4. We change the distribution at the *source* of the edge by substituting $c_b \leftarrow c_{a_b}$. We update the placements of the operands at node a and *backwards-propagate* the change through the DAG.
5. We check the weight of the DAG. If it has gone up, we abandon the change and mark the edge a $\to$ b as "attempted". Otherwise, we accept the change.

We stop optimising if the weight of the DAG becomes zero. This, however, is rare. Otherwise, we iterate the algorithm a fixed, small number of times each time we encounter a particular context, attempting to eliminate the costliest remaining residual communication. This is particularly suitable for runtime systems where we wish to only spend a strictly limited time optimising whenever the algorithm is invoked.

Once we have begun optimising, we use our value numbering scheme [2] for recognising previously encountered contexts and no longer use our default placement strategy for such nodes, but rather use the results of the last optimisation. Thus, we have the chance of improving on a placement scheme every time a particular context is encountered.

Summary. The fact that our replication descriptors have two key properties means that we have been able to propose an algorithm for optimising data replication which is exactly analogous to our previous affine alignment optimisation algorithm. The algorithm aims to minimise the overall communication cost arising from data replication. It works incrementally, attempting to eliminate the costliest communications at each stage. We review related work in Section 5.

4 Evaluation

We have implemented the techniques described in this paper in our DESO library of parallel linear algebra routines. In this section, we show performance results for an implementation of the Conjugate Gradient iterative algorithm [1] which uses our library (see [2] for a source code sample). Table 1 splits the overall time spent by our benchmark into different categories; in particular, *point-to-point* communication accounts for transpose operations and *collective* communication for reductions and broadcasts.

- We achieve very encouraging parallelisation speedup: 13.03 for 16 processors.
- Affine alignment optimisation alone achieves a reduction by a factor of about 2 in point-to-point communication.

Table 1. Time in milliseconds for 10 iterations of conjugate gradient, with a 3600×3600 parameter matrix (about 100 MB) on varying numbers of processors. N denotes timings without any optimisation, A timings with affine alignment optimisation only, and R timings with affine alignment and replication optimisation. *O-Speedup* shows the speedup due to our optimisations, and *P-Speedup* the speedup due to parallelisation. The platform is a cluster of 350MHz Pentium II workstations with 128MB RAM, running Linux 2.0.36 (TCP patched), connected by two channel-bonded 100Mb/s ethernet cards per machine through a Gigabit switch and using mpich-1.1.1. Averages of 10 runs; the standard deviation is about 1% of the reported figures.

	P	Compu-tation	Runtime Overhead	Communication Pt-to-Pt	Communication Collective	Optimi-sation	Total Σ	O-Speedup	P-Speedup
N	1	4351.92	7.10	0.00	0.24	0.00	4359.26	1.00	1.00
A	1	4359.11	7.22	0.00	0.25	6.43	4372.99	1.00	1.00
R	1	4340.46	7.39	0.00	0.25	11.01	4359.11	1.00	1.00
N	4	1108.62	12.00	57.18	95.85	0.00	1273.66	1.00	3.42
A	4	1114.36	10.77	28.78	80.89	6.85	1241.64	1.03	3.52
R	4	1095.75	10.21	12.63	60.12	16.41	1195.12	1.07	3.65
N	9	467.35	11.77	51.28	83.90	0.00	614.30	1.00	7.10
A	9	464.51	11.52	27.08	72.49	7.12	582.71	1.05	7.50
R	9	463.53	10.57	14.32	65.29	16.64	570.34	1.08	7.64
N	16	238.28	12.50	41.22	72.82	0.00	364.81	1.00	11.95
A	16	237.94	12.01	25.00	62.88	7.17	345.00	1.06	12.68
R	16	235.07	10.09	8.92	64.22	16.18	334.48	1.09	13.03

- Performing the replication optimisation algorithm from this paper in addition to affine alignment optimisation results in a further factor 2.0–2.8 reduction in point-to-point communication. In addition, collective communication is decreased by about 10%. The two key motivations for this work were that handling replication correctly results in cheaper affine realignments and in fewer broadcasts.
- The data in Table 1 were obtained with optimisation running on every iteration of the CG loop. The optimisation times we achieve show that firstly, our replication algorithm takes roughly the same time as affine alignment optimisation, and, secondly, that it is feasible to execute both at runtime in this way. However, we have previously described a technique [2] that allows us to *re-use* the results of previous optimisations at runtime. Applying this technique here will cause the overall optimisation time to become insignificant. We plan to implement this shortly.
- Conjugate Gradient has $O(N^2)$ computation complexity, but only $O(N)$ communication complexity. This means that for relatively small numbers of processors with a fairly large problem size, such as in Table 1, the overall speedups that can be achieved by optimising communication are small. We expect our optimisations to have greater overall benefit on more fine-grain problems and problems with a higher communication complexity.

5   Related Work

Affine Alignment Optimisation. Feautrier [6] proposes a compile-time method for automatic distribution which works for static-control programs. This method minimises communication between *virtual* processors, i.e. it deals with the affine alignment stage of parallel data placement only. The method does not address replication; for lower-dimensional loops, some processors are assumed to remain idle. Further, the placement functions in [6] are static. In contrast, our method allows for dynamic realignments and dynamic changes in replication, and will attempt to schedule such operations in an optimal way.

Chatterjee et al. [5] give a comprehensive theoretic treatment of the alignment problem, including axis-, stride- and offset-alignment. Our affine alignment descriptors are very similar to those of Chatterjee et al., though we impose slightly fewer restrictions.

Optimising Replicated Alignments. To our knowledge, the only previous work on optimising replicated alignments is by Chatterjee et al. [4]. They use a representation which permits replicating data not just on entire template axes, but also on subsets of template axes. However, this refinement is not taken into account in their optimisation algorithm. On the other hand, it appears that our use of augmentation, together with carefully chosen alignment, permits us to handle a range of replication patterns, as illustrated in Section 2.3 which the representation in [4] was not intended for. We consider the strongest point of our representation to be the two properties of closure under composition and invertibility.

Chatterjee et al. propose to use replication labelling, where data is labelled either replicated or non-replicated, and network flow is used to find an optimal labelling. In comparison, we use a more finely differentiated representation and cost model for replication. While Chatterjee et al. therefore solve a slightly simpler problem than we do, their proposed algorithm finds the optimum solution to the problem as they formulate it. Our algorithm, solving a harder problem, is heuristic and incremental, seeking to eliminate the costliest communications as quickly as possible. This makes our algorithm particularly suitable to runtime optimisation, without restricting its potential of finding the optimum solution with a larger investment in time.

6   Conclusion

We have presented an efficient technique for optimising data replication:

- We propose a mathematical representation for replication which satisfies the properties of closure under composition and invertibility.
- These two properties of our replication descriptors allow us to propose an optimisation algorithm for data replication which is exactly analogous to previously published algorithms for optimising affine alignment.

- Our optimisation algorithm is efficient enough to be used in a runtime system, but we believe that its simplicity should also make it attractive for compile-time optimisers.

Future Work. This work can be extended in a number of ways. By taking account of affine placements while optimising replication, and vice-versa, we should be able to detect overall placement strategies which are more efficient still than what we can obtain by optimising both separately. For example, using skewed placements for the results of non-replicated reductions may allow us to eliminate some affine re-alignments which appear inevitable when the result of the reduction is replicated.

Through most of this paper we have assumed a two-dimensional processor array. This works well for BLAS, but we should evaluate our techniques for the one-dimensional and higher-dimensional cases. A more difficult issue is how to mix different processor arrangements within a single computation.

Acknowledgements. This work is partially supported by a United Kingdom Engineering and Physical Sciences Research Council (EPSRC) Studentship for Olav Beckmann. Special thanks to colleagues at UCSD for their hospitality during Paul Kelly's sabbatical. We thank Steven Newhouse, Keith Sephton and the Imperial College Parallel Computing Centre for the use of their Beowulf cluster and AP3000, and Scott Baden and NPACI for SP2 access. We thank Ariel Burton from Imperial College for supplying a lightweight, accurate timing mechanism under Linux [3] and for pointing out some 'performance bugs' in the TCP implementation of 2.0.x Linux kernels.

References

1. R. Barrett, M. Berry, T. Chan, J. Demmel, J. Donato, J. Dongarra, V. Eijkhout, R. Pozo, C. Romine, and H. van der Vorst. *Templates for the Solution of Linear Systems: Building Blocks for Iterative Methods.* Society for Industrial and Applied Mathematics (SIAM), Philadelphia, PA, USA, 1994.
2. O. Beckmann and P. H. J. Kelly. Efficient interprocedural data placement optimisation in a parallel library. In D. O'Hallaron, editor, *LCR98: Fourth International Workshop on Languages, Compilers and Run-time Systems for Scalable Computers*, volume 1511 of *LNCS*, pages 123–138. Springer-Verlag, May 1998.
3. A. N. Burton and P. H. J. Kelly. Tracing and reexecuting operating system calls for reproducible performance experiments. *Journal of Computers and Electrical Engineering—Special Issue on Performance Evaluation of High Performance Computing and Computers*, 1999. To appear.
4. S. Chatterjee, J. R. Gilbert, and R. Schreiber. Mobile and replicated alignment of arrays in data-parallel programs. In *Proceedings of Supercomputing '93*, pages 420–429, Nov. 1993.
5. S. Chatterjee, J. R. Gilbert, R. Schreiber, and S.-H. Teng. Automatic array alignment in data-parallel programs. In *Twentieth Annual ACM SIGPLAN-SIGACT Symposium on Principles of Programming Languages, Charleston, South Carolina, January 10–13, 1992*, pages 16–28. ACM Press, 1993.

6. P. Feautrier. Toward automatic distribution. *Parallel Processing Letters*, 4(3):233–244, 1994.
7. J. A. Green. *Sets and Groups*. Routledge & Kegan Paul, second edition, 1988.
8. C. H. Koelbel, D. B. Loveman, R. S. Schreiber, G. L. Steele Jr., and M. E. Zosel. *The High Performance Fortran Handbook*. MIT Press, Cambridge, MA, USA, Jan. 1994.
9. V. Kumar, A. Grama, A. Gupta, and G. Karypis. *Introduction to Parallel Computing*. Benjamin/Cummings, 1993.
10. C. L. Lawson, R. J. Hanson, D. R. Kincaid, and F. T. Krogh. Basic Linear Algebra Subprograms for Fortran usage. *ACM Transactions on Mathematical Software*, 5(3):308–323, Sept. 1979.
11. Z. Li. Array privatization for parallel execution of loops. In *1992 International Conference on Supercomputing, Washington, DC*, pages 313–322. ACM Press, 1992.
12. L. Snyder. *A Programmer's Guide to ZPL*. Department of Computer Science and Engineering, University of Washington, Seattle, WA 98195, Jan. 1999. Verion 6.3.
13. S. A. M. Talbot. *Shared-Memory Multiprocessors with Stable Performance*. PhD thesis, Department of Computing, Imperial College London, U.K., 1999.

Accurate Data and Context Management in Message-Passing Programs *

Dhruva R. Chakrabarti and Prithviraj Banerjee

Center for Parallel and Distributed Computing
ECE Dept., Northwestern University
2145 Sheridan Road, Evanston, IL 60208-3118
{dhruva, banerjee}@ece.nwu.edu

Abstract. This paper presents a novel scheme for maintaining accurate information about distributed data in message-passing programs. The ability to maintain dynamically the data-to-processor mapping as well as the program contexts at which state changes occur enable a variety of sophisticated optimizations. The algorithms described in this paper are based on the static single assignment (SSA) form of message-passing programs which can be used for performing many of the classical compiler optimizations during automatic parallelization as well as for analyzing user-written message-passing programs. Reaching definition analysis is performed on SSA-structures for determining a suitable communication point. The scheme addresses possible optimizations and shows how appropriate representation of the data structures can substantially reduce the associated overheads. Our scheme uniformly handles arbitrary subscripts in array references and can handle general reducible control flow. Experimental results for a number of benchmarks on an IBM SP-2 show a conspicuous reduction in inter-processor communication as well as a marked improvement in the total run-times. We have observed up to around 10-25% reduction in total run-times in our SSA-based schemes compared to non-SSA-based schemes on 16 processors.

1 Introduction

Static Single Assignment (SSA) [8] has been used for performing various kinds of compiler optimizations including code motion, constant propagation, elimination of partial redundancies and detection of program equivalence. While SSA was originally used for sequential programs manipulating scalars, it has been recently used for handling arrays [10,6]. Furthermore, it is being increasingly used for parallel programs with the aim to apply the classical optimizations to parallel programs too. [13,16,6] present Array SSA forms for explicitly parallel programs with various models of memory consistency, with event-based synchronization or mutual exclusion, with parallel sections or indexed parallel constructs. Many

* This research was partially supported by the National Science Foundation under Grant NSF CCR-9526325, and in part by DARPA under Contract DABT-63-97-0035.

of these above-mentioned concepts can be carried over to analyses performed for automatic parallelization. [10] uses precise element-level data flow information for array variables in the form of Array SSA and shows how this form can be used to enable parallelization of loops free of loop-carried true data dependences. Our paper presents an SSA form for message passing-programs and shows how sophisticated optimizations including global communication optimization can be performed using SSA-based analyses. We present algorithms to convert a sequential program into SSA form for message-passing programs and then use reaching definition analyses (RDA) [7] to compute a suitable communication point. The SSA-form that we present for message-passing programs can be used for performing many of the classical compiler optimizations not only during automatic parallelization but also while analyzing user-written parallel programs. The classical optimizations, however, are not the focus of this paper and will not be discussed here any more.

```
// Array b initialized here
1: do i = 1, n
2:     ... = b(i+1)
3:     ... = b(i+2)
4: enddo
(a) Original Form
```

```
1: B_0[...] = ...
2: @B_0[...] = ()
3: @B_{1-6}[...] = ⊥
4: do i ∈ myIters
5:     B_1 = Φ_d(B_5, B_0)
6:     @B_2 = U_r(localize(i + 1))
7:     Inter-processor comm. into B_2
8:     B_3 = Φ_r(B_2, B_1)
9:     ... = B_3(localize(i + 1))
10:    @B_4 = U_r(localize(i + 2))
11:    Inter-processor comm. into B_4
12:    B_5 = Φ_r(B_4, B_3)
13:    ... = B_5(localize(i + 2))
14: enddo
15: B_6 = Φ_d(B_5, B_0)
(b) SSA form
```

Fig. 1. SSA Form for a Code Segment having a Read of a Distributed Variable

This paper provides an efficient framework for SSA-based analysis of message-passing programs while focusing on the analyses required for write of a distributed variable. We assume the use of the SPMD execution model and the owner-computes rule in the context of execution on distributed memory machines. The SSA-form for read of distributed variables can be found in detail in [3]. While the analysis for a *read* is similar to a write, there are some important differences. First, since a read may result in inter-processor communication, the analyses for read involve generation of a communication schedule. In addition, while the processor set having valid data becomes smaller owing to a distributed write, this set is likely to expand for a distributed read. While this paper focuses on applying element-level SSA-analyses for writes to distributed arrays irrespective of the subscripts used, Figure 1 shows an intermediate SSA-form of a code segment containing read of a distributed variable. Note that since the data is distributed across processors and since a read statement may potentially access off-processor elements, some data may need to be received in the local buffer of a processor before it can proceed with the actual reading of the data. Once the communication requirements are analyzed, the data is received in a temporary array, B_2. A new definition of the array b, B_3, is generated by merging the old values in the array b with the newly-received values, as shown in line 8. This Φ function is called Φ_r to distinguish it from Φ_d. Line 9 contains the actual read from the newly generated definition. The transformation for the other read statement is similar. It may be noted that a merge of the old elements and the newly-received off-processor elements is essential for various optimizations. If no merge function is added for the read statements, a processor's view of the data will be restricted to its own local data space. Owing to the insertion of merge functions for read, it is possible to capture the state of the data in a certain processor at every point in the SPMD program. This enables optimizations not only on the data owned by a processor but also on the valid off-processor data present in a certain processor. For instance, it enables sophisticated communication optimizations. Note that the function U_r on line 10 has an implicit use of the reaching definition B_3. So if the second read statement in the loop accesses an off-processor data element received by the first read statement, it need not be communicated again. Our scheme can handle general reducible control flow and provides a basis for performing global preprocessing and communication optimizations.

The rest of the paper is organized as follows. Section 2 contains the definitions of various structures and functions used in later sections of the paper. Section 3 provides transformations that result owing to write of a distributed array. Section 4 explains how various optimizations are supported by the SSA-form presented in the previous sections. Section 5 presents some experimental results on an IBM SP-2, Section 6 discusses the related existing work while Section 7 presents the conclusions of our work.

2   Definitions of Relevant Data Structures

2.1   Structure of an @ Array

We capture the semantics of Φ functions using the concept of an @ array similar to that used in [10]. However, in addition to information about iteration vector maintained in [10], we maintain data-to-processor mapping and the basic block identity in an @ array corresponding to a certain definition.

Processor Structure: Assuming that there are P processors, the processor structure contains an array of P 1-bit entries with possible values of 1 and 0. A 1 in entry i indicates that processor i has the most recent value of the corresponding data element while a value 0 indicates otherwise. Our scheme is conservative in the sense that if the validity of an off-processor data element is not determined accurately, the corresponding bit is reset to 0.

Identity of Basic Block: We assume that the statements in a program are organized into basic blocks so that every statement has a basic block number. We use a control flow graph similar to that described in [8]. The merge functions operating on data elements obtained through different basic blocks require a distinguishing identity in order to resolve conflicts and this is why the identity of the basic block is maintained.

Iteration Vector: This field is similar to the one used in [10] and helps resolve conflicts during merging for accesses to the same variable. The iteration vector is a point in the iteration space and can be represented as $i = (i_1, \ldots, i_n)$, where i_k denotes the kth iteration variable. We assume that loops are single-entry and normalized.

2.2   Functions Modifying @ Arrays: Placement and Semantics

In the case of read or write to a distributed variable, an @ array has to be created for the variables modified. Note that for a distributed variable, a read may imply obtaining off-processor elements into a local buffer which in turn implies modification of the local buffer. The functions used for creation of the @ arrays are referred to as U_r and U_w for read and write respectively.

1. U_r: This function is inserted just before the corresponding Φ_r (explained below) for every read of a distributed variable. This function accepts the address of the new @ array, the iteration vector, the basic block identity corresponding to the definition, a communication schedule and the address of the reaching @ array definition as parameters. It computes the entries required for the processor structure, copies the iteration vector and the basic block identity obtained as parameters into the newly created @ variable and updates the communication schedule.

2. U_w: This function is inserted just after the corresponding write of a distributed variable. This function accepts the address of the new @ array, the iteration vector, the basic block identity corresponding to the definition and the address of the reaching @ array definition as parameters. It computes the entries required for the processor structure and copies the iteration vector and the basic block identity obtained as parameters into the newly created @ variable. Besides placement, U_w differs from U_r in the way the processor structure is computed for the corresponding @ variable — in addition, no communication schedule is updated for U_w since no inter-processor communication is required for a write to a distributed variable.

2.3 Φ Functions: Placement and Semantics

This section deals with the placement and semantics of Φ functions. As is the case in scalar SSA, the placement and semantics of Φ functions should ensure that each use of a variable refers to a unique definition of the variable. The initial placement that we are presenting in this section uses the same concept as that used in scalar SSA [8] and array SSA [10]. However, as we will explain, we require extensions owing to the complexities introduced by inter-processor communication in a distributed memory environment.

Notations :
ps: processor structure, iv: iteration vector, bbi: basic block identity
$A_{x+2} = \Phi(A_x, A_{x+1}, iv)$

1:$k = minimumComponent(A_x.iv, A_{x+1}.iv)$
2:$\forall$ i$\in$ both A_x and A_{x+1}
3:    $A_{x+2}[i].iv = iv$
4:    **if** $(@A_x[i].iv_k \succ @A_{x+1}[i].iv_k)$
5:       Assign the *ps* and *bbi* structures of $@A_x[i]$ to $@A_{x+2}[i]$
6:    **elsif** $(@A_x[i].iv_k \prec @A_{x+1}[i].iv_k)$
7:       Assign the *ps* and *bbi* structures of $@A_{x+1}[i]$ to $@A_{x+2}[i]$
8:    **elsif** $(@A_x[i].bbi \succ @A_{x+1}[i].bbi)$
9:       Assign the *ps* and *bbi* structures of $@A_x[i]$ to $@A_{x+2}[i]$
10:   **else**
11:       Assign the *ps* and *bbi* structures of $@A_{x+1}[i]$ to $@A_{x+2}[i]$
12:   **endif**
13:**endfor**
22:$\forall$ i$\in$ either A_x or A_{x+1}
23:    propagate corresponding *ps* and *bbi* values to A_{x+2}
24:    $A_{x+2}[i].iv = iv$
25:**endfor**

Fig. 2. Semantics of Φ function

Definition and Placement: We require three kinds of Φ functions. Though the semantics of the different Φ functions are the same, the analyses need to distinguish between them in order to carry out various optimizations.

1. Φ_r: A Φ_r function is inserted immediately before each read of a distributed variable. The reader may consider a read of a distributed variable as similar to a write to a distributed variable in some senses, since in both the cases, the data values for the array as a whole (including both local and off-processor data in the local buffer) may be modified. The Φ_r functions are intended to ensure that any subsequent use of the variable refers to a unique name containing updated values.

2. Φ_w: A Φ_w function is inserted immediately after the corresponding U_w function. This function merges the new definitions owing to the write with the definitions available prior to the write. A Φ_w function will be introduced after every write to a distributed variable unless it can be ensured that all the data values including any off-processor element information maintained in a processor are totally killed by the definition.

3. Φ_d: A Φ_d function is inserted at exactly the same locations as inserted by scalar SSA, namely at the dominance frontiers. The purpose of this function, Φ_d, is to combine values propagated along different control paths.

Semantics: The semantics of the Φ functions, which always choose the most recent values, are shown in Figure 2. The input parameters of the Φ function, A_x and A_{x+1}, refer to the successive definitions of the array A obtained from distinct control paths. The input parameter iv refers to the iteration vector corresponding to the dominance frontier. Line 1 in Figure 2 computes the length of the smaller of the iteration vectors obtained from A_x and A_{x+1}. This is because only the common components of the iteration vectors will be compared in lines 4 and 6 in Figure 2. As Figure 2 shows, the iteration vector and the identity of the basic block are taken into consideration in this order in order to resolve any potential conflicts. Let us consider the case dealt with in lines 4-5 in Figure 2, where the iteration vector component in $A_x[i]$ is greater than that in $A_{x+1}[i]$. This means that the definition $A_x[i]$ is more recent than A_{x+1}. Consequently, the processor structure, the basic block identity corresponding to the definition $A_x[i]$ are copied to $A_x[i+2]$. Note that the Φ function sets the iteration vector of the new definition to the one corresponding to the dominance frontier. This is essential for determining the value later in time when iteration vectors obtained from disjoint loops are compared against each other using the algorithm in Figure 2. In addition, the original basic block identity of a certain reference is preserved throughout the program states. More details can be found in [3].

3   SSA Form for Write of a Distributed Variable

3.1   Basic Implementation of SSA Semantics

Let us consider the write to a distributed array B in line 2 of Figure 3(a). In line 6 in Figure 3(b), a new array, B_2, is created and all writes occur to this array. As shown in line 7 of Figure 3(b), an update of the corresponding @ array element is added immediately after the write to the distributed array element. This update captures not only the change in the processor-configuration of valid data maintained by processors, it also stores adequate information for resolving conflicts among processors. Finally, line 8 does an element-by-element merge of the modified definitions with the definitions available prior to the modification. This merge involves manipulation of the corresponding @ arrays.

The following are the steps performed for handling of a write of a distributed array variable (say $A(f(i))$).

- Let A_x be the unique definition reaching the concerned write of the distributed array A assuming SSA-renaming.
- We assume that the SSA-analysis for the access $f(i)$ has been performed so that we don't worry about $f(i)$ any more in this algorithm. A function call, $U_w(localize(f(i)), iv, bbi)$ is inserted for handling the write of a distributed

```
                1:B_0[...] = ...
                2:@B_0[...] = ()              1:B_0[...] = ...
                3:@B_{1-3}[...] = ⊥           2:@B_0[...] = ()
1:do i = 1, n   4:do i ∈ myIters              3:@B_{1-2}[...] = ⊥
2:   B(f(i)) = ... 5:   B_1 = Φ_d(B_0, B_3)   4:do i ∈ myIters
3:enddo         6:   B_2(Localize(f(i))) = ...  5:   @B_1 = U_w(...)
                7:   @B_2 = U_w(localize(f(i)))  6:enddo
(a) Serial Code 8:   B_3 = Φ_w(B_1, B_2)      7:@B_2 = Combine_w(@B_1, @B_0)
                9:enddo
                                             (c) Optimized Code
                (b) Corresponding SSA Form
```

Fig. 3. Code Transformation for Write to a Distributed Variable

array variable. While iv is the iteration vector and bbi the basic block identity corresponding to the write statement, A_{x+1} is the new @-array generated by this function call.

- $localize(f(i))$ refers to the own sets, send and receive sets and other relevant data structures that are required to capture the access structure of references. The methods for computing these sets is not discussed in this paper but can be found in [4].

- The basic block identity and the iteration vector corresponding to the write statement are copied to the appropriate structures in the @-array.

- If the access $A(f(i))$ is regular and the array A is distributed using a regular distribution, every processor determines the elements that are written to by other processors. Every processor computes the corresponding local indices of such global elements modified by some other processor. If any of those local elements is maintained by a processor, it invalidates its own copy by modifying the processor entry corresponding to itself in the @-array. It may be noted that this step does not require any inter-processor communication for regular accesses. This step ensures that a processor will never use a data element if it is dirty. However, this also implies that even if a data element is dirty and a processor maintains an invalid value, the value will not be updated as long as the result of a computation is not affected. If a processor having an invalid value for the data element attempts to use it at a later point of time, it will have to be fetched from the remote owner processor before it can be used. If a processor having an invalid value never attempts to use it, it will never be fetched.

- If the access $A(f(i))$ is irregular, expensive inter-processor communication is required in order for a processor to determine whether any of the off-processor elements maintained by it in its local buffer has been rendered dirty by the write. The other option is to arbitrarily invalidate all off-processor entries corresponding to that particular array variable present in a certain processor. We have chosen the latter option. We do so because this avoids any immediate inter-processor communication — if such data elements are attempted to be used by the processor at a later point of time, they will have to be fetched. We feel that on an average, some of the locally maintained off-processor elements will have been modified by the remote owner processor while some others unmodified will probably never be used again by the local processor and this is why we use such an approach.

3.2   Optimized Implementation of SSA Semantics

The Φ functions used by us are associative and this allows various optimizations such as copy-propagation, loop-invariant code motion etc. which in turn allow reduction in Φ function computations or repositioning of Φ functions. The resulting code segment is shown in Figure 3(c). The call to the function U_w in line 5 generates a new @-array B_1 for the elements $localize(f(i))$. This function accepts the address of the new @-array, the iteration vector and the basic block identity corresponding to the definition as parameters. It computes the entries required for the processor structure and copies the iteration vector and the basic block identity corresponding to the definition as parameters into the newly created @-variable. The way the processor structures are determined and the values that are assigned to them are explained later in detail. Line 7 uses the $Combine_w$ function to merge the newly obtained @-array values with the @-array values obtained prior to the definition. The exact algorithm for this $Combine_w$ function is presented later.

We describe here the methodology used for assigning the various fields to the SSA structures for a write to an array variable.

- Let us consider Figure 4(b) and Figure 4(c) in order to understand the updates required for an irregular write. $LocalRef(R, p)$ refers to the local references accessed by the reference R by the processor p. In Figure 4(c), B refers to the new @-array generated by the function call U_w. Lines 1-2 assign the basic block identity and the iteration vector corresponding to the write statement to the appropriate fields of the @-array for the elements written to by the executing processor. Lines 3-5 invalidate the data-to-processor fields corresponding to remote processors for the elements written to by the executing processor. In Figure 4(b), the function $Combine_{w_{irreg}}$ creates the updated @-variable as the result of the irregular write reference. This function accepts, as parameters, the @-array (denoted by $@A_{x+1}$) generated immediately before this function call and the @-array (denoted by $@A_x$) whose definition reaches $@A_{x+1}$. The resulting new @-array is denoted by $@A_{x+2}$. As is clear from Figure 4(b), the function $Combine_{w_{irreg}}$ effectively resets the values of the @-array to its initial state — this is a conservative update and is employed to avoid expensive inter-processor communication. In Figure 4(b), R_L refers to the corresponding write reference and $Extent(A, p)$ refers to the elements of array A owned by processor p at a local address domain.
- The algorithm shown in Figure 4(c) is used to update the processor configuration of the data values in the case of a regular write and is no different from the algorithm used for an irregular write. Figure 4(a) shows the algorithm for generating the updated @-array elements following a regular write. Lines

$$@A_{x+2} = Combine_{w_{reg}}(@A_{x+1}, @A_x)$$

$$@A_{x+2} = Combine_{w_{irreg}}(@A_{x+1}, @A_x)$$

1: $\forall i \in @A_{x+1}$

2: $@A_{x+2}[i].bbi = @A_{x+1}[i].bbi$

3: $@A_{x+2}[i].iv = @A_{x+1}[i].iv$

4: $@A_{x+2}[i].ps = @A_{x+1}[i].ps$

5: **endfor**

6: $\forall p_r$ other than myId

7: $TempRef(R_L) = TempRef(R_L)$

$\cup GlobRef(R_L, p_r)$

8: **endfor**

9: $\forall i \in (@A_x - @A_{x+1})$

10: $@A_{x+2}[i].ps = @A_x[i].ps$

11: $@A_{x+2}[i].bbi = @A_x[i].bbi$

12: $@A_{x+2}[i].iv = @A_x[i].iv$

13: **if** i $\in localize(TempRef(R_L))$

14:   $@A_{x+2}[i].ps[myId] = 0$

15:   $@A_{x+2}[i].bbi = @A_{x+1}[i].bbi$

16:   $@A_{x+2}[i].iv = @A_{x+1}[i].iv$

17: **endif**

18: **endfor**

(a) Combine function for regular write

1: $\forall p$

2:   $@A_{x+2}[Extent(A, myId)].ps[p] = 0$

3: **endfor**

4: $@A_{x+2}[Extent(A, myId)].ps[myId] = 1$

5: $@A_{x+2}[Extent(A, myId)].bbi = R_L.bbi$

6: $@A_{x+2}[Extent(A, myId)].iv = R_L.iv$

(b) Combine function for irregular write

$$@B = U_w(localize(f(i)), bbi, iv)$$

1: $@B[LocalRef(R_L, myId)].bbi = bbi$

2: $@B[LocalRef(R_L, myId)].iv = iv$

3: $\forall p$

4:   $@B[LocalRef(R_L, myId)].ps[p] = 0$

5: **endfor**

6: $@B[LocalRef(R_L, myId)].ps[myId] = 1$

(c) Update Function for Distributed Write

Fig. 4. Functions Required for a Distributed Write

1-5 copy the values from A_{x+1} to A_x since these reflect the updated state of the @-array for the elements referenced by the regular write. The rest of the function deals with the rest of the elements of the definition reaching the current one. Note that the reaching definition is denoted by the @-array A_x. As shown in lines 6-8, $TempRef(R_L)$ collects all the elements (at a global address domain) that have been referenced by remote processors. If any of these elements is contained in $@A_x$, the corresponding data-to-processor state for the executing state is invalidated and the basic block identity and the iteration vector fields are set to values corresponding to the write reference — otherwise, the old state is allowed to propagate through. This is shown in lines 9-18 in Figure 4(a).

It may be observed from the above algorithms that an element-level data-to-processor mapping is maintained. While the algorithms presented above often refer to the elements of the array in an *enumerated* manner, the actual implementation uses analytical expressions, sets and efficient operations on them to minimize the computation overheads.

4   SSA-Based Optimizations

[17] has shown how *use-def* chains can be used in an SSA implementation in order to improve optimization and parallelism in a program. While [17] shows the use of *use-def* chains in the case of scalars, the same concepts can be used for

arrays as well. Note that for arrays, the same name is used for all the elements of the array and consequently separate use-def chains for different elements of an array are not necessary. More details can be found in [3].

4.1 Maintaining Regularity in Data Structures

All information is stored in the form of sets whenever possible. This includes the data-to-processor mapping of distributed data, the basic block identity information and the iteration vector associated with the corresponding accesses. While this way of maintaining information contributes to efficient manipulation of various computation and communication sets and results in amortization of storage needs, it also poses a number of implementation challenges as detailed in [3].

4.2 Determining the Inspection and Communication Point

The SSA-form that we have presented for message-passing programs is typically used at an intermediate code generation stage for performing various optimizations. However, if some of the analyses cannot be resolved at compile-time, some of the SSA-structures can be incorporated in the generated code as inspectors [15] to be executed at run-time.

We use instance-wise reaching definition analyses to determine the placement of inspectors and communication calls. Instance-wise reaching definition allows us to compute, for every instance of a statement R containing a read of reference r, the set of instances of all assignments S assigning to reference r, such that there is a program path from each instance of S to the instance of R being free of any modification of r [7]. Let us consider the statement R containing the access $A(B(f))$, requiring inspection. A and B are arrays while f is a function, either affine in terms of the enclosing loop variables or an indirect function in terms of index arrays. In order to determine the point of inspection for array A, we need to compute the definitions of each of the elements contained in $B(f)$ that are reaching use of $B(f)$ in statement R free of any modification of the corresponding element. Once this is determined, the inspector for accesses to array A in R can be placed after the definitions. In order to determine the inter-processor communication point, we have to compute the instance-wise reaching definition point for the array elements we consider for communication. For instance, in the case of statement R containing the access $A(B(f))$, we compute the definitions of each of the elements contained in $A(B(f))$ that are reaching use of $A(B(f))$ in statement R free of any modification of the corresponding element. Once this is determined, the inter-processor communication calls for accesses to array A in R can be placed after the definitions.

Figure 5 presents the algorithm for generating the inspection point and the communication point for a certain reference. Let us consider the reference, R, $X_1(X_2(X_3(\ldots(X_n(f))\ldots)))$. I_i and C_i refer to the inspection point and communication point respectively for the reference X_i in reference R and are computed

```
1:X₁(X₂(X₃(...(Xₙ(f))...))): Data access R
2:I(i): Inspection point for reference Xᵢ
3:C(i): Communication point for reference Xᵢ
4:S(D): Statement Number corresponding to definition D
5:I(n) = 1
6:for (i = n − 1; i >= 0; i − −)
7:    found = false
8:    while (not found)
9:    begin
10:        Traverse use-def chain for instance-wise reaching defn. D for Xᵢ₊₁ in R
11:        if (D is Φ_w-type or U_w-type or initial write)
12:            found = true
13:            if (i > 0)
14:                I(i) = S(D)
15:            endif
16:            C(i + 1) = S(D)
17:        endif
18:    end
19:    C(i + 1) = max(C(i + 1), I(i + 1))
20:    if (i > 0)
21:        I(i) = max(I(i), I(i + 1), C(i + 1))
22:    endif
23:endfor
```

Fig. 5. Algorithm to Generate Inspection Point and Communication Point

by the algorithm presented in Figure 5. $S(D)$ denotes the statement number corresponding to the definition D and is assumed to be available to the algorithm. We assume that f is a function independent of any arrays and its value is available at statement labeled 1. This assumption does not affect the generality of the algorithm. Intuitively, the algorithm finds out the inspection point and then the communication point for every reference X_i starting from $i = n$ to $i = 1$. Note that line 10 finds the reaching definition, D, using instance-wise reaching definition analysis for a certain reference. Line 11 checks whether the definition D is generated out of a Φ_w function or U_w function or whether it is an initializing write. This is essential since we want to hoist the inspection or communication to a point where the data elements have been changed owing to a write. Note that this is the only point where the global view of an array changes as opposed to other functions which generate new definitions but either change only the local view of data or the local state. This is an instance where maintaining different names for various Φ functions helps. For any X_i, the inspection point is the maximum of the statement numbers of the reaching definitions of all X_j, where $i + 1 \leq j \leq n$, and the communication points of all X_j, where $i + 1 \leq j \leq n$. This is shown in line 21 in Figure 5. This algorithm tries aggressive hoisting of inspectors and inter-processor communication points. At a later point, we plan to investigate into the related issues discussed in [5] that have to be considered during hoisting of communication.

5   Experimental Results

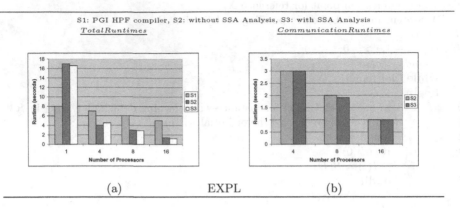

(a)   EXPL   (b)

Fig. 6. Comparative Runtimes

We present comparative results for three schemes — (1) code generated by the PGI compiler [1], (2) code generated by the PARADIGM compiler without SSA analysis and (3) code generated using SSA analysis. We are in the process of automating the SSA-framework in a compiler and a run-time library — while the library has been automated, the top-level SSA-code was generated by hand (with possible calls to the run-time library) in compliance with the SSA-principles in a way that would be produced by a compiler. Schemes 2 and 3 use the *PILAR* library [12] for implementation of any run-time preprocessing structures that may be required. It has been shown in [4] that run-time resolution using the PILAR library obtains good results for hybrid applications — it may be noted that scheme 2 is a state-of-the-art technique with sophisticated optimizations and performs as well or better than other existing techniques. This is why we present results for programs with and without SSA analysis, both built on the PILAR library. A number of benchmarks have been considered and the arrays have been block-distributed unless otherwise mentioned. The platform chosen was a 16-processor *IBM SP-2* running *AIX 4.3* and all experiments used the *high performance communication switch* and the *SP-2 user space library*.

2-D Explicit Hydrodynamics (EXPL, from Livermore kernel) [14] has nine 1024x7 arrays accessed inside doubly perfectly nested loops, all enclosed within the same non-partitionable outer loop. This kernel contains only regular accesses. Figure 6(a,b) present the experimental results. This kernel is different from the others in the sense that all the analysis (including those for SSA) can be done at compile-time and so the overheads owing to SSA-analysis are minimal. This manifests in the total runtimes as very good performance for S3 for 4, 8 and 16 processors. However, there isn't much scope for global optimizations and so the performance of S2 and S3 are practically similar, with slight differences arising out of differences in implementation.

The LU Decomposition routine [11] factors a square non-singular matrix A into a lower triangular matrix L and a upper triangular matrix U such that

$A = LU$. This program contains a number of regular and irregular accesses — an important characteristic which makes this program different from the previous benchmark is that many of the left-hand-sides are irregular since the elements of the sparse matrix have to be modified. The code uses a sparse matrix of dimension 256 represented in compressed sparse row (CSR) format. The PGI HPF compiler was not able to parallelize the program properly and has hence been excluded from the results presented. Figure 7(a) shows the total run-times for the schemes with and without SSA analysis. Note that the scheme S3 attains a better global optimization of preprocessing structures other than better communication optimization in this kind of an algorithm. The speedups for both the schemes are modest largely owing to the presence of irregular writes. S3 obtains around 10% reduction in total run-times compared to S2 on 16 processors in the case of this benchmark.

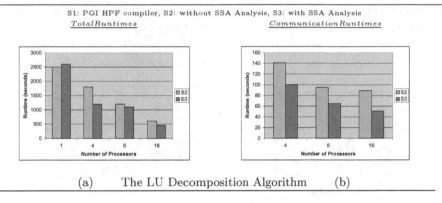

(a)   The LU Decomposition Algorithm   (b)

Fig. 7. Comparative Runtimes

We have used the Conjugate Gradient Algorithm [11] for sparse matrices for comparing the different schemes. The code consists of sparse matrices represented in CSR format. The code used here consists of a number of single-dimensional arrays with every dimension of size 2048. Figure 8(a,b) present the total run-times and the time spent in inter-processor communication for the Conjugate Gradient Algorithm. As is seen from the results, the SSA-based optimizations help obtain a better performance.

The results indicate that the scheme using SSA analysis obtains lower run-times compared to other schemes as the number of processors increases. Preprocessing overheads tend to increase a bit for SSA-analysis and this explains the higher run-times for the 1-processor experiments. However, since SSA-analysis also allows global optimization of preprocessing structures, the overheads associated with SSA-analysis are not prohibitive as the number of processor increases.

6   Related Work

Static Single Assignment (SSA) [8] has been used for performing various kinds of compiler optimizations including code motion, constant propagation, elimination of partial redundancies and detection of program equivalence. While SSA was originally used for sequential programs manipulating scalars, it has been recently used for handling arrays [10,6]. [10] uses a precise element-level data flow information for array variables in the form of Array SSA and shows how this form can be used to enable parallelization of loops free of loop-carried true data dependences. While this scheme deals with parallelization at an abstract level, our scheme considers parallelization of message-passing programs for distributed memory machines. [13,16,6] present Array SSA forms for explicitly parallel programs with various models of memory consistency, with event-based synchronization or mutual exclusion, with parallel sections or indexed parallel constructs. The scheme presented in our paper can deal with many of the issues that typically need to be handled in order to obtain performance out of message passing programs to be executed on distributed memory machines.

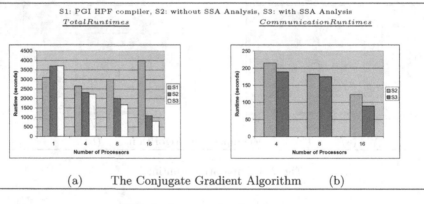

S1: PGI HPF compiler, S2: without SSA Analysis, S3: with SSA Analysis

TotalRuntimes   *CommunicationRuntimes*

(a)   The Conjugate Gradient Algorithm   (b)

Fig. 8. Comparative Runtimes

A number of schemes use data flow analysis in addressing optimization of inter-processor communication for distributed memory machines. [2] presents a uniform framework where data decompositions, computation decompositions and the data flow information are all represented as systems of linear inequalities and uses analyses based on LUT. [18] can optimize inter-processor communication for unconstrained array references using the GIVE-N-TAKE code placement framework. While this provides global analysis on the control flow graph, it treats arrays as indivisible units. [9] combines dependence analysis and data flow analysis based on the GIVE-N-TAKE framework and performs more extensive optimizations. [12] explains how compile-time analysis can be used to generate optimized code for hybrid references. However, this analysis is loop-based and so global inter-processor communication optimization is not performed in this scheme.

7 Conclusions

A new scheme, based on static single assignment, has been presented in this paper for optimizing message passing programs to be executed on distributed memory machines. The scheme addresses possible optimizations and shows how appropriate representation of the data structures can substantially reduce the associated overheads. Experimental results for a number of benchmarks on an IBM SP-2 show a conspicuous reduction in inter-processor communication as well as a marked improvement in the total run-times. We have observed up to around 10-25% reduction in total run-times in our SSA-based schemes compared to non-SSA-based schemes on 16 processors. More extensive analyses and optimizations will be pursued in the future.

References

1. *pghpf Version 2.2,The Portland Group, Inc.,1997.*
2. S. P. Amarasinghe and M. S. Lam. Communication Optimization and Code Generation for Distributed Memory Machines. In *Proceedings of the SIGPLAN'93 Conference on Programming Language Design and Implementation*, June 1993.
3. D. R. Chakrabarti and P. Banerjee. SSA-Form for Message Passing Programs. Technical Report CPDC-TR-9904-005, Center for Parallel & Distributed Computing (http://www.ece.nwu.edu/cpdc), Northwestern University, April 1999.
4. D. R. Chakrabarti, N. Shenoy, A. Choudhary, and P. Banerjee. An Efficient Uniform Run-time Scheme for Mixed Regular-Irregular Applications. In *Proceedings of The 12th ACM International Conference on Supercomputing (ICS'98)*, July 1998.
5. S. Chakrabarti, M. Gupta, and J. Choi. Global Communication Analysis and Optimization. In *Proc. ACM SIGPLAN Conference on Programming Language Design and Implementation*, May 1996.
6. J. F. Collard. Array SSA for Explicitly Parallel Programs, http://www.prism.uvsq.fr/ jfcollar/assaepp.ps.gz. Technical report, CNRS and PRiSM, University of Versailles.
7. J. F. Collard. The Advantages of Instance-wise Reaching Definition Analyses in Array (S)SA. In *Proceedings of LCPC'98, Eleventh International Workshop on Languages and Compilers for Parallel Computing, Chapel Hill, NC, USA*, August 1998.
8. R. Cytron, J. Ferrante, B. K. Rosen, M. Wegman, and F. K. Zadeck. Efficiently Computing Static Single Assignment Form and the Control Dependence Graph. *ACM Transactions on Programming Languages and Systems*, pages 451–490, October 1991.
9. K. Kennedy and N. Nedeljkovic. Combining Dependence and Data-Flow Analyses to Optimize Communication. In *Proceedings of the 9th International Parallel Processing Symposium*, April 1995.
10. K. Knobe and V. Sarkar. Array SSA Form and its Use in Parallelization. In *ACM Symposium on Principles of Programming Languages*, pages 107–120, January 1998.
11. V. Kumar, A. Grama, A. Gupta, and G. Karypis. Introduction to Parallel Computing. *Benjamin-Cummings*, 1994.
12. A. Lain. Compiler and Run-time Support for Irregular Computations. Technical report, PhD thesis, University of Illinois at Urbana-Champaign, 1995.

13. J. Lee, S. Midkiff, and D. A. Padua. Concurrent Static Single Assignment Form and Constant Propagation for Explicitly Parallel Programs. In *Workshop on Languages and Compilers for Parallel Computing*, August 1997.
14. F. McMohan. The Livermore Fortran kernels : A computer test of the numerical performance range. Technical report, Lawrence Livermore National Laboratory, Livermore, CA, Tech. Rep. UCRL-53745, December 1986.
15. J. Saltz, K. Crowley, R. Mirchandaney, and H. Berryman. Run-time Scheduling and Execution of Loops on Message Passing Machines. *Journal of Parallel and Distributed Computing*, April 1990.
16. H. Srinivasan, J. Hook, and M. Wolfe. Static Single Assignment Form for Explicitly Parallel Programs. In *20th ACM Symposium on Principles of Programming Languages*, pages 260–272, January 1993.
17. E. Stoltz, M. P. Gerlek, and M. Wolfe. Extended SSA with Factored Use-Def Chains to Support Optimization and Parallelism. In *Proc. Hawaii International Conference on Systems Sciences, Maui, Hawaii*, January 1994.
18. R. v. Hanxleden and K. Kennedy. Give-N-Take – A balanced code placement framework. In *Proceedings of the SIGPLAN '94 Conference on Programming Language Design and Implementation*, June 1994.

An Automatic Iteration/Data Distribution Method Based on Access Descriptors for DSMM*

Angeles G. Navarro and Emilio L. Zapata

Dept. de Arquitectura de Computadores,
Universidad de Málaga, Spain
{angeles,ezapata}@ac.uma.es

Abstract. Nowadays NUMA architectures are widely accepted. For such multiprocessors exploiting data locality is clearly a key issue. In this work, we present a method for automatically selecting the iteration/data distributions for a sequential F77 code, while minimizing the parallel execution overhead (communications and load unbalance). We formulate an integer programming problem to achieve that minimum parallel overhead. The constraints of the integer programming problem are derived directly from a graph known as the *Locality-Communication Graph* (*LCG*), which captures the memory locality, as well as the communication patterns, of a parallel program. In addition, our approach use the *LCG* to automatically schedule the communication operations required during the program execution, once the iteration/data distributions have been selected. The aggregation of messages in blocks is also dealt in our approach. The TFFT2 code, from NASA benchmarks, that includes non-affine access functions and non-affine index bounds, and repeated subroutine calls inside loops, has been correctly handled by our approach. With the iteration/data distributions derived from our method, this code achieves parallel efficiencies of over 69% for 16 processors, in a Cray T3E, an excellent performance for a complex real code.

1 Introduction

Current multiprocessor architectures tend to focus on the distributed-shared memory paradigm, which allows machines to be highly scalable without losing simplicity in the programming model. We focus on loop level parallelism where the parallel loop iterations in the program are distributed among the available processors. Due to the NUMA organization of these machines and the fact that access time to remote memory is much higher than to local memory, exploiting data locality in the program is clearly a key issue. In practice, exploiting data locality means selecting an efficient data distribution in which the data are placed in the local memory of the processors needing them. Since to place the data

---

* This work was supported by the Ministry of Education and Science (CICYT) of Spain (TIC96-1125-C03) and by the European Union (EU ESPRIT IV Working Group No. 29488)

statically in the local memories of processors that need them, is not always possible, the solution in these cases is to minimize the number of accesses to remote memory (communications). Achieving a good load balance is also highly desirable in order to attain high performance in the parallel execution of the program.

In this paper, we present a method to automatically select the iteration/data distributions of a code, that minimizes the parallel execution overhead: communications and load unbalance. We base our distribution method on a graph called the *Locality-Communication Graph* (*LCG*) that captures the memory locality exhibited by a program. Our iteration/data distribution approach formulates an integer programming problem from the *LCG*. The variables, in this problem, are the size of the chunks of parallel iterations that are going to be scheduled on each processor, following a BLOCK_CYCLIC scheme. The objective function of our integer programming problem has two terms: i) the *load unbalance*, where we have develop a cost function that estimates the difference of execution times between the slower and the faster processor (we consider here rectangular and triangular loops); and ii) the *communications overhead* where we have develop other cost function that estimates the maximum time that processors spend in data redistributions or updating of the overlap regions. The constraints of the integer programming problem are derived directly from the *LCG*, and actually, they express the data locality requirements for each array and the affinity relations between different array references. In addition, our approach uses the *LCG* to automatically schedule the communication operations required during the program execution, once the iteration/data distributions have been selected. The aggregation of messages in blocks is also dealt in our approach.

We make the following contributions in this paper: i) we have developed an analytical model of the parallel execution overhead, where we consider communications and load unbalance; ii) we show, by measurements in a Cray T3E, that our analytical model gives a good approximation of the real overhead; iii) we present an iteration/data distribution method formulated as an integer programming problem, that attempts to derive the best distribution of a code such that the parallel execution overhead is minimized. This approach is more general than previous [2,6,4,1] in the sense that we cover a large class of programs, including programs consisting of multiple subroutines, containing non-perfectly nested loops, and loops with non-affine array references and non-affine loop bounds; iv) we show, by measurements in a MIPS R10000, that the use of the integer programming does not increase the compilation time significantly; and v) we present experimental results of the iteration/data distributions derived for a real code, that show the efficiency of our method.

The organization of the paper is as follows. In Section 2 we summarize some key concepts in order to build the *LCG* of a code. In Section 3 we formulate our iteration/data distribution method as an integer programming problem where the objective function and the constraints are computed from the *LCG* of the code. In Section 4, once the integer programming problem has been solved, our method defines the iteration/data distributions for the code. Next, in Section 5 we describe how our method schedules the communications routines. Finally, in Section 6 we conduct some experiments to evaluate how our objective function is modeling the parallel overhead and to check in real codes the effectiveness of the derived iteration/data distributions from our method.

2   Locality Analysis Based on Access Descriptors

We assume that the program contains a collection of DO loop nests (henceforth called *phases*) where at most one level of parallelism is exploited in each nest. IF statements, WHILE loops, DO loops and other constructs control the execution of the loop nests. Our techniques are based on the *Linear Memory Access Descriptor (LMAD)* introduced in [9], which can be accurately computed in relatively complex situations such as array reshaping resulting from subroutine calls and non-affine expressions in subscript expressions and loop bounds.

To generate descriptors of memory access patterns we assume that loops have been normalized and all arrays have been converted into one-dimensional arrays in the way it is traditionally done by conventional compilers. First, we compute the *array reference descriptor (ARD)* of each reference to array X_j in a phase. The ARD captures the memory access pattern of an array X_j occurrence within a phase. Once we have obtained the ARDs for array X_j in a phase, we build the *phase descriptor (PD)* that represents all the accesses to array X_j in a phase, taking into account all occurrences of X_j in the phase. A PD, including PDs that represent non-linear subscript expressions, can be simplified by applying several transformation operations. Detailed descriptions of all these operations can be found in [7] and [8].

2.1   Iteration Descriptor

To describe the elements of array X_j accessed by one iteration, say i, of the parallel loop in phase F_k, we use the *iteration descriptor (ID)*. The ID represents a super-set of all elements of array X_j accessed in such parallel iteration. A simple way to compute an ID is from the corresponding PD [7]. The ID of array X_j can describe some access sub-regions with storage symmetry. For each type of storage symmetry we define a *distance*: a) *Shifted storage*: two array sub-regions with the same access pattern, but shifted can be represented by a single ID term. In this situation, we define the *shifted storage distance*, Δ_d; b) *Reverse storage*: this represents two array sub-regions that are accessed with a reverse access pattern (this means that one access function is increasing and the other is decreasing with respect to the parallel loop index). In this case, we define the *reverse storage distance*, Δ_r; c) *Overlapping storage*: this represents two array sub-regions which are partially overlapped. In this case, we calculate the *overlapping distance*, Δ_s.

2.2   Memory Access Locality Analysis

In developing our analysis and transformation algorithms, we have assumed:
i) The total number of processors, H, to be involved in the execution of the

program is known at compile time; ii) The iterations of each parallel loops are statically distributed between the H processors involved in the execution of the code following a BLOCK-CYCLIC pattern.

The first part of our approach is to identify when it is possible to distribute iterations and data in such a way that all accesses to an array X_j are to local memory. For this, we use the information provided by the IDs of each array. We call this part of the algorithm *memory access locality analysis*. In the locality analysis we have identified two types of conditions to assure the locality of accesses: on the first hand, the *intra-phase locality condition*, which sets in each phase and for each array the data that must be located in the local memory of processor that executes a parallel iteration to avoid communications inside the phase. And on the other hand, the *inter-phase locality condition*, which determines if it is possible to find a chunk of parallel iterations in two phases, such that they cover the same local sub-region of an array. For more detail see [7]. The goal of this analysis is to compute the *Locality-Communication Graph (LCG)* a representation that captures the memory locality exhibited by a program in the form of a graph.

The *LCG* contains a directed, connected subgraph for each array X_j in the program. Each node in these subgraphs corresponds to a phase accessing the array represented by the subgraph. Notice that these phases do not have to include outermost DO loops. That is, the phases could be inside one or more DO loops. The nodes are connected according to the program control flow. We assign an attribute to each node of the *LCG* identifying the type of memory access for that array in the corresponding phase. When the memory access for an array X_j in a phase is write only, the associated node in the X_j subgraph is marked with the attribute W; when the memory access is read only, the attribute is R; and finally, for read and write accesses, the attribute is R/W. A special case arises when array X_j is privatizable in a phase (we restrict the definition of privatizable array given in [3] because we consider that the value of X_j is not lived after the execution of F_k): then the corresponding node is marked with attribute P. Fig. 2 (a) shows the *LCG* for a fragment of TFFT2 code from the NASA benchmarks. This *LCG* comprises two subgraphs, one for array X and another one for array Y. Each one of them contains 8 nodes (phases). On each subgraph the edges connecting nodes are also annotated with additional labels: L, which means that is possible to exploit memory access locality between the connected nodes (because the inter-phase locality condition is fulfilled), and C, when there is not possible to assure such memory access locality. This C label stands from "communication", due to the lack of memory access locality implies non local accesses. In these cases, the communication operations will be placed just after the execution of the source phase and before the execution of the target phase. In the cases where an edge connects a node with attribute P we say that connected phases are *un-coupled* [7], which means that the values of the corresponding array are defined independently on each one of these phases. Thus, the corresponding edge is removed (the dashed edges in Fig. 2 (a)).

3   Problem Formulation

In the second part of our approach, we have developed techniques to schedule parallel iterations and distribute the shared arrays across the local memories to minimize the parallel execution overhead due to load unbalance and communications. In our approach, the data distribution may change dynamically from phase to phase. When remote accesses are unavoidable, our techniques can identify them to subsequently generate communication primitives. Actually, the communication operation is implemented in our model via a *put* operation. This operation is an example of what is known as single-sided communication primitives.

Our iteration/data distribution problem is going to be formulated as an integer programming problem. We can see in Fig. 2 (a) that each (k, j) node has been associated with a variable p_{kj}. This variable represents the size of each chunk of parallel iterations that are going to be scheduled on each processor for phase F_k. The objective function is the parallel overhead and the goal is to find the iteration distributions such that parallel overhead is minimized. That objective function is subject to lineal constraints derived from the LCG of the program. And those constraints reflect the data locality and affinity requirements. We assume that the base iteration distribution is a generic CYCLIC(p_{kj}) (BLOCK_CYCLIC). Thus, the solution of the integer programming problem gives us the size p_{kj} of each chunk of parallel iterations for each phase F_k. For example, if $p_{kj} = 1$, a CYCLIC iteration distribution has been selected. If $p_{kj} = \left\lceil \frac{u_{k1}+1}{H} \right\rceil$ (where u_{k1} is the upper bound of the parallel loop), then a BLOCK distribution has been selected. In other case, a general CYCLIC(p_{kj}) iteration distribution has been selected. Now we can formalize the objective function and the constraints of our integer programming problem.

3.1   Constraints

The constraints of the integer programming problem are:

1. *Locality constraints.* They are derived for each pair of nodes $((k, j), (g, j)) \in LCG$ connected with L. Locality constraint guarantees that when p_{kj} and p_{gj} parallel iterations are scheduled in phase F_k and phase F_g, respectively, all accesses to array X_j cover a common data sub-region [7].
2. *Load balance constraints.* For each node $(k, j) \in LCG$, these constraints set the limits for the size of the chunks that are going to be scheduled on each processor.
3. *Storage constraints.* For each node $(k, j) \in LCG$ where the shifted storage, or the reverse storage, is found, the data sub-region covered by a chunk of p_{kj} parallel iterations and for all processors, must be smaller than the corresponding distance.
4. *Affinity constraints.* All the nodes which belong to the same phase in the LCG must have the same size of chunk. These constraints express the affinity relations between the different array references in a phase. This translates

into the following: $\forall j \quad p_{kj} = p_k$. From now, we will refer to p_k as the size of chunk of parallel iterations which will define the CYCLIC(p_k) iteration distribution of phase F_k.

Table 1 illustrates all the constraints for the LCG of the TFFT2 code example, where H is the number of processors and P and Q are constant input parameters.

Table 1. Objective function and Constraints for TFFT2

	X	Y
o.f.	$\text{Min}\left\{ \sum\limits_{j=1:2} \sum\limits_{k=1:8} D^k(X_j, p_{kj}) + C^{kg}(X_j, p_{kj}) \right\}$	
Locality	$p_{31} = p_{41}$ $P \cdot p_{41} = Q \cdot p_{51} \quad p_{51} = p_{61}$ $p_{61} = p_{71} \quad 2 \cdot Q \cdot p_{71} = p_{81}$	$p_{12} = Q \cdot p_{22}$ $P \cdot p_{32} = Q \cdot p_{52}$ $2 \cdot Q \cdot p_{62} = p_{82}$
Load bal.	$1 \leq p_{11}, p_{81} \leq \left\lceil \dfrac{P \cdot Q}{H} \right\rceil$ $1 \leq p_{31}, p_{41} \leq \left\lceil \dfrac{Q}{H} \right\rceil$ $1 \leq p_{21}, p_{51}, p_{61}, p_{71} \leq \left\lceil \dfrac{P}{H} \right\rceil$	$1 \leq p_{12}, p_{82} \leq \left\lceil \dfrac{P \cdot Q}{H} \right\rceil$ $1 \leq p_{32}, p_{42} \leq \left\lceil \dfrac{Q}{H} \right\rceil$ $1 \leq p_{22}, p_{52}, p_{62}, p_{72} \leq \left\lceil \dfrac{P}{H} \right\rceil$
Storage	$p_{81} \cdot H \leq \Delta_d^{81} = P \cdot Q$ $p_{81} \cdot H \leq \dfrac{\Delta_r^{81}(1)}{2} = \dfrac{P \cdot Q}{2}$ $p_{81} \cdot H \leq \dfrac{\Delta_r^{81}(2)}{2} = \dfrac{2 \cdot P \cdot Q}{2}$	$p_{12} \cdot H \leq \Delta_d^{12} = P \cdot Q$ $Q \cdot p_{22} \cdot H \leq \Delta_d^{22} = P \cdot Q$ $p_{82} \cdot H \leq \Delta_d^{81} = P \cdot Q$ $p_{82} \cdot H \leq \dfrac{\Delta_r^{81}(1)}{2} = \dfrac{P \cdot Q}{2}$ $p_{82} \cdot H \leq \dfrac{\Delta_r^{81}(2)}{2} = \dfrac{2 \cdot P \cdot Q}{2}$
Affinity	$p_{11} = p_{12} \quad p_{21} = p_{22} \quad p_{31} = p_{32} \quad p_{41} = p_{42}$ $p_{51} = p_{52} \quad p_{61} = p_{62} \quad p_{71} = p_{72} \quad p_{81} = p_{82}$	

3.2 Objective Function

The *objective function* represents the overhead (in seconds) of the parallel execution. The aim of our integer programming problem is the minimization of such an overhead:

$$\text{Min}\left\{ \sum_j \sum_k D^k(X_j, p_k) + C^{kg}(X_j, p_k) \right\} \tag{1}$$

where j traverses all the subgraphs in the LCG and k all the phases. In Fig. 1 we show the objective function of the TFFT2 code, that traverses two arrays and eight phases. $D^k(X_j, p_k)$ represents the *load unbalance cost function* of array X_j in phase F_k. $C^{kg}(X_j, p_k)$ represents the *communications cost function* of array X_j between the phases F_k and F_g. Both cost functions will be described next.

Load Unbalance Cost Function. In this paper we assume that there are no conditional executions in a phase. We compute the load unbalance cost function, $D^k(X_j, p_k)$, of a phase F_k, as the difference between the time consumed by the most loaded processor and the least loaded one. Clearly, this cost function depends on p_k. In addition, we have taken into account , in order to compute the cost function, if the phase is *rectangular* (neither the lower bound nor the upper bound of sequential loops depend on the loop index of the parallel loop) or *triangular*. A more detailed description is found in [8].

Communications Cost Function. The second source of overhead is due to the edges labeled with C, that connect the phases F_k and F_g $(g > k)$. They represent communications between phases that do not verify the inter-phase locality condition, so a redistribution, or updating of the overlap regions, must take place between them. In these cases we compute the communications cost function, $C^{kg}(X_j, p_k)$, which is defined as the time consumed in the communications that takes place between the execution of such phases. The communications cost for N messages of n elements, for a single-step communications routine, is:

$$C^{kg}(X_j, p_k) = N \cdot \left\{ \sigma + \frac{1}{\omega} \cdot n \right\} \tag{2}$$

where σ represents the *startup time* and ω represents the bandwidth of the communication routine. In the communications cost function, N and n depend on the communications pattern.

We consider two patterns: the *Frontier Communications pattern* and the *Global Communications pattern*. The Frontier Communications pattern happens when the overlapping storage is detected in a node (h, j) of the X_j subgraph. In this case, part of the ID for array X_j is replicated in the local memory of at least two processors. So, when in a phase F_k, there are writes in the overlap region of array X_j, replicated data must be kept coherent by means of communications routines. Such communications routines are generated by the processor that updates date of the overlap region. The Global Communications pattern occurs in the remaining situations where an edge of the LCG is labeled with C, and the overlapping storage is not detected in any node of the X_j subgraph. In such cases a redistribution for array X_j, between phases F_k and F_g, must take place.

In order to get the solution of the integer programming problem of the TFFT2 example (Table 1), we have invoked a mixed-integer non-linear programming (MINLP) solver of GAMS[5]. The values of p_k are shown in Fig. 1.

$$p_1 = p_{11} = p_{12} = \frac{P \cdot Q}{H} \qquad p_2 = p_{21} = p_{22} = \frac{P}{H}$$
$$p_3 = p_{31} = p_{32} = \frac{Q}{4 \cdot H} \qquad p_4 = p_{41} = p_{42} = \frac{Q}{4 \cdot H}$$
$$p_5 = p_{51} = p_{52} = \frac{P}{4 \cdot H}; \qquad p_6 = p_{61} = p_{62} = \frac{H}{4 \cdot H}$$
$$p_7 = p_{71} = p_{72} = \frac{P}{4 \cdot H} \qquad p_8 = p_{81} = p_{82} = \frac{P \cdot Q}{2 \cdot H}$$

Fig. 1. Solution for the integer programming problem of TFFT2 code

4 Iteration/Data Distribution Selection

Once the integer programming problem has been solved, we know the iteration distribution for each phase F_k, CYCLIC(p_k). The next step is the definition of a data distribution suitable for each phase.

We can define for each array X_j a mapping function that allocates the data accessed on a chunk of size p_k in a phase F_k, in the local memory of processor that executes the chunk. We will call that mapping function the *data distribution function* for array X_j. All phases of a j-th LCG subgraph that are connected consecutively with L edges define a **chain**. We note that the iteration distributions of all the phases of a chain cover the same data region of array X_j. This is due to the phases of a chain verify the locality constraints. So, the data distribution of all phases which belong to the chain is the same. In fact, we can select one of the data distribution functions of array X_j, from a phase that belongs to a chain, as the data distribution function of the chain. In the LCG the chains of an array X_j are separated by C (or dashed) edges. Therefore, a data redistribution (or allocation) procedure of an array X_j only takes place before the first phase of the chain.

Let's assume that phase F_k is in a chain and that array X_j is accessed in that phase. We define the data distribution function for array X_j in phase F_k as:

$$\psi^k(X_j) = cyclic\left(p_k, \delta_P^k, \mathcal{S}^k(X_j), \delta_S^k\right) \tag{3}$$

where:

- p_k is the size of the chunk in the BLOCK_CYCLIC iteration distribution of phase F_k;
- δ_P^k represents the parallel stride of array X_j in phase F_k;
- $\mathcal{S}^k(X_j)$ is the number of elements of array X_j allocated in the local memory of the processor for each parallel iteration;
- δ_S^k represents the sequential stride of the array X_j in the chain.

The parameters δ_P^k, $\mathcal{S}^k(X_j)$ and δ_S^k are computed from the ID of array X_j in phase F_k (see [8]).

The data distribution function can be extended to incorporate the storage distances [8]. Figure 2(b) shows the parameters (Equation 3) of all the data distribution functions for arrays X and Y, with $H = 4$, $P = 64$ and $Q = 32$, in our TFFT2 code.

An algorithm, for the computation of array X_j positions that must be allocated in the local memory of each processor, is shown next. Let $\psi^k(X_j) = cyclic\left(p_k, \delta_P^k, \mathcal{S}^k(X_j), \delta_S^k\right)$ be the data distribution function for array X_j in phase F_k, that is the first phase of a chain. Let p be the first parallel iteration of a chunk. And let's suppose that such an iteration is scheduled in processor PE. The X_j array positions which must be allocated in the local memory of processor PE, for that chunk, are computed as:

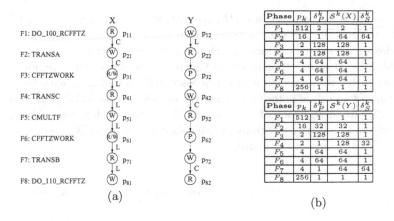

(a)

(b)

Fig. 2. TFFT2: (a) *LCG*; (b) Parameters of the data distribution functions (X and Y)

```
1.   do l_C^k = p  to p + p_k - 1
2.      do l_P^k = 0  to l_{Pmax}^k - 1
3.         do l_S^k = 0  to S^k(X_j) - 1
4.            X_j((l_C^k + l_P^k) · δ_P^k + l_S · δ_S^k)
5.            if ∃Δ_d^{kj} then   X_j((l_C^k + l_P^k) · δ_P^k + l_S · δ_S^k + Δ_d^{kj})
6.            if ∃Δ_r^{kj} then   X_j(Δ_r^{kj} - (l_C^k + l_P^k) · δ_P^k + l_S · δ_S^k)
7.            if ∃Δ_s^{kj} then   X_j((l_C^k + l_P^k) · δ_P^k + l_S · δ_S^k + Δ_s^{kj})
8.         enddo
9.      enddo
10.  enddo
```

We can note that the storage distances have been taken into account in this allocation procedure. This procedure must be carried out for each chunk of parallel iterations scheduled in processor PE. In this way, the data which are going to be requested on each chunk, are allocated in the local memory of PE.

5   Communications Generation

In this Section we outline how to automatically generate the communications routines for array X_j when there is a C edge in the j-th subgraph of the *LCG*. The basic communication primitive that we are going to use is *shmem_iput*.

Let's suppose that phases F_k and F_g are connected by a C edge in the j-th subgraph of the *LCG*, being $\psi^k(X_j)$ and $\psi^g(X_j)$ the data distribution functions for array X_j in such phases.

Fig. 3 shows an algorithm to generate the communications routine when the C edge has the pattern of Global Communications (redistribution). The communications routine generation for the Frontier Communications pattern is explained in [8]. In Fig. 3, $NC(PE)$ is the number of chunks scheduled in processor PE and *stride_block* is the number of memory positions of array X_j that must be skipped on each chunk of phase F_k. We can see that all array positions that are allocated in the memory of processor PE are traversed following the $\psi^k(X_j)$ data distribution function. For simplicity's sake in the expressions, we are using the global index of the array positions, which are represented with ind_{global}. For such a variable, the B index is pointing to the first position of each region of data associated with a chunk scheduled in processor PE. In addition, with the P index the ind_{global} variable is pointing to the first position of the subregion associated with each parallel iteration of that chunk. With the S index, the ind_{global} variable traverses all the array positions of the subregion of array X_j associated with each parallel iteration of the chunk.

1.   **do** $B = PE \cdot stride\_block$ **to** $(NC(PE) - 1) \cdot stride\_block \cdot H + PE \cdot stride\_block,$ $H \cdot stride\_block$
2.   **do** $P = 0$ **to** $p_k - 1$
3.   **do** $S = 0$ **to** $\mathcal{S}^k(X_j) - 1$
4. $ind_{global} = B + P \cdot \delta_P^k + S \cdot \delta_S^k$
5. $X_j(target) = X_j' \left(\frac{ind_{global}}{\delta_S^g} + mod(ind_{global}, \delta_S^g) \right)$
6. $X_j(source) = X_j(ind_{global})$
7. $PE_{remote} = mod \left(\left[\frac{ind_{global}}{S^g \cdot \delta_S^g \cdot p_g} + mod(\frac{ind_{global}}{p_g}, \delta_S^g) \right], H \right)$
8. $shmem\_iput(X_j(target), X_j(source), \delta_S^g, \delta_S^k, 1, PE_{remote})$
9.   **enddo**
10.   **enddo**
11. **enddo**

Fig. 3. Generation of communications routine (array X_j) between phases F_k and F_g for the Global Communications pattern

X_j' represents a temporal buffer, where a copy of data which must be allocated in the memory of processor PE_{remote}, is maintained. The data in this buffer are allocated following the data distribution function $\psi^g(X_j)$. After the execution of the communications routine, and before the execution of F_g, each temporal buffer X_j' can be dumped on the local positions of X_j. Doing this, we have reallocated the data in the local memories in such a way that $\psi^g(X_j)$ is now the data distribution function for X_j.

An optimization of the communications algorithm shown in Fig. 3, is the elimination of the P loop. This happens when the messages can be aggregated in blocks of size p_k. Another optimization possibility is the elimination of the S loop, that happens when the messages can be aggregated in blocks of size $\mathcal{S}^k(X_j)$. The conditions under those aggregations can take place are described in [8].

6   Experimental Results

This Section has two goals. First, to evaluate the objective function that we have proposed in Section 3. That function is an estimation of the parallel execution overhead. In Section 6.1 we propose a simple code example for what we have compared our estimation of the parallel overhead times and the real overhead times. These estimated and real overhead times have been obtained for a Cray T3E. In addition, it is important to understand how each overhead source that we are considering (load unbalance and communications) influences the final selection of the p_k size in the CYCLIC(p_k) distributions. The contribution of each overhead term of the objective function is also discussed in Section 6.1. The second goal consists in applying our iteration/data distribution method to real codes. The iteration/data distributions selected by the method have been hand coded, and the resulting parallel codes have been executed in a Cray T3E. With these experiments we can probe in Section 6.2 the effectiveness of the iteration/data distributions found with our method.

6.1 Validation of Objective Function

In Fig. 4 we show a small code example with two phases (two nested loops in this case). Each parallel iteration of F_1 traverses the X rows and each parallel iteration of F_2 traverses the X columns. u1 and u2 represent the upper bounds of parallel loops in F_1 and F_2, respectively; v and w represent the upper bounds of sequential loops in F_1 and F_2. When we apply the locality analysis procedure in order to build the LCG of this code, the edge connecting F_1 and F_2 is labeled with C. This means that communications operations are necessary between these phases. The Global communication pattern happens here because this is a redistribution case (Section 3.2). Let us recall that the goal in our integer programming problem is to find the p_k size of the parallel chunks that are going to be scheduled on each processor, such that the overhead of the parallel execution is minimized. Once p_k is found, we can derive the data distribution function for each array, as we saw in Section 4.

```
F1: doall J=0 to u1              F2: doall I=0 to u2
       do I=0 to v                      do J=0 to w
          X((I+1)*N+J)=X(I*N+J) ...        ... = X(I*N+J)
          ...                              X(I*N+J)= ...
       enddo                            enddo
    enddo                            enddo
```

Fig. 4. Code example with two phases. There are communications between phases F_1 and F_2 for array X

For the example of Fig. 4, the objective function (the parallel execution overhead) is:

$$\sum_{k=1}^{2} D^k(X, p_k) + C^{12}(X, p_1) \tag{4}$$

where $D^k(X, p_k)$ represents the load unbalance cost function for phase F_k ($k = 1, 2$); and $C^{12}(X, p_1)$ represents the communications cost function for the redistribution between phases F_1 and F_2; p_1 and p_2 are the variables that represent the size of parallel chunks for phases F_1 and F_2, respectively. Initially, let us suppose N=256, H=4, and u1=u2=N-1.

Load Unbalance Cost Function. In [8], we summarize the load unbalance cost functions for array X_j, depending on whether F_k is a rectangular phase, or a triangular phase. Let us now suppose that F_1 is rectangular phase, with v=N-2, in the code example of Fig. 4. For such a case, the particular expression for the load unbalance cost function is:

$$D^1(X, p_1) = (p_1 \cdot I^1 \cdot Ref^1(X)) \cdot b_1 \tag{5}$$

here, $I^1 = N-1$, represents the number of sequential iterations executed on each parallel iteration; $Ref^1(X)$ represents the time consumed by accesses to X on each iteration of I^1; b_1 is a Boolean variable: when the number of chunks in phase F_k is an integer multiple of H, then $b_1 = 0$, which means that there is no load unbalance. Otherwise, $b_1 = 1$. Fig. 5(a) shows the estimated vs. measured load unbalance cost function for the rectangular phase F_1. The Y-axis represents the load unbalance overhead time in seconds. The X-axis represents all possible solutions for p_1. The solid line is the estimated load unbalance (Equation 5) for a Cray T3E. The dashed line is the measured load unbalance in the Cray T3E. In Figure 5(a) we see that when F_1 is a rectangular phase, the load unbalance overhead is minimum for: $p_1 = \{1, 2, 4, 5, 8, 11, 13, 16, 17, 22, 23, 32, 33, 34, 35, 36, 64\}$. These are the values of p_1 such that $\lceil \frac{u_1+1}{p_1} \rceil$ (the number of chunks) is an integer multiple of $H = 4$. We note that the measured load unbalance has a similar behavior that the estimated one, and they present the minimums for the same values of p_1.

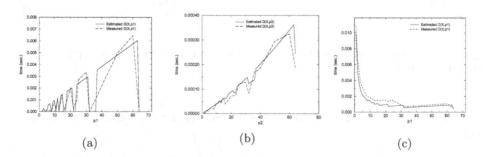

(a)   (b)   (c)

Fig. 5. (a) $D^1(X, p_1)$ estimated and measured when F_1 is a rectangular phase; (b) $D^2(X, p_2)$ estimated and measured when F_2 is a triangular phase; (c) $C^{12}(X, p_1)$ estimated and measured

Let's now suppose, in the code example of Fig. 4, that F_2 is a triangular phase, with w=I. Now, the particular expression for the load unbalance cost function is:

$$D^2(X, p_2) = \left(\left(\frac{d_2 \cdot u_2 + 1}{p_2 \cdot H} + e_2 \right) \cdot p_2^2 + e_2 \cdot p_2 \right) \cdot \frac{1}{d_2} \cdot Ref^2(X) \qquad (6)$$

where $Ref^2(X)$ represents the time consumed by accesses to X; e_2 and d_2 are two variables that verify: when the number of chunks in phase F_2 is an integer multiple of H, then $e_2 = 0$ and $d_2 = 1$. Otherwise, $e_2 = 1$, and $d_2 = 2$. Fig. 5(b) shows the estimated vs. measured load unbalance cost function for the triangular phase F_2. Here, the Y-axis represents the load unbalance overhead time in seconds and the X-axis represents all posible solutions for p_2. The solid line is the estimated load unbalance (Equation 6) for a Cray T3E and the dashed line is the measured load unbalance in the Cray T3E. In Figure 5(b) we see that when F_2 is a triangular phase, the load unbalance overhead is minimum for $p_2 = 1$. The ripple in the figures appears in those values of p_2 where the number of chunks, $\left\lceil \frac{u_2+1}{p_2} \right\rceil$, is an integer multiple of H. Again, we can see that the measured cost function has a similar behavior that the estimated one, and they present the same minimums. We can note that the measured load unbalance overhead is slightly lower than the estimated, although for the minimum values, the differences are below 10^{-5} seconds.

Communications Cost Function. For the example of Fig. 4, our method has detected the Global communications pattern. Thus, in the general case, with $n = 1$, the communications cost function expression is:

$$C^{12}(X, p_1) = \left\lceil \frac{u_1 + 1}{H \cdot p_1} \right\rceil \cdot \left(\mathcal{S}^1(X) \cdot p_1 \right) \cdot \left\{ \sigma + \frac{1}{\omega} \right\} . \qquad (7)$$

From this equation we can check that the minimum communications overhead in our example code is in $p1 = \{1, 2, 4, 8, 16, 32, 64\}$, while $p2 = [1 : 64]$. Another important observation is that p_2 does not affect the communications overhead. The computation of p_2 will be derived from the unbalance cost function for F_2 and from the constraints of our integer programming problem.

The code example of Fig. 4, with $\mathcal{S}^1(X) = N$, and $\mathcal{S}^2(X) = N$, verifies the conditions for aggregation of messages in blocks of size $n = p_1$. For this case, the communications cost function ([8]) is:

$$C^{12}(X, p_1) = \left\lceil \frac{u_1 + 1}{H \cdot p_1} \right\rceil \cdot \left(\mathcal{S}^1(X) \right) \cdot \left\{ \sigma + \frac{1}{\omega} \cdot p_1 \right\} . \qquad (8)$$

Fig. 5(c) shows the estimated vs. measured communication cost function with message aggregation in the Cray T3E. The Y-axis represents the communication overhead time in seconds. The solid line is the estimated communication overhead (Equation 8) and the dashed line is the measured communication overhead. In Figure 5(c) we can see that the minimum communications overhead is now in $p1 = 64$, while $p2 = [1 : 64]$. So, one consequence of the aggregation of messages is that the minimum communications overhead is in the larger p_1 such that $\left\lceil \frac{u_1+1}{p_1} \right\rceil$ is an integer multiple of H. Now, we note that the measured communications overhead is slightly greater than the estimated one, although again, for the minimum values, the differences are below 10^{-5} seconds ($< 10\%$).

Fig. 6 (a) and (b) summarizes the total overhead due to the communications and the load unbalance of each phase, and for two different configurations of the phases F_1 and F_2, in our code example (Fig. 4). Both figures represent the parallel overhead times (in seconds), estimated for a Cray T3E. As messages can be aggregated in blocks of size $n = p_1$, we use the Equation 8 as the communications cost function of our code. We can note that the main contribution of overhead is due to communications, especially for small values of p_1. But, when the size of p_1 increases, the communication overhead decreases, and the load unbalance overhead becomes determinant, mainly, when F_1 is a triangular phase. In this last situation (case of Fig. 6(b)), smaller values of p_1 lead to minimize the overhead. Thus, the selection of p_1 is a trade off between communications and load unbalance, depending on the kind of phase: the minimum overhead is for $p_1 = 64$, when F_1 is rectangular, and for $p_1 = 16$, when F_1 is triangular. The values for p_2 depends only on the load unbalance overhead. When F_2 is a rectangular phase (Fig. 6(a)), there are several solutions such that the overhead is minimized. That solutions are those in which the number of chunks is an integer multiple of the number of processors. However, when F_2 is a triangular phase (Fig. 6(b)), there is just one solution leading to a minimum overhead: $p_2 = 1$.

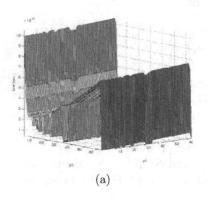 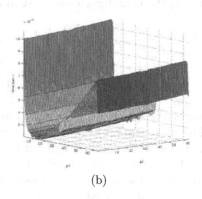

(a)   (b)

Fig. 6. Estimated total overhead $C^{12}(X, p_1) + D^1(X, p_1) + D^2(X, p_2)$ in a Cray T3E: (a) F_1 and F_2 are rectangular; (b) F_1 and F_2 are triangular

In order to compute the iterations/data distributions of our example of Fig. 4, we have formulated the integer programming problem of the code. In order to get the solution, we have invoked a MINLP solver of GAMS[5]. The solution has been obtained in just 30 ms (10 ms in the compilation and generation step plus 20 ms in the execution step) in a MIPS R10000 at 196 MHz. Using this tool, p_1 took the previously discussed values, and $p2$ always took the value 1.

6.2   Iteration/Data Distribution for Real Codes

The iteration/data distribution method presented in this paper has been applied to the TFFT2 code, which performs real-to-complex, complex-to-complex, and complex-to-real FFTs. Thus, this code includes non-affine access functions and non-affine index bounds, which are correctly handled by our approach. In addition, the repeated subroutine calls inside loops form a deeply nested loop structure. Our method was successfully applied across the inter-procedural bounds. The parallelization procedure was the following: first, the Polaris parallelizer [3] marked the parallel loops; then, the LCG of the code was built; next, the integer programming problem was derived. Here again, we used a MINLP solver of GAMS to obtain the iteration/data distributions of each phase, getting the solution on 150 ms, in a MIPS R10000 at 196 MHz; finally, the obtained distributions were hand coded, including the communications generation for the C edges of the LCG. The experimental efficiencies of the parallel code, executed in the Cray T3E are 85%, 84%, 77%, 75% and 69% for 1, 2, 4, 8 and 16 processors respectively. With our BLOCK_CYCLIC iteration distributions (Figure 1) and data distributions (Figure 2(b)) we exploit locality without communications for the 77% of sequential coverage. Our method has also exploited locality by privatizing the array Y in the phases F_3 and F_6. These results corroborate the effectiveness of the data distributions and the control of communications operations derived with our method.

7   Conclusions

The access descriptor notation, ARD, is a powerful array access representation that can be easily handled by the compiler. One of its applications is the building of the Locality-Communication Graph (LCG) of a program. This LCG efficiently captures the data locality of the program. Using the LCG we have developed a method to automatically find the CYCLIC(p_k) iteration/data distributions which minimize the parallel overhead of the program (objective function). Preliminary experiments in a Cray T3E show us that the modeled parallel overhead is very similar to the real one. The main conclusion here is that our objective function gives a sufficient criterion to select an efficient iteration/data distribution in real codes. In addition, our method uses the LCG to automatically schedule communications and to perform message aggregation.

A real code, the TFFT2 from NASA benchmarks, that includes non-affine access functions and non-affine index bounds, and repeated subroutine calls inside loops, has been correctly handled by our approach. The version of the code, parallelized with the iteration/data distributions derived from our method, achieves parallel efficiencies of over 69% for 16 processors, in a Cray T3E. This result states that with our method, the automatic selection of iteration/data distributions, and the control over communications operations, lead to excellent performance with complex real codes.

References

1. J.M. Anderson and M.S. Lam. Global optimizations for parallelism and locality on scalable parallel machines. In *Proceedings of SIGPLAN'93 Conference on Programming Language Design and Implementation (PLDI)*, Alburquerque, New Mexico, June 1993.
2. D. Bau, I. Kodukula, V. Kotlyar, K. Pingali, and Stodghill. Solving alignment using elementary linear algebra. In K. Pingali et al., editor, *Proceedings of LCPC'94*, number 892 in LNCS. Springer Verlag, Ithaca, N.Y., August 1994.
3. W. Blume, R. Doallo, R. Eigenmann, J. Grout, J. Hoeflinger, T. Lawrence, J. Lee, D. Padua, Y. Paek, W. Pottenger, L. Rauchwerger, and P. Tu. Parallel programming with Polaris. *IEEE Computer*, pages 78–82, Dec 1996.
4. J. Garcia, E. Ayguade, and J. Labarta. Dynamic data distribution with control flow analysis. In *Proceedings of Supercomputing*, Pittsburgh, PA, November 1996.
5. http://www.gams.com/Default.htm.
6. K. Kennedy and U. Kremer. Automatic data layout using 0-1 integer programming. In *Int'l Conf. Parallel Architectures and Compilation Techniques*, Montréal, Canada, Aug. 1994.
7. A. Navarro, R. Asenjo, E. Zapata, and D. Padua. Access descriptor based locality analysis for distributed-shared memory multiprocessors. In *International Conference on Parallel Processing (ICPP'99)*, pages 86–94, Aizu-Wakamatzu, Japan, September 21–24 1999.
8. Angeles G. Navarro and E.L. Zapata. An automatic iteration/data distribution method based on access descriptors for DSM multiprocessors. Technical Report UMA-DAC-99/07, Department of Computer Architecture, University of Málaga, 1999.
9. Y. Paek, J. Hoeflinger, and D. Padua. Simplification of array access patterns for compiler optimizations. In *Proceedings of the SIGPLAN Conference on Programming Language Design and Implementation*, June 1994.

Inter-array Data Regrouping

Chen Ding and Ken Kennedy

Rice University
Houston TX 77005, USA

Abstract. As the speed gap between CPU and memory widens, memory hierarchy has become the performance bottleneck for most applications because of both the high latency and low bandwidth of direct memory access. With the recent introduction of latency hiding strategies on modern machines, limited memory bandwidth has become the primary performance constraint and, consequently, the effective use of available memory bandwidth has become critical. Since memory data is transferred one cache block at a time, improving the utilization of cache blocks can directly improve memory bandwidth utilization and program performance. However, existing optimizations do not maximize cache-block utilization because they are *intra-array*; that is, they improve only data reuse within single arrays, and they do not group useful data of multiple arrays into the same cache block. In this paper, we present *inter-array data regrouping*, a global data transformation that first splits and then selectively regroups all data arrays in a program. The new transformation is optimal in the sense that it exploits inter-array cache-block reuse when and only when it is always profitable. When evaluated on real-world programs with both regular contiguous data access, and irregular and dynamic data access, inter-array data regrouping transforms as many as 26 arrays in a program and improves the overall performance by as much as 32%.

1 Introduction

As modern single-chip processors have increased the rate at which they execute instructions, performance of the memory hierarchy has become the bottleneck for most applications. In the past, the principal challenge in memory hierarchy management was in overcoming latency, but computation blocking and data prefetching have ameliorated that problem significantly. As exposed memory latency is reduced, the bandwidth constraint becomes dominant because the limited memory bandwidth restricts the rate of data transfer between memory and CPU regardless of the speed of processors or the latency of memory access. Indeed, we found in an earlier study that the bandwidth needed to achieve peak performance levels on intensive scientific applications is up to 10 times greater than that provided by the memory system[7]. As a result, program performance is now limited by its effective bandwidth; that is, the rate at which operands of a computation are transferred between CPU and memory.

L. Carter and J. Ferrante (Eds.): LCPC'99, LNCS 1863, pp. 149–163, 2000.
© Springer-Verlag Berlin Heidelberg 2000

The primary software strategy for alleviating the memory bandwidth bottleneck is cache reuse, that is, reusing the buffered data in cache instead of accessing memory directly. Since cache consists of non-unit cache blocks, sufficient use of cache blocks becomes critically important because low cache-block utilization leads directly to both low memory-bandwidth utilization and low cache utilization. For example for cache blocks of 16 numbers, if only one number is useful in each cache block, 15/16 or 94% of memory bandwidth is wasted, and furthermore, 94% of cache space is occupied by useless data and only 6% of cache is available for data reuse.

A compiler can improve cache-block utilization, or equivalently, cache-block spatial reuse, by packing useful data into cache blocks so that all data elements in a cache block are consumed before it is evicted. Since a program employs many data arrays, the useful data in each cache block may come from two sources: the data within one array, or the data from multiple arrays. Cache-block reuse within a single array is often inadequate to fully utilize cache blocks. Indeed, in most programs, a single array may never achieve full spatial reuse because data access cannot always be made contiguous in every part of the program. Common examples are programs with regular, but high dimensional data, and programs with irregular and dynamic data. When non-contiguous access to a single array is inevitable, the inclusion of useful data from other arrays can directly increase cache-block reuse.

This paper presents *inter-array data regrouping*, a global data transformation that first splits and then selectively regroups all data arrays in a program. Figure 1 gives an example of this transformation. The left-hand side of the figure shows the example program, which traverses a matrix first by rows and then by columns. One of the loops must access non-contiguous data and cause low cache-block utilization because only one number in each cache block is useful. Inter-array data regrouping combines the two arrays by putting them into a single array that has an extra dimension, as shown in the right-hand side of Figure 1. Assuming the first data dimension is contiguous in memory, the regrouped version guarantees at least two useful numbers in each cache block regardless the order of traversal.

In addition to improving cache spatial reuse, data regrouping also reduces the page-table (TLB) working set of a program because it merges multiple arrays into a single one. Otherwise, a program may touch too many arrays, causing overflow of TLB. On modern machines, TLB misses are very harmful to performance because CPU cannot continue program execution during a TLB miss.

Inter-array data regrouping can also improve communication performance of shared-memory parallel machines. On these machines, cache blocks are the basis of data consistency and consequently the unit of communication among parallel processors. Good cache-block utilization enabled by inter-array data regrouping can amortize the latency of communication and fully utilize communication bandwidth.

The rest of the paper is organized as follows. The next section formulates the problem of inter-array data regrouping and presents its solution. Section

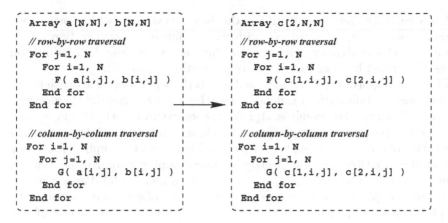

Fig. 1. Example of Inter-array Data Regrouping

3 evaluates the transformation on two well-known kernels and two real-world applications. Section 4 discusses related work, and Section 5 concludes.

2 Inter-array Data Regrouping

This section first describes the necessary program analysis for data regrouping, then gives the regrouping algorithm, proves its optimality, and finally discusses three extensions of the regrouping problem and presents their solutions as well.

2.1 Program Analysis

Given a program, a compiler identifies in two steps all opportunities of inter-array data regrouping. The first step partitions the program into a sequence of computation phases. A computation phase is defined as a segment of the program that accesses data larger than cache. A compiler can automatically estimate the amount of data access in loop structures with the technique given by Ferrante et al[8].

The second step of the analysis identifies sets of compatible arrays. Two arrays are compatible if their sizes differ by at most a constant, and if they are always accessed in the same order in each computation phase. For example, the size of array $A(3, N)$ is compatible with $B(N)$ and with $B(N - 3)$ but not with $C(N/2)$ or $D(N, N)$. The access order from $A(1)$ to $A(N)$ is compatible with $B(1)$ to $B(N)$ but not with the order from $C(N)$ to $C(1)$ or from $D(1)$ to $D(N/2)$. The second criterion does allow compatible arrays to be accessed differently in different computation phases, as long as they have the same traversal order in the same phase[1].

---

[1] In general, the traversal orders of two arrays need not to be the same as long as they maintain a consistent relationship. For example, array A and B have consistent

The second step requires identifying the data access order within each array. Regular programs can be analyzed with various forms of array section analysis. For irregular or dynamic programs, a compiler can use the data-indirection analysis described by Ding and Kennedy (in Section 3.2 of [6]).

The other important job of the second step is the separation of arrays into the smallest possible units, which is done by splitting constant-size data dimensions into multiple arrays. For example, $A(2, N)$ is converted into $A1(N)$ and $A2(N)$.

After the partitioning of computation phases and compatible arrays, the formulation of data regrouping becomes clear. First, data regrouping transforms each set of compatible arrays separately because grouping incompatible arrays is either impossible or too costly. Second, a program is now modeled as a sequence of computation phases each of which accesses a subset of compatible arrays. The goal of data regrouping is to divide the set of compatible arrays into a set of new arrays such that the overall cache-block reuse is maximized in all computation phases.

2.2   Regrouping Algorithm

We now illustrate the problem and the solution of data regrouping through an example—the application *Magi* from DOD, which simulates the shock and material response of particles in a three-dimensional space (based on smoothed particle hydrodynamics method). Table 1 lists the six major computation phases of the program as well as the attributes of particles used in each phase. Since the program stores an attribute of all particles in a separate array, different attributes do not share the same cache block. Therefore, if a computation phase uses k attributes, it needs to load in k cache blocks when it accesses a particle.

Table 1. Computation phases of a hydrodynamics simulation program

Computation phases	Attributes accessed
1 *constructing interaction list*	`position`
2 *smoothing attributes*	`position, velocity, heat, derivate, viscosity`
3 *hydrodynamic interactions 1*	`density, momentum`
4 *hydrodynamic interactions 2*	`momentum, volume, energy, cumulative totals`
5 *stress interaction 1*	`volume, energy, strength, cumulative totals`
6 *stress interaction 2*	`density, strength`

Combining multiple arrays can reduce the number of cache blocks accessed and consequently improve cache-block reuse. For example, we can group *position* and *velocity* into a new array such that the ith element of the new array contains the position and velocity of the ith particle. After array grouping, each particle

---

traversal order if whenever $A[i]$ is accessed, $B[f(i)]$ is accessed, where $f(x)$ is a one-to-one function.

reference of the second phase accesses one fewer cache blocks since *position* and *velocity* are now loaded by a single cache block. In fact, we can regroup all five arrays used in the second phase and consequently merge all attributes into a single cache block (assuming a cache block can hold five attributes).

However, excessive grouping in one phase may hurt cache-block reuse in other phases. For example, grouping *position* with *velocity* wastes a half of each cache block in the first phase because the *velocity* attribute is never referenced in that phase.

The example program shows two requirements for data regrouping. The first is to fuse as many arrays as possible in order to minimize the number of loaded cache blocks, but at the same time, the other requirement is not to introduce any useless data through regrouping. In fact, the second requirement mandates that two arrays should not be grouped unless they are always accessed together. Therefore, the goal of data regrouping is to partition data arrays such that (1) two arrays are in the same partition only if they are always accessed together, and (2) the size of each partition is the largest possible. The first property ensures no waste of cache, and the second property guarantees the maximal cache-block reuse.

Although condition (1) might seem a bit restrictive in practice, we note that many applications use multiple fields of a data structure array together. Our algorithm will automatically do what the Fortran 77 hand programmer does to simulate arrays of data structures: implement each field as a separate array. Thus it should be quite common for two or more arrays to always be accessed together. In Section 2.4 we discuss methods for relaxing condition (1) at the cost of making the analysis more complex.

The problem of optimal regrouping is equivalent to a set-partitioning problem. A program can be modeled as a set and a sequence of subsets where the set represents all arrays and each subset models the data access of a computation phase in the program.

Given a set and a sequence of subsets, we say two elements are *buddies* if for any subset containing one element, it must contain the other one. The *buddy* relation is reflexive, symmetric, and transitive; therefore it is a partition. A buddy partitioning satisfies the two requirements of data regrouping because (1) all elements in each partition are buddies, and (2) all buddies belong to the same partition. Thus the data regrouping problem is the same as finding a partitioning of buddies. For example in Table 1, array *volume* and *energy* are buddies because they are always accessed together.

The buddy partitioning can be solved with efficient algorithms. For example, the following partitioning method uses set memberships for each array, that is, a bit vector whose entry i is 1 if the array is accessed by the ith phase. The method uses a radix sort to find arrays with the same set memberships, i.e. arrays that are always accessed together. Assuming a total of N arrays and S computation phases, the time complexity of the method is $O(N * S)$. If a bit-vector is used for S in the actual implementation, the algorithm runs in $O(N)$ vector steps. In this sense, the cost of regrouping is linear to the number of arrays.

2.3 Optimality

Qualitatively, the algorithm groups two arrays when and only when it is always profitable to do so. To prove, consider on the one hand, data regrouping never includes any useless data into cache, so it is applied only when profitable; on the other hand, whenever two arrays can be merged without introducing useless data, they are regrouped by the algorithm. Therefore, *data regrouping exploits inter-array spatial reuse when and only when it is always profitable.*

Under reasonable assumptions, the optimality can also be defined quantitatively in terms of the amount of memory access and the size of TLB working set. The key link between an array layout and its overall data access is the concept called *iteration footprint*, which is the number of distinct arrays accessed by one iteration of a computation phase. Assuming an array element is smaller than a cache block but an array is larger than a virtual memory page, then the iteration footprint is equal to the number of cache blocks and the number of pages accessed by one iteration. The following lemma shows that data regrouping minimizes the iteration footprint.

Lemma 1. *Under the restriction of no useless data in cache blocks, data regrouping minimizes the iteration footprint of each computation phase.*

Proof. After buddy partitioning, two arrays are regrouped when and only when they are always accessed together. In other words, two arrays are combined when and only when doing so does not introduce any useless data. Therefore, for any computation phase after regrouping, no further array grouping is possible without introducing useless data. Thus, the iteration footprint is minimal after data regrouping.

The size of a footprint directly affects cache performance because the more distinct arrays are accessed, the more active cache blocks are needed in cache, and therefore, the more chances of premature eviction of useful data caused by either limited cache capacity or associativity. For convenience, we refer to both cache capacity misses and cache interference misses collectively as *cache overhead misses*. It is reasonable to assume that the number of cache overhead misses is a non-decreasing function on the number of distinct arrays. Intuitively, a smaller footprint should never cause more cache overhead misses because a reduced number of active cache blocks can always be arranged so that their conflicts with cache capacity and with each other do not increase. With this assumption, the following theorem proves that a minimal footprint leads to minimal cache overhead.

Theorem 1. *Given a program of n computation phases, where the total number of cache overhead misses is a non-decreasing function on the size of its iteration footprint k, then data regrouping minimizes the total number of overhead misses in the whole program.*

Proof. : Assuming the number of overhead misses in the n computation phases is $f_1(k_1), f_2(k_2), \ldots, f_n(k_n)$, then the total amount of memory re-transfer is proportional to $f_1(k_1) + f_2(k_2) + \ldots + f_n(k_n)$. According to the previous lemma,

$k_1, k_2, \ldots, k_n$ are the smallest possible after regrouping. Since all functions are non-decreasing, the sum of all cache overhead misses is therefore minimal after data regrouping.

The assumption made by the theorem covers a broad range of data access patterns in real programs, including two extreme cases. The first is the worst extreme, where no cache reuse happens, for example, in random data access. The total number of cache misses is in linear proportion to the size of the iteration footprint since each data access causes a cache miss. The other extreme is the case of perfect cache reuse where no cache overhead miss occurs, for example, in contiguous data access. The total number of repeated memory transfer is zero. In both cases, the number of cache overhead misses is a non-decreasing function on the size of the iteration footprint. Therefore, data regrouping is optimal in both cases according to the theorem just proved.

In a similar way, data regrouping minimizes the overall TLB working set of a program. Assuming arrays do not share the same memory page, the size of the iteration footprint, i.e. the number of distinct arrays accessed by a computation phase, is in fact the size of its TLB working set. Since the size of TLB working set is a non-decreasing function over the iteration footprint, the same proof can show that data regrouping minimizes the overall TLB working set of the whole program.

A less obvious benefit of data regrouping is the elimination of useless data by grouping only those parts that are used by a computation phase of a program. The elimination of useless data by array regrouping is extremely important for applications written in languages with data abstraction features, as in, for example, C, C++, Java and Fortran 90. In these programs, a data object contains lots of information, but only a fraction of it is used in a given computation phase.

In summary, the regrouping algorithm is optimal because it minimizes all iteration footprints of a program. With the assumption that cache overhead is a non-decreasing function over the size of iteration footprints, data regrouping achieves maximal cache reuse and minimal TLB working set.

2.4   Extensions

The previous section makes two restrictions in deriving the optimal solution for data regrouping. The first is disallowing any useless data, and the second is assuming a static data layout without dynamic data remapping. This section relaxes these two restrictions and gives modified solutions. In addition, this section expands the scope of data regrouping to minimizing not only memory reads but also memory writebacks.

Allowing Useless Data. The base algorithm disallows regrouping any two arrays that are not always accessed together. This restriction may not always be desirable, as in the example program in the left-hand side of Figure 2, where array A and B are accessed together for in the first loop, but only A is accessed in the second loop. Since the first loop is executed 100 times as often as the second loop, it is very likely that the benefit of grouping A and B in the first exceeds the overhead of introducing redundant data in the second. If so, it is profitable to relax the prohibition on no useless data.

Allowing useless data   Allowing dynamic data remapping

```
for step=1, t                    for step=1, t
   for i=1, N                       for i=1, N
      Foo(A[i], B[i])                  Foo(A[i], B[i])
   end for                          end for
end for                          end for

for i=1, N                       for step=1, t
   Bar(A[i])                        for i=1, N
end for                             Bar(A[i])
                                    end for
                                 end for
```

Fig. 2. Examples of extending data regrouping

However, the tradeoff between grouping fewer arrays and introducing useless data depends on the precise measurement of the performance gain due to data regrouping and the performance loss due to redundant data. Both the benefit and cost are program and machine dependent and neither of them can be statically determined. One practical remedy is to consider only frequently executed computation phases such as the loops inside a time-step loop and to apply data regrouping only on them.

When the exact run-time benefit of regrouping and the overhead of useless data is known, the problem of optimal regrouping can be formulated with a weighted, undirected graph, called a *data-regrouping graph*. Each array is a node in the graph. The weight of each edge is the run-time benefit of regrouping the two end nodes minus its overhead. The goal of data regrouping is to pack arrays that are most beneficial into the same cache block. However, the packing problem on a data-regrouping graph is NP-hard because it can be reduced from the G-partitioning problem[12].

Allowing Dynamic Data Regrouping. Until now, data regrouping uses a single data layout for the whole program. An alternative strategy is to allow dynamic regrouping of data between computation phases so that the data layout of a particular phase can be optimized without worrying about the side effects in other phases. For example, in the example program in the right-hand side of Figure 2, the best strategy is to group A and B at the beginning of the program and then separate these two arrays after the first time-step loop.

For dynamic data regrouping to be profitable, the overhead of run-time data movement must not exceed its benefit. However, the exact benefit of regrouping and the cost of remapping are program and machine dependent and consequently cannot be determined by a static compiler. As in the case of allowing useless data, a practical approach is to apply data regrouping within different time-step loops and insert dynamic data remapping in between.

When the precise benefit of regrouping and the cost of dynamic remapping is known, the problem can be formulated in the same way as the one given by Kremer[13]. In his formulation, a program is separated into computation phases. Each data layout results in a different execution time for each phase plus the cost of changing data layouts among phases. The optimal layout, either dynamic or static, is the one that minimizes the overall execution time. Without modification, Kremer's formulation can model the search space of all static or dynamic data-regrouping schemes. However, as Kremer has proved, finding the optimal layout is NP-hard. Since the search space is generally not large, he successfully used 0-1 integer programming to find the optimal data layout. The same method can be used to find the optimal data regrouping when dynamic regrouping is allowed.

Minimizing Data Writebacks. On machines with insufficient memory bandwidth, data writebacks impede memory read performance because they consume part of the available memory bandwidth. To avoid unnecessary writebacks, data regrouping should not mix the modified data with the read-only data in the same cache block.

To totally avoid writing back read-only data, data regrouping needs an extra requirement. Two arrays should not be fused if one of them is read-only and the other is modified in a computation phase. The new requirement can be easily enforced by a simple extension. For each computation phase, split the accessed arrays into two disjoint subsets: the first is the set of read-only arrays and the second is the modified arrays. Treat each subset as a distinctive computation phase and then apply the partitioning. After data regrouping, two arrays are fused if and only if they are always accessed together, and the type of the access is either both read-only or both modified. With this extension, data regrouping finds the largest subsets of arrays that can be fused without introducing useless data or redundant writebacks.

When redundant writebacks are allowed, data regrouping can be more aggressive by first combining data solely based on data access and then separating read-only and read-write data within each partition. The separation step is not easy because different computation phases read and write a different set of arrays. The general problem can be modeled with a weighted, undirected graph, in which each array is a node and each edge has a weight labeling the combined effect of both regrouping and redundant writebacks. The goal of regrouping is to pack nodes into cache blocks to maximize the benefit. As in the case of allowing useless data, the packing problem here is also NP-hard because it can be reduced from the G-partitioning problem[12].

3   Evaluation

3.1   Experimental Design

We evaluate data regrouping both on regular programs with contiguous data traversal and on irregular programs with non-contiguous data access. In each class, we use a kernel and a full application. Table 2 and Table 3 give the description of these four applications, along with their input size. We measure the overall performance except *Moldyn*, for which we measure only the major computation subroutine *compute_force*. The results of *Moldyn* and *Magi* were partially reported in [6] where data regrouping was used as a preliminary transformation to data packing.

Table 2. Program description

name	description	access pattern	source	No. lines
Moldyn	molecular dynamics simulation	irregular	CHAOS group	660
Magi	particle hydrodynamics	irregular	DoD	9339
ADI	alternate-direction integration	regular	standard kernel	59
Sweep3D	nuclear simulation	regular	DOE	2105

Table 3. Data inputs

application	input size	source of input	exe. time
Moldyn	4 arrays, 256K particles, 1 iteration	random initialization	53.2 sec
Magi	84 arrays, 28K particles, 253 cycles	provided by DoD	885 sec
ADI	3 arrays, 1000x1000 per array , 10 iterations	random initialization	2.05 sec.
Sweep3D	29 arrays, 50x50x50 per array	provided by DoE	56 sec.

The test programs are measured on a single MIPS R10K processor of SGI Origin2000, which provides hardware counters that measure cache misses and other hardware events with high accuracy. The processor has two caches: the first-level (L1) cache is 32KB with 32-byte cache blocks and the second-level (L2) cache is 4MB with 128-byte cache blocks. Both are two-way set associative. The processor achieves good latency hiding through dynamic, out-of-order instruction issue and compiler-directed prefetching. All applications are compiled with the highest optimization flag except *Sweep3D* and *Magi*, where the user specified -O2 to preserve numerical accuracy. Prefetching is turned on in all programs.

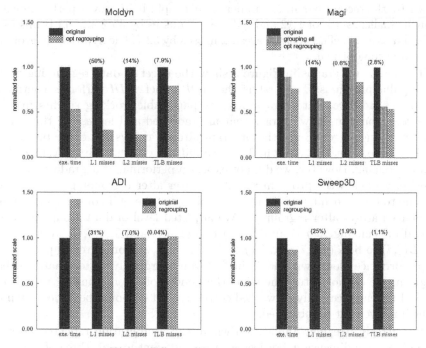

Fig. 3. Effect of Data Regrouping

3.2 Effect of Data Regrouping

Each of the four graphs of Figure 3 shows the effect of data regrouping on one of the applications; it shows the changes in four pairs of bars including the execution time, the number of L1 and L2 cache misses, and the number of TLB misses. The first bar of each pair is the normalized performance (normalized to 1) of the original program, and the second is the result after data regrouping. Application *Magi* has a set of 26 compatible arrays. Its graph has an additional bar in each cluster, which shows the performance of grouping all 26 arrays. All graphs report the miss rate of the base program, but the reduction is on the number of misses, not on the miss rate. The miss rate here is computed as the number of misses divided by the number of memory loads.

Data regrouping achieves significant speedups on the two irregular applications, *Moldyn* and *Magi*, as shown by the upper two graphs in Figure 3. Since both applications mainly perform non-contiguous data access, data regrouping improves cache-block reuse by combining data from multiple arrays. For *Moldyn* and *Magi* respectively, data regrouping reduces the number of L1 misses by 70% and 38%, L2 misses by 75% and 17%, and TLB misses by 21% and 47%. As a result, data regrouping achieves a speedup of 1.89 on *Moldyn* and 1.32 on *Magi*.

Application *Magi* has multiple computation phases, and not all arrays are accessed in all phases, as shown by Table 1. Data regrouping fuses 26 compatible arrays into 6 arrays. Blindly grouping all 26 arrays does not perform as well, as shown by the second bar in the upper-right graph: it improves performance by a much smaller factor of 1.12 and reduces L1 misses by 35% and TLB misses by 44%, and as a side effect, it increases L2 misses by 32%. Clearly, blindly grouping all data is sub-optimal.

The lower two graphs in Figure 3 show the effect of data regrouping on the two regular programs. The first is the *ADI* kernel. *ADI* performs contiguous data access to three data arrays, and its page-table working set fits in TLB. Data regrouping fuses two arrays that are modified and leaves the third, read-only array unchanged. Since the program already enjoys full cache-block reuse and incurs no capacity misses in TLB, we did not expect an improvement from data regrouping. However, we did not expect a performance degradation. To our surprise, we found the program ran 42% slower after regrouping. The problem was due to the inadequate dependence analyzer of the SGI compiler in handling interleaved arrays after regrouping. We adjusted level of data grouping so that instead of changing $X(j,i)$ and $B(j,i)$ to $T(1,j,i)$ and $T(2,j,i)$, we let $X(j,i)$ and $B(j,i)$ to be $T(j,1,i)$ and $T(j,2,i)$. The new version of regrouping caused no performance slowdown and it in fact ran marginally faster than the base program. We cannot determine what the benefit of the regrouping would be if the SGI dependence analyzer worked correctly. But it should be no less than the slight improvement we observed.

Sweep3D is a regular application where the computation repeatedly sweeps through a three-dimensional object from six different angles, three of which are diagonal. A large portion of data access is non-contiguous. In addition, *Sweep3D* is a real application with a large number of scalars and arrays and consequently, its performance is seriously hindered by a high miss rate of 1.1%. However, the data layout seem to be highly hand-optimized because any relocation of scalar and array declarations we tried ended up in an increase in TLB misses.

Currently, we perform a limited regrouping, which combines eight arrays into two new ones. The limited regrouping reduces the overall L2 misses by 38% and TLB misses by 45%. The execution time is reduced by 13%. The significant speedup achieved by data grouping demonstrates its effectiveness for highly optimized regular programs.

In summary, our evaluation has shown that data regrouping is very effective in improving cache spatial reuse and in reducing cache conflicts and TLB misses for both regular and irregular programs, especially those with a large number of data arrays and complex data access patterns. For the two real-world applications, data regrouping improves overall performance by factors of 1.32 and 1.15.

4   Related Work

Many data and computation transformations have been used to improve cache spatial reuse, but inter-array data regrouping is the first to do so by selectively combining multiple arrays. Previously existing techniques either do not combine multiple arrays or do so in an indiscriminate manner that often reduces cache-block reuse instead of increasing it.

Kremer[13] developed a framework for finding the optimal static or dynamic data layout for a program of multiple computation phases[13]. He did not consider array regrouping explicitly, but his formulation is general enough to include any such transformations, however, at the expense of being an NP-hard problem. Data regrouping simplifies the problem by allowing only those transformations that always improve performance. This simplification is desirable for a static compiler, which cannot quantify the negative impact of a data transformation. In particular, data regrouping takes a conservative approach that disallows any possible side effects and at the same time maximizes the potential benefit.

Several effective techniques have been developed for improving spatial reuse within single data arrays. For regular applications, a compiler can rearrange either the computation or data to employ stride-one access to memory. Computation reordering such as loop permutations was used by Gannon et al.[9], Wolf and Lam[18], and McKinley et al[16]. Without changing the order of computation, Mace developed global optimization of data "shapes" on an operation dag[15]. Leung studied a general class of data transformations—unimodular transformations— for improving cache performance[14]. Beckman and Kelly studied run-time data layout selection in a parallel library[2]. The combination of both computation and data restructuring was explored by Cierniak and Li[5] and then by Kandemir et al[11]. For irregular and dynamic programs, run-time data packing was used to improve spatial reuse by Ding and Kennedy[6]. None of these techniques addressed the selective grouping of multiple data arrays, neither did they exploit inter-array cache reuse. However, these techniques are orthogonal to data regrouping. In fact, they should be always preceded by data regrouping to first maximize inter-array spatial reuse, as demonstrated by Ding and Kennedy in [6] where they combined data regrouping with data packing.

Data placement transformations have long been used to reduce data interference in cache. Thabit packed simultaneously used data into non-conflicting cache blocks[17]. To reduce cache interference among array segments, a compiler can make them either well separated by padding or fully contiguous by copying. Data regrouping is different because it reorganizes not scalars or array segments but individual array elements. By regrouping elements into the same cache block, data grouping guarantees no cache interference among them. Another important difference is that data regrouping is conservative, and it does not incur any memory overhead like array copying and padding.

Data transformations have also been used to avoid false data sharing on parallel machines with shared memory. The transformations group together data that is local to each processor. Examples include those of Anderson et al.[1] and of Eggers and Jeremiassen[10]. Anderson et al. transformed a single loop nest at a time and did not fuse multiple arrays; Eggers and Jeremiassen transformed a single parallel thread at a time and fused all data it accesses. However, blindly grouping local data wastes bandwidth because not all local data is used in a given computation phase. Therefore, both data transformations are sub-optimal compared to data regrouping, which selectively fuses multiple arrays for maximal cache spatial reuse and cache utilization.

Besides the work on arrays, data placement optimizations have been studied for pointer-based data structures[3,4]. The common approach is to first find data objects that are frequently accessed through profiling and then place them close to each other in memory. In contrast to data regrouping, they did not distinguish between different computation phases. As a result, these transformations are equivalent to grouping all frequently accessed objects in the whole program. As in the case of greedy regrouping by Eggers and Jeremiassen[10], the result is sub-optimal.

5   Conclusions

In this work, we have developed inter-array data regrouping, a global data transformation that maximizes overall inter-array spatial reuse in both regular and dynamic applications. The regrouping algorithm is compile-time optimal because it regroups arrays when and only when it is always profitable. When evaluated on both regular and irregular applications including programs involving a large number of arrays and multiple computation phases, data regrouping combines 8 to 26 arrays and improves overall performance by factors of 1.15 and 1.32. Similar regrouping optimization can also improve cache-block utilization on shared-memory parallel machines and consequently improve their communication performance.

The significant benefit of this work is that of enabling a user to write machine-independent programs because a compiler can derive the optimal data layout regardless of the initial data structure specified by the user. Since the choice of global array layout depends on the computation structure, manual data regrouping by a user would defeat the modularity of a program. Therefore, data regrouping is a perfect job for an automatic compiler, and as shown by this work, a compiler can do it perfectly.

Acknowledgement. We would like to thank anonymous referees of LCPC'99 for their careful review and very helpful comments. Special thanks to our assigned committee member, Larry Carter, who corrected a technical error of the paper and helped in improving the discussion of the optimality of data regrouping.

References

1. J. Anderson, S. Amarasinghe, and M. Lam. Data and computation transformation for multiprocessors. In *Proceedings of the Fifth ACM SIGPLAN Symposium on Principles and Practice of Parallel Programming*, Santa Barbara, CA, July 1995.
2. O. Beckmann and P.H.J. Kelly. Efficient interprocedural data placement optimisation in a parallel library. In *Proceedings of the Fourth Workshop on Languages, Compilers, and Run-time Systems for Scalable Computers*, May 1998.

3. B. Calder, K. Chandra, S. John, and T. Austin. Cache-conscious data placement. In *Proceedings of the Eighth International Conference on Architectural Support for Programming Languages and Operating Systems (ASPLOS-VIII)*, San Jose, Oct 1998.

4. T.M. Chilimbi, B. Davidson, and J.R. Larus. Cache-conscious structure definition. In *Proceedings of SIGPLAN Conference on Programming Language Design and Implementation*, 1999.

5. M. Cierniak and W. Li. Unifying data and control transformations for distributed shared-memory machines. In *Proceedings of the SIGPLAN '95 Conference on Programming Language Design and Implementation*, La Jolla, June 1995.

6. C. Ding and K. Kennedy. Improving cache performance in dynamic applications through data and computation reorganization at run time. In *Proceedings of the SIGPLAN '99 Conference on Programming Language Design and Implementation*, Atlanta, GA, May 1999.

7. C. Ding and K. Kennedy. Memory bandwidth bottleneck and its amelioration by a compiler. Technical report, Rice University, May 1999. Submitted for publication.

8. J. Ferrante, V. Sarkar, and W. Thrash. On estimating and enhancing cache effectiveness. In U. Banerjee, D. Gelernter, A. Nicolau, and D. Padua, editors, *Languages and Compilers for Parallel Computing, Fourth International Workshop*, Santa Clara, CA, August 1991. Springer-Verlag.

9. D. Gannon, W. Jalby, and K. Gallivan. Strategies for cache and local memory management by global program transformations. In *Proceedings of the First International Conference on Supercomputing*. Springer-Verlag, Athens, Greece, June 1987.

10. Tor E. Jeremiassen and Susan J. Eggers. Reducing false sharing on shared memory multiprocessors through compile time data transformations. In *Proceedings of the Fifth ACM SIGPLAN Symposium on Principles and Practice of Parallel Programming*, pages 179–188, Santa Barbara, CA, July 1995.

11. M. Kandemir, A. Choudhary, J. Ramanujam, and P. Banerjee. A matrix-based approach to the global locality optimization problem. In *Proceedings of International Conference on Parallel Architectures and Compilation Techniques*, 1998.

12. D. G. Kirkpatrick and P. Hell. On the completeness of a generalized matching problem. In *The Tenth Annual ACM Symposium on Theory of Computing*, 1978.

13. U. Kremer. *Automatic Data Layout for Distributed Memory Machines*. PhD thesis, Dept. of Computer Science, Rice University, October 1995.

14. S. Leung. Array restructuring for cache locality. Technical Report UW-CSE-96-08-01, University of Washington, 1996. PhD Thesis.

15. M.E. Mace. *Memory storage patterns in parallel processing*. Kluwer Academic, Boston, 1987.

16. K. S. McKinley, S. Carr, and C.-W. Tseng. Improving data locality with loop transformations. *ACM Transactions on Programming Languages and Systems*, 18(4):424–453, July 1996.

17. K. O. Thabit. *Cache Management by the Compiler*. PhD thesis, Dept. of Computer Science, Rice University, 1981.

18. M. E. Wolf and M. Lam. A data locality optimizing algorithm. In *Proceedings of the SIGPLAN '91 Conference on Programming Language Design and Implementation*, Toronto, Canada, June 1991.

Iteration Space Slicing for Locality

William Pugh and Evan Rosser

Department of Computer Science
Univ. of Maryland
College Park, MD 20742
{pugh,ejr}@cs.umd.edu

Abstract. Improving data locality in programs which manipulate arrays has been the subject of a great deal of research. Much of the work on improving data locality examines individual loop nests; other work includes transformations such as loop fusion, which combines loops so that multiple loop nests can be transformed as a single loop nest. We propose a data-driven method to optimize locality across multiple loop nests. Our technique achieves loop fusion-like results even when normal loop fusion is illegal without enabling transformations. Given an array whose locality should be optimized, it also finds other calculations that can profitably be executed with the computation of that array.

1 Introduction

Program slicing [12] is an analysis that answers questions such as "Which statements might affect the computation of variable v at statement s?" or "Which statements depend on the value of v computed in statement s?". The answers computed by program slicing are generally a set of statements, and the variables considered are generally either scalars or entire arrays. We introduce the idea of *iteration spacing slicing*: we refine program slicing to ask questions such as "Which iterations of which statements might affect the value of elements $1:10$ of array A in iterations I of statement s?" or "Which iterations of which statements depend on the value computed by iterations I of statement s?". In addition, we can specify any subset of an array to be the variable of interest, rather than treating any assignment to the array as an assignment to every location. The slice can be executed to produce the same values for those elements that the full unsliced computation would produce.

We can produce an iteration space slice for programs where loop bounds and array subscripts are affine functions of outer loop bounds and symbolic constants. Iteration set descriptions can be very specific, such as $\{[k,i] : 1 \le k < i \le n\}$, and dependences can be described using relations such as $\{[k,i,i] \to [i,i'] : 1 \le$

This work was supported National Science Foundation grants ACI9720199 and CCR9619808.

L. Carter and J. Ferrante (Eds.): LCPC'99, LNCS 1863, pp. 164–184, 2000.

$k < i < i' \leq n$}. These sets and relations can be represented and manipulated using the Omega library [3].

Iteration space slicing is not simply a new kind of dependence analysis technique. Data dependence analysis finds pairs of statement instances which access the same memory, and that information can be used to analyze communication or prove legality of transformations. Iteration space slicing takes dependence information as input to find *all* statement instances from a given loop nest which must be executed to produce the correct values for the specified array elements. We can think of the slice as following chains of dependences (i.e. transitive dependences) to reach all statement instances which can affect the result. For example, while dependence information by itself can identify the endpoints of an interprocessor communication, slicing can identify everything that has to be done before that communication can take place.

The key step in calculating an iteration space slice is to calculate the transitive closure of the data dependence graph of the program [5]; the transitive dependences then are applied to the iterations of interest to produce the slice. Instead of edges being between statements in the graph, edges are actually between iterations of the statements; therefore, we need to compute the transitive closure of an infinite graph, because the iteration spaces may have symbolic bounds. In previous work [5], we presented techniques for doing this and have implemented them within the Omega library. Computing iteration space slices that are exact in all cases is impossible [5,10]. However, we can compute upper or lower bounds on a slice, as required. Alternative representations that would be cruder but faster could also be used, although we do not examine them in this paper.

Because it extracts some subset of the statements in a loop body and a subset of the loop nest's iterations, iteration space slicing can be thought of as a finer-grained approach than many existing transformations, which might act on all statements in a loop, or all iterations of an individual statement. A slice includes all and only those statement instances which must be executed to produce the correct output (up to the precision of the transitive closure computation). It is a data-driven technique in that an optimizer does not work with the loop structure, but instead specifies which data should be computed.

In previous work [10], we described several applications of iteration space slicing and focused on using slicing for optimizing communication generated by data-parallel compilers for message-passing machines.

Improving data locality in programs which manipulate arrays has been the subject of a great deal of research. In this paper, we present an approach to locality optimization based on iteration space slicing. We first outline the optimization in general terms, then give a series of examples which demonstrate its application. More details are available in Rosser's thesis [11].

2   Backward Slicing for Locality

In scientific programs, it is often the case that computing an array element depends only on a handful of other array elements (possibly of other arrays). One approach to improving data reuse would be to break an array into pieces, and then in sequence, compute each piece, along with all other array elements that contribute to its value. Since the values needed to compute an array element would be computed shortly before they are used, we could hope that they would be in fast cache memory. In other words, we want to transform the program to *produce* the array one partition at a time. We can use backward slicing to derive the code that produces each piece of the array.

As with any application of slicing, the slicer must be given the program segment to slice, the array elements of interest, and the point at which their values are desired. In this case, the array elements should represent one partition of the array being optimized, and we are interested in their values at the end of the program segment. We do not describe methods for determining the program segment to slice or the array partitions; such decisions are important but beyond the scope of this work.

We take a backward slice with respect to the criteria. The array partitions are parameterized (e.g., "column K of array A" is parameterized by K), so the resulting slice is generic; that is, it could be used to produce any partition of the array, by setting the parameters to the appropriate value.

The techniques we use for computing iteration space slices are described elsewhere [5,10,11]. It is done within the Omega library [3], a sophisticated library for reasoning about dependence relations and iteration sets. The slices we compute are always valid, but are not always exact: a slice may be of the form "definitely iterations i and $i - 1$, and maybe iterations $1 \ldots i - 2$." Depending on how the slice is being used, any "maybe" portion of the slice is used or excluded as appropriate. In general, our techniques produce exact slices when taking the transitive closure of simple dependences (constant distances or direction vectors); for more general affine dependences (such as $\{[i, j] \rightarrow [i + j, j + x]\}$), we often produce inexact slices.

When we derive a slice, we obtain a symbolic iteration set for each statement in the slice (e.g., slice i includes iterations $\{[i'] : 1 \le i' < i\}$ of statement S_1 and iterations $\{[i'] : 1, i - 1 \le i' \le i\}$ of statement S_2. Give iteration sets for each statement, we can generate efficient code that iterates over the selected iterations, preserving the original relative order [4]. We then surround the slice with a loop that enumerates all partitions of the array. Thus, the entire loop will compute all partitions of the array.

Because the slice represents a transformation derived from the program's data dependences, it is difficult to characterize in general the kinds of results that locality slicing achieves. In this section, we describe the approach and uses of locality slicing through a series of examples which demonstrate key aspects of the transformation.

```
for i = 1 to n  // Loop 1          for K = 1 to n
   a[i] = i                           a[K] = K
for i = 1 to n  // Loop 2             b[K] = a[K]
   b[i] = a[i]                        c[K] = b[K]
for i = 1 to n  // Loop 3
   c[i] = b[i]
```

Original Code   Sliced Code

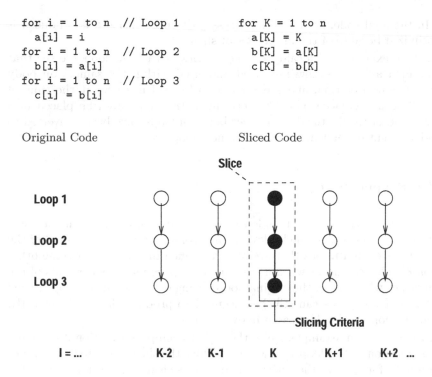

Fig. 1. Following transitive dependences

2.1   Using a Single Backward Slice

A simple example appears in Figure 1. This code computes the array a, then computes the array b using a, then computes the array c using the array b. Each array is computed in a separate loop.

Suppose we wish to partition the c array by elements, and produce it one element at a time, across the entire set of three loops. We need to create a slice which can produce any representative element of c. The slice should be backwards, since we want to find everything necessary for correct production of the element, and it should be movable, since we want to execute the slice as part of a program optimization. We compute the slice for a generic location K of array c and its final value after the third loop; then we generate a loop over values of K. In this example, c[K] is written during iteration K of the surrounding loop, so we can also think of this as slicing backwards from that iteration.

Thus, for c[K], the constructed slice includes iteration K of all three statements, and no other computations. Finally, we create a loop to enumerate each partition of the array with index variable K. A key feature of this example is that accesses to array a are included in the slice, even though we did not specify any references to it in the input to the slicer, and c is not directly dependent on its value. In the final code, however, the access pattern by which a is produced is also optimized because of the properties of slicing.

When we examine the locality characteristics of the new loop, we see that elements of a and b are now produced and used within the same loop body during the same iteration, and are certain to be still in cache at the time of the use. If scalar replacement [1] is performed, they may even be placed in a register. In other words, the dependences between loops have been converted to loop-independent dependences within the new loop body.

2.2   Overlapping Slices

In the previous example, we were able to construct new loops using only a single backward slice. Sometimes, the backward slice computed for a partition K of the array contains computations that are also contained in the slice for some other partition K'. This can occur when a statement accesses multiple elements of the same array, or when one of the original loops being optimized has a loop-carried dependence. These slices can still be executed to produce the array correctly, but computation will be duplicated between them.

Figure 2 shows an example. Here, the slice to compute iteration K of loop 3 contains iteration K-1 of loop 1; however, so does the slice generated to produce iteration K-1 of loop 3. In the generated code, it is clear that work is duplicated between slices, and some statement instances will be executed more than once.

When work is duplicated, we can perform a subtraction on the slice to eliminate the redundant code. We can use simple subtraction of tuple sets for this purpose, since the slice is represented as a set of statements, each with an iteration set. To subtract one slice from another, for each statement, we simply subtract its iteration set from that of the other slice. Since we are slicing for some representative iteration K, we can subtract out all computations which occur for any iteration K' < K. The resulting slices are now disjoint, and no work is redundant. Because we are using movable slices, all variables ever assigned in a slice have the correct value upon exiting the slice, so it is safe to simply delete the later, redundant computations, as they would have computed the same value.

Until now, we have not discussed the order of executing slices, but in the examples we have been producing array partitions in increasing order. In fact, since each slice execution produces all the values it needs, the slices can be executed in any order. (This property of slicing led Weiser to propose slicing for parallelization in the original program slicing paper [12].)

It is the fact that each slice is self-contained that makes the reordering possible. But it is the duplication of code (when necessary) between slices that gives us the property of being self-contained, therefore making the slices disjoint imposes an ordering on the slices. The subtraction of all K' < K assumes that all previous slices have been completed, and so when executed, partitions must be produced in increasing order.

```
for i = 1 to n                          for K = 1 to n
  a[i] = i                                for i = max(K-1,1) to K
for i = 1 to n                              a[i] = i
  b[i] = a[i] + a[i-1]                   b[K] = a[K] + a[K-1]
for i = 1 to n                          c[K] = b[K]
  c[i] = b[i]
```

Original Code   Sliced Code

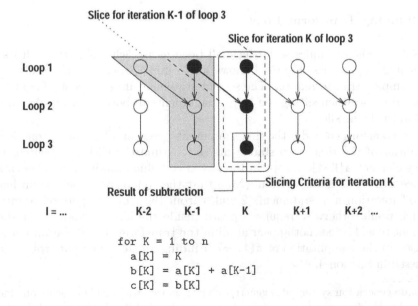

Fig. 2. Redundant computation due to overlapping slice

```
for K = 1 to n
  a[K] = K
  b[K] = a[K] + a[K-1]
  c[K] = b[K]
```

Fig. 3. Corrected results, after subtracting previous slices

```
for i = 1 to n  // Loop 1        for K = 1 to n-1
   a[i] = i                         a[K+1] = K+1
for i = 1 to n  // Loop 2           b[K] = a[K+1]
   b[i] = a[i+1]                     c[K] = b[K]
for i = 1 to n  // Loop 3        b[n] = a[n+1]
   c[i] = b[i]                   c[n] = b[n]
```

Original Code   Sliced Code

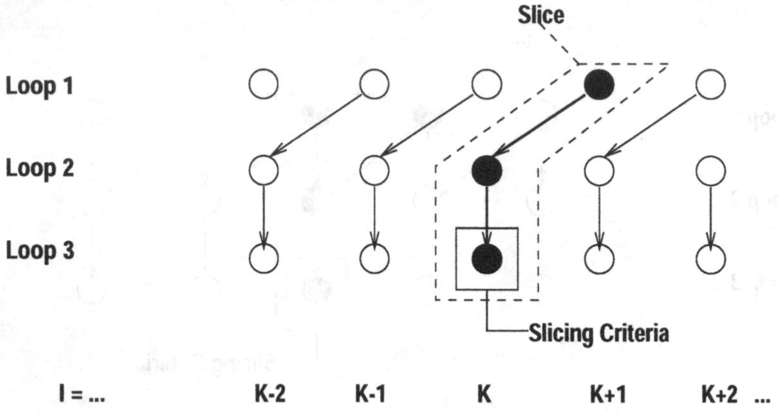

Fig. 4. Slicing resulting in bumping a loop

2.3   Bumping Transformations

The results of the examples so far have all been easily achievable through less sophisticated approaches. Figure 4 shows an example where slicing results in a more complex transformation. The second statement uses element a[i+1] to compute b[i], so when slicing the loop, assignments to both elements they are located in the same slice.

In the transformed code, the first statement is essentially running one iteration ahead of the other two statements. Each time the slice is executed, it produces element a[K+1], except in the last slice, which produces no elements of a since a[n+1] is never written. (Note that the code generation system has peeled off iteration n of statements 2 and 3 from the loop; it splits off iterations which would otherwise require a guard inside the loop.)   Notice that the assignment to a[1] does not appear at all in the transformed code, because it is never used in the computation of c[1..n]. Finding a place to execute this code is discussed in Section 4.

The code generation system also generates outer guards when code appears outside a loop. In this case, none of the code should be executed if n is less than 1. In the examples, these guards are omitted for brevity.

Loop fusion could not have been directly applied in this situation, because elements of a would have been read by the second statement before they were written by the first, violating a flow dependence from the original code. Because the slicer derives the set of elements which have to be correctly computed in order to produce each element of c, the sliced code correctly uses the newly-written values in a.

Figure 5 shows an example requiring subtraction which results in bumping.

2.4   Other Differences from Fusion

In some cases when simple loop fusion would be possible, slicing does not always produce the same results. In Figure 6, as in Figure 4, dependences are again not between like-numbered iterations of the original loops. But in this case, fusion is legal. Slicing, however, bumps one of the loops (in the opposite direction of Figure 4) due to the pattern of reuse. In the traditionally-fused loop, the reuse created by fusion is separated by one iteration of the fused loop, but the reuse created by slicing is within the same iteration. This may ease the application of scalar replacement; no loop unrolling or shifting of values between registers would be necessary to put the element a[K-1] into a register.

The calculation of a[n] does not appear in the final slice, although it is computed in the original program. That is because the value a[n] is never read by any statement in the slice. In general, the slice may not include the entire set of computations in the original program; we only know that it will include everything needed to compute the slicing criteria correctly. In the Section 4.2, we will discuss placement of left-over code in the general case.

3   Forward Slicing for Locality

We can also use forward slicing to try to improve locality. Given a partitioning of an array, we can slice forward from the definition of the array, capturing all uses. Ideally, the partition of the array used as a criteria will stay in cache during all of its uses.

Consider again Figure 1. Initially, we used backward slicing to ask how to produce a partition of array c, for the values it should have after the third loop. Using forward slicing, we can instead can ask what computations depend on a partition of the a array, for the values written to it in the first statement. In this case, using forward slicing on a yields results identical to taking a backward slice on the array c. Forward slicing can also yield results similar to backward slicing (using different criteria) for Figures 4 and 6.

In Section 2.2, we noted that when doing backwards slicing, an iteration might appear in two different slices. To avoid duplicate work, we want it to appear in only one. It must be done before either slice can complete, so we execute it as part of the earlier slice and exclude it from the later slice.

In doing forward slicing, if an iteration appears in two slices, it depends on computations in both, and so cannot be executed until parts of each slice have

```
for i = 1 to n  // Loop 1        a[1] = 1
  a[i] = i                       for K = 1 to n-1
for i = 1 to n  // Loop 2          a[K+1] = K+1
  b[i] = a[i-1] + a[i+1]          b[K] = a[K-1] + a[K+1]
for i = 1 to n  // Loop 3         c[K] = b[K]
  c[i] = b[i]                    b[n] = a[n-1] + a[n+1]
                                 c[n] = b[n]
```

Original Code   Sliced Code

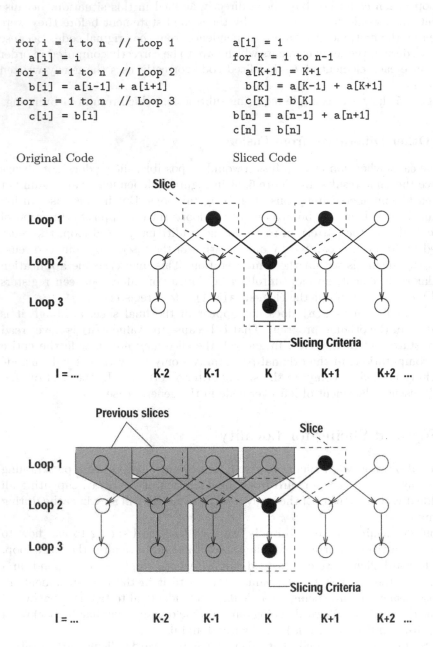

Fig. 5. Using subtraction can result in bumping

```
for i = 1 to n  // Loop 1          // Slice 1
    a[i] = i                       b[1] = a[0]
for i = 1 to n  // Loop 2          c[1] = b[1]
    b[i] = a[i-1]                  // Slices K = 2 through n
for i = 1 to n  // Loop 3          for K = 2 to n
    c[i] = b[i]                        a[K-1] = K-1
                                       b[K] = a[K-1]
                                       c[K] = b[K]
        Original Code              // code not in any slice
                                   a[n] = n
```

Sliced Code

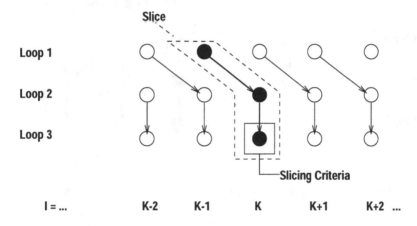

Fig. 6. Results which differ from loop fusion

executed. If the slices are being executed sequentially, it should be executed as part of the later slice and excluded from the earlier slice. In this case, subtracting duplicate computations is a matter of correctness rather than avoiding duplicate work; otherwise, executing the partitions in increasing order would violate data dependences.

Figure 7 duplicates the code of 2, but uses a forward slice based on the values of a written in the first statement. Notice that iteration K+1 of the second and third loops is included. However, they should not be executed as part of the slice for a[K], since they also depend on a[K+1]. After subtraction, those two iterations are removed, and the forward slicing results are the same as those achieved with backward slicing.

4   Iterative Slicing

In this section, we will discuss how to combine forward and backward slicing to obtain better results.

```
for i = 1 to n              for K = 1 to n
  a[i] = i                    a[K] = K
for i = 1 to n                b[K] = a[K] + a[K-1]
  b[i] = a[i] + a[i-1]        c[K] = b[K]
for i = 1 to n
  c[i] = a[i]
```

Original Code   Code after slicing
                              and subtraction

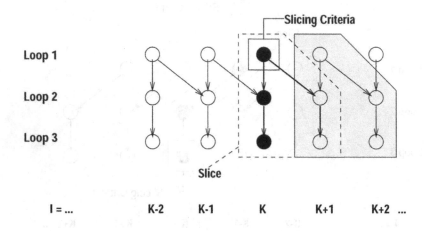

Fig. 7. Forward Slicing Overlap

It is possible for a slice created using either the forward or backward methods to include only a subset of the program's statement iterations; there are leftover parts of the program that are not ordered by this technique. In order to execute the entire program correctly, we need to find a placement for this code.

In the backward slicing case, because of the properties of backward slicing, we know that correct execution of the sliced code cannot depend on these "leftovers" (otherwise they would be included in the slice.) However, there may be dependences from the slices to the leftover code. So one safe technique for executing it is to place it after execution of the backward slices. Similarly, code leftover from forward slicing can be executed before execution of the forward slices.

However, this placement may not produce good locality. Assume that we have taken a backward slice on a segment of code. We know that all computations needed to compute the value of the slicing criteria are already in the slice. But performing that computation brings a number of array elements into the cache, and those array elements may also be used in the leftover code. We would like to

```
for i = 1 to n  // Loop 1
  a[i] = i
for i = 1 to n  // Loop 2
  b[i] = a[i]
for i = 1 to n  // Loop 3
  c[i] = a[i]
```

Original Code

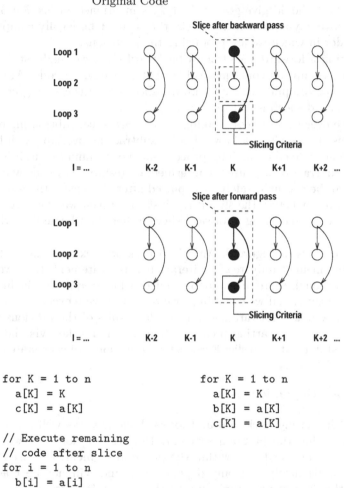

```
for K = 1 to n          for K = 1 to n
  a[K] = K                a[K] = K
  c[K] = a[K]             b[K] = a[K]
                          c[K] = a[K]

// Execute remaining
// code after slice
for i = 1 to n
  b[i] = a[i]
```

Code after   Code after
backward pass   forward pass

Fig. 8. Capturing additional uses with iterative slicing

perform any uses of those array elements while they are still in the cache, which means interleaving them with the iterations already in the slice.

We can use additional passes of slicing to achieve this effect. Suppose we have taken a backward slice that we want to improve. We can use the iterations contained in that slice as the input to another pass of forward slicing. The result will identify and bring into the slice all uses of arrays written in the backward slice. Any new statement instances added must use array elements referenced in the backward slice, so executing them as part of the new slice (which is a superset of the previous slice) should give good locality. As mentioned in Section 3, we then need to remove any statement instances that cannot be legally computed yet, given the order in which we are producing the partitions.

After computing a forward slice from a backward slice, we might still have leftover iterations. Again, we could place them before the sliced code. Alternatively, we could now compute a new backward slice, where the slicing criteria consists of the forward slice just made.

We can iterate over this process – taking a backward slice, subtracting overlaps with previous slices, taking a forward slice, subtracting overlaps with later slices – until we reach a fixed point. This process may not terminate, but it is safe to stop after any subtraction and use the intermediate results. Any code which is not in the slice can be executed safely; it is placed after the slice if the last slice taken was backward, or before the slice if the last slice taken was forward. The process can also be started using a forward slice, rather than beginning with a backward slice.

An example appears in Figure 8. An initial pass of backward slicing from iteration K of statement 3 only reaches iteration K of statement 1. However, we can see that although there are no dependences which require its inclusion, statement 2 uses array a, and we could improve reuse if it were executed as part of the slice. We now take a forward slice, using the results of the previous pass of backward slicing as our starting point. Statement 2 is reached via the flow dependence from statement 1, so slice K consists of iteration K of each statement.

4.1   Using Input Dependences

This method of alternating backward and forward slices works well for arrays that are written within the program segment. However, it does not work as well for arrays which are read-only within the program segment, because those references will not be involved in any dependences, and will not be reached when exploring the dependence graph (unless there are references in the same statement which are reachable.) So, the slice still may not contain all uses of array elements which were merely read and not written in the original slice. For arrays which are written in the slice, uses which occur before writes can also be missed.

For example, in Figure 9, an array x is used in both the second and third statements, but is not written in any of the three statements. There is no dependence connecting statement 2 with statements 1 or 3, so it is not reached by

```
for i = 1 to n  // Loop 1
  a[i] = i
for i = 1 to n  // Loop 2
  b[i] = x[i]
for i = 1 to n  // Loop 3
  c[i] = a[i] + x[i]
```

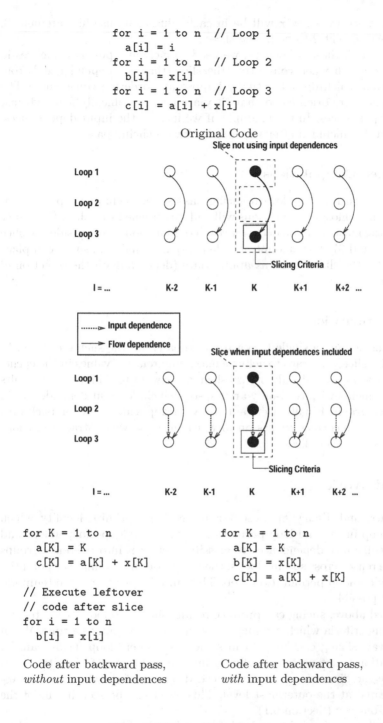

Original Code

for K = 1 to n
  a[K] = K
  c[K] = a[K] + x[K]

// Execute leftover
// code after slice
for i = 1 to n
  b[i] = x[i]

Code after backward pass,
without input dependences

for K = 1 to n
  a[K] = K
  b[K] = x[K]
  c[K] = a[K] + x[K]

Code after backward pass,
with input dependences

Fig. 9. Slicing with input dependences

the slicer. But since we know x will be in cache due to its use in statement 3, we would like statement 2 to be in the slice.

In order to catch those references, we need to include input dependences in the dependence graph when computing the slice (that is, "dependences" from a read to a read, which do not actually impose any ordering constraint.) The input dependences are oriented so that they are lexicographically forward, just as for other dependences. In the example, if we include the input dependences, then statement 2 is included after the first backward slicing pass.

4.2   Unrelated Computations

After making forward and backward slicing passes, and including input dependences in the slicer, most computations will end up attached to a slice. Boundary iterations are the most common occurrence of computations still outside the slice (as in Figures 4 and 6). The amount of code is usually small and so we can place it before or after the sliced code, as appropriate (depending on the direction of the last slice.)

4.3   Final Formulation

We began by using only a single backward slice based on the slicing criteria. In the final locality slicer, we want to achieve maximum reuse of values in the cache, so we use iterative backward and forward slicing. We want to achieve good results for program segments with read-only arrays, so we include input dependences in the dependence graph. Finally, we want to avoid duplicate work for backward slices, and prevent incorrect results on forward slices, so we subtract iterations which overlap with other slices.

5   Related Work

McKinley, Carr, and Tseng [8] present a method to optimize locality which incorporates loop fusion and loop permutation. They use loop-independent and short-constant-distance dependences to classify references into reference groups which indicate reuse across specific loops; they then use this estimate of potential locality to guide a loop permutation step. They fuse loops to improve temporal locality where possible.

As discussed above, slicing can produce results similar to loop fusion techniques when using criteria which produce arrays a row or column at a time. When used in this way, slicing can be used in some cases where loop fusion cannot. Loop permutation is not necessary when using slicing for loop fusion; the loops which traverse the dimension being produced drop out of the slice, and are essentially recreated at the outermost level. This effect can be seen in one of the case studies, Tomcatv (Section 6.1).

McKinley et al use dependences both for legality checking and to guide their optimizations. Rather than using dependence information for legality checking, slicing uses data dependences to directly derive a legal computation. However, we do not have a method of estimating profitability of various possible locality slices in order to guide our technique. The profitability depends on the complicated interaction of our transformation with other compiler transformations such as register tiling.

Yoshida et al [13] describe some techniques for partitioning computations based on something that is essentially the transitive closure of dependences (although they do not call it that). However, their technique was used to minimize communication in a distributed program, rather than improve cache locality. They also ignored intra-loop dependences (and their impact on the transitive closure) and their techniques only were intended for (and only worked for) stencil computations.

5.1   Data Shackling

Kodukula, Ahmed, and Pingali [6] propose data shackling as a data-centric locality transformation. Data shackling shares some aspects of locality slicing. Both techniques break a computation down into partitions of iterations to be executed, and enumerate those partitions, hopefully obtaining good reuse within a partition, and ignoring reuse between partitions. They are also both data-driven techniques; that is, the compiler specifies which data should be optimized (along with other information), rather than directly transforming control structures.

They differ in the method by which they produce those iteration partitions. The results of the two techniques are not directly comparable, although in some cases they produce the same answers.

To produce the iteration sets to loop over, data shackling selects a program segment to optimize, and a partitioning of an array into blocks. For each statement, a reference is chosen to "shackle" to a block of the array. The transformed code enumerates the blocks; when a block becomes "current", for each statement, all iterations such that the chosen reference touches the current block are executed. A partitioning is illegal if an iteration would appear in more than one partition, or if executing the partitions sequentially does not respect the data dependences of the program.

It is also possible to apply a Cartesian product of shackles. In that case, each combination of blocks is enumerated, and only those iterations which satisfy both shackles are executed.

When using data shackling, the compiler has more decisions to make than when using locality slicing. Once a reference has been chosen for one statement, compatible references must be chosen for other statements in order to make the transformation legal. In some cases, there are compositions of data shackles which are legal, but the individual shackles would be illegal by themselves. So the compiler needs to rely on heuristics not only to decide what arrays to optimize, but also how to combine shackles for legality and performance. In addition, shackling assumes that every statement accesses the array being shackled. When there are such statements, shackling must choose "dummy references" to attach to those statements so that they are transformed. Care must be taken in selecting dummy references, since a poor choice of dummy references can make a shackle illegal.

Iteration space slicing requires the compiler to employ heuristics to choose what arrays to optimize, but not for finding legal combinations of transformations. However, in cases where dependences require it, a large amount of work may be done in the first slice, essentially executing the code untransformed.

Another difference is that data shackling always orders all of the statement instances in the original code, and so does not have to address the problem of placing code which falls outside the transformation. Slicing will simply leave out code which has no data dependences connecting it to the array being optimized.

Data shackling has the most freedom when transforming code which contains few dependences, because there are fewer legality restrictions. Statements which are not connected by a dependence but appear in the same loop nest can be transformed identically by choosing the appropriate shackles for each.

Locality slicing, on the other hand, works comparatively better at transforming codes which contain more dependences. It can find transformations that would be very difficult for other techniques to find, and given little guidance (e.g., generate C by columns) may determine the legal way to slice the code. When there are few dependences, slicing may take longer to find all computations to be included in a slice, and will break apart computations which are connected by no dependences. As mentioned before, in some cases this may improve performance due to decreased contention in the cache.

6   Case Studies

In the case studies, we focus on the use of locality slicing to expand the region across which reuse can be achieved via fusion-like transformations, relying on a later phase such as tiling or data shackling to improve reuse across outer loops.

In the case studies, the slicing criteria and program regions to slice were chosen by hand. Our goal for the case studies was to identify cases in which loop fusion techniques were unable to fuse loops, but which appeared to be attractive candidates. In order to achieve fusion-like effects, we restricted the set of possible partitionings to those which fix a single subscript of the array, thus producing a subarray at a time (usually a row or column). This approach tends to "fuse" any loops which traverse that dimension of the array, and place the "fused" loop outermost.

In order to test the technique, we attempted to achieve fusion-like effects on the largest possible program segment. In some cases, our goal of achieving the most fusion does not yield an inner loop with good spatial locality; the innermost loop does not stride along cache lines, with successive accesses often touching the same line, but across them, where successive accesses never touch the same line. This decreases the amount of cache-line reuse rather than increasing it. In those cases, we transposed the arrays in order to create stride-1 access in the innermost loop; any such changes are mentioned for the specific programs.

We should warn the reader that the effectiveness of these transformations in practice depends crucially on interactions with the compiler used to compile the transformed source code. For Tomcatv, the transformed code ran well on a Sun workstation but interacted poorly with the SGI compiler. For SWIM, we got good performance with the SGI compiler, but poor interaction with the Sun compiler. We are investigating these interactions and hope to have a better handle on them.

Table 1. Tomcatv performance and simulations, Sun Ultra-1/170

	Original	Sliced
Time (seconds)	411	333
L1 References (millions)	19807	18836
L1 Misses (millions)	2666	2193
L2 References (millions)	7446	4884
L2 Misses (millions)	516	233

Table 2. Tomcatv performance changes, Original to Sliced, on Sun

Factor	Change	Cycles each	Total difference in cycles
Time	78 seconds	170 million	13.3 billion
L2 misses	283 million	42	11.9 billion
L1 misses	473 million	3	1.4 billion
Memory refs	971 million	1	970 million

6.1   Tomcatv

Tomcatv is a program from the SPEC CFP95 floating point benchmark suite. Tomcatv is an iterative computation, with an outer timestep loop and a series of inner loop nests. A set of arrays is computed each time through the outer timestep loop, and each of the inner loop nests scans some subset of the arrays. In all, the arrays used are scanned up to five times in a single iteration of the time step loop. Our goal was to reduce this to a single scan of the rows or columns of each array.

The arrays are two dimensional, so if we consider only slices to produce entire rows or columns of the arrays at a time, there are two choices. If slicing to produce a row at a time, it is only possible to reduce this to three scans rather than five (the fourth inner loop nest which traverses the rows runs backwards and carries a dependence.) If slicing to produce columns at a time, it is indeed possible to reduce all scans of all arrays to a single scan over the columns of those arrays, producing them one at a time, with several scans over the elements in a column as it is produced. Traditional transformations are not able to improve reuse across as large a portion of the program. The first loop nest must be peeled and bumped by 1 in order to make the transformation legal. The loops which are "fused" by the slice correspond to the inner loops in each of the nests, as well as some single loops between them, so permutation would be necessary as well. Scalar and array expansion must be performed before slicing the code to break storage dependences.

Unfortunately, however, producing by columns is the wrong order for improving locality: this results in non-stride-1 access in the innermost loops, so each successive access to an array touches a different cache line. If we permit transposing the major arrays, this is a more sensible transformation, as the innermost loops now touch successive memory locations.

In order to do this transformation, we need only ask the slicer to produce columns of the X and Y arrays. In the transformed code, other arrays (RX, RY, D, DD, AA) are produced a column at a time without having to describe any desired access pattern for them, because the dependence pattern requires it.

To get a better sense of how slicing affects cache hit rates on this code, we performed cache simulations. Simulations were run using cachesim5, an application of the Shade instrumentation system from Sun [2]. Experiments were run on an Sun Ultra-1/170 with Solaris 2.5. Results appear in Table 1; run times are measured from normal executions, and cache statistics were gathered with cachesim5 simulations of the Ultra-1's cache (16K level one data cache and 512K level two unified cache.) The compiler again was Sun f77 version 3.0.1 with option -fast. The sliced code performed approximately 19% better than the original code in runtime. Simulation results show an improvement at both level one and level two. The number of level one misses is reduced approximately 19% and the number of level two misses is reduced about 55%. The cache miss penalties at level one and level two are 3 and 42 cycles, respectively [9,7].

Table 3. SWIM results on SGI Octane

	Original	Sliced
Execution time (sec)	145.4	130.9
Megaflops achieved	79.7	88.6
Loads (millions)	7,574	7,604
Stores (millions)	3,117	3,100
L1 Misses (millions)	1,020	929
L2 Misses (millions)	223	187

A breakdown of performance differences appears in Table 2. The difference in cache behavior together with the reduced number of loads is adequate to explain the performance difference between the two programs. The level two cache misses have a much greater impact than the other factors. The Ultra-1 is able to continue working in the presence of one cache miss (but not two) so cache miss penalties can sometimes be hidden. Therefore, given worst case behavior, the cache misses alone can explain the performance between the two codes; however, there may be other performance factors involved (for example, differences in instruction scheduling or TLB misses.)

Finally, we also ran on the Sun a version of Tomcatv with the arrays transposed but no other modifications, and a transposed and interchanged version. Neither version was competitive in performance, and we do not report their results here.

6.2   SWIM

We also looked at the SPEC95 benchmark SWIM. In this code, there are three main routines, CALC1, CALC2, and CALC3, which are called in an outer loop. Each routine has only one call site, so inlining is typical.

After inlining, it is attractive to fuse the loops from CALC1 and CALC2 in order to improve temporal locality. However, loop fusion is prevented both by intervening code (which also writes boundaries of the arrays), and dependences which would be violated (for instance, the loop nest from CALC1 writes CU(I+1,J) and the loop nest from CALC2 reads CU(I+1,J+1).)

Slicing is able to create a new loop which contains all of the array assignments in the two loops and the intervening code such that they execute in a fused fashion. An inner loop remains from the main loop nests from each subroutine. The slicing criteria is on columns of the arrays UNEW, PNEW, and VNEW, backwards from the end of CALC2's main loop nest.

We ran the transformed code and compared its speed against the original code on the SGI Octane. All programs were compiled with f77 and the option -Ofast=ip30. Results appear in Table 3. All numbers were collected using SGI's perfex tool. The sliced code performed approximately 10% faster than the unsliced code, and had better cache performance. In this case, the number of loads and stores executed by the two versions were comparable, so cache hit rates are a more reliable measure of performance. The number of level one cache misses was reduced by 9%, and level two cache misses was reduced by 16%.

7   Future Work

In work so far, we have primarily examined locality slicing using criteria which fix a certain array dimension and produce the array one subarray at a time. In future work, we hope to examine the effectiveness of using more general partitionings of arrays. In particular, we would like to examine the use of tiling-like partitions as criteria. This approach offers the possibility of combining in one step fusion-like transformations, which increase the scope of possible reuse, and tiling transformations, which improve reuse across single loop nests.

Another area of research is in selection of criteria. While slicing reduces the number of decisions to be made by the compiler, the selection can still be difficult. Heuristics used by other locality optimization techniques might be helpful in selecting arrays and partitionings for the criteria. Because slicing gives a great deal of flexibility in the segment of the program to be optimized, there are interesting issues to be addressed there as well. The program segment being sliced is one of the determiners of the cache footprint of the transformed program, so care must be taken in selecting it.

References

1. D. Callahan, S. Carr, and K. Kennedy. Improving register allocation for subscripted variables. In *ACM SIGPLAN '90 Conference on Programming Language Design and Implementation*, June 1990.
2. B. Cmelik and D. Keppel. Shade: a fast instruction-set simulator for execution profiling. *ACM SIGMETRICS Performance Evaluation Review*, 22(1):128–137, May 1994.
3. W. Kelly, V. Maslov, W. Pugh, E. Rosser, T. Shpeisman, and D. Wonnacott. The Omega Library interface guide. Technical Report CS-TR-3445, Dept. of Computer Science, University of Maryland, College Park, Mar. 1995. The Omega library is available from http://www.cs.umd.edu/projects/omega.
4. W. Kelly, W. Pugh, and E. Rosser. Code generation for multiple mappings. In *The 5th Symposium on the Frontiers of Massively Parallel Computation*, pages 332–341, McLean, Virginia, Feb. 1995.
5. W. Kelly, W. Pugh, E. Rosser, and T. Shpeisman. Transitive closure of infinite graphs and its applications. *International J. of Parallel Programming*, 24(6):579–598, Dec. 1996.
6. I. Kodukula, N. Ahmed, and K. Pingali. Data-centric multi-level blocking. In *ACM SIGPLAN '97 Conference on Programming Language Design and Implementation*, June 1997.
7. S. S. Lumetta, A. M. Mainwaring, and D. E. Culler. Multi-protocol active messages on a cluster of smp's. In *Proceedings of SC '97*, Nov. 1997.
8. K. McKinley, S. Carr, and C.-W. Tseng. Improving data locality with loop transformations. *ACM Trans. on Programming Languages and Systems*, 18(4):424–453, 1996.
9. S. Microsystems. The ultrasparctm processor technology white paper. Technical Report WPR-0021, Sun Microsystems, 1998. Available from http://www.sun.com/microelectronics/whitepapers/.
10. W. Pugh and E. Rosser. Iteration space slicing and its application to communication optimization. In *Proceedings of the 1997 International Conference on Supercomputing*, July 1997.
11. E. J. Rosser. *Fine Grained Analysis of Array Computations*. PhD thesis, Dept. of Computer Science, The University of Maryland, Sept. 1998.
12. M. Weiser. Program slicing. *IEEE Transactions on Software Engineering*, pages 352–357, July 1984.
13. A. Yoshida, K. Koshizuka, and H. Kasahara. Data-localization for fortran macro-dataflow computation using partial static task assignment. In *Proceedings of the 1996 International Conference on Supercomputing*, pages 61–68, May 1996.

A Compiler Framework for
Tiling Imperfectly-Nested Loops *

Yonghong Song and Zhiyuan Li

Department of Computer Sciences
Purdue University
West Lafayette, IN 47907
{songyh,li}@cs.purdue.edu

Abstract. This paper presents an integrated compiler framework for tiling a class of nontrivial imperfectly-nested loops such that cache locality
is improved. We develop a new memory cost model to analyze data reuse
in terms of both the cache and the TLB, based on which we compute
the tile size with or without array duplication. We determine whether
to duplicate arrays for tiling by comparing the respective *exploited reuse
factors*. The preliminary results with several benchmark programs show
that the transformed programs achieve a speedup of 1.09 to 3.82 over
the original programs.

1   Introduction

This paper considers loop tiling [16] as a technique to improve data locality.
Previous tiling techniques are generally limited to perfectly-nested loops. Unfortunately, many important loops in reality are imperfectly nested. In our recent
work [11], we define a class of imperfectly-nested loops and present a set of algorithms to tile such loops with *odd-even array duplication*. In this paper, we
make the following new contributions:

- We develop a memory cost model to analyze data reuse in terms of both the
  cache and the TLB, based on which we compute the tile size with or without
  array duplication. We determine whether to duplicate arrays for tiling by
  comparing the respective *exploited reuse factors*. (In [11], we considered only
  the cache, and we always duplicated arrays without a cost analysis.)
- We present an integrated compiler framework for tiling the class of nontrivial
  imperfectly-nested loops considered in [11] such that data locality is improved for both the cache and the TLB. (In [11], we presented only a subset of
  the key algorithms.)

The rest of the paper is organized as follows. In Section 2, we define our
program model and review basic concepts in our tiling techniques. We present
our memory cost model and a tile-size selection scheme in Section 3. Section 4

---

* This work is sponsored in part by National Science Foundation through grants CCR-
9975309, CCR-950254, MIP-9610379 and by Purdue Research Foundation.

L. Carter and J. Ferrante (Eds.): LCPC'99, LNCS 1863, pp. 185–200, 2000.

```
DO T = 1, ITMAX
  DO J₁ = L₁ + b₁ * T, U₁ + b₁ * T
    ...
    ... ← B[...]
    ...
  END DO
  ...
  DO Jₘ = Lₘ + bₘ * T, Uₘ + bₘ * T
    ...
    B[...] ← ...
    ...
  END DO
END DO
        (a) Program Model
```

```
DO JJ = f₃(SLOPE),
       f₄(SLOPE), NSTEP
  DO T = g₃(JJ, SLOPE, NSTEP),
         g₄(JJ, SLOPE, NSTEP)
    DO J₁ = L₁'', U₁''
      ...
      ... ← B[...]
      ...
    END DO
    ...
    DO Jₘ = Lₘ'', Uₘ''
      ...
      B[...] ← ...
      ...
    END DO
  END DO
END DO
  (c) After Tiling without Duplication
```

```
DO JJ = f₁(SLOPE), f₂(SLOPE), NSTEP
  DO  T   =   g₁(JJ, SLOPE, NSTEP),
         g₂(JJ, SLOPE, NSTEP)
    IF MOD(T, 2).EQ.1) THEN
      DO J₁ = L₁', U₁'
        ...
        ... ← B[...]
        ...
      END DO
      ...
      DO Jₘ = Lₘ', Uₘ'
        ...
        B'[...] ← ...
        ...
      END DO
    ELSE
      DO J₁ = L₁', U₁'
        ...
        ... ← B'[...]
        ...
      END DO
      ...
      DO Jₘ = Lₘ', Uₘ'
        ...
        B[...] ← ...
        ...
      END DO
    END IF
  END DO
END DO
     (b) After Tiling with Duplication
```

Fig. 1. Program Model and Various Intermediate Code Shapes during Transformation

compares tiling with and without duplication. In Section 5, we present our integrated framework. We then evaluate our framework in Section 6. Related work is presented in Section 7, followed by a conclusion in Section 8.

2 Preliminaries

2.1 Program Model

Our program model [11] is shown in Figure 1(a). The T-loop body contains m loops, J_1, J_2, ..., J_m ($m \geq 1$), at the next inner level. We call these loops the J loops. Each J loop may contain arbitrary program constructs. Without loss of generality, all loops are assumed to have step 1. We require each loop J_i to take the form of $L_i + b_i * T$ and $U_i + b_i * T$ as the lower and upper bounds respectively, where L_i and U_i are T-invariants and b_i is a nonnegative known constant. To make the presentation clean, $ITMAX$ is assumed here to be an even number. In order to support array duplication, we require that any flow dependence should have the distance of either 0 or 1 at the loop level T. This is commonly true for the applications of our focus, which repeatedly access the same arrays. Existing compiler techniques for *array privatization* can determine

DO $T = 1, ITMAX$
  DO $J_1 = 2, N - 1$
    DO $I_1 = 2, N - 1$
      $L(I_1, J_1) = (A(I_1 + 1, J_1) + A(I_1 - 1, J_1)$
        $+ A(I_1, J_1 + 1) + A(I_1, J_1 - 1))/4$
    END DO
  END DO
  DO $J_2 = 2, N - 1$
    DO $I_2 = 2, N - 1$
      $A(I_2, J_2) = L(I_2, J_2)$
    END DO
  END DO
END DO

(a)

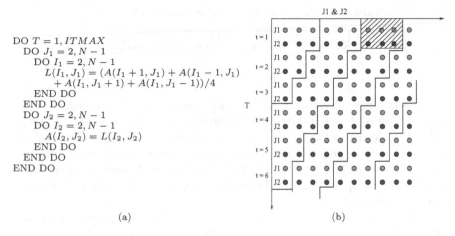

(b)

Fig. 2. Code and Iteration Subspace of Jacobi Kernel

whether such a condition on flow dependences is satisfied (see [4] for a list of references). In Figure 1(a), we assume that B always gets its value from the previous T iteration, i.e., with flow dependence distance of 1.

For simplicity of exposition, in this paper we consider tiling for the J loops only, even though they may contain inner loops. The techniques proposed here, however, can be extended to include loops within the J loops, as in [11]. Several known simple transformations, such as code sinking [11,16] and creation of single-iteration loops, can be used to transform an imperfectly-nested loop to conform to our program model.

2.2   Basic Concepts

In [11], we develop a set of compiler algorithms to tile the loops conforming to our program model (Figure 1(a)). The key to our scheme is to find a uniform tile *slope* such that all flow dependences carried by T are satisfied and to find an *offset* for each tiled inner loop such that all flow dependences within the same T iteration are also satisfied. The tile shape, as the result, guarantees that no flow dependences will exist from a later-executed tile to an earlier-executed tile. Anti- and output dependences which exist from later-executed tiles to earlier-executed ones are eliminated by a technique called *odd-even duplication* of arrays. This technique can be useful for reducing the skewing factor of tiles, hence it can potentially increase data reuse.

For our program model, Figure 1(b) shows the final tiled code after odd-even duplication, where *SLOPE* represents the uniform slope angle and *NSTEP* stands for the tile size. We call *JJ* the *tile-controlling loop* and T the *tile-sweeping loop*. Figures 2(a) and (b) shows the code and the iteration subspace of Jacobi kernel respectively. In Figure 2(b), the shaded rectangle is called a *tile* and the area between two stair-case lines is called a *tile traversal* in this paper. Two tiles are called *consecutive* if they belong to the same tile traversal and the difference

Table 1. Parameters of the Cache and the TLB

Notation	C_s	C_b	T_s	T_b
Description	Cache size	Cache block size	TLB size	TLB block size

of their corresponding T values is 1. The slope angle, $SLOPE$, equals to the maximum number of J loop iterations left-shifted between two consecutive tiles. While $SLOPE$ determines the relative position between different tiles, the *offset* value characterizes the relative position between different J loops within the same tile. In Figure 2(b), $SLOPE$ equals 1, $NSTEP$ equals 3, and the *offsets* are equal to 0 for both loops J_1 and J_2. After tiling (Figure 1(b)), each JJ iteration defines one tile traversal.

Alternatively, the compiler can choose a greater skewing factor without array duplication. Since array duplication increases the working set, whether it truely increases data reuse or whether it performs better than no duplication must be verified by the compiler. In the next section, we introduce a memory cost model for such verification.

3   A Memory Cost Model and Tile-Size Selection

Different levels of reuse [14] exist in our program model: *reuse carried by T, reuse between different J loops, reuse carried by a particular J loop* and *reuse within one iteration of a J loop*. Our goal is to maximize the reuse carried by T. Note that our method improves the temporal locality without sacrificing the original spatial locality in the innermost loop, since the access order in the innermost loop is not changed.

If the tile size $NSTEP$ is chosen properly, then any repeated data referenced within the same tile traversal should be a cache hit and a TLB hit. Except the first reference, all references to the same memory location within the same tile traversal should be a cache hit and a TLB hit. To be more specific, the tiled loop nest should have the following properties:

- **Property 1:** Any repeated reference to the same memory location within the same tile should be a cache hit and a TLB hit.
- **Property 2:** The overlapping data [1] between two consecutive tiles should be kept within the cache and the TLB when the execution proceeds from one tile to the next.

Next, we construct a memory cost model to characterize the cache and the TLB and we derive a scheme to select the optimal tile size for our loop transformation, assuming that Properties 1 and 2 hold. (Later on in this section, we will discuss how to preserve these two properties.) Table 1 lists the key sizes measured in the number of data elements. We assume the LRU replacement

---

[1] Within a tile traversal, the exact J-iterations executed in T and $T + 1$ overlap partially if $SLOPE$ is greater than 0, as in the case of Jacobi (Figure 2(b)).

policy both for the fully-associative cache and for the fully-associative TLB. Let $\gamma_1 = min\{L_i | 1 \leq i \leq m\}$ and $\gamma_2 = max\{U_i | 1 \leq i \leq m\}$ represent the minimum and the maximum of J_i index values in the original loop nest. Let $\gamma = \gamma_2 - \gamma_1 + 1$ be the length of the range of all legal J_i loop index values. For simplicity, we assume that the size of the data set accessed within each T iteration is T-invariant, denoted by W. We make three assumptions in our estimation of the cache and TLB misses:

- **Assumption 1**: The data set size W is greater than the cache size and the TLB size and $ITMAX$ is large.
- **Assumption 2**: There exist no cache and TLB reuse between different tile traversals.
- **Assumption 3**: Spatial locality is fully exploited in the innermost loops.

Many numerical applications have large data set and require many time steps. Therefore Assumption 1 is reasonable. Assumption 2 is reasonable because, if $ITMAX$ is large and the tiles are skewed, it is very likely for a tile traversal to overwrite cache lines whose old data could otherwise be reused in the next tile traversal. For regular applications, programmers and compilers normally write or transform the programs in such styles that Assumption 3 is naturally satisfied. From Assumption 1, we can derive $NSTEP \ll \gamma$ and $NSTEP \ll (ITMAX-1)*SLOPE$.

We estimate the cache misses in the original loop nest (Figure 1(a)) as $ITMAX * \frac{W}{C_b}$ and the TLB misses as $ITMAX * \frac{W}{T_b}$.

For the tiled loop nest, we estimate the cache misses as follows. We assume all b_i $(1 \leq i \leq m)$ in the loop bound expression to be 0 for simplicity. (The case with nonzero b_i can be covered by a more lengthy discussion.) Assume that, after odd-even array duplication as shown in Figure 1(b), the data size of the T loop becomes $\mu W, 1 \leq \mu \leq 2$. The average data size accessed in a single loop tile equals $D = \frac{\mu W}{\gamma} * NSTEP$. The iteration space of the tile-controlling loop JJ spans from γ_1 to $\gamma + \gamma_1 + SLOPE *(ITMAX-1)$ with the step value $NSTEP$, and each JJ value identifies one tile traversal. With Assumptions 1 to 3, we can then estimate the number of cache misses by considering three different cases.

- **Case 1**: $\gamma = (ITMAX-1) * SLOPE$.
  This case is illustrated by Figure 3(a). In this case, the tile traversals defined by $JJ \leq \gamma_1 + \gamma - NSTEP$ will not execute to the $ITMAX$th T-iteration. The tile traversal defined by $\gamma_1 + \gamma - NSTEP < JJ \leq \gamma_1 + \gamma$ is the first to reach the $ITMAX$th T-iteration. The tile traversals defined by $JJ > \gamma_1 + \gamma$ will start executing at $T > 1$. The tile traversal defined by $JJ = \gamma_1$ will incur cache misses of $\frac{D}{C_b}$. The tile traversal defined by $JJ = \gamma_1 + NSTEP$ will incur cache misses of $\frac{D}{C_b} * 2$, and so on. Hence we have the following:
  - The cache misses in all the tile traversals defined by $JJ \leq \gamma_1 + \gamma - NSTEP$ equal to $\frac{D}{C_b} * (1 + 2 + \ldots + \lfloor \frac{\gamma - NSTEP}{NSTEP} \rfloor)$.
  - Similarly, the cache misses in all the tile traversals defined by $\gamma_1 + \gamma < JJ$ amount to $\frac{D}{C_b} * (1 + 2 + \ldots + \lfloor \frac{\gamma - NSTEP}{NSTEP} \rfloor)$.

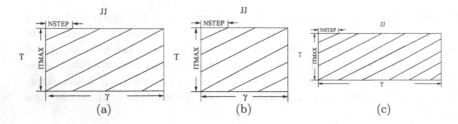

Fig. 3. Illustration of Different Scenarios to Calculate the Cache Misses

- Similarly, the cache misses in the tile traversal defined by $\gamma_1 + \gamma - NSTEP < JJ \leq \gamma_1 + \gamma$ amount to $\frac{D}{C_b} * \frac{\gamma}{NSTEP}$.

Adding up the three numbers of the above, the total number of cache misses in the tiled loop nest approximates $\frac{D}{C_b} * (\frac{\gamma}{NSTEP})^2$.

- **Case 2:** $\gamma < (ITMAX\text{-}1)*SLOPE$.

This case is illustrated by Figure 3(b). In this case, one of the tile traversals defined by $JJ > \gamma_1 + \gamma$ first reaches the $ITMAX$th T-iteration. Similar to Case 1, we derive the following:

- The cache misses in all the tile traversals defined by $JJ \leq \gamma_1 + \gamma$ amount to $\frac{D}{C_b} * (1 + 2 * \ldots + \lfloor \frac{\gamma}{NSTEP} \rfloor)$.
- The cache misses in all the tile traversals defined by $\gamma_1 + \gamma < JJ \leq (ITMAX\text{-}1)*SLOPE + \gamma_1$ amount to
  $\frac{D}{C_b} * \frac{\gamma}{NSTEP} * \lceil \frac{(ITMAX\text{-}1)*SLOPE - \gamma}{NSTEP} \rceil$.
- The cache misses in all the tile traversals defined by $(ITMAX\text{-}1)*SLOPE + \gamma_1 < JJ$ amount to $\frac{D}{C_b} * (1 + 2 * \ldots + \lfloor \frac{\gamma}{NSTEP} \rfloor)$.

Adding up the three numbers above, the total number of cache misses in the tiled loop nest approximates $\frac{D}{C_b} * \frac{\gamma}{NSTEP} * \frac{(ITMAX\text{-}1)*SLOPE}{NSTEP}$.

- **Case 3:** $\gamma > (ITMAX\text{-}1)*SLOPE$.

This case is illustrated by Figure 3(c). In this case, one of the tile traversals defined by $JJ \leq \gamma_1 + \gamma - NSTEP$ first reaches the $ITMAX$th T-iteration. Similar to Case 1, we derive the following:

- The cache misses in all the tile traversals defined by
  $JJ \leq \gamma_1 + (ITMAX\text{-}1)*SLOPE - NSTEP$ amount to $\frac{D}{C_b} * (1 + 2 + \ldots + \lfloor \frac{(ITMAX\text{-}1)*SLOPE - NSTEP}{NSTEP} \rfloor)$.
- The cache misses in all the tile traversals defined by
  $\gamma_1 + (ITMAX\text{-}1)*SLOPE - NSTEP < JJ \leq \gamma + \gamma_1$ amount to $\frac{D}{C_b} * \frac{NSTEP + (ITMAX\text{-}1)*SLOPE}{NSTEP} * \lceil \frac{\gamma - (ITMAX\text{-}1)*SLOPE + NSTEP}{NSTEP} \rceil$.
- The cache misses in all the tile traversals defined by $\gamma + \gamma_1 < JJ$ amount to $\frac{D}{C_b} * (1 + 2 + \ldots + \lfloor \frac{(ITMAX\text{-}1)*SLOPE - NSTEP}{NSTEP} \rfloor)$.

Adding up the three numbers above, the total number of cache misses in the tiled loop nest approximates $\frac{D}{C_b} * \frac{(ITMAX\text{-}1)*SLOPE}{NSTEP} * \frac{\gamma}{NSTEP}$.

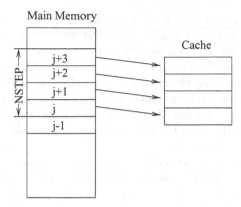

Fig. 4. An Illustration to Select a Proper Tile Size

In summary of the above three cases, the total number of cache misses in the tiled loop nest approximates

$$\frac{D}{C_b} * \frac{(ITMAX\text{-}1) * SLOPE}{NSTEP} * \frac{\gamma}{NSTEP}. \tag{1}$$

With previously defined $D = \frac{\mu W}{\gamma} * NSTEP$, Equation (1) can be simplied to

$$\frac{W * (ITMAX\text{-}1)}{C_b} * \frac{\mu * SLOPE}{NSTEP}. \tag{2}$$

Following similar steps, we approximate the total number of TLB misses in the tiled loop nest to

$$\frac{W * (ITMAX\text{-}1)}{T_b} * \frac{\mu * SLOPE}{NSTEP}. \tag{3}$$

In Equations (2) and (3), $ITMAX$, W, C_b and T_b are all T-invariant. In order to reduce the cache misses and the TLB misses, $NSTEP$ should be large and $SLOPE$ should be small. For a given loop nest and a given machine architecture, the number of cache and TLB misses is completely determined by $\frac{\mu * SLOPE}{NSTEP}$. In this paper, we call its reciprocal, $\lceil \frac{NSTEP}{\mu * SLOPE} \rceil$, the *exploited reuse factor*. Therefore, the greater exploited reuse factor, the smaller the number of the cache and TLB misses. We choose the final tiling scheme from all the tiling schemes either with or without array duplication such that it has the largest exploited reuse factor.

In the discussions above, we assume that Properties 1 and 2 are preserved in our estimation of the number of cache misses and TLB misses. We now discuss how to preserve these two properties and, at the same time, to maximize the exploited reuse factor, $\lceil \frac{NSTEP}{\mu * SLOPE} \rceil$.

Property 1 can be preserved by imposing the *working set constraint*, i.e., the amount of data accessed within a single tile should not exceed the cache size and the TLB size. Furthermore, array padding [7] is performed such that the accessed data within a tile are evenly allocated within the cache to minimize the set conflicts. In order to accommodate inaccuracy in array padding and the fact that instructions and data compete for the unified (L2) cache, we follow the industrial practice of utilizing the effective cache size [15], which is smaller than the real cache. (As in our previous work [11], we choose the effective cache size factor $\alpha = 0.3$ in our experiments. Since TLB is fully associative in practice, we choose the effective TLB size to be 0.75, which is considerably greater than the effective cache size factor.)

Figure 4 illustrates how Property 2 is preserved. Suppose that $NSTEP$ equals 4 and $SLOPE$ equals 1 and that the tile executed in a T-loop iteration consists of four consecutive J-loop iterations, denoted by j, $j + 1$, $j + 2$ and $j + 3$ for each J loop. Suppose the data accessed by these four iterations exactly fit in the data cache [2]. In the next T-loop iteration, the tile will contain the iterations $j - 1$, j, $j + 1$ and $j + 2$. Assuming data accessed in consecutive J iterations have consecutive addresses, then a subset of the data accessed in the last tile will be replaced. Since we assume a fully-associative cache, the data accessed previously in j will be replaced. Note that we assume a fully-associative TLB with LRU replacement policy. If the data accessed in a tile which contains iteration j through $j + 3$ exactly fit in the TLB in a particular T-loop iteration, then the TLB entry accessed previously in j will be replaced in the next tile when T increases by 1.

We now determine the tile size, $NSTEP$, as follows. Let κ represent the maximum number of J iterations whose data can fit in both the cache and the TLB under the working set constraint. The tile size is chosen to be $NSTEP = \kappa - SLOPE$. This ensures that, within the same tile traversal, data shared by two consecutive tiles will not be replaced before used by the latter tile [3].

4   Tiling with or without Duplication

In our framework, the compiler tries tiling both with and without odd-even array duplication, and picks the one with a greater exploited reuse factor. Figure 1(b) shows the tiled code with duplication. Note that the computation of the tile size $NSTEP$ is now based on our new memory cost model in Section 3, not simply based on the working-set constraint as in [11].

The profitability test is as follows.

1. Condition $NSTEP > SLOPE$ must be satisfied.

---

[2] For a cache with limited set associativity, this may not be true because, within a tile, the references from different arrays may map to the same cache locations, which may cause one portion of the cache to be undersubscribed and the other portion oversubscribed. We expect that data transformation techniques such as padding [7, 10] can relieve this problem.

[3] For directly-mapped caches, if the TLB is fully-utilized, the tile size should also be $\kappa - SLOPE$, otherwise, it is simply κ. For all other set-associative caches, the tile size should be $\kappa - SLOPE$.

2. Let $NSTEP1 = max\{offset[v] + |d_J| - offset[u]\ |u, v$ are nodes in $G_l, <$
   $u, v >$ is any anti- or output dependence edge with $d_T = 0.\}$, $NSTEP2$
   $= max\{offset[v] + |d_J| - offset[u] - SLOPE\ |u, v$ are nodes in $G_l, < u, v >$ is
   any anti- or output dependence edge with $d_T = 1.\}$.
   Condition $NSTEP > max\ (NSTEP1,\ NSTEP2)$ must be satisfied.

Condition 1 makes $NSTEP$ large enough to allow potential temporal reuse across T iterations. Condition 2 prevents any anti- or output dependence from crossing backward more than one tile boundary. If the final loop nest passes profitability test, profitability $p = TRUE$ and the exploited reuse factor $r = \lceil \frac{NSTEP}{\mu * SLOPE} \rceil$ are returned. Otherwise, profitability $p = FALSE$ is returned.

Alternative to odd-even duplication, we can conservatively select $SLOPE$ and *offsets* such that no backward dependences (flow, anti- and output) exist from a later tile to an earlier tile. The form of the tiled code without duplication is shown in Figure 1(c). The main difference from tiling with odd-even duplication is that, when we compute $SLOPE$ and *offsets* [11], we examine not only the flow dependences but also the anti- and output dependences. If the loop nest is tiled without duplication, the profitability test above no longer needs to check Condition 2.

For example, if Jacobi kernel is tiled with duplication, $SLOPE$ equals to 1, and the offset values for both J_1 and J_2 equal 0. If it is tiled without duplication, however, $SLOPE$ equals 2, the offset value for J_2 equals 0 and 1 for J_1.

5   An Integrated Framework

In this section, we present our integrated compiler framework to tile imperfectly-nested loops.

Figure 5 presents the sketch of the framework. The compiler first needs to select a candidate loop (sub)nest which fits our program model. The compiler identifies all loops each of which may be labeled as the T loop. We say these are the T *candidates*. The compiler then computes all the dependence information associated with each T candidate [11].

If a loop nest contains more than one T candidate, the compiler orders the T candidates to form a priority queue, Q, based on the *reuse factor* which is defined as the maximum number of times any element is referenced by a loop repeatedly at the given loop level [14,16]. In case that two T candidates have the same reuse factor, if one is nested within the other, the inner one has a higher priority. Otherwise, the order can be arbitrary. The compiler takes one T candidate, say T_1, from Q. If T_1 can be tiled successfully, the tiling process terminates for the given loop nest. Otherwise, the compiler picks the next T candidate, until Q is empty.

For each T candidate, T_1, the compiler first computes all the compatible sets [4]. If the number of compatible sets exceeds the maximum number of per-

---

[4] The concept of compatible set, the algorithm to compute the compatible set and a running example to illustrate our framework is available in a long version of this paper in http://www.cs.purdue.edu/homes/li/publications.html.

Input: a loop nest.
Output: a transformed loop nest if the algorithm succeeds or the restored original loop nest
    if the algorithm aborts.
Procedure:
    Compute a set of T candidates, say $TPool$, and dependence information associated
      with each T candidate.
    Order the T candidates in $TPool$ to form a priority queue Q.
    do
      if (Q is empty) aborts.
      Extract a T loop from Q, say T_1.
      Compute the *compatible sets* for T_1, say $comSets$.
      if ($|comSets| > max\,\{s_i + 1 | 1 \leq i \leq m\}$) continue to the next do iteration.
      for each compatible set $cset$ **do**
        Transform the loop nest according to $cset$.
        if (this transformation cannot be realized) continue to the next compatible set.
        Construct J-loop distance subgraph.
        Transform the loop nest with duplication with the exploited reuse factor r_1
          and the profitability p_1 returned.
        Transform the loop nest without duplication with the exploited reuse factor r_2
          and the profitability p_2 returned.
        if (p_1) perform real transformation with duplication if p_2 is $FALSE$ or $r_1 > r_2$.
        if (p_2) perform real transformation without duplication if p_1 is $FALSE$ or $r_2 \geq r_1$.
        if (p_1 or p_2) return from the procedure.
      end for
    end do
    abort.

Fig. 5. A Sketch of Compiler Framework to Tile Imperfectly-Nested Loops

fectly-nested loop levels with T_1, then tiling T_1 is unlikely to be profitable, and
the compiler moves to the next T candidate. Otherwise, the compiler examines
all the compatible sets with T_1 as the T loop, starting from column-compatible
ones, as follows.

For each compatible set, *cset*, the compiler first tries to transform the loop
nest according to *cset* by loop permutation and array transpose. If such transformations are impossible, the compiler continues to the next compatible set.
Otherwise, the J-loop distance subgraph is constructed [11]. The compiler then
tries to tile with and without odd-even duplication. If both tiling schemes are
profitable, then the one with more exploited reuse is favored. If neither is profitable, the compiler continues to the next compatible set.

6 Experimental Evaluation

We are implementing the new framework presented above in the Panorama compiler [4]. To pre-evaluate their effectiveness, we have manually applied this framework to two well-known numerical kernels, Jacobi and Livermore Loop LL18,
and two SPEC95 benchmarks `tomcatv` and `swim` [12], which run on two processors. One is a MIPS R5K processor within an SGI workstation, and the other
is a single MIPS R10K processor within an SGI Origin 2000 multiprocessor.
The R5K processor has a 32KB 2-way L1 data cache, a 512KB 2-way unified
L2 cache and a 48-entry fully-associative unified TLB. Each TLB entry represents an 8KB page. The R10K processor has a 32KB 2-way L1 data cache, a
4MB 2-way unified L2 cache and a 64-entry fully-associative unified TLB. Each

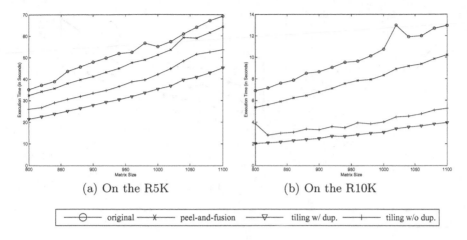

(a) On the R5K   (b) On the R10K

| ─⊖─ original | ─✕─ peel-and-fusion | ─▽─ tiling w/ dup. | ─+─ tiling w/o dup. |

Fig. 6. Execution Time (in Seconds) of Jacobi on the R5K and R10K with Various Matrix Size

TLB entry also represents an 8KB page [5]. Both machines have a random replacement policy. Moreover, the MIPS R10K performs out-of-order instruction execution, provides data prefetching instructions, and permits multiple pending cache misses. The native compiler is MIPSpro F77 compiler. We turn on the "-O3" switch for the original code, but turn off the tiling switch in the compiler for all the other schemes. The "-O3" option enables a number of loop transformations including interchange, fusion, fission and tiling. For peel-and-fusion, we also apply padding to reduce cache set conflicts and choose the tile size such that the working set for any array within a single tile can fit in one partition [7], where both the real cache size and effective cache size are used in experiments and the better results are taken as the final one. We use both the real cache size and the effective cache size and take the better result as the final one. We apply a speculation scheme [11] to overcome the convergence test in Jacobi and in tomcatv. The basic idea of speculation is to partition the whole T iteration space into several chunks, so tiling can be applied to each individual chunk. Checkpointing is performed before executing a new chunk. The convergence test is performed after the execution of a chunk. In case of convergence test failure, the latest checkpoint is restored and the execution is completed by the untiled version.

The Jacobi Kernel. We fix ITMAX to 100 and vary the input matrix size arbitrarily from 800 to 1100 incremented by 20. *SLOPE* equals 1 for with duplication and equals 2 for without duplication. Figure 6(a) and (b) show the

---

[5] The R10K machine used here has a larger L2 cache and a faster clock than the one used in our previous work [11]. We achieve a higher speedup with the new techniques in this paper.

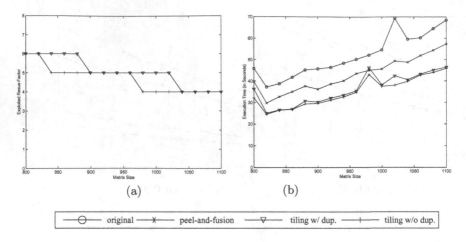

Fig. 7. The Exploited Reuse Factor and Execution Time (in Seconds) of LL18 on the R10K with Various Matrix Size

performance result for different versions of Jacobi code on the R5K and R10K respectively.

NSTEP is computed based on the scheme presented in Section 3. The compiler chooses tiling with duplication since it yields a greater exploited reuse factor. The data for non-duplication tiling is presented for comparison.

The final code of Jacobi does not increase the memory usage because forward substitution eliminates the usage of L [11]. Figure 6 shows that tiling with duplication performs better than the other three schemes. On the R10K, the transformed programs achieve a speedup of 3.27 to 3.82 over the original code and achieve a speedup of 2.56 to 2.81 over peel-and-fusion. On the R5K, the transformed programs achieve a speedup of 1.52 to 1.73 over the original code and achieves a speedup of 1.41 to 1.51 over peel-and-fusion.

The LL18 Kernel. We fix ITMAX to 100 and choose the same input matrix sizes as for Jacobi. With two arrays, *ZR* and *ZZ*, duplicated, *SLOPE* is computed as 2. The memory requirement increases by 18%. Without duplication, *SLOPE* equals 3. Figure 7(a) shows the exploited reuse factor for the schemes with and without duplication on the R10K. The compiler favors tiling with duplication when N equals to 840, 860, 880, 980, 1000 and 1020. The compiler favors tiling without duplication for all the other cases where the exploited reuse factors are equal.

Figure 7(b) shows the performance result for various versions of LL18 on the R10K. For the schemes with and without duplication, the difference between the exploited reuse factors is at most 1, predicting a similar performance. The execution time of the code transformed with the two schemes is indeed very close except for $N = 800, 980$ and 1020. Although our framework does not choose the best solution for all cases, the result of the transformed code still outperforms

Table 2. Execution Time(in Seconds) of `swim`

Test Program	R10K		R5K	
	Exec. Time	Speedup	Exec. Time	Speedup
Orig. Prog.	92.66	1.00	625	1.00
Trans. Prog.	58.55	1.58	573	1.09

the original code with a speedup of 1.13 to 1.64, and it outperforms peel-and-fusion with a speedup of 1.16 to 1.30 except $N = 980$, where it degrades the performance by 3% compared with peel-and-fusion. With such a large data set and our chosen effective cache factor, our framework cannot profitably perform tiling on the R5K. With a smaller size of data set, however, we get results similar to what are shown in Figure 7.

The Tomcatv Program. Two arrays, X and Y, among the 7 N-by-N arrays in `tomcatv`, are duplicated by the duplication algorithm, increasing the memory usage by 29%. On the R10K, $NSTEP$ equals 33 if we tile with duplication and it equals 41 without duplication. On the R5K, it equals 3 with or without duplication. Since $SLOPE = 1$ with duplication and $SLOPE = 2$ without duplication, the compiler chooses tiling with duplication for both machines.

Using the reference input data, `tomcatv` always runs to the maximum time step, i.e., 750. On the R10K, the original program completes in 116 seconds. The transformed program with duplication completes in 81 seconds and the one without duplication completes in 86 seconds, a speedup of 1.43 and 1.34 respectively. On the R5K, the original program completes in 732 seconds. The transformed program with duplication completes in 451 seconds and 528 seconds with and without duplication respectively, giving a speedup of 1.62 and 1.39. We also run `tomcatv` with peel-and-fusion, where the transformed code takes 132 and 677 seconds on the R10K and the R5K and achieves a speedup of 0.87 and 1.08 respectively over the original program.

The Swim Program. In `swim`, $SLOPE$ equals 2 and $NSTEP$ equals 45 and 3 for the R10K and the R5K respectively. No arrays need to be duplicated to decrease $SLOPE$. Table 2 shows the performance results, where "Orig. Prog." stands for the original program, and "Trans. Prog." represents the transformed program. On the R5K the speedup by tiling is lower than on the R10K. We suspect that, for the R5K, the small $NSTEP$ value, hence the small overlap of iteration points between consecutive tiles in the same tile traversal, has made our tiling results more sensitive to the cache set conflicts. Peel-and-fusion does not apply directly to `swim` due to long backward dependence distances.

6.1   Cache Miss Measurement

On the R10K, in addition to execution time, we also measure the secondary cache misses using *perfex* library based on R10K performance counters. Table 3 shows the result, where 'LS' stands for the number of dynamic load-store instructions, 'SM' for the number of misses for the secondary cache, and 'MR' for the secondary cache miss ratio. We show the results for the Jacobi and LL18 with N arbitrarily chosen as 1000. We also show results for tomcatv and swim using the reference data. In Jacobi, even with checkpointing, the number of dynamic load-store instructions are reduced due to forward substitution. In all four test programs the secondary cache miss rate is dramatically reduced by our tiling scheme. The gain in temporal locality across T iterations offsets the loss due to more memory requirements after array duplication.

Table 3. Secondary Cache Utilization of Jacobi, LL18, tomcatv and swim

(LS and SM are counters in millions)

Test Program	Original			Peel-and-Fusion			Duplication			Non-duplication		
	LS	SM	MR	LS	SM	MR	LS	SM	MR	LS	SM	MR
Jacobi (N = 1000)	553.5	24.9	0.045	648.5	12.5	0.019	451.1	0.45	0.0010	671.7	0.53	0.0008
LL18 (N = 1000)	2767.4	99.7	0.036	2762.7	56.3	0.020	3400.8	12.8	0.0038	3403.2	15.1	0.0044
tomcatv	10809.2	177.1	0.016	10052.3	142.4	0.014	8335.2	51.2	0.0061	8151.4	73.1	0.0090
swim	11701.2	167.1	0.014	-	-	-	9280.4	5.0	0.0005	9280.4	5.0	0.0005

7   Related Work

Kodukula *et al.* propose *data shackling* [5], which blocks the arrays based on data flow analysis and then forms new loop nests to compute block-by-block. Although it can handle certain imperfectly-nested loops, their method does not apply to the stencil computations handled in our work, because updating one block will destroy the boundary data necessary for its adjacent blocks.

Manjikian *et al.* present peel-and-fusion and apply padding to eliminate cache set conflict within a tile [7]. Their method can partially fuse the adjacent loops within the same T loop and tile the fused loops, but it only exploits locality within the same T loop iteration. Our offset computation bears some similarity to their peel-factor computation, but they consider dependences within the same T-iteration only, while we further consider dependences across T-iterations.

Bacon *et al.* develop a padding algorithm for selecting efficient padding amount, which takes into account both cache and TLB in a single framework [1]. Their method mainly applies to the innermost loop. More recently, Rivera and Tseng present a set of padding heuristics which are used to perform inter- and intra-array padding [10]. Padding and tiling are generally viewed as two complementary techniques.

In our framework, any repeated reference to a memory location within the same tile will be a cache hit and a TLB hit, so the working set for that tile will determine the number of cache misses and TLB misses. Ferrante *et al.* provide closed-form formulae that bound the number of array accesses and the number of cache lines accessed within a loop nest, thus providing an estimate of the number of cache misses in a loop nest [2]. Their method applies to perfectly-nested loops only. Temam *et al.* presents an algorithm to estimate the number of cache misses, especially interference misses [13], for a perfectly-nested loop nest. Ghost *et al.* develop a cache miss equation (CME) to count the number of cache misses in order to guide optimization [3] for a perfectly-nested loop. Our work in this paper covers more complex loop nests, including imperfectly-nested loops and skewed tiles.

Mitchell *et al.* use matrix multiplication as an example to show that both the TLB misses and the cache misses must be considered simultaneously in order to achieve the best performance [9], although they provide no formal algorithms to select tile sizes.

Kodukula and Pingali propose a matrix-based framework to represent transformations of imperfectly-nested loops [6] including permutation, reversal, skewing, scaling, alignment, distribution and jamming, but not including tiling.

McCalpin and Wonnacott introduce the notion of *machine balance* vs. *compute balance*, and they develop a scheme called *time skewing* which adopts a value-based flow analysis to optimize for memory locality [8]. Their method first performs full array expansion and forward substitution, and it then recompresses the expanded array while preserving data dependences. Their current method handles a subset of the imperfectly-nested loops represented by our program model.

8   Conclusion and Future Work

In this paper, we have extended our previous work [11] on tiling imperfectly-nested loops. We present a framework to systematically select and tile a loop nest from a number of candidates, based on a memory cost model which considers both the cache and the TLB. Preliminary experimental results show the transformed programs run faster by 9% to 282% than those optimized by the native compiler only.

Our work may be further improved in a number of ways. The scheme for ordering the T candidates may be improved further. We also need to better understand the interaction between the TLB and the multiple levels of cache memories, and the competition between instructions and data for unified L2 cache, among other issues, which can affect the tile-size selection.

References

1. D. Bacon, J.-H. Chow, D. Ju, K. Muthukumar, and V. Sarkar. A compiler framework for restructuring data declarations to enhance cache and tlb effectiveness. In *Proceedings of CASCON'94*, Toronto, Ontario, October 1994.
2. J. Ferrante, V. Sarkar, and W. Thrash. On estimating and enhancing cache effectiveness. In *Proceedings of 4th International Workshop on Languages and Compilers for Parallel Computing*, August 1991. Also in *Lecture Notes in Computer Science*, U. Banerjee, D. Gelernter, A. Nicolau, and D. Padua, eds., pp. 328-341, Springer-Verlag, Aug. 1991.

3. Somnath Ghosh, Margaret Martonosi, and Sharad Malik. Precise miss analysis for program transformations with caches of arbitrary associativity. In *Proceedings of the 8th ACM Conference on Architectural Support for Programming Languages and Operating Systems*, pages 228–239, San Jose, California, October 1998.

4. Junjie Gu, Zhiyuan Li, and Gyungho Lee. Experience with efficient array data flow analysis for array privatization. In *Proceedings of the 6th ACM SIGPLAN Symposium on Principles and Practice of Parallel Programming*, pages 157–167, Las Vegas, NV, June 1997.

5. Induprakas Kodukula, Nawaaz Ahmed, and Keshav Pingali. Data-centric multi-level blocking. In *Proceedings of ACM SIGPLAN Conference on Programming Language Design and Implementation*, pages 346–357, Las Vegas, NV, June 1997.

6. Induprakas Kodukula and Keshav Pingali. Transformations of imperfectly nested loops. In *Proceedings of Supercomputing*, November 1996.

7. Naraig Manjikian and Tarek Abdelrahman. Fusion of loops for parallelism and locality. *IEEE Transactions on Parallel and Distributed Systems*, 8(2):193–209, February 1997.

8. John McCalpin and David Wonnacott. *Time Skewing: A Value-Based Approach to Optimizing for Memory Locality*. http://www.haverford.edu/cmsc/davew/cache-opt/cache-opt.html.

9. Nicholas Mitchell, Karin Högstedt, Larry Carter, and Jeanne Ferrante. Quantifying the multi-level nature of tiling interactions. *International Journal of Parallel Programming*, 26(6):641–670, December 1998.

10. Gabriel Rivera and Chau-Wen Tseng. Eliminating conflict misses for high performance architectures. In *Proceedings of the 1998 ACM International Conference on Supercomputing*, pages 353–360, Melbourne, Australia, July 1998.

11. Yonghong Song and Zhiyuan Li. New tiling techniques to improve cache temporal locality. In *Proceedings of ACM SIGPLAN Conference on Programming Language Design and Implementation*, pages 215–228, Atlanta, GA, May 1999.

12. Standard Performance Evaluation Corporation, Vols. 1-9. *SPEC Newsletter*, 1989-1997.

13. O. Temam, C. Fricker, and W. Jalby. Cache interference phenomena. In *Proceedings of ACM SIGMETRICS Conference on Measurement and Modeling of Computer Systems*, pages 261–271, Nashville, TN, May 1994.

14. Michael E. Wolf and Monica S. Lam. A data locality optimizing algorithm. In *Proceedings of ACM SIGPLAN Conference on Programming Languages Design and Implementation*, pages 30–44, Toronto, Ontario, Canada, June 1991.

15. Michael E. Wolf, Dror E. Maydan, and Ding-Kai Chen. Combining loop transformations considering caches and scheduling. In *Proceedings of the 29th Annual IEEE/ACM International Symposium on Microarchitecture*, pages 274–286, Paris, France, December 1996.

16. Michael Wolfe. *High Performance Compilers for Parallel Computing*. Addison-Wesley Publishing Company, 1995.

Parallel Programming with Interacting Processes

Peiyi Tang[1] and Yoichi Muraoka[2]

[1] Department of Mathematics and Computing
University of Southern Queensland
Toowoomba 4350 Australia
[2] School of Science and Engineering
Waseda University
Tokyo 169 Japan

Abstract. In this paper, we argue that interacting processes (IP) with multiparty interactions are an ideal model for parallel programming. The IP model with multiparty interactions was originally proposed by N. Francez and I. R. Forman [1] for distributed programming of reactive applications. We analyze the IP model and provide the new insights into it from the parallel programming perspective. We show through parallel program examples in IP that the suitability of the IP model for parallel programming lies in its programmability, high degree of parallelism and support for modular programming. We believe that IP is a good candidate for the mainstream programming model for the both parallel and distributed computing in the future.

Keywords: *Programming Models, Parallel Programming, Interacting Processes, Multiparty Interactions, Programmability, Maximum Parallelism, Modular Programming.*

1   Introduction

The concept of parallel computing for high performance has been around for decades. While the technology of hardware and architecture has allowed to build powerful scalable parallel machines like CM-5, SP/2 and AP3000, the software to run those machines remains scarce. Parallel programming has proved to be hard. The productivity of parallel software development is still low. One of the reasons for the gap between parallel software and machines is the lack of appropriate model for parallel programming.

The parallel programming models currently accepted include the explicit communication model, the distributed shared-memory model and the data-parallel model [2]. All these models try to deal with the fact that an individual processor of a scalable parallel machine cannot hold the entire memory space of large problems. The data space of a large problem has to be distributed among physical local memories of the parallel processors.

The explicit communication model uses the abstraction of direct communication to allow one processor to access the memory space of another processor.

L. Carter and J. Ferrante (Eds.): LCPC'99, LNCS 1863, pp. 201–218, 2000.

Careful design and implementation of parallel programs in the explicit communication model can produce efficient parallel codes. However, programming with explicit communication is proved to be tedious and error-prone, even using machine-independent interfaces such as PVM [3] and MPI [4]. This programming model is regarded as assembly language programming for parallel machines.

The distributed shared-memory model is based on the abstraction of virtual shared memory [5] built on physically distributed memories. Virtual shared memory can be implemented in hardware as in Stanford DASH machine or through software [6], providing an illusion of shared memory space. Programming with distributed shared-memory is easier than explicit communication. However, parallel programs in this model do not have enough information about data locality to facilitate compiler's optimization of memory access. The synchronization mechanism in this model usually includes barriers and locks. Barrier synchronization can be inflexible and is often stronger than necessary. Handling locks directly is tricky as shown in many thread packages such as Pthread [7] and Java [8].

In the data-parallel model [9], data domains are divided into sub-domains assigned to and operated on by different processors in parallel. The drawback of this model is that it offers little support for programming applications with irregular data sets. It is unlikely that it would become a mainstream model for general-purpose parallel programming in the future.

We believe that an ideal model for the mainstream general-purpose parallel and distributed programming should

- make programming easy (programmability),
- facilitate expressing maximum parallelism in applications (expression of parallelism), and
- support modular programming for large and complicated real-world applications (modularity).

Note that both shared-memory and explicit communication are abstractions close to machine architectures. It is hard to program at such a low level [2].

Interacting processes (IP) with multiparty interactions are a coordinated distributed programming model for interactive applications proposed by N. Francez and I. R. Forman [1]. The model has only three fundamental abstractions: process, synchronous multiparty interaction, and team and role. Processes are objects for concurrency. Synchronous multiparty interactions are objects to achieve *agreement* among concurrent processes. Agreement about values of variables and effect of synchronization is essential for reasoning about parallel and distributed programs[1]. Multiparty interactions allow processes to access non-local data with

---

[1] The authors of [1] believe that agreement is fundamental and more important than communication in distributed programming. They said:

> In order to appreciate the importance of multiparty interactions, one must understand the essence of the problem of designing and implementing concurrent systems. It is a mistake to think in terms of communication; instead, one must go beyond this narrow view and conceive the problem in terms of agre-

strong agreement. Combined with guard selection and iteration, they allow programmers to establish the agreement about the states of the parallel processes easily.

The support for modular distributed and parallel programming in IP is provided through *teams* and *roles*. A team is a module to encapsulate concurrency and interactions among the processes in it. It can be instantiated and referenced like an ordinary object. Roles in a team are formal processes to be enroled[2] by actual processes from outside of the team. Enrolements, like function calls in sequential programming models, can pass actual parameters. Therefore, teams can be used as parallel modules to build large parallel and distributed applications

The IP model is extremely powerful for programming distributed reactive applications. The purpose of this paper is to argue that IP is also an ideal model for parallel programming. In section 3, we present the IP programs for three typical problems in parallel computing to demonstrate the suitability of the model for parallel programming. We then provide the analysis and argument why the IP model is ideal for parallel programming in Section 4. We first introduce the IP model and its notations in Section 2. Section 5 concludes the paper with a short summary.

2   IP Model and Notations

In this section, we introduce the IP programming model and its notations. More details of the model can be found in [1].

2.1   Teams and Processes

In IP, a program consists of a number of modules called *teams*, one of which is the main program. Each team consists of *processes* or *roles*. The main program contains only processes. A process in a team is a separate thread of execution and it starts to run as soon as the team is instantiated. A role is a formal process to be enroled by actual processes. It starts to run only when an actual process outside the team enroles it.

The processes (or roles) of the same type share the common code and are distinguished by the indices used as the process identifier. For example, we can use $\|_{i=0,n-1}$ **process** P_i to declare n processes of type P in a team. The code for processes of P can use the index i as the process identifier for the process. One way to implement the processes of the same type in a team is to create an array of threads and use the array index as the process identifier. The code of a type of process (role) follows the process (role) declaration. For example, the code for a team T which consists of n processes of type P and m roles of type R is written as follows:

---

ement. ... Of course, communication is part of the problem, but no language can rise to the challenge without recognizing that *agreement* is an abstraction that must be achieved.

We believe that this argument also applies to parallel programming.

[2] This is a new word suggested by Francez and Forman to mean "enter a role".

team $T()$ ::

[

   $\|_{i=0,n-1}$ **process** $P_i()$ ::

     $\vdots$ (the code for processes P)

   $\|_{j=0,m-1}$ **role** R_j ::

     $\vdots$ (the code for roles R)

]

The subscripted names such as P_i and R_j are introduced to simplify the presentation of IP pseudo codes. Of course, a team can declare many process (role) types, each of which can have multiple instantiations.

The code of each process or role type is a sequence of assignments, **for** and **if** statements[3], function and procedure calls from the sequential programming model as well as *interaction statements*, and enhanced CSP-like [10] guard selection and iteration statements.

2.2 Variables

A team can declare team variables which all processes (roles) declared in the team can read and write. Therefore, team variables are shared variables in the team. Team variables also include the formal parameters of the team to be bound to actual parameters when the team is instantiated.

Apart from team variables, each process or role can declare its own local variables. These variables are "local" in the sense that (1) they can be updated only by the process which declares them and (2) they reside in the local memory space of the process. Other processes or roles in the team can read them through interaction statements to be described shortly. This implies that the scope of these local variables is the entire team. These local variables are something between shared variables and strictly local variables with the scope being the declaring processes. You can call them "controlled shared variables" or "semi-local variables", but we simply call them local variables in IP.

Quite often the processes of the same type need to declare similar local variables. Again, we can use the process identifier to distinguish them. For example, n processes of type P can declare local variables with the same name k indexed by the process identifier i as follows:

   $\|_{i=0,n-1}$ **process** $P_i()$ ::
     int k_i;

     $\vdots$ (the code for processes P)

---

[3] The original IP notations do not have **for** and **if** statements. However, they can be easily realized by using guard iteration and selection statements in IP. We include them in the IP notations to improve readability.

Again, the subscripted names k_i are used to simplify the pseudo code presentation. They can be implemented by a distributed array across the processes and k_i is actually $k[i]$.

2.3   Interaction Statement

Within a team of an IP program, the synchronization and coordination among the concurrent processes or roles are captured by *multiparty interactions*. A multiparty interaction is defined by (1) a name and (2) p parties, each of which represents an *participant* of the interaction and is characterized by the code to be executed by the participant during the interaction. (Multiparty interactions are called interactions in the rest of the paper.) A process can *participate* in an interaction by executing an *interaction statement* of format $a[...]$, where a is the name of the interaction and the square brackets enclose the code to be executed by the participating process during the interaction.

An interaction a with p parties will not be executed until there are p processes ready to participate in it.

The code within the square brackets for each participating process of the interaction is a set of assignments whose left-hand sides are local variables of the process only. The right-hand expressions can contain non-local variables of other participating processes. The execution of the interaction is atomic, meaning that the right-hand expressions use the old values of the variables involved and the new values of the left-hand variables are visible only after the interaction is completed.

```
process P ::
  int x, y;
      ⋮                    process Q ::           process R ::
                             int z;                  int w;
  x = 2;                        ⋮                       ⋮
  y = 1;                     z = 3;                   w = 4;
  a[x = z + w, y = x + z];   a[z = w + y];           a[w = x + y - z];
  print x; print y;          print z;                print w;

      ⋮                         ⋮                       ⋮
```

Fig. 1. Example of Multiparty Interaction

Figure 1 shows an example of three-party interaction named a in which processes P, Q and R participates. Processes P, Q and R have local variables $\{x, y\}$, $\{z\}$ and $\{w\}$, respectively. The three interaction statements of a are executed atomically in parallel when all the controls of P, Q and R reach them. The values of x and y printed by P after the interaction is 7 and 5, respectively. Note that the assignment to y uses the old value of x, 2, instead of the new value, 7.

Similarly, the values of z and w printed by Q and R after the interaction is 5 and 0, respectively.

The interaction in IP is an extension of rendezvous type of synchronization in Ada to allow synchronization among an arbitrary number of processes. It is also an extension of synchronous communication in Milner's CCS model [11] to allow synchronous communication among a group of arbitrary number of processes.

2.4   Guard Selection and Iteration

The IP model has CSP-like guard selection and iteration statements [10] enhanced with the interaction statements described above. The format of enhanced guard selection statements is as follows:

$$[B_1\&a_1[...] \to S_1 \square \cdots \square B_n\&a_n[...] \to S_n]$$

In the k-th guard $(1 \le k \le n)$, B_k is a boolean predicate of local variables called *guarding predicate* and $a_k[...]$ an interaction statement called *guarding interaction*; both are optional. S_k is a sequence of statements of any type.

A guard is *ready* if its guarding predicate is true. At least one guard must be ready in a guard selection statement. The guarding interaction of a ready guard is *enabled* if all the guards with the same interaction in other processes are also ready. An enabled guarding interaction can be selected for execution. If many guarding interactions in a guard selection statement are enabled, only one of them can be selected. Whether an enabled guarding interaction is actually selected depends on the result of coordination among the processes involved. If none of the enabled interactions is selected, the process is blocked. Figure 2

Fig. 2. Coordination for Selecting Enabled Interactions

shows an example of three guarding interactions, a, b and c, involving processes P, Q and R. Each of a, b and c has two parties. All the guarding interactions are enabled when P, Q and R are executing the guard selection statements, because there are no guarding predicates in the guards. However, only one of a, b and c can be selected for execution in this example. If a is selected, process Q is blocked and processes P and R execute it. Symmetrically, if b is selected to be executed by P and Q, R is blocked.

After a guarding interaction is selected and executed, the sequence of statements denoted S_k following the right arrow are executed.

The guard iteration statement is similar and of format:

$$*[B_1 \& a_1[...] \to S_1 \square \cdots \square B_n \& a_n[...] \to S_n]$$

The difference is that the enclosed guard selection will be executed repeatedly until none of the guarding predicates is true.

As an example of guard iteration, a team to encapsulate the interactions in the dining philosophers problem is shown in Figure 3(a). In this problem, a dining philosopher sitting in a round dining table needs to pick up the two forks (or chopstics) at his/her both sides before he/she can eat. Each philosopher alternates between "thinking" and "eating". In this team, we use n processes,

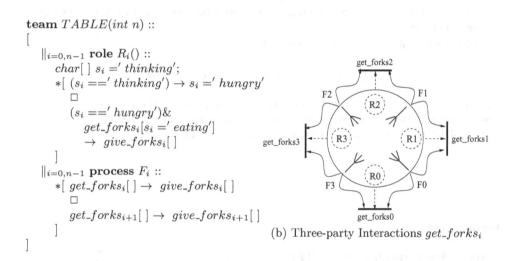

```
team TABLE(int n) ::
[
    ‖i=0,n−1 role Ri() ::
        char[ ] si =′ thinking′;
        *[ (si ==′ thinking′) → si =′ hungry′
           □
           (si ==′ hungry′)&
              get_forksi[si =′ eating′]
              → give_forksi[ ]
        ]
    ‖i=0,n−1 process Fi ::
        *[ get_forksi[ ] → give_forksi[ ]
           □
           get_forksi+1[ ] → give_forksi+1[ ]
        ]
]
```

(b) Three-party Interactions get_forks_i

(a) Team of Dining Philosophers

Fig. 3. IP Module for Dining Philosophers Problem

F_i, to simulate the n forks, because they are part of the table and ready to be used as soon as the table is set up (instantiated). To simulate more general situations where possibly different philosophers can sit at the same table position at different times, we chose to use n roles, R_i, to code the behavior of philosopher and let philosopher processes outside the team enrole these roles.

There are n three-party interactions named get_forks_i and another n three-party interactions named $give\_forks_i$ to encapsulate the interprocess synchronization[4]. Again, we use subscripted names for the interactions here to simplify presentation. The participants of interaction get_forks_i and $give\_forks_i$ are R_i, F_i and F_{i-1}[5]. Figure 3(b) illustrates the three-party interactions get_forks_i (thick bars) and their participating processes and roles.

When interaction get_forks_i is enabled and selected for execution, the philosopher process enroling (invoking) R_i gets both forks managed by F_i and F_{i-1} and eats. Since a philosopher process gets both forks in one atomic action, deadlock is not possible.

2.5 Roles and Their Enrolement

Roles in a team are formal processes to be enroled by actual processes. A role can be enroled by only one process at at a time. When multiple processes try to enrole a role, only one can succeed.

The code of the role is executed by the enroling process in the context of the team. The enroling process can pass parameters to the role, in much the same way as function calls with parameters. The enrolement is finished when the code of the role exits.

The format of enrolement statement is

$$< role\_name > @ < team\_designator > (< actual\_parameters >)$$

Figure 4(a) shows an IP main program which creates a dining table team of size n and n philosopher processes to enrole the n roles in the team repeatedly. Figure 4(b) illustrates the enrolements with dash lines for the team of size 4.

team $MAIN$ $(int\ n)$ ::
[
  team designator $table = TABLE(n)$;
  $\|_{k=0,n-1}$ **process** P_k ::
    for $(;;)$ $R_k@table()$;
]

(a) Main Program

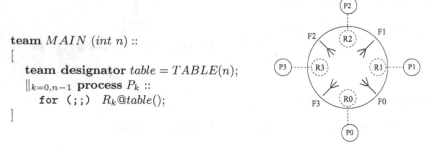

(d) Enrolements of Roles

Fig. 4. Simulation of Dining Philosophers Problem

---

[4] One weakness of IP syntax is that it lacks explicit declaration of multiparty interactions.

[5] All the addition and subtraction in the indexes are modulo arithmetic operations with respect to n.

We could create twice as many philosopher processes as the number of dining positions in the table and let two philosophers to compete to eat in the same position. The code would be as follows:

team $MAIN$ $(int\ n)$ ::
[
   team designator $table = TABLE(n)$;
  $\|_{k=0,2n-1}$ **process** P_k ::
    for (; ;) $R_{k \bmod n}@table()$;
]

3 IP Parallel Programming Examples

To demonstrate the suitability of IP for parallel programming, we present three IP parallel programs in this section. They are parallel sorting, parallel dynamic programming for optimal binary search tree and parallel successive over-relaxation (SOR). The algorithms for parallel sorting and parallel SOR are from [12]. The dynamic programming algorithm for optimal binary search tree is described in [13].

3.1 Parallel Sorting

To sort an array of n elements, $b[1..n]$, the odd-even transposition parallel sorting algorithm [12] goes through $\lceil n/2 \rceil$ iterations. In each iteration, each odd element $b[j]$ (j is odd) is compared with its even neighbor element $b[j+1]$ and the two are exchanged if they are out of order. Then each even element $b[i]$ (i is even) is compared and exchanged with its odd neighbor element $b[i+1]$ if necessary.

The algorithm can be easily implemented in IP with n parallel processes, each of which holds a data element. The compares and exchanges can be done through the interactions between neighbor processes.

The IP program for the parallel sorting is as follows, assuming the type of data to be sorted is **char**:

team $OESort(int\ n,\ char[\ ]\ b)$ ::
[
  $\|_{j=0,n-1}$ **process** P_j ::
    $char\ a_j = b[j]$;
    for (int i = 1; i <= $\lceil n/2 \rceil$; i++) {
      //odd compare and exchange
      if $(j < n - 1 \wedge odd(j))$
        $comp_j[a_j = \min(a_j, a_{j+1})]$;
      else if $(j > 0 \wedge even(j))$
        $comp_{j-1}[a_j = \max(a_{j-1}, a_j)]$;

      //even compare and exchange

```
    if (j < n − 1 ∧ even(j))
        comp_j[a_j = min(a_j, a_{j+1})];
    else if (j > 0 ∧ odd(j))
        comp_{j−1}[a_j = max(a_{j−1}, a_j)];
    }
    b[j] = a_j;
]
```

Here, each process P_j holds a data element, a_j. The odd compares and exchanges are done through interactions $comp_j$ (j is odd, i.e. $odd(j)$ is true) between processes P_j and P_{j+1}. All these compares and exchanges can be done in parallel, because they use different interactions $comp_j$ (j is odd). The even compares and exchanges are similar.

Figure 5 illustrates the execution of this IP program for a char array: $b[\,] = \{'D','C','B','A'\}$. The boxes in the figure represent the three interactions, $comp_0$, $comp_1$ and $comp_2$, reused many times. The dotted vertical lines show the progress of the processes (from top to bottom).

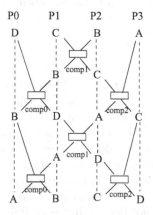

Fig. 5. Example of OESort

It can be proved that after passing through k pairs of odd and even interactions, the data held by each process is no farther than $n − 2k$ positions away from its final sorted position. After process P_j finishes $\lceil n/2 \rceil$ iterations, the data which it holds in a_j must have passed through $\lceil n/2 \rceil$ pairs of odd and even interactions. Therefore, the array is sorted when all processes are terminated.

Note that there is no global barrier synchronization across all processes in this program. The interactions and their synchronization are restricted between adjacent processes.

3.2   Optimal Binary Search Trees

As the second example, we present the IP program to find the optimal binary search tree (BST). Given n keys, $K_1 < \cdots < K_n$, with their probability of occurrence, $p_1, \cdots, p_n$, the problem is to find the binary search tree for those keys so that the average search time is minimized.

The optimal binary search tree problem is best solved by dynamic programming [13]. The optimal BST with n keys can be obtained if the optimal BSTs with $n - 1$ consecutive keys have been found. Let the optimal BST containing $j - i + 1$ keys, $K_i, \cdots, K_j$ ($j \geq i - 1$), be denoted $BST_{i,j}$ and its mean search time $MST_{i,j}$. Note that $BST_{i,i-1}$ is an empty tree and, thus, $MST_{i,i-1} = 0$. $BST_{1,n}$ can be obtained by comparing n binary search trees with the root nodes holding different keys K_l ($l = 1, \cdots, n$), and $BST_{1,l-1}$ and $BST_{l+1,n}$ as their left and right subtrees. The mean search time for $BST_{1,n}$ with root node K_l is

$$(MST_{1,l-1} + \sum_{k=1}^{l-1} p_k) + p_l + (MST_{l+1,l} + \sum_{k=l+1}^{n} p_k)$$

Therefore, the optimal mean search time $MST_{1,n}$ is as follows:

$$MST_{1,n} = \min_{1 \leq l \leq n} (MST_{1,l-1} + MST_{l+1,n}) + \sum_{k=1}^{n} p_k$$

Subtrees $BST_{1,l-1}$ and $BST_{l+1,n}$ can be found recursively in the same way. In general, the formula to find $MST_{i,j}$ is as follows:

$$MST_{i,j} = \min_{i \leq l \leq j} (MST_{i,l-1} + MST_{l+1,j}) + \sum_{k=i}^{j} p_k \qquad (1)$$

The working data structure for finding $MST(1, n)$ is an $(n+1) \times (n+1)$ upper-triangular matrix M as shown in Figure 6. The matrix element $M[i][j]$ is used to store $MST(i, j)$ ($i \leq j$). Note that the index ranges of the first and second dimensions of M are $[1..(n + 1)]$ and $[0..n]$, respectively. $M[k][k]$ ($1 \leq k \leq n$) and $M[k][k - 1]$ ($1 \leq k \leq n + 1$) are initialized to p_k and 0, respectively. The dynamic programming algorithm computes $M[i][j]$ ($1 \leq i < j \leq n$) by using vectors[6] $M[i][(i - 1)..(j - 1)]$ and $M[(i + 1)..(j + 1)][j]$ in M according to Equation (1). Figure 6(a) uses thick bars to show vectors $M[i][(i - 1)..(j - 1)]$ and $M[(i + 1)..(j + 1)][j]$, both of which contain $(j - i + 1)$ elements. Obviously, the computations of $M[i][j]$ on the diagonal $j - i = k$ ($1 \leq k \leq n - 1$) can be done in parallel, because they are data-independent. The result of the algorithm is stored in an $(n - 1) \times (n - 1)$ integer matrix R, where $R[i][j]$ ($2 \leq i \leq j \leq n$) is the index of the root node of optimal binary search tree $BST_{i,j}$.

---

[6] Given a two-dimensional matrix $A[\ ][\ ]$, we use $A[i][j_1..j_2]$ to denote the sub-vector on the i-th row ($A[i][j_1], \cdots, A[i][j_2]$). Similarly, the sub-vector on the j-th column ($A[i_1][j], \cdots, A[i_2][j]$) is denoted $A[i_1..i_2][j]$.

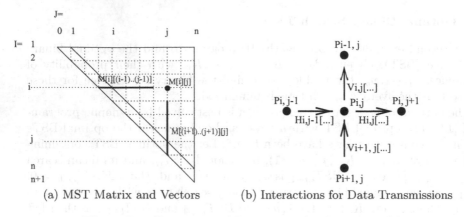

(a) MST Matrix and Vectors   (b) Interactions for Data Transmissions

Fig. 6. Data Structure and Interactions for Computing BST

We let each $MST_{i,j}$ be computed by a separate process $P_{i,j}$. The matrix M is implemented through local vectors in these processes. Each $P_{i,j}$ has two local vectors $h_{i,j}$ and $v_{i,j}$ both with $j - i + 2$ elements. The index range of $h_{i,j}$ is $[(i-1)..j]$. Its sub-vector $h_{i,j}[(i-1)..(j-1)]$ is used to store $M[i][(i-1)..(j-1)]$ and element $h_{i,j}[j]$ is used to store $M[i][j]$ computed. Similarly, the index range of $v_{i,j}$ is $[i..(j+1)]$. Its sub-vector $v_{i,j}[(i+1)..(j+1)]$ is used to store $M[(i+1)..(j+1)][j]$. Element $v_{i,j}[i]$ is the same as $h_{i,j}[j]$ and used to store $M[i][j]$.

Basically, each process $P_{i,j}$ does three things in sequence during its life time:

1. It inputs $M[i][(i-1)..(j-1)]$ from $P_{i,j-1}$ and $M[(i+1)..(j+1)][j]$ from $P_{i+1,j}$ and stores them in $h_{i,j}[(i-1)..(j-1)]$ and $v_{i,j}[(i+1)..(j+1)]$, respectively.
2. It computes $MST_{i,j}$ using (1) and stores it in both $h_{i,j}[j]$ and $v_{i,j}[i]$. It also stores the index of the root node of $BST_{i,j}$ in $R[i][j]$.
3. It outputs $h_{i,j}[(i-1)..j)]$ and $v_{i,j}[i..(j+1)]$ to $P_{i,j+1}$ and $P_{i-1,j}$, respectively.

The data transmissions from $P_{i,j}$ to $P_{i,j+1}$ and $P_{i-1,j}$ are done through the interactions named $H_{i,j}$ and $V_{i,j}$, respectively. Figure 6(b) illustrates the data transmissions in which $P_{i,j}$ is involved and the corresponding interactions used.

The IP program to compute the optimal binary search tree is as follows:

```
team OptimalBST(int n,
            float[1..n] p,
            float[1..(n + 1)][0..n] M,
            int[2..n][2..n] R)
[
   ||i=1,n-1  j=2,n  j≥i+1 process P_{i,j} ::
      float[(i − 1)..j] h_{i,j};
      float[i..(j + 1)] v_{i,j};
      boolean h_in, v_in  =  false;
      boolean h_out, v_out  =  false;
      float mst; int root;
```

```
    if (j = i + 1) { //take initial values
        h_{i,j}[(i − 1)..(j − 1)] = M[i][(i − 1)..(j − 1)];
        v_{i,j}[(i + 1)..(j + 1)] = M[(i + 1)..(j + 1)][j];
    }
    else  //input from P_{i,j−1} and P_{i+1,j}
        *[ (j > i + 1 ∧ ¬h_in) &
            H_{i,j−1}[h_{i,j}[(i − 1)..(j − 1)] = h_{i,j−1}[(i − 1)..(j − 1)] ]
            →  h_in = true

        □

        (j > i + 1 ∧ ¬v_in) &
            V_{i+1,j}[v_{i,j}[(i + 1)..(j + 1)] = v_{i+1,j}[(i + 1)..(j + 1)] ]
            →  v_in = true
    ];
```

$$mst = \min_{l=i}^{j}(h_{i,j}[l − 1] + v_{i,j}[l + 1]) + \sum_{k=i}^{j} p[k];$$
$root =$ the value of l which makes the mst above;
$h_{i,j}[j] = v_{i,j}[i] = mst;$

```
    //output local vectors to P_{i,j+1} and P_{i−1,j}
    *[ (j < n ∧ ¬h_out) & H_{i,j}[ ]  →  h_out = true
        □
        (i > 1 ∧ ¬v_out) & V_{i,j}[ ]  →  v_out = true
    ];
```

$R[i, j] = root; M[i, j] = mst;$
]

Note that the assignments in the square brackets of interactions $H_{i,j−1}$ and $V_{i+1,j}$ are vector assignment statements.

3.3   Parallel SOR

Successive Over-Relaxation (SOR) is a sequential iterative method to solve partial differential equations using finite difference. This method is also known as the Gauss Seidel method. It has faster convergence rate than the Jacobi method, which requires only $en/3$ iterations to reduce the error by a factor $10^{−e}$ for a problem of n^2 grid points. A parallel SOR algorithm called *odd-even ordering with Chebyshev acceleration* has the same convergence rate as the Gauss Seidel method [12].

Consider an $(n+2) \times (n+2)$ array $a[0..(n+1)][0..(n+1)]$ for the grid points in the parallel SOR. Each iteration has two phases to first update even grid points $a[i][j]$ ($i + j$ is even) and then odd grid points $a[i][j]$ ($i + j$ is odd), both using the values of neighbor grid points. Figure 7(a) uses hollow and filled circles to show the even and odd grid points, respectively. The updates in each phase can be done in parallel because there are no data dependencies between them. Since the computing formula and data access pattern are the same in both phases, it is better to encapsulate them in a common module. The IP model provides a

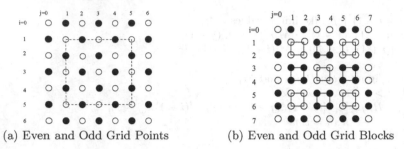

(a) Even and Odd Grid Points   (b) Even and Odd Grid Blocks

Fig. 7. Even and Odd Grid Points and Blocks

perfect framework to do this through its parallel module, team. The IP program of the team to update even or odd grid points is as follows:

Team $Update(int\ n)$
[
  $\|_{i=0,n+1}\ _{j=0,n+1}$ **role** $W_{i,j}(float\ b,\ boolean\ eo)$ ::
  $float\ a_{i,j} = b;$
  $boolean\ eastDone, southDone, westDone, northDone = false;$

  if ($(eo \wedge even(i+j) \vee \neg eo \wedge odd(i+j)) \wedge 0 < i,j < n+1$)
    $C_{i,j}[a_{i,j} = \frac{a_{i-1,j}+a_{i,j-1}+a_{i+1},a_{i,j+1}}{4}];$ //update $a_{i,j}$
  else if $(eo \wedge odd(i+j) \vee \neg eo \wedge even(i+j)$) {

    //decide which neighbors to pass $a_{i,j}$
    if $(i == 0)\ northDone = true;$
    else if $(i == n+1)\ southDone = true;$
    else if $(j == 0)\ westDone = true;$
    else if $(j == n+1)\ eastDone = true;$

    // pass $a_{i,j}$ to all neighbors
    $*[(\neg northDone \wedge i > 0)\ \&\ C_{i-1,j}[\ ] \rightarrow northDone = true$
    □
      $(\neg eastDone \wedge j < n+1)\ \&\ C_{i,j+1}[\ ] \rightarrow eastDone = true$
    □
      $(\neg southDone \wedge i < n+1)\ \&\ C_{i+1,j}[\ ] \rightarrow southDone = true$
    □
      $(\neg westDone \wedge j > 0)\ \&\ C_{i,j-1}[\ ] \rightarrow westDone = true$
    ];
  }
  $b = a_{i,j};$
]

    There are $(n+2) \times (n+2)$ formal processes, $W_{i,j}$, each of which holds a grid point value $a_{i,j}$. Depending on the situation, $W_{i,j}$ either updates its $a_{i,j}$ using the grid points of its neighbors or contributes the value of $a_{i,j}$ to the neighbors for their grid points updates. The data exchange and computing for updating

$a_{i,j}$ are done through interaction $C_{i,j}$. Boolean variables *eastDone, southDone, westDone* and *northDone* are used to make sure that the value of $a_{i,j}$ is used by all its neighbors before the code exits. If the argument *eo* of $W_{i,j}$ is true, even grid points are updated; otherwise odd grid points are updated.

The main IP program for the parallel SOR is as follows.

```
team ParallelSOR(int n, float[ ][ ] A, int e) ::
[
    //create a team of Update
    team designator update = new Update(n);

    ||ᵢ₌₀,ₙ₊₁ ⱼ₌₀,ₙ₊₁ process Pᵢ,ⱼ ::
        float aᵢ,ⱼ = A[i, j];
        for (int k = 1; k <= ⌈en/3⌉; k++) {
            Wᵢ,ⱼ@update(aᵢ,ⱼ, true);
            Wᵢ,ⱼ@update(aᵢ,ⱼ, false)
        };
        if (0 < i, j < n + 1) A[i, j] = aᵢ,ⱼ
]
```

This program creates a team of *Update* and $(n+2) \times (n+2)$ processes $P_{i,j}$. During each iteration, process $P_{i,j}$ enroles $W_{i,j}$ of the team twice with same data argument $a_{i,j}$, but different boolean values for the second argument.

The IP program above can be easily extended to the blocked parallel SOR as illustrated in Figure 7(b). The grid points are grouped into blocks. The even and odd blocks are update alternatively. The updates of all even (odd) blocks can be done in parallel. The updates of grid points within each block are done sequentially as in the Gauss-Seidel method.

4 Suitability of IP for Parallel Programming

In this section, we analyze the IP programming model and show why it is a good model for parallel programming.

A good model for parallel programming should be easy to program, allow to express the maximum parallelism and support modular programming.

4.1 Ease-of-Programming

Since processes in IP are allowed to *read* non-local variables of other processes in a team, the union of the all local variables forms a shared name space. Since each variable can be updated only by its local process, data race is not possible in this shared name space. For instance, the local variables $a_{i,j}$ of all roles in team *Update* in the parallel SOR example form a shared name space for the grid points. As in the shared memory model [5], explicit interprocess data communication is not necessary.

Another feature of memory access in IP is that it restricts non-local variables accesses in interaction statements. All the code sections outside of interactions statements use only local variables and shared team variables. Combined with the synchrony and atomicity of the interaction statement in IP, this controlled non-local variables access enables programmers to establish the agreement about values of all local variables easily. Consider the IP program for parallel SOR in Section 3.3 for instance. The programmer can easily establish the following agreement about all grid points values:

– Each grid point $a_{i,j}$ is updated $\lceil en/3 \rceil$ times, once for each iteration.
– The update of grid point $a_{i,j}$ by an even process in the k-th iteration uses the values of the grid points of its odd neighbors calculated in the $(k-1)$-th iteration (or the initial grid values if $k = 1$). The update of grid point $a_{i,j}$ by an odd process in the k-th iteration uses the values of the grid points of its even neighbors calculated in the same k-th iteration.
– The new value of each grid point $a_{i,j}$ calculated in an iteration is used to calculate the grid points of its all neighbors before it is updated in the next iteration.

Another reason for the ease-of-programming of IP is that it maintains the sequential programming model as a sub-model of computing for processes. With the agreement on the global view of the values of all local variables established by synchronous and atomic interaction statements, the reasoning about code sections outside interaction statements are purely sequential. We believe that this sub-model of sequential computation is very important for the ease of programming. While the real world is inherently parallel and distributed, each individual process in it is still sequential. Although some functions of human brains are parallel in nature (e.g., recognition of a human face), the reasoning process by human is mainly sequential. This is probably one of the reasons why some high-level parallel programming paradigms that conceal sequential computations (e.g. functional or logic programming) have never been widely accepted.

4.2   Parallelism and Efficiency

A good parallel programming model should also allow compilers to generate efficient parallel codes. To achieve this, the following qualities of the model are important.

– Programmers should be able to express the maximum parallelism in applications and algorithms.
– Programmers should be able to provide sufficient information about data distribution to enable compilers to optimize memory access and data communication.

Maximum Parallelism

The IP model supports the expression of maximum parallelism through its multiparty interaction and enhanced guard statements. Barrier synchronization

[6,14,15] in the shared-memory parallel programming model is, in fact, a special case of multiparty interaction, where all the codes in the square brackets of the interaction statements are empty and the participants include all the parallel processes. Multiparty interaction is, therefore, more flexible and enforces synchronization only among the relevant processes. In the both examples of parallel sorting and parallel SOR, synchronization occurs only among the processes that engage in the data flows and no global barrier synchronization is used. By using multiparty interactions we can minimize synchronization and maximize asynchrony in the parallel program. The cost of synchronization of multiparty interaction is also less than that of barrier synchronization involving all processes.

The IP model supports the expression of maximum parallelism also through its enhanced guard statement which allows enabled guarding interactions to be selected for execution in the nondeterministic order. For instance, in the parallel SOR example in Section 3.3 each process $P_{i,j}$ has to pass the value of its grid point $a_{i,j}$ to its neighbor processes through the interactions. The enhanced guard iteration statement does not specify any order of execution for these interactions. This allows the interactions to be completed in the shortest time. The same argument applies to the example of parallel optimal binary search tree in Section 3.2. Each process $P_{i,j}$ takes two inputs through interactions $H_{i,j-1}$ and $V_{i+1,j}$ before computing its $MST_{i,j}$. The enhanced guard iteration allows these inputs to take place in any order.

Memory Locality Information

Locality of memory access has a significant impact on the performance of parallel codes. In abstract high-level parallel programming models, the memory locality information is usually lost in the abstract address space such as virtual shared memory. The compilers have use to the run-time memory access patterns to optimize the memory access and it is a difficult task. As a result, abstract high-level models can hardly be implemented efficiently [2].

The IP model retains the memory locality information while providing the shared name space through restricted accesses in interaction statements. It seems to strike a good balance between the easy-of-programming through shared name space and the efficient compiler implementation.

4.3 Support for Modular Programming

Support for modular programming is essential for any programming model if it is to be used to develop large complicated applications. The IP model provides true parallel modules to encapsulate concurrency and interactions among the processes. Processes in a parallel module are first-class objects and can be parameterized. In the example of parallel SOR in Section 3.3 for instance, the parallel computation of new values for grid points as well as the interaction and data communication among the neighbor processes are all encapsulated in a parallel module which is used twice in each iteration.

The parallel modules in the IP model allow parallel algorithms and design patterns to be re-used. This enables parallel programmers to develop large complicated parallel applications in accordance with the well-established software engineering methodologies.

5   Conclusion

We have presented three parallel programs in the IP programming model to demonstrate the suitability of this model for parallel programming. We analyze the IP model and provide the new insights into it from the parallel programming perspective. We have shown that that IP with multiparty interaction is an ideal model for parallel programming. It suitability lies in its ease-of-programming, its capability to express the maximum parallelism and its support for modular parallel programming.

References

1. Nissim Francez and Ira R Forman. *Interacting Processes – A Multiparty Approach to Coordinated Distributed Programming.* Addison-Wesley, 1996.
2. D.B. Skillicorn and D. Talia. Models and languages for parallel computation. *ACM Computer Surveys,* 30(2):123–169, June 1998.
3. A. Geist, A. Beguelin, J. Dongarra, and W. Jiang at el. *PVM: Parallel Virtual Machine - A User guide and Tutorial for Network Parallel Computing.* MIT Press, 1994.
4. W. Gropp, E. Lusk, and A. Skjellum. *MPI: Portable Parallel Programming with the Massage Passing Interface.* MIT Press, 1994.
5. K. Li and P. Hudak. Memory coherence in shared virtual memory systems. *ACM Transactions on Computer Systems,* 7(4):321–359, 1989.
6. C. Amza, A.L. Cox, S. Dwarkadas, and P. Keleher at el. Treadmarks: Shared memory computing on networks of workstations. *IEEE Computer,* 29(2):18–28, 1996.
7. Bradford Nichols, Dick Buttlar, and Jacqueline Proulx Farrell. *Pthreads Programming: POSIX Standard for Better Multiprocessing.* O'Reilly Associates, Inc., 1996.
8. Doug Lea. *Concurrent Programming in Java: Design Principles and Patterns.* Addison-Wesley Longman, Inc., 1996.
9. High Performance Fortran Forum. High performance fortran language specification. *Scientific Programming,* 1(1-2):1–170, 1993.
10. C.A.R. Hoare. *Communication Sequential Processes.* Prentice Hall, 1985.
11. Robin Milner. *Communication and Concurrency.* Prentice-Hall, 1989.
12. Michael J. Quinn. *Designing Efficient Algorithms for Parallel Computers.* McGraw-Hill Book Company, 1987.
13. C.H. Nevison, D.C. Hyde, G.M. Schneider, and P.T. Tymann. *Laboratories for Parallel Computing.* Jones and Bartlett Publishers, 1994.
14. Peter Carlin, Mani Chandy, and Carl Kesselman. The compositional c++ language definition. Technical Report http://globus.isi.edu/ccpp/lang_def/cc++-def.html, California Technology Institute, 1993.
15. Parallel Fortran Forum. Parallel fortran from x3h5, version 1. Technical report, X3H5, 1991.

Application of the Polytope Model
to Functional Programs

Nils Ellmenreich, Christian Lengauer, and Martin Griebl

Fakultät für Mathematik und Informatik
Universität Passau
{nils,lengauer,griebl}@fmi.uni-passau.de

Abstract. We propose an approach to the static parallelization of functional programs. In past work, implicit parallelism in functional programs has mostly been dynamic, i.e., implemented by parallel graph reduction. In a special application domain, scientific computing, a static parallelization method has been successful, which is based on a mathematical execution model, the polytope model. Since scientific computations are usually phrased imperatively, the study of the polytope model has focused on imperative programs. We show that the polytope model also applies to functional programs.

We describe the prerequisites for adapting the polytope model to Haskell, a non-strict functional language. Automatically generated parallel code in a subset of Haskell consists of instructions for an abstract parallel machine (APM). In future work, APM code can be translated further to native code for a parallel machine.

We demonstrate a parallelization in the polytope model on a functional program for LU decomposition.

1 Introduction

Many benefits of functional programming languages have been stressed and exploited, but one expectation, the easy exploitation of implicit parallelism, has not yet been fulfilled. Based on the dominance of dynamic data structures in functional programs, the dominant approach to implicit parallelism has been dynamic as well, mainly via parallel graph rewriting [24]. Problems with the fine granularity of the generated parallelism and the overhead caused in detecting and administering it, have posed a serious challenge to significant gains in performance.

In one specific domain of imperative programming, scientific computation, a static approach to the detection and exploitation of implicit parallelism has made much progress recently. This progress is based on the use of a mathematical model, the polytope model [10,18], which happens to be a suitable basis for automatic optimizing search methods for the best parallelism with respect to some objective function like execution length, number of processors, number of communications or communication links, etc.

L. Carter and J. Ferrante (Eds.): LCPC'99, LNCS 1863, pp. 219–235, 2000.

Many scientific algorithms are based on matrices. This is where the polytope model excels. Many (not all) matrix algorithms can also be easily formulated in a functional language – even more simply if the language has a non-strict semantics, since no total evaluation order need be defined. This circumstance is quite helpful in the parallelization process, since a total order would stand in its way, anyway. Therefore, we can benefit on two accounts from the use of a non-strict functional language: simplicity of programming and simplicity of parallelization.

Since a matrix is more suitably represented as a static array than a dynamic list, we need a functional language which supports the array. Our choice is the predominantly non-strict functional language Haskell [23]. The sequential efficiency of Haskell's multi-threaded single-assignment arrays is far behind imperative implementations, but the final result of our parallelization will be imperative target code with the usual, efficient single-threaded array implementation.[1]

We demonstrate by example that the formal specification of a scientific problem can be stated immediately in a functional language –more directly than in an imperative language– and that the polytope model can be used to derive a parallel implementation which incurs no run time overhead in detecting the parallelism.

2   The Basics of the Polytope Model

The polytope model provides a framework for the automatic parallelization of specific parts of a program. For traditional imperative languages, these are loop nests with array computations in the body. Here, we consider an equivalent control structure in functional languages, the *array comprehension* [7]. It describes a list of index-value pairs which initalizes an array. The list is in comprehension form, similar to the mathematical set notation. As an example, the comprehension [(a,2*a) | a <- [1..10]] yields a list of ten pairs, the second member having the double value of the first. Our joint name for both of these iterative structures is *loop nest*.

The characteristics of an program fragment suitable for treatment with a parallelizer based on the polytope model are:

- The program is a loop nest whose body consists of array definition(s).
- Loop bounds and array index expressions are affine and may contain other variables which are constant within the loop nest.
- Other than array definitions, only conditionals/guards and function calls are analyzed in the loop body. In the imperative parallelization, the latter are treated as read and write accesses to all parameters.

The determination of the parallelism inherent in the loop nest and the generation of semantically equivalent, parallel code proceed as follows:

---

[1] Here, we only get to a prototype in Glasgow Parallel Haskell, but APMs will get us further.

- Data dependences are calculated. They associate accesses of different operations on the same array element. If such dependences exist, they impose a partial ordering on the operations. A sequential loop nest is in fact a specific traversal of the *index space*, a subset of $\mathbb{Z}^n$ with one point for each combination of loop variable values, which preserves this ordering.
- The task of "scheduling" is to find a function mapping all operations to points in time. This is also called the *time mapping*. The optimization aspect is to map every operation to the earliest possible time without violating the data dependences. If there is any parallelism in the program, there will be more than one operation scheduled at the same time.
- The dual mapping, the "allocation", assigns the operations to specific processing elements (PE). This is called the *space mapping*. One goal is to optimize data locality on the PEs, thus reducing communication. Ideally, one would like this to be adjusted to the schedule for optimal results, but in general this is not feasible.
- A code generation procedure performs a program transformation of the original source code into parallel target code by using the *space-time mapping*.

Intuitively speaking, the index space of the original loop nest is skewed by means of a coordinate transformation in such a way that there exist some dimensions to which no dependence arrows are parallel. These dimensions may be enumerated in parallel, the others are enumerated in sequence. The resulting loop nest has an time-optimal schedule with respect to the restrictions of the model.

3   The Polytope Model in Action

The parallelization of our example, LU decomposition, has been a subject of study before. Chen [3] used the polytope model to transform uniform recurrence equations to make space and time explicit. Our source program is closer to the problem specification than Chen's recurrence equations are. It contains non-uniform dependences, which is an increased challenge not only for the space-time mapping [8] but especially for the generation of parallel code [13].

We use Haskell and its array comprehensions in our demonstration. Currently, the comprehension notation is required for the syntactic analysis of the source program. We have a loop parallelizer, LooPo [12], which comprises a test suite for different parallelization strategies based on the polytope model. It can parallelize loop nests written in Fortran or C. Some steps of the parallelization process (dependence analysis, scheduling, allocation) are language-independent; the respective modules can be used for our purposes, and we have done so in this example.

3.1   The Example: LU-Decomposition

Our example algorithm is the LU decomposition of a non-singular square matrix $A = (a_{ij})$, $(i, j = 1, \ldots, n)$. The result consists of one lower triangular matrix

```
lu_decomp:: Array (Int,Int) Float -> (Array (Int,Int) Float,
                                      Array (Int,Int) Float)
lu_decomp a = (l ,u)
  where
  l:: Array (Int,Int) Float
  l = array ((1,1), (n,n))
    [ ((i,j), a!(i,j) - sum [ l!(i,k)*u!(k,j) | k <- [1..j-1]])
     | i <- [1..n], j <- [1..n] , j<=i ]

  u:: Array (Int,Int) Float
  u = array ((1,2), (n,n))
    [ ((i,j), (a!(i,j)-sum [ l!(i,k)*u!(k,j) | k <- [1..i-1]])/l!(i,i))
     | j <- [2..n], i <- [1..n], i<j ]

  (_ , (n, _)) = bounds a
```

Fig. 1. Haskell code for LU decomposition

$L = (l_{ij})$, with unit diagonal, and one upper triangular matrix $U = (u_{ij})$, whose product must be A. L and U are defined constructively as follows [11]:

$$l_{ij} = a_{ij} - \sum_{k=1}^{j-1} l_{ik} u_{kj}, j \leq i, \ i = 1, 2, \ldots, n$$

$$u_{ij} = \frac{a_{ij} - \sum_{k=1}^{i-1} l_{ik} u_{kj}}{l_{ii}}, j > i, \ j = 2, \ldots, n$$

The Haskell implementation used for this example is shown in Figure 1.

3.2 Dependence Analysis

Data dependences between computations impose a partial order which any evaluation order must follow. The aim of the dependence analysis is to obtain this partial order by inspecting the source code. We present a simple algorithm to determine the dependences between array elements in array computations of a Haskell program.

The array elements in Haskell are usually defined by an array comprehension. Within this definition, other arrays may be used, making the relation *depends_on* transitive. In the case of mutually recursive definitions, the induced graph of this relation contains a cycle. The aim is now to find all weakly connected components within this graph, as all arrays within such a component set are in a dependence relation and, therefore, their computations are parallelized simultaneously.

The first task is to determine these array component sets, given the Haskell program. This is done by the algorithm in Figure 2. The algorithm is most conveniently presented in an imperative style, with one informal "statement" per line.

Input: – Haskell-program with array definitions
Output: – Array component sets S_i, $i \in \mathbb{N}$

1. Construct a list L of all arrays in the program.
2. **while** there exists an unmarked array A in L **do**
3.   Construct the weakly connected component
          S_A of arrays which includes A.
4.   Mark all arrays of set S_A in list L
5. **output** all S_i

Fig. 2. Array component set determination

The second task is to determine all dependences within a set. They will be used later on for the parallelization of all computations in the set. The informal algorithm for the dependence analysis is presented in Figure 3.

Input: – Haskell-program with array definitions
              – Component set S
Output: – Set of all dependences with index spaces of set S

1. **foreach** array A in S
2.   **foreach** array A' of S used in the definition of A
3.   construct a dependence A' $\rightarrow$ A; add it to set D,
              together with appropriate index space.
4. **output** D

Fig. 3. Dependence Analysis Algorithm

The determination of the index space in Step 3 has to consider possible boolean restrictions of generators in Haskell's list comprehension. The original polytope model [18] is restricted to index spaces with affine bounds. For simplicity, we use this model in the context of this paper, i.e., the predicates may only be affine relations of index variables. Extensions of the polytope model can deal with general **IF** statements [5], which correspond to arbitrary boolean predicates in our context.

Arr	No	Source	Dest.	Restr.	Restricted Index Space
L	1	$l(i,k)$	$l(i,j)$	$j \le i$	$(i,j,k) \in \{1,\ldots,n\} \times \{1,\ldots,i\} \times \{1,\ldots,(j-1)\}$
	2	$u(k,j)$	$l(i,j)$		
U	3	$l(i,k)$	$u(i,j)$	$i < j$	$(i,j,k) \in \{1,\ldots,(j-1)\} \times \{2,\ldots,n\} \times \{1,\ldots,(i-1)\}$
	4	$u(k,j)$	$u(i,j)$		
	5	$l(i,i)$	$u(i,j)$		

Fig. 4. Dependences in the LU example

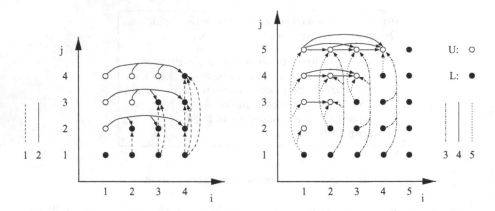

Fig. 5. Dependences between array elements

When applying the dependence algorithm to the LU example, we obtain one component set S comprising A and the two mutually recursive arrays L and U, both requiring elements of A; see Figure 4. This set of dependences describes a partial order on the index space of L and U. The figure contains, for each array, the referenced array elements (of itself and others), the restriction imposed on the original array's domain definition (an affine relation) and the restricted index space of the dependence. To get an idea of the structure of the dependences, Figure 5 contains a graphical presentation of the data space with L's dependences on the left and U's dependences on the right. The numbers next to the different types of lines in the legend correspond to the dependence numbers in Figure 4. The reason for the different dimensionality of data and index space is in our case the intermediate list generated by k, which is summed up. Dependences and index spaces are input for a scheduling algorithm which is described in the next section.

3.3 Schedule and Allocation

Using the Feautrier scheduler [8] of LooPo to calculate an optimal schedule for the dependences above, we obtain:

$$\theta_l(i,j) = 2 * (j - 1)$$
$$\theta_u(i,j) = 2 * (i - 1) + 1$$

This schedule honours the fact that the definitions of L and U are mutually recursive, so that their overall computation is interleaved.

The mapping of computations which are performed at the same time to virtual processors is defined by the allocation function. Finding a valid function is not difficult, since every mapping from the set of parallel computations to the natural numbers will do. The difficulty is to find a sensible function which minimizes the number of communications. This is done by placing dependences on single processors, i.e., allocating a computation on the same processor as a previous computation it depends on. Then, the data item can simply stay in the local memory of the processor. Up to now, no provably optimal algorithm for generating an allocation has been found, but some heuristic algorithms have been proposed [9,6].

We use LooPo's Feautrier allocator to compute suitable allocation functions for the LU example:

$$\sigma_l(i,j) = i$$
$$\sigma_u(i,j) = j$$

Now we combine schedule and allocation to a single transformation matrix, which is used to perform a coordinate transformation of the index pairs (i,j) into (t,p), which corresponds to the enumeration of time and processors. The scheduler generates a schedule for each computation so that we have two matrices, one for L and one for U. Generally, the relation $T \cdot \binom{i}{j} + d = \binom{t}{p}$ holds, in this case, denoting a mapping from the index space $\{(i,j) \mid (i,j) \in \mathbb{N}_+^2\}$ to the target space $\{(t,p) \mid (t,p) \in \mathbb{N}^2\}$. We obtain:

$$T_L = \begin{pmatrix} 0 & 2 \\ 1 & 0 \end{pmatrix} \;;\; d_L = \begin{pmatrix} -2 \\ 0 \end{pmatrix} \;;\; T_U = \begin{pmatrix} 2 & 0 \\ 0 & 1 \end{pmatrix} \;;\; d_U = \begin{pmatrix} -1 \\ 0 \end{pmatrix}$$

This matrix presentation combines the data necessary for the coordinate transformation.

To see the effect on the index space, Figure 6(a) presents the computations of L and U in a single index space (their domains do not intersect, so that they could even be stored in a single matrix). In this example, we choose a value of 5 for n. The data points which are independent of each other lie on the same dotted schedule line. The target space in Figure 6(b) depicts the points after the coordinate transformations. Data items with the same schedule now have the same value t, meaning that they are computed at the same time. Thus, as a result of the parallelization, the computation of the LU decomposition has been accelerated from 25 to 9 virtual time units (n^2 compared to $2n - 1$), where one unit is the time to compute a single data item. This time unit depends on the level of abstraction we have chosen here. In the Haskell program in Figure 1, each computation of L and U contains the summation of a list whose length is $O(n)$. Taking this into account, a refined parallel solution requires about $3n$ time units, which corresponds to Chen's solution [3].

3.4   Space-Time Mapped Haskell Code

At this point, we have analyzed the source program to obtain a set of parallelizable array definitions, we have determined the data dependences between array elements, and we have found scheduling and allocation functions to specify when and where computations are to be performed. The final task is the generation of a parallel target program, which is semantically equivalent to the source program, by using schedule and allocation to specify the parallel behaviour explicitly.

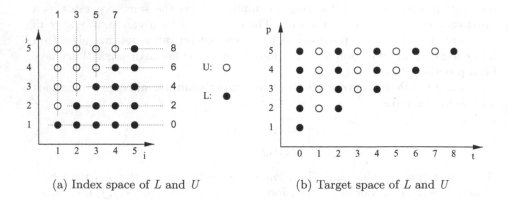

(a) Index space of L and U (b) Target space of L and U

Fig. 6. Before and after the space-time mapping

In the polytope model, the central step in the transformation of the source program into a parallel target program is the space-time mapping, as specified by the schedule and allocation. This coordinate transformation yields new names for the comprehension variables, as they now denote processor number and time.

Figure 7 contains the result of the coordinate transformation for our example, as defined in Section 3.3. This is still pseudocode, although it is legal Haskell and it can be executed with the same results as the program in Figure 1. It does not contain explicit directives for parallelism or communication.

```
lu_decomp_trafo_sy:: Array (Int,Int) Float -> (Array (Int,Int) Float,
                                               Array (Int,Int) Float)
lu_decomp_trafo_sy a =  (l ,u)
  where
  l:: Array (Int,Int) Float
  l = array ((1,1), (n,n))
    [((p,t'div'2+1) , a!(p,t'div'2+1)
                      - sum ([ l!(p,k)*u!(k,t'div'2+1)
                              | k <- [1..t'div'2]]))
     |t <- [0,2..(2*n-2)], p <- [t'div'2+1..n], t'div'2+1 <= p]

  u:: Array (Int,Int) Float
  u = array ((1,2), (n,n))
     [(((t+1)'div'2, p), (a!((t+1)'div'2, p)
                          - sum ([ l!((t+1)'div'2,k)*u!(k,p)
                                  | k <- [1..(t-1)'div'2]]))
        / l!((t+1)'div'2, (t+1)'div'2))
      | t <- [1,3..(2*n-3)], p <- [(t+3)'div'2..n], (t+1)'div'2 < p]

  (_ , (n, _)) = bounds a
```

Fig. 7. Transformed Haskell code for LU decomposition

4   Abstract Parallel Machines

Our aims were to choose a framework which is flexible enough to be adapted to the specific needs of our parallelization method and which allows for sufficient possibilities to tune the result. We believe that a suitable collection of abstract parallel machines (APMs) [22] fits these needs best. The idea is to perform a sequence of program transformations, each being a bit more specific, to convert an abstract presentation of an algorithm into low-level executable code for a parallel machine.

Each machine has a dedicated instruction set. It is possible to design a family of APMs, each coded in Haskell and on a different level of abstraction. The semantic equivalence of two APMs can be proved via equational reasoning. Then, APM programs equivalent to the source program can be derived automatically and are executable at any level of abstraction.

At certain levels of abstraction, different APMs may reflect different design options regarding implementation details not visible before. Then, the family of APMs can be arranged in a tree structure, which may be extended to an acyclic directed graph. The executability of every APM program is very important to us since it makes the difference between a monolithic compiler and our APM framework, where every intermediate stage is accessible and examinable. An important part of this work will be the comparison of effects of different design decisions.

The general APM model introduced by [22] comprises a set of *sites*, representing abstract processors, which have an internal state and a computation function, and which may communicate asynchronously.

Figure 8 depicts the structure of the APM model. It does not fit cleanly into Flynn's taxonomy. It is possible to write a synchronous parallel program in SPMD fashion, as well as asynchronous MIMD code. However, the full generality of MIMD cannot be achieved since the general communication pattern could be non-deterministic, possibly causing deadlock, and Haskell is deterministic. This is no drawback since we avoid non-determinism by statically generating a deterministic communication pattern.

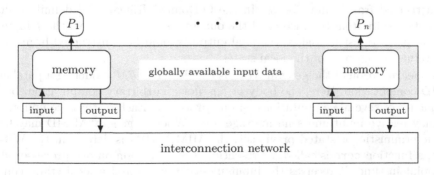

Fig. 8. Structure of the APM

The higher-level APMs can be implemented directly in sequential Haskell – leaving it to the lazy run time system to find the correct evaluation order, which is determined by the data dependences on the computations and communications. The evaluation control has to be made explicit when the code is compiled for a parallel architecture. The advantage of this approach is that code with an undetermined degree of parallelism can already be expressed on an APM. On the other hand, the drawback is that information about explicit parallelism, in case it exists already, is not expressed and has to be kept separate from the code. Nevertheless, the use of APMs allows for combination with other techniques while maintaining the potential of incorporating dynamic (i.e., not statically determined) methods into the space-time mapping model.

4.1   Formal Specification of an APM

The global function in the APM framework, `parop`, represents a parallel operation. It requires the local state for each processor, which contains all local data, and the overall system input, which is arranged in a list since it may be more than one item. The outputs are local states after the computation paired with the output of each processor, which together comprise the result of the operation.

Without going into much detail, `parop` calls two families of functions: f_i and g_i for every processor i. f_i is the *site computation function*, taking the initial state and the input for processor i and yielding the final state and the output. Here, the output can be viewed as interprocessor messages. The distribution of these messages is performed by the *coordination function* g_i, which uses the system input and all outputs (messages) of the fs and generates the input for processor i. The list comprehension calling the f_i can be thought of being parallel, although in a sequential setting it may not be. The data dependence graph on the functions is cyclic – each f-input is constructed from the collection of all f-outputs. Haskell's lazy run time system has to work out a legal evaluation order and the programmer must make sure that there is one. As we have seen in Section 2, our parallelization technique is quite helpful in that it parallelizes the source program with respect to the data dependences. Finally, `parop`'s output is constructed from a function g_0. In the O'Donnell/Rünger [22] definition, it draws its results from the history of the outputs of f_i. In our view, the f-input and -output are just messages, the final output should be constructed from the final values, being part of the local states.

A specialization of the general APM is the *MIMD APM* modeling a parallel MIMD computation. Here, the body of f is not an arbitrary computation, but a sequence of several computations on one processor. Each of these computations may receive input and send messages out. Whereas general MIMD may be non-deterministic, as stated previously, the MIMD APM is deterministic. Within f, a function `core` is called, representing a computation on one processor at one point in time. It receives the input message queue and a local state, consumes part of the input, and returns the unconsumed input, the updated state and some output messages. All message passing is subject to lazy evaluation.

```
parop:: [State] -> [SysInput] -> ([State], [SysOutput])
parop ss xs = (sis, ys)
   where (sis,ais) =
               (unzip [ f proc (state, g i v)
                       | (proc,state) <- (zip [p_lower..p_upper] ss)])

            -- Here is a change of the APM definition
            -- we want to retrieve the final output from the final
            -- local states, not the history of communications
            ys:: [SysOutput]
            ys =  g_0 sis
            v:: ([SysInput],[F_Output])
            v = (xs,ais)
```

Fig. 9. The parop-function of the MIMD APM

Our implementation of the MIMD **parop** is shown in Figure 9. Instead of providing a separate implementation of f and g for every processor, we employ the SPMD model and enrich these functions with an additional parameter denoting the processor number. Whether an APM is instantiated with a user program via insertion of functions into a Haskell template or by parameterization of all program-dependent parts is, in our view, an implementation detail.

4.2 LU-Decomposition on the MIMD APM

Recall that the result of a parallelization based on the polytope model is a space-time mapping of operations, which can be used directly to construct MIMD code. The implemented MIMD APM has a one-dimensional processor field – there is one space and one time dimension. In case the parallelization process produced more than one of either dimension or more processors than physically available, a separate tiling [16] phase is necessary. The number of processors can remain a variable until the start of execution of the program. Our example requires only one dimension of each and we assume, for the sake of simplicity, that enough processors are available.

Therefore, specializing the MIMD APM for our parallelized version of the LU decomposition goes like this:

- Define types for state, input and output of both the system and the f functions.
- Implement the f functions with the computation and code to consume the input; return the output.
- Implement g to reflect the specific communication pattern.

As for the types, the state comprises the three arrays A, L and U; system input is just the dimension of the array; input and output type of f range over messages, each containing a computed value of either L or U. Our definition of some of the types is presented in Figure 10.

```
-- Arrays A, L and U
type State =
    (Array (Int,Int) Float,Array (Int,Int) Float,Array (Int,Int) Float)

-- dimensionality of A
type SysInput = Int

-- here: the locally computed row of L resp. U
type SysOutput = ([((Int,Int), Float)], [((Int,Int),Float)])

type Msg = Value
-- value is a pair: (source time, (index, value))
type Value = (Time, ((Int,Int), Float))

type F_output_item = Value
type F_input_item = Msg

type F_Input = [F_input_item] -- Type of Input of f's
type F_Output = [F_output_item] -- Output of one f

-- input type for core function
type Core2Core = (State,F_Input,F_Output)

f :: Proc -> (State, F_Input) -> (State, F_Output)
f p (inp_state, input) =  (final_state, foutput)
    where
    old_to_new_state:: [Core2Core -> Core2Core]
    old_to_new_state = [ core p time
                       | time <- [t_lower..t_upper]]

    states:: [Core2Core]
    states = foldl combi
                [(inp_state,input,empty_foutput)] old_to_new_state

    combi:: [Core2Core] -> (Core2Core -> Core2Core) -> [Core2Core]
    combi [] f = error "combi: empty state"
    combi ss@(x:xs) f = ((f (head ss))):ss

    (final_state, foutput) =
            case (head states):: Core2Core of
                (state,[], output) -> (state, output)
                otherwise -> error "f: unconsumed input mesgs!"
```

Fig. 10. Excerpts of MIMD APM Code

Besides **parop**, the most interesting function is f, which initiates the sequence of MIMD computations on one processor. To do that, the function **core** is called, which performs the computation at a given space-time point. **core** is the central expression of the user's array comprehension, in imperative terms the *loop body*. Partially applied, (**core p time**) has type **Core2Core -> Core2Core**. The input (and output) type contains values which are passed from *core to core*, namely local state and message queues. The first list comprehension constructs a list of these functions, where the output of one has to be fed as input into the next one. The fold operation does exactly that. Its result is a prepended list of states whose first element is the final state after all computations have finished. This last state is returned and contributes to the **parop** output.

The complete Haskell program for LU decomposition on the MIMD APM can be obtained from us on request. In another project, our group is already developing a parallelizing compiler for divide-and-conquer programs in a Haskell-like language [15], so that we are confident in pursuing this goal with Haskell APMs and the polytope model.

4.3   More APMs

At this point, we have generated the code by hand. We are going to design a few more APMs at lower levels of abstraction, down to the level of C. The goal is that a parallelizing compiler will perform the successive translations along the sequence of APMs automatically. This approach has the advantage that, although one family of APMs is used for a restricted class of problems, other families for different problem classes can be defined, and APMs of distinct families can be combined at some lower level. This helps to integrate different parallelization techniques into a single system and support the parallel implementation of a general-purpose language.

Figure 11 depicts the structure of APMs needed by a parallel compilation system. In this paper, we have followed the path to the right. From the MIMD APM, it might be advantageous to devise several more intermediate APMs until the target language C+MPI is reached.

Up to now, no specific cost model has been designed to direct and evaluate the APM transformations. However, we believe this to be of minor importance since we rely on the optimality of the polyhedral model, albeit on the conceptual level.

5   Experimental Results

When compiling down to executable code, the APM tree enables us to aim at more than one target language and, thus, compare different ones. The polytope model provides us with very specific information of what is to be computed where and when. This calls for explicit parallel constructs in the target languages – otherwise parallelism may be lost. Although we would like to reuse other

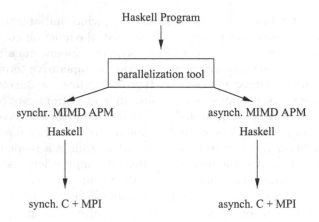

Fig. 11. Tree of APMs

code generators, most user-level parallel languages do not meet the above requirements. Therefore, in the end, we are targeting C+MPI, but this work is not yet completed.

To get some indication of whether our approach is worth-while, we have run parallel simulations of the transformed LU program of Figure 7 in Glasgow Parallel Haskell (GPH) [19]. We have split the outer list comprehension with two generators into two nested comprehensions. With the use of GPH strategies, we have declared one as sequential, the other as parallel. The simulation was performed on the *GranSim* simulator, which is part of the Glasgow Haskell Compiler (GHC). We used GHC 2.10 on a Sun SPARC to simulate an eight-processor MIMD distributed memory machine. In GPH, the run-time system is making the decision of whether a parallel annotation leads to a new thread and whether this thread is allocated a dedicated processor to gain parallelism. Despite the overhead this involves, the simulation with a 30×30 input array yielded significant amounts of parallelism. Preliminary experiments indicated an average parallelism of 3.6 to 4.9 on eight processors, depending on the simulated machine's properties. While we are aware that a simulation contains a lot of uncertainties, this gives us the confidence that we are on the right track.

6   Related Work

Not surprisingly, the combination of functional and parallel programming is a popular topic of research. We are interested in an automatic parallelization.

Probably most relevant for scientific computing is SISAL [2], a strict and lately even higher-order language developed at Lawrence Livermore National Labs, which was designed to motivate former FORTRAN programmers to use the functional programming paradigm to gain reliability and expressive power without losing too much efficiency. SISAL lacks several features of a modern functional language like an advanced type system with polymorphism. Also,

SISAL has a strict semantics. We use a non-strict semantics, which helps in supporting array parallelism in the presence of referential transparency [7].

Another project aimed at scientific computing was Crystal at Yale University [4]. Similarly to parallel versions of Fortran used in scientific computing today, Crystal is based on the principle of data alignment, but in a more general way. This admits ideas of the polytope model, but Crystal does not contain an optimizing search for a schedule or allocation. The target language of Crystal is Fortran or C with communication directives. Crystal also supports parallelization outside the polytope model, e.g., on trees. Some primitive optimizations can be performed automatically, like the parallelization of reductions.

More tightly connected with the polytope model is ALPHA [17], a functional language based on recurrence relations which is not general-purpose and does not use sophisticated allocation algorithms. Originally, ALPHA was meant to support VLSI chip design, with target code in VHDL. Later a preliminary code generation backend for C was drafted [25,26]. Current intentions are to carry this work further and also link ALPHA more earnestly to general-purpose functional programming.

NESL [1] is a language which permits the exploitation of implicit parallelism contained in nested list comprehensions and some built-in functions. Our approach is different in that it can parallelize different expressions together and is not restricted to lists. NESL's parallelism is dynamic, ours is static.

The MIT group of Arvind and Nikhil first designed Id [20], a data flow language whose main contributions were the introduction of I- and M-structures, which are used to provide efficient, indexed data structures for a parallel environment at the cost of destroying some semantic properties of the language. More recent work adapts the ideas of Id to a Haskell dialect, pH [21] (parallel Haskell). The language differs from Haskell in replacing lazy with lenient evaluation and accepting impurities in the referential transparency for the sake of efficient parallelism. The main difference to our work is that we maintain the purely functional semantics of Haskell.

Finally, Glasgow Parallel Haskell (GPH) [19] is an extension of the Glasgow Haskell Compiler and uses explicit annotations to evaluate expressions in parallel. We have and will use it for prototyping, but since it addresses the entire Haskell language via parallel graph rewriting, we hope that we can be more efficient for our restricted application domain.

7   Conclusions

We have attempted to demonstrate that the polytope model has the potential of supporting functional parallelism in the application area of scientific computing. The use of this model can free the programmer from having to think about parallelism. Remember that Figure 1 is where the coding work of the programmer is going to stop. The rest of the development will be an automatic process, maybe, with a few hints of the programmer on what choice to take.

Here, the application domain we have focussed on is scientific computing. As mentioned before, we are also applying the static space-time mapping approach to another domain, divide-and-conquer algorithms [14,15], but not employing the polytope model, since it yields at best linear execution time. For parallel divide-and-conquer, sublinear execution time is possible. We have taken an APM-like approach by defining a hierarchy of divide-and-conquer skeletons – again, all executable functions in Haskell [15]. The most concrete skeleton can be translated directly to C+MPI.

The significance of dynamic approaches like parallel graph reduction [24] remains high. Many problems cannot be cast in the regular dependence structure which is the prerequisite for a static space-time mapping. Then there are the irregular problems whose dependence structure cannot be determined before run time.

Acknowledgements. Thanks to John O'Donnell for inspiration and helpful comments and Paul A. Feautrier for fruitful discussions. Both contacts were supported by DAAD exchange grants under the programmes ARC and PRO-COPE.

References

1. G. E. Blelloch, S. Chatterjee, J. C. Hardwick, J. Sipelstein, and M. Zagha. Implementation of a portable nested data-parallel language. In *Principles and Practices of Parallel Programming*, pages 102–111, 1993.

2. A. P. W. Böhm, R. R. Oldehoeft, D. C. Cann, and J. T. Feo. *SISAL Reference Manual, Language Version 2.0*. Colorado State University – Lawrence Livermore National Laboratory, 1992.

3. M. C. Chen. Placement and interconnection of systolic processing elements: A new LU-decomposition algorithm. In *Proc. IEEE Int. Conf. on Computer Design (ICCD'86)*, pages 275–281. IEEE Press, 1986.

4. M. C. Chen, Y. Choo, and J. Li. Crystal: Theory and pragmatics of generating efficient parallel code. In B. K. Szymanski, editor, *Parallel Functional Languages and Compilers*, Frontier Series, chapter 7. ACM Press, 1991.

5. J.-F. Collard. Automatic parallelization of while-loops using speculative execution. *Int. J. Parallel Programming*, 23(2):191–219, 1995.

6. M. Dion and Y. Robert. Mapping affine loop nests: New results. In B. Hertzberger and G. Serazzi, editors, *High-Performance Computing & Networking (HPCN'95)*, LNCS 919, pages 184–189. Springer-Verlag, 1995.

7. N. Ellmenreich, M. Griebl, and C. Lengauer. Applicability of the polytope model to functional programs. In H. Kuchen, editor, *Proc. 7th Int. Workshop on Functional and Logic Programming*. Institut für Wirtschaftsinformatik, Westf. Wilhelms-Universität Münster, Apr. 1998.

8. P. Feautrier. Some efficient solutions to the affine scheduling problem. Part I. One-dimensional time. *Int. J. Parallel Programming*, 21(5):313–348, 1992.

9. P. Feautrier. Toward automatic distribution. *Parallel Processing Letters*, 4(3):233–244, 1994.

10. P. Feautrier. Automatic parallelization in the polytope model. In G.-R. Perrin and A. Darte, editors, *The Data Parallel Programming Model*, LNCS 1132, pages 79–103. Springer-Verlag, 1996.
11. C. F. Gerald. *Applied Numerical Analysis*. Addison-Wesley, 2nd edition, 1978.
12. M. Griebl and C. Lengauer. The loop parallelizer LooPo—Announcement. In D. Sehr, U. Banerjee, D. Gelernter, A. Nicolau, and D. Padua, editors, *Languages and Compilers for Parallel Computing (LCPC'96)*, LNCS 1239, pages 603–604. Springer-Verlag, 1997.
13. M. Griebl, C. Lengauer, and S. Wetzel. Code generation in the polytope model. In *Proc. Int. Conf. on Parallel Architectures and Compilation Techniques (PACT'98)*, pages 106–111. IEEE Computer Society Press, 1998.
14. C. A. Herrmann and C. Lengauer. On the space-time mapping of a class of divide-and-conquer recursions. *Parallel Processing Letters*, 6(4):525–537, 1996.
15. C. A. Herrmann and C. Lengauer. Transformation of divide & conquer to nested parallel loops. In H. Glaser, P. Hartel, and H. Kuchen, editors, *Programming Languages: Implementation, Logics, and Programs (PLILP'97)*, LNCS 1292, pages 95–109. Springer-Verlag, 1997.
16. F. Irigoin and R. Triolet. Supernode partitioning. In *Proceedings of the Fifteenth Annual ACM SIGACT-SIGPLAN Symposium on Principles of Programming Languages*, pages 319–329. ACM, 1988.
17. H. Le Verge, C. Mauras, and P. Quinton. The ALPHA language and its use for the design of systolic arrays. *J. VLSI Signal Processing*, 3:173–182, 1991.
18. C. Lengauer. Loop parallelization in the polytope model. In E. Best, editor, *CONCUR'93*, Lecture Notes in Computer Science 715, pages 398–416. Springer-Verlag, 1993.
19. H.-W. Loidl and P. W. Trinder. Engineering large parallel functional programs. In C. Clack, K. Hammond, and T. Davie, editors, *Implementation of Functional Languages (IFL 97)*, LNCS 1467. Springer-Verlag, September 1997.
20. R. S. Nikhil. Id (Version 90.1) Reference Manual. CSG-Memo-284-2, MIT, Computation Structures Group, 1991.
21. R. S. Nikhil, Arvind, J. Hicks, S. Aditya, L. Augustsson, J.-W. Maessen, and Y. Zhou. pH Language Reference Manual, Version 1.0. CSG-Memo-369, Computation Structures Group, MIT, 1995.
22. J. O'Donnell and G. Rünger. A methodology for deriving abstract parallel programs with a family of parallel abstract machines. In C. Lengauer, M. Griebl, and S. Gorlatch, editors, *EuroPar'97: Parallel Processing*, LNCS 1300, pages 662–669. Springer-Verlag, 1997.
23. S. Peyton-Jones and J. Hughes (editors). Haskell 98, A Non-Strict, Purely Functional Language, February 1999. http://www.haskell.org/onlinereport.
24. R. Plasmeijer and M. v. Eekelen. *Functional Programming and Parallel Graph Rewriting*. International Computer Science Series. Addison-Wesley, 1993.
25. P. Quinton, S. Rajopadhye, and D. Wilde. Derivation of data parallel code from a functional program. In *Proc. 9th Int. Parallel Processing Symposium (IPPS'95)*, pages 766–772. IEEE Computer Society Press, Apr. 1995.
26. D. K. Wilde. *From ALPHA to Imperative Code: A Transformational Compiler for an Array Based Functional Language*. PhD thesis, Department of Computer Science, Oregon State University, July 1995.

Multilingual Debugging Support for Data-Driven and Thread-Based Parallel Languages

Parthasarathy Ramachandran and Laxmikant V. Kale'

Department of Computer Science
University of Illinois at Urbana Champaign
1304 W. Springfield Ave. Urbana, IL 61801
Email: kale@cs.uiuc.edu, Phone (217) 244-0094

Abstract. Current debugging support is inadequate for debugging programs written in data-driven and multithreaded parallel programming languages. Yet such languages are essential for attaining high-performance in the next generation of parallel applications, which tend to be dynamic and irregular in their structure. Also, such applications can often benefit from a multi-paradigm approach, where individual modules are programmed using different parallel paradigms to fit their computational structure. We present a methodology, and its embodiment in a debugging tool, that supports the requirements of programmers writing data-driven applications.

1 Introduction

Data driven execution is a technique that allows parallel programs to adapt to dynamically varying, often unpredictable, computation structures. In traditional programming models such as message-passing via MPI, or data-parallel (loop-parallel) programming via HPF [10] and openMP, processors typically execute actions in a relatively pre-ordained manner. Although techniques such as self-scheduled loops in OpenMP and asynchronous wild-card receives in MPI provide some support for dynamic behavior, it is often inadequate for more complex applications (See [6]). In any case, data-driven execution provides an alternative programming style specifically aimed at handling dynamic behavior adaptively.

A simple example of a data-driven paradigm is that of user-level threads that send messages to each other via the usual send-receive constructs (e.g. Chant [3]). A single processor may have a number of such user level threads. When a running thread blocks at a receive, another thread may be resumed if the data *it* was waiting for is available. Such threads allow one to express the logic of each subcomputation cleanly while overlapping the useful computation in one thread with potential idle time in another. Data driven object languages (e.g. Charm++ [9]) also provide such adaptive overlap, as do handler-based paradigms such as Split-C [2], Active Messages [14], and MultiPol [15]. Several other paradigms, such as divide-and-conquer, functional programming, and master-slave, also require the ability to schedule multiple ready entities on each processor. As the complexity of the parallel applications tackled has been increasing, the need

L. Carter and J. Ferrante (Eds.): LCPC'99, LNCS 1863, pp. 236–250, 2000.

for such data-driven paradigms has increased. Applications such as molecular dynamics and operations research, and strategies such adaptive refinement of structured and non-structured meshes, exhibit such dynamic behavior which is efficiently tackled using data-driven techniques. Further, as data-driven approaches often address distinct performance or program-structuring requirements, it is often necessary, or at least beneficial, to allow modules written using different paradigms to coexist in a single application.

One of the difficulties in developing data-driven applications is the lack of adequate debugging support for these paradigms. A number of projects have produced useful parallel debugging tools [12,13,1,11], but none of these tools adequately cater to the needs of data-driven or multithreaded applications; for example, it is not easy to examine the set of ready (user-level) threads, or the pool of method invocation messages waiting to be executed. This paper describes the debugging techniques we have developed for data-driven applications, and the tool we built that embodies them.

Our debugger allows programmers to freeze a data-driven program, to inspect its state in a language-specific manner, and to conduct source level debugging with traditional tools such as gdb in an integrated fashion. Support for multiparadigm programming is built in to the debugger framework. To provide such support for a new language (or paradigm or library), the framework provides a powerful set of hooks in the form of callbacks. The debugger, which is in use on parallel machines as well as clusters, is made easier to use via a convenient GUI interface.

In the next section we describe the general data-driven paradigm in some detail, and specifically state how multiple data-driven paradigms are supported in an interoperable fashion by the Converse runtime system. The scheduler-level debugging techniques, specifically useful for data-driven programs, are described in Section 3. The overall debugger architecture is described in Section 4. Integration of gdb-style source-level debugging in described in Section 5. The implementation issues and techniques are addressed briefly in Section 6. The paper concludes with a summary of its contributions.

2   Converse Design Overview

The Converse runtime framework was designed to support data-driven execution. It provides components that make it easy to implement new data-driven languages and paradigms, with full portability across a wide range of parallel machines (e.g, Unix, Linux and Windows workstation clusters, Origin 2000, IBM SP, Intel's ASCI Red, etc.). It allows multiple data-driven paradigms to interoperate with each other, as well as with traditional paradigms.

All data-driven languages [1] have some form of a scheduler at their core. It may be expressed as an explicit "polling" routine in MultiPol, or be implicit

---

[1]   * We will use the word "language" to mean a parallel programming paradigm, whether it is implemented as a library in an existing sequential language or as a new language with its own syntax.

as in a thread scheduler, and in *message driven execution* supported in early systems such as Charm [8]. (The original interrupt-based Active Messages can be thought of as an exception, but a common current use of active messages appears to be in the form of "optimistic active messages", which are identical to message-driven execution). Converse provides a scheduler component that can be customized if necessary, and can be explicitly invoked to support interoperability with traditional paradigms such as MPI. The scheduler interacts with a pool of "generalized messages", each of which specifies a handler function and includes arbitrary amounts of data. These messages may stand for a ready (user-level) thread, a previously posted handler, a message sent to a ready thread, or an asynchronous method invocation, for example. The mixing of multi-lingual entities in this general scheduler's queue provides for interoperability. Each "message" may, optionally, have a priority associated with it. The paradigms that do not required priorities may schedule their entities for immediate execution in FIFO order, without having to pay any overhead due to the support for priorities.

Converse provides several other components that make it easier to build a new data-driven paradigm. The load balancer module moves user-specified entities (e.g. objects) across processors as needed. A threads package, which separates the scheduler and synchronization operations from the essential thread operations (of encapsulating the stack, and supporting suspension and resumption) is especially useful for many data-driven paradigms. Also supported are global pointers with remote get and put operations, support for "clusters of SMP nodes" machine model, various mechanisms for inter-processor communication, along with many commonly needed libraries. For further details, the reader is encouraged to refer [4,5].

In the context of parallel debugging, the most important feature of the Converse system is its scheduler, and it support for multilingual handlers. In the next few sections, we describe how the debugging framework interacts with the scheduler and achieves its functionality.

3   Scheduler Level Multi-paradigm Debugging

Many issues need to be considered while providing support for debugging at the level of scheduling events. A solution needs to comprise a framework that seamlessly supports diverse programming paradigms and languages, while catering to the needs of data-driven execution.

3.1   Current Debugging Support is Inadequate

Freezing the scheduler's event loop to capture a state of the executing program on a particular (or all) processor is extremely important while debugging a parallel program.

The scheduler-event level debugging that we are proposing complements source level debugging provided by traditional tools. One question that naturally arises is: can the traditional tools (e.g. gdb) be used for this purpose? After all, the scheduler itself is another part of the code, and so one can set breakpoints inside it. However, there are several difficulties with this approach.

1. The design of the event loop of a particular higher level language (or runtime system) is not known to the application programmer. It is hence difficult to set breakpoints at a specific location to freeze the event loop.
2. Even if it were possible to set a breakpoint in the event loop, this breakpoint will be triggered for all events passing through the event loop. This makes rapid focus on the problem difficult, since the programmer will typically have to manually step through each iteration of the event loop, even when they are interested in the situation when a specific type of thread is about to be executed, or a particular method of a data-driven object is about to be called.
3. It is not enough to merely break out of execution in the event loop. All the processors are continuously sending messages to each other, and breaking out of the event loop will mean that the other administrative duties performed by the event loop will not be done. This can create other error conditions, which may make the programmer lose focus of the problem at hand.
4. In the context of a multi-paradigm program, and a genetic runtime system such as Converse, another challenge arises. The scheduler, common to all data driven paradigms/libraries/languages (simply called "languages" in the rest of the paper) being used in a given program, views the ready-to-execute entities (called "messages" for brevity) uniformly. Each one of them is presented to it as a block of memory, with a short standard-form header on it. Only the structure of this header is common across all languages. The rest of the data structure of each message (or ready-to-execute entry) is fully determined by each language itself. Thus, in case of Charm++, the message encodes the destination object, the method being invoked, and the parameters. In the entity is a ready thread, the message simply includes the thread ID. For a Chant message, it may include the message tag, and message data. So, although the scheduler has a list of all ready to run entities, there is no simple mechanism to identify and display the contents in a fashion meaningful to the user.

3.2 Our Approach

Our debugger provides the following facilities that aid scheduler level debugging.

– *Freeze-Thaw* : *Freeze* allows the program execution to be arbitrarily frozen, so that a snapshot of its state can be taken and studied. Similarly, *Thaw* allows the suspended program to continue on its execution.
– *Scheduler level breakpoints* can be set, and the program execution can be continued until breakpoints are reached.

– *Language entities* can be viewed, when the program has been paused by either of the above mechanisms. Language specific entities, like objects and messages can be inspected for their contents.

In a Converse program, requesting a *Freeze* on a processor (or all processors) would cause the Converse scheduler to stop all processing of Converse messages, and would make it active to only debugger messages. All subsequently arriving Converse messages are queued for later processing. Similarly, a *Thaw* resumes the scheduler loop.

The debugger makes the following information available to the programmer:

A static list of named ptential breakpoints where the scheduler may pause. For example, for Charm++, such a list will include a set of classname:: method name pairs, for each of the methods that can be asynchronously (i.e. via the scheduler) invoked. In a language such as Cid, this may be the list of names of functions that can be invoked via a future. Using this list, a programmer could specify a set of scheduler-level breakpoints, and allow the program to run until the breakpoint is reached. Alternatively, the programmer has the choice to step through the program execution, stopping at each scheduler-level potential breakpoint (i.e. at each scheduling event).

Once the execution on one (or all) processors has been frozen, the user may view the list of entities in the scheduler's queue on a frozen processor (for example, this may include remote method invocations, and ready threads). The user may also view the list of non-scheduler entities on that processor. These may include the set of data driven objects (in Charm++) or the set of sleeping threads, for example. Notice that, since Converse allows multi-paradigm parallel programming, these entities may be heterogeneous in their format, as they arise from multiple distinct languages. The debugger ensures that the programmer can observe entities belonging to the different languages being used in the application in a single snapshot. As the set of such entities may be large, it shows a brief 1-line header for each entity, and if the user asks, it shows the "full content" of that entity. The definition of what constitutes the brief header and what constitutes the fill content is left to the lnaguage implementor. For Charm++ scheduler entries, for example, the header shows the className::methodName pair, where as the content shows the parameter values.

3.3   Debugging Support for a New Languge

The effort to register a new language with the debugger runtime system is straightforward. *Freeze* and *Thaw* are provided by the debugger runtime itself, and hence no effort needs to be made on part of the language implementation.

The language however does need to specify how the contents of program entities will be interpreted. This is done by registering appropriate functions with the debugger runtime system. In order to define the granularity of execution steps (and consequently the list of all possible language breakpoints), the language needs to register functions that will generate the *symbol table* for the language, and will also determine, for a given message, whether it is a step point or a break point. Section 5.2 discusses the mechanism and the steps required to implement a new language in greater detail.

4   Architecture of the System

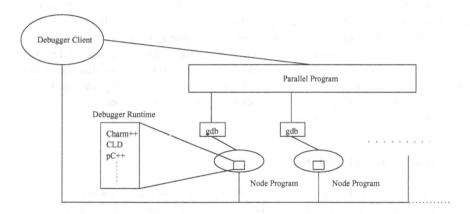

Fig. 1. System Architecture

Figure 1 details the generic architecture of the debugging framework. Further sections explain refinements to this model in the case of traditional parallel machines and the network of workstations.

The debugger client could reside on any machine that has network connectivity to the machines where the parallel program is running. The debugger client uses the Converse Client Server (CCS) Interface (see Section 6.1) to communicate with the parallel program during its execution.

The debugger runtime resides on each of the nodes of the parallel program. It is the part that communicates information back to the debugger client using the CCS interface. The gdb interface resides in tandem with the node programs. It uses ordinary TCP connectivity to communicate with the debugger client.

The major parts of the system are as follows:

Debugger Client: The debugger client is responsible for providing an appropriate user interface for high-level (scheduler event) functions, such as activating program freeze-thaw, displaying contents of parallel program entities, setting language-level (event) breakpoints, and stepping through event execution. It also provides a uniform interface for executing GDB commands, including source code view commands, setting source code breakpoints, and displaying stack traces.

Debugger Runtime: This module maintains information about the status of the executing parallel program. Node specific details (i.e., information specific to the node program executing on that processor) are periodically collected. Various parallel language-specific information, such as the contents of various language entities are provided for view. Static information, such as the symbol tables of each of the languages used, is also available. It allows the setting and reaching of language level breakpoints, and allows the programmer to step through the parallel program execution. The granularity of stepping is entirely up to the programmer. Asynchronous freezing and thawing of parallel program execution is made available to the programmer. Facilities are provided to incorporate support for any new language implemented on top of Converse.

GDB interface: This module allows the GNU debugger to attach itself to a node program, in order to permit the integration of our scheduler-level debugging facilities with traditional source level debugging support provided by *gdb*. This helps in the case of source code level debugging, where functionalities such as setting breakpoints, stepping and continuing execution, watching variables, and in general any source code level debugging action can be performed. The implementation of this module differs between the network of workstations and the traditional parallel machines.

5   Implementation Issues

We next describe a few important implementation issues. First, we describe the debugging support integrated into the Converse runtime, and then how this support can be used to implement debugging support for a new "language". Some performance optimizations necessary for smooth debugging experience are then described. The debugger framework is built using the client-server interface provided by Converse.

5.1   Debugger Runtime

The debugger runtime resides in Converse and is responsible for maintaining debugging information about the diverse currently functional entities in the parallel program. It is important to note that a Converse program is typically multilingual, and hence a large number of entities, each from different languages may be coexisting simultaneously. Information needs to be maintained about all these entities in the most efficient manner. The debugger handles two kinds of entities: scheduled entities (method invocations, ready threads, etc.) and local entities (such as objects, or function activation records).

Local entities/Objects: Languages having C++ objects as one of their abstractions use ordinary C++ polymorphism to represent the content of objects. The debugger runtime defines 2 virtual member functions of a special _object class, namely showHeader() and showContent(). Languages such as Charm++

redefine these two functions to interpret their particular language objects. The method used to interpret raw object memory is up to the implementation of the function, which may be defined by the end user. (showHeader must return a short string, whereas showContent may return a string of arbitrary length containing new-lines.

Whenever a new object (of any language) is created, it is registered with the debugger runtime. When the object is destroyed, it is deregistered. Hence the debugger runtime maintains the current functional set of objects in the system. Whenever the list of objects is desired by the debugger client, then the debugger runs through its data structures, and applies the showHeader() function to each of the registered objects. Once a particular object is selected for complete view, the debugger runtime applies the showContent() function to the object and returns it to the client.

For non-C++ languages, the objects are registered and deregistered as above, with a different registration function. At registration, the language provides names of the functions the runtime must call to identify the header and contents of individual objects.

Scheduled entities: Each scheduled entitiy is represented by a Converse message either in the scheduler's queue or the network queue. For each Converse handler registered by a language, it also registers callback functions for showing a brief header for the message and the detailed contents of the message, when needed. Whenever the client desires the list of messages present in the system queues, the runtime enumerates the system queues and runs the header function on each of the messages in the queue. This result is then returned back to the user. Once the user requests the content of a particular message, the content function is applied to it, and the result is passed back to the client program.

The debugger client may request a freeze on the program execution. When this happens, the debugger runtime moves into the frozen state, where the main event loop responds only to messages from the debugger client. All other messages (coming from other processors, or locally generated at the same processor) are queued up in a special system queue. As soon as the debugger client requests a thaw in program execution, the main event loop resumes processing ordinary messages. First the messages queued up in the special queue are processed, and the incoming messages are processed next.

Breakpoints: Each language registers its potential breakpoints by defining a *symbol table* for itself. Recall that Converse message headers include an index of the handler to be executed for each message. Each language registers one of more such handlers. But each handler may represent multiple distinct user level entities. (E.g. a single Charm++ handler is responsible for handling method invocations to all types of its objects). To allow users to set breakpoints at user level entities (such as individual methods), the system allows the language to define multiple potential breakpoints for each converse handler in the form of the symbol table.

The symbol table is the collection of all possible scheduler-level breakpoints that exist for the language. When the user requests the system's symbol table information on the client side, the debugger runtime runs through all the languages (actually, all the Converse handlers) registered, concatenates their symbol tables, and creates a comprehensive symbol table. The user then has the ability to select a subset of the displayed breakpoints as his current breakpoint list. The debugger runtime remembers each set breakpoint simply with a pair of numbers: i'th breakpoint of the j'th language.

Each new language registers its symbol table with the debugger runtime, and also provides pointers to a callback function that aid the debugger runtime to keep track of language level breakpoints.

To determine whether a particular message represents a set breakpoint, the debugger runtime passes the message to the callback function associated with its Converse handler index, which returns the relative index of the entity within the language's symbol table. This helps the system identify if that particular breakpoint is set. Thus, if the scheduler is about to schedule a "message" representing a Charm++ method invocation, it simply notices that the message belongs to "language number 3", assuming Charm++ handler's index is 3. It passes the message to the function registered by Charm++, asking it to see which breakpoint it represents. This function, written by the Charm++ implementor, understands the format of Charm++ messages, decodes the class-method pair indicated by it, looks it up in the symbol table, and returns the index in its symbol table (say 7). Now the debugger simply checks its table of set breakpoints to see if "the 7th breakpoint of the 3rd language" has been set by the user earlier, and freezes program execution on that processor if so.

In addition to implementing runtimes for data-driven languages, Converse can also be used to write parallel libraries directly. It is also possible for any such Converse library (in contrast to a language runtime) to define a set of breakpoints for the diverse messages that it handles. This is because a Converse library can be thought of as a multilingual program where each type of Converse message represents a different "language".

If the user has requested that the program continue until the next breakpoint, then the debugger runtime checks every message being processed to see if it represents a breakpoint that has been set. If it does, the debugger client is duly notified, and the program goes into the freeze state. The check ceases to happen when the user requests a program thaw.

A similar mechanism is used to implement stepping through the program execution. If program stepping has been enabled, each message being processed causes the debugger runtime to send a notification to the debugger client. The program then goes into the freeze state. A program thaw disables the stepping mode in the program.

5.2 Implementing Debugging Support for a New Language

Once a new language is implemented on top of the Converse runtime system, it is a very small step to allow debugging functionality to be integrated into the language. For each type of scheduler entity the language may generate (and enqueue in Converse's scheduler's queue), it must register functions to showHeader() and showContent(), either directly, or via the virtual inheritance mechanism mentioned above. For each runtime entity (such as objects and threads) it wants to be made visible to the programmer, it must provide such showHeader() and showContent() functions as well. Finally, it must also register a function that returns the "symbol table" — the list of scheduler-level breakpoints — and a function to be used for interpreting the scheduler entry to figure out which one of the registered breakpoints it stands for.

5.3   Performance Optimizations

A running multilingual parallel program potentially has a large number of currently functional entities. When the client freezes the program and requests state information, this large amount of information has to be sent to it, leading to several problems.

- Network delays can result in a large delay to transfer data between the parallel program and the client. Since debugger client requests are mostly blocking calls, this results in a large response time for the user.
- Large amount of data transfer also means that large amounts of memory need to be allocated. This could result in thrashing, and memory allocation failure on the parallel program side as well as the client side.
- The GUI (Java AWT) components take an inordinately long time to display large amounts of data, leading to slow response time.

A solution to this problem is *chunking*, which takes advantage of the fact that the human user is able to digest only a screenful of information at a time. Both the debugger runtime (on the parallel program side) and the debugger client obtain and display data in chunks. The client hence asks for (and displays) a small fraction of the data initially, and on demand, sends a CCS request to the debugger runtime for more data. The debugger runtime keeps track of the amount of data requested so far, and hence also has to allocate and send only small amounts of memory. This approach solves problems associated with memory allocation, network delays, and Java garbage collection, and leads to an increased response time.

Processing time for data collection by the debugger runtime is high if there are large number of currently functional entities. This is because a number of system data structures (like the Converse runtime scheduler queue) need to be traversed, and data needs to be collected for each existing entity. This leads to increased response time on the client end.

The solution to this problem is *caching*. This method exploits high user response delay. That is, there is a finite (and quite large) delay between the time the user requests a program freeze, and the point when the user requests debugging information of current functional entities in the program. The debugger runtime uses this time in collecting this information, and caching it in its data structures, so that they can be immediately returned to the client on demand. The cached data is freed once the client requests a thawing action to be performed on the program. This method results in increased response time for the user.

Other optimization mechanisms include the use of hash tables for storing debugging information in the debugger runtime. Also, when the program is run in the non-debugging mode, the debugger runtime is completely inactive, and hence no extra overhead is incurred.

5.4   Converse Client Server Interface

The debugger is implemented using Converse's Client-Server interface (CCS). This interface allows an external program to contact an executing parallel program. Once this connection is established, it can pass data into and get data out of the parallel program.

CCS Client side Protocol

- The parallel program prints out its IP address and port number to be contacted, on its standard output, which can be passed on to the intermediary automatically. Other methods for communicating this information are also feasible.
- The client calls CcsConnect(). This step is a two-way handshake between the client and the parallel program. This call allows the client to get information about contacting the individual node programs. As far as the client is concerned, the interface to the call CcsConnect() is uniform. Hence the client need not know whether the parallel program is executing on a network of workstations or a traditional parallel machine.
- The client does a CcsSendRequest() to one (or more) node programs of the parallel program. Each call to CcsSendRequest() sends a message (signifying a particular request type) to the specified node program. This call is non-blocking.
- The client does a CcsRecvResponse() from a particular node program. In this step, it waits for a reply to a previously issued request. It is important to note that the CCS Interface does not maintain any state about issued and pending requests. It is the responsibility of the client to wait at an appropriate time for an appropriate reply to an earlier request. The CcsRecvResponse() call could be blocking or non-blocking. In case of a non-blocking call, it takes an additional parameter specifying the timeout delay after which it ceases to wait for a reply.

CCS Server Side (Parallel program side) Protocol

- The parallel program needs to implement a handler that will carry out the action on receiving a particular CCS message. This handler could be an existing Converse handler, or there could be new handlers defined solely for the purpose of acting on CCS messages.
- The parallel program needs to register the above described handler with the system. This step associates the handler with the request type specified during registration. The call used for this purpose is CcsRegisterHandler().
- In case the parallel program needs to send a reply to the client, it uses the CcsSendReply() call.

6   Integration with Source Code Level Debugging Tools

The contribution of our work is recognizing the need for scheduler-level debugging techniques in data-driven execution, especially in a multi-paradigm context, and developing debugging mechanisms to support it. However, it is clearly not sufficient to have purely scheduler-event level debugging facilities; they must be used in conjunction with the source-level debugging tools, such as gdb. Rather than use such a tool separately from our scheduler-level debugger, we integrate such traditional debuggers within a single GUI based implementation. The interface with existing sequential debuggers is briefly described next.

Converse has node programs running on every involved processor. The source level debugger attaches itself to these node programs and communicates with an intermediary component which relays commands to the debugger client through a TCP connection, as shown in figure 2.

This intermediary takes on different forms depending on whether the platform is a traditional parallel machine or a network of workstations, as shown in figure 3. On networks of workstations, converse programs are run through a host program. In this case, the host program plays the role of intermediary.

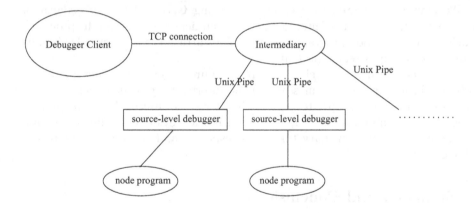

Fig. 2. GDB Interface Architecture for Workstation Clusters

Many traditional parallel machines, however, do not use a host program, and hence this architecture would not work. Thus, it is necessary to distribute the functionality of the host program (with regard to its actions for source debugging) over a number of proceses (each running on the processor where its corresponding node program runs).

On traditional parallel machines, the node programs are executed by wrapper programs, and so the "intermediary" is distributed across each of the *wrapper* programs. The wrapper program now spawns a source debugger process, and starts the node program as a child process of the debugger process. The wrapper programs play the role of the host program on every node. All source code

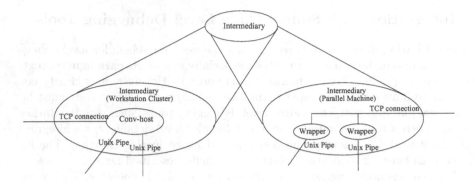

Fig. 3. GDB Interface Architecture for Parallel Machines

debugging related communication, initiated by the client, goes to the wrapper program. The wrapper program then conveys the appropriate command to its child source debugger process. When a response is obtained, the wrapper program sends it back to the client.

We have implemented this architecture using GNU's debugger (*gdb*) as a source-level debugger. The intermediary communicates with the gdb processes which control the node programs through pipes attached to the standard input (stdin) and output streams (stdout).

Whenever the debugger client desires a source code debugging command to be performed, it sends a message to the intermediary, which then passes a command into the appropriate pipe. This allows the appropriate gdb process to obtain the command, and the command is then evaluated, and a response is generated. The intermediary takes this response, and returns it back to the debugger client.

7   Summary and Conclusions

Debugging programs written in data driven parallel programming paradigms, such as message-passing threads and data-driven objects, is challenging because of the presence of its system scheduler, which implicitly transfers control between different user level execution units. This is especially difficult in a multi-paradigm parallel program, written using multiple data-driven parallel languages. We presented a methodology for debugging such programs, based on breakpoints at scheduler events, and observation of the entities in the scheduler's queue, and other run-time entities. We've developed implementation techniques for supporting such debugging, and incorporated them in a GUI based debugger. We are integrated the functionality of traditional debugging tools, such as gdb, within this debugger. The scheduler based debugging capabilities are complementary to such traditional debuggers. A comprehensive framework has been developed that allows any new language implemented on top of Converse to make use of these debugging facilities, by registering and implementing a few callback functions. Such functions have been implemented for Charm++, a language that supports C++ objects with asynchronous method invocation. In addition, they have been implemented for a couple of Converse libraries, to demonstrate the multi-paradigm utility of our framework. The debugger client, which is implemented in Java, can attach to any running converse program via the Internet. Using the Web based parallel program interaction tools developed by our group, we plan to make the debugger accessible via a browser such as Netscape. Adding authentication mechanisms to the attachment process is also being considered. Extending the GUI capabilities of the client, and developing debugging support for several other data driven paradigms will further help to demonstrate the broad utility of this framework.

References

1. D. Cheng and R. Hood. A portable debugger for parallel and distributed programs. In *Proceedings of Supercomputing '94*, pages 723–732, Washington, D.C, November 1994.
2. D.E. Culler, A. Dusseau, S.C. Goldstein, A. Krishnamurthy, S. Lumetta, T. von Eicken, and K. Yelick. Parallel Programming in Split-C. In *Proc. Supercomputing '93*, 1993.
3. M. Haines, D. Cronk, and P. Mehrotra. On the design of Chant: A talking threads package. In *Proceedings of Supercomputing 1994*, Washington D.C., Nov 1994.
4. L. V. Kale, Milind Bhandarkar, Robert Brunner, and Joshua Yel on. Multiparadigm, Multilingual Interoperability: Experience with Conver se. In *Proceedings of 2nd Workshop on Runtime Systems for Parallel Progr amming (RTSPP) Orlando, Florida - USA*, Lecture Notes in Computer Science, March 1998.
5. L. V. Kale, Milind Bhandarkar, Narain Jagathesan, Sanjeev Krishnan, and Joshua Yelon. Converse: An Interoperable Framework for Parallel Programming. In *Proceedings of the 10th International Parallel Processing Symposium*, pages 212–217, Honolulu, Hawaii, April 1996.
6. L. V. Kalé and Attila Gursoy. Modularity, reuse and efficiency with message-driven libraries. In *Proc. 27th Conference on Parallel Processing for Scientific Computing*, pages 738–743, February 1995.
7. L. V. Kalé and Sanjeev Krishnan. Charm++: Parallel Programming with Message-Driven Objects. In Gregory V. Wilson and Paul Lu, editors, *Parallel Programming using C++*, pages 175–213. MIT Press, 1996.
8. L.V. Kalé. The Chare Kernel parallel programming language and system. In *Proceedings of the International Conference on Parallel Processing*, volume II, pages 17–25, August 1990.
9. L.V. Kalé and Sanjeev Krishnan. Charm++ : A portable concurrent object oriented system based on C++. In *Proceedings of the Conference on Object Oriented Programmi ng Systems, Languages and Applications*, September 1993.
10. C.H. Koelbel, D.B. Loveman, R.S. Schreiber, G.L. Steele Jr., and M.E. Zosel. *The High Performance Fortran Handbook*. MIT Press, 1994.
11. S.S. Lumetta and D.E. Culler. The Mantis Parallel Debugger. Technical report, University of California at Berkeley, Computer Science Division.

12. John May and Francine Berman. Panorama: A portable, extensible parallel debugger. In *Proceedings of ACM/ONR Workshop on Parallel and Distributed Debugging*, pages 96–106, San Diego, California, May 1993.
13. S. Sistare, D. Allen, R. Bowker, K. Jourdenais, J .Simmons, and R. Title. A Scalable Debugger for massively parallel message passing p rograms. *IEEE Parallel and Distributed Technology: Systems and Applic ations*, 2(1):50–6, Summer 1994.
14. T. von Eicken, D. E. Culler, S. C. Goldstein, and K. E. Schauser. Active messages: A mechanism for integrated communication and computation. In David Abramson and Jean-Luc Gaudiot, editors, *Proceedings of the 19th Annual International Symposium on Computer Architecture*, pages 256–267, Gold Coast, Australia, May 1992. ACM Press.
15. Chih-Po Wen, Soumen Chakrabarti, Etienne Deprit, Arvind Krishnamurthy, and Katherine Yelick. Run-time support for portable distributed data structures. In *Third Workshop on Languages, Compilers, and Run-Time Systems for Scalable Computers*, Rensselaer Polytechnic Institute, NY, May 1995.

An Analytical Comparison of the I-Test and Omega Test

David Niedzielski and Kleanthis Psarris

Division of Computer Science
The University of Texas at San Antonio
San Antonio, Texas 78249
email:psarris@cs.utsa.edu

Abstract. The Omega test is an exact, (worst case) exponential time data dependence test. The I-Test is a polynomial time test, but is not always exact. In this paper we show the fundamental relationship between the two tests under conditions in which both tests are applicable. We show that Fourier-Motzkin Variable Elimination (FMVE), upon which the Omega test is based, is equivalent to the Banerjee Bounds Test when applied to single-dimensional array reference problems. Furthermore, we show the Omega Test's technique to refine Fourier-Motzkin Variable Elimination to integer solutions (dark shadow) is equivalent to the I-Test's refinement of the Banerjee Bounds Test (the interval equation). Finally, under the conditions we specify, we show the I-Test delivers an inconclusive answer if and only if the Omega test would require an exhaustive search to produce an exact answer (the so-called "Omega Test Nightmare").

1 Introduction

Sequential programs can fully utilize parallel machines if they can be automatically transformed into parallel programs. Additionally, improvements in program performance can be obtained by certain program transformations. For example, loop reordering can improve the locality of memory references, allowing more references to be satisfied from cache. It is the responsibility of the compiler to identify areas of the program that can be transformed, vectorized, and/or parallelized. A common source of such potential parallelism occurs in nested loops. An r-nested loop accessing a d-dimensional array follows is shown in Figure 1.

A *dependence* exists between two statements S_1 and S_2 if both reference the same element and at least one of them writes it. If S_1 writes an element that is later read by S_2, the dependence is classified as a *flow* dependence. If S_2 reads an element that is later written by S_1, then an *antidependence* exists from statement S_2 to S_1. If both S_1 and S_2 write the element, the dependence is termed an *output* dependence. Since a dependence between S_1 and S_2 may arise in different iterations of the common loops, we treat the loop iteration variables referenced in S_1 as being different variables from those referenced in S_2, subject to common loop bounds. Thus, when analyzing dependences arising

L. Carter and J. Ferrante (Eds.): LCPC'99, LNCS 1863, pp. 251–270, 2000.

```
for  x₁ = L₁ to U₁
   for  x₂ = L₂ to U₂
         ⋮
      for  xᵣ = Lᵣ to Uᵣ
```
$S_1:$ $\quad$ $A[f_1(x_1, x_2, \ldots, x_r), f_2(x_1, x_2, \ldots, x_r), \ldots, f_d(x_1, x_2, \ldots, x_r)] = \ldots$
$S_2:$ $\quad$ $\ldots = A[f_1'(x_1, x_2, \ldots, x_r), f_2'(x_1, x_2, \ldots, x_r), \ldots, f_d'(x_1, x_2, \ldots, x_r)]$
```
      endfor
         ⋮
   endfor
endfor
```

Fig. 1. Example of a nested loop

from a statement pair nested in r common loops, the problem will involve n unique variables (where $n = 2r$). Furthermore, variables x_i and $x_{i+r}(1 \le i \le r)$ are different instances of the same loop iteration variable, and so $L_{i+r} = L_i$ and $U_{i+r} = U_i$.

The compiler must employ a *dependence test* to determine if statements S_1 and S_2 can address the same element of array A. To do so, the test must take into consideration not only the subscript expressions $f_1(), f_2(), \ldots, f_d()$, $f_1'(), f_2'(), \ldots, f_d'()$, but also the loop iteration variable bounds $L_1, L_2, \ldots, L_n$, $U_1, U_2, \ldots, U_n$. That is, the dependence test must determine if there are integer values $i_1, i_2, \ldots, i_n$ such that

$$
\begin{aligned}
f_1(i_1, i_2, \ldots, i_r) &= f_1'(i_{r+1}, i_{r+2}, \ldots, i_n) \\
f_2(i_1, i_2, \ldots, i_r) &= f_2'(i_{r+1}, i_{r+2}, \ldots, i_n) \\
\vdots \qquad\qquad & \qquad \vdots \qquad\qquad \vdots \\
f_d(i_1, i_2, \ldots, i_r) &= f_d'(i_{r+1}, i_{r+2}, \ldots, i_n)
\end{aligned}
\tag{1}
$$

and

$$
\begin{aligned}
L_1 &\le i_1 \le U_1 \\
L_2 &\le i_2 \le U_2 \\
\vdots \quad &\vdots \quad \vdots \\
L_n &\le i_n \le U_n
\end{aligned}
\tag{2}
$$

Additional dependence information may allow more aggressive optimizations. For example, if the test is able to determine the distance vectors (i.e. the values of $i_k - i_{r+k}(1 \le k \le r)$) or direction vectors (i.e. the signs of $i_k - i_{r+k}(1 \le k \le r)$) that produce a dependence, the compiler may be able to partially parallelize or reorder the loops.

Most dependence tests (including those we consider in this paper) require that the subscripts $f_1(), f_2(), \ldots, f_d(), f_1'(), f_2'(), \ldots, f_d'()$ be *affine* expressions of the enclosing loop iteration variables. Such tests dependence must determine if integer solutions exist to the system of constrained linear equations that result from the equations in (1), and the constraints from the bounds on the loop iteration variables considered in (2). Often, a dependence test first converts the system of constrained linear equations into an equivalent system involving only linear inequalities. The dependence problem is thus a form of integer programming, an NP-complete problem.

If no two subscript expressions have any loop iteration variables in common, the subscripts are said to be *uncoupled*. In this case, each of the d array dimensions can be tested independently, and dependence disproved if any individual test disproves dependence.

Numerous dependence tests have been developed, which can in general be classified as either expensive and exact, or efficient and approximate. Approximate tests give exact answers under frequently occurring conditions, but may produce inconclusive otherwise. The exact tests always produce exact answers, but may require exponential time to do so.

For example, the Omega test [10], which extends a technique known as Fourier-Motzkin Variable Elimination (FMVE), is a generally-applicable exact test with (rare) worst case exponential-time complexity ([5]). On the other hand, the "I-Test"[6], is an approximate test which extends the widely-used Banerjee bounds and GCD tests. It runs in polynomial time, and produces exact answers in most cases encountered in practice [9]. However, the I-Test places conditions on the dependence problem, which if not met, may cause it to produce inconclusive answers.

1.1 Limitations of the I-Test

The I-Test considers only a single dimension of a multi-dimensional array subscript at a time. If the subscripts are not coupled, the I-Test tests each dimension independently, and returns a "no" answer if any individual test produces a "no" answer, and produces a "yes" answer if all individual tests produce "yes" answers. Otherwise, the I-Test returns a "maybe" answer.

If the subscripts are coupled, the I-Test again tests each dimension independently. As before, if any individual test produces a "no" answer, the I-Test returns a "no" answer to the dependence problem. However, in all other cases the I-Test returns a "maybe" answer.

As detailed in Section 4.3, the I-Test requires that the coefficients of the loop iteration variables be relatively small compared to loops bounds. Although this condition is almost always met in practice, it requires at least one variable coefficent be ± 1 after normalization (see Section 3.2). If this is not the case, the I-Test simply reverts to the Banerjee bounds test, which produces only "no" or "maybe" answers.

Finally, at present the I-Test requires that loop limits and variable coefficients be known and constant in order to produce exact answers.

In order to draw meaningful comparisons between the Omega and I-Test tests, we assume in this paper the following conditions:

1. The array being referenced is single dimensional, or multi-dimensional with uncoupled subscripts

2. Loop limits and variable coefficients are known and constant
3. After normalization, at least one variable in each equation has a coefficient of ± 1

We say that under these conditions, the I-Test is "applicable", although the I-Test can produce exact "no" answers even if none of the preceding conditions are satisfied. Additionally, when comparing the Banerjee test with FMVE, we assume that conditions 1 and 2 are met.

1.2 Outline of Paper

This paper compares the I-Test and Omega tests under the 3 previous conditions. We show that under these conditions, the I-Test gives an inconclusive (maybe) answer if and only if the Omega test requires exponential time to produce an exact answer.

We also compare the Banerjee Test and FMVE. We show that when conditions 1 and 2 are met, the two tests effectively use the same variable-elimination algorithm and produce identical results.

In Section 2, we introduce the notation to be used in the remainder of the paper. In Section 3, we describe FMVE and the Banerjee tests, give examples of their execution, and show their equivalence. Likewise, in Section 4, we describe and compare the Omega Test and I-Test, and give examples of their execution.

In discussing the tests in these sections, we assume the dependence problem involves a single dimensional array. In Section 5, we discuss the case of a multi-dimensional array with uncoupled subscripts.

2   Notation

The dependence tests examine pairs of linear subscript expressions $f_k()$ and $f_k'()$, where $1 \leq k \leq d$, and d is the number of dimensions in the array. Each of these expressions consists of one or more of the terms $a_1 x_1, a_2 x_2, \ldots, a_n x_n$ (where x_k is a loop iteration variable), plus (optionally) a constant. In order for a dependence to exist, corresponding subscript expressions must be equal, or

$$f_j(x_1, x_2, \ldots, x_r) = f_j'(x_{r+1}, x_{r+2}, \ldots, x_n) \qquad (1 \leq j \leq d) \qquad (3)$$

Since we assume uncoupled subscripts, each variable x_k appears in at most one of the d subscript expressions, and we consider each of the d subscripts as an independent problem. We thus can express the dependence problem as a set of d independent constrained linear equalities of the form:

$$\sum_{1 \leq i \leq n} a_i x_i = c \qquad (4)$$

In the following sections, we examine how the various tests deal with a single such inequality, and discuss multi-dimensional arrays in a later section.

The set of indices of the loop iteration variables being manipulated will be referred to as $\{V\}$, where $0 \notin \{V\}$, and let $|V| = n$. Assume, without loss of generality, that for $1 \leq i \leq n-1$, $a_i \leq a_{i+1}$. We express this linear equation as the equivalent inequality

$$c \leq \sum_{i \in \{V\}} a_i x_i \leq c \tag{5}$$

We express the bounds on loop iteration variables as:

$$
\begin{array}{ccc}
L_1 \leq x_1 \leq U_1 \\
L_2 \leq x_2 \leq U_2 \\
\vdots \quad \vdots \quad \vdots \\
L_n \leq x_n \leq U_n
\end{array}
\tag{6}
$$

where for $i \in \{V\}$, $L_i \leq U_i$. Finally, we let $\{S\}$ be the set of inequalities, and let $s = |S|$.

3   Comparison of FMVE and Banerjee Bounds

3.1   The Mechanics of FMVE

Fourier-Motzkin variable elimination [1,2,3] solves systems of linear inequalities by eliminating variables one at a time. Conceptually, eliminating a variable finds the $n-1$ dimensional shadow cast by an n dimensional object. When choosing which variable to eliminate, we choose the variable whose coefficient has the smallest absolute value. It eliminates a variable x_k by comparing all upper bounds on x_k to all lower bounds on x_k. In general, given the following upper bound $U \in \{S\}$ on x_k:

$$\sum_{i \in \{V\}} a_i x_i \leq 0$$

(where $a_k > 0$), and the following lower bound $L \in \{S\}$ on x_k:

$$\sum_{i \in \{V\}} a'_i x_i \leq 0$$

(where $a'_k < 0$), we combine the two limits and obtain:

$$\sum_{i \in \{V\}-\{k\}} a_k a'_i x_i \leq |a'_k| a_k x_k \leq \sum_{i \in \{V\}-\{k\}} a'_k a_i x_i \tag{7}$$

The equality in one fewer dimension that results from this comparison is therefore

$$\sum_{i \in \{V\}-\{k\}} a_k a'_i x_i \leq \sum_{i \in \{V\}-\{k\}} a'_k a_i x_i \tag{8}$$

If this inequality is inconsistent, we report that no real solution to the system exists.

Once all lower bounds on x_k have been compared to all upper bounds on x_k, the resulting inequalities can be added to $\{S\}$, those containing x_k can be removed from $\{S\}$, and k can be removed from $\{V\}$. FMVE continues eliminating variables in this fashion until either a contradiction is reached, or until all variables have been eliminated.

Because of the conditions we specify in Section 1.1, the generalized procedure for eliminating a variable outlined above are simplified. Under these conditions, when we eliminate a variable $x_k(k \in \{V\})$ via FMVE, there will only be two expressions in $\{S\}$ involving x_k, namely

$$c_L \leq \sum_{i \in V} a_i x_i \leq c_U \tag{9}$$

$$L_k \leq x_k \leq U_k \tag{10}$$

where c_L, c_U, L_k, and U_k are integers, and $L_k \leq U_k$. Assume for now that $c_L \leq c_U$. If $a_k > 0$, we express (9) as

$$c_L - \sum_{i \in \{V\}-\{k\}} a_i x_i \leq a_k x_k \leq c_U - \sum_{i \in \{V\}-\{k\}} a_i x_i \tag{11}$$

Comparing the lower limit on the LHS of (11) to the upper limit in (11) produces the trivial inequality $c_L \leq c_U$. Likewise, comparing the lower limit on the LHS of (10) to the upper limit on the RHS of (10) produces $L_k \leq U_k$, We shall see in the next section that the dark shadow inequality may cause these initial comparisons to produce a contradiction.

Comparing the lower limit in (11) to the upper limit in (10) produces

$$c_L - \sum_{i \in \{V\}-\{k\}} a_i x_i \leq a_k U_k \quad \Rightarrow \quad c_L - a_k U_k \leq \sum_{i \in \{V\}-\{k\}} a_i x_i \tag{12}$$

Next, we compare the upper limit in the RHS of (11) to the lower limit in the LHS of (10), yielding

$$a_k L_k \leq c_U - \sum_{i \in \{V\}-\{k\}} a_i x_i \quad \Rightarrow \quad \sum_{i \in \{V\}-\{k\}} a_i x_i \leq c_U - a_k L_k \tag{13}$$

Combining (12) and (13), we see that when $a_k > 0$, the elimination of variable x_k produces:

$$c_L - a_k U_k \leq \sum_{i \in \{V\}-\{k\}} a_i x_i \leq c_U - a_k L_k \tag{14}$$

If $a_k < 0$, we express (9) as

$$-c_U + \sum_{i \in \{V\}-\{k\}} a_i x_i \leq |a_k| x_k \leq -c_L + \sum_{i \in \{V\}-\{k\}} a_i x_i \tag{15}$$

and compare upper and lower bounds with (10). As before, the lower limit in the LHS of (15) combined with the upper limit in the RHS of (15) produce $c_L \leq c_U$. Comparing the lower limit in (15) to the upper limit in (10) produces

$$-c_U + \sum_{i \in \{V\}-\{k\}} a_i x_i \leq |a_k| U_k \quad \Rightarrow \quad \sum_{i \in \{V\}-\{k\}} a_i x_i \leq c_U + |a_k| U_k \tag{16}$$

Comparing the upper limit in (15) to the lower limit in (10) produces

$$|a_k|L_k \leq -c_L + \sum_{i \in \{V\}-\{k\}} a_i x_i \quad \Rightarrow \quad |a_k|L_k + c_L \leq \sum_{i \in \{V\}-\{k\}} a_i x_i \qquad (17)$$

Combining (16) with (17) when $a_k < 0$, the elimination of x_k yields:

$$c_L + |a_k|L_k \leq \sum_{i \in \{V\}-\{k\}} a_i x_i \leq c_U + |a_k|U_k \qquad (18)$$

3.2   Normalization

Whenever we eliminate a variable and obtain an inequality $c_L \leq \sum_{i \in \{V\}} a_i x_i \leq c_U$ which needs to be added to $\{S\}$, we can potentially produce a contradiction by *normalizing* the inequality. Let $g = GCD(a_1, a_2, \ldots, a_n)$. If $g > 1$, we divide each $a_i (i \in \{V\})$ by g, replace c_L by $\lceil c_L/g \rceil$, and c_U by $\lfloor c_U/g \rfloor$. If this produces a contradiction, we report that no integer solution exists, otherwise, we add the normalized inequality to $\{S\}$.

3.3   Relationship of the Bounds

Referring to (9), we assumed earlier that $c_L \leq c_U$ prior to eliminating a variable x_k from $\{V\}$. As each variable is eliminated from $\{V\}$, c_L and c_U are adjusted to account for the coefficient and bounds of the eliminated variable. We now prove that at every stage of the elimination process, $c_L \leq c_U$. By "stage", we mean the point prior to eliminating the next variable x_k from $\{V\}$.

Lemma 1. *At every phase of the FMVE process, $c_L \leq c_U$.*

Proof. We use induction on α, which we define as the number of variables we have thus far eliminated. Initially, $\alpha = 0$, (because no variables have been eliminated). At this point, (9) is identical to (5), $c_L = c_U = c$, and clearly $c_L \leq c_U$, so the basis is trivially established.

For the inductive step, assume that after α eliminations, we next decide to eliminate x_k, and the two equalities in $\{S\}$ containing x_k are those in (9) and (10). By the inductive hypothesis, $c_L \leq c_U$. Assume $a_k \geq 0$. By (14), the elimination will produce a new inequality

$$c_L - a_k U_k \leq \sum_{i \in \{V\}-\{k\}} a_i x_i \leq c_U - a_k L_k \qquad (19)$$

We need to show that $c_L - a_k U_k \leq c_U - a_k L_k$. This is obvious, since

$$c_L - a_k U_k \leq c_U - a_k L_k$$
$$\Leftrightarrow \quad c_L - c_U \leq a_k U_k - a_k L_k$$
$$\Leftrightarrow \quad c_L - c_U \leq a_k(U_k - L_k)$$

This latter equality is true, since $c_L \leq c_U \Rightarrow c_L - c_U \leq 0$, and $L_k \leq U_k \Rightarrow U_k - L_k \geq 0$. Now assume $a_k < 0$. By (18), the elimination will produce a new inequality

$$c_L + |a_k|L_k \leq \sum_{i \in \{V\}-\{k\}} a_i x_i \leq c_U + |a_k|U_k \qquad (20)$$

We see that $c_L + |a_k|L_k \leq c_U + a_k U_k$, since

$$c_L + |a_k|L_k \leq c_U + |a_k|U_k$$
$$\Leftrightarrow \quad c_L - c_U \leq |a_k|U_k - |a_k|L_k$$
$$\Leftrightarrow \quad c_L - c_U \leq |a_k|(U_k - L_k)$$

As before, this latter equality is true, since $c_L \leq c_U \Rightarrow c_L - c_U \leq 0$, and $L_k \leq U_k \Rightarrow U_k - L_k \geq 0$. $\qquad\qquad\qquad\qquad\qquad\qquad\qquad\qquad\square$

3.4   Example of FMVE

We illustrate with an example. Given the following linear equation and set of loop bounds:

$$x + 4y + 7z - 34 = 0, \text{ where:} \qquad \begin{array}{c} 0 \leq x \leq 15 \\ -5 \leq y \leq 10 \\ 3 \leq z \leq 12 \end{array}$$

we first create the equivalent system of linear inequalities:

$$\begin{array}{rcl} 34 \leq x + 4y + 7z & \leq & 34 \\ 0 \leq \quad x & \leq & 15 \\ -5 \leq \quad y & \leq & 10 \\ 3 \leq \quad z & \leq & 12 \end{array} \qquad (21)$$

Since $a_x = 1$, we first eliminate x from the system. Expressing the first inequality in terms of x, produces:

$$\begin{array}{rcl} 34 - 4y - 7z \leq x & \leq & 34 - 4y - 7z \\ 0 \leq x & \leq & 15 \\ -5 \leq y & \leq & 10 \\ 3 \leq z & \leq & 12 \end{array} \qquad (22)$$

Comparing upper and lower bounds on x yields:

Lower Bound	Upper Bound	Combination	Result
$34 - 4y - 7z \leq x$	$x \leq 34 - 4y - 7z$	$34 - 4y - 7z \leq x \leq 34 - 4y - 7z$	$0 \leq 0$
$34 - 4y - 7z \leq x$	$x \leq 15$	$34 - 4y - 7z \leq x \leq 15$	$19 \leq 4y + 7z$
$0 \leq x$	$x \leq 34 - 4y - 7z$	$0 \leq x \leq 34 - 4y - 7z$	$4y + 7z \leq 34$
$0 \leq x$	$x \leq 15$	$0 \leq x \leq 15$	$0 \leq 15$

The first and last result are consistent and involve only constant terms, and so are ignored. Combining the middle two results yields the inequality $19 \leq 4y + 7z \leq 34$. We add this to the inequalities contained in (22), and remove from (22) the two inequalities involving x.

In any event, the elimination of x produces the following system:

$$19 \leq 4y + 7z \leq 34$$
$$-5 \leq \quad y \quad \leq 10$$
$$3 \leq \quad z \quad \leq 12$$

We next eliminate y. Rewriting in terms of y gives

$$-7z + 19 \leq 4y \leq -7z + 34$$
$$-5 \leq y \leq \qquad 10$$
$$3 \leq z \leq \qquad 12$$

Comparing lower and upper bounds on y:

Lower Bound	Upper Bound	Combination	Result
$-7z + 19 \leq 4y$	$4y \leq -7z + 34$	$-7z + 19 \leq 4y \leq 7z + 34$	$19 \leq 34$
$-7z + 19 \leq 4y$	$y \leq 10$	$-7z + 19 \leq 4y \leq 40$	$-21 \leq 7z$
$-5 \leq y$	$4y \leq -7z + 34$	$-20 \leq 4y \leq -7z + 34$	$7z \leq 54$
$-5 \leq y$	$y \leq 10$	$-5 \leq y \leq 10$	$0 \leq 15$

This adds the inequality $-21 \leq 7z \leq 54$, which normalizes to $-3 \leq z \leq 7$:

$$-3 \leq z \leq 7$$
$$3 \leq z \leq 12$$

We next eliminate z:

Lower Bound	Upper Bound	Combination	Result
$-3 \leq z$	$z \leq 7$	$-3 \leq z \leq 7$	$-3 \leq 7$
$-3 \leq z$	$z \leq 12$	$-3 \leq z \leq 12$	$-15 \leq 0$
$3 \leq z$	$z \leq 7$	$3 \leq 7$	$0 \leq 4$
$3 \leq z$	$z \leq 12$	$3 \leq z \leq 12$	$3 \leq 12$

The final inequality is $-15 \leq 0 \leq 4$. Since we have eliminated all variables and have not reached any contradictions, we conclude that the original system of linear inequalities has a real solution.

3.5   The Banerjee Bounds Test

The Banerjee bounds test [4] finds the minimum and maximum value a constrained linear expression can assume. We begin with a linear inequality in the form of (5), and a set of variable bounds in the form of (6). For each term $a_i x_i$ in the inequality, we calculate $Min(a_i x_i)$ and $Max(a_i x_i)$, and subtract these values from the RHS and LHS, respectively, of the inequality. After doing so, we eliminate the term $a_i x_i$ from the inner expression. As with FMVE, we normalize the inequality if the GCD of the coefficients is greater than 1. If this produces a contradiction, we report that no integer solution exists. When all the terms have been processed, we are left with an inequality of the form:

$$c - \sum_{i \in \{V\}} Max(a_i x_i) \leq 0 \leq c - \sum_{i \in \{V\}} Min(a_i x_i)$$

if this inequality holds, we report that a real solution exists. Otherwise, we report no real solution exists.

The Banerjee bounds test defines r^+ (the *positive part*) and r^- (the *negative part*) of a real number r as follows:

$$r^+ = \begin{cases} r, & \text{if } r \geq 0 \\ 0, & \text{if } r < 0 \end{cases}$$

$$r^- = \begin{cases} 0, & \text{if } r > 0 \\ r, & \text{if } r \leq 0 \end{cases}$$

The functions $Min(a_i x_i)$ and $Max(a_i x_i)$ are defined as:

$$Min(a_i x_i) = a_i{}^+ L_i + a_i{}^- U_i$$
$$Max(a_i x_i) = a_i{}^+ U_i + a_i{}^- L_i$$

3.6 Example of Banerjee Bounds Test

Using the same example as in FMVE, the Banerjee bounds proceeds as follows:

$$
\begin{aligned}
34 &\leq x + 4y + 7z \leq 34 \\
34 - (15 + 0) \leq\ & 4y + 7z \quad \leq 34 - (0 + 0) \\
19 - (40 + 0) \leq\ & 7z \qquad \leq 34 - (-20 + 0) \\
-21 \leq\ & 7z \qquad \leq 54
\end{aligned}
\tag{23}
$$

We normalize the last constraint to produce $-3 \leq z \leq 7$:

$$
\begin{aligned}
-3 - (12 + 0) &\leq 0 \leq 7 - (3 + 0) \\
\Rightarrow \qquad -15 &\leq 0 \leq 4 \qquad \Leftarrow
\end{aligned}
\tag{24}
$$

Note that the final inequality is identical to that obtained via FMVE. We proceed to show that this will be true in general.

3.7 Equivalence of FMVE and Banerjee Bounds

Lemma 2. *Under the restrictions in Section 1.1, the variable elimination steps performed by the Banerjee bounds test and FMVE are equivalent, and thus the tests produce identical answers.*

Proof. We use induction on α, the number of variables eliminated so far. We show the inequalities produced after every variable elimination are identical.

For the basis ($\alpha = 0$), FMVE and Banerjee begin with the same inequality, shown in (5).

Now assume that after α variables have been eliminated, the LHS and RHS of the inequality are the same using both FMVE and Banerjee. For consistency, we refer the the LHS of the inequality as c_L, and the RHS as c_U. We next eliminate variable x_k. There are two cases to consider. If $a_k \geq 0$, Banerjee proceeds as follows:

$$c_L - Max(a_k x_k) \leq \sum_{i \in \{V\}-\{k\}} a_i x_i \leq c_U - Min(a_k x_k)$$

$$\Rightarrow \quad c_L - (a_k{}^+ U_k + a_k{}^- L_k) \leq \sum_{i \in \{V\}-\{k\}} a_i x_i \leq c_U - (a_i{}^+ L_i + a_i{}^- U_i)$$

$$\Rightarrow \quad c_L - (a_k U_k + 0) \leq \sum_{i \in \{V\}-\{k\}} a_i x_i \leq c_U - (a_k L_k + 0) \tag{25}$$

$$\Rightarrow \quad c_L - a_k U_k \leq \sum_{i \in \{V\}-\{k\}} a_i x_i \leq c_U - a_k L_k$$

This result is identical to that produced by FMVE, shown in (14). If $a_k < 0$, Banerjee performs the following:

$$c_L - Max(a_k x_k) \leq \sum_{i \in \{V\}-\{k\}} a_i x_i \leq c_U - Min(a_k x_k)$$

$$\Rightarrow \quad c_L - (a_k{}^+ U_k + a_k{}^- L_k) \leq \sum_{i \in \{V\}-\{k\}} a_i x_i \leq c_U - (a_i{}^+ L_i + a_i{}^- U_i)$$

$$\Rightarrow \quad c_L - (0 + a_k L_k) \leq \sum_{i \in \{V\}-\{k\}} a_i x_i \leq c_U - (0 + a_k U_k) \tag{26}$$

$$\Rightarrow \quad c_L + |a_k| L_k \leq \sum_{i \in \{V\}-\{k\}} a_i x_i \leq c_U + |a_k| U_k$$

This result is identical to that produced by FMVE, shown in (18). We conclude that FMVE and Banerjee are equivalent.   □

4   Comparison of the Omega and I-Tests

4.1   Overview of the Omega Test

The Omega Test [10,11] refines FMVE to *integer* solutions. Given upper and lower bounds U and L, respectively, on x:

$$bx \leq UL \leq ax$$

We combine the two inequalities, obtaining:

$$bL \leq abx \leq aU$$

This does not imply that an *integer* multiple of ab exists between the upper and lower bounds. However, suppose no integer multiple exists. Then there is an integer i such that:

$$abi < bL \leq aU < ab(i+1)$$

Since both abi and bL are both multiples of b, and both aU and $ab(i+1)$ are both multiples of a, and $ab(i+1) - abi = ab$, we have

$$bL - abi \geq b$$
$$ab(i+1) - aU \geq a$$
$$aU - bL \leq ab - a - b$$

We see that if the difference between the upper and lower bounds on abx exceeds $ab - a - b$, we are guaranteed an integer multiple of ab falls somewhere between them. Specifically, an integer solution must exist if:

$$aU - bL > ab - a - b$$
$$\Rightarrow aU - bL \geq ab - a - b + 1$$

$$\Rightarrow aU - bL \geq (a - 1)(b - 1) \qquad (27)$$

The inequality shown in (27), called the "dark shadow" inequality, is the Omega test extension to FMVE.

Conceptually, FMVE calculates the real $n - 1$ dimensional shadow cast by an n dimensional polyhedron. Unfortunately, we cannot be sure which integer points (if any) in this real shadow correspond to integer points in the original object. The "dark shadow" inequality calculates a sub-shadow wherein every integer point corresponds to an integer point in the original object. If you imagine the original polyhedron as being translucent, the "dark shadow" is the shadow under the object where the polyhedron is of at least unit thickness. The Omega test essentially calculates two shadows per every variable elimination: one to calculate the real shadow, the other to calculate the "dark shadow". It is claimed that the cost of the additional shadow calculation is minimal, since it involves the addition of a constant term to each inequality. After a variable x_k has been eliminated, a check is made to see if the dark shadow calculation has produced a contradiction. If it has not, we continue eliminating variables. If we manage to eliminate all variables without producing a contradiction in the dark shadow calculation, we know that an integer solution must exist to the original system of linear equations, and we report "yes".

If the dark shadow inequality during the elimination of the variable x_k produces a contradiction, we know that the dark shadow is empty. We then check if the real shadow is also empty by resorting to standard FMVE. If the real shadow is empty, we know that no real solution exists, and we report "no". If we cannot disprove the existence of real solutions, we know that if an integer solution exists, there must be a pair of constraints $L \leq ax_k$ and $bx_k \leq U$ such that

$$bL \leq abx_k \leq aU \leq ab - a - b + bL$$

That is, the distance between the upper and lower bounds on x_k were too small to guarantee an integer solution existed between them. That being the case, if an integer solution exists, it must be "tightly nestled" between some pair of upper and lower bounds on x_k. The Omega test then chooses the largest coefficient b in some upper bound on x_k, and for each lower bound $L \leq ax_k$, recursively creates and solves a new problem with the original constraints plus the equality constraint $L + i = ax_k$ for $(0 \leq i \leq \frac{ab-a-b)}{b})$. Although expensive, this recursive search is rarely needed in practice.

Note that if either $a = 1$ or $b = 1$, the dark shadow will be identical to the real shadow, because the dark inequality $(a - 1)(b - 1) = 0$. This is termed an *exact* projection. When such projections occur, the Omega test will produces the same result as FMVE. In our case, there will only be a single comparison affected by the addition of the dark shadow inequality, namely, the comparison between the lower bound on the LHS of (11) to the upper bound in the RHS of (11).

4.2   Example of the Omega Test

The Omega test is similar to that of FMVE, except that two shadows are calculated. When the comparison of an upper and lower bound in the real shadow calculation produces an inequality

$$bL \leq abx \leq aU \qquad \Rightarrow \qquad bL \leq aU$$

The corresponding dark shadow inequality is produced by simply adding the extra constraint to the new inequality:

$$bL + (a - 1)(b - 1) \leq aU$$

Using the FMVE example, we begin with:

$$
\begin{aligned}
34 \leq\ & x + 4y + 7z \leq 34 \\
0 \leq\ & x && \leq 15 \\
-5 \leq\ & y && \leq 10 \\
3 \leq\ & z && \leq 12
\end{aligned}
\tag{28}
$$

Rewriting the inequalities in terms of x:

$$
\begin{aligned}
34 - 4y - 7z \leq\ & x \leq 34 - 4y - 7z \\
0 \leq\ & x \leq && 15 \\
-5 \leq\ & y \leq && 10 \\
3 \leq\ & z \leq && 12
\end{aligned}
\tag{29}
$$

Comparing upper and lower bounds on x produces the same results as in FMVE, because the coefficient of x is 1, and $(1 - 1)(1 - 1) = 0$:

Lower Bound	Upper Bound	Combination	Result
$34 - 4y - 7z \leq x$	$x \leq 34 - 4y - 7z$	$34 - 4y - 7z(+0) \leq x \leq 34 - 4y - 7z$	$0 \leq 0$
$34 - 4y - 7z \leq x$	$x \leq 15$	$34 - 4y - 7z(+0) \leq x \leq 15$	$19 \leq 4y + 7z$
$0 \leq x$	$x \leq 34 - 4y - 7z$	$0(+0) \leq x \leq 34 - 4y - 7z$	$4y + 7z \leq 34$
$0 \leq x$	$x \leq 15$	$0(+0) \leq x \leq 15$	$0 \leq 15$

We next eliminate y. Rewriting the inequalities, we have:

$$
\begin{aligned}
-7z + 19 \leq\ & 4y \leq -7z + 34 \\
-5 \leq\ & y \leq && 10 \\
3 \leq\ & z \leq && 12
\end{aligned}
$$

We compare bounds on y. The dark shadow inequality in the first row is $(9 = (4 - 1)(4 - 1))$.

Lower Bound	Upper Bound	Combination	Result
$-7z + 19 \leq 4y$	$4y \leq -7z + 34$	$-28z + 76(+9) \leq 16y \leq -28z + 136$	$85 \leq 136$
$-7z + 19 \leq 4y$	$y \leq 10$	$-7z + 19(+0) \leq 4y \leq 40$	$-21 \leq 7z$
$-5 \leq y$	$4y \leq -7z + 34$	$-20(+0) \leq 4y \leq -7z + 34$	$7z \leq 54$
$-5 \leq y$	$y \leq 10$	$-5(+0) \leq y \leq 10$	$0 \leq 15$

We normalize the resulting equality $-21 \leq 7z \leq 54$ to produce $-3 \leq 7z \leq 7$, yielding:
$$-3 \leq z \leq 7$$
$$3 \leq z \leq 12$$

We next eliminate z. The dark inequality addition is $0 = (1-1)(1-1)$:

Lower Bound	Upper Bound	Combination	Result
$-3 \leq z$	$z \leq 7$	$-3(+0) \leq z \leq 7$	$-3 \leq 7$
$-3 \leq z$	$z \leq 12$	$-3(+0) \leq z \leq 12$	$-15 \leq 0$
$3 \leq z$	$z \leq 7$	$3(+0) \leq 7$	$0 \leq 4$
$3 \leq z$	$z \leq 12$	$3+0 \leq z \leq 12$	$3 \leq 12$

As before, the final inequality is $-15 \leq 0 \leq 4$. Since we have eliminated all variables and have not reached any contradictions, we conclude that the dark shadow is not empty, and report that integer solutions exist.

If a contradiction had been encountered during the calculation of the real shadow, we would have reported no real solution exists. However, if the contradiction arose as a result of the dark shadows inequality, the Omega test would have resorted to standard FMVE to see if real solutions could be ruled out. If they could not be ruled out, the Omega test would have begun the recursive search outlined above.

4.3   Overview of the I-Test

The I-Test [6,7,8] extends the Banerjee bounds in the same fashion as the Omega test extends FMVE: it adds a condition which, if met, allows a variable to be eliminated from the system. Conceptually, it performs the same calculations done in the Banerjee bounds: eliminating a term at a time from the center of a linear equality in the form of (11), and subtracting the term's maximum and minimum value from the LHS and RHS, respectively, of the inequality. In I-Test terminology, the upper and lower bounds form an "interval equation", which is a set of linear equations that are *all* guaranteed to have integer solutions as long as a specific relationship exists between the length of the interval and the magnitude of the coefficient being moved. This relationship is as follows:

Let U and L be the current RHS and LHS, respectively, of the inequality in (11). We can move a term $a_i x_i$ from the center to either side of the inequality if

$$|a_i| \leq U - L + 1 \tag{30}$$

This requires that at least one term of the original linear equation has a coefficient of ± 1. As long as the coefficients meet this requirement, we continue eliminating them. If we remove all the terms and the interval equation contains 0, we announce that an integer solution exists. Otherwise, no integer solution exists. If we reach a point where a term cannot be moved, we continue moving terms and normalizing the resulting equations anyway (essentially reverting to the Banerjee bounds test), in the hope of disproving real solutions. If the result produces a contradiction, we know no real solutions exist. Otherwise, we know a real solution exists, but are unsure if an integer solution exists. In this case, the I-Test returns a "maybe" answer.

Note that the I-Test performs the same calculations as a term-by-term application of the Banerjee bounds test, except that before moving a term, we check the magnitude of the coefficient against the length of the gap between the bounds. If all the terms qualify, the end interval equation will be identical to that produced by the standard Banerjee bounds test.

4.4   Example of the I-Test

We use the interval equation format

$$\sum_{i \in \{V\}} a_i x_i = [L, U]$$

This is to be understood as the set of linear equations

$$\sum_{i \in \{V\}} a_i x_i = L$$
$$\sum_{i \in \{V\}} a_i x_i = L + 1$$
$$\vdots \quad \vdots \quad \vdots$$
$$\sum_{i \in \{V\}} a_i x_i = U - 1$$
$$\sum_{i \in \{V\}} a_i x_i = U$$

where as long as the requirement in (30) is met, all equations are guaranteed to have an integer solution. If this condition is not met, then the bounds have the same meaning as in Banerjee: the region in which a real solution potentially exists.

We use the same example as in FMVE:

$$x + 4y + 7z - 34 = 0, \text{ where: } \quad \begin{array}{c} 0 \le x \le 15 \\ -5 \le y \le 10 \\ 3 \le z \le 12 \end{array}$$

And eliminate terms as follows:

$$
\begin{array}{llc}
x + 4y + 7z - 34 = [0, 0] & \text{(Initial equation)} & \\
x + 4y + 7z = [34, 34] & \text{(Move the constant)} & \\
4y + 7z = [19, 34] & (|1| \le 0 - 0 + 1) & \checkmark \\
7z = [-21, 54] & (|4| \le 34 - 19 + 1) & \checkmark \\
z = [-3, 7] & \text{(Normalize the interval)} & \\
0 = [-15, 4] & (|1| \le 4 - (-15) + 1) & \checkmark
\end{array}
$$

Since $-15 \le 0 \le 4$, the I-Test returns a "yes" answer, meaning that integer solutions definitely exist to this system.

4.5   Equivalence of the Omega and I-Tests

The Omega and I-Test are based upon the same principle. To show the tests are equivalent, we need to compare the dark shadows inequality in (27) and the I-Test condition in (30).

Recall that when we eliminate a variable x_i, we compare pairs of upper and lower bounds on x_i. The bounds are those described in (11) and (10). Of the four comparisons we have to make, three involve coefficients of x_i that are equal to 1. Recall that in this case the dark inequality is inconsequential, since when either $a = 1$ or $b = 1$ in (27), the dark inequality adds 0.

In only one comparison does the dark inequality play any role, and that is in the comparison of the upper bound in (11) to the lower bound in (11). This is precisely where the I-Test compares the coefficient b to the range of the interval $U - L + 1$ to decide whether it was legal to move the term from the center to either side of the inequality. When the Omega test performs this comparison, the coefficient of x_i is same in both bounds (b). In this case, the dark inequality becomes $bU - bL \geq (b-1)^2$. We must prove that the tests the Omega and I-Tests use for deciding whether integer solutions are guaranteed are exactly equivalent. In other words, that the dark shadow inequality

$$bU - bL \geq (b - 1)^2$$

and the I-Test's check

$$b \leq U - L + 1$$

are equivalent. Note that the coefficient b is positive. If the coefficient is negative, we simply reverse signs and swap the LHS and RHS of the inequality. To begin, we state and prove a simple lemma:

Lemma 3. *If b and x are integers, and $b \geq 1$, $bx \geq (b-1)^2$ is true if and only if $x \geq b - 1$.*

Proof (if part).

$$bx \geq (b - 1)^2$$
$$bx \geq b^2 - 2b + 1$$
$$x \geq b - 2 + \tfrac{1}{b}$$

We see that when b is at its minimum value of 1, the fraction in the RHS of the last equality becomes 1, and x becomes $b - 1$. As b approaches infinity, x *asymptotically* approaches $b - 2$. Therefore, the smallest *integer* value x can assume is $b-1$. To illustrate, we substitute $b-2$ for x and produce a contradiction:

$$b(b - 2) \geq (b - 1)^2$$
$$b^2 - 2b \geq b^2 - 2b + 1$$
$$0 \geq 1$$

We now substitute $b-1$ for x:

$$b(b-1) \geq (b-1)^2$$
$$b^2 - b \geq b^2 - 2b + 1$$
$$b \geq 1$$

Thus we conclude that for integer b and x where $b \geq 1$, if $bx \geq (b-1)^2$, then $x \geq b-1$.

Proof (only if).

$$x \geq b - 1$$
$$bx \geq b(b-1) \quad (31)$$
$$bx \geq b^2 - b$$

We also have

$$b^2 - b \geq (b-1)^2$$
$$b^2 - b \geq b^2 - 2b + 1 \quad (32)$$
$$b \geq 1$$

And so we have $b^2 - b \geq (b-1)^2$ whenever $b \geq 1$. Combining (31) and (32) we conclude that for integer b and x where $b \geq 1$, if $x \geq b-1$, then $bx \geq (b-1)^2$. $\square$

We can now see why the two tests are identical: The dark shadows inequality

$$bU - bL \geq (b-1)^2$$

can be rewritten as

$$b(U - L) \geq (b-1)^2$$

Substituting $U - L$ for x, we know by Lemma 3 that the dark shadows inequality is exactly equal to the I-Test's

$$U - L + 1 \geq b$$

since

$$bU - bL \geq (b-1)^2 \quad \text{Dark shadows inequality when } a = b$$
$$\Rightarrow \quad b(U - L) \geq (b-1)^2 \quad \text{Factoring the } b$$
$$\Rightarrow \quad U - L \geq b - 1 \quad \text{Using Lemma 3 with } x = (U - L)$$
$$\Rightarrow U - L + 1 \geq b \quad \text{Move the 1: I-Test condition}$$

and

$$U - L + 1 \geq b \quad \text{I-Test condition}$$
$$\Rightarrow \quad U - L \geq b - 1 \quad \text{Move the 1}$$
$$\Rightarrow \quad b(U - L) \geq (b-1)^2 \quad \text{Using Lemma 3 with } x = (U - L)$$
$$\Rightarrow \quad bU - bL \geq (b-1)^2 \quad \text{Multiply through by b: dark shadows inequality}$$

The equivalence between the I-Test condition and the dark shadows inequality when the coefficients in both bounds are equal (as is always the case when comparing the upper and lower bounds in (11)) is intuitively obvious if we revisit the discussion at the beginning of this section.

If both coefficients are équal, then given upper and lower bounds on x:

$$bx \leq UL \leq bx$$

We can combine the two inequalities directly, and obtain

$$L \leq bx \leq U$$

Recall that this does not imply that an *integer* multiple of b exists between the upper and lower bounds. Again, suppose no integer multiple exists. Then there exists an integer i such that:

$$bi < L \leq bx \leq U < b(i+1)$$

Clearly, if the distance between the upper and lower bounds is greater than or equal to $b - 1$, then an integer multiple *must* exist between the two bounds.

We now state formally the implication of the above.

Theorem 1. *Under the conditions in Section 1.1:*

1. *If the I-Test returns a "yes" answer, the Omega test will return a "yes" answer.*
2. *If the I-Test returns a "no" answer, the Omega test will return a "no" answer"*
3. *If the I-Test returns a "maybe" answer, the Omega test will return a "yes" or "no", but only after exhaustively searching between the upper and lower bounds on some variable x_k.*

Proof. For the first part, if the I-Test returns a "yes" answer, it is because all terms passed the I-Test's checks, and the resulting interval equation contained 0. If this is true, then by Lemma 3 all terms would pass the "dark shadows" inequality as well. Furthermore, because all the remaining comparisons involve a coefficient of 1, the calculation of the dark shadow will be identical to that of FMVE, which in turn is identical to Banerjee bounds. Since the I-Test's final interval is exactly equal to that obtained by the Banerjee bounds test, the Omega test would also find no contradiction, and return "yes".

The second part is similar to the first. If the I-Test returned "no", it is because either all terms were moved and 0 did not lie between the interval bounds, or because a term could not be moved, but the Banerjee bounds test found that no real solutions existed. In the former case, Lemma 3 ensures that the Omega test would also move all terms and produce the same results as FMVE, which are same results as Banerjee. Since the I-Test's final interval is exactly equal to that obtained by the Banerjee bounds test, the Omega test would make the same observation as the I-Test, and return "no". In the latter case, the Omega test would also be unable to move the same term, and would revert to FMVE to try to rule out real solutions. If the Banerjee bounds test ruled out real solutions, FMVE would as well, and the Omega test would return "no".

For the last part, if the I-Test produced a maybe answer, it is because some term $a_k x_k$ did not pass the I-Test's check, and furthermore, Banerjee bounds was unable to disprove real solutions. By Lemma 3, we again know that the Omega test would also detect a contradiction in the real shadow's calculation after moving $a_k x_k$, and would attempt to disprove the existence of real solution by checking the real shadow produced by FMVE. Since the Banerjee bounds test was unable to rule out real solutions, FMVE would also be unable to do so. Thus, the Omega test would begin exhaustively searching bounds on x_k for a integer solution.   □

5 Multidimensional Arrays

The previous results apply to multidimensional arrays provided the subscript expressions are uncoupled. If so, then *regardless of the number of array dimensions*, when any of the tests we've considered eliminates a variable x_k, there are only two inequalities in the set S that contain x_k: (1) the inequality describing the loop limits on x_k:

$$L_k \leq x_k \leq U_k$$

and (2) the single inequality resulting from the subscript expression in which x_k appears:

$$c_L \leq \sum_{i \in V} a_i x_i \leq c_U$$

The tests we've considered will simply make a single pass through the variables in order of non-descending coefficients. As each variable is considered, the tests will attempt to eliminate it from one of the d subscript expressions in which it appears.

6 Conclusion

This paper demonstrates the symmetry between FMVE and the Banerjee bounds test, and between their extensions, the Omega Test and I-Test, respectively. We specified a number of restrictions on the dependence problem so that both sets of tests would be applicable.

We show that FMVE and the Banerjee bounds test proceed in lockstep fashion in determining whether real solutions exist to a set of linear inequalities (Lemma 2), although some of the bounds comparisons FMVE makes would be irrelevant under the restrictions we specify.

Likewise, we see the Omega test's extension to FMVE mirroring the I-Test's extension to the Banerjee Bounds test. We see that the dark shadow inequality $(aU - bL \geq (a-1)(b-1))$ is exactly the same as the I-Test's $U - L + 1 \geq b$ restriction under the conditions set forth in Section 1.

Finally, we see the correspondence between the answers given by the I-Test and Omega tests. We also note that the Omega test always produces a yes/no answer, but may have to resort to an expensive sequential search of variable bounds in order to produce this answer. We show that the I-Test gives an inconclusive (maybe) answer if and only if the Omega test requires exponential time to produce an exact answer.

Although the types of dependence problems permitted under the restrictions we specify in Section 1 predominate in practice [9], they nonetheless place the Omega Test/FMVE at a disadvantage, since we exclude all cases where the Omega test is applicable, but the I-Test is not. Furthermore, the I-Test/Banerjee Bounds test will be faster than the Omega test under these conditions, because the latter would make extraneous bounds comparisons that are inconsequential under the restrictions we specify.

References

1. Williams, H.P. (1976). Fourier-Motzkin Elimination Extension to Integer Programming Problems. *Journal of Combinatorial Theory (A)*, 21:118-123.
2. Williams, H.P. (1983). A Characterisation of All Feasible Solutions to an Integer Program. *Discrete Applied Mathematics*, 5:147-155.
3. Wolfe, Michael (1996). *High Performance Compilers for Parallel Computing*, Redwood City, Ca.: Addison-Wesley Publishing Company.
4. U. Banerjee (1988). *Dependence Analysis for SuperComputing*, Norwell, Mass.: Kluwer Academic Publishers.
5. U. Banerjee (1997). *Dependence Analysis*, Boston, Mass.: Kluwer Academic Publishers. p. 106
6. Psarris, Kleanthis, David Klappholz, and Xiangyun Kong (1991). On the Accuracy of the Banerjee Test. *Journal of Parallel and Distributed Computing*, June, 12(2):152-158.
7. Kong, Xiangyun, Psarris Kleanthis, and David Klappholz (1991). The I-Test: An Improved Dependence Test for Automatic Parallelization and Vectorization. *IEEE Transactions on Parallel and Distributed Systems*, July, 2(3): 342-349.
8. Psarris, Kleanthis, Xiangyun Kong, and David Klappholz (1993). The Direction Vector I-Test. *IEEE Transactions on Parallel and Distributed Systems*, November, 4(11):1280-1290.
9. Psarris, Kleanthis, and Santosh Pande (1994). An Empirical Study of the I-Test for Exact Data Depedence. *1994 International Conference on Parallel Processing* August, 1994
10. Pugh, William (1991) The Omega Test: A Fast and Practical Integer Programming Algorithm for Dependence Analysis. *Supercomputing '91*
11. Pugh, William (1992). A Practical Algorithm for Exact Array Dependence Analysis. *Communications of the ACM*, August, 35(8): 102-114.

The Access Region Test [*]

Jay Hoeflinger[1] and Yunheung Paek[2]

[1] Center for Simulation of Advanced Rockets, University of Illinois at
Urbana-Champaign
[2] Department of Electrical Engineering, Korea Advanced Institute of Science &
Technology

Abstract. Traditional loop-based dependence analysis techniques have
limitations when non-affine expressions are used, when interprocedural
analysis is required, or when analysis of non-loops is needed. In this
work, we return to first principles to devise a more general parallelism
detection strategy, which includes a dependence analysis technique which
removes some of these limitations. We show how to do interprocedural
dependence testing between arbitrary sections of code as well as loops,
using a technique which includes privatization and recognition of induc-
tions and reductions. We also present the results of recent experiments
that we conducted to test the effectiveness of our algorithm on a variety of actual programs. The results are still preliminary, but are quite
encouraging.

1 Introduction

Most methods for finding dependences between array references within loops
rely on an equation-solving paradigm. In this paradigm, the pair of subscript
expressions for two array reference sites being checked for dependence are equa-
ted. Then an attempt is made to determine whether the equation can have a
solution, subject to constraints on the values of variables in the program, such as
loop indices. In the general case, a linear system is solved to determine whether
the same memory location can be accessed in different loop iterations.

Traditional methods were mainly designed to detect dependences in a loop.
They use a *dependence graph* to represent the dependence relationship between
all pairs of memory references within a loop. These memory references occur at
discrete points within the loop, thus we say that these methods are *point-to-point*
dependence tests.

1.1 Loop-Based Point-to-Point Dependence Analysis

Two of the earliest point-to-point dependence tests were the GCD Test and
the Banerjee Test [2]. In practice, these were simple, efficient, and successful

---

[*] This work is supported in part by Army contract DABT63-95-C-0097; Army contract N66001-97-C-8532; NSF contract MIP-9619351; and a Partnership Award from
IBM and the NJIT SBR program. This work is not necessarily representative of the
positions of the Army or the Government.

at determining dependence, since most subscript expressions occurring in real scientific programs are very simple. However, the simplicity of the tests results in some limitations. For instance, they are not effective for determining dependence for multidimensional arrays with *coupled* subscripts, as stated in [7]. Several *multiple-subscript* tests have been developed to overcome this limitation: the multidimensional GCD Test [2], the λ-test [10], the Power Test [17], and the Delta Test [7].

The above tests are exact in commonly occurring special cases, but in some cases are still too conservative. The Omega Test [13] provides a more general method, based on sets of constraints, capable of handling dependence problems as integer programming problems.

All of the just-mentioned tests have the common problem that they cannot handle subscript expressions which are non-affine. Non-affine subscript expressions occur in irregular codes (subscripted-subscript access), in FFT codes (subscripts frequently involving 2^I), and as a result of compiler transformations (induction variable closed forms and inline expansion of subroutines). To solve this problem, Pugh, et al.[14] enhanced the Omega test with techniques for replacing the non-affine terms in array subscripts with symbolic variables. This technique does not work in all situations, however. The Range Test [3,4] was built to provide a better solution to this problem. It handles non-affine subscript expressions without losing accuracy. Overall, the Range Test is almost as effective as the Omega Test and sometimes out-performs it, due mainly to its accuracy for non-affine expressions [3]. One critical drawback of the Range Test is that it is not a multiple-subscript test, and so is not effective for handling coupled-subscripts.

Clearly, there is room for a new dependence test to address these shortcomings.

1.2 Interprocedural Dependence Analysis with Access Summaries

Interprocedural dependence testing demands new capabilities from dependence tests. Point-to-point testing becomes unwieldy across procedure boundaries, and so has given way to dependence testing using summaries of the accesses made in subroutines.

The use of access summaries for dependence analysis was previously proposed by several researchers such as Balasundaram, et al.[1] and Tang [15]. Several notations have been developed and used for representing access summaries. Most notable are *triplet notation* [8] and sets of linear constraints [1,5,15].

1.3 Dependence Testing Gives Way to Parallelism Detection

While dependence testing has been studied exhaustively, a topic which has not been adequately addressed is a unified method of **parallelism detection**, which not only finds dependences, but categorizes them for easy removal with important compiler transformations.

Table 1. Traditional data dependence definition

Earlier access	Read	Write	Read	Write
Later access	Read	Read	Write	Write
Dependence Type:	Input	Flow	Anti	Output

Eigenmann, et al [6] studied a set of benchmark programs and determined that the most important compiler analyses needed to parallelize them were array privatization, reduction and induction (idiom) analysis, and dependence analysis for non-affine subscript expressions, and that all of those must be done in the presence of strong symbolic interprocedural analysis.

The need for a new dependence testing technique prompts us to go back to first principles, rethink what data dependence means and ask whether dependence analysis can be done **with compiler transformations in mind**.

The key contribution of this paper is the description of a *general interprocedural parallelism detection* technique. It includes a general dependence analysis technique, described in Section 4, called the *Access Region Test* (ART). The ART is a multiple-subscript, interprocedural, summary-based test, combining privatization and idiom recognition. It represents memory locations in a novel form called a *Linear Memory Access Descriptor* (LMAD)[12], described in Section 3. We implemented the ART in the Polaris compiler [4] and experimented with ten benchmark codes. The results of our preliminary experiments are presented in Section 5.

2   Summarizing Memory Access Patterns for Dependence Analysis

The traditional notion of data dependence is based on classifying the relationship between two accesses to the same memory location, relating the type of each access (Read or Write) and the order of the accesses. A data dependence arc is a directed arc from an earlier instruction to a later instruction, both of which access a single memory location in a program. The four types of arcs are determined as shown in Table 1.

Input dependences can be safely ignored when doing parallelization. Anti and output dependences (also called *memory-related* dependences) can be removed by using more memory, usually by privatizing the memory location involved. Flow dependences (also called true dependences) can sometimes be removed by transforming the original code through techniques such as induction variable analysis and reduction analysis [16].

A generalized, notion of data dependence between arbitrary sections of code can be built by returning to first principles. Instead of considering a single instruction as a memory reference point, we can consider an arbitrary sequence of instructions as an indivisible memory referencing unit. The only thing we require is that the memory referencing unit be executed entirely on a single processor. We refer to this memory referencing unit as a *dependence grain*.

Table 2. Write-order summary scheme for loops and arbitrary grains. RO=ReadOnly, WF=WriteFirst, RW= ReadWrite.

Access	RO	RW	WF
Dep. Type	Input	Flow	Anti/Output

For loops

	RO later	WF later	RW later
RO earlier	Input	Anti/Output	Flow
WF earlier	Flow	Anti/Output	Flow
RW earlier	Flow	Anti/Output	Flow

For arbitrary dependence grains

If we want to know whether two dependence grains may be executed in parallel, then we must do dependence analysis between the grains. Since a single grain may access the same memory address many times, we must summarize the accesses in some useful way and relate the type and order of the accesses to produce a *representative dependence* for the memory address between the two grains.

Definition 1. *A* **representative dependence arc** *is a single dependence arc for a particular memory address showing the order in which two dependence grains must be executed to preserve the sequential semantics of accesses to that address.*

There are many possible ways to summarize memory accesses. The needs of the analysis and the desired precision determine which way is appropriate. To illustrate this idea, we describe the *write-order summary* scheme, which underlies the Access Region Test.

2.1   The Write-Order Summary Scheme

When the dependence grains are loop iterations, the dependence problem is a special case of the more general problem in that a single section of code (the loop body) represents all dependence grains. This simplifies the dependence analysis task.

We can classify an access to a memory location in a loop iteration as to whether it is read-only or not. If it is read-only, there is no dependence. If it is not read-only, then there is at least one write to the location within the iteration. If the write is done before any other access, and a dependence exists within the loop for that location, then the location may be privatized to remove the dependence. To discern these cases, we can classify memory locations in three classes: ReadOnly (only reads to the location), WriteFirst (a write happens first in the grain), and ReadWrite (either a read happens first in the grain, followed by a write, or the order is unknown), as shown in Table 2.

Using the write-order summary scheme for non-loop dependence grains, any locations which are read-only in both grains would correspond to an input dependence, those which are write-first in the later grain would correspond to a memory related dependence (since it is written first in the later grain, the later grain need not wait for any value from the earlier grain), and all others would correspond to a flow dependence. This is illustrated on the right in Table 2.

```
for I = 1 to N {
    if (P) { A(I) = ··· }
    if (Q) { ··· = A(I) }
}
```

Fig. 1. Only through logical implication can the compiler determine the ordering of accesses to array A in the loop.

2.2   Establishing an Order Among Accesses

Knowing the order of accesses is crucial to the write-order summarization scheme, so we must establish an ordering of the accesses within the program. If a program contained only straight-line code, establishing an ordering between accesses would be trivial. One could simply sweep through the program in "execution-order", keeping track of when the accesses happen. But branching statements and unknown variables make it more difficult to show that one particular access happens before another.

For example, consider the loop in Figure 1. The write to A(I) happens before the read of A(I) only if both P and Q are true. But if Q is true and P is false, then the read happens without the write having happened first. If P and Q have values which are unknown and unrelated, then the compiler has no way of knowing which ordering will occur at execution time, and must act conservatively - classifying A(I) as ReadWrite. On the other hand, if the compiler can show that P and Q are related and that in fact Q *implies* P, the compiler can know that the write happened first. So, for code involving conditional branches, the major tool the compiler has in determining the ordering is *logical implication*.

To facilitate the use of logical implication to establish execution order, the representation of each memory reference must potentially have an *execution predicate* attached to it. In fact, the access in Figure 1 could be classified as ReadOnly with the condition $\{\neg P \wedge Q\}$, WriteFirst with condition $\{P\}$ and ReadWrite if P and Q contain a loop-variant component.

Definition 2. *The* **execution predicate** *is a boolean-valued expression, attached to the representation of a memory reference, which specifies the condition(s) under which the reference actually takes place. An execution predicate P will be denoted as* $\{P\}$.

2.3   Using Summary Sets to Store Memory Locations

We can classify a set of memory locations according to their access type by adding a symbolic representation of them to the appropriate *summary set*.

Definition 3. *A* **summary set** *is a symbolic description of a set of memory locations.*

We have chosen to use Linear Memory Access Descriptors (LMADs), described in Section 3, to represent memory accesses within a summary set. To represent memory accesses in the write-order summary scheme, according to Table 2, requires three summary sets for each dependence grain: ReadOnly (RO), ReadWrite (RW), and WriteFirst (WF).

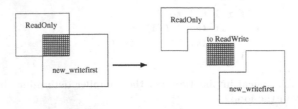

Fig. 2. The intersection of earlier ReadOnly accesses with later WriteFirst accesses - the result is a ReadWrite set.

$t_{WF} \leftarrow WF_n - WF$	$t_{RO} \leftarrow RO_n - RO$	$t_{RW} \leftarrow RW_n - WF$
$t_{WF} \leftarrow t_{WF} - RW$	$t_{RO} \leftarrow t_{RO} - WF$	$t_{RW} \leftarrow t_{RW} - RW$
$RW \leftarrow RW \cup (t_{WF} \cap RO)$	$t_{RO} \leftarrow t_{RO} - RW$	$RW \leftarrow RW \cup (t_{RW} \cap RO)$
$RO \leftarrow RO - (t_{WF} \cap RO)$	$RO \leftarrow RO \cup t_{RO}$	$RO \leftarrow RO - (t_{RW} \cap RO)$
$t_{WF} \leftarrow t_{WF} - (t_{WF} \cap RO)$		$t_{RW} \leftarrow t_{RW} - (t_{RW} \cap RO)$
$WF \leftarrow WF \cup t_{WF}$		$RW \leftarrow RW \cup t_{RW}$

Fig. 3. Classification of new summary sets RO_n, WF_n, and RW_n into the existing summary sets RO, WF, and RW. The t_x are temporary sets.

2.4   Classification of Memory References

Each memory location referred to in the program must be entered into one of these summary sets, in a process called *classification*. A program is assumed to be a series of nested elementary contexts[**]: *procedures, simple statements*, if *statements, loops*, and call *statements*. Thus, at every point in the program, there will be an enclosing context and an enclosed context.

The contexts are traversed in "execution order". The summary sets of the enclosing context are built by (recursively) calculating the summary sets for each enclosed context and distributing them into the summary sets of the enclosing context. We can determine memory locations in common between summary sets by an intersection operation, as illustrated in Figure 2.

Classification takes as input the current state of the three summary sets for the enclosing context (RO, WF, and RW) and the three new summary sets for the last enclosed context which was processed (RO_n, WF_n, and RW_n) and produces updated summary sets for the enclosing context. The sets for the enclosed context are absorbed in a way which maintains proper classification for each memory location. For example, a memory location which was RO in the enclosing context (up to this point) and is WF or RW in the newly-calculated enclosed context becomes RW in the updated enclosing context. The steps of classification can be expressed in set notation, as shown in Figure 3.

[**] If the programming language does not force this through its structure, then the program will have to be transformed into that form through a *normalization* process.

Program Context Classification. Simple statements are classified in the obvious way, according to the order of their reads and writes of memory. All statements within an `if` context are classified in the ordinary way, except that the *if-condition* P is applied as an execution predicate to the statements in the `if` block and $\neg P$ is applied to the statements in the `else` block. Descriptors for the `if` and `else` blocks are then intersected and their execution predicates are *or*'ed together, to produce the result for the whole `if` context.

Classifying the memory accesses in a loop is a two-step process. First, the summary sets for a single iteration of the loop must be collected by a scan through the loop body in execution order. They contain the symbolic form of the accesses, possibly parameterized by the index of the loop. Next, the summary sets must be *expanded* by the loop index so that at the end of the process, the sets represent the locations accessed during the entire execution of the loop.

The expansion process can be illustrated by the following loop:

```
do I = 1, 100
    A(I) =  . . .
end do
```

For a single iteration of the surrounding loop, the location `A(I)` is write-first. When `A(I)` is expanded by the loop index `I`, the representation `A(1:100)` results. Summary sets for `while` loops can be expanded similarly, but we must use a basic induction variable as a loop index and represent the number of iterations as "unknown". This expansion process makes it possible to avoid traversing the back-edges of loops for classification.

Classification for a `call` statement involves first the calculation of the access representation for the text of the `call` statement itself, calculation of the summary sets for the procedure being called, matching formal with actual parameters, and finally translating the summary sets involved from the called context to the calling context (described further in Section 3.3).

3   Representing Array Accesses in Summary Sets

To manipulate the array access summaries for dependence analysis, we needed a notation which could precisely represent a collection of memory accesses. A previous study [12] gave us a clear picture of the strengths and weaknesses of existing notations. It also gave us the requirements the notation should meet to support efficient array access summarization.

- Complex array subscripts should be represented accurately. In particular, non-affine expressions should be handled because time-critical loops in real programs often contain array references with non-affine subscripts.
- The notation should have simplification operations defined for it, so that complex accesses could be changed to a simpler form.
- To facilitate fast and accurate translation of access summaries across procedure boundaries, non-trivial *array reshaping* at a procedure boundary should be handled efficiently and accurately.

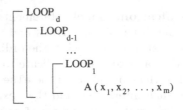

Fig. 4. An m-dimensional array reference in a d-loop nest.

To meet these requirements, we introduced a new notation, called the *Linear Memory Access Descriptor*, which is detailed in the previous literature [9,11,12]. Due to space constraints, this section will only briefly discuss a few basics of the LMAD necessary to describe our dependence analysis technique in Section 4.

3.1   Representing the Array Accesses in a Loop Nest

If an array is declared as an m-dimensional array:

$$\text{A}(L_1 : U_1, L_2 : U_2, \cdots, L_m : U_m),$$

and referenced in the program with an array name followed by a list of *subscripting expressions* in a nested loop, as in Figure 4, then implicit in this notation is an *array subscripting function* F_m which translates the array reference into a set of offsets from a base address in memory:

$$F_m(x_1, x_2, \cdots, x_m) = (x_1(\mathbf{i}) - L_1)\lambda_1 + (x_2(\mathbf{i}) - L_2)\lambda_2 + \cdots + (x_m(\mathbf{i}) - L_m)\lambda_m$$

where $\mathbf{i}$ refers to the set of loop indices for the surrounding nested loops, $\mathbf{i} = (i_1, i_2, \cdots, i_d)$ and λ_k refers to a set of constants determined by the rules of the programming language.

As the nested loop executes, each loop index i_k moves through its set of values, and the subscripting function F_m generates a sequence of offsets from the base address, which we call the **subscripting offset sequence**:

$$F_m(x_1, x_2, \cdots, x_m)|_{i_d, i_{d-1}, \cdots, i_1} = S_1, S_2, \cdots, S_n$$

The isolated effect of a single loop index on F_m is a sequence of offsets which can **always** be **precisely represented** in terms of

– its starting offset,
– the expression representing the difference between two successive offsets, and
– the total number of offsets in the sequence.

For example, consider a non-affine subscript expression:

```
real A(0:*)
do I = 1, N
   A(2**I)
end do
```

The subscripting offset sequence is:

$$F_1(2^I)\big|_I = 2, 4, 8, 16, \cdots$$

The difference between two successive values can be easily expressed. To be clear, the difference is defined to be *the expression to be added to the Ith member of the sequence to produce the $I + 1$th member of the sequence*:

$$S_{I+1} - S_I = 2^I.$$

So, this sequence may be precisely represented as a sequence starting with 2, differing between members by 2^I, with N members.

3.2 Components of an LMAD

We refer to the subscripting offset sequence generated by an array reference, due to a single loop index, as a *dimension* of the access. We use this as the *dimension* of an LMAD.

Definition 4. *A **dimension** of an LMAD is a representation of the subscripting offset sequence for a set of memory references. It consists of*

- *a starting value, called the **base offset***
- *a difference expression, called the **stride**, and*
- *the number of values in the sequence, represented as a **dimension index**, taking on all integer values between 0 and a **dimension-bound** value.*

Notice that the access produced by an array reference in a nested loop has as many dimensions as there are loops in the nest. Also, the dimension index of each dimension may be thought of as a *normalized* form of the actual loop index occurring in the program when the LMAD is originally constructed by the compiler from the program text.

In addition to the three expressions described above for an LMAD dimension, a *span* expression is maintained for each dimension. The span is defined as the difference between the offsets of the last and first elements in the dimension. The span is useful for doing certain operations and simplifications on the LMAD (for instance detecting *internal overlap*, as described in Section 4.2), however it is only accurate when the subscript expressions for the array access are *monotonic*.

A single base offset is stored for the whole access. An example of an array access, its access pattern in memory, and its LMAD may be seen in Figure 5.

The LMAD for the array access in Figure 4 is written as

$$\mathcal{A} \, _{\sigma_1, \quad \sigma_2, \quad \cdots, \sigma_d}^{\delta_{1[i_1 \leq u_1]}, \delta_{2[i_2 \leq u_2]}, \cdots, \delta_{d[i_d \leq u_d]}} + \tau,$$

with a series of d comma-separated strides $(\delta_1 \cdots \delta_d)$ as superscripts to the variable name and a series of d comma-separated spans $(\sigma_1 \cdots \sigma_d)$ as subscripts to the variable name, with a base offset (τ) written to the right of the descriptor. The dimension index is only included in the written form of the LMAD if it is needed for clarity. In that case,

$$[index \leq dimension\text{-}bound]$$

is written as a subscript to the appropriate stride.

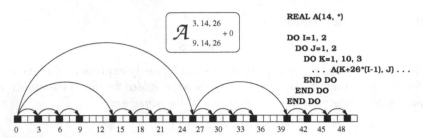

Fig. 5. A memory access diagram for the array A in a nested loop and the Access Region Descriptor which represents it.

3.3 Interprocedural Translation of an LMAD

A useful property of the LMAD is the ease with which it may be translated across procedure boundaries. Translation of array access information across procedure boundaries can be difficult if the declaration of a formal array parameter differs from the declaration of its corresponding actual parameter. Array access representations which depend on the declared dimensionality of an array (as most do) are faced with converting the representation from one dimensionality to another when array reshaping occurs. This is not always possible without introducing complicated mapping functions. This is the *array reshaping problem.*

When LMADs are used to represent the accesses, however, the array reshaping problem disappears. The LMAD notation is not dependent upon the declared dimensionality of the array. When a subroutine is called by reference, the base address of the formal array parameter is set to be whatever address is passed in the actual argument list. Any memory accesses which occur in the subroutine would be represented in the calling routine in their LMAD form relative to that base address. Whenever it is desired to translate the LMAD for a formal argument into the caller's context, we simply translate the formal argument's variable name into the actual argument's name, and add the base offset of the actual parameter to that of the LMAD for the formal parameter. For example, if the actual argument in a Fortran code is an indexed array, such as

                    `call X( A(2*I+1) )` ! `Real A(1:100)`

then the offset from the beginning of the array A for the actual argument is $2I$. Suppose that the matching formal parameter in the subroutine X is Z and the LMAD for the access to Z in X is

$$\mathcal{Z} \; {}^{10,200}_{100,400} + 10.$$

When the access to Z, in the subroutine, is translated into the calling routine, then the LMAD would be represented in terms of variable A as follows:

$$\mathcal{A} \; {}^{10,200}_{100,400} + 10 + 2I,$$

which results from simply adding the offset after the renaming of Z to A. Notice that A now has a two-dimensional access even though it is declared to be one-dimensional.

4   The Access Region Test

In this section, we first describe the general dependence analysis method, called the *Access Region Test*, based on intersecting LMADs. The general method can detect data dependence between any two arbitrary sections of code. Then, we show a simplification of the general method which works for loop parallelization.

4.1   General Dependence Testing with Summary Sets

Given the symbolic summary sets RO_1, WF_1, and RW_1 (as discussed in Section 2.3), representing the memory accesses for an earlier (in the sequential execution of the program) dependence grain, and the sets RO_2, WF_2, and RW_2 for a later grain, it can be discovered whether any locations are accessed in both grains by finding the intersection of the earlier and later summary sets. Any non-empty intersection represents a dependence between grains. However, some of those dependences may be removed by compiler transformations.

If any of the following are non-empty: $RO_1 \cap WF_2$, $WF_1 \cap WF_2$, $RW_1 \cap WF_2$, or $RO_1 \cap RW_2$, then they represent dependences which can be removed by privatizing the intersecting regions.

If $RW_1 \cap RW_2$ is non-empty, and all references involved are in either induction form or reduction form, then the dependence may be removed by induction or reduction transformations.

If any of the other intersections: $WF_1 \cap RO_2$, $WF_1 \cap RW_2$, or $RW_1 \cap RO_2$ are non-empty, then they represent non-removable dependences.

4.2   Loop Dependence Testing with the ART

As stated in Section 2.1, dependence testing between loop iterations is a special case of general dependence testing, described in Section 4.1. Loop-based dependence testing considers a loop iteration to be a dependence grain, meaning all dependence grains have the same summary sets.

Once we expand the summary sets by the loop index (Section 1), cross-iteration dependence can be noticed in three ways: within one LMAD, between two LMADs of one summary set, or between two of the summary sets.

Overlap within a Single LMAD. Internal overlap within an LMAD occurs when loop-index expansion causes its subscripting offset sequence to contain at least one duplicated offset. This would indicate a cross-iteration dependence. This condition can be easily checked during the classification process and flagged in the LMAD.

Intersection of LMADs within a Summary Set. Even though two LMADs in the same summary set do not intersect initially, expansion by a loop index could cause them to intersect. Such an intersection would represent a cross-iteration dependence. Such an intersection within RO would be an input dependence, so this summary set need not be checked.

Intersection of Two Summary Sets. There are only three summary sets to consider in loop dependence testing, instead of six (because there is only one dependence grain), so there are only three intersections to try, instead of the eight required in Section 4.1. After expansion by the loop index, the following intersections must be done:

$$RO \cap WF$$
$$RO \cap RW$$
$$WF \cap RW$$

An intersection between any pair of the sets RO, WF, and RW involves at least one read and one write operation, implying a dependence.

Within WF, internal overlaps or intersection between LMADs can both be removed by privatization. Within RW, internal overlaps or intersection between LMADs can be removed if all references involved are in induction or reduction form.

4.3   The Loop-Based Access Region Test Algorithm

For each loop L in the program, and its summary sets RO, WF, and RW, expanded by the loop index of L as described in Section 1, the ART does the following:

- Check for internal overlap (an overlap flag is set by the expansion due to the loop index of L) of any LMAD in WF or RW. Any found within WF can be removed by privatization. Any found in RW is removed if all references involved are in either induction or reduction form. Once overlap for an LMAD is noted, its overlap flag is reset.
- Check for non-empty intersection between any pair of LMADs in WF (removed by privatization) or RW (possibly removed by induction or reduction, as above).
- For all possible pairs of summary sets, from the group RO, WF, and RW, check for any non-empty intersection between two LMADs, each pair containing LMADs from different sets. Any intersection found here is noted as a dependence and moved to RW.

If no non-removable dependences are found, the loop may be declared parallel. Wherever uncertainty occurs in this process, demand-driven deeper analysis can be triggered, or run-time tests can be generated.

4.4   Generality of the ART

The Access Region Test is a general, conservative dependence test. By design, it can discern three types of dependence: input, flow, and memory-related. It cannot distinguish between anti and output dependence, but that is because for our purposes it was considered unimportant - both types of dependence can be removed by privatization transformations. For other purposes, a different classification scheme can be formulated, with appropriate summary sets, to produce the required information, much as data flow analysis can be used to solve different data flow problems.

Table 3. A comparison of the current version of the ART, the Range test, and the Omega test. A line labeled "X − Y" refers to the number of loops which test X could parallelize and test Y could not. All other loops in the codes were parallelized identically by all tests.

codes	tfft2	trfd	mdg	flo52	hydro2d	bdna	arc2d	tomcatv	swim	ocean
ART − Range	7	0	5	0	0	11	0	0	0	8
Range − Omega	×	6	6	1	3	0	0	0	0	76
ART − Omega	>7	6	11	1	3	11	0	0	0	84
Omega − Range	×	0	1	0	0	6	0	0	0	8

4.5   A Multi-dimensional Recursive Intersection Algorithm

Intersecting two arbitrary LMADs is very complex and probably intractable. But if two LMADs to be compared represent accesses with the same strides, which has been quite often true in our experiments with real programs, then they are similar enough to make the intersection algorithm tractable. We have developed a multi-dimensional, recursive algorithm for intersecting LMADs. Space constraints prevent us from presenting it here, but it may be found in [9].

5   Comparison with Other Techniques

We implemented a preliminary version of the ART in *Polaris* [4], a parallelizing compiler developed at Illinois, and experimented with ten benchmark codes. In these experiments, it was observed that the ART is highly effective for programs with complex subscripting expressions, such as ocean, bdna, and tfft2. Table 3 shows a summary of the experimental results that were obtained at the time we prepared this paper.

The numbers of loops additionally parallelized by the ART are small, but some of these are time-critical loops which contain complex array subscripting expressions. For instance, in ocean, the eight additional parallelized loops were pieces of the most important loop, ftrvmt_109 found in clones of ftrvmt. Also, our previous experiments, reported in [11], showed that the ART applied by hand increased the parallel speedup for tfft2 by factor of 7.4 on the Cray T3D 64 processors.

As can be expected, the ART, the Omega Test, and the Range Test all find equivalent parallelism for the codes with only simple array subscripting expressions, such as tomcatv, arc2d and swim, as shown in Table 3.

The ART has an advantage over the tests discussed in Section 1, in two ways:

− It handles coupled subscripts, which are a problem for the Range Test, and non-affine expressions, which are a problem for most other tests.
− The test is accurate interprocedurally since LMADs may be translated precisely across procedure boundaries.

```
                                   SUBROUTINE FFTZ2 (IS, L, M, U, X, Y)
DIMENSION U(1), X(1), Y(1)         DIMENSION U(*), X(*),
DO I=0,2**(M/2)-1                  DIMENSION Y(0:2**(L-1)-1, 0:1, 0:2**(M-L)-1, 0:1)
   CALL CFFTZWORK (IS, M-M/2,       DO I=0,2**(M-L)-1
                   U(1+3*2**(1+M)/2),    DO K=0,2**(L-1)-1
                   Y(1+I*2**(1+M-M/2)),     ... = X(1+K+I*2**(L-1))
                   X)                        ... = X(1+K+I*2**(L-1)+2**M)
END DO                                       ... = X(1+K+I*2**(L-1)+2**(M-1))
SUBROUTINE CFFTZWORK (IS, M, U, X, Y)        ... = X(1+K+I*2**(L-1)+2**(M-1)+2**M)
DIMENSION U(1), X(1), Y(1)                   Y(K,0,I,0) = ...
DO LO=1, (M+1)/2                             Y(K,0,I,1) = ...
   CALL FFTZ2 (IS,2*LO-1, M, U, X, Y)        Y(K,1,I,0) = ...
   CALL FFTZ2 (IS,2*LO  , M, U, Y, X)        Y(K,1,I,1) = ...
END DO                                    END DO
                                   END DO
```

Fig. 6. A simplified excerpt from the benchmark program tfft2, which the ART can determine to be free of dependences.

To separate the value of the ART from the value of the LMAD, it is instructive to consider the question of whether other dependence tests might be as powerful as the ART if they represented memory accesses with the LMAD notation. The answer to this question is "no".

Take as an example the Omega Test. The mechanism of the Omega Test is only defined for affine expressions. The user of the Omega Test must extract the linear coefficients of the loop-variant values (loop indices, etc), plus provide a set of constraints on the loop-variants. The LMADs partially fill the role of the constraints, but if non-affine expressions are used, there is no way to extract linear coefficients for the non-affine parts. So even using the LMAD, the Omega Test could not handle non-affine subscript expressions because its mechanism is simply not well-defined for such expressions.

Likewise, if the Range Test were to use the LMAD to represent value ranges for variables, that still would not change its basic mechanism, which makes it a single-subscript test, unable to handle coupled-subscripts.

Figure 6 shows an example, from the tfft2 benchmark code, which neither the Omega Test nor the Range Test can find independent due to the apparent complexity of the non-affine expressions involved, yet the ART *can* find them independent interprocedurally at the top-most loop.

6   Conclusion

This paper describes a new classification technique for recursively summarizing memory accesses interprocedurally in a program. This technique is used to formulate a specific type of interprocedural data dependence analysis, starting from first principles, which combines privatization and idiom recognition with parallelization. The resulting Access Region Test eliminates some of the limitations which encumber the loop-based, linear system-solving data dependence paradigm.

References

1. V. Balasundaram and K. Kennedy. A Technique for Summarizing Data Access and its Use in Parallelism Enhancing Transformations. *Proceedings of the SIGPLAN Conference on Programming Language Design and Implementation*, June 1989.
2. U. Banerjee. *Dependence Analysis*. Kluwer Academic Publishers, Norwell, MA, 1997.
3. W. Blume. *Symbolic Analysis Techniques for Effective Automatic Parallelization*. PhD thesis, Univ. of Illinois at Urbana-Champaign, Dept. of Computer Science, June 1995.
4. W. Blume, R. Doallo, R. Eigenmann, J. Grout, J. Hoeflinger, T. Lawrence, J. Lee, D. Padua, Y. Paek, W. Pottenger, L. Rauchwerger, and P. Tu. Parallel Programming with Polaris. *IEEE Computer*, 29(12):78–82, December 1996.
5. B. Creusillet and F. Irigoin. Interprocedural Array Region Analyses. In *Lecture Notes in Computer Science*. Springer Verlag, New York, New York, August 1995.
6. R. Eigenmann, J. Hoeflinger, and D. Padua. On the Automatic Parallelization of the Perfect Benchmarks. *IEEE Transactions on Parallel and Distributed Systems*, pages 5–23, January 1998.
7. G. Goff, K. Kennedy, and C. Tseng. Practical Dependence Testing. In *Proceedings of the ACM SIGPLAN 91 Conference on Programming Language Design and Implementation*, pages 15–29, June 1991.
8. P. Havlak and K. Kennedy. An Implementation of Interprocedural Bounded Regular Section Analysis. *IEEE Transactions on Parallel and Distributed Systems*, 2(3):350–360, July 1991.
9. J. Hoeflinger. *Interprocedural Parallelization Using Memory Classification Analysis*. PhD thesis, Univ. of Illinois at Urbana-Champaign, Dept. of Computer Science, August, 1998.
10. Z. Li, P. Yew, and C. Zhu. An Efficient Data Dependence Analysis for Parallelizing Compilers. *IEEE Transactions on Parallel and Distributed Systems*, 1(1):26–34, January 1990.
11. Y. Paek. *Automatic Parallelization for Distributed Memory Machines Based on Access Region Analysis*. PhD thesis, Univ. of Illinois at Urbana-Champaign, Dept. of Computer Science, April 1997.
12. Y. Paek, J. Hoeflinger, and D. Padua. Simplification of Array Access Patterns for Compiler Optimizations. *Proceedings of the SIGPLAN Conference on Programming Language Design and Implementation*, June 1998.
13. W. Pugh. A Practical Algorithm for Exact Array Dependence Analysis. *Communications of the ACM*, 35(8), August 1992.
14. W. Pugh and D. Wonnacott. Nonlinear Array Dependence Analysis. Technical Report 123, Univ of Maryland at College Park, November 1994.
15. P. Tang. Exact Side Effects for Interprocedural Dependence Analysis. In *1993 ACM International Conference on Supercomputing, Tokyo, Japan*, pages 137–146, July 1993.
16. M. Wolfe. *High Performance Compilers for Parallel Computing*. Addison-Wesley Publishing Co., New York, 1996.
17. M. Wolfe and C. Tseng. The Power Test for Data Dependence. *IEEE Transactions on Parallel and Distributed Systems*, September 1992.

A Precise Fixpoint Reaching Definition Analysis for Arrays

Jean-François Collard[1] and Martin Griebl[2]

[1] CNRS - PriSM. University of Versailles
45 avenue des Etats-Unis. 78035 Versailles. France.
jfc@prism.uvsq.fr
[2] FMI. University of Passau
Innstr 32. 94032 Passau. Germany.
griebl@fmi.uni-passau.de

Abstract. This paper describes a precise reaching definition (RD) analysis tuned for arrays.

RD analyses are of two kinds. The first group, Maximal Fixed Point (MFP) analyses, considers arrays as indivisible objects and does not contrast the side-effects of separate instances of writes. Its main benefit, however, is its wide applicability (e.g. to any unstructured program). On the other hand, analyses based on integer linear programming are able to pinpoint, for a given read instance, which instance of which write reference actually defined the read value. They are, however, restricted to limited classes of programs.

Our analysis tries to take the best of both worlds by computing, in an iterated MFP framework, instancewise RDs of array elements.

1 Introduction

Over the past decade, two different frameworks have been succesful in reaching definition analysis.

The first one is based on abstract interpretation, with one main feature being an iterative propagation of data-flow information until a maximal fixed point (MFP) is reached [1]. Its main benefit is its wide applicability, e.g., to any unstructured program. Its drawback is that the granularity of control and data units is pretty coarse: statements as well as arrays are usually considered as atomic units, i.e., these analyses do not distinguish between different array *cells*, or between different run-time *instances* of a statement, e.g., caused by loops.

The second framework is tailored for arrays and is able to pinpoint, for a given read instance, which instance of which write reference actually defined the read value. Methods in this framework are typically based on integer linear programming (ILP) and may be caracterized by their use of symbolic solvers to precisely analyze arrays elementwise. However, they are usually restricted to very limited classes of programs.

Of course, this classication is rough, and several works are closely related (for related work of the two frameworks cf. Section 3 and 4). But none of them, to

L. Carter and J. Ferrante (Eds.): LCPC'99, LNCS 1863, pp. 286–302, 2000.
© Springer-Verlag Berlin Heidelberg 2000

the best of our knowledge, answers (if possible) the following question: given a run-time instance of a read reference in a possibly unstructured program (e.g., containing gotos), which instance of which write statement defines the read value?

To answer this question, this paper tries to take the best of both worlds. This is not simply a philosophical issue, but it has also practical relevance: the instancewise analysis described in this paper combines the applicability of the first framework with the power of the second framework. Furthermore, since the analysis is based on iterative propagation on the program's control-flow graph, it makes instancewise analysis closer to abstract interpretation and, hence, may allow in the future, to extend to arrays other well-known data-flow analyses, not just reaching definitions.

2   A Motivating Example

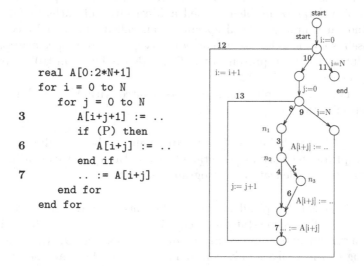

Fig. 1. Program piter and its Control-Flow Graph.

Consider program piter in Figure 1. (Its Control-Flow Graph (CFG) appears in the same figure but will be discussed later on. Note that we model statements as *edges* instead of nodes, following the findings of Knoop et al. [11]. Our analysis, however, applies to the traditional definition of CFGs as well.)

Since reaching definition analyses of the MFP framework consider array A as a one indivisible object and statements **3**, **6** and **7** as atomic units, the result of the analysis will be: both, **3** or **6**, can be reaching definitions for the read of A in **7**.[1]

---

[1] Things are even worse for dataflow analyses based on lexical names of variables. Then, A[i+j] is considered as a variable name (a string with 6 characters), and A[i+j+1] is considered as a separate variable (another string, with 8 characters).

However, the information we want to achieve on the example is:

- At which iterations of i and j may **7** read an *uninitialized* value? In other words, which instances of **7** may be reached by no definition? (The answer is none of them, except perhaps for the very first.)
- Which instances of **3** and/or **6** reach a given, parametric instance (i, j) of **7**?

After having revisited the two frameworks in more detail in the next two sections, we shall derive our new method in Section 5, and afterwards come back to this example in more detail.

3   The MFP Framework

Traditional RD analyses are based on iterative resolution of dataflow equations. More precisely, they rely on a global (i.e., with respect to all possible paths) specification of a dataflow problem, called a Meet-Over-all-Paths (MOP) specification, and on a practical local specification, called Maximal Fixed Point (MFP) whose resolution is iterative. The equality of the MOP specification and the MFP solution has been proven in the Coincidence Theorem [10], extended to the interprocedural case in [12].

We detail below the current drwabacks associated with MFP techniques or with MOP specifications.

Array Cells. No MFP technique we know of distinguishes between different array elements, except for the work in [8] detailed below. However, this is a big issue in, e.g., automatic parallelization or program verification.

Instances of Statements. Typically, different elements of arrays are referenced at different instances of the same statement, e.g., inside a loop. Hence, the desire for elementwise array analysis enforces an *instancewise* analysis. Or, the other way round: as long as the analysis only considers scalar variables, all the instances of a scalar assignment write into the same memory location. However, this does not hold for arrays, as the example in Figure 1 shows: the first instance of **3** writes into A[1], the second into A[2], etc. Hence the need for an instancewise RD analysis.

A paper by Duesterwald et al. [8] is close to our goal. That paper extends the classical framework so as to express, in limited cases, the instances of reaching definitions. Array subscripts must be affine functions of one variable only (the counter of the innermost loop). Moreover, multidimensional arrays are linearized, which requires that array bounds are known numerically at analysis time.

They consider nests with a single loop (or the innermost loop only), and derive, for the read in a given iteration i, the distance d such that the defining write instance occurred at iteration $i - d$. The set of possible values for d is

---

Definitions of the latter can therefore never reach use of the former. See [6] for details.

limited to an integer lattice (a range of integer values, plus a bottom *bot* element and a top $\top$, to denote the iteration count of the loop). Unfortunately, this set of values may not be expressive enough in some cases.

Precision on the Control-flow. Another issue is how precisely control-flow is taken into account. In MFP, all possible paths in the control-flow graph are considered to be valid (in the intraprocedural case), independently of the possible outcomes of predicates in `ifs`, `whiles`, etc. However, this may lead to a big loss in precision.

```
1   if P(..) then x := 0
3   if P(..) then x := 1
5   y := x
```

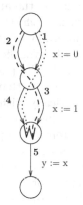

Fig. 2. Impossible execution paths.

To see why, consider the example in Figure 2, and assume predicate P does not depend on x. Then, depending on the outcomes, the execution flows either through both **1** and **3**, or through none of them. In both cases, the definition of x in **1** never can reach **5**.

In the MOP framework, all possible paths are considered. For instance, the two paths denoted with dashed lines in Figure 2 (i.e., paths **1.4** and **2.3**). These paths, however, never correspond to an actual execution. Our analysis takes advantage of a symbolic solver, Omega [14], to avoid this loss of precision. In particular, Omega provides *uninterpreted functions* that allow to manipulate functions on which we have little or no knowledge. On an uninterpreted function F, Omega is able to perform logic operations such as simplifying $F(x) \geq 0 \vee F(x) \leq 0$ to true, or simplifying $F(x) \geq 0 \wedge F(x) < 0$ to false. Such operations are exactly what we need to derive precise reaching definitions on the program in Figure 2 (coding for example $P(..)$ with $F(..) \geq 0$).

4   The ILP Framework

Originally, the instancewise array dataflow analysis based on integer linear programming (ILP) was designed for nested `for` loops whose bounds are affine expressions w.r.t. surrounding loop counters and symbolic constants. The loop body had to consist of assignments to arrays whose indices also had to be affine expressions in outer loop indices and symbolic constants [9]. In this setting, an *iteration vector* of a statement S is the vector which consists of the indices of all loops surrounding S, ordered outside-in. Every run-time "incarnation" of S is a separate instance of S which we precisely identify by S and the iteration vector i. We denote such an instance with $\langle S, i \rangle$. The *iteration domain* $D(\mathbf{s})$ of a statement S is the set of all iteration vectors of S. The iteration domain turns out to be convex (a polytope), and the order in which the iteration vectors are generated by the loop nest is the lexicographic order on the iteration vectors.

In the meantime, the analysis has been extended to more general but structured loops, such as `while` loops. Then, the iteration domain is not a polytope anymore but an unbounded polyhedron.

In other works, the flexibility of the basic idea has also been proved by extensions to explicitliy parallel programs [5] or even to recursive programs [4]. However, it turns out that the effort for solving the integer linear programs increases dramatically with the size of the input program.

In addition, since the basic approach relies on the structure of the input program, an extension to programs without any structure, e.g., containing arbitrary `goto`s, is not straight forward. Current methods in this framework [9, 3,15] would just fail. A simple way out would be to use a preprocessing phase for structuring the program. However, this leads, in general, to significant code duplication. Furthermore, in an interactive compiler environment, the user will not be able to recognize his or her program.

5   Our MFP Technique for Instancewise Reaching Definition Analyses

Section 5.1 defines what an instance-based analysis means when arbitrary `goto`s appear. We then formally define the dataflow equations we solve. An intuitive view of the resolution process is given in Section 5.3, and the algorithm is formally given in Section 5.4. Convergence properies of the algorithm are discussed in Section 5.5.

5.1   How to Label Instances and Define the Execution Order in the Presence of gotos?

Structured Programs. An example of such a structured program is when `goto`s build nested loops, as in Figure 3.

Edge **4** (between n4 and n5) should be labeled by the iteration vector built from the number of **3**s and the number of **2**s, in this order, and assuming the count of **2** is re-initialized to 0 each time **5** is taken.

How Can We Tell a Program is "Structured"? Natural loops do not correspond to the loops we want to detect. Consider for instance Figure 5. The

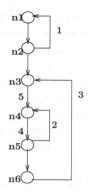

Fig. 3. `gotos` building a structured program.

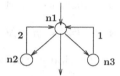

Fig. 4. A graph were loops are ambiguous

natural loop [1] for **3** includes nodes n1, n2, n3 and n4, and edges **1**, **2**, **3**, **4** and **5**, and therefore surrounds the loop on **2**. However, we should not consider the two loops here as nested.

Structural analysis [13] does not provide the information we need either. Consider the example in Figure 4, taken from [13]. Structural analysis detects that this flow graph corresponds to two nested `while` loops. Which loop is innermost, however, depends on the order edges are visited. For our purpose, it would not make much sense in such cases to enforce a nest structure and to derive information about the lexicographic order of an index vector. Therefore, when `gotos` appear in a program segment, and when no separate analysis states otherwise, we handle this segment according to the following section.

Unstructured Program Segments. To precisely identify statement instances in the presence of backward edges, we would need to capture the exact sequence of traversed edges. One way to do this would be to reason on execution traces, or on words built on the alphabet of backward edges. For example, an instance of **4** in Figure 5 could be labeled with a word in {**2, 3**}*. Previous papers of ours explored this way [4], and our experience is that such a labeling scheme is too complex to be usefulwith current compilation techniques.

Therefore, we pick the following trade-off: statements are labeled by the (unordered) list of edge counts, that is, by the *number of times* each edge was traversed *since the unstructured part was entered*. For instance, an instance of **4** in Figure 5 is labeled by (**#2,#3**), where **#2** and **#3** denote the number of times edges **2** and **3** are traversed, respectively. Clearly, the information we lose with this labeling is the order in which these edges are traversed.

One obvious question is how to choose the edges we should consider for a given instance. Let us remark that we may label a statement instance by an additional edge counter, even if traversing this edge does not lead to distinct instances. Inversely, if we "forget" such an edge, we will just have a semi-instancewise analysis, where several instances are collapsed into "super-instances". The simplest and most general solution, however, is to label a statement **s** with the edge counts of all back-edges whose natural loops include statement **s**.

What is then the Execution Order on Instances? When programs are structured, the execution order is the same as if the loops had been made explicit, i.e., the order is the lexicographical order on vectors built from the edge counts. For example, the order between two instances of **4** from Figure 3 is:

$$\langle 4, \#2', \#3' \rangle \prec \langle 4, \#2, \#3 \rangle \iff \#2' < \#2 \lor (\#2' = \#2 \land \#3' < \#3)$$

However, now consider Figure 5. Obviouly, the lexicographical order on the

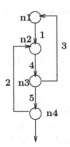

Fig. 5. Control-flow graph of an unstructured programs.

numbers of edge traversals does not correctly capture the order anymore. What we can say, however, is that a given execution will have one single trace, i.e., one single path along edges **3** and **2**. To see this, consider an instance of **4** reached after traversing **3**, **3** again, then **2**, which we denote by a word built by concatenating edge labels: **3.3.2.4**. Then, previous incarnations of **4** occured just after **1**, denoted ϵ.**4** (ϵ is the empty label), then at **3.4**, and then at **3.3.4**.

What we see is that the execution enforces that the numbers of occurences of all shared back edges must be ordered by $\leq$. That is:

$$\langle 4, \#2', \#3' \rangle \prec \langle 4, \#2, \#3 \rangle \Leftrightarrow \#2' \leq \#2 \land \#3' \leq \#3$$

The General Case. In general, a program segment may feature intermingled structured and unstructured parts. Each part should be handled according to the appropriate execution order described above. Consider for example the CFG in

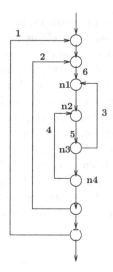

Fig. 6. Control-flow graph of an unstructured programs.

Figure 6. An appropriate index for instances of Statement **5** is ($\#1,\#2,\#3,\#4$). (Other indices are acceptable too, e.g. ($\#1,\#2,\#4,\#3$)). Remember that these edge counts are reinitialized to 0 when the unstructured program part is entered, i.e., each time edge **6** is traversed.

To capture the execution order, we need to use the fact that Edges **1** and **2** make a structured part, and edges **3** and **4** make a nonstructured part. Therefore, the correct order is defined in two steps:

1. The index vector is cut into subvectors, each subvector corresponding to a structured or unstructured part. Subvectors corresponding to a structured part are compared by the lexicographic order $\ll$, those corresponding to an unstructured part are compared by pointwise $\leq$. Each comparison gives $<, =,$ or $>$. (Note that the case of uncomparability does not appear for instances of the same execution.) For instance, in the running example, vectors are compared lexicographically on the first two components, and with pointwise $\leq$ on the last two. E.g., (4, 0, 2, 3) and (4, 1, 2, 2) yield $(<, >)$.
2. Two vectors are ordered if their first respective subvectors are ordered by $<$, or if the first two subvectors are ordered by $(=, <)$, or if the first three are ordered by $(=,=,<)$, etc.

5.2   MFP Formulation

Typically, the data-flow facts are given by the elements of a complete (not necessarily finite) lattice of finite height, the data-flow functions by transformations on these lattices, which in practice are monotonic or even distributive. Formally, the dataflow analysis is defined by a lattice $\mathcal{C}$ and a *local semantic functional* $[\![\ ]\!] : E \to (\mathcal{C} \to \mathcal{C})$ on graph edges E. This functional gives abstract meaning to the (elementary) statements of a program in terms of a transformation on a complete lattice $(\mathcal{C}, \sqcap, \sqsubseteq, \bot, \top)$ with least element $\bot$ and greatest element $\top$.

For a flow graph G, let $pred(n)$ and $succ(n)$ denote the set of all immediate predecessors and successors of a node n, and let $source(\mathbf{e})$ and $dest(\mathbf{e})$ denote the source and the destination node of an edge $\mathbf{e}$. A *finite path* in G is a sequence $e_1 \ldots e_q$ of edges such that $dest(\mathbf{e}_j) = source(\mathbf{e}_{j+1})$ for $j \in \{1, \ldots, q-1\}$. It is a path from m to n, if $source(\mathbf{e}_1) = m$ and $dest(\mathbf{e}_q) = n$. Additionally, $p[i, j]$, where $1 \le i \le j \le q$, denotes the *subpath* $e_i, \ldots, e_j$ of p. Finally, $\mathbf{P}[m, n]$ denotes the set of all finite paths from m to n. Without loss of generality we assume that every node $n \in N$ lies on a path from start to end.

The point of the *maximal-fixed-point (MFP)* approach is to iteratively approximate the greatest solution of a system of equations which specifies the consistency between conditions expressed in terms of data-flow information of $\mathcal{C}$:

$$\mathbf{info}(n) = \sqcap \{ [\![(m, n)]\!] (\mathbf{info}(m)) \mid m \in pred(n) \} \quad \textit{if } n \ne \text{end} \qquad (1)$$

The initial value for $n = \text{end}$ is defined later.

Checking that our MFP coincides with its MOP is an interesting theoretical issue left for future work. In particular, the coincidence theorem states that the algorithmic MFP-solution is equal to (coincides with) the expected result specified by MOP if all semantic functionals are distributive.

5.3   Intuitive Overview of Our Algorithm

We present an MFP algorithm to compute definitions reaching a given read instance. Basically, this algorithm boils down to propagating up the control flow graph a set which contains three kinds of information:

- The identity of definitions that can reach a given read of some memory location. These definition instances are described by (in)equalities on loop counters and symbolic constants. When these (in)equalities are not affine, an affine approximation will be made along the lines of [3].
- A conjunction of predicates collected while traversing ifs and whiles
- A predicate that captures the execution order on computations (more precisely, a disjunct of the lexicographical order. See below.)

We start with a conservative information. Then, when we encounter an assignment when walking up the control-flow graph, local semantic functionals collect the effects of assignments, and the lattice element we obtain contains only those definitions that are not killed.

The last point above serves to avoid iterating along a loop in the control flow graph. When a loop comes from an iterative control structure (a for or while loop), direct computation of the global effect is applied: we take benefit of the property of the loop, "guessing" the result in one step, which can therefore be considered as a special case of widening [7]. This fact is detailed in Section 5.5 to guarantee convergence.

The algorithm, therefore, considers 3-tuples (α, e, p), and computes the solution as a recurrence $(\alpha^{(n+1)}, e^{(n+1)}, p^{(n+1)}) = [\![\mathbf{s}_n]\!](\alpha^{(n)}, e^{(n)}, p^{(n)})$, where $\mathbf{s}_n$ is the n-th statement we encounter.

5.4   Formalization

Let us consider a single array A. Its range is $\mathsf{Range(A)}$. The iterationwise reaching definition (IRD) problem is restricted here to one statement $\mathbf{r}$ reading array A. The problem is defined as follows: given one instance $\langle \mathbf{r}, r \rangle$ of the read, give the set of assignment instances whose definitions may reach $\langle \mathbf{r}, r \rangle$. Obviously, the result has to be parameterized with r. If $\mathbf{s}$ is an assignment to A, then let $f_{\mathbf{s}} : D(\mathbf{s}) \to \mathsf{Range(A)}$ be the subscript function in the left-hand expression.

We now define the three features, hinted to in the previous section, which are propagated up the control flow graph.

Accesses to array elements. Intuitively, set S codes which statement instance writes in which array element[2]:

$$S = \{(a, \langle \mathbf{s}, x \rangle) \ : \ a \in \mathsf{Range(A)}, \mathbf{s} \in E, x \in D(\mathbf{s})\}$$

This set associates to element a of array A an instance of a statement. Intuitively, for a given instance of a read reference, an element of this set will tell which is the reaching definition. Note that, instead of giving the "vector" of the solutions for all elements of A, the result is parameterized by a.

Predicate on execution. This predicate is built from the conjunction of predicates copied from conditionals. They are not interpreted yet. For instance, the execution predicate for **1** and **3** in Figure 2 is just P. Let $\mathcal{T}$ be the set of all syntactically possible predicates.

Execution order. In addition, we have to capture the fact that the write executes before the read. The relative order between the write instance and the read instance will be given by a predicate on the iteration vectors of the instances. E.g., we will first look for definitions in the current iteration, so a predicate will initially captures that $x = r$. (i.e., component-wise, if n is the minimum of the dimensions of x and r: $\forall i, 1 \leq i \leq n, x_i = r_i$). Similar predicates code previous iterations of parts of, or all surrounding loops. These predicates have the form $p_k(x, r) = (\forall i, 1 \leq i \leq k : x_i = r_i) \wedge (x_{k+1} < r_{k+1})$. We denote with $\mathcal{P}$ the set of such predicates on iteration vectors.

The lattice is then the set of all parts in S augmented with set $\mathcal{P}$:

$$\mathcal{C} = 2^S \times \mathcal{T} \times \mathcal{P},$$

---

[2] To make equations easier to read, we often denote conjunction with a comma instead of $\wedge$.

so the information **info** attached to a node is a triple $(\alpha, e, p) \in \mathcal{C}$. **Except when predicate e is needed, this triple will be simply denoted with (α, p).**

These predicates also define the *lexicographic order* $\ll$ on vectors:

$$x \ll y \ =_{df} \ \exists k, \ 0 \leq k < n, \ p_k(x, y)$$

where n, again, is the lowest dimensionality of the two vectors: $n = \min(|x|, |y|)$.

The lexicographic order on vectors gives the order on statement instances. Indeed, two instances are executed in sequence if their iteration vectors are lexicographically ordered, or if these vectors (restricted to shared surrounding loops) are equal and the statements themselves appear in order in the program text. Formally:

$$\langle \mathbf{s}, x \rangle \prec \langle \mathbf{t}, y \rangle \ =_{df} \ (x \ll y) \vee (x[1..N_{\mathbf{s},\mathbf{t}}] = y[1..N_{\mathbf{s},\mathbf{t}}] \wedge \mathbf{s} \text{ appears before } \mathbf{t})$$

where $N_{\mathbf{s},\mathbf{t}} = \min(x, y)$.

The partial order $\sqsubseteq$ is defined as follows: $\forall (\alpha, p), (\alpha', p') \in \mathcal{C}$, we have:

$$(\alpha, p) \sqsubseteq (\alpha', p') =_{df} \{a : \exists u, (a, u) \in \alpha\} \subseteq \{a : \exists u, (a, u) \in \alpha'\}$$
$$\wedge \ ((a, u) \in \alpha \wedge (a, u') \in \alpha') \Rightarrow u \preceq u'$$

Intuitively, two elements in the lattice are ordered if all the array elements defined by the 'smaller' are also defined by the 'larger', and if the reaching definitions given by the 'larger' are executed later than the reaching definitions of the 'smaller'.

The merge operator $\sqcap$ is similar to union, except that two writes competing for the definition of the same array element are filtered according to the order $\prec$:

$$(\alpha, p) \sqcap (\beta, p) = (\{(x, v) \ : \ \exists v, (x, v) \in \alpha, \ \neg \exists w, (x, w) \in \beta, \ p(w) = tt, \ v \prec w\}$$
$$\cup \{(x, w) \ : \ \exists w, (x, w) \in \beta, \ p(w) = tt, \ \neg \exists v, (x, v) \in \alpha, \ w \prec v\} \ , p)$$
$$\Downarrow \text{ Since } p \text{ is associated to both } \alpha \text{ and } \beta$$
$$= (\{(x, v) \ : \ \exists v, (x, v) \in \alpha, \ \neg \exists w, (x, w) \in \beta, \ v \prec w\}$$
$$\cup \{(x, w) \ : \ \exists w, (x, w) \in \beta, \ \neg \exists v, (x, v) \in \alpha, \ w \prec v\} \ , p)$$

Notice that the predicates of two objects merged by $\sqcap$ must have equal predicates (intuitively, this is because the merge point is at a single nesting depth).

After having defined which information must be propagated and how two states of information can be merged, we now have to define how the various statements influence this information. The corresponding local semantic functional is defined as follows:

For assignments: The semantic functional gives the elements of A defined by the current statement during the last possible (i.e., complying with the predicate in $\mathcal{P}$) iteration x. Let us first define

$$W(\mathbf{s}) = \{(a, \langle \mathbf{s}, x \rangle) \ : \ a \in \mathsf{Range}(\mathsf{A}), \ x \in D(\mathbf{s}), a = f_{\mathbf{s}}(x)\} \tag{2}$$

which captures the effect of **s** on array A. The functional is then:

$$\forall (\alpha, p) \in \mathcal{C}, \ [\![\, s\,]\!](\alpha, p) = (\alpha, p) \square W(s) \tag{3}$$

Operator $\square$ adds to the set α of (array element, definition) pairs a new pair if an instance satisfying p is a reaching definition. Adding a new pair is thus only possible if the definition associated to the corresponding array element is older, or if there is no such definition yet. This operator is reminiscent from the one proposed by Barthou [2]:

$$\square : \mathcal{C} \rightarrow 2^{S} \rightarrow \mathcal{C}$$

$$(\alpha, p) \square \beta = \left(\begin{array}{l} \{(x, v) \ : \ (x, v) \in \alpha, \ \neg \exists w, \ (x, w) \in \beta, \ p(w) = tt, \ v \prec w\} \\ \cup \{(x, w) \ : \ (x, w) \in \beta, \ p(w) = tt, \ \neg \exists v, \ (x, v) \in \alpha \cup \beta, \ p(v), \ w \prec v\} \end{array}, p \right)$$

For statements incrementing loop counters: If **s** is the increment statement of loop counter i, then predicate p has to code that the value i' of i for writes becomes smaller than the value i for the read. In other words, the effect of **s** is to change from predicate p_k to predicate p_{k-1}:

$$\forall (\alpha, p_k) \in \mathcal{C}, \ [\![\, s\,]\!](\alpha, p_k) = (\alpha, p_{k-1}) \tag{4}$$

For conditionals: When entering a conditional predicated with P, P (resp. $\neg P$) is added (by conjunction) to the previous predicate in the **then** (resp. in the **else**) branch.

$$\forall (\alpha, e, p) \in \mathcal{C}, \ [\![\, s_{\mathsf{then}}\,]\!](\alpha, e, p) = (\alpha, e \wedge P, p) \tag{5}$$

$$\forall (\alpha, e, p) \in \mathcal{C}, \ [\![\, s_{\mathsf{else}}\,]\!](\alpha, e, p) = (\alpha, e \wedge \neg P, p) \tag{6}$$

5.5   Solving the Dataflow Equations Iteratively

We start with **info**(start) $= (\{(a, \perp) \ : \ a \in \mathsf{Range}(\mathtt{A})\}, p_0)$ and propagate up the control-flow graph.

Since our lattice of dataflow facts is of unbounded height, we have to make sure our semantic functionals never follow an infinite and monotonically increasing sequence. Doing so is here very simple: A back edge is traversed as many times as there are surrounding loops, plus 1. So it is $O(n^2)$ with n being the maximal nesting depth of the program. Before it is traversed, it means this edge is not traversed between the instances of the writes and of the reads we consider (intuitively, reads and writes are in the same iteration w.r.t. this edge). However, traversing the back edge in the analysis corresponds to traversing the edge once *or more* at the current depth of the nest. (intuitively, we consider all the write instances from previous iterations along that edge.)

This scheme is exactly the one used in [9] for structured programs, and suffers no loss in precision. Concerning unstructured programs, however, we might lose some precision. We are not able, for the moment, to quantify this loss.

6 Back to the Example

Let us consider the example in Figure 1 and compute the instancewise reaching definition for an instance (i, j) of **7**. The effects of assigments **3** and **6** are, respectively:

$$W(3) = \{(a, \langle \mathbf{3}, i', j' \rangle) : a = i' + j' + 1 = i + j, 0 \le i', j' \le N\}$$

and:

$$W(6) = \{(a, \langle \mathbf{6}, i', j' \rangle) : a = i' + j' = i + j, 0 \le i', j' \le N, P(i', j')\}$$

Initially, all elements of A have an undefined reaching write:

$$\alpha^{(0)} = \{(a, \perp), 0 \le a \le 2N + 1\}$$

Predicate p initially says that we look for definitions in the same iteration. I.e., the iteration vector (i', j') of the write has to be equal to iteration vector (i, j) of the read:

$$p^{(0)} = p_2 = (i' = i \land j' = j)$$

Walking up edge **6** gives the first iterate, denoted by $(\alpha^{(1)}, p^{(1)})$ as explained in Section 5.3. From (3) we have:

$$(\alpha^{(1)}, p^{(1)}) = [\![\, \mathbf{6}\,]\!](\alpha^{(0)}, p^{(0)}) = (\alpha^{(0)}, p_2) \square W(6)$$
$$= (\{(a, \langle \mathbf{6}, i, j \rangle) : a = i + j, 0 \le i, j \le N, P(i, j)\}, p_2)$$

Up the fall-through edge **4**: no effect, so:

$$[\![\, \mathbf{4}\,]\!](\alpha^{(0)}, p_2) = (\alpha^{(0)}, p_2)$$

Merging at the confluence of **4** and **5**:

$$(\alpha^{(2)}, p^{(2)}) = State(n_2)$$
$$= [\![\, \mathbf{4}\,]\!](\alpha^{(0)}, p_2) \cup [\![\, \mathbf{5}\,]\!](\alpha^{(1)}, p^{(1)})$$
$$= \left(\begin{array}{l} \{(a, \langle \mathbf{6}, i, j \rangle) : a = i + j, 0 \le a \le 2N + 1, P(i, j)\} \\ \cup \{(a, \perp) : 0 \le a \le 2N + 1\} \end{array} , p_2 \right)$$

Up Edge **3**:

$$(\alpha^{(3)}, p^{(3)}) = [\![\, \mathbf{3}\,]\!](State(n_2))$$
$$= (\alpha^{(2)}, p^{(2)}) \square W(3)$$
$$= \left(\begin{array}{l} \{(a, \langle \mathbf{6}, i, j \rangle) : a = i + j, 0 \le a \le 2N + 1, P(i, j)\} \\ \cup \{(a, \perp) : 0 \le a \le 2N + 1\} \end{array} , p_2 \right) \square W(3)$$

But p_2 implies that equality $i' + j' + 1 = i + j$ in $W(3)$ cannot be verified. So:

$$(\alpha^{(3)}, p^{(3)}) = State(n_1) = State(n_2) = (\alpha^{(2)}, p^{(2)})$$

Traversing Edge **13** change the order predicate: Applying (4):

$$[\![\,\mathbf{13}\,]\!](State(n_1)) = (\alpha^{(3)}, p_1)$$

$$= \left(\begin{array}{l} \{(a, \langle \mathbf{6}, i, j\rangle) : a = i + j, 0 \le a \le 2N + 1, P(i,j)\} \\ \cup \{(a, \bot) : 0 \le a \le 2N + 1\} \end{array} , i' = i \wedge j' < j \right)$$

Back to node n_3:

$$(\alpha^{(4)}, p^{(4)}) = State(n_3) = [\![\,\mathbf{6}\,]\!](\alpha^{(3)}, p_1) = (\alpha^{(3)}, p_1) \square W(\mathbf{6})$$

Since we cannot simultaneously have $i' = i \wedge j' < j$ (from p_1) and $i' + j' = i + j$ (from $W(\mathbf{6})$), $(\alpha^{(4)}, p^{(4)}) = (\alpha^{(3)}, p_1)$.

Back to node n_2: since edges $\mathbf{4}, \mathbf{5}$ and $\mathbf{6}$ have no effect on $(\alpha^{(4)}, p^{(4)})$, and since the merge operator is just plain union, we have:

$$(\alpha^{(5)}, p^{(5)}) = (\alpha^{(3)}, p_1)$$

Walking up edge **3**, we take advantage of the definition of $\square$ which requires that j' must be maximal. First, to be maximal compared with the previously found writes, we have to require that $\langle \mathbf{6}, i, j\rangle$ is not executed, i.e., $\neg P(i,j)$. Second, j' must be maximal also among the new writes with $j' < j$. Hence we have $j' = j - 1$ for $j > 0$. Thus, we have $\{(a, \langle \mathbf{3}, i, j-1\rangle) : 1 \le a \le 2N + 1, a = i + j, j \ge 1, \neg P(i,j)\}$. :

$$(\alpha^{(5)}, p^{(5)}) = [\![\,\mathbf{3}\,]\!](\alpha^{(3)}, p_1)$$

$$= \left(\begin{array}{l} \{(a, \langle \mathbf{6}, i, j\rangle) : a = i + j, 0 \le a \le 2N + 1, P(i,j)\} \\ \cup \{(a, \bot) : 0 \le a \le 2N + 1\} \end{array} , i' = i \wedge j' < j \right) \square W(\mathbf{3})$$

$$= \left(\begin{array}{l} \{(a, \langle \mathbf{6}, i, j\rangle) : a = i + j, 0 \le a \le 2N + 1, P(i,j)\} \\ \cup \{(a, \langle \mathbf{3}, i, j-1\rangle) : 1 \le a \le 2N + 1, a = i + j, j \ge 1, \neg P(i,j)\}, i' = i \wedge j' < j \\ \cup \{(a, \bot) : j = 0, a = i\} \end{array} \right)$$

Up edge **12**:

$$(\alpha^{(6)}, p^{(6)}) = [\![\,\mathbf{12}\,]\!](\alpha^{(5)}, p^{(5)}) = (\alpha^{(5)}, p_0)$$

Going back up **6**,

$$(\alpha^{(7)}, p^{(7)}) = [\![\,\mathbf{6}\,]\!](\alpha^{(6)}, p^{(6)})$$

$$= \left(\begin{array}{l} \{(a, \langle \mathbf{6}, i, j\rangle) : a = i + j, 0 \le a \le 2N + 1, P(i,j)\} \\ \cup \{(a, \langle \mathbf{3}, i, j-1\rangle) : 1 \le a \le 2N + 1, a = i + j, j \ge 1, \neg P(i,j)\}, i' < i \\ \cup \{(a, \bot) : j = 0, a = i\} \end{array} \right) \square W(\mathbf{6})$$

Let us consider the three subsets[3] to be compared with $W(\mathbf{6})$.

- No definition in the first subset definitely kills the effect of **6** because of uninterpreted predicate P.
- The second subset definitely kills effects of $W(\mathbf{6})$ if $j \ge 1$. For $j = 0$, $\square$ makes sure that only definitions in $W(\mathbf{6})$ that are not killed by other definitions in $W(\mathbf{6})$ are added. In this case, definition $\langle \mathbf{6}, i-1, 1\rangle$ may reach $\langle \mathbf{7}, i, 0\rangle$, $i \ge 1$.

---

[3] Beware that $\square$ does not work this way, since $\max((S_1 \cup S_2), S_3)$ is not equal to $\max(S_1, S_3) \cup \max(S_2, S_3)$.

- The definitions in the last subset are just bottoms, so they do not prevent any new definitions, so $W(\mathbf{6})$ wins again. (Notice that writes in $W(\mathbf{6})$ will not eliminate the last subset of bottoms, since instances of $\mathbf{6}$ may themselves *not* execute.)

We get:

$$
(\alpha^{(7)}, p^{(7)}) = \left(
\begin{aligned}
&\{(a, \langle \mathbf{6}, i, j \rangle) : a = i + j, 0 \le a \le 2N + 1, P(i, j)\} \\
&\{(a, \langle \mathbf{6}, i - 1, 1 \rangle) : a = i, 1 \le i \le N, j = 0, P(i - 1, 1))\} \\
&\cup\{(a, \langle \mathbf{3}, i, j - 1 \rangle) : 1 \le a \le 2N + 1, a = i + j, j \ge 1, \neg P(i, j)\} \\
&\cup\{(a, \bot) : j = 0, a = i\}
\end{aligned}
\right)^{, i' < i}
$$

Up edge $\mathbf{3}$, we have $(\alpha^{(8)}, p^{(8)}) = [\![\,\mathbf{3}\,]\!](\alpha^{(7)}, p^{(7)})$, which is equal to:

$$
\left(
\begin{aligned}
&\{(a, \langle \mathbf{6}, i, j \rangle) : a = i + j, 0 \le a \le 2N + 1, P(i, j)\} \\
&\{(a, \langle \mathbf{6}, i - 1, 1 \rangle) : a = i, 1 \le i \le N, j = 0, P(i - 1, 1))\} \\
&\cup\{(a, \langle \mathbf{3}, i, j - 1 \rangle) : 1 \le a \le 2N + 1, a = i + j, j \ge 1, \neg P(i, j)\} \\
&\cup\{(a, \bot) : j = 0, a = i\}
\end{aligned}
\right)^{, i' < i} \square W(\mathbf{3}),
$$

that is:

$$
(\alpha^{(8)}, p^{(8)}) = \left(
\begin{aligned}
&\{(a, \langle \mathbf{6}, i, j \rangle) : a = i + j, 0 \le a \le 2N + 1, P(i, j)\} \\
&\{(a, \langle \mathbf{6}, i - 1, 1 \rangle) : a = i, 1 \le i \le N, j = 0, P(i - 1, 1))\} \\
&\cup\{(a, \langle \mathbf{3}, i, j - 1 \rangle) : 1 \le a \le 2N + 1, a = i + j, j \ge 1, \neg P(i, j)\}, i' < i \\
&\cup\{(a, \langle \mathbf{3}, i - 1, j \rangle) : 1 \le a \le 2N + 1, a = i, i \ge 1, j = 0\} \\
&\cup\{(a, \bot) : i = 0, j = 0, a = 0\}
\end{aligned}
\right)
$$

$$\tag{7}$$

Notice how precise and informative this result is:

- Only one array element (`A[0]`) may be uninitialized when read. Moreover, we know this read is the very first instance of statement $\mathbf{7}$ ($i = 0, j = 0$).
- For a parametric instance $\langle \mathbf{7}, i, j \rangle$, $\alpha^{(8)}$ gives all the definition instances that may reach this use. This result has the same precision as with methods in [3, 15, 2].

7   Implementation

The analysis presented in this paper is developped on top of two compiler platforms: LooPo, developped at the University of Passau, and SUIF, from Stanford. A preliminary phase has been implemented for each of these platforms, the one for LooPo in Passau and the one for SUIF in Versailles. This phase takes the output of the parser and generates the control flow graph annotated with Omega relations.

The CFG is then the input to the analysis itself, which propagates reaching definitions as described above. This analysis phase is common to both implementations, i.e., the same files are used in the LooPo- and the SUIF-version of the analysis.

A preliminary version may be found at

http://www.prism.uvsq/~jfc/scff/scff.html

The LooPo version will be released soon. Please check:

http://brahms.fmi.uni-passau.de/cl/loopo/

Don't expect, however, to find a robust, production-quality compiler pass. The current implementation just serves as a prototype to check the analysis on simple examples.

A subtle difference between the result derived in the previous section and the output of our software is that most reaching definitions are guarded by uninterpreted function in the software. For instance, the fourth subset of $\alpha^{(8)}$ in (7) could be guarded by a predicate corresponding to cases where the predicate of instance of **6** is *false*. Therefore, the result of the software can be considered as *more precise* than (7).

8   Conclusions

In this paper we presented two frameworks for reaching definition analysis: one based on iteratively solving data-flow equations, and one based on integer linear programming techniques. We combined both techniques and, thus, got an analysis which rejoins the flexibility of the first and the precision of the second framework.

Furthermore, our analysis method scales very well to larger programs (in contrast to the techniques based on integer linear programming), mainly for two reasons:

- Using a bottom-up traversal of the control-flow graph guarantees that we first focus on possible reaching definitions "close" to the read. The order in which we traverse the control-flow graph allows us to stop as soon as we have found a write for every read we are interested in; writes which execute earlier and are rewritten, are never considered by our method.
- Our analysis is flexible enough to trade off between precision and analysis time, e.g., by ignoring loops and colleting the respective instances in super-instances as indicated in Section 5.1, or by stopping the propagation of data-flow information, adding all not yet considered writes as possible reaching definitions for still undefined array cells.

In our prototype implementation, it turned out that induction variable recognition is crucial for the precision in unstructured programs. Further experiments will show how to select a good balance between analysis time and precision, i.e., depending on the purpose of the analysis, in which parts of the program it makes sense to do the analysis as tight as possible, and in which parts an approximation is sufficient.

Acknowledgment. We would like to thank Jens Knoop for several discussions that gave the initial motivation for this work [6]. Part of the sofware was implemented by Andreas Dischinger and Ivan Djelic.

References

1. A. V. Aho, R. Sethi, and J. D. Ullman. *Compilers: Principles, Techniques and Tools.* Addison-Wesley, Reading, Mass, 1986.
2. D. Barthou. *Array Dataflow Analysis in Presence of Non-affine Constraints.* PhD thesis, Univ. Versailles, February 1998.
3. D. Barthou, J.-F. Collard, and P. Feautrier. Fuzzy array dataflow analysis. *Journal of Parallel and Distributed Computing*, 40:210–226, 1997.
4. A. Cohen and J.-F. Collard. Instance-wise reaching definition analysis for recursive programs using context-free transductions. In *PACT'98*, Paris, France, October 1998.
5. J.-F. Collard and M. Griebl. Array dataflow analysis for explicitly parallel programs. *Parallel Processing Letters*, 1997.
6. J.-F. Collard and J. Knoop. A comparative study of reaching definitions analyses. Technical Report 1998/22, PRiSM, U. of Versailles, 1998.
7. P. Cousot and R. Cousot. Comparing the Galois connection and widening/narrowing approaches to abstract interpretation. In M. Bruynooghe and M. Wirshing, editors, *4th Int. Symp. on Prog. Lang. Implem. and Logic Prog (PLILP'92)*, volume 631 of *LNCS*, pages 269–295, Leuven, Belgium, August 1992.
8. E. Duesterwald, R. Gupta, and M.-L. Soffa. A practical data flow framework for array reference analysis and its use in optimization. In *ACM SIGPLAN'93 Conf. on Prog. Lang. Design and Implementation*, pages 68–77, June 1993.
9. P. Feautrier. Dataflow analysis of scalar and array references. *Int. Journal of Parallel Programming*, 20(1):23–53, February 1991.
10. J. B. Kam and J. D. Ullman. Monotone data flow analysis frameworks. *Acta Informatica*, 7:309 – 317, 1977.
11. J. Knoop, D. Koschützki, and B. Steffen. Basic–block graphs: Living dinosaurs? In *Proc. of the 7th International Conference on Compiler Construction (CC'98)*, LNCS, Lisbon, Portugal, 1998.
12. J. Knoop and B. Steffen. The interprocedural coincidence theorem. In *Proc. of the 4th International Conference on Compiler Construction (CC'92)*, number 641 in LNCS, Paderborn, Germany, 1992.
13. S. S. Muchnick. *Advanced Compiler Design & Implementation.* Morgan Kaufmann, 1997.
14. W. Pugh and D. Wonnacott. Going beyond integer programming with the omega test to eliminate false data dependences. Technical Report CS-TR-3191, U. of Maryland, December 1992.
15. D. Wonnacott and W. Pugh. Nonlinear array dependence analysis. In *Proc. Third Workshop on Languages, Compilers and Run-Time Systems for Scalable Computers*, 1995. Troy, New York.

Demand-Driven Interprocedural Array Property Analysis*

Yuan Lin and David Padua

Department of Computer Science, University of Illinois at Urbana-Champaign
{yuanlin,padua}@uiuc.edu

Abstract. Many optimization techniques rely on the analysis of array subscripts. Current compilers often give up optimizations when arrays are subscripted by index arrays and treat the index arrays as unknown functions at compile-time. However, recent empirical studies of real programs have shown that index arrays often possess some properties that can be used to derive more precise information about the enclosing loops. In this paper, we present an index array analysis method, called array property analysis, which computes array properties by back-propagating queries along the control flow of the program. This method integrates the array data-flow analysis with interprocedural analysis and the demand-driven approach.

1 Introduction

Most loop optimization techniques rely on the analysis of array subscripts. When arrays are subscripted by index arrays[1], current compilers are forced to make conservative assumptions and give up optimizations or apply run-time methods at the cost of significant execution overhead. Index arrays are used extensively in sparse computation codes and also appear in some dense/regular programs. In order to optimize these programs, more aggressive compile-time methods to analyze the index arrays are desired. Having more precise information on index arrays at compile-time not only can enable more optimizations and transformations, but also can lead to more efficient run-time methods.

The compile-time analysis of index arrays has been facilitated by two recent developments. First, recent empirical studies of real programs [4,17] have shown that the use of index arrays often follows a few patterns. By identifying these patterns at compile-time, more precise analysis can be accomplished. Second, recent progress in interprocedural analysis [7,12,14,16], array data flow analysis [10,9, 11,23], and demand-driven approaches [8,26] have enabled the more efficient and more powerful whole program analysis required by index array analysis.

---

* This work is supported in part by Army contract DABT63-95-C-0097; Army contract N66001-97-C-8532; NSF contract MIP-9619351; and a Partnership Award from IBM. This work is not necessarily representative of the positions or policies of the Army or Government.

[1] In this paper, we call the array that appears in the subscripts of other arrays the *index array* and the indirectly accessed array the *host array*.

L. Carter and J. Ferrante (Eds.): LCPC'99, LNCS 1863, pp. 303–317, 2000.

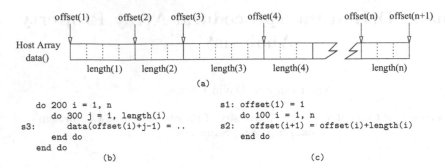

Fig. 1. Example of closed-form distance

In this paper, we present an index array analysis method, called *array property analysis*. By performing a whole program analysis, array property analysis can automatically identify whether an index array possesses one of several key properties. These key properties are used in the analysis of the subscripts of the host array to produce more accurate analysis results. We discuss these key properties and show how to use a demand-driven approach to do whole program analysis.

This paper makes three principal contributions. First, this paper describes how to use compile-time techniques to derive properties of index arrays and how to use the properties in array subscript analysis. Second, this paper presents an efficient whole program analysis that integrates demand-driven approach, interprocedural analysis, and structure-based array dataflow analysis. Third, this paper describes a prototype implementation of this analysis in the Polaris parallelizing compiler and presents experimental results demonstrating its effectiveness.

2   The Problem

2.1   Array Property Analysis

While it is true that the values of index arrays usually are not available until run-time, oftentimes we can get more precise results if global program analysis is performed. In their study of the Perfect Benchmarks, Blume and Eigenmann found that index arrays usually had some detectable properties [4]. By knowing these properties, compilers often can avoid making conservative assumptions. Results similar to those of Blume and Eigenmann also were obtained by the authors in a study of several sparse and irregular programs [17].

In sparse and irregular programs, index arrays are extensively used. The use of index arrays tends to have a few fixed patterns. For example, when a sparse matrix is stored in the Compressed Column Storage(CCS) format, the non-zero elements of the matrix are stored in a one-dimensional host array. The host is divided into several segments, as illustrated in Fig. 1(a). Each segment corresponds to a column. Two index arrays are used here. Index array offset()

points to the starting position of each segment, and index array `length()` gives the length of each segment. Figure 1(b) shows a common loop pattern using the `offset()` and `length()` arrays. The loop traverses the host array segment by segment. Figure 1(c) shows a common pattern used to define `offset()`. It is easy to see that loop `do 200` does not carry any dependences if $length(i) \geq 0$, because

$$offset(i) + length(i) - 1 < offset(i+1), \text{ where } 1 \leq i < n.$$

This is guaranteed by the fact that

$$offset(i+1) - offset(i) = length(i), \text{ where } 1 \leq i \leq n,$$

which can be derived from Fig. 1(c).

Given an array, if the difference of the values of any two consecutive elements can always be represented by a closed-form expression, we say the array has a **closed-form distance** [5]. The array `offset()` in Fig. 1 has a closed form distance, which is `length()`. Having a closed-form distance is just one of the five properties of index arrays that can be exploited by compilers. The other four are:

- **Injectivity** An array $a()$ is injective if $a(i) \neq a(j)$ when $i \neq j$.
- **Monotonicity** An array $a()$ is monotonically non-decreasing if $a(i) \leq a(j)$, $i < j$. It is monotonically non-increasing if $a(i) \geq a(j)$, $i < j$.
- **Closed-form Value** An array has a closed-form value if all the values of the array elements can be represented by a closed-form expression at compile-time.
- **Closed-form Bound** An array has a closed-form bound if closed-form expression is available at compile-time for either the lower bound or the upper bound of the elements' values in this array.

We want to know if an index array has any of the above properties. This can be described as an *available property* problem. A property of a variable x is *available* at a point p if the execution of the program along any path from the initial node to p guarantees that x has this property. This, in general, is undecidable. In real programs, however, the index arrays seldom are modified once they are defined, which allows us to take the following approach: when we analyze an indirectly accessed array reference, we check all the reaching definitions of the index arrays. We examine the program pattern of each definition. If all the definition sites imply that the index array has any of the properties, and none of the statements in between the definition sites and the use site redefines any variables that are used to express the property, then we say that the property is available at the use site. Otherwise, we assume it is not available.

There are two other issues that must be addressed. First, we must do the analysis interprocedurally. Index arrays usually are used to store data structure information. Most real programs read the input data and construct the data structure in one procedure, and perform the major numerical computation based on the data structure in another procedure. This means that index arrays often are defined in one procedure but used in other procedures. In such cases, the reaching definitions can be found only interprocedurally. Second, we want the analysis to be demand-driven. The cost of interprocedural array reaching definition analysis and property checking is high. However, only the arrays that are used as index arrays require this analysis. Thus, we perform the analysis only when we meet an index array; and, heuristically, we check only the property that the use site suggests. For example, a use site like s3 in Fig. 1 strongly indicates that the distance of offset() is length(). Thus, in this case, we only need to check the property of closed-form distance.

2.2   Dataflow Model

We model our demand-driven analysis of the available property as a query propagation problem [8]. A query is a tuple $(n, section)$, where n is a statement and $section$ is an array section[2] for the index array. Given an index array and a property to be checked, a query $(n, section)$ raises the question whether the index array elements in $section$ always have the desired property when the control reaches the point after n. For example, the query $(st1, [1 : n])$ in Fig. 2 asks whether $a(i) = (i - 1) * i/2$ for $1 \le i \le n$ after statement $st1$.

A query is propagated along the reverse direction of the control flow until it can be verified to be $true$ or $false$. Let
- $OUT(S)$ be the section of index array elements to be examined at statement S,
- $GEN(S)$ be the section of the index array elements that possess the desired property because of the execution of statement S,
- $KILL(S)$ be the section of the index array elements that are verified not to have the property because of the execution of S,
- $IN(S)$ be the section of the index array elements that cannot be determined to possess the property by examining S and, thus, should be checked again at the predecessors of S, and
- $DES(S)$ be the section of index array elements in $OUT(S)$ that are verified not to have the property because of the execution of S.
The general dataflow equations for the reverse query propagation are shown in Fig. 3. For a property query $(st, section)$, initially, $OUT(st) = section$ and $OUT(s) = \emptyset$ for all statements other than st.

If, after the propagation finishes, we have $IN(entry) \ne \emptyset$, where $entry$ is the entry statement of the program, or there exists a statement s such that $DES(s) \ne \emptyset$, then the answer to the original query is $false$. Otherwise the answer is $true$. $IN(entry) \ne \emptyset$ means that some elements in the original $section$ are not defined along some path from the program entry to statement st; thus, not all the elements in $section$ have the desired property. If, for some statement s, we have $DES(s) \ne \emptyset$, then some element in the original $section$ has been found not to have the desired property because of the execution of s. Hence, in either case, the answer to the query is $false$.

---

[2] An array section can be represented as either a convex region [25], an abstract data access [3,21], or a regular section [13]. Our method is orthogonal to the representation of the array section. Any representation can be used as long as the aggregation operation in Sect. 3.4 is defined.

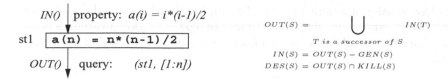

IN() property: $a(i) = i*(i-1)/2$

st1 $a(n) = n*(n-1)/2$

OUT() query: $(st1, [1:n])$

$$OUT(S) = \bigcup_{T \text{ is a successor of } S} IN(T)$$

$$IN(S) = OUT(S) - GEN(S)$$

$$DES(S) = OUT(S) \cap KILL(S)$$

Fig. 2. A sample query   **Fig. 3.** Dataflow equations

3   The Method

3.1   Program Representation

We represent the program in a hierarchical control graph (HCG), which is similar to the *hierarchical supergraph* [11]. Each statement, loop, and procedure is represented by a node, respectively. There also is a section node for each loop body and each procedure body. Each section node has a single entry node and a single exit node. There is a directed edge from one node to the other at the same hierarchical layer if the program control can transfer from one to the other. Figure 4 shows an HCG example. We assume that the only loops in the program are **do** loops, and we deliberately delete the back edges from the **end do** nodes to the **do** nodes. Hence, the HCG is a hierarchical directed acyclic graph.

3.2   Overview of The Method

Our method consists of three parts, as shown in Fig. 5. The *QueryGenerator* is incorporated in the test methods that require detailed analyses of index arrays. The *QueryGenerator* issues a query when the test needs to verify whether an index array has a certain property at a certain point. The *QueryChecker* accepts the query and then uses *QuerySolver* to traverse the program in the reverse direction of the control flow to verify the query. It uses the *PropertyChecker* to get the *GEN* and *KILL* information. The *QueryChecker* returns *true* to *Query-Generator* if it can determine that the property is available; otherwise it returns *false*.

The *QueryGenerate* and the *PropertyChecker* are closely related to the test problem and the properties being checked. We will show how to construct these two parts by using a case study in Sect. 4. In this section, we focus on the

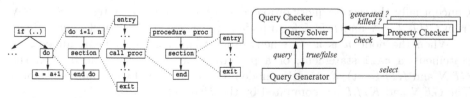

Fig. 4. An HCG example

Fig. 5. The components of array property analysis

QuerySolver, which is a generic method. To simplify the discussion, in this paper we assume no parameter passing, that values are passed by global variables only, and that if constant numbers are passed from one procedure to another, the callee is cloned.

3.3 The Query Solver

Given a query $(n_{query}, section_{query})$ and a root node n_{root} that dominates n_{query}, *QuerySolver* returns a tuple $(anykilled, section_{remain})$. The *anykilled*, which is a boolean, is *true* if some element in $section_{query}$ might be killed when the program is executed from n_{root} to n_{query}. When *anykilled* is *false*, $section_{remain}$ gives the array elements that are neither generated nor killed from n_{root} to n_{query}. In order to check if the index array elements in $section_{query}$ at node n_{query} have the desired property, *QueryChecker* invokes *QuerySolver* with the n_{root} being the entry node of the whole program. If *anykilled* is *true* or *anykilled* is *false* but $section_{remain}$ is not empty, then we know the index array does not have the desired property. Otherwise, it has the desired property.

The algorithm for *QuerySolver* is shown in Fig. 6. A worklist is used. Each element in the worklist is a query. The algorithm takes a query $(n, sect)$ from the worklist. The query $(n, sect)$ asks whether any array element in *sect* can have the desired property immediately after the execution of n. This is checked by the reverse query propagation *QueryProp*. *QueryProp* returns a tuple (DES, IN), whose meaning was given in Sect. 2.2. If *DES* is not empty, then the answer to the original query is assumed to be *false* and the algorithm returns. When *DES* is empty, new queries are constructed from the *IN* sets of the predecessors of n and are inserted into the worklist. This process repeats until the worklist becomes empty or the root node is met.

The worklist is a priority queue. All the elements are sorted in the reverse topological order$(rTop)$ of its node in the control flow graph. Therefore, a node is not checked until all its successors have been checked. This ensures that the query presented to a node is composed from the queries propagated by its successors.

Queries are inserted into the list by using $add_{\cup}()$. The general $add_{op}()$, where *op* can be either $\cap$ or $\cup$, is defined as: if there exists a query $(n, section')$ in the worklist, then replace $(n, section')$ with $(n, section \ op \ section')$; otherwise, insert $(n, section)$ into the *worklist* according to the $rTop$ order.

3.4 Reverse Query Propagation

Conceptually, the reverse query propagation *QueryProp* computes *DES* and *IN* from *OUT*, *GEN* and *KILL* for a node n according to the dataflow equations.

When the node n is a statement other than a **do** statement, an **end do** statement, a **call** statement, or a procedure head, the side-effects (i.e., the *GEN* and *KILL* set) of executing node n can be derived by examining n alone. The *GEN* and *KILL* are computed by the *PropertyChecker*.

In other cases, it is not possible to apply the dataflow equations directly. These cases are: 1) when n is a do node, 2) when n is a **do** header, 3) when n

Method: $QuerySolver(query, n_{root})$
Input: 1) a query $(n_{init}, sect_{init})$
              2) a root node n_{root} that
                 dominates n_{init}
Output: $(anykilled, sect_{remain})$
Begin:
$worklist := \emptyset$;
$add_{\cup}((n_{init}, sect_{init}), worklist)$;
while $worklist \neq \emptyset$ do
  remove an element $(n, sect)$ from $worklist$;
  if (n is n_{root}) then break ;
  $(DES, IN) := QueryProp(n, sect)$;
  if ($DES \neq \emptyset$) then
    return $(true, IN)$;
  if ($IN \neq \emptyset$) then
    for each node $m \in pred(n)$
      $add_{\cup}((m, IN), worklist)$;
    end for
  end if
end while
return $(false, sect)$;
End

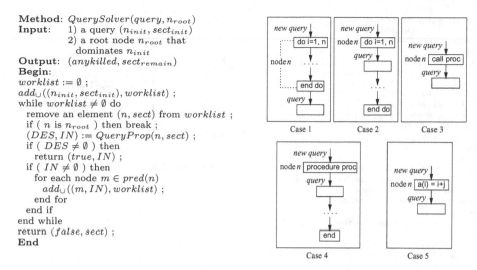

Case 1   Case 2   Case 3

Case 4   Case 5

Fig. 6. QuerySolver   **Fig. 7.** The five cases

is a `call` statement, and 4) when n is a procedure head. All the four cases, as well as the one in the previous paragraph, are illustrated in Fig. 7. Each case is handled by a different reverse query propagation method.

Loop Analysis. Cases 1 and 2 involve loops. To summarize the effect of executing the loops, aggregation methods such as the one proposed by Gross and Steenkiste [10] (for one dimensional arrays) or by Gu et al. [11] (for multiple dimensional arrays) are used to aggregate the array access. Consider an array section expression, $section_i$, which contains the loop index i. Let low be the lower bound of the loop and up be the upper bound. $Aggregate_{low \leq i \leq up}(section_i)$ computes the section spanned by the loop index across the iteration space.

In case 1, the initial query comes from outside the loop. The key is to summarize the effect of executing the whole loop ($SummarizeLoop$). Let n be the node corresponding to the loop body, i be the loop index, $(Kill_i, Gen_i)$ be the effect of executing the loop body, up be the upper bound of loop m, and low be the lower bound of loop m. Then

$$Kill = Aggregate_{low \leq i \leq up}(Kill_i)$$
$$Gen = Aggregate_{low \leq i \leq up}(Gen_i - Aggregate_{i+1 \leq j \leq up}(Kill_j))$$

When $Kill$ and Gen are computed, the dataflow equations can be applied.

$(Kill_i, Gen_i)$ is computed by the $SummarizeSection$ method shown in Fig. 8. $SummarizeSection$ back-propagates the $Kill$ and Gen set from the exit node to the entry node. It also uses a worklist, the element (n, gen) of which represents the array section gen that is being generated as a result of the execution of the program from the exit of node n to the exit of the program section. The method uses $SummarizeSimpleNode$, $SummarizeProcedure$, and

Method: $SummarizeSection(n)$
Input: A section node n
Output: $(Kill, Gen)$
Begin:
Let n_{entry} be the entry node of section n.
Let n_{exit} be the exit node of section n.
$Gen := \emptyset, Kill := \emptyset, WorkList := \emptyset$;
$add_\cap((n_{exit}, \emptyset), Worklist)$;
while $WorkList \neq \emptyset$ do
  remove an element (n, gen') from $Worklist$;
  if $(n = n_{entry})$ then
    $Gen := gen'$;
    break ;
  end if
  if (n is a **call** statement) then
    $(kill, gen) := SummarizeProcedure(n)$;
  else if (n is a do node) then
    $(kill, gen) := SummarizeLoop(n)$;
  else
    $(kill, gen) := SummarizeSimpleNode(n)$;
  end if
  if (n dominates n_{exit}) $Gen := gen'$;
  if ($kill = [-\infty, \infty]$) then
    $Kill := kill$;
    break ;
  end if
  $Kill := Kill \cup (kill - gen')$;
  for each $m \in pred(n)$
    $add_\cap((m, gen' \cup gen), WorkList)$;
  end for
end while
return $(Kill, Gen)$;
End

Fig. 8. *SummarizeSection*

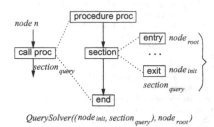

$QuerySolver((node_{init}, section_{query}), node_{root})$

Fig. 9. Reusing *QuerySolver* for Case 3

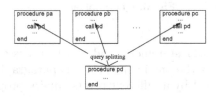

Fig. 10. Query splitting

SummarizeLoop recursively depending on the type of statements used in the loop body. *SummarizeProcedure* summarizes the effect of calling a procedure. Without considering parameter boundings, *SummarizeProcedure* can be computed by using *SummarizeSection* on the section node representing the body of the procedure being called.

In case 2, the initial query comes from one iteration of the loop. In this case, we aggregate not only the GEN and $KILL$ set, but also the IN set. First, we compute the effects of executing the previous iterations of the loop. Then, we use the dataflow equations to get the IN_i and DES_i set for this iteration. Because we are interested in whether DES is empty or not, DES can be safely set to $[-\infty, \infty]$ when DES_i is not empty. Finally, if DES_i is empty, the IN_i is aggregated. The algorithm is:

1. Let n be the section node of the loop body, and assume n_i represents the ith iteration of the loop, perform $(Kill_i, Gen_i) = SummarizeSection(n_i)$.
2. Let up be the upper bound of loop, low be the lower bound of loop, and $sect$ be the array section in the given query. If $sect \cap Aggregate_{low \leq j \leq (i-1)}(Kill_j)$ is not empty, then set DES to $[-\infty, \infty]$, IN to $\emptyset$, and return.
3. Set IN to $Aggregate_{low \leq i \leq up}(sect - Aggregate_{low \leq j \leq (i-1)}(Gen_j))$ and DES to $\emptyset$. Return.

Interprocedural Analysis. The interprocedural reverse query propagation also involves two cases (i.e., cases 3 and 4 in Fig. 7).

In case 3, the node n is a `call` statement. We construct a new query problem with the initial query node being the exit node of the callee and the root node being the entry node of the caller, as illustrated in Fig. 9. We can reuse *QuerySolver* to propagate the query in a demand-driven way. *QuerySolver* can early-terminate once any array element in the query section is found not to have the desired property or all of them are found to have the property.

In case 4, the node n is the entry node of a procedure. If n is not the program entry, then the query will be propagated into the callers of this procedure. We use a query splitting method illustrated in Fig. 10.

Suppose the property query at the entry node n of a procedure *proc* is $(n, sect_{query})$, and the call sites of *proc* are $n_1, n_2, n_3, ...,$ and n_m. If n is the program entry, then the array elements in $sect_{query}$ are not generated in this program and, as a result, the property analysis can terminate with the answer being *false*. Otherwise, the query is split into m sub-queries, each of which has a set of initial queries as $\{(n', sect_{query}) | n' \in pred(n_i)\}$. The original query has the result *true* when all the sub-queries terminate with the result *true*. Otherwise, the initial query has the result *false*.

3.5   Memoization

Processing a sequence of k queries requires k separate invocations of *Query-Checker*, which may result in repeated evaluations of the same intermediate queries. Similarly, because a procedure may be called multiple times in a program, the summarization methods also may repeat several times for the same node. These repeated computations are avoided by using *memoization* [1]. In our analysis, we choose to memoize the *QueryChecker* and the *Summarize* because they are most likely to be invoked repeatedly with the same input. Summarization methods are called independently of the query sections. Memoization tends to be more effective for summarizations than *QuerySolver* and *QueryProp*, which depend not only on the index array and the property to be checked, but also on the query section, which often varies from instance to instance.

3.6   Cost Analysis

Let $|N|$ be the number of HCG nodes and $|E|$ be the number of edges in a program. We assume $|E| = O(|N|)$ because we are working on structured programs. For a single query, memoizing the summarization methods requires a storage space of size $O(|N|)$. To determine the time complexity, we consider the number of array section operations (intersection, union, subtraction and aggregation) and the number of *PropertyCheck* methods. The latter is $O(|N|)$ as *PropertyCheck* is invoked only in *SummarizeSimpleNode*. *PropertyCheck* is executed once at most for each node because of the memoization. The array section operations are performed for each edge in the query propagation methods and the summarization methods. The number is $O(n_{inlined})$ for query propagation methods and $O(|N|)$ for summarization methods, where $n_{inlined}$ is the number of statement nodes if the program is fully inlined. Hence, the complexity of execution time is $O((C_{pc} + C_{as}) * |N| + C_{as} * n_{inlined})$, where C_{pc} is the cost of a *PropertyCheck* and C_{as} is the cost of an array section operation. Because we make approximations when property check cannot be performed locally or when array sections become complicated, both C_{pc} and C_{as} can be considered constants here.

4   Examples of a Query Generator and a Property Checker

Of the three major components of array property analysis, the *QueryChecker* is a generic method, while the *QueryGenerator* and the *PropertyChecker* are specific to the base problem, such as dependence tests or privatization tests, and specific to the potential property the array is likely to hold. In this section, we use a data dependence test problem to illustrate how to construct a *QueryGenerator* and a *PropertyChecker*.

4.1   Generating Demands

A new dependence test, called the *offset-length* test [19], has been designed to disprove data dependences in loops where indirectly accessed arrays are present and the index arrays are used as offset arrays and length arrays, such as the offset() and the length() in Fig. 1. The *offset-length* test needs array property analysis to verify the relationship between the *offset* arrays and the *length* arrays. Therefore, the *offset-length* test serves as a query generator.

We test whether a data dependence exists between two array accesses $a(f())$ and $a(g())$ with a dependence direction vector $(=_1, =_2, ..., =_{t-1}, \neq_t, *, ..., *))$ in a loop nest. We assume that the index arrays in the loop nest are arrays of the t outermost loops only.

We first compute both the ranges of values of $f(i_1, ..., i_t, *, ..., *)$ and $g(i_1, ..., i_t, *, ..., *)$ when $i_1, i_2, ..., i_t$ are kept fixed. Because the index arrays are arrays of only the outermost t loops, the loop indices $i_1, i_2, ..., i_t$ and the index arrays can be treated as symbolic terms in the range computation. If, except for the index arrays, $f()$ or $g()$ is an affine function of the loop indices, the range can be calculated by substituting the loop indices with their appropriate loop bounds, as by *Banerjee's test*. Otherwise, the ranges be calculated with the method used in some nonlinear data dependence tests, such as the *Range test*.

If the ranges of $f(i_1, ..., i_t, *, ..., *)$ and $g(i_1, ..., i_t, *, ..., *)$ can be represented as $[x(i_t) + f_{low}, x(i_t) + y(i_t) + f_{up}]$ and $[x(i_t) + g_{low}, x(i_t) + y(i_t) + g_{up}]$, respectively, where $x()$ and $y()$ are two index arrays, and
$$f_{low} = e(i_1, ..., i_{t-1}) + c_1, \quad f_{up} = e(i_1, ..., i_{t-1}) - d_1,$$
$$g_{low} = e(i_1, ..., i_{t-1}) + c_2, \quad g_{up} = e(i_1, ..., i_{t-1}) - d_2,$$

$e(i_1, ..., i_{t-1})$ is an expression of indices i_1, i_2,...,i_{t-1} and index arrays of the outermost $t-1$ loops, and c_1 and c_2 are some non-negative integers, d_1 and d_2 are some positive integers, then there is no loop carried dependence between the two array accesses if index array $x()$ has a closed-form distance $y()$ and the values of $y()$ are non-negative.

4.2   Checking Properties

Given a property to be verified and an assignment statement, the property checker *PropertyChecker* checks whether the assignment will cause any array elements to be generated or killed. Properties, such as injectivity and closed-form bounds, can be checked by using the *single-indexed array analysis* [18]. In this subsection, we show how to use a simple pattern matching technique to check the *closed-form distance*.

Suppose the given property to be verified is
$$x(i+1) = x(i) + y(i), \text{ for } 1 \le i \le n - 1.$$
The *PropertyChecker* can take the following steps to inspect an assignment statement.

1. If the left-hand side (LHS) of the assignment is neither the array $x()$ nor the array $y()$, then nothing is generated or killed.
2. If the LHS is an array element $x(i)$, then the assignment and the other statements in the surrounding loops are checked to see if they match any of the following two patterns shown below. If not, then all elements of $x()$ are killed. Otherwise, $x(i)$ is generated.

```
                                   t = ...
   x(1) = ...                      do i = 1, n
   do i = 2, n                         x(i) = t
       x(i) = x(i-1) + y(i-1)          t = t + y(i)
   end do                          end do

        (a)                             (b)
```

3. otherwise (this includes the case when the LHS is an array element of $y()$ and the case when the LHS is an array element of $x()$ but the subscript is not a simple index), all elements of $x()$ are killed.

In general, the *closed-form distance* can be detected by using abstract interpretation, such as the recurrence recognition method proposed by Z. Ammarguellat and W. Harrison [2]. Compared with abstract interpretation, our pattern matching method is simplified and, thus, conservative. However, we found this simplification to be very effective in practice. For most cases, *PropertyChecker* never needs more sophisticated methods to get precise results.

5   Implementation and Experimental Results

Array property analysis can enable deeper analysis in many parts of an optimizing compiler. To evaluate its effectiveness, we measured its impact in finding

Table 1. Programs used in our experiment. CFV - closed-form value, CFB - closed-form bound, CFD - closed-form distance, PRIV - privatization test, DD - data dependence test.

Program	Loops	Indirectly Accessed Arrays		Property and Test	$\%_{seq}$	$\%_{par}$	Whole Program	Array Property Analysis	%
		Host	Index						
TRFD	INTGRL/do_140	x	ia	CFV/DD	5%	$24\%_{32}$	181.3s	8.1s	4.5%
DYFESM	SOLXDD/do_4 SOLXDD/do_10 SOLXDD/do_30 SOLXDD/do_50 HOP/do_20	xdd, z r, y z xdd xdplus, xplus, xd	pptr, iblen	CFD/DD	20%	$7\%_8$	302.3s	19.4s	6.4%
BDNA	ACTFOR/do_240	xdt	ind	CFB/PRIV	32%	$63\%_{32}$	465.7s	31.2s	6.7%
P3M	PP/do_100	x0, ind0 r2, ind	jpr	CFB/PRIV	74%	$76\%_8$	73.1s	8.0s	10.9%

more parallelism. We implemented the demand-driven interprocedural array property analysis in our Polaris parallelizing compiler. We also extended the original data dependence test and privatization test so that they can heuristically generate property queries when they meet index arrays.

Table 1 shows the four programs used in our experiments. TRFD, BDNA and DYFESM are from the Perfect Benchmark suite. P3M is a particle-mesh program from NCSA. Column two shows the loops with indirectly accessed arrays that now can be parallelized by Polaris using array property analysis. The properties of the index arrays and the tests in which the properties can be used are listed in column five. Column six shows the percentage of total sequential program execution time accountable to the loops in column two. And, column seven shows the percentage of total parallel program execution time accountable to these loops if the loops are not parallelized (the number after the % sign is the number of processors used). The program execution time was measured on an SGI Origin2000 with 56 195MHz R10k processors. One to thirty-two processors were used. The compilation times of the programs using Polaris are shown in columns eight through ten. Array property analysis increases the compilation time by 4.5% to 10.9%[3]. These data were measured on a Sun Enterprise 4250 Server with four 248MHz UltraSPARC-II processors.

Figure 11 shows the speedups of these programs. We compare the speedups of the programs generated by Polaris, with and without array property analysis, and the programs compiled using the automatic parallelizer provided by SGI. DYFESM used a tiny input data set and suffered from the overhead introduced by parallelization. The performance of all three versions worsened when multiple processors were used. Better results were possible when large input sets were used. Loop INTGRL/do_140 in TRFD accounted for only 5% of the total sequential execution time. However, parallelizing it still increased the speedups from five to six when 16 processors were used. For BDNA and P3M, speedups improved significantly.

---

[3] The data of P3M is for subroutine PP only.

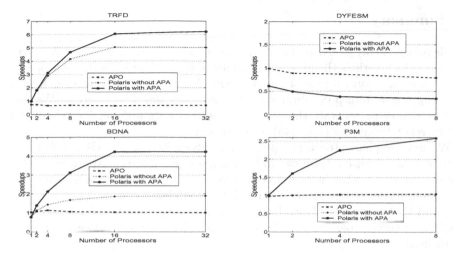

Fig. 11. Speedups: APA - array property analysis, APO - using the automatic paral-lelization option in the SGI F77 compiler

6   Related Work

Two different studies, done by Z. Shen et al. [24] and P. Petersen et al. [22], have found that index arrays are a significant source of imprecision in dependence testing. B. Blume et al. studied the Perfect Benchmarks and found detecting index array properties to be important [4]. The same conclusion also was achieved by the authors in a study of several sparse/irregular Fortran programs [17].

Our approach of modeling a demand for property checking as a set of queries was inspired by the work of E. Duesterwald et al. [8]. They proposed a general framework for developing demand-driven interprocedural data flow analyzers. They use an iterative method to propagate the queries and can handle only scalars. We use a more efficient structural analysis and work on arrays, which is possible because we have a more specific problem.

Array data flow analysis has been extensively studied [10,9,11,23]. In all studies, exhaustive analysis is used. The idea of representing array elements by an array section descriptor and using aggregations to summarize the elements accessed by a loop was first proposed by Callahan and Kennedy [6], and was used in our method of handling arrays in loops. Another class of array data flow analysis methods uses the framework of data dependence and can provide fine-grain instance-wise information [9,23]. However, this approach is difficult to use in whole program analysis.

Compile-time analysis of index arrays also was studied by K. McKinley [20] and K. Kennedy et al. [15]. They investigated how user assertions about the index arrays could be used in dependence tests. The user assertions correspond to the properties in our work. They focus on how to use the properties, while we focus on how to get the properties automatically. Their work complements ours when the properties are undetectable at compile-time.

7 Summary

In this paper, we presented an index array analysis method, called array property analysis, which verifies the property of an array by back-propagating a property query along the control flow of the program. This method integrates demand-driven approach, interprocedural analysis, and array dataflow analysis. We also illustrated how to generate the property query in a data dependence test and how to verify the property by pattern matching.

We have implemented array property analysis in our Polaris parallelizing compiler and measured its impact in finding more parallelism. Experiments with four real programs that have indirectly accessed arrays showed that array property analysis improved the precision of data dependence tests and privatization tests and that eight more loops in the four programs were found parallel. The speedups of three programs were improved considerablely when these loop were parallelized.

References

1. Harold Abelson, Gerald Jay Sussman, and Julie Sussman. *Structure and Interpretation of Computer Programs*. The MIT Press, San Francisco, California, 1985.
2. Z. Ammarguellat and W. L. Harrison, III. Automatic recognition of induction variables and recurrence relations by abstract interpretation. In *Proceedings of '90 PLDI*, pages 283–295, June 1990.
3. V. Balasundaram and K. Kennedy. A technique for summarizing data access and its use in parallelism-enhancing transformations. In *Proceedings of the Conference on Programming Language Design and Implementation*, Portland, OR, June 1989.
4. W. Blume and R. Eigenmann. An overview of symbolic analysis techniques needed for the effective parallelization of the perfect benchmarks. In *Proceedings of the 23rd International Conference on Parallel Processing. Volume 2: Software*, pages 233–238, FL, USA, August 1994.
5. William Joseph Blume. *Symbolic analysis techniques for effective automatic parallelization*. PhD thesis, University of Illinois at Urbana-Champaign, June 1995.
6. David Callahan and Ken Kennedy. Compiling programs for distributed-memory multiprocessors. *The Journal of Supercomputing*, 2(2):151–169, October 1988.
7. Béatrice Creusillet and Francois Irigoin. Interprocedural array region analysis. In *Eighth International Workshop on Languages and Compilers for Parallel Computing*, pages 4–1 to 4–15. Ohio State Uni., August 1995.
8. Evelyn Duesterwald, Rajiv Gupta, and Mary Lou Soffa. A practical framework for demand-driven interprocedural data flow analysis. *ACM Transactions on Programming Languages and Systems*, 19(6):992–1030, November 1997.
9. P. Feautrier. Dataflow analysis of scalar and array references. *International Journal of Parallel Programming*, 20(1):23–52, February 1991.
10. T. Gross and P. Steenkiste. Structured dataflow analysis for arrays and its use in an optimizing compiler. *Software Practice and Experience*, 20(2):133–155, February 1990.
11. Junjie Gu, Zhiyuan Li, and Gyungho Lee. Symbolic array dataflow analysis for array privatization and program parallelization. In *Proceedings of the 1995 Supercomputing Conference, December 3–8, 1995, San Diego, CA, USA*, 1995.

12. M. W. Hall, B. R. Murphy, and S. P. Amarasinghe. Interprocedural analysis for parallelization: Design and experience. In *SIAM Conference on Parallel Processing for Scientific Computing*, February 1995.

13. P. Havlak. *Interprocedural Symbolic analysis*. PhD thesis, Rice University, May 1994.

14. P. Havlak and K. Kennedy. Experience with interprocedural analysis of array side effects. *IEEE Transactions on Parallel and Distributed Systems*, 2(3), July 1991.

15. K. Kennedy, K. S. McKinley, and C.-W. Tseng. Analysis and transformation in the ParaScope Editor. In *Proceedings of the 1991 ACM International Conference on Supercomputing*, Cologne, Germany, June 1991.

16. Zhiyuan Li and Pen-Chung Yew. Interprocedural analysis for parallel computing. In *1988 International Conference on Parallel Processing*, volume II, pages 221–228, St. Charles, Ill., August 1988.

17. Y. Lin and D. Padua. On the automatic parallelization of sparse and irregular fortran programs. In *Proc. of 4th Workshop on Languages, Compilers, and Runtime Systems for Scalable Computers (LCR98)*, volume 1511 of *Lecture Notes in Computer Science*, pages 41–56. Springer-Verlag, Pittsburgh, PA, 1998.

18. Y. Lin and D. Padua. Analysis of irregular single-indexed arrays and its applications in compiler optimizations. Technical Report CSRD-TR-1566, Dept. of Computer Science, University of Illinois at Urbana-Champaign, October 1999.

19. Y. Lin and D. Padua. Detecting properties of arrays by using a demand-driven and interprocedural approach. Technical Report CSRD-TR-1567, Dept. of Computer Science, University of Illinois at Urbana-Champaign, October 1999.

20. K. S. McKinley. Dependence analysis of arrays subscripted by index arrays. Technical Report TR91-162, Dept. of Computer Science, Rice University, June 1991.

21. Yunheung Paek, Jay Hoeflinger, and David Padua. Simplification of array access patterns for compiler optimizations. In *Proceedings of the ACM SIGPLAN'98 Conference on Programming Language Design and Implementation (PLDI)*, pages 60–71, Montreal, Canada, 17–19 June 1998.

22. Paul M. Petersen and David A. Padua. Static and dynamic evaluation of data dependence analysis techniques:. *IEEE Transactions on Parallel and Distributed Systems*, 7(11):1121–1132, November 1996.

23. William Pugh and David Wonnacott. An exact method for analysis of value-based array data dependences. In *Proceedings of the Sixth Annual Workshop on rogramming Languages and Compilers for Parallel Computing*, December 93.

24. Z. Shen, Z. Li, and P. C. Yew. An empirical study on array subscripts and data dependencies. In *International Conference on Parallel Processing, Vol. 2: Software*, pages 145–152, Pennsylvania, USA, August 1989.

25. R. Triolet, F. Irigoin, and P. Feautrier. Direct parallelization of call statements. In *Proceedings of the SIGPLAN'86 Symposium on Compiler Construction*, pages 176–185, Palo Alto, CA, July 1986.

26. P. Tu and D. Padua. Gated SSA-Based demand-driven symbolic analysis for parallelizing compilers. In *Conference proceedings of the 1995 International Conference on Supercomputing*, Barcelona, Spain, July 3-7, 1995, pages 414–423, 1995.

Language Support for
Pipelining Wavefront Computations*

Bradford L. Chamberlain, E. Christopher Lewis, and Lawrence Snyder

Department of Computer Science and Engineering
University of Washington
Seattle, WA 98195-2350 USA
{brad,echris,snyder}@cs.washington.edu

Abstract. Wavefront computations, characterized by a data dependent flow of computation across a data space, are receiving increasing attention as an important class of parallel computations. Though sophisticated compiler optimizations can often produce efficient pipelined implementations from sequential representations, we argue that a language-based approach to representing wavefront computations is a more practical technique. A language-based approach is simple for the programmer yet unambiguously parallel. In this paper we introduce simple array language extensions that directly support wavefront computations. We show how a programmer may reason about the extensions' legality and performance; we describe their implementation and give performance data demonstrating the importance of parallelizing these codes.

1   Introduction

Wavefront computations are characterized by a data dependent flow of computation across a data space. Though the dependences imply serialization, wavefront computations admit efficient, parallel implementation via pipelining [6,21]. Wavefront computations frequently appear in scientific applications, including solvers and dynamic programming codes; and recently, the ASCI (Accelerated Strategic Computing Initiative) SWEEP3D benchmark has received considerable attention as an important wavefront computation [10,20]. The Fortran 77 and Fortran 90 SPECfp92 Tomcatv code fragments in Figures 1(a) and (b) represent typical wavefront computations.

The growing interest in wavefront computations raises the question of how they may be best expressed and realized on parallel machines. Choosing not to distribute array dimensions across which a wavefront travels is the simplest solution. For example, if only the second dimension of the arrays in the Tomcatv code fragment in Figure 1 is distributed, the entire computation is parallel. This is not a general solution, for other components of the computation may prefer different distributions, perhaps due to surface-to-volume issues or wavefronts traveling along orthogonal dimensions. If we assume that any dimension of each array may be distributed, we must use pipelining to exploit parallelism in wavefront computations.

---

* This research was supported in part by DARPA Grant F30602-97-1-0152, NSF Grant CCR-9710284 and the Intel Corporation.

L. Carter and J. Ferrante (Eds.): LCPC'99, LNCS 1863, pp. 318–332, 2000.

```
        DO 100 i = 2 , n-1
          DO 100 j = 2 , n-2
            r=aa(j,i)*d(j-1,i)
            d(j,i)=1.0/(dd(j,i)-aa(j-1,i)*r)
            rx(j,i)=rx(j,i)-rx(j-1,i)*r
            ry(j,i)=ry(j,i)-ry(j-1,i)*r
   100 CONTINUE
```

(a)

```
   DO 100 j = 2 , n-2
     r(2:n-1)=aa(j,2:n-1)*d(j-1,2:n-1)
     d(j,2:n-1)=1.0/(dd(j,2:n-1)-aa(j-1,2:n-1)*r(2:n-1))
     rx(j,2:n-1)=rx(j,2:n-1)-rx(j-1,2:n-1)*r(2:n-1)
     ry(j,2:n-1)=ry(j,2:n-1)-ry(j-1,2:n-1)*r(2:n-1)
 100 CONTINUE
```

(b)

Fig. 1. Fortran 77 (a) and Fortran 90 (b) wavefront code fragments from SPECfp92 Tomcatv benchmark.

There are three approaches to pipelining wavefront codes: (i) the *explicit* approach requires the programmer to write an explicitly parallel program (*e.g.*, Fortran 77 plus MPI [18]) exploiting pipelining, (ii) the *optimization-based* approach permits the programmer to write a sequential representation of the wavefront computation, from which the compiler produces a pipelined implementation, and (iii) the *language-based* approach provides the programmer with language-level abstractions that permit the unambiguous representation of wavefront computations that are candidates for pipelining.

The explicit approach is potentially the most efficient, because the programmer has complete control over all performance critical details. This control comes at the cost of added complexity that the programmer must manage. For example, the core of the ASCI SWEEP3D benchmark is 626 lines of code, only 179 of which are fundamental to the computation. The remainder are devoted to tiling, buffer management, and communication; different dimensions of the 4-dimensional problem are treated asymmetrically, despite problem-level symmetry, obscuring the true logic of the computation. Furthermore, the explicit approach will probably not exhibit portable performance, because the pipelined computation may be highly tuned to a particular machine.

The optimization-based approach appears to be the simplest for programmers, as they may exploit a familiar sequential representation of the computation. Researchers have described compiler techniques by which pipelined code may be generated from sequential programs [8,17]. Unfortunately, significant performance will be lost if a compiler does not perform this optimization. As a result, the optimization-based approach does not have portable performance either, because different compilers may or may not implement the optimization. Even if all compilers do perform the transformation, there is a question of how well they perform it. Programmers may have to write code to a particular idiom that a particular compiler recognizes and optimizes, again sacrificing portability. Programmers cannot be certain that pipelined code will be generated, thus they lack complete information to make informed algorithmic decisions. In any case, we are aware of only one commercial High Performance Fortran (HPF) [7,11] compiler that even attempts to pipeline wavefront codes, and there are many circumstances under which it is unsuccessful [13].

The language-based approach provides a simple representation of the wavefront computation, yet unambiguously identifies the opportunity for pipelining to both the programmer and the compiler. The programmer can be certain that the compiler will generate fully parallel pipelined code. In the best case, all three approaches will result in comparable parallel performance; but the programmer only has guarantees for the explicit and language-based approaches, while the optimization-based approach requires faith in the compiler to perform the transformation. On the other hand, to exploit the language-based approach, programmers must learn new language concepts. In this paper, we introduce two modest extensions to array languages that provide language-level support for pipelining wavefront computations. The extensions have no impact on the rest of the language (*i.e.*, existing programs need not change and do not suffer performance degradation). Though our extension can be applied to any array language, such as Fortran 90 [1] or HPF [7,11], we describe it in terms of the ZPL parallel array language [19].

This paper is organized as follows. In the next section, we describe our array language extension to support wavefront computations in ZPL. Sections 3 and 4 describe its implementation and parallelization, respectively. Performance data is presented in Section 5, and conclusions and future work are given in the final section.

2 Array Language Support for Wavefront Computation

This section describes array language support for wavefront computations in the context of the ZPL parallel array language [19]. Previous studies demonstrate that the ZPL compiler is competitive with hand-coded C with MPI [3] and that it generally outperforms HPF [14]. The compiler is publicly available for most modern parallel and sequential platforms [22]. The language is in active use by scientists in fields such as astronomy, civil engineering, biological statistics, mathematics, oceanography, and theoretical physics. Section 2.1 gives a very brief summary of the ZPL language, only describing the features of the language immediately relevant to this paper. Section 2.2 introduces our language extension.

2.1 Brief ZPL Language Summary

ZPL is a data parallel array programming language. It supports all the usual scalar data types (*e.g.*, integer, float, char), operators (*e.g.*, math, logical, bit-wise), and control structures (*e.g.*, if, for, while, function calls). As an array language, it also offers array data types and operators. ZPL is distinguished from other array languages by its use of *regions* [4]. A region represents an index set and may precede a statement, specifying the extent of the array references within its dynamic scope. The region is said to *cover* statements of the same rank within this scope. By factoring the indices that participate in the computation into the region, explicit array indexing (*i.e.*, slice notation) is eliminated. For example, the following Fortran 90 (slice-based) and ZPL (region-based) array statements are equivalent.

```
for j := 2 to n-2 do                              [2..n-2,2..n-1] scan
[j,2..n-1] begin                                       r=aa*d'@north;
           r=aa*d@north;                                d=1.0/(dd-aa@north*r);
           d=1.0/(dd-aa@north*r);                       rx=rx-rx'@north*r;
           rx=rx-rx@north*r;                            ry=ry-ry'@north*r;
           ry=ry-ry@north*r;                           end;
           end;
end;
```

               (a)   (b)

Fig. 2. ZPL representations of the Tomcatv code fragment from Figure 1. (a) Using an explicit loop to express the wavefront. (b) Using a scan block and the prime operator. Arrays r, aa, d, dd, rx and ry are all $n \times n$.

```
a(n/2..n,n/2:n) = b(n/2:n,n/2:n) + c(n/2:n,n/2:n)        [n/2..n,n/2..n] a = b + c;
```

Regions can be named and used symbolically to further improve readability and conciseness. When all array references in a statement do not refer to exactly the same set of indices, array operators are applied to individual references, selecting elements from the operands according to some function of the covering region's indices. ZPL provides a number of array operators (*e.g.*, shifts, reductions, parallel prefix operations, broadcasts, general permutations), but for this discussion, we will only discuss the shift operator. The shift operator, represented by the @ symbol, shifts the indices of the covering region by some offset vector, called a *direction*, to determine the indices of its argument array that are involved in the computation. For example, the following Fortran 90 and ZPL statements perform the same four point stencil computation from the Jacobi Iteration. Let the directions north, south, west, and east represent the programmer defined vectors $(-1, 0)$, $(1, 0)$, $(0, -1)$, and $(0, 1)$, respectively.

```
a(2:n+1,2:n+1) = (b(1:n,2:n+1)+b(3:n+2,2:n+1)+b(2:n+1,1:n)+b(2:n+1,3:n+2))/4.0
            [2..n+1,2..n+1] a := (b@north + b@south + b@west + b@east) / 4.0;
```

Figure 2(a) contains a ZPL code fragment representing the same computation as the Fortran 90 Tomcatv code fragment in Figure 1(b). The use of regions improves code clarity and compactness. Note that though the scalar variable r is promoted to an array in the array codes, we have previously demonstrated compiler techniques by which this overhead may be eliminated via array contraction [12].

2.2 Wavefront Computation in ZPL

Semantics. Array language semantics dictate that the right-hand side of an array statement must be evaluated before the result is assigned to the left-hand side. As a result, the compiler will not generate a loop that carries a non-lexically forward true data dependence (*i.e.*, a dependence from a statement to its self or a preceding statement). For example, the ZPL statement in Figure 3(a) is implemented by the loop nest in 3(b). The compiler determines that the i-loop must iterate from high to low indices in order to

$$[2..n,1..n] \ a := 2 * a@north;$$

```
for i ← n downto 2 do
  for j ← 1 to n do
    a_{i,j} ← 2 * a_{i-1,j}
```

$$a = \begin{matrix} 1 & 1 & 1 & 1 & 1 \\ 2 & 2 & 2 & 2 & 2 \\ 2 & 2 & 2 & 2 & 2 \\ 2 & 2 & 2 & 2 & 2 \\ 2 & 2 & 2 & 2 & 2 \end{matrix}$$

(a)   (b)   (c)

$$[2..n,1..n] \ a := 2 * a'@north;$$

```
for i ← 2 to n do
  for j ← 1 to n do
    a_{i,j} ← 2 * a_{i-1,j}
```

$$a = \begin{matrix} 1 & 1 & 1 & 1 & 1 \\ 2 & 2 & 2 & 2 & 2 \\ 4 & 4 & 4 & 4 & 4 \\ 8 & 8 & 8 & 8 & 8 \\ 16 & 16 & 16 & 16 & 16 \end{matrix}$$

(d)   (e)   (f)

Fig. 3. ZPL array statements (a and d) and the corresponding loop nests (b and e) that implement them. The arrays in (c and f) illustrate the result of the computations if array a initially contains all 1s.

ensure that the loop does not carry a true data dependence. If array a contains all 1s before the statement in 3(a) executes, it will have the values in Figure 3(c) afterward.

In wavefront computations, the programmer wants the compiler to generate a loop nest with non-lexically forward loop carried true data dependences. We introduce a new operator, called the *prime* operator, that allows a programmer to reference values written in previous iterations of the loop nest that implement the statement containing the primed reference. For example, the ZPL statement in Figure 3(d) is implemented by the loop nest in 3(e). In this case, the compiler must ensure that a loop carried true data dependence exists due to array a, thus the i-loop iterates from low to high indices. If array a contains all 1s before the statement in 3(d) executes, it will have the values in Figure 3(f) afterward. In general, the directions on the primed array references define the orientation of the wavefront.

The prime operator alone cannot represent wavefronts such as the Tomcatv code fragment in Figure 2(a), because it only permits loop carried true dependences from a statement to itself. We introduce a new compound statement, called a *scan block*, to allow multiple statements to participate in a wavefront computation. Primed array references in a scan block refer to values written by any statement in the block, not just the statement that contains it. For example, the ZPL code fragment in Figure 2(b) uses a scan block and the prime operator to realize the computation in Figure 2(a) without an explicit loop. The array reference d'@north refers to values from the previous iteration of the loop that iterates over the first dimension. Thus the primed @north references imply a wavefront that travels from north to south. Just as in existing array languages, a non-primed reference refers to values written by lexically preceding statements, within or outside the scan block.

The scan blocks we have looked at thus far contain only cardinal directions (*i.e.*, directions in which only one dimension is nonzero, such as north, south, east and west). When non-cardinal directions or combinations of orthogonal cardinal directions appear with primed references, the character of the wavefront is less obvious. Below, we describe how programmers may interpret these cases.

The notation may at first appear awkward. It is important to note, however, that experienced ZPL programmers are already well accustomed to manipulating arrays atomically and shifting them with the @-operator. They must only learn the prime operator, which is motivated by mathematical convention where successor values are primed. In the same vein, array languages such as Fortran 90 can be extended to include the prime operator.

Assumptions and Definitions. At this point, we give several assumptions and definitions that will be exploited in the subsequent discussion. We assume that all dimensions of each array may be distributed, and the final decision is deferred until application startup time. In addition, we assume that the dimension(s) along which the wavefront travel, the wavefront dimension(s), are decided at compile time. Define function f, where i and j are integers, as follows.

$$f(i,j) = \begin{cases} 0 & \text{if } i = j = 0 \\ \pm & \text{if } ij < 0 \\ + & \text{if } ij \geq 0 \text{ and } (i > 0 \text{ or } j > 0) \\ - & \text{if } ij \geq 0 \text{ and } (i < 0 \text{ or } j < 0) \end{cases}$$

Given two directions, $u = (u_1, \ldots, u_d)$ and $v = (v_1, \ldots, v_d)$, of size d we construct a size d *wavefront summary vector*[1] (WSV), $w = (w_1, \ldots, w_d)$, by letting $w_i = f(u_i, v_i)$ for $1 \leq i \leq d$. In a similar manner, all of the directions that appear with primed array references may be considered to form a single wavefront summary vector. We say that a wavefront summary vector is *simple* if none of its components are $\pm$. For example, WSV($\{(-1,0),(-2,0)\}$) = $(-,0)$, WSV($\{(-1,0),(-2,0),(-1,2)\}$) = $(-,+)$, WSV($\{(-1,0),(0,-1)\}$) = $(-,-)$, and WSV($\{(-1,0),(1,-2)\}$) = $(\pm,-)$. All but the final example are simple.

Legality. There are a number of statically checked legality conditions. (i) Primed arrays in a scan block must also be defined in the block; (ii) the directions on primed references may not over-constrain the wavefront, as discussed below; (iii) all statements in a scan block must have the same rank (*i.e.*, they are implemented by a loop nest of the same depth)—this precludes the inclusion of scalar assignment in a scan block; (iv) all statements in a scan block must be covered by the same region; and (v) parallel operators' operands other than the shift operator may not be primed; this is essential because array operators are pulled out of the scan block during compilation.

An over-constrained scan block is one for which a loop nest can not be created that respects the dependences from the shifted array references. For example, primed @north and @south references over-constrain the scan block because they imply both north-to-south and south-to-north wavefronts, which are contradictory. In general, the programmer constructs a wavefront summary vector from the directions used with primed array references in order to decided whether the scan block is over-constrained.

---

[1] The observant reader will recognize many similarities in this presentation to standard data dependence properties and algorithms. We have avoided a technical presentation in order to streamline the programmer's view.

Simple wavefront summary vectors, the common case, are always legal, for a wavefront may travel along any non-zero dimension, always referring to values "behind it."

Wavefront Dimensions and Parallelism. For performance reasons programmers may wish to determine along which dimensions of the data space wavefronts travel, called *wavefront dimensions*, so that they may understand which dimensions benefit from pipelined parallelism. The dependences do not always fully constrain the orientation of the wavefront, so we give a set of simple rules to be used by the programmer to approximate wavefront dimensions. Again, the programmer examines the wavefront summary vector and considers three cases: (i) the WSV contains at least one 0 entry, (ii) the WSV contains no 0 entries and at least one ± entry, and (iii) the WSV contains only + and − entries. In case (i), all of the dimensions associated with + or − entries benefit from pipeline parallelism, and all the 0 entry dimensions are completely parallel. In case (ii), all but the ± entries benefit from pipelined parallelism. In case (iii), all but the leftmost entry benefits from pipelined parallelism. The leftmost entry is arbitrarily selected to minimize the impact of pipelining on cache performance.

Examples. We will use a single code fragment with different direction instantiations to illustrate how programmers may reason about their wavefront computations.

```
a := (a'@d1 + a'@d2)/2.0;
```

Example 1: Let d1=d2=(-1,0). The WSV is $(-,0)$, which is simple, so the wavefront is legal (*i.e.*, not over-constrained). The first dimension is the wavefront dimension, and the second dimension is completely parallel.
Example 2: Let d1=(-1,0) and d2=(0,-1). The WSV is $(-,-)$, which is simple, so the wavefront is legal. The wavefront could legally travel along either the first or second dimension, but we have defined it to travel along the second. There will be pipelined parallelism in the second dimension, but the first will be serialized.
Example 3: Let d1=(-1,0) and d2=(1,1). The WSV is $(\pm,+)$, which is not simple. Nevertheless the wavefront is legal because there exists a loop nest that respects the dependences. The second dimension is the wavefront dimension.
Example 4: Let d1=(0,-1) and d2=(0,1). The wavefront summary vector is $(0,\pm)$, which is not simple. The wavefront is not legal because no loop nest can respect the dependence is the second dimension. The scan block is over-constrained and the compiler will flag it as such.

Summary. We have presented a simple array language extension that permits the expression of loop carried true data dependences, for use in pipelined wavefront computations. It is simple for programmers to reason about the semantics, legality and parallel implications of their wavefront code. In fact, programmers need not actually compute wavefront summary vectors, for they will normally be trivial. For example, only the direction north=(-1,0) appears in the Tomcatv code fragment of Figure 2(b). This trivially begets the WSV $(-,0)$, indicating that the second dimension is completely parallel and the first is the wavefront dimension.

Contrast this with an optimization-based approach, where the programmer must be aware of the compiler's optimization strategy in order to reason about a code's potential parallel performance. Without this knowledge, the programmer is ill-equipped to make design decisions. For example, suppose a programmer writes a code that performs both north-south and east-west wavefronts. The programmer may opt to distribute only one dimension and perform a transposition between each north-south and east-west wavefront, eliminating the need for pipelining. This may be much slower than a fully pipelined solution, guaranteed by our language-level approach.

3   Implementation

This section describes our approach to implementing primed array references and scan blocks in the ZPL compiler. Below we describe how loop structure is determined and naive communication is generated.

The ZPL compiler identifies groups of statements that will be implemented as a single loop nest, essentially performing loop fusion. The data dependences (true, anti and output) that exist between these statements determine the structure of the resulting loop nest (which loop iterates over each dimension of the data space and in what direction). The ZPL and scalar code fragment in Figure 3(a) illustrates this. Notice that the i-loop iterates from high to low indices in order to preserve the loop carried anti-dependence from the statement to itself.

3.1   Deriving Loop Structure

In previous work we have defined *unconstrained distance vectors* to represent array-level data dependences, and we have presented an algorithm to decide loop structure given a set of intra-loop unconstrained distance vectors [12]. Traditional distance vectors are inappropriate for use in this context because they are derived from loop nests, which are not created until after our transformations have been performed. Because array statements are implemented with a loop nest in which a single loop iterates over the same dimension of all arrays in its body, we can characterize dependences by dimensions of the array rather than dimensions of the iteration space. Unconstrained distance vectors are more abstract than traditional (constrained) distance vectors because they separate loop structure from dependence representation. Though unconstrained distance vectors are not fully general, they can represent any dependence that may appear in a scan block.

The prime operator transforms what an array language would otherwise interpret as an anti-dependence into a true dependence. In order to represent this, the unconstrained distance vectors associated with primed array references are simply negated. The algorithm for finding loop structure is unchanged.

3.2   Communication Generation

Next, we consider naive communication generation for scan blocks. We assume that all parallel operators except shift are pulled out of scan blocks and assigned to temporary arrays. Furthermore, we assume that all arrays in a scan block are aligned and block

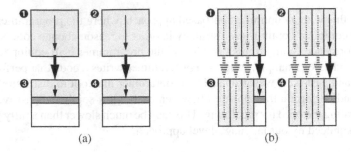

(a)   (b)

Fig. 4. Illustration of the data movement and parallelism characteristics of wavefront computations with (a) naive and (b) pipelined communication.

distributed in each dimension, so communication is only required for the shift operator. This last assumption is the basis of ZPL's *WYSIWYG performance model* [2]. There are obvious extensions for cyclic and block-cyclic distributions. Each processor blocks, waiting to receive all the data it needs to compute its portion of the scan block. When all the data is received by a processor, it computes its portion of the scan block, and sends the necessary data on to the next processor(s) in the wave. The communication has the effect of serializing all the computation along the direction of the wavefront. Figure 4(a) illustrates this interprocessor communication. Though this naive implementation does not exploit any parallelism along the wavefront dimension, the next section describes and analyzes a parallel implementation exploiting pipelining.

4   Parallelization by Pipelining

In the implementation described above, a processor finishes computing on its entire portion of a scan block before data is sent on to later processors in the wavefront computation. As a result, there is no parallelism along the *wavefront dimension*—the dimension along which the wavefront travels. Suppose a north-to-south wavefront computation is performed on an $n \times n$ array block distributed across a 2×2 processor mesh as in Figure 4(a). Processors 3 and 4 must wait for processors 1 and 2 to compute their $\frac{n^2}{4}$ elements before they may proceed. Furthermore, processors 1 and 2 may then need to wait for the others to complete.

Alternatively, the wavefront computation may be *pipelined* in order to exploit parallelism [8,15,17,21]. Specifically, a processor may compute over a *block* of its portion of the data space, transmit some of the data needed by subsequent processors, then continue to execute its next block. The benefit of this approach is that it allows multiple processors to become involved in the computation as soon as possible, greatly improving parallelism. Figure 4(b) illustrates this. Processors 3 and 4 only need to wait long enough for processors 1 and 2 to compute a single block ($\frac{n^2}{4} \times \frac{1}{4} = \frac{n^2}{16}$ elements) each. They can then immediately begin computing blocks of their portions of the scan block.

Smaller blocks increase parallelism at the expense of sending more messages. Several researchers have considered the problem of weighing this tradeoff in order to find the optimal block size. Hiranandani *et al.* developed a model that assumes constant cost communication [9], while Ohta *et al.* model communication as a linear function of message size [16]. In other words, the cost of transmitting a message of n words is given by $\alpha + \beta n$, where α is the message startup cost and β is the per-word communication cost. We present an analysis using this model to demonstrate its improved accuracy versus the constant cost communication model.

Assume that a wavefront is moving along the first dimension of a 2-dimensional $n \times n$ data space, as in the code of Figure 2(b). Let the data space be block distributed across p processors in the first dimension; for simplicity we do not distribute the second dimension. Let α and β be the startup and per-element costs of communication, respectively, and b be the block size. Also we assume that all times are normalized to the cost of computing a single element in the data space. The total computation and communication times of a pipelined implementation are given below.

$$T^{\text{pipe}}_{\text{comp}} = \frac{nb}{p}(p-1) + \frac{n^2}{p} \qquad T^{\text{pipe}}_{\text{comm}} = (\alpha + \beta b)\left(\frac{n}{b} + p - 2\right)$$

The first term of $T^{\text{pipe}}_{\text{comp}}$ gives the time to compute $p - 1$ blocks of size $\frac{nb}{p}$, at which point the last processor may begin computing. The second term gives the time for the last processor to compute on its $\frac{n^2}{p}$ elements. The first factor of $T^{\text{pipe}}_{\text{comm}}$ is the cost of transmitting each b element message. The second factor gives the number of messages on the critical path. A total of $p - 1$ messages are required before the last processor has received any data, and then the last processor receives another $\frac{n}{b} - 1$ messages. In order to find the value of b that minimizes this time, we differentiate the sum of $T^{\text{pipe}}_{\text{comp}}$ and $T^{\text{pipe}}_{\text{comm}}$ with respect to b, let this equation equal 0 and solve for b.

$$-\frac{\alpha n}{b^2} + \beta(p-2) + \frac{n(p-1)}{p} = 0 \quad \Longrightarrow \quad b = \sqrt{\frac{\alpha n p}{(p\beta + n)(p-1)}} \approx \sqrt{\frac{\alpha n}{p\beta + n}} \qquad (1)$$

This approximate equation for b tells us that as α grows, the optimal b grows, because a larger startup communication cost must be offset by a reduction in the number of messages. As β grows, the optimal b decreases, because a larger per-element communication cost decreases the relative per-message startup cost. As p grows, the optimal b decreases, because there are more processor to keep busy. As n grows, the optimal b becomes less sensitive to the relative values of α, β, and p. Equation (1) reduces to the constant communication cost equation of Hiranandani *et al.* when we let $\beta = 0$ (*i.e.*, $b = \sqrt{\alpha}$). This simplified model gives no insight into the relative importance and roles of α, β, n, and p.

In order to assess the value of the added accuracy of modeling communication costs as a function of message size, we compare speedup derived from the two approaches to empirical data from the Cray T3E in Figure 5(a). *Model1* assumes that $\beta = 0$ (*i.e.*, like Hiranandani's model), and *Model2* is the more general model described above. First, observe that *Model2* more closely tracks the observed speedup. *Model1* predicts that $b = 39$ is the optimal block size, while *Model2* predicts $b = 23$, which is in fact better. For this particular problem, n is relatively large making speedup not especially sensitive to the exact value of b. If we assume large problem sizes, the assumption that $\beta = 0$ is not

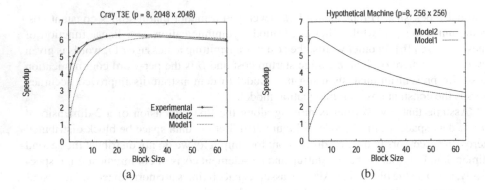

Fig. 5. Model evaluations. *Model1* and *Model2* are identical except that the former assumes that $\beta = 0$, *i.e.*, it ignores the per-element communication cost. (a) Modeled versus experimental speedup due to pipelining of Tomcatv wavefront computation. (b) A demonstration of the value of modeling the per-word cost (β) of communication.

an unreasonable one. For smaller problem sizes *Model1* is ineffective because the relative value of α and β becomes increasingly more important. This is particularly a problem on modern machines such as the Cray T3E on which β dominates communication costs. Figure 5(b) illustrates this problem with *Model1*. We use hypothetical values for α and β to illustrate a worst case scenario, so experimental data is not included. In this case, *Model1* does not accurately reflect speedup, and it suggests that the optimal block size is $b = 20$ versus $b = 3$ in *Model2*. We can expect the speedup with a block size of 20 versus 3 to be considerably less. The situation is even worse for larger numbers of processors.

5   Performance Evaluation

In this section we demonstrate the potential performance benefits of providing scan blocks in an array language. We conduct experiments on the Cray T3E and the SGI PowerChallenge using the Tomcatv and SIMPLE [5] benchmarks. For each experiment, we consider the program as a whole, and we consider two components of each that contain a single wavefront computation. Our extensions drastically improve the performance of the two wavefront portions of code in each benchmark, which results in significant overall performance enhancement. We use the following compilers in these experiments: Portland Group, Inc. pghpf version 2.4-4, Cray cf90 version 3.0.2.1, and University of Washington ZPL 1.14.3.

5.1   Cache Benefits

Before we evaluate the parallel performance of wavefront codes, we will examine cache performance implications on a single processor. Consider the code fragment without scan blocks in Figure 2(a), and assume the arrays are allocated in column-major-order. For the code to have acceptable cache behavior, the compiler must implement the four

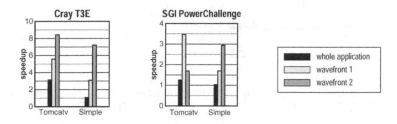

Fig. 6. Potential uniprocessor speedup due to scan blocks from improved cache behavior.

statements with a single loop nest and then interchange the compiler generated loop with
the user loop. After these transformations, the inner loop iterates over the elements of
each column, exploiting spatial locality. Despite the fact that loop interchange is a well
understood transformation, there are certain circumstances where it fails. For example,
for these codes, at the default optimization level (*-O1*) the pghpf compiler produces
Fortran 77 code that the back end compiler is unable to optimize. The Cray Fortran 90
compiler, on the other hand, is successful. The programmer cannot be certain one way
or the other.

With this in mind, we experimentally compare the performance of array language
codes with and without our language support for wavefront computations. Figure 6 graphs the speedup of the former over the latter. These experiments are on a single node
of each machine, so the speedup is entirely due to caching effects. On the Cray T3E,
the wavefront computations alone (the two grey bars) speedup by up to $8.5\times$, resulting
in an overall speedup (black bars) of $3\times$ for Tomcatv and 7% for SIMPLE. Tomcatv
experiences such a large speedup, because the wavefront computations represent a significant portion of the program's total execution time. The SGI PowerChallenge graph
has similar characteristics except that the speedups are more modest (up to $4\times$). This is
because the PowerChallenge has a much slower processor than the T3E, thus the relative
cost of a cache miss is less, so performance is less sensitive to cache behavior than on
the T3E.

5.2   Parallelization Benefits

Performance enhancements like those presented below have also been demonstrated for
optimization-based approaches to parallelizing wavefront computations [9]. When the
optimization is successful, it can produce efficient parallel code. The data below gives
a sense for the performance that may be lost if the optimization is not performed, either
because its analysis is thwarted by an extraneous dependence or it is not implemented
in the compiler. The language-based approach has the advantage that the programmer
can be certain that the compiler is aware of the opportunity for pipelining, because the
phrasing of the computation is unambiguously parallel. We are aware of no commercial
HPF compilers that pipeline wavefront computations.

We are in the process of implementing the parallelization strategy described in Section 4 in the ZPL compiler. For this study, we have performed the pipelining transformations by hand on Tomcatv and SIMPLE to assess its impact. Figure 7 presents speedup

330   B.L. Chamberlain, E.C. Lewis, and L. Snyder

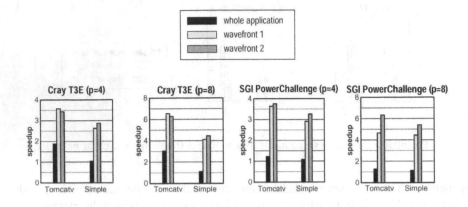

Fig. 7. Speedup of pipelined parallel codes versus nonpipelined codes. All arrays are distributed entirely across the dimension along which the wavefront travels.

data due to pipelining alone. Speedup is computed against a fully parallel version of the code without pipelining, thus the bars representing whole program speedup (black bars) are speedup beyond an already highly parallel code. The bars representing speedup of the wavefront computations (grey bars) are serial without pipelining, so the baseline in their case does not benefit from parallelism. We would like the grey bars to achieve speedup as close to the number of processors as possible. In all cases the speedup of the wavefront segments approaches the number of processors, and the overall program improvements are large in several cases (up to $3\times$ speedup). The smallest overall performance improvements are still greater than 5 to 8%. Though the absolute speedup improves as the number of processors increases, the efficiency decreases. This is because we have kept the problem size constant, so the relative cost of communication increases with the number of processors.

6 Conclusion

Wavefront computations are becoming increasingly important and complex. Though previous work has developed techniques by which compilers may produce efficient pipelined code from serial source code, the programmer is left to wonder whether the optimization was successful or whether the optimization is even implemented in a particular compiler. In contrast, we have extended array languages to provide language-level support for wavefront codes, thus unambiguously exposing the opportunity for pipelining to both the programmer and the compiler. The extensions do not impact the rest of the language, and they permit programmers to simply reason about their codes' legality and potential performance. We have given a simple analysis that gives insight into the roles of machine parameters, problem size, and processor configuration in determining the optimal block size for pipelining. In addition, we have presented experimental data for the Tomcatv and SIMPLE benchmarks on the Cray T3E and SGI PowerChallenge demonstrating the potential performance lost when pipelining is not performed.

Currently, we are in the process of fully implementing these language extensions in the ZPL compiler. Because the optimal block size is a function of non-static parameters such as problem size and computation cost, we will develop dynamic techniques for calculating it. We will investigate the quality of block size selection using only static and profile information. We will also develop a benchmark suite of wavefront computations in order to evaluate our design and implementation and investigate their properties, such as dynamism of optimal block size.

Acknowledgments. We thank Sung-Eung Choi and Samuel Guyer for their comments on drafts of this paper. This research was supported by a grant of HPC time from the Arctic Region Supercomputing Center.

References

1. Jeanne C. Adams, Walter S. Brainerd, Jeanne T. Martin, Brian T. Smith, and Jerrold L. Wagener. *Fortran 90 Handbook*. McGraw-Hill, New York, NY, 1992.
2. Bradford L. Chamberlain, Sung-Eun Choi, E Christopher Lewis, Calvin Lin, Lawrence Snyder, and W. Derrick Weathersby. ZPL's WYSIWYG performance model. In *Third IEEE International Workshop on High-Level Parallel Programming Models and Supportive Environments*, pages 50–61, March 1998.
3. Bradford L. Chamberlain, Sung-Eun Choi, E Christopher Lewis, Lawrence Snyder, W. Derrick Weathersby, and Calvin Lin. The case for high-level parallel programming in ZPL. *IEEE Computational Science and Engineering*, 5(3):76–85, July–September 1998.
4. Bradford L. Chamberlain, E Christopher Lewis, Calvin Lin, and Lawrence Snyder. Regions: An abstraction for expressing array computation. In *ACM SIGAPL/SIGPLAN International Conference on Array Programming Languages*, pages 41–49, August 1999.
5. W. Crowley, C. P. Hendrickson, and T. I. Luby. The SIMPLE code. Technical Report UCID-17715, Lawrence Livermore Laboratory, 1978.
6. Ron Cytron. Doacross: Beyond vectorization for multiprocessors. In *International Conference on Parallel Processing*, pages 836–844, 1986.
7. High Performance Fortran Forum. *High Performance Fortran Language Specification, Version 2.0.* January 1997.
8. Seema Hiranandani, Ken Kennedy, and Chau-Wen Tseng. Compiler optimizations for Fortran D on MIMD distributed-memory machines. In *Supercomputing '91*, pages 96–100, Albuquerque, NM, November 1991.
9. Seema Hiranandani, Ken Kennedy, and Chau-Wen Tseng. Evaluation of compiler optimizations for Fortran D on MIMD distributed-memory machines. In *International Conference on Supercomputing*, pages 1–14, Washington, DC, July 1992.
10. K. R. Koch, R. S. Baker, and R. E. Alcouffe. Solution of the first-order form of three-dimensional discrete ordinates equations on a massively parallel machine. *Transactions of the American Nuclear Society*, 65:198–9, 1992.
11. Charles H. Koelbel, David B. Loveman, Robert S. Schreiber, Guy L. Steele Jr., , and Mary E. Zosel. *The High Performance Fortran Handbook*. The MIT Press, Cambridge, Massachusetts, 1993.
12. E Christopher Lewis, Calvin Lin, and Lawrence Snyder. The implementation and evaluation of fusion and contraction in array languages. In *ACM SIGPLAN Conference on Programming Language Design and Implementation*, pages 50–59, June 1998.
13. E Christopher Lewis and Lawrence Snyder. Pipelining wavefront computations: Experiences and performance. Submitted for publication, November 1999.

14. C. Lin, L. Snyder, R. Anderson, B. Chamberlain, S. Choi, G. Forman, E. Lewis, and W. D. Weathersby. ZPL vs. HPF: A comparison of performance and programming style. Technical Report 95–11–05, Department of Computer Science and Engineering, University of Washington, 1994.
15. Ton A. Ngo. *The Role of Performance Models in Parallel Programming and Languages*. PhD thesis, University of Washington, Department of Computer Science and Engineering, 1997.
16. Hiroshi Ohta, Tasuhiko Saito, Masahiro Kainaga, and Hiroyuki Ono. Optimal tile size adjustment in compiling general DOACROSS loop nests. In *International Conference on Supercomputing*, pages 270–9, Barcelona, Spain, 1995.
17. Anne Rogers and Keshav Pingali. Process decomposition through locality of reference. In *ACM SIGPLAN Conference on Programming Language Design and Implementation*, pages 69–80, June 1989.
18. Marc Snir, Steve Otto, Steven Huss-Lederman, David Walker, and Jack Dongarra. *MPI—The Complete Reference*. The MIT Press, Cambridge, Massachusetts, 2nd edition, 1998.
19. Lawrence Snyder. *The ZPL Programmer's Guide*. The MIT Press, Cambridge, Massachusetts, 1999.
20. David Sundaram-Stukel and Mark K. Vernon. Predictive analysis of a wavefront application using LogGP. In *Seventh ACM SIGPLAN Symposium on Principles and Practice of Parallel Programming*, May 1999.
21. Michael Wolfe. *High Performance Compilers for Parallel Computing*. Addison-Wesley, Redwood City, CA, 1996.
22. ZPL Project. ZPL project homepage. *http:/www.cs.washington.edu/research/zpl*.

The Data Mover: A Machine-Independent Abstraction for Managing Customized Data Motion

Scott B. Baden[1] and Stephen J. Fink[2]

[1] University of California, San Diego,
Department of Computer Science and Engineering,
9500 Gilman Drive, La Jolla, CA 92093-0114 USA
baden@cs.ucsd.edu
http://www.cse.ucsd.edu/users/baden
[2] IBM Thomas J. Watson Research Center,
P.O. Box 704,Yorktown Heights, NY 10598 USA
sjfink@us.ibm.com

Abstract. This paper discusses the Data Mover, an abstraction for expressing machine-independent customized communication algorithms arising in block-structured computations. The Data Mover achieves performance that is competitive with hand-coding in MPI, but enables application-specific optimization to be expressed using intuitive geometric set operations that encapsulate low-level details.

1 Introduction

Scientific applications are characteristically receptive to performance optimizations that employ knowledge about the structure, data access patterns, and initial data of the underlying computation. An important class of such applications is block-structured, with an underlying representation comprising sets of multi-dimensional arrays. This class of applications includes finite difference (stencil) methods and blocked numerical linear algebra. On a multicomputer many block-structured applications carry out systematic patterns of communication that may be characterized as sets of atomic multidimensional regular section moves: panel broadcasts within subsets of processor geometries [9] total exchange [10] and halo updates [11]. More elaborate patterns include multi-phase communication [1], periodic boundary conditions, and irregularly blocked data, possibly organized into levels [7]. Two of these patterns appear in Fig. 1.

On a multicomputer, communication interfaces like MPI [12] support many of the above communication algorithms. For example, MPI provides a data type mechanism to express regular sections with strides, communication domains to configure processor geometries, and a variety of global communication primitives. But MPI has limitations. Support for irregular problems is lacking, and irregular data structures incur high software overheads in the form of bookkeeping. In addition, the quality of MPI implementations varies widely, hindering efforts to

L. Carter and J. Ferrante (Eds.): LCPC'99, LNCS 1863, pp. 333–349, 2000.

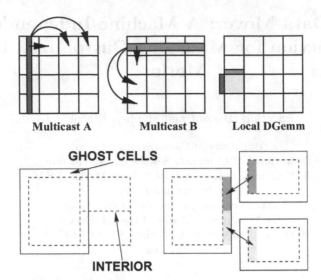

Fig. 1. Many scientific applications carry out systematic patterns of communication involving regular array sections. The example on the top is from blocked matrix multiply, which performs panel broadcasts within row and columns of processors configured in a 2-dimensional geometry. The example on the bottom employs halo updates in an irregular multiblock stencil-based computation.

write portable codes with good performance. This is true because development cost constraints may compel software providers to implement only a subset of MPI efficiently, or because the hardware may not support the required functionality [13]. For example, many of today's MPI installations do not understand MPI datatypes; the user achieves better performance by explicitly packing and unpacking data into contiguous buffers. Significantly, the MPI standard does not mandate the ability to overlap communication with computation–even if the hardware can support it–and many commercial implementations fail to do so.

The requirement that a communication library offer portability with performance poses difficult challenges. On multicomputers with SMP nodes, it is possible to realize overlap using mixed-mode programming involving threads and message passing [1,3,15]. However, the interactions of threads and message passing leads to complex program design, and many users lack the background or time to experiment with such advanced programming techniques. The problem becomes even more daunting when we consider that other communication interfaces besides MPI may be available, e.g. IBM's LAPI [17], the VIA standard [18], or even single sided communication. In the face of these myriad options, we cannot effectively deliver portability with performance if we rely on the native communication substrate alone. We argue that a higher level model is needed instead.

In this paper, we present a simple model of machine-independent communication called the Data Mover. The Data Mover provides an interface for expressing

customized collective communication patterns for block-structured scientific calculations. As a compiler or programmer target, the Data Mover model has the
following advantages over lower level communication models such as MPI.

1. *Abstraction:* the model supports a concise, high-level description of a communication pattern.
2. *Expressive power:* the model can express a larger set of collective patterns.
3. *Separation of concerns:* the programmer or compiler can separate the expression of correct programs from implementation policies affecting performance.

The Data Mover supports meta-data types and a geometric model for encoding data-dependence patterns arising in block structured computations. The
Data Mover model supports application-specific optimizations through direct
manipulation of communication meta-data (e.g. inspector-executor analysis [19]),
and object-oriented inheritance mechanisms.

We have implemented the Data Mover as part of the KeLP framework [1,4].
A carefully designed Mover implementation can take advantage of installation-
specific capabilities of the underlying communication substrate, or work around
limitations of the substrate or its implementation. For example, we have implemented a Mover for multicomputers with SMP nodes, which runs as a proxy.
This implementation of the Mover can mask communication on architectures
that do not support overlap via non-blocking message passing [1,2].

The rest of the paper is organized as follows. In the next section we describe
the Data Mover communication model. Section 3 presents empirical results, and
section 4 a discussion, including related work. Section 5 concludes the paper and
suggests future research directions.

2   The Data Mover Communication Model

The Data Mover has been implemented as part of the KeLP infrastructure.
While a complete discussion of KeLP lies beyond the scope of this paper, we
describe portions of the KeLP model relevant to the ensuing discussions. We
refer the reader to a recent paper [4] or to the KeLP web site.[1]

KeLP supports collections of block-structured data distributed across multiple address spaces. Some examples are shown in Fig. 1. At the core of KeLP are
two capabilities: user-level meta-data, and a collective model of communication.
To support this model, KeLP provides two kinds abstractions: meta-data and
instantiators, which are listed in Table 1. KeLP meta-data objects represent the
abstract structure of some facet of the calculation, such as data decomposition,
communication, or controlled execution under mask. Instantiation objects carry
out program behavior based on information contained in meta-data objects; they
allocate storage or move data.

---

[1] http://www.cse.ucsd.edu/groups/hpcl/scg/kelp.html.

Table 1. A brief synopsis of the KeLP instantiator and meta-data abstractions.

Meta-Data Abstractions		
Name	Definition	Interpretation
Point	$< \text{int } p_0, \text{int } p_1, \dots \text{int } p_{d-1} >$	A point in Z^d
Map	$f : \{0, \dots k-1\} \to Z$	An integer mapping
Region	$< \text{Point } P_l, \text{Point } P_h >$	A rectangular subset of Z^d
FloorPlan	$< \text{Array of Region, Map} >$	A set of Regions, each with an integer *owner*
MotionPlan	List of $< \text{Region } R_s, \text{int } i, \text{Region } R_d, \text{int } j >$	Block-structured communication pattern between two FloorPlans
Instantiators		
Name	Description	
Grid	A multidimensional array whose index space is a Region	
XArray	An array of Grids; structure represented by a FloorPlan	
Mover	An object that atomically performs the data motion pattern described by a MotionPlan	

2.1   Meta-data Abstractions

There are four meta-data abstractions: the *Region, FloorPlan, Map,* and *MotionPlan*. The Region represents a rectangular subset of Z^d ; i.e., a regular section with stride one. KeLP provides the *Region calculus,* a set of high-level geometric operations to help the programmer manipulate Regions. Typical operations include *grow* and *intersection,* which appear in Fig. 2. The Map class implements a function $Map : \{0, \dots, k-1\} \to Z$, for some integer k. That is, for $0 \le i \le k$, $Map(i)$ returns an integer. The Map forms the basis for node assignments in KeLP partitioning. The FloorPlan consists of a Map along with an array of Regions. It is a table of meta-data that represents a potentially irregular block data decomposition. An example of a FloorPlan is depicted in Fig. 3. The MotionPlan implements a dependence descriptor, e.g., a communication schedule. The programmer builds and manipulates MotionPlans using geometric Region calculus operations, a process to be described shortly.

2.2   Storage Model

KeLP defines two storage classes: *Grid* and *XArray.* A Grid is a node-level object that lives in the address space of a single node.[2] For example, the Fortran 90 array `real A(3:7,-5:-1)` corresponds to a KeLP two-dimensional Grid of reals, with region `A.region()` `==` `[3:7,-5:-1]` . An XArray is a distributed array of Grids whose structure is represented by a FloorPlan. All elements must have the

---

[2] This restriction is made in the interest of efficiency, since KeLP does not assume the existence of a global shared memory. A Grid that spanned multiple nodes would, in effect, define a shared-memory address space across all nodes.

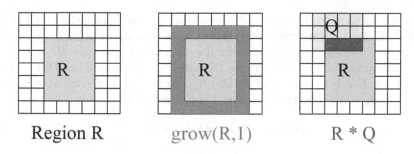

Region R   grow(R,1)   R * Q

Fig. 2. Examples of Region calculus operations grow and intersection *. Q and R are regions. Grow(R,1) expands the Region R by one unit in all directions, and is commonly used to grow a halo region for stencil computations. We can intersect one region with another to determine data dependencies requiring communication.

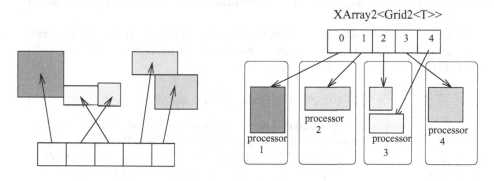

Fig. 3. Example of a FloorPlan (left) and XArray (right). The arrows on the right denote processor assignments, not pointers.

same number of spatial dimensions, but the index set of each Grid component (a KeLP Region) can be different. Grid components can have overlapping Regions, but they do not share memory. The application is responsible for managing any such sharing explicitly, and for interpreting the meaning of such overlap. An XArray is a collective object, and must be created from The number of XArray elements may be greater than the number of physical nodes or processors, and the mapping of XArray elements to processors may be many-to-one. This capability is useful in managing locality when load balancing irregular problems.

2.3   The Data Mover

The Data Mover supports a collective communication model that performs block transfers of regular array sections between two XArrays. There are three steps to expressing under the model: 1) build a MotionPlan describing the collective data dependence pattern; 2) construct a *Mover* object by associating the MotionPlan with the XArrays to be moved; and 3) carry out the communication to satisfy the dependencies by invoking Mover member functions. To understand the operation of the MotionPlan and Mover, we use the following notation. Let D and S be two XArrays, $D[i]$ be element i of D, and $S[j]$ element j of S ($D[i]$ and $S[j]$ are Grids). Let R_s and R_d be two Regions. Then, the notation

$$(D[i] \ \ on \ R_d) \Leftarrow (S[j] \ \ on \ R_s) \tag{1}$$

denotes a dependence between two rectangular sections of XArray elements $D[i]$ and $S[j]$. Informally, we may think of this dependence as being met by executing the following block copy operation: copy the values from $S[j]$, over all the indices in R_s, into $D[i]$, over the indices in R_d. We assume that R_d and R_s contain the same number of points, though their shapes may be different. The copy operation visits the points in R_d and R_s in a consistent systematic order, e.g., column-major order, and performs a coordinate shift when copying the data if $R_s \neq R_d$.

A MotionPlan encodes a set of dependencies expressed in the above form. The MotionPlan M is a list containing n entries, denoted $M[k]$ for $0 \leq k \leq n-1$. Each entry is a 4-tuple of the following form:

$$\langle RegionR_s, \ int \ i, \ RegionR_d, \ int \ j \rangle. \tag{2}$$

The components of the 4-tuple describe dependence (and hence communication) in a manner consistent with the previous discussion. We use the *copy()* member function to augment the MotionPlan with new entries. An example of MotionPlan construction appears in Fig. 4. We instantiate a Mover object μ by associating a MotionPlan M with two XArrays:

$$Mover \ \mu \ = \ Mover(M, \ S, \ D). \tag{3}$$

The result is an object μ with two operations, *start()* and *wait()*. Informally, data motion commences with a call to *start()*. This call is asynchronous and returns immediately. The *wait()* member function is used to detect when all communication has completed. In particular, when *wait()* returns, the Mover will have executed the following communication operation for each $M[k]$:

$$(D[M[k] @ i] \ \ on \ M[k] @ R_d) \Leftarrow (S[M[k] @ j] \ \ on \ M[k] @ R_s), \tag{4}$$

where we select the entries of the $M[k]$ 4-tuple with the @ qualifier: $M[k] @R_d$, $M[k] @ i$, and so on. Since the specific order of transfers is not defined, correctness must not depend on that ordering. We build a Mover for each data motion pattern to be executed. In cases where source and destination are the same XArray, we have an endogenous copy, which is useful in halo updates. An example of MotionPlan construction for an endogenous copy is shown in Fig. 4. A sample application kernel appears in Fig. 5.

```
FloorPlan2 U;
int NGHOST;
MotionPlan M;
foreach U(i) IN  U
   I = grow( U(i), -NGHOST )
   foreach U(j) IN U, j != i
      Region2 R = I * U(j)
      M.Copy( U(i)*R, U(j)* R)
   end for
end for
```

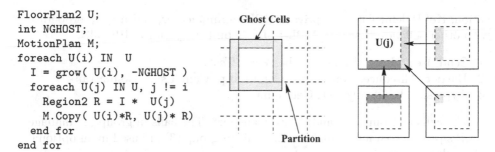

Fig. 4. MotionPlan construction for a halo update (left). The grow( ) operation trims off the ghost cells (right), which are NGHOST cells deep. A graphical depiction of MotionPlan construction appears on the right.

```
( 1)     FloorPlan3 F =  BuildFloorPlan( );
( 2)     XArray3<Grid3<double> > U(F);
( 3)     MotionPlan3 M = BuildMotionPlan( );
( 4)     Mover3<Grid3<double>, double> Mvr(U, U, M );
( 5)     while (not converged) {
( 6)         Mvr.start( );
( 7)          Mvr.wait( );
( 8)         for ( nodeIterator ni(F);  ni;  ++ni ) {
( 9)             int i = ni( );
(10)             _serialRelax( U(i) );
         }
     }
```

Fig. 5. A KeLP coding example: 3D iterative solver. MotionPlan construction is shown in Fig. 4.

2.4 Implementation

The KeLP infrastructure implements all the above abstractions as first-class C++ objects. In a typical KeLP program, the user constructs one or more FloorPlans, which are later used to build XArrays. FloorPlans and XArrays are replicated on all processors. However, the data in an XArray is not replicated, only the meta-data. A presence flag determines whether or not a process actually has a copy of the data for a particular Grid. Though this solution is not scalable–the replicated meta-data storage grows as the square of the number of nodes–the meta-data are compact and consume very little memory. For example, a 3-dimensional FloorPlan with 100,000 entries would consume only 2.4 Megabytes of memory at 4 bytes per integer. Consequently, we have not not encountered any difficulties in practice.

The Mover implementation deserves special attention, since it performs inspector/executor analysis of the data motion pattern, and issues message-passing calls and memory copies to effect data motion. The KeLP implementation of the Mover uses MPI point-to-point messages to carry out the Mover's communication. KeLP defines its own private MPI communicator, and may interoperate with other software that uses MPI. KeLP is built on just 16 MPI calls:

1. Send, Recv, Irecv, Probe, Iprobe, Wait, Test
2. Barrier, Allreduce, Comm_free, Comm_dup, Comm_size, Comm_rank
3. Type_size, Errhandler_set, Get_count

The calls in group (1) handle data transport. The calls in group (2) manage KeLP's private communicator, and the calls in group (3) are used in an optional safety-checking mode.

The Data Mover is implemented as a templated class. The Mover constructor does some preliminary communication analysis, determining which data transfers may be satisfied locally, and which must be transmitted via a message. The remaining analysis is triggered by calls to the start() and wait() member functions, and falls into two phases. Phase 1 performs the following operations on each node:

1. Allocate message buffers for incoming and outgoing messages.
2. Post for incoming non-blocking messages from other nodes.
3. Pack outgoing data into message buffers, where necessary.
4. Send non-blocking messages to other nodes.
5. Perform local memory-to-memory copies for XArray elements assigned to the same process.

The second phase performs the remaining work. While incoming messages are expected:

1. Poll until an incoming message arrives.
2. Unpack the detected message data into the target XArray element.
3. Free the message buffer.

Notably, the KeLP Mover allocates all message buffers dynamically–at the time the call to the start() member function is made. It frees the buffers when the call to wait() completes. This strategy was designed to avoid tying up temporary buffer storage at the cost of adding a small fixed overhead to each message passed. However, it does not affect peak communication bandwidth [1]. As shown in the next section, this added overhead is significant only when the problem size is small relative to the number of processors. As discussed in the next section, the MPI implementation is likely communication-bound in this regime as well.[3]

In exchange for maintaining global information about communication, a Mover implementation can effect various optimizations. For example, the KeLP Mover implementation avoids buffer-packing for contiguous data. That is, if source or destination data happens to lie contiguously in memory, then the Mover will send or receive the data directly from the original storage locations. Using object-oriented inheritance mechanisms it is also possible to derive specialized Movers

---

[3] Alternatively, one could implement a Mover constructor to preallocate the message buffers, and avoid the recurring overhead.

that perform message aggregation, combining multiple messages with a common destination; message packetization, to handle flow control; or update forms of data transport, that perform an operation like addition while moving the data. These specialized Movers meet specific needs of an application or an architecture, and can work around defects in the underlying communication substrate [1,4].

As mentioned previously, the KeLP implementation supports asynchronous execution of the Mover activity by providing the start() and wait() member functions, which asynchronously initiate and rendezvous collective communication. Different invocations of the start() member function are guaranteed not to interfere so long as they do not incur any race conditions. For example, the following code executes correctly so long as the Movers do not access common data. (Even a single synchronous Mover invocation can incur race conditions if some MotionPlan entries overlap.):

```
Mover mvr1, mvr2;
mvr1.start();
mvr2.start();
mvr1.wait();
mvr2.wait();
```

The implementation realizes communication overlap with either MPI asynchronous messages or by dedicating a proxy thread exclusively to communication. The proxy thread approach is particularly effective on multicomputers with SMP nodes, since the implementation can temporarily assign a physical processor to the Mover, without directly impacting other processors. A distinguished user thread on each node communicates with the proxy using shared queues; see Fink's Ph.D. dissertation [1] for additional details.

3   Results

In this section we provide empirical evidence demonstrating that the convenience of the Data Mover's higher-level abstraction does not come at the expense of performance. We measure two different implementations of the Mover running on different distributed memory architectures. We find that the performance of applications written using the Mover are competitive with equivalent versions written with MPI. We look at four applications: Redblack3D, Red Black Gauss-Seidel relaxation in three dimensions on a 7-point stencil; two NAS benchmarks [21] NAS-MG, which solves the 3D Poisson equation using multigrid V cycles, and NAS-FT, which solves the time-dependent diffusion equation in three dimensions using an FFT; and SUMMA [22] which performs blocked matrix multiply.

The applications we have chosen represent a diverse range of communication patterns encountered in block-structured applications. Redblack3D performs halo updates; NAS-MG performs halo updates with periodic boundary conditions, and it also transfers data between multigrid levels. NAS-FT performs a massive 3D array transpose (total exchange), while SUMMA broadcasts horizontal and vertical slices of data within rows and columns of a two-dimensional processor geometry.

The KeLP applications were written in a mix of C++ and Fortran 77. KeLP calls were made from C++, and all numerical computation was carried out in Fortran. The hand-coded versions were implemented somewhat differently from their KeLP equivalents, except for RedBlack3D. Redblack3D had a similar organization to the KeLP version, allocating storage in C++, and performing numerical computation in Fortran. It also allocated all message buffers dynamically. The NAS benchmarks, v2.1, were written in Fortran only. All message buffers and other data structures were allocated statically, as the problem size and number of processors had to be fixed at compile time (By contrast, the KeLP versions allow the problem size and number of processors to be run time inputs). SUMMA [22] was written entirely in C, but invoked a vendor supplied matrix multiply routine (The IBM `essl` routine `dgemm`). All storage was statically allocated.

We report results on two systems: an IBM SP2, located at the San Diego Supercomputer Center, and IBM ASCI Blue Pacific CTR, located at Lawrence Livermore National Laboratory. The SP2 has 160 MHz Power-2 SC thin nodes with 256 Megabytes of memory per node, running AIX 4.2. We compiled C++ using `mpCC`, with compiler options `-O -Q -qmaxmem=-1`, and compiled Fortran 77 using `mpxlf`, and compiler options `-O3 -qstrict -u -qarch=auto -qtune= auto`. The IBM ASCI Blue Pacific CTR employs clustered technology. Each node is a 4-way Symmetric Multiprocessor (SMP) based on 332 MHz Power PC 604e processors, sharing 1.5 Gigabytes of memory and running AIX 4.3.1. We compiled C++ with `mpCC_r`, using the compiler options `-O3 -qstrict -Q -qmaxmem=-1 -qarch=auto -qtune=auto`, and compiled Fortran 77 using `mpxlf_r` with compiler options `-O3 -qstrict -u -qarch=auto -qtune= auto`. We ran with KeLP version 1.2.95 on the SP2,[4] and used a prototype of KeLP, AKA KeLP2.0 [1,2], on the CTR system.

3.1 IBM SP2

On the SDSC SP2 we ran with the following problem sizes. We ran Redblack3D on a fixed size 360^3 mesh, NAS-MG on a 256^3 mesh, NAS-FT on a $256 \times 256 \times 128$ mesh. The SUMMA computations multiplied square matrices. We linearly increased the amount of work with the number of processors, such that number of floating point operations per node was fixed at approximately 3.4×10^8, i.e. we increase the linear dimension of the matrix by $2^{1/3}$ when we double the number of processors.

We observe that the performance of the applications running with the KeLP Mover is competitive with the equivalent MPI encodings. These results are shown in Fig. 6, and corroborate previous findings on the Cray T3E [1]. The Data Mover's higher level of abstraction does not substantially hinder performance.

---

[4] http://www.cse.ucsd.edu/groups/hpcl/kelp.

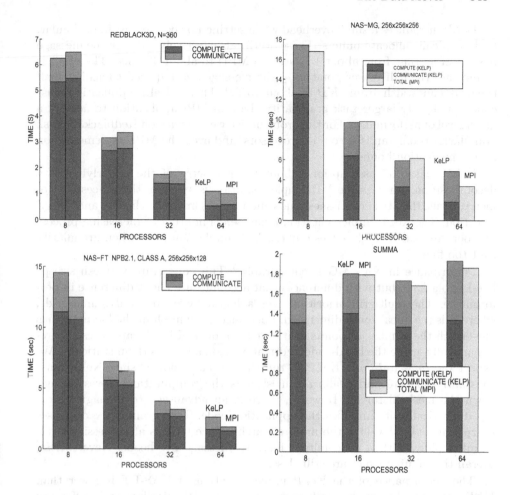

Fig. 6. Comparative performance of equivalent KeLP and MPI codes running on the IBM SP2. *Communicate* gives the time spent waiting on communication.
The problem sizes are fixed, except for SUMMA, where the work increases with the number of processors: N=1400, 1800, 2200, and 2800 on 8, 16, 32, and 64 processors, respectively.

We note that KeLP enjoys a slight performance advantage with RedBlack3D, which diminishes as the number of processors increases. At 64 processors, the MPI version runs slightly faster, taking less time to communicate than the KeLP version. (Local computation times are always smaller in KeLP, but the differences aren't significant.) Since both the hand-coded and KeLP version of RedBlack3D allocate message buffers dynamically, the difference in performance is attributed to miscellaneous overheads in the KeLP run time library, and to the differing dynamic communication patterns generated by the respective codes.

KeLP introduces a small overhead when setting up the Movers, in particular, to dynamically allocate buffers. These overheads effectively increase the message passing start time from about 13 $\mu sec.$ (in MPI) to about 40 $\mu sec.$ The effect is to increase the half power point $n_{1/2}$-the message size required to achieve half the peak bandwidth–from $4KB$ to about $16KB$. Thus, a KeLP application must choose a slightly larger task granularity than an MPI application to achieve a given level of performance. For the problem size we run with on Redblack3D, task granularity is only an issue on 64 processors, and even the MPI implementation is communication bound.

KeLP makes no assumptions about the geometry of the underlying data decomposition, whereas the MPI implementation is aware of the processor geometry. Thus, the MPI code issues sends and receives in the X, then Y, and then Z direction. The KeLP implementation issues sends in order of increasing process number, and surprisingly edges out the MPI implementation when granularity isn't too fine.

Performance in NAS MG is comparable.[5] This code employs mesh sweeps like Redblack3D, but with differences that account for a slight difference in performance. The multigrid algorithm uses a hierarchy of log N dynamic grids, where N is the linear mesh dimension. Each successive mesh in the hierarchy has one-eighth the number of points of its predecessor. KeLP allocates these arrays dynamically, while the hand-coded Fortran version allocates them statically. We expect the *computation* in KeLP to run slightly more slowly, since KeLP must constantly allocate and deallocate meshes as the computation moves up and down the mesh hierarchy. However, there is an advantage to managing storage dynamically: it simplifies the application code. Task granularity decreases sharply at higher levels of the mesh hierarchy, since meshes at successive levels shrink rapidly, with a concomitant increase Message overheads. Nevertheless, overall the running times are still close.

The performance of the KeLP implementation of NAS-FT is lower than MPI's, though the two are still reasonably close. We attribute the difference to a naive implementation of a massive 3D transpose. The MPI version uses All_to_all, which is presumably optimized for the architecture. In contrast, the KeLP implementation results in a message being sent for each pair of communicating tasks. Perhaps we could improve the KeLP transpose using a more efficient algorithm when running on larger number of processors, and we plan to investigate this. Another possibility is to enable the KeLP Mover to recognize the transpose pattern and invoke an appropriate primitive in the underlying communication substrate, where doing so led to reduced communication times. The user's programming would not need to change.

Performance of the KeLP and MPI implementations of SUMMA are comparable. We use a non-scaling, linear time broadcast algorithm, and the effect can be seen as we increase the number of processors. Again, our naive implementation is could probably be improved. However, the effect is relatively benign,

---

[5] Unfortunately, we were unable to break out the computation time in the hand-coded NAS version in time for publication.

since broadcasts involve rows or columns of processors rather than all the processors, so communication time varies only as the square root of the number of processors.

3.2 ASCI Blue Pacific

The Mover interface simplifies the implementation of more complex algorithms. For example, in order to improve utilization of SMP nodes, we have restructured each of the applications described here to overlap communication with computation A full discussion of these restructured algorithms [1] is beyond the scope of this paper, but we present results from Redblack3D on the ASCI Blue-Pacific CTR. We ran with cubical domains, scaling the problem with the number of nodes to maintain a ratio of approximately 2 million unknowns per node. We ran with the KeLP2.0 prototype [3,1,2], which uses a proxy implemented as an extra thread to handle communication. Results reveal that the overlapped KeLP2 Mover is able to improve performance significantly. The use of communication overlap improves performance by as much as 19% on 64 nodes (256 processors). Results are shown in Fig. 7. These results corroborate similar findings by Fink running on a cluster of Digital AlphaServer 2100 SMPs and on a cluster of UltraSPARC SMPs [1,2].[6]

4 Discussion

Our experiences with the KeLP Data Mover have been positive, and indicate this higher-level abstraction is able to match the performance of hand-coded MPI, and in some cases exceed it. The Mover's versatility in supporting communication overlap on an SMP-based illustrates the importance of separating correctness concerns from policy decisions that affect performance.

The Data Mover resembles an MPI persistent communication object. However, KeLP provides inspector-executor analysis, which is particularly useful in irregular problems, and it also provides first-class support for multidimensional arrays, via user-defined metadata and a geometric region calculus. KeLP avoids MPI's awkward data type mechanism to handle strides of non-contiguous faces that would entail registering a separate data type for each stride appearing in the data. More generally, the KeLP meta-data abstractions, e.g. the Region calculus, provide a more intuitive and concise notation for expressing and managing customized communication domains.

Communication libraries like KeLP have been used in compilers or exist as middleware for compiler or application library builders. ADLIB provides high-level, array-based collective communication [23]. This C++ class library, built on top of MPI, provides runtime support for HPF and more generally may be used directly for distributed data parallel programming. ADLIB supports irregular

---

[6] The overlapped Mover was also observed to improve the performance of the other three benchmarks discussed earlier in this section.

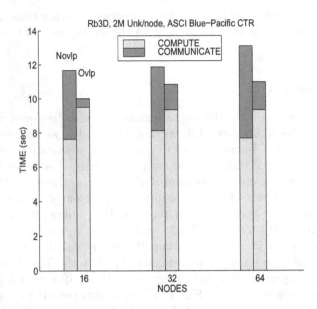

Fig. 7. Communication overlap on the ASCI Blue Pacific CTR running a 3D iterative stencil method. In the overlapped (Ovlp) implementation, KeLP runs the Mover as a proxy thread on a dedicated processor. Compared with the non-overlapped strategy (Novlp), running times improved by 8.7%, 14%, and 19%, 16, 32, and 64 nodes, respectively. The performance of the largest run was about 3.6 Gigaflops. The number of nodes is given on the x-axis, total times (sec.) on the y-axis. *Communicate* gives the time spent waiting on communication, *Compute* the time spent in local computation. Computation time increases under overlap, since the proxy consumes processor cycles that could otherwise be devoted to computation.

communication via general gather/scatter. ARMCI is a library that provides a remote memory copying of non-contiguous data sets, with optimizations for multidimensional array slices [28]. BSP [29] is a communication library which like KeLP, employs global information to improve communication performance, though it is not specialized to provide a geometric Region Calculus.

Chamberlain, Choi, and Snyder describe the IRONMAN abstraction, which separates the expression of data transfer from the underlying implementation. In some cases this library was able to improve performance over MPI and PVM by making machine-specific optimizations [24]. Bala et al. Describe CCL, a portable and tunable Collective Communication Library [25] Like KeLP, CCL is designed to run on top of an existing point-to-point message-passing interface. CCL supports a variety of collective operations, similar in spirit to what is now provided by MPI. The issue of multi-dimensional array support is not addressed.

5   Conclusions

We have demonstrated that the Data Mover is an effective abstraction for expressing a variety of communication patterns in block-structured applications. The Data Mover facilitates inspector-executor analysis, which is useful in irregular applications. It is also useful on systems providing true shared memory or single-sided communication; expensive global barrier synchronization may be replaced by a weaker and less costly form that enables processors to synchronize with point-to-point signals. In some cases it may be desirable to manage data motion explicitly [26], and the KeLP Mover implementation can take advantage of shared memory if doing so improves performance.

KeLP currently runs on a variety of architectures including the IBM SP2, IBM ASCI Blue-Pacific, SGI-Cray Origin 2000, Cray T3E, and clusters of workstations running under Solaris, Linux, and Digital Unix. An interesting possibility is to employ a Grid aware message passing layer like MPICH-G [20], that would enable KeLP applications in turn to be Grid aware.

We are currently investigating generalizations of KeLP that permit users to supply their own implementation of storage containers, or to replace message passing calls by alternative means of data transport including: single-sided communication, multi-method communication I/O, and resource brokers. This version of KeLP, also known as "Abstract KeLP" is currently under investigation.

Acknowledgments. The authors wish to thank Jonathan May and Bronis de Supinski, with the Center for Applied Scientific Computing at Lawrence Livermore National Laboratory, for the many illuminating discussions about the ASCI Blue-Pacific machine, and to Paul Kelly and Jarmo Rantakokko for advice on how to improve this paper.

This research was performed while the second author was with the Computer Science Department at UCSD, and supported by the DOE Computational Science Graduate Fellowship Program. Scott B. Baden was supported by NSF contract ASC- 9520372 and NSF contract ACI-9619020, National Partnership for Advanced Computational Infrastructure. Work on the ASCI Blue-Pacific CTR machine was performed under the auspices of the US Dept of Energy by Lawrence Livermore National Laboratory Under Contract W07405-Eng-48. Computer Time on the IBM SP2 located at the San Diego Supercomputer Center was provided by SDSC and by a Jacobs School of Engineering Block grant. Thanks go to Richard Frost for assistance in building the KeLP distribution, and in providing KeLP tutorials to the user community.

References

1. Fink, S. J.: Hierarchical Programming for Block–Structured Scientific Calculations. Doctor dissertation, Dept. of Computer Science and Engineering, University of California, San Diego (1998)

2. Baden, S.B. and Fink, S. J.: Communication Overlap in Multi-tier Parallel Algorithms. In Proc. SC '98,
   http://www.supercomp.org/sc98/TechPapers/sc98_FullAbstracts/Baden708/INDEX.HTM. IEEE Computer Society Press (1998)
3. Fink, S. J. and Baden, S.B.: Runtime Support for Multi-tier Programming of Block-Structured Applications on SMP Clusters. In: Ishikawa, Y., Oldehoeft, R, Reynders, J.V.W., and Tholburn, M. (eds.): Scientific Computing in Object-Oriented Parallel Environments. Lecture Notes in Computer Science, Vol. 1343. Springer-Verlag, Berlin Heidelberg New York (1997) 1–8
4. Baden, S.B. and Fink, S. J., and Kohn, S. R.: Efficient Run-Time Support for Irregular Block-Structured Applications. *J. Parallel Distrib. Comput.* 50(1998) 61–82
5. Howe, J., Baden, S. B., Grimmett, T., and Nomura, K.: Modernization of Legacy Application Software. In Kågström, B., Dongarra, J, Elmroth, E., and Wasniewski, J. (eds.): Applied Parallel Computing: Large Scale Scientific and Industrial Problems: 4th International Workshop. Lecture Notes in Computer Science, Vol. 1541. Springer-Verlag, Berlin, Heidelberg New York (1997) 255–262
6. Kohn, S. R. and Baden, S.B.: A Parallel Software Infrastructure for Structured Adaptive Mesh Methods. In Proc. Supercomputing '95,
   http://www.sc98.org/sc95/proceedings/507_SKOH/SC95.HTM. IEEE Computer Society Press (1995)
7. Kohn, S.R., Weare, J. H., Ong, M. E. G., and Baden, S. B.: Software Abstractions and Computational Issues in Parallel Structured Adaptive Mesh Methods for Electronic Structure Calculations. In: Baden, S. B., Chrisochoides, N., Norman, M., and Gannon, D. (eds.): Workshop on Structured Adaptive Mesh Refinement Grid Methods. Lecture Notes in Mathematics, in press. Springer-Verlag, Berlin, Heidelberg New York (1999)
8. Saltz, J., Sussman, A., Graham, S., Demmel, J., Baden, S., and Dongarra, J.: Programming Tools and Environments. Communications of the ACM 41 (1998) 64–73
9. J. Choi, A. Cleary , J. Demmel, I. Dhillon , J. Dongarra, S. Hammarling, G. Henry, S. Ostrouchov , A. Petitet, K. Stanley , D. Walker, and R. C. Whaley: ScaLAPACK: A Portable Linear Algebra Library for Distributed Memory Computers - Design Issues and Performance. In Proc. Supercomputing '96, http://www.sc98.org/sc96/proceedings/SC96PROC/DONGARRA/INDEX.HTM. IEEE Computer Society Press (1996)
10. Kumar, V., Grama, A., Gupta, A., and Karypis, G: Introduction to Parallel Computing: Design and Analysis of Algorithms. Benjamin Cummings (1993)
11. Foster, I. Designing and Building Parallel Programs. Addison-Wesley (1995)
12. MPI Forum: The Message Passing Interface (MPI) Standard. http://www-unix.mcs.anl.gov/mpi/index.html (1995)
13. Sohn, A. and Biswas, R.: Communication Studies of DMP and SMP Machines. Technical Report, NAS, NASA Ames Research Center (1997)
14. MPI Forum: MPI-2: Extensions to the Message-Passing Interface. http://www-unix.mcs.anl.gov/mpi/index.html (1997)
15. Gropp, W.W. and Lusk, E. L.: A Taxonomy of Programming Models for Symmetric Multiprocessors and SMP Clusters. In Giloi, W. K. and Jahnichen, S., and Shriver, B. D. (eds.): Programming Models for Massively Parallel Computers. IEEE Computer Society Press (1995) 2–7

16. Lumetta, S.S, Mainwaring, A.M. and Culler, D. E. Multi-Protocol Active Messages on a Cluster of SMPs. In Proc. SC '97, http://www.sc98.org/sc97/proceedings/TECH/LUMETTA/INDEX.HTM. IEEE Computer Society Press (1997)

17. IBM Corp: Understanding and Using the Communication Low-Level Application Programming Interface (LAPI). In IBM Parallel System Support Programs for AIX Administration Guide, GC23-3897-04, http://ppdbooks.pok.ibm.com:80/cgi-bin/bookmgr/bookmgr.cmd/BOOKS/ sspad230/9.1 (1997)

18. P. Buonadonna, A. Geweke, and D. Culler. An Implementation and Analysis of the Virtual Interface Architecture. In Proc. SC '98, http://www.supercomp.org/sc98/TechPapers/sc98_FullAbstracts/   Buonadonna893/INDEX.HTM. IEEE Computer Society Press (1998)

19. Agrawal, A., Sussman, A, and Saltz, J.: An Integrated Runtime and Compile-Time Approach for Parallelizing Structured and Block Structured Applications. IEEE Transactions on Parallel and Distributed Systems 6 (1995) 747–754

20. Foster, I., and Karonis, N.T.: A Grid-Enabled MPI: Message Passing in Heterogeneous Distributed Computing Systems. In Proc. SC '98, http://www.supercomp.org/sc98/TechPapers/sc98_FullAbstracts/Foster1125 /index.htm. IEEE Computer Society Press (1998)

21. NAS, NASA Ames Research Center: The NAS Parallel Benchmarks. http://www.nas.nasa.gov/Software/NPB/ (1997).

22. Geign, R. v. d., and Watts, J.: SUMMA: Scalable Universal Matrix Multiplication Algorithm. Concurrency: Practice and Experience, 9(1997) 255–74

23. Carpenter, B., Zhang, G., and Wen, Y.: NPAC PCRC Runtime Kernel (Adlib) Definition. Northeast Parallel Architectures Center, Syracuse Univ., http://www.npac.syr.edu/users/dbc/Adlib (1998)

24. Chamberlain, B. L. Choi, S.-E., and Snyder, L.: A Compiler Abstraction for Machine Independent Parallel Communication Generation. In Li, Z., et al. (eds): Proc. Workshop on Languages and Compilers for Parallel Computation (1997) 261–276

25. Bala, V., et al.: CCL: A Portable and Tunable Collective Communication Library for Scalable Parllel Computers. IEEE. Trans. On Parallel and Distributed Sys., 6(1995) 154–164

26. Mukherjee, S. S., et al.: Efficient Support for Irregular Applications on Distributed Memory Machines. In 5th SIGPLAN Symposium on Principles and Practice of Parallel Programming (PPoPP) (1995) 68-79

27. Culler, D., Dusseau, A, Goldstein, S., Krishnamurthy, A., Lumetta, S, von Eicken, T., and Yelick, K. Parallel Programming in Split-C. In Conf. Proc. Supercomputing '93. IEEE Computer Society Press (1993)

28. Nieplocha, J. and Carpenter, B.: ARMCI: A Portable Remote Memory Copy Library for Distributed Array Libraries and Compiler Run-time Systems. In Proc. 3rd Workshop on Runtime Systems for Parallel Programming (RTSPP) of International Parallel Processing Symposium IPPS/SPDP '99, San Juan, Puerto Rico (1999)

29. Donaldson, S., Hill, J., and Skillicorn, D.: BSP Clusters: High-Performance, Reliable and Very Low Cost. Oxford University Computing Laboratory Technical Report PRG-5-98, http://www.cs.queensu.ca/home/skill/papers.html (1998).

Optimization of Memory Usage Requirement for a Class of Loops Implementing Multi-dimensional Integrals [*]

Chi-Chung Lam[1], Daniel Cociorva[2], Gerald Baumgartner[1], and P. Sadayappan[1]

[1] Department of Computer and Information Science
The Ohio State University, Columbus, OH 43210
{clam,gb,saday}@cis.ohio-state.edu
[2] Department of Physics
The Ohio State University, Columbus, OH 43210
cociorva@pacific.mps.ohio-state.edu

Abstract. Multi-dimensional integrals of products of several arrays arise in certain scientific computations. In the context of these integral calculations, this paper addresses a memory usage minimization problem. Based on a framework that models the relationship between loop fusion and memory usage, we propose an algorithm for finding a loop fusion configuration that minimizes memory usage. A practical example shows the performance improvement obtained by our algorithm on an electronic structure computation.

1 Introduction

This paper addresses the optimization of a class of loop computations that implement multi-dimensional integrals of the product of several arrays. Such integral calculations arise, for example, in the computation of electronic properties of semiconductors and metals [1,7,15]. The objective is to minimize the execution time of such computations on a parallel computer while staying within the available memory. In addition to the performance optimization issues pertaining to inter-processor communication and data locality enhancement, there is an opportunity to apply algebraic transformations using the properties of commutativity, associativity and distributivity to reduce the total number of arithmetic operations. Given a specification of the required computation as a multi-dimensional sum of the product of input arrays, we first determine an equivalent sequence of multiplication and summation formulae that computes the result using a minimum number of arithmetic operations. Each formula computes and stores some intermediate results in an intermediate array. By computing the intermediate results once and reusing them multiple times, the number of arithmetic operations can be reduced. In previous work, this operation minimization problem was proved to be NP-complete and an efficient pruning search strategy was proposed [10].

The simplest way to implement an optimal sequence of multiplication and summation formulae is to compute the formulae one by one, each coded as a set of perfectly nested loops, and to store the intermediate results produced by each formula in an intermediate array. However, in practice, the input and intermediate arrays could be so large that

---

[*] Supported in part by the National Science Foundation under grant DMR-9520319.

L. Carter and J. Ferrante (Eds.): LCPC'99, LNCS 1863, pp. 350–364, 2000.

they cannot fit into the available memory. Hence, there is a need to fuse the loops as a means of reducing memory usage. By fusing loops between the producer loop and the consumer loop of an intermediate array, intermediate results are formed and used in a pipelined fashion and they reuse the same reduced array space. The problem of finding a loop fusion configuration that minimizes memory usage without increasing the operation count is not trivial. In this paper, we develop an optimization framework that appropriately models the relation between loop fusion and memory usage. We present an algorithm that finds an optimal loop fusion configuration that minimizes memory usage.

Reduction of arithmetic operations has been traditionally done by compilers using the technique of common subexpression elimination [4]. Chatterjee et al. consider the optimal alignment of arrays in evaluating array expression on massively parallel machines [2,3]. Much work has been done on improving locality and parallelism by loop fusion [8,14,16]. However, this paper considers a different use of loop fusion, which is to reduce array sizes and memory usage of automatically synthesized code containing nested loop structures. Traditional compiler research does not address this use of loop fusion because this problem does not arise with manually-produced programs. The contraction of arrays into scalars through loop fusion is studied in [6] but is motivated by data locality enhancement and not memory reduction. Loop fusion in the context of delayed evaluation of array expressions in APL programs is discussed in [5] but is also not aimed at minimizing array sizes. We are unaware of any work on fusion of multi-dimensional loop nests into imperfectly-nested loops as a means to reduce memory usage.

The rest of this paper is organized as follows. Section 2 describes the operation minimization problem. Section 3 studies the use of loop fusion to reduce array sizes and presents algorithms for finding an optimal loop fusion configuration that minimizes memory usage under the static memory allocation model. Due to space limitations, the extensions of the framework to the dynamic memory allocation model and to parallel machines are omitted in this paper but can be found in [13]. Section 4 provides conclusions.

2 Operation Minimization

In the class of computations considered, the final result to be computed can be expressed as multi-dimensional integrals of the product of many input arrays. Due to commutativity, associativity and distributivity, there are many different ways to obtain the same final result and they could differ widely in the number of floating point operations required. The problem of finding an equivalent form that computes the result with the least number of operations is not trivial and so a software tool for doing this is desirable.

Consider, for example, the multi-dimensional integral shown in Figure 1(a). If implemented directly as expressed (i.e. as a single set of perfectly-nested loops), the computation would require $2 \times N_i \times N_j \times N_k \times N_l$ arithmetic operations to compute. However, assuming associative reordering of the operations and use of the distributive law of multiplication over addition is satisfactory for the floating-point computations, the above computation can be rewritten in various ways. One equivalent form that only requires $2 \times N_j \times N_k \times N_l + 2 \times N_j \times N_k + N_i \times N_j$ operations is given in Figure 1(b).

$$W[k] = \sum_{(i,j,l)} A[i,j] \times B[j,k,l] \times C[k,l]$$

(a) A multi-dimensional integral

$$
\begin{aligned}
f_1[j] &= \sum_i A[i,j] \\
f_2[j,k,l] &= B[j,k,l] \times C[k,l] \\
f_3[j,k] &= \sum_l f_2[j,k,l] \\
f_4[j,k] &= f_1[j] \times f_3[j,k] \\
W[k] = f_5[k] &= \sum_j f_4[j,k]
\end{aligned}
$$

(b) A formula sequence for computing (a)

$f_5 \sum_j$

$f_4 \times$

$f_1 \sum_i$ $f_3 \sum_k$

$A[i,j]$ $f_2 \times$

$B[j,k,l]$ $C[k,l]$

(c) An expression tree representation of (b)

Fig. 1. An example multi-dimensional integral and two representations of a computation.

It expresses the sequence of steps in computing the multi-dimensional integral as a sequence of formulae. Each formula computes some intermediate result and the last formula gives the final result. A formula is either a product of two input/intermediate arrays or a integral/summation over one index, of an input/intermediate array. A sequence of formulae can also be represented as an expression tree. For instance, Figure 1(c) shows the expression tree corresponding to the example formula sequence.

The problem of finding a formula sequence that minimizes the number of operations has been proved to be NP-complete [10]. A pruning search algorithm for finding such a formula sequence is given below.

1. Form a list of the product terms of the multi-dimensional integral. Let X_a denote the a-th product term and $X_a.dimens$ the set of index variables in $X_a[...]$. Set r and c to zero. Set d to the number of product terms.
2. While there exists an summation index (say i) that appears in exactly one term (say $X_a[...]$) in the list and $a > c$, increment r and d and create a formula $f_r[...] = \sum_i X_a[...]$ where $f_r.dimens = X_a.dimens - \{i\}$. Remove $X_a[...]$ from the list. Append to the list $X_d[...] = f_r[...]$. Set c to a.
3. Increment r and d and form a formula $f_r[...] = X_a[...] \times X_b[...]$ where $X_a[...]$ and $X_b[...]$ are two terms in the list such that $a < b$ and $b > c$, and give priority to the terms that have exactly the same set of indices. The indices for f_r are $f_r.dimens = X_a.dimens \cup X_b.dimens$. Remove $X_a[...]$ and $X_b[...]$ from the list. Append to the list $X_d[...] = f_r[...]$. Set c to b. Go to step 2.
4. When steps 2 and 3 cannot be performed any more, a valid formula sequence is obtained. To obtain all valid sequences, exhaust all alternatives in step 3 using depth-first search.

3   Memory Usage Minimization

In implementing the computation represented by an operation-count-optimal formula sequence (or expression tree), there is a need to perform loop fusion to reduce the sizes of the arrays. Without fusing the loops, the arrays would be too large to fit into the available memory. There are many different ways to fuse the loops and they could result in different memory usage. This section addresses the problem of finding a loop fusion configuration for a given formula sequence that uses the least amount of memory. Section 3.1 introduces the memory usage minimization problem. Section 3.2 describes some preliminary concepts that we use to formulate our solutions to the problem. Sections 3.3 presents an algorithm for finding a memory-optimal loop fusion configuration under static memory allocation model. Section 3.4 illustrates how the application of the algorithm on an example physics computation improves its performance.

3.1 Problem Description

Consider again the expression tree shown in Figure 1(c). A naive way to implement the computation is to have a set of perfectly-nested loops for each node in the tree, as shown in Figure 2(a). The brackets indicate the scopes of the loops. Figure 2(b) shows how the sizes of the arrays may be reduced by the use of loop fusions. It shows the resulting loop structure after fusing all the loops between A and f_1, all the loops among B, C, f_2, and f_3, and all the loops between f_4 and f_5. Here, A, B, C, f_2, and f_4 are reduced to scalars. After fusing all the loops between a node and its parent, all dimensions of the child array are no longer needed and can be eliminated. The elements in the reduced arrays are now reused to hold different values at different iterations of the fused loops. Each of those values was held by a different array element before the loops were fused (as in Figure 2(a)). Note that some loop nests (such as those for B and C) are reordered and some loops within loop nests (such as the j-, k-, and l-loops for B, f_2, and f_3) are permuted in order to facilitate loop fusions.

For now, we assume the leaf node arrays (i.e., input arrays) can be generated one element at a time (by the gen$v$ function for array v) so that loop fusions with their parents are allowed. This assumption holds for arrays in which the value of each element is a function of the array subscripts, as in many arrays in the physics computations that we work on. As will be clear later on, the case where an input array has to be read in or produced in slices or in its entirety can be handled by disabling the fusion of some or all the loops between the leaf node and its parent.

Figure 2(c) shows another possible loop fusion configuration obtained by fusing all the j-loops and then all the k-loops and l-loops inside them. The sizes of all arrays except C and f_5 are smaller. By fusing the j-, k-, and l-loops between those nodes, the j-, k-, and l-dimensions of the corresponding arrays can be eliminated. Hence, B, f_1, f_2, f_3, and f_4 are reduced to scalars while A becomes a one-dimensional array.

In general, fusing a t-loop between a node v and its parent eliminates the t-dimension of the array v and reduces the array size by a factor of N_t. In other words, the size of an array after loop fusions equals the product of the ranges of the loops that are not fused with its parent. We only consider fusions of loops among nodes that are all transitively related by (i.e., form a transitive closure over) parent-child relations. Fusing loops between unrelated nodes (such as fusing siblings without fusing their parent) has no effect on array sizes. We also restrict our attention for now to loop fusion configurations that do not increase the operation count.

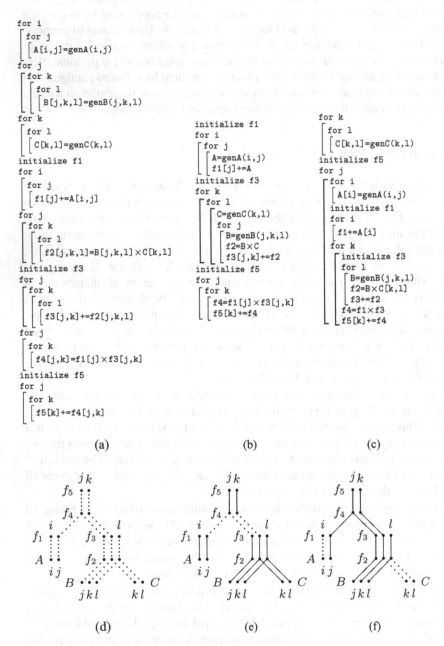

```
for i
  for j
    A[i,j]=genA(i,j)
for j
  for k
    for l
      B[j,k,l]=genB(j,k,l)
for k
  for l
    C[k,l]=genC(k,l)
initialize f1
for i
  for j
    f1[j]+=A[i,j]
for j
  for k
    for l
      f2[j,k,l]=B[j,k,l]×C[k,l]
initialize f3
for j
  for k
    for l
      f3[j,k]+=f2[j,k,l]
for j
  for k
    f4[j,k]=f1[j]×f3[j,k]
initialize f5
for j
  for k
    f5[k]+=f4[j,k]
```

(a)

```
initialize f1
for i
  for j
    A=genA(i,j)
    f1[j]+=A
initialize f3
for k
  for l
    C=genC(k,l)
    for j
      B=genB(j,k,l)
      f2=B×C
      f3[j,k]+=f2
initialize f5
for j
  for k
    f4=f1[j]×f3[j,k]
    f5[k]+=f4
```

(b)

```
for k
  for l
    C[k,l]=genC(k,l)
initialize f5
for j
  for i
    A[i]=genA(i,j)
  initialize f1
  for i
    f1+=A[i]
  for k
    initialize f3
    for l
      B=genB(j,k,l)
      f2=B×C[k,l]
      f3+=f2
    f4=f1×f3
    f5[k]+=f4
```

(c)

(d)   (e)   (f)

Fig. 2. Three loop fusion configurations for the expression tree in Figure 1.

In the class of loops considered in this paper, the only dependence relations are those between children and parents, and array subscripts are simply loop index variables[1]. So, loop permutations, loop nests reordering, and loop fusions are always legal as long as child nodes are evaluated before their parents. This freedom allows the loops to be permuted, reordered, and fused in a large number of ways that differ in memory usage. Finding a loop fusion configuration that uses the least memory is not trivial. We believe this problem is NP-complete but have not found a proof yet.

Fusion graphs. Let T be an expression tree. For any given node $v \in T$, let $subtree(v)$ be the set of nodes in the subtree rooted at v, $v.parent$ be the parent of v, and $v.indices$ be the set of loop indices for v (including the summation index $v.sumindex$ if v is a summation node). A loop fusion configuration can be represented by a graph called a *fusion graph*, which is constructed from T as follows.

1. Replace each node v in T by a set of vertices, one for each index $i \in v.indices$.
2. Remove all tree edges in T for clarity.
3. For each loop fused (say, of index i) between a node and its parent, connect the i-vertices in the two nodes with a *fusion edge*.
4. For each pair of vertices with matching index between a node and its parent, if they are not already connected with a fusion edge, connect them with a *potential fusion edge*.

Figure 2 shows the fusion graphs alongside the loop fusion configurations. In the figure, solid lines are fusion edges and dotted lines are potential fusion edges, which are fusion opportunities not exploited. As an example, consider the loop fusion configuration in Figure 2(b) and the corresponding fusion graph in Figure 2(e). Since the j-, k-, and l-loops are fused between f_2 and f_3, there are three fusion edges, one for each of the three loops, between f_2 and f_3 in the fusion graph. Also, since no loops are fused between f_3 and f_4, the edges between f_3 and f_4 in the fusion graph remain potential fusion edges.

In a fusion graph, we call each connected component of fusion edges (i.e., a maximal set of connected fusion edges) a *fusion chain*, which corresponds to a fused loop in the loop structure. The *scope of a fusion chain c*, denoted $scope(c)$, is defined as the set of nodes it spans. In Figure 2(f), there are three fusion chains, one for each of the j-, k-, and l-loops; the scope of the shortest fusion chain is $\{B, f_2, f_3\}$. The scope of any two fusion chains in a fusion graph must either be disjoint or a subset/superset of each other. Scopes of fusion chains do not partially overlap because loops do not (i.e., loops must be either separate or nested). Therefore, any fusion graph with fusion chains whose scopes are partially overlapping is illegal and does not correspond to any loop fusion configuration.

Fusion graphs help us visualize the structure of the fused loops and find further fusion opportunities. If we can find a set of potential fusion edges that, when converted to fusion edges, does not lead to partially overlapping scopes of fusion chains, then we can perform the corresponding loop fusions and reduce the size of some arrays. For

---

[1] When array subscripts are not simple loop variables, as many researchers have studied, more dependence relations exist, which prevent some loop rearrangement and/or loop fusions. In that case, a restricted set of loop fusion configurations would need to be searched in minimizing memory usage.

example, the i-loops between A and f_1 in Figure 2(f) can be further fused and array A would be reduced to a scalar. If converting all potential fusion edges in a fusion graph to fusion edges does not make the fusion graph illegal, then we can completely fuse all the loops and achieve optimal memory usage. But for many fusion graphs in real-life loop configurations (including the ones in Figure 2), this does not hold. Instead, potential fusion edges may be mutually prohibitive; fusing one loop could prevent the fusion of another. In Figure 2(e), fusing the j-loops between f_1 and f_4 would disallow the fusion of the k-loops between f_3 and f_4. Although a fusion graph specifies what loops are fused, it does not fully determine the permutations of the loops and the ordering of the loop nests.

3.2 Preliminaries

So far, we have been describing the fusion between a node and its parent by the set of fused loops (or the loop indices such as $\{i, j\}$). But in order to compare loop fusion configurations for a subtree, it is desirable to include information about the relative scopes of the fused loops in the subtree. **Scope and fusion scope of a loop.** The *scope of a loop* of index i in a subtree rooted at v, denoted $scope(i, v)$, is defined in the usual sense as the set of nodes in the subtree that the fused loop spans. That is, if the i-loop is fused, $scope(i, v) = scope(c) \cap subtree(v)$, where c is a fusion chain for the i-loop with $v \in scope(c)$. If the i-loop of v is not fused, then $scope(i, v) = \emptyset$. We also define the *fusion scope of an i-loop* in a subtree rooted at v as $fscope(i, v) = scope(i, v)$ if the i-loop is fused between v and its parent; otherwise $fscope(i, v) = \emptyset$. As an example, for the fusion graph in Figure 2(e), $scope(j, f_3) = \{B, f_2, f_3\}$, but $fscope(j, f_3) = \emptyset$.

Indexset sequence. To describe the relative scopes of a set of fused loops, we introduce the notion of an *indexset sequence*, which is defined as an ordered list of disjoint, non-empty sets of loop indices. For example, $f = \langle \{i, k\}, \{j\} \rangle$ is an indexset sequence. For simplicity, we write each indexset in an indexset sequence as a string. Thus, f is written as $\langle ik, j \rangle$. Let g and g' be indexset sequences. We denote by $|g|$ the number of indexsets in g, $g[r]$ the r-th indexset in g, and $Set(g)$ the union of all indexsets in g, i.e. $Set(g) = \bigcup_{1 \le r \le |g|} g[r]$. For instance, $|f| = 2$, $f[1] = \{i, k\}$, and $Set(f) = Set(\langle j, i, k \rangle) = \{i, j, k\}$. We say that g' is a *prefix* of g if $|g'| \le |g|$, $g'[|g'|] \subseteq g[|g'|]$, and for all $1 \le r < |g'|$, $g'[r] = g[r]$. We write this relation as $prefix(g', g)$. So, $\langle \rangle, \langle i \rangle, \langle k \rangle, \langle ik \rangle, \langle ik, j \rangle$ are prefixes of f, but $\langle i, j \rangle$ is not. The *concatenation* of g and an indexset x, denoted $g + x$, is defined as the indexset sequence g'' such that if $x \neq \emptyset$, then $|g''| = |g| + 1$, $g''[|g''|] = x$, and for all $1 \le r < |g''|$, $g''[r] = g[r]$; otherwise, $g'' = g$.

Fusion. We use the notion of an indexset sequence to define a *fusion*. Intuitively, the loops fused between a node and its parent are ranked by their fusion scopes in the subtree from largest to smallest; two loops with the same fusion scope have the same rank (i.e. are in the same indexset). For example, in Figure 2(f), the fusion between f_2 and f_3 is $\langle jkl \rangle$ and the fusion between f_4 and f_5 is $\langle j, k \rangle$ (because the fused j-loop covers two more nodes, A and f_1). Formally, a fusion between a node v and $v.parent$ is an indexset sequence f such that

1. $Set(f) \subseteq v.indices \cap v.parent.indices$,

2. for all $i \in Set(f)$, the i-loop is fused between v and $v.parent$, and
3. for all $i \in f[r]$ and $i' \in f[r']$,
   a) $r = r'$ iff $fscope(i, v) = fscope(i', v)$, and
   b) $r < r'$ iff $fscope(i, v) \supset fscope(i', v)$.

Nesting. Similarly, a *nesting* of the loops at a node v can be defined as an indexset sequence. Intuitively, the loops at a node are ranked by their scopes in the subtree; two loops have the same rank (i.e. are in the same indexset) if they have the same scope. For example, in Figure 2(e), the loop nesting at f_3 is $\langle kl, j \rangle$, at f_4 is $\langle jk \rangle$, and at B is $\langle jkl \rangle$. Formally, a nesting of the loops at a node v is an indexset sequence h such that

1. $Set(h) = v.indices$ and
2. for all $i \in h[r]$ and $i' \in h[r']$,
   a) $r = r'$ iff $scope(i, v) = scope(i', v)$, and
   b) $r < r'$ iff $scope(i, v) \supset scope(i', v)$.

By definition, the loop nesting at a leaf node v must be $\langle v.indices \rangle$ because all loops at v have empty scope.

Legal fusion. A legal fusion graph (corresponding to a loop fusion configuration) for an expression tree T can be built up in a bottom-up manner by extending and merging legal fusion graphs for the subtrees of T. For a given node v, the nesting h at v summarizes the fusion graph for the subtree rooted at v and determines what fusions are allowed between v and its parent. A fusion f is legal for a nesting h at v if $prefix(f, h)$ and $set(f) \subseteq v.parent.indices$. This is because, to keep the fusion graph legal, loops with larger scopes must be fused before fusing those with smaller scopes, and only loops common to both v and its parent may be fused. For example, consider the fusion graph for the subtree rooted at f_2 in Figure 2(e). Since the nesting at f_2 is $\langle kl, j \rangle$ and $f_3.indices = \{j, k, l\}$, the legal fusions between f_2 and f_3 are $\langle \rangle$, $\langle k \rangle$, $\langle l \rangle$, $\langle kl \rangle$, and $\langle kl, j \rangle$. Notice that all legal fusions for a node v are prefixes of a *maximal legal fusion*, which can be expressed as $MaxFusion(h, v) = \max\{f \mid prefix(f, h) \text{ and } set(f) \subseteq v.parent.indices\}$, where h is the nesting at v. In Figure 2(e), the maximal legal fusion for C is $\langle kl \rangle$, and for f_2 is $\langle kl, j \rangle$.

Resulting nesting. Let u be the parent of a node v. If v is the only child of u, then the loop nesting at u as a result of a fusion f between u and v can be obtained by the function $ExtNesting(f, u) = f + (u.indices - Set(f))$. For example, in Figure 2(e), if the fusion between f_2 and f_3 is $\langle kl \rangle$, then the nesting at f_3 would be $\langle kl, j \rangle$.

Compatible nestings. Suppose v has a sibling v', f is the fusion between u and v, and f' is the fusion between u and v'. For the fusion graph for the subtree rooted at u (which is merged from those of v and v') to be legal, $h = ExtNesting(f, u)$ and $h' = ExtNesting(f', u)$ must be *compatible* according to the condition: for all $i \in h[r]$ and $j \in h[s]$, if $r < s$ and $i \in h'[r']$ and $j \in h'[s']$, then $r' \leq s'$. This requirement ensures an i-loop that has a larger scope than a j-loop in one subtree will not have a smaller scope than the j-loop in the other subtree. If h and h' are compatible, the resulting loop nesting at u (as merged from h and h') is h'' such that for all $i \in h''[r'']$ and $j \in h''[s'']$, if $i \in h[r]$, $i \in h'[r']$, $j \in h[s]$, and $j \in h'[s']$, then $[r'' = s'' \Rightarrow r = s \text{ and } r' = s']$ and $[r'' \leq s'' \Rightarrow r \leq s \text{ and } r' \leq s']$. Effectively, the loops at u are re-ranked by their combined scopes in the two subtrees to form h''. As an example, in Figure 2(e), if the fusion between f_1 and f_4 is $f = \langle j \rangle$ and the fusion between f_3 and f_4 is $f' = \langle k \rangle$, then $h = \mathit{ExtNesting}(f, f_4) = \langle j, k \rangle$ and $h' = \mathit{ExtNesting}(f', f_4) = \langle k, j \rangle$ would be incompatible. But if f is changed to $\langle \rangle$, then $h = \mathit{ExtNesting}(f, f_4) = \langle jk \rangle$ would be compatible with h', and the resulting nesting at f_4 would be $\langle k, j \rangle$. A procedure for checking if h and h' are compatible and forming h'' from h and h' is provided in Section 3.3.

The "more-constraining" relation on nestings. A nesting h at a node v is said to be *more or equally constraining than* another nesting h' at the same node, denoted $h \sqsubseteq h'$, if for all legal fusion graph G for T in which the nesting at v is h, there exists a legal fusion graph G' for T in which the nesting at v is h' such that the subgraphs of G and G' induced by $T - \mathit{subtree}(v)$ are identical. In other words, $h \sqsubseteq h'$ means that any loop fusion configuration for the rest of the expression tree that works with h also works with h'. This relation allows us to do effective pruning among the large number of loop fusion configurations for a subtree in Section 3.3. It can be proved that the necessary and sufficient condition for $h \sqsubseteq h'$ is that for all $i \in m[r]$ and $j \in m[s]$, there exist r', s' such that $i \in m'[r']$ and $j \in m'[s']$ and $[r = s \Rightarrow r' = s']$ and $[r < s \Rightarrow r' \leq s']$, where $m = \mathit{MaxFusion}(h, v)$ and $m' = \mathit{MaxFusion}(h', v)$. Comparing the nesting at f_3 between Figure 2(e) and (f), the nesting $\langle kl, j \rangle$ in (e) is more constraining than the nesting $\langle jkl \rangle$ in (f). A procedure for determining if $h \sqsubseteq h'$ is given in Section 3.3.

3.3 Static Memory Allocation

Under the static memory allocation model, since all the arrays in a program exist during the entire computation, the memory usage of a loop fusion configuration is simply the sum of the sizes of all the arrays (including those reduced to scalars). Figures 3 shows a bottom-up, dynamic programming algorithm for finding a memory-optimal loop fusion configuration for a given expression tree T. For each node v in t, it computes a set of solutions $v.\mathit{solns}$ for the subtree rooted at v. Each solution s in $v.\mathit{solns}$ represents a loop fusion configuration for the subtree rooted at v and contains the following information for s: the loop nesting $s.\mathit{nesting}$ at v, the fusion $s.\mathit{fusion}$ between v and its parent, the memory usage $s.\mathit{mem}$ so far, and the pointers $s.\mathit{src1}$ and $s.\mathit{src2}$ to the corresponding solutions for the children of v.

The set of solutions $v.\mathit{solns}$ is obtained by the following steps. First, if v is a leaf node, initialize the solution set to contain a single solution using **InitSolns**. Otherwise, take the solution set from a child $v.\mathit{child1}$ of v, and, if v has two children, merge it (using **MergeSolns**) with the compatible solutions from the other child $v.\mathit{child2}$. Then, prune the solution set to remove the inferior solutions using **PruneSolns**. A solution s is *inferior* to another unpruned solution s' if $s.\mathit{nesting}$ is more or equally constraining than $s'.\mathit{nesting}$ and s does not use less memory than s'. Next, extend the solution set by considering all possible legal fusions between v and its parent (see **ExtSolns**). The size of array v is added to memory usage by **AddMemUsage**. Inferior solutions are also removed.

Although the complexity of the algorithm is exponential in the number of index variables and the number of solutions could in theory grow exponentially with the size of the expression tree, the number of index variables in practical applications is usually

MinMemFusion (T):
    InitFusible (T)
    foreach node v in some bottom-up traversal of T
        if $v.nchildren = 0$ then
            $S1 =$ InitSolns (v)
        else
            $S1 = v.child1.solns$
            if $v.nchildren = 2$ then
                $S1 =$ MergeSolns $(S1, v.child2.solns)$
            $S1 =$ PruneSolns $(S1, v)$
        $v.solns =$ ExtendSolns $(S1, v)$
    $T.root.optsoln =$ the single element in $T.root.solns$
    foreach node v in some top-down traversal of T
        $s = v.optsoln$
        $v.optfusion = s.fusion$
        $s1 = s.src1$
        if $v.nchildren = 1$ then
            $v.child1.optsoln = s1$
        else
            $v.child1.optsoln = s1.src1$
            $v.child2.optsoln = s1.src2$

InitFusible (T):
    foreach $v \in T$
        if $v = T.root$ then
            $v.fusible = \emptyset$
        else
            $v.fusible = v.indices \cap v.parent.indices$

InitSolns (v):
    $s.nesting = \langle v.fusible \rangle$
    InitMemUsage (s)
    return $\{s\}$

MergeSolns $(S1, S2)$:
    $S = \emptyset$
    foreach $s1 \in S1$
        foreach $s2 \in S2$
            $s.nesting =$ MergeNesting $(s1.nesting, s2.nesting)$
            if $s.nesting \neq \langle \rangle$ then   // if $s1$ and $s2$ are compatible
                $s.src1 = s1$
                $s.src2 = s2$
                MergeMemUsage $(s1, s2, s)$
                AddSoln (s, S)
    return S

PruneSolns $(S1, v)$:
    $S = \emptyset$
    foreach $s1 \in S1$
        $s.nesting =$ MaxFusion $(s1.nesting, v)$
        AddSoln (s, S)
    return S

ExtendSolns $(S1, v)$:
    $S = \emptyset$
    foreach $s1 \in S1$
        foreach prefix f of $s1.nesting$
            $s.fusion = f$
            $s.nesting =$ ExtNesting $(f, v.parent)$
            $s.src1 = s1$
            $size =$ FusedSize (v, f)
            AddMemUsage $(v, f, size, s1, s)$
            AddSoln (s, S)
    return S

AddSoln (s, S):
    foreach $s' \in S$
        if Inferior (s, s') then
            return
        else if Inferior (s', s) then
            $S = S - \{s'\}$
    $S = S \cup \{s\}$

MergeNesting (h, h'):
    $g = \langle \rangle$
    $r = r' = 1$
    $x = x' = \emptyset$
    while $r \leq |h|$ or $r' \leq |h'|$
        if $x = \emptyset$ then
            $x = h[r + +]$
        if $x' = \emptyset$ then
            $x' = h'[r' + +]$
        $y = x \cap x'$
        if $y = \emptyset$ then
            return $\langle \rangle$ // h and h' are incompatible
        $g = g + y$
        $y = x - x'$
        $x' = x' - x$
        $x = y$
    end while
    return g // h and h' are compatible

$h \sqsubseteq h'$:   // test if h is more/equally constraining
    than h'
    $r' = 1$
    $x' = \emptyset$
    for $r = 1$ to $|h|$
        if $x' = \emptyset$ then
            if $r' > |h'|$ then
                return false
            $x' = h'[r' + +]$
        if $h[r] \not\subseteq x'$ then
            return false
        $x' = x' - h[r]$
    return true

InitMemUsage (s):
    $s.mem = 0$

AddMemUsage $(v, f, size, s1, s)$:
    $s.mem = s1.mem + size$

MergeMemUsage $(s1, s2, s)$:
    $s.mem = s1.mem + s2.mem$

Inferior $(s, s') \equiv$
    $s.nesting \sqsubseteq s'.nesting$ and $s.mem \geq s'.mem$

FusedSize $(v, f) \equiv$
    $\prod_{(i \in v.indices - \{v.sumindex\} - f)} N_i$

ExtNesting $(f, u) \equiv f + (u.indices - \text{Set } (f))$

MaxFusion $(h, v) \equiv$
    $\max\{f \mid \text{prefix}(f, h)$ and $\text{Set } (f) \subseteq v.parent.$
    $indices\}$

Set $(f) \equiv \bigcup_{1 \leq r \leq |f|} f[r]$

Fig. 3. Algorithm for static memory allocation.

small and there is indication that the pruning is effective in keeping the size of the solution set in each node small.

The algorithm assumes the leaf nodes may be freely fused with their parents and the root node array must be available in its entirety at the end of the computation. If these assumptions do not hold, the **InitFusible** procedure can be easily modified to restrict or expand the allowable fusions for those nodes.

v	line	src	nesting	fusion	ext-nest	memory usage	opt
A	1		$\langle ij \rangle$	$\langle ij \rangle$	$\langle ij \rangle$	1	√
B	2		$\langle jkl \rangle$	$\langle jkl \rangle$	$\langle jkl \rangle$	1	√
C	3		$\langle kl \rangle$	$\langle kl \rangle$	$\langle kl, j \rangle$	1	
	4		$\langle kl \rangle$	$\langle k \rangle$	$\langle k, jl \rangle$	15	√
	5		$\langle kl \rangle$	$\langle l \rangle$	$\langle l, jk \rangle$	40	
	6		$\langle kl \rangle$	$\langle \rangle$	$\langle jkl \rangle$	600	
f_1	7	1	$\langle ij \rangle$	$\langle j \rangle$	$\langle j, k \rangle$	1+1=2	
	8	1	$\langle ij \rangle$	$\langle \rangle$	$\langle jk \rangle$	1+100=101	√
f_2	9	2,3	$\langle kl, j \rangle$	$\langle kl, j \rangle$	$\langle kl, j \rangle$	(1+1)+1=3	
	10	2,4	$\langle k, jl \rangle$	$\langle k, jl \rangle$	$\langle k, jl \rangle$	(1+15)+1=17	√
	11	2,5	$\langle l, jk \rangle$	$\langle l, jk \rangle$	$\langle l, jk \rangle$	(1+40)+1=42	
	12	2,6	$\langle jkl \rangle$	$\langle jkl \rangle$	$\langle jkl \rangle$	(1+600)+1=602	
f_3	13	10	$\langle k, jl \rangle$	$\langle k, j \rangle$	$\langle k, j \rangle$	17+1=18	√
	14	12	$\langle jkl \rangle$	$\langle jk \rangle$	$\langle jk \rangle$	602+1=603	
f_4	15	7,14	$\langle j, k \rangle$	$\langle j, k \rangle$	$\langle j, k \rangle$	(2+603)+1=606	
	16	8,13	$\langle k, j \rangle$	$\langle k, j \rangle$	$\langle k, j \rangle$	(101+18)+1=120	√
	17	8,14	$\langle jk \rangle$	$\langle jk \rangle$	$\langle jk \rangle$	(101+603)+1=705	
f_5	18	16	$\langle k, j \rangle$	$\langle \rangle$	$\langle \rangle$	120+40=160	√

Fig. 4. Solution sets for the subtrees in the example.

To illustrate how the algorithm works, consider again the empty fusion graph in Figure 2(d) for the expression tree in Figure 1(c). Let $N_i = 500$, $N_j = 100$, $N_k = 40$, and $N_l = 15$. There are $2^3 = 8$ different fusions between B and f_2. Among them, only the full fusion $\langle jkl \rangle$ is in B.*solns* because all other fusions result in more constraining nestings and use more memory than the full fusion and are pruned. However, this does not happen to the fusions between C and f_2 since the resulting nesting $\langle kl, j \rangle$ of the full fusion $\langle kl \rangle$ is not less constraining than those of the other 3 possible fusions. Then, solutions from B and C are merged together to form solutions for f_2. For example, when the two full-fusion solutions from B and C are merged, the merged nesting for f_2 is $\langle kl, j \rangle$, which can then be extended by full fusion (between f_2 and f_3) to form a full-fusion solution for f_2 that has a memory usage of only 3 scalars. Again, since this solution is not the least constraining one, other solutions cannot be pruned. Although this solution is optimal for the subtree rooted at f_2, it turns out to be non-optimal for the entire expression tree. Figure 4 shows the solution sets for all of the nodes. The "src" column contains the line numbers of the corresponding solutions for the children. The "ext-nest" column shows the resulting nesting for the parent. A $\sqrt{}$ mark indicates the solution forms a part of an optimal solution for the entire expression tree. The fusion graph for the optimal solution is shown in Figure 5(a).

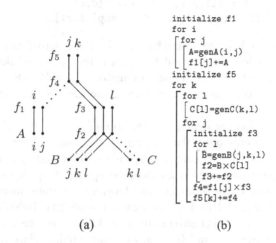

```
initialize f1
for i
  ⎡for j
  ⎢  ⎡A=genA(i,j)
  ⎣  ⎣f1[j]+=A
initialize f5
for k
  ⎡for l
  ⎢  ⎡C[l]=genC(k,l)
  ⎢  for j
  ⎢  ⎡initialize f3
  ⎢  ⎢for l
  ⎢  ⎢  ⎡B=genB(j,k,l)
  ⎢  ⎢  ⎢f2=B×C[l]
  ⎢  ⎢  ⎣f3+=f2
  ⎢  ⎢f4=f1[j]×f3
  ⎣  ⎣f5[k]+=f4
```

(a)   (b)

Fig. 5. An optimal solution for the example.

Once an optimal solution is obtained, we can generate the corresponding fused loop structure from it. The following procedure determines an evaluation order of the nodes:

1. Initialize set P to contain a single node $T.root$ and list L to an empty list.
2. While P is not empty, remove from P a node v where $v.optfusion$ is maximal among all nodes in P, insert v at the beginning of L, and add the children of v (if any) to P.
3. When P is empty, L contains the evaluation order.

Putting the loops around the array evaluation statements is trivial. The initialization of an array can be placed inside the innermost loop that contains both the evaluation and use of the array. The optimal loop fusion configuration for the example expression tree is shown in Figure 5(b).

3.4   An Example

We illustrate the practical application of the memory usage minimization algorithm on the following example formula sequence which can be used to determine self-energy in electronic structure of solids. It is optimal in operation count and has a cost of 1.89×10^{15} operations. The ranges of the indices are $N_k = 10, N_t = 100, N_{RL} = N_{RL1} = N_{RL2} = N_G = N_{G1} = 1000,$ and $N_r = N_{r1} = 100000$.

```
f1[r,RL,RL1,t] = Y[r,RL] * G[RL1,RL,t]
f2[r,RL1,t] = sum RL f1[r,RL,RL1,t]
f5[r,RL2,r1,t] = Y[r,RL2] * f2[r1,RL2,t]
```

```
f6[r,r1,t]     = sum RL2 f5[r,RL2,r1,t]
f7[k,r,r1]     = exp[k,r] * exp[k,r1]
f10[r,r1,t]    = f6[r,r1,t] * f6[r1,r,t]
f11[k,r,r1,t]  = f7[k,r,r1] * f10[r,r1,t]
f13[k,r1,t,G]  = fft r f11[k,r,r1,t] * exp[G,r]
f15[k,t,G,G1]  = fft r1 f13[k,r1,t,G] * exp[G1,r1]
```

In this example, array Y is sparse and has only 10% non-zero elements. Notice that the common sub-expressions Y, exp, and f_6 appear at the right hand side of more than one formula. Also, f_{13} and f_{15} are fast Fourier transform formulae. Discussions on how to handle sparse arrays, common sub-expressions, and fast Fourier transforms can be found in [12,13].

Without any loop fusion, the total size of the arrays is 1.13×10^{14} elements. If each array is to be computed only once, the presence of the common sub-expressions and FFTs would prevent the fusion of some loops, such as the r and $r1$ loops between f_6 and f_{10}. Under the operation-count restriction, the optimal loop fusion configuration obtained by the memory usage minimization algorithm for static memory allocation requires memory storage for 1.10×10^{11} array elements, which is 1000 times better than without any loop fusion. But this translates to about 1,000 gigabytes and probably still exceeds the amount of memory available in any computer today. Thus, relaxation of the operation-count restriction is necessary to further reduce to memory usage to reasonable values. Discussions on heuristics for trading arithmetic operations for memory can be found in [13].

We perform the following simple transformations to the DAG and the corresponding fusion graph.

- Two additional vertices are added: one for a k-loop around f_{10} and the other for a t-loop around f_7. These additional vertices are then connected to the corresponding vertices in f_{11} with additional potential fusion edges to allow more loop fusion opportunities between f_{11} and its two children.
- The common sub-expressions Y, exp, and f_6 are split into multiple nodes. Also, two copies of the sub-DAG rooted at f_6 are made. This will overcome some constraints on legal fusion graphs for DAGs.

The memory usage minimization algorithm for static memory allocation is then applied on the transformed fusion graph. The fusion graph and the loop fusion configuration for the optimal solution found are shown in Figure 6. For clarity, the input arrays are not included in the fusion graph. The memory usage of the optimal solution after relaxing the operation-count restriction is significantly reduced by a factor of about 100 to 1.12×10^9 array elements. The operation count is increased by only around 10% to 2.10×10^{15}. The best hand-optimized loop fusion configuration produced by domain experts also has some manually-applied transformations to reduce memory usage to 1.12×10^9 array elements and has 5.08×10^{15} operations. In comparison, the optimal loop fusion configuration obtained by the algorithm shows a factor of 2.5 improvement in operation count while using the same amount of memory.

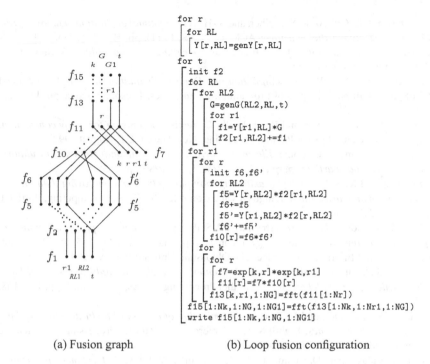

(a) Fusion graph   (b) Loop fusion configuration

Fig. 6. Optimal loop fusions for the example formula sequence.

4 Conclusion

In this paper, we have considered an optimization problem motivated by some computational physics applications. The computations are essentially multi-dimensional integrals of the product of several arrays. In practice, the input arrays and intermediate arrays could be too large to fit into the available amount of memory. It becomes necessary to fuse the loops to eliminate some dimensions of the arrays and reduce memory usage. The problem of finding a loop fusion configuration that minimizes memory usage was addressed in this paper. Based on a framework that models loop fusions and memory usage, we have presented an algorithm that solves the memory optimization problem. Work is in progress on the optimization and the implementation of the algorithms in this paper. We also plan on developing an automatic code generator that takes array partitioning and loop fusion information as input and produces the source code of a parallel program that computes the desired multi-dimensional integral.

References

1. W. Aulbur, *Parallel implementation of quasiparticle calculations of semiconductors and insulators*, Ph.D. Dissertation, Ohio State University, Columbus, October 1996.
2. S. Chatterjee, J. R. Gilbert, R. Schreiber, and S.-H. Teng, *Automatic array alignment in data-parallel programs*, 20th Annual ACM SIGACTS/SIGPLAN Symposium on Principles of Programming Languages, New York, pp. 16–28, 1993.

3. S. Chatterjee, J. R. Gilbert, R. Schreiber, and S.-H. Teng, *Optimal evaluation of array expressions on massively parallel machines*, ACM TOPLAS, 17 (1), pp. 123–156, Jan. 1995.
4. C. N. Fischer and R. J. LeBlanc Jr, *Crafting a compiler*, Menlo Park, CA:Benjamin/Cummings, 1991.
5. L. J. Guibas and D. K. Wyatt, *Compilation and Delayed Evaluation in APL*, Fifth Annual ACM Symposium on Principles of Programming Languages, Tucson, Arizona, pp. 1–8, Jan. 1978.
6. G. Gao, R. Olsen, V. Sarkar, and R. Thekkath, *Collective loop fusion for array contraction*, Languages and Compilers for Parallel Processing, New Haven, CT, August 1992.
7. M. S. Hybertsen and S. G. Louie, *Electronic correlation in semiconductors and insulators: band gaps and quasiparticle energies*, Phys. Rev. B, 34 (1986), pp. 5390.
8. K. Kennedy and K. S. McKinley, *Maximizing loop parallelism and improving data locality via loop fusion and distribution*, Languages and Compilers for Parallel Computing, Portland, OR, pp. 301–320, August 1993.
9. C. Lam, D. Cociorva, G. Baumgartner, and P. Sadayappan, *Memory-optimal evaluation of expression trees involving large objects*, Technical report no. OSU-CISRC-5/99-TR13, Dept. of Computer and Information Science, The Ohio State University, May 1999.
10. C. Lam, P. Sadayappan, and R. Wenger, *On optimizing a class of multi-dimensional loops with reductions for parallel execution*, Parallel Processing Letters, Vol. 7 No. 2, pp. 157–168, 1997.
11. C. Lam, P. Sadayappan, and R. Wenger, *Optimization of a class of multi-dimensional integrals on parallel machines*, Eighth SIAM Conference on Parallel Processing for Scientific Computing, Minneapolis, MN, March 1997.
12. C. Lam, P. Sadayappan, D. Cociorva, M. Alouani, and J. Wilkins, *Performance optimization of a class of loops involving sums of products of sparse arrays*, Ninth SIAM Conference on Parallel Processing for Scientific Computing, San Antonio, TX, March 1999.
13. C. Lam, *Performance optimization of a class of loops implementing multi-dimensional integrals*, Technical report no. OSU-CISRC-8/99-TR22, Dept. of Computer and Information Science, The Ohio State University, Columbus, August 1999.
14. N. Manjikian and T. S. Abdelrahman, *Fusion of Loops for Parallelism and Locality*, International Conference on Parallel Processing, pp. II:19–28, Oconomowoc, WI, August 1995.
15. H. N. Rojas, R. W. Godby, and R. J. Needs, *Space-time method for Ab-initio calculations of self-energies and dielectric response functions of solids*, Phys. Rev. Lett., 74 (1995), pp. 1827.
16. S. Singhai and K. MacKinley, *Loop Fusion for Data Locality and Parallelism*, Mid-Atlantic Student Workshop on Programming Languages and Systems, SUNY at New Paltz, April 1996.

Compile-Time Based Performance Prediction*

Calin Cascaval, Luiz DeRose, David A. Padua, and Daniel A. Reed

Department of Computer Science
University of Illinois at Urbana-Champaign
{cascaval,derose,padua,reed}@cs.uiuc.edu

Abstract. In this paper we present results we obtained using a compiler to predict performance of scientific codes. The compiler, Polaris [3], is both the primary tool for estimating the performance of a range of codes, and the beneficiary of the results obtained from predicting the program behavior at compile time. We show that a simple compile-time model, augmented with profiling data obtained using very light instrumentation, can be accurate within 20% (on average) of the measured performance for codes using both dense and sparse computational methods.

1 Introduction

In this paper we present the compiler-related part of the Delphi project whose goal is to predict performance of codes when executed on multiprocessor and distributed platforms. The project will integrate several components, such as compilers, resource managers, dynamic instrumentation tools, and performance prediction and visualization tools, into a unique environment targeted for high performance computing.

The part of the project presented in this paper focuses on compiler techniques for performance prediction of parallel codes and machines. By using these techniques, a compiler becomes a useful tool to support machine design and program tuning either by itself or as part of performance visualization tools, such as SvPablo [8]. Furthermore, accurate compile-time performance prediction techniques are of crucial importance for the compiler itself to select the best possible transformations during the code optimization pass.

Powerful techniques for performance prediction are quite important due to the difficulties programmers and compilers encounter in achieving peak performance on high-end machines. The complexity is exacerbated in new architectures, which have multi-level memory hierarchies and exploit speculative execution, making the achievement of a large fraction of the peak performance of these systems even harder.

---

* This work is supported in part by Army contract DABT63-95-C-0097; Army contract N66001-97-C-8532; NSF contract MIP-9619351; and a Partnership Award from IBM. This work is not necessarily representative of the positions or policies of the Army or Government.

L. Carter and J. Ferrante (Eds.): LCPC'99, LNCS 1863, pp. 365–379, 2000.
© Springer-Verlag Berlin Heidelberg 2000

One of the main challenges we face is to find a general methodology that allows the performance prediction of arbitrary codes, including irregular applications, for any arbitrary input data. In this paper, we describe a simple strategy for performance prediction that we have implemented in the Polaris source-to-source translator [3]. The strategy leads to symbolic expressions generated by the compiler for each loop of the program being analyzed. These expressions integrate the prediction of CPU execution time and the prediction of cache behavior and can make use of both compile-time and profiling information.

Examples of optimizing transformations that should be controlled by performance prediction results are: parallelization of loops based on the tradeoff between the amount of work in the loop and the overhead of running the loop in parallel; loop interchange, a classical loop optimization that affects data locality and parallelism overhead in non-obvious ways. Even a gross estimate of the performance of a program segment can enable the compiler to decide if the optimizing transformation is beneficial.

Our work is performed at the high level language representation, which allows us to keep the models simple and relatively hardware independent. We have validated our performance prediction models on sequential programs using the SPEC95 benchmarks and some sparse matrix codes on the SGI's R10000 and Sun's UltraSparc IIi processors. It was quite surprising to see how well our simple strategy worked for our test cases.

The remainder of this paper is organized as follows. In Sect. 2 we describe our compiler-driven prediction model. In Sect. 3 we present the experimental results. In Sect. 4 we discuss related work, and we conclude in Sect. 5.

2   Compiler Driven Prediction

In the approach described in this paper, the compiler extracts information from the source code and generates symbolic expressions representing the execution time of different program segments. For the cases where we do not have compile-time information, either run-time profiling [6] provides the necessary data or simple approximations [1] can be used.

The target computer can be an existing machine or a proposed architecture. Although for many users the total execution time will be the main figure of interest, we believe that other values, such as number of cache misses, can be used profitably to drive compiler transformations. Along the same lines, for architectures with multiple heterogeneous processors, such as FlexRAM [16], compile-time performance prediction can be used to decide where to execute the code: in the main processor which has a larger, slower cache and less bandwidth to the main memory, or in the Processor-In-Memory (PIM) which has a smaller but faster cache and it is implemented in the memory chip.

In Fig. 1, we present an overview of the prediction environment. In this environment, the compiler analyzes the source code and synthesizes the symbolic expressions representing performance data from the application. It also instruments the code to extract profiling information. The code can be run with different data sets to extract the profiling data used as parameters for the performance expressions. The compiler uses the profiling data to evaluate the performance expressions – although, symbolic expressions comparisons are also possible, which in turn will be used to control program optimizations. In our environment, since Polaris is a source-to-source parallelizing compiler, the optimized program will be an optimized and parallelized Fortran source. Also, the profiling data can be used along with hardware costs to resolve the symbolic expressions and the results displayed using a performance visualization tool.

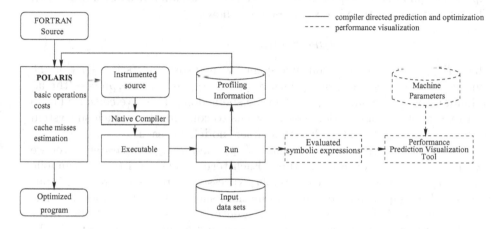

Fig. 1. Compiler-based prediction environment

We present first the machine model supported by our performance prediction model, then the targeted application domain and, finally, the prediction model itself.

2.1 Models

Machine Model. The architecture supported by our prediction model assumes one or more CPUs that execute code stored in memory. The processor could be a simple in-order single issue architecture or a more complex, multiple issue out-of-order processor. The memory consists of a hierarchy of memory levels (caches), each having different characteristics.

Program Model. The type of applications to be evaluated in this project are scientific Fortran programs. The codes used in our experiments include dense matrix computations from the SPECfp95 benchmark suite [18], and sparse matrix codes from SpLib, a library of sparse functions for linear algebra [4].

Since we want to handle a wide range of codes, our compiler must be able to handle programs with complex control flow, such as imperfectly nested loops, loops with early exits and conditionals, and while loops. We are willing to trade

some prediction accuracy for the ability to handle efficiently any program structure. The approach that we have taken, detailed in the following section, is to
have several models that we can apply depending on the amount of compile-time
information available. In case we do not have enough compile-time information,
run-time profiling can be used to obtain the necessary data.

Performance Prediction Model. The performance prediction model uses
analytical and experimental information. The compiler synthesizes performance
expressions and instruments the code to extract values unknown at compile-time.
The total execution time is decomposed as follows:

$$T_{total} = T_{CPU} + T_{MEM} + T_{COMM} + T_{I/O} \tag{1}$$

where T_{CPU} is the computation time spent by the processor itself, T_{MEM} is the
time spent accessing the memory hierarchy, T_{COMM} is the interprocess/thread
communication time, and $T_{I/O}$ is the time spent doing I/O. We consider (1) to
be a reasonable decomposition that allows us to concentrate on each subsystem
(CPU, memory, I/O) and work with simpler models for each.

We shall detail the how we estimate T_{CPU} and T_{MEM} separately after we
describe some of the common features. Each term in (1) consists of a symbolic
expression, i.e., a mathematical formula expressed in terms of program input
values and perhaps some profiling information, such as branch frequencies. The
expressions also involve parameters representing characteristics of the target
machine and are a function of the source code and input data. To factor in the
data sets, the compiler will place very light instrumentation in the program,
and the user or the prediction environment will run the program such that it
can collect information on the input data, and substitute it in the symbolic
expressions.

For example, the loop in Fig. 2 performs a sparse matrix vector multiplication
($Y = A \times X$) and the matrix A is stored in compressed sparse row storage (row
i is stored in consecutive locations of A beginning at $ia(i)$ and the column of
the element stored in $A(k)$ is $ja(k)$). Since the number of iterations of loop L2
depends on the input data, the compiler will not be able to estimate how many
times statement S2 is executed without information on the input data. To obtain
this information, the compiler will add instrumentation after loop L2 to compute
the number of iterations, place a symbolic variable for the number of iterations
in the prediction formula, and let the dynamic phase compute the actual value
that depends on the data set. This interaction is illustrated by the path marked
with solid arrows in Fig. 1.

2.2 Compile-Time Prediction

In the static phase of the prediction, the compiler goes through the Abstract
Syntax Tree (AST) of the program and collects information about operations.
Recall that all our evaluations are done at source code level. The compiler combi-
nes this information in symbolic expressions for statements, loops, and routines,

```
L1          do i = 1, m
S1              Y(i) = 0.0d0
L2              do k = ia(i), ia(i+1)-1
S2                  Y(i) = Y(i) + A(k) * X(ja(k))
            end do
        end do
```

Fig. 2. Sparse matrix vector multiplication

depending on the level at which we want to predict performance. The compiler also places instrumentation statements for the dynamic phase wherever it does not have enough information, such as loop bounds, branch frequencies, etc.

Basic Operations. The sub-model for T_{CPU} in (1) estimates the time spent by the processor doing computation. It counts the number of operations executing in the CPU's functional units, including load and store operations assuming no cache misses. In addition, it considers as basic operations intrinsic functions, such as $SQRT$ (many current processors have functional units that execute square root operations) or trigonometric functions, as well as function calls and loop overheads.

To reduce the number of independent variables in the symbolic expressions, operations may be grouped together based on the operation type and the data size on which they operate. For example, we group together single precision addition and multiplication since, on most current architectures, these instructions have similar latencies being executed in the same or identical functional units. We distinguish between multiplication and division since the division operation usually has longer latency than other operations. However, the grouping is not fixed so that we can accommodate other architectures with different designs. T_{CPU} can be expressed as:

$$T_{CPU} = CycleTime \times \sum_i^{\#groups} (k_i \times C_i), \qquad (2)$$

where k_i are symbolic expressions representing the number of operations in group i, and C_i represents the hardware cost for the operations in group i. The hardware costs C_i can be obtained either from the processor's manual and design specifications, or by using microbenchmarking [21]. The latter is usually the most convenient way to get the values associated with intrinsic functions and loop overheads.

Using simple symbolic arithmetic, these expressions are combined to generate the cost of operation in each statement. The expressions corresponding to the statements are then combined and augmented with coefficients obtained from the dynamic phase (e.g., loop bounds and branch frequencies), to produce cost expressions for several levels of granularity in the program (blocks of statements, loops, procedures) until a unique expression is generated for the entire program.

Although this is a very simple strategy, it has proven reasonably accurate when no compiler optimizations are applied, as can be seen in the experimental results presented in Sect. 3. Dependence graph information could be used to improve prediction accuracy on modern processors that exploit instruction level parallelism (ILP).

In order to accurately predict the performance for optimized codes we have to apply, or at least approximate, the optimizations performed by the native compiler in our restructurer. We have chosen to approximate these optimizations by using the following heuristics applied at high level source code:

- *Eliminate loop invariants.* This is a simple optimization applied by all optimizing compilers and it can be done at high level.
- *Consider only the floating point operations.* This is based on the observation that, in scientific codes, the useful computation is done in floating point, and in optimized code integer operations are used mostly for control flow and index computation and are usually removed from the innermost loops. We do take into account the control flow in the form of loop overheads.
- *Ignore all memory accesses that are not array references.* The reason for this heuristic is that scalar references occur relatively infrequently in scientific codes and, if they do, current architectures often have enough registers to buffer them.
- *Overlap operations.* For multiple issue architectures with multiple functional units, we must allow operations in different categories to overlap execution. For example, on the R10000 processor, there can be 6 instructions issued in one cycle: 2 integer operations, 2 floating point operations, 1 memory operation and 1 branch.

Using these approximations we obtain a lower bound on the processor's execution time.

Memory Hierarchy Model. The term T_{MEM} in (1) estimates the time spent accessing memory locations in the memory hierarchy. As we mentioned before, when estimating the the execution time of basic operations we assume all memory references are cache hits in the first level cache. However, many accesses are not served from the first level cache, in part because applications have data sets much larger than the cache.

T_{MEM} can be expressed as follows:

$$T_{MEM} = CycleTime \times \sum_{i}^{\#levels} (M_i \times C_i), \tag{3}$$

where M_i represents the number of accesses that miss in the ith level of the memory hierarchy, and C_i represents the penalty (in machine cycles) for a miss in the ith level of the memory hierarchy. C_i is computed using microbenchmarking, as in [19].

The compiler computes the number of array references in each statement and aggregates the values across blocks of statements, loops, and procedures. We do not include scalar references in this version of the model because, as mentioned above, we assume that the register files and the first level caches in most current processors are large enough to hold the majority of scalars. We propose two models to estimate the number of cache misses, which are used according to how much compile-time information is available.

Stack Distances Model. This model is based on the stack histogram obtained from a stack processing algorithm [5,17] and requires accurate data dependence distance information [2]. The stack processing algorithm works on a program trace, where the elements in the trace can be memory locations, cache lines or virtual pages, and builds a stack as follows: for each element in the trace, check if the element is present in the stack. If it is, store the distance from the top of the stack where the element was found (the stack distance) and move the element on the top of the stack. If the element is not found, store ∞ as the stack distance and push the element on the top of the stack. The stack histogram is the distribution of the number of references at different stack distances. Stack algorithms have been used to simulate memory and cache behavior of programs [17,15,23,25,24].

We have devised a compile-time algorithm to compute the stack histogram. The compiler will label each data dependence arc (including input dependences) with the number of distinct memory locations accessed between the source and the sink of the dependence. The dependence with the minimum label will give the stack distance δ for the reference that is the sink of the data dependence arc. We also compute the number of times a static reference is accessed, A_δ. The number of cache misses for the cache at level i with cache size S_i is computed using the formula:

$$M_i = \sum_{\delta=S_i}^{\infty} A_\delta \qquad (4)$$

In order to take into account spatial locality, we adjust the number of accesses when the dependence between two references that could potentially share a cache line satisfies the sharing conditions [5].

Indirect Accesses Model. When data dependence vectors are not available, we must approximate the number of cache lines that are spanned by the array references using other methods. This situation occurs mostly when indirect accesses are present in the code; therefore, we call this model the *indirect accesses model*, although it can be applied to any loop. In this model, we obtain the number of misses by multiplying each array reference A_j with the array element size e_j, and dividing the sum by the number of bytes for each block size in the memory hierarchy. Thus, M_i can be expressed as:

$$M_i = (\sum_j A_j \times e_j)/BlockSize_i \qquad (5)$$

When indirect accesses are involved, we need to apply a correction to the estimation since there could be many accesses to the same element. For example, many of the accesses to array X in statement S2 in Fig. 2 can map to the same element, depending on the value of the array element $ja(k)$. Therefore, we approximate the number of accesses with the minimum between the number of accesses and the size of the array. If the size is not known at compile time, the compiler can obtain it by run-time profiling.

For both models, the expressions are computed symbolically and we use profiling data to replace the parameters that depend on the input data set.

2.3   Putting it All Together

The static phase of the prediction is completed when the compiler instruments the code with the symbolic expressions for performance estimation. In the next phase, dynamic prediction, we compile the instrumented code using a native compiler and run the code in order to gather the run-time profiling data. Note that to obtain profiling data, the code need not run on the architecture for which we are predicting performance, therefore, the prediction model is not constrained by the existence of the architecture.

After the dynamic phase is completed, results are merged with the architectural parameters determined through microbenchmarking (or supplied by the user in case the architecture under study is not available) and can be used to guide compiler optimizations, and/or to be displayed using a performance prediction visualization tool, as mentioned at the beginning of this section.

3   Experimental Results

We have implemented the prediction model using the Polaris source-to-source restructurer [3]. Polaris contains implementations of most of the classical optimizations. It also has a dependence analysis pass that computes distance vectors whenever possible. We are using Polaris to analyze codes from the SPECfp95 benchmarks [18] and the Indiana University SpLib package, which is part of the Linear System Analyzer [4].

In Table 1 we present a summary of the loops analyzed and estimated by Polaris for the SPECfp95 benchmarks. For each benchmark, in the first two columns, we show the total number of loops that are present in the program and the number of loops that do not containing I/O, thus the loops that we considered in this paper. The next columns show the distribution of the estimated loops based on the amount of compile-time information available. "Full" means that Polaris was able to compute the data dependence distance vectors for all array references in the loop. "Partial", means that while all the dependence distances were computed, some of the dependences have non-constant distances. For both these cases we can apply the stack distances model to predict the number of cache misses. For the second case we assume that accesses take place at the minimum distance. "Missing" represents the case in which Polaris could not compute the dependence distances for all the array references, and therefore the indirect accesses model is the only strategy that can be applied to predict performance. "Profiling" is the case in which the compiler needs run-time data due to unknown branch frequencies. For multiply nested loops, each loop of the

Table 1. Compile-time Stack Distances Accuracy

Benchmark	Total Loops	Estimated Loops	Compile-time Information			Profiled
			Full	Partial	Missing	
APPLU	168	149	137	8	0	4
APSI	298	231	175	29	7	20
HYDRO2D	165	158	124	15	6	13
MGRID	57	47	46	0	1	0
SU2COR	117	82	56	11	1	14
SWIM	24	24	24	0	0	0
TOMCATV	16	12	11	1	0	0
TURB3D	70	60	40	2	13	5
WAVE5	362	334	223	51	19	41
Total	1277	1097	836	117	47	97
Percentage		85.90%	76.21%	10.67%	4.28%	8.84%

nest counts in only one category. For example, if the innermost loop of a doubly nested loop can be analyzed precisely, but the outermost can not, the innermost loop will be counted in the "full" column, and the outermost will be counted in the "missing" column. Both loops are part of the total and estimated loops.

To validate our model, we have conducted experiments on the MIPS R10000 processor and the UltraSparc IIi processor. The R10k processor is a 4 issue out-of-order superscalar architecture, with 32 KB on-chip L1 cache and 1 MB–4 MB off-chip L2 cache. In one cycle, the R10K can execute up to two integer instructions, two floating point instruction, one memory operation and one branch. Both caches are two way set-associative. The UltraSparc is a 4 issue in-order superscalar processor. It can execute up to two integer, two floating point, one memory and one branch operation per cycle. The caches, both the 16 KB on-chip L1 cache and the 256 KB off-chip L2 cache, are direct mapped.

In the following figures we present the prediction accuracy of our strategy. The accuracy is computed as the predicted execution time divided by the measured execution time. For cache predictions the accuracy is computed as the predicted number of misses divided by the actual number of misses measured using hardware counters. Thus, in both cases, the closer to 100%, the better the prediction.

In Fig. 3 we present the accuracy of predictions using the indirect accesses model for unoptimized loops in the SpLib package. Each bar in the graphs represents the performance accuracy for one of the following data sets: a sparse matrix of 1128 × 1128 with 13360 non-zero elements (the left bar in each group), and a 20284 × 20284 sparse matrix with 452752 non-zero elements (the right bar in each group). Figure 3(a) displays prediction accuracy for the L1 cache with respect to actual cache misses measured using the hardware counters on the R10k processor. The accuracy is within 25% for most of the loops. The loop do1 in subroutine LUSOLT shows somewhat less accuracy, due the fact that our model does not account for conflict misses. Figure 3(b) shows execution time prediction accuracy. The accuracy of the prediction remains within 25% for most of the loops. The results for the optimized codes are somewhat worse, especially for the small data set. We attribute this to interloop reuse, which our indirect accesses model does not capture.

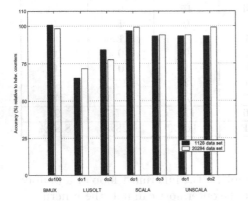

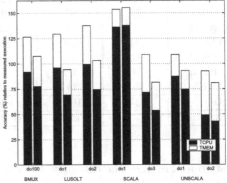

(a) L1 cache prediction using the indirect accesses model. Each bar represents a different data size.

(b) Execution time prediction using the indirect accesses model. For each loop the two bars represent different data sets.

Fig. 3. Prediction accuracy for loops in SpLib for two input data sets on the R10k

To predict the execution time for the SPECfp95 benchmarks we have used the following strategy: for all the loops that we can estimate (loops that do not contain I/O) we use the compiler to estimate the number of operations and then use (2) to obtain T_{CPU}. We also estimate the number of cache misses, for both levels of cache, using both the stack distances model and the indirect accesses model. If the stack distances model cannot be applied because not enough compile-time information is available, we apply the indirect accesses model. We convert the number of misses into execution time using (3). To get the overall figures for the benchmarks, we multiply the predicted execution time for each loop by the number of times it is executed, and then sum these times to get the execution time. We compute the actual execution time similarly, using measured execution times for each loop.

In Fig. 4 we present the cache estimation accuracy for both levels of cache on the R10000 processor for a set of loops in the TOMCATV benchmark. The left bars (black) represent the actual number of cache misses measured using hardware counters, while the right bars (white), represent the predicted number of cache misses. The prediction is very accurate for most of the cases. The two exceptions, the prediction for loop do100 in the L1 cache does not capture all the inter-array conflict misses; and the prediction for loop do60 in the L2 cache does not capture some of the spatial locality. However, as we shall see in Fig. 5, it will not affect adversely the overall execution time.

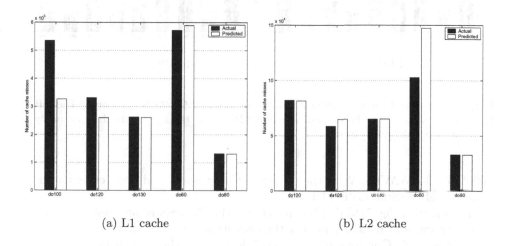

(a) L1 cache   (b) L2 cache

Fig. 4. Cache prediction accuracy for the TOMCATV benchmark on the R10k

We present results for codes optimized using the default level of optimization for the native compiler, which is O3 for the SparcWorks Fortran compiler and O2 for the MipsPro Fortran compiler. In Fig. 5 we present prediction accuracy for the SPEC95fp benchmarks. For each benchmark we show two bars, one which uses the indirect memory access estimation model (left), and the other one which uses the stack distances model (right). The two sections of each bar represent the percentage of CPU execution time and the percentage of memory hierarchy access time, respectively.

The results in Fig. 5(a) show prediction accuracy for the R10k processor. The indirect accesses model does not perform well in these codes since it does not account for much of the reuse present in dense computations. The stack distances model prediction (right bars) is, for most of the benchmarks within 20% of the actual execution time. The three exceptions, HYDRO2D, SU2COR and WAVE5 exhibit interloop reuse and our compile time model does not capture it at the present time. However, we have used a run-time implementation of the stack distances model to quantify the amount of interloop reuse, and with that method the prediction accuracy was 142% for HYDRO2D, 108% for SU2COR

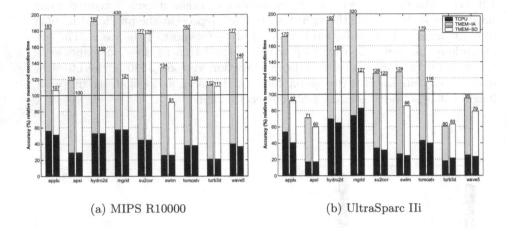

(a) MIPS R10000   (b) UltraSparc IIi

Fig. 5. Execution time prediction accuracy for the SPECfp95 benchmarks. The left bars show results using the indirect access model, while the right bars show accuracy using the stack distances model

and 110% for WAVE5. With those figures, the average prediction error for the entire set of benchmarks is 14%.

The chart in Fig. 5(b) displays results for the UltraSparc processor. For this processor we tend to under-predict the execution time, the average prediction error being 27%. One reason is that both levels of cache on this processor are direct mapped. Since our compiler model works for fully associative caches, there are many conflict misses that we do not capture. However, there are methods such as the one presented in [15], that allow approximating the number of cache misses for a set associative cache from the number of misses for a fully associative cache. Again, using the run-time implementation of the stack distances model, the average prediction error for the entire set of benchmarks on the processor drops to 20%.

4   Related Work

The need for good tools to estimate the application performance has been, and continues to be, high on the desire list of many application developers and compiler writers. While most of the performance prediction estimates have relied on simulations, there have been a few attempts to predict performance at compile time, mostly for applications running on multiprocessor systems. We summarize a few of these attempts, and explain how our work makes use of those results and how our work contrasts with some of the other methods.

Saavedra et al. [21,20,19] has done extensive work in the area of performance prediction for uniprocessors. In [21], the authors present the microbenchmarking concept to measure architectural parameters. We use the same microbenchmarking approach to estimate operation costs (including intrinsic functions) and cache latencies. In [20], they present an abstract machine model that characterizes the architecture and the compiler. Their early model does not consider memory hierarchy effects. They do consider such effects in [19], but not using compile-time prediction. Their estimation of the number of cache misses relies on the measurements for the SPEC92 benchmarks presented in [13].

Sarkar [22] presents a counter-based approach to determine the average execution time and the variance in execution time for programs. His approach relies on a *program database* to collect information about execution frequencies of basic blocks. However, in estimating the execution time of the program, he assumes known basic block costs. We could use the same control flow based method to count frequencies of execution for the basic blocks, including their optimizations to minimize the number of counters; however we also would need to compute the basic block costs, and the memory hierarchy penalties. We could create the program database from our symbolic expressions.

Fahringer [10,9,11] describes P^3T, a performance estimation tool. He uses the Vienna Fortran Compilation System as an interactive parallelizing compiler, and the *WeightFinder* and P^3T tools to feedback performance information to both the compiler and the programmer. While our goals are similar, the works differ in the approach taken. Fahringer uses pattern matching benchmarking based on a library of kernels to estimate execution time. A program is parsed to detect existing kernels and pre-measured run-times for the discovered kernels are accumulated to yield the overall execution time. The prediction relies heavily on the quality and completeness of the kernel library. To estimate cache behavior the author classifies the array accesses with respect to cache reuse. An estimated upper bound of the number of cache lines accessed inside a loop is computed. Misses for loops can be aggregated for predicting procedures and entire programs.

We cannot readily compare the accuracies of the two methods, as Fahringer presents experimental results for HPF programs only and, therefore, uses message passing, while our work is targeted to programs running on shared memory machines.

Ghosh *et al.* [14] have introduced the *Cache Miss Equations* (CMEs) as a mathematical framework that precisely represents cache misses in a loop nest. They count the cache misses in a code segment by analyzing the number of solutions present for a system of linear Diophantine equations extracted from reuse vectors, where each solution corresponds to a potential cache miss. Although solving these linear systems is difficult, the authors claim that mathematical techniques for manipulating the equations allow them to relatively easily compute and/or reduce the number of possible solutions without solving the equations.

One of the first attempts to use profiling information in order to improve compiler optimizations was trace scheduling for very long instruction word (VLIW) processors [12,7], which uses profile data to optimize execution of the most probable code execution paths. More recently, Chang *et al.* [6] have developed an optimizing compiler that uses profiling information to assist classic code optimizations. The compiler contains two new components, an execution profiler and a profile-based code optimizer. The execution profiler inserts probes into the input program, executes the input program for several inputs, accumulates profile information, and supplies this information to the optimizer. The profile-based code optimizer uses the profile information to expose new optimization opportunities that are not visible to traditional global optimization methods.

5   Conclusions

The prediction environment presented in this paper integrates a compiler derived model with run-time instrumentation to estimate performance for scientific codes. We have presented the compiler-driven performance prediction model, which although very simple, is able to predict performance of codes in the SPECfp95 benchmark suite with 20% error margin on complex architectures. This model can also be extended to shared multiprocessor codes because our compiler is a parallelizing source-to-source translator.

We use the results of the compiler-driven performance prediction in two ways. First, the compiler can use the performance prediction results to guide optimizations. Examples are deciding if a parallel loop is worth running in parallel based on the sequential execution time and the overhead to run the loop in parallel. Second, the performance prediction results can be displayed using performance visualization tools and the performance data can be related back to the high level source code based on information provided by the compiler.

References

1. T. Ball and J. R. Larus. Branch prediction for free. In *Proceedings of the ACM SIGPLAN Conference on Programming Languages Design and Implementation '93*, pages 300–313, 1993.
2. U. Banerjee. *Dependence analysis*. Kluwer Academic Publishers, 1997.
3. W. Blume, R. Doallo, R. Eigenmann, J. Grout, J. Hoeflinger, T. Lawrence, J. Lee, D. Padua, Y. Paek, W. Pottenger, L. Rauchwerger, and P. Tu. Parallel Programming with Polaris. *IEEE Computer*, December 1996.
4. R. Bramley, D. Gannon, T. Stuckey, J. Villacis, J. Balasubramanian, E. Akman, F. Breg, S. Diwan, and M. Govindaraju. *The Linear System Analyzer*, chapter PSEs. IEEE, 1998.
5. C. Cascaval and D. A. Padua. Compile-time cache misses estimation using stack distances. In preparation.
6. P. P. Chang, S. A. Mahlke, and W.-M. W. Hwu. Using profile information to assist classic compiler code optimizations. *Software Practice and Experience*, 21(12):1301–1321, December 1991.
7. R. P. Colwell, R. P. Nix, J. J. O'Donnell, D. B. Papworth, and P. K. Rodman. A VLIW architecture for a trace scheduling compiler. In *Proceedings of ASPLOS II*, pages 180–192, Palo Alto, CA, October 1987.
8. L. DeRose, Y. Zhang, and D. A. Reed. SvPablo: A multi-language performance analysis system. In *10th International Conference on Computer Performance Evaluation - Modelling Techniques and Tools - Performance Tools'98*, pages 352–355, Palma de Mallorca, Spain, September 1998.

9. T. Fahringer. Evaluation of benchmark performance estimation for parallel Fortran programs on massively parallel SIMD and MIMD computers. In *IEEE Proceedings of the 2nd Euromicro Workshop on Parallel and Distributed Processing*, Malaga, Spain, January 1994.

10. T. Fahringer. *Automatic Performance Prediction of Parallel Programs*. Kluwer Academic Press, 1996.

11. T. Fahringer. Estimating cache performance for sequential and data parallel programs. Technical Report TR 97-9, Institute for Software Technology and Parallel Systems, Univ. of Vienna, Vienna, Austria, October 1997.

12. J. A. Fisher. Trace scheduling: A technique for global microcode compaction. *IEEE Transactions on Computers*, C(30):478–490, July 1981.

13. J. D. Gee, M. D. Hill, and A. J. Smith. Cache performance of the SPEC92 benchmark suite. In *Proceedings of the IEEE Micro*, pages 17–27, August 1993.

14. S. Ghosh, M. Martonosi, and S. Malik. Precise Miss Analysis for Program Transformations with Caches of Arbitrary Associativity. In *Proceedings of ASPLOS VIII*, San Jose, CA, October 1998.

15. M. D. Hill and A. J. Smith. Evaluating associativity in cpu caches. *IEEE Transactions on Computers*, 38(12):1612–1630, December 1989.

16. Y. Kang, M. Huang, S.-M. Yoo, Z. Ge, D. Keen, V. Lam, P. Pattnaik, and J. Torrellas. FlexRAM: Toward an advanced intelligent memory system. In *International Conference on Computer Design (ICCD)*, October 1999.

17. R. L. Mattson, J. Gecsei, D. Slutz, and I. Traiger. Evaluation techniques for storage hierarchies. *IBM Systems Journal*, 9(2), 1970.

18. J. Reilly. SPEC95 Products and Benchmarks. *SPEC Newsletter*, September 1995.

19. R. Saavedra and A. Smith. Measuring cache and tlb performance and their effect on benchmark run times. *IEEE Transactions on Computers*, 44(10):1223–1235, October 1995.

20. R. H. Saavedra-Barrera and A. J. Smith. Analysis of benchmark characteristics and benchmark performance prediction. Technical Report CSD 92-715, Computer Science Division, UC Berkeley, 1992.

21. R. H. Saavedra-Barrera, A. J. Smith, and E. Miya. Machine characterization based on an abstract high-level language machine. *IEEE Transactions on Computers*, 38(12):1659–1679, December 1989.

22. V. Sarkar. Determining average program execution times and their variance. In *Proceedings of the ACM SIGPLAN Conference on Programming Languages Design and Implementation '89*, pages 298–312, Portland, Oregon, July 1989.

23. R. A. Sugumar and S. G. Abraham. Set-associative cache simulation using generalized binomial trees. *ACM Trans. Comp. Sys.*, 13(1), 1995.

24. J. G. Thompson and A. J. Smith. Efficient (stack) algorithms for analysis of write-back and sector memories. *ACM Transactions on Computer Systems*, 7(1), 1989.

25. W.-H. Wang and J.-L. Baer. Efficient trace-driven simulation methods for cache performance analysis. *ACM Transactions on Computer Systems*, 9(3), 1991.

Designing the Agassiz Compiler for Concurrent Multithreaded Architectures

B. Zheng[1], J.Y. Tsai[2], B.Y. Zang[3], T. Chen[1], B. Huang[3], J.H. Li[3], Y.H. Ding[3]
J. Liang[1] , Y.Zhen[1], P.C. Yew[1], and C.Q. Zhu[1]

[1] Computer Sci. and Eng. Department, University of Minnesota, MPLS, MN 55108
[2] Hwelett-Packard Company Cupertino, CA 95014
[3] Institute of Parallel Processing, Fudan University, Shanghai, P.R. China

Abstract. In this paper, we present the overall design of the Agassiz compiler [1]. The Agassiz compiler is an integrated compiler targeting the concurrent multithreaded architectures [12,13]. These architectures can exploit both loop-level and instruction-level parallelism for general-purpose applications (such as those in SPEC benchmarks). They also support various kinds of control and data speculation, runtime data dependence checking, and fast synchronization and communication mechanisms. The Agassiz compiler has a loop-level parallelizing compiler as its front-end and an instruction-level optimizing compiler as its back-end to support such architectures. In this paper, we focus on the IR design of the Agassiz compiler and describe how we support the front-end analyses, various optimization techniques, and source-to-source translation.

1. Introduction

VLSI technology will allow hundreds of millions of transistors on a single chip in a couple of years. Exploiting parallelism at various granularity levels on a single chip for higher performance will soon become a reality, and even a necessity, for both uniprocessors and multiprocessors. As a matter of fact, with the recent introduction of concurrent multithreaded architectures [12,13], the line dividing traditional uniprocessors and multiprocessors for single-chip architectures has gradualy disappeared. A lot of parallel processing technologies, including parallelizing compiler technology, can be leveraged and extended to the more general-purpose applications typified by the industry-standard SPEC benchmark programs. In those applications, the dominant programming languages are still Fortran and C because of their requirement of high performance.

The traditional parallel processing technology has primarily been focussed on scientific applications dominated by a large number of floating operations and well-structured arrays and loops. To extend this technology to general-purpose applications, we need to face several new challenges which are common in those applications. They include: (1) a large number of integer operations; (2) a large number of pointers and very flexible data structures; (3) many *do-while* loops and *do-across* loops; (4) many loops with a small number of loop iterations, or a small loop body. Many of these challenges cannot be met by the compiler or the processor architecture alone. It requires a careful study and evaluation on the tradeoff between architecture and compiler design. It also requires aggressive exploitation of both instruction-level and loop-level parallelism.

L. Carter and J. Ferrante (Eds.): LCPC'99, LNCS 1863, pp. 380–398, 2000.
© Springer-Verlag Berlin Heidelberg 2000

In this paper, we focus on the design of the Agassiz compiler, which is an integrated compiler targeting concurrent multithreaded architectures (such as Multiscalar [12] and Superthreaded processors [13, 14]). These architectures support both loop-level (LLP) and instruction-level (ILP) parallelism. They also support various kinds of control and data speculation, run-time data dependence checking for complicated pointers and data structures, and very fast communication and synchronization mechanisms.

The Agassiz compiler has been designed with several goals in mind:

- Support both loop-level and instruction-level parallelization. It includes a front-end loop-level source-to-source parallelizing compiler, and a back-end instruction-level optimizing compiler. Each of those compilers has its own intermediate representations (IR). A mechanism (see Section 2) is provided to integrated both front-end and back-end compilers to produce highly optimized code. This mechanism also allows other front-end and back-end compilers to be integrated into the Agassiz compiler.
- Support multiple languages, such as C and Fortran. It has two levels of intermediate representation (IR) in the front-end: the Raw-IR which is more language-specific, and the Real-IR which is more language independent. They facilitate program analysis and optimization while maintaining useful language-specific information for more efficient analysis and optimization (see Section 2).
- Support large applications, such as SPEC benchmarks, which might have hundreds of procedures and tens of thousands of lines of code. Time- and space-efficient algorithms have to be used to control the total analysis time and the IR size. Furthermore, extensive interprocedural analysis and optimization have to be performed.
- Support end-to-end compilation from the source code to the final target machine code generation for high performance. Potential overhead incurred during the loop parallelization, such as during induction variable optimization and loop transformation, are marked in the IR. This allows such overhead to be removed and the loop cleaned up when it is determined to be unparallelizable in later compiler passes.
- Provide robust and easy-to-use components to support collaborative development effort. Our kernel has been designed with a high-level intermediate representation, an interface to back-end compilers, and layers of functionality. Data structures in the kernel are encapsulated by C++ classes. Any access to these data structures is under the control of a consistency-maintenance mechanism. We also add a built-in pointer-specific error detection mechanism to avoid potential dangling pointers and memory leakage. Layers of functionality make the kernel easy to use for those who work on the compiler.

In this paper, we present the overall design of the Agassiz compiler with an emphasis on (1) the design of its IR to facilitate front-end analyses, optimizations, and source-to-source translation, and (2) its analysis and optimization techniques to parallelize C and Fortran programs for concurrent multithreaded architectures.

The remainder of this paper is organized as follows. In Section 2, we present an overview of the Agassiz compiler. Section 3 addresses some issues in designing our program IR, while Section 4 discusses its implementation issues. We describe the implemented analysis and optimization techniques that are important to support concurrent multithreaded code generation in Section 5. Some related works are discussed in Section 6. Finally, Section 7 draws conclusions and discusses ongoing works.

2. Overview of the Agassiz Compiler

As shown in Figure 1, the Agassiz Compiler currently has six major components: (1) a parser to generate a language-independent intermediate representation (Real-IR) from sources; (2) a front-end analyzer; (3) a parallel source code generator targeting concurrent multithreaded processors, or shared-memory multiprocessors; (4) an unparser to generate annotated source from the IR; (5) a high-level information (HLI) generator; and (6) a back-end ILP (instruction-level parallelism) optimizing compiler (based on gcc).

The parser first converts a C or a Fortran program into a language-specific intermediate representation, called Raw-IR. It uses a high-level abstract syntax tree that preserves all the language dependent features in the program. The main purpose of using Raw-IR is to separate the language-dependent parsing and semantic checking from later analyses and transformations. It then tries to eliminate some but not all language specific constructs, such as the side-effect expressions in C programs and the *entry* statements in Fortran programs, and convert the Raw-IR to a more language-independent internal representation, called Real-IR. During the process, it also tries to "normalize" the intraprocedural control flow in the programs to facilitate later analysis. For example, it will convert a code section with a backward *goto* statement into a loop structure; rearrange code segments to reduce the number of *goto* statements; eliminate *entry* statements as mentioned above. It also links global symbols used in different source files.

The front-end analyzer then performs interprocedural pointer analysis and scalar data flow analysis. It also performs scalar optimizations to improve the code, and to prepare for the later parallelization. These optimizations include control-flow and data flow dead code elimination, constant folding, constant propagation, copy propagation, indirection removal, non-zero-iteration loop recognition, loop invariant code motion, and induction variable substitution. The output of the front-end analyzer is an optimized program with annotated data flow information, which could then be used in later phases.

The parallelizer, which currently is targeted for concurrent multithreaded architectures, performs further analyses to generate parallel codes. The analyses performed in this stage include privatizable scalar analysis, data dependence analysis, and *Doall* and *Doacross* loop analysis. It will then generate parallelized code for the target machines. The parallelized code, still in its Real-IR form, can be either fed into the unparser or the HLI generator. The unparser generates an annotated source program. The HLI generator, on the other hand, exports important high-level information, such as alias information, loop-carried data dependence information and interprocedural Ref/Mod information to a file with a standardized format, called HLI

(High-Level program Information) [4]. It can then be imported into and used by the back-end ILP optimizing compiler.

The back-end ILP compiler is currently a modified version of gcc. It first parses the annotated source program and generates its internal representation RTL. It then augments its RTL with the imported HLI information. An extensive utility library has been developed to facilitate the use and the maintenance of HLI [4]. It provides utility functions to inquire and to update the associated HLI without the need to know the detail of the HLI format. The analysis and optimization algorithms in the original gcc are modified so that they can operate on the extended RTL and utilize the HLI information. The back-end optimizer finally produces executable codes for the target machines, currently an execution-driven simulator based on the SimpleScalar [3] for the Superthreaded processors and many existing superscalar processors.

3. The Design of IR

The target programming languages as well as the intended compiler analyses and optimizations drive the design of the compiler internal representation. In this section, we focus on issues related to the IR (i.e. Real-IR) design for front-end analyses and optimizations. We also address how our IR supports multiple languages and some software engineering considerations.

3.1 Choosing an Appropriate Intermediate Representation Level

We use abstract syntax trees (AST) to represent the statements and the expressions in a program. The AST representation allows us to represent high-level control structures, such as loops and branches, explicitly by their components. For example, we represent a do-loop by its index, step, lower bound, upper bound, and loop-body. Using AST representation supports structure-based (or syntax-based) analysis techniques as well as loop-oriented parallelization.

We also retain the high-level operators defined in the source language in our IR. An alternative approach is to encode the high-level operators into simpler operators, such as the operators used in machine instructions. For example, SUIF encodes the assignment operator into operators *ldc*, *cpy*, *lod*, *memcpy* and *str*, according to the semantics of the assignment operations. Encoding the assignment operator this way simplifies the machine code generation, but complicates the high-level analyses and optimizations. For example, finding all dereferences to a pointer p involves only a search of all expression "*p" in an IR that preserves high-level operators. However, if the dereference operators are encoded into operators *lod*, *memcpy* and *str*, finding the dereferences to the pointer p becomes more complicated. Furthermore, if later analysis determines that the pointer p definitely points to j, we may want to replace all dereferences to p with j in the IR. Performing this optimization in an IR retaining the dereference operator is simply a replacement of all "*p" with j. However,performing similar optimization to the statement "$i = {}^*p$" using a lower-level IR, we need to change the whole instruction from "*lod* $i = p$" to "*cpy* $i = j$". This change is not local to the operand "*p"; it affects the encoding of its higher-level instructions ($i = {}^*p$).

384   B. Zheng et al.

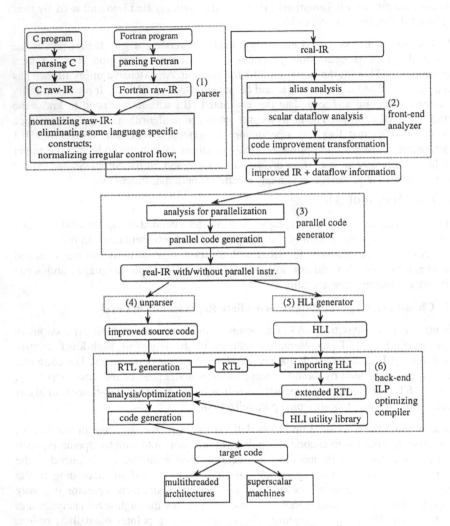

Figure 1: An overview of the Agassiz Compiler

Source code	SUIF-1 IR
int i, j, *p, *q;	
i = 2;	ldc i , 2
i = j;	cpy i , j
i = *p;	lod i , p
*q = *p;	memcpy q , p
*q = j;	str q , j

Figure 2: An Example Program and Its SUIF-1 IR

Our IR retains variable accesses, array and structure references, and complicated array/structure access expressions, such as *s.a[1].f*, without dissecting them into simpler expressions using temporary variables. In doing this, we retain variable type, array size, array dimension, and structure field types information in the IR. Such information is critical for efficient scalar/array data flow analysis, data dependence analysis, and alias analysis.

3.2 Supporting Multiple Languages

Supporting multiple languages, such as C and Fortran, is also an important consideration in the design of our IR. Our IR is expressive enough to capture the details of all the language constructs defined in the target languages. However, to simplify later analyses and optimizations, we avoid putting unnecessary language specific constructs into IR while retaining only critical language specific information. The following C- and Fortran-specific language features are considered:

- Loop structures. The C language provides three loop structures: *for-loop*, *while-loop* and *do-while-loop*. The only loop construct in the Fortran is *do-loop*. Our real-IR contains three loop structures: Fortran-like *do-loop* and C-like *while-loop* and *do-while-loop*. If a *for-loop* has an index with a lower bound, an upper bound and a step, and the index is not modified inside the loop, the *for-loop* is converted into a *do-while-loop*. Otherwise, it is converted to a *while-loop*. This transformation preserves the high-level information in the original *for-loop*.

- Side-effect operators. Our IR does not include any side-effect operators because they may complicate later analyses and optimizations. All expressions with side-effect operators are transformed into equivalent expressions without side-effect operators. This is done in the raw-IR normalization phase.

- Parameter passing modes for procedures. The parameters are passed-in-by-value in C, but passed-in-by-reference in Fortran. Theoretically, it is possible to use pointers as passed-in-by-value parameters to replace the passed-in-by-reference parameters. However, in later analyses, a passed-in-by-value pointer parameter can be treated very differently from a passed-in-by-reference parameter. For instance, in alias analysis, the passed-in-by-reference induced aliases cannot be changed during an execution of a subroutine while the pointer-induced aliases can. Using pointers to replace passed-in-by-reference parameters can cause more pseudo aliases, especially when a less precise alias analysis algorithm is chosen due to efficiency consideration. For this reason, we keep the above two parameter passing modes in our IR.

- Goto statements. Fortran provides *goto*, *compute-goto*, and *assign-goto* statements while C has only *goto* statements. A *compute-goto* statement can be transformed into nested *goto* statements. Thus, we only provide *goto* and *assign-goto* representations in IR. Furthermore, to simplify later analyses and optimizations, there is a control-flow *normalization* phase during the conversion from Raw-IR to Real-IR which eliminates *goto* statements as much possible. It also marks a program segment with *un-normalized goto* statements and *goto* targets as an unstructured program segment. This allows later analyses to apply different algorithms to analyze well-structured program segments and unstructured program segments.

- I/O statements. The I/O statements in Fortran can be very complicated. To avoid handling such I/O statements in the front-end, our real-IR provides a high-level construct to represent the variables read/written in the I/O statements, and mask the detail of these I/O statements in the later analysis.

- Storage overlapping. Fortran has the *common* and *equivalence* constructs to specify the storage overlapping among different variables. C has the *union* constructs for the same purpose. Our IR represents these constructs in a uniform way. It uses a *(block-name, offset)* pair to represent an element of the above constructs.

- Entry statement. An *entry* statement in Fortran is used to specify an additional entry point of a subroutine. To simply analyses and optimizations, we eliminate *entry* statements by creating a version of the function for each entry statement during the control flow normalization.

- Alternative return. A Fortran subroutine with *alternative return* statements is transformed into an equivalent subroutine without *alternative return* statements. This is done by introducing an additional parameter to the subroutine which indicates a program point in the caller as a return point of the subroutine call. An *if* statement is also added immediately after each call-site to the subroutine. This *if* statement issues a *goto* to a specific return point according to the return value of the additional parameter.

3.3 Supporting Source-to-Source Translation

Supporting source-to-source translation also imposes additional requirement to the IR. First, we want to reduce the machine and other environment dependent features in our generated source program for portability. A Compatible Compiler Preprocessor (CPP) may inject machine and compiler dependent features to a program in three ways: (1) inclusion of system header files; (2) expanding system dependent macros; and (3) including or excluding parts of the program according to system dependent preprocessing directives. To identify the system dependent features included in the system header files, we attach the name of the header file on each line inlined from the header file in IR. This allows the unparser to filter them out and keep them from being included in the generated source program. Second, we want the output source program looks similar to the original source program for readability. Our IR records the file name of each subroutine so that the unparser can output one source file for each original source file.

3.4 Software Engineering Considerations

We implement the IR in C++ because it allows data encapsulation. Layers of functionality can be built on top of each class, thus enable easy access and manipulation of the data structures while maintaining their consistency. However, as in C, the pointer mechanism in C++ can cause two most common errors in such programs: dangling pointers and dangling memory objects. In a large software program which is being implemented and maintained by many people, pointers can become *dangling* when the objects they point to are somehow freed in some other part of the software. A dereference to a dangling pointer can cause an error which is very difficult to detect, especially when the free operation is far from the dereference operator in the program. A dangling memory object is a dynamically allocated memory object which is no longer reachable because there is no pointer points to it anymore. A dangling memory object can waste memory space, which can become a problem when we are dealing with very large application programs. To help avoiding these two errors, we provide high-level classes to manipulate pointer data structures so that the users cannot use unconstrained pointers on IR objects (see Section 4).

Our IR also provides an *Annotation* class (as in SUIF) for extensibility. Users can attach other information to any IR element by adding annotations to it. However, it is the users' responsibility to maintain the consistency of the annotated information.

4. Implementation and Evaluation of IR

In this section, we discuss some implementation issues of our IR. We also describe the utility functions provided in our IR to facilitate program analysis and optimizations. We also present some preliminary experimental data regarding our IR implementation.

4.1 Detecting Pointer-Related Errors

We apply the reference counting technique [10] to detect pointer-related errors such as dangling pointers and memory leakage. This technique requires an additional field, *reference count*, for each object that may be pointed to by pointers. The *reference count* records the number of pointers pointing to the object, thus indicating whether the object is in use or not.

To facilitate this error detection mechanism, we include a *reference count* field in our base class, *AgassizBase*. All other classes that require a *reference count* are derived from this super class. We then design a class template *Pointer<A>*, where parameter A is a derived class of *AgassizBase*, to manipulate the reference count. We refer an object in the class *Pointer<A>* as an *agassiz-pointer* and an object of type "A * " as a C++ *raw-pointer*. The only data field encapsulated in the template *Pointer<A>* is *mpoPointer*, which is a raw-pointer of type "A*". This template keeps track of the reference count for the data structure being pointed to by its member *mpoPointer*, and allocates and deallocates the storage accordingly. More specifically, when a value is assigned to or created through *mpoPointer*, the reference count of its old points-to target is decreased by one while the reference count of its new points-to target is incremented by one. Dynamic objects are allocated via member functions in the template. These dynamic objects are automatically deallocated by the template when the object's reference count becomes zero, thus avoiding memory leakage. Furthermore, an object will not be deleted unless its reference count becomes zero.

Not deleting an Agassiz object with a non-zero reference count can avoid dangling pointers

Another class called *GenericPointer* is designed to replace the use of type "void *" in our programs. Type *"void *"* is a frequently used type in C++ because it provides the flexibility to define a pointer that can points to objects of different classes. To provide similar capability as type "void *", the class *GenericPointer* encapsulates a raw-pointer to an object of the class *AgassizBase*. It also manipulates the reference count of the *AgassizBase* object it points to as the class template *Pointer<A>* does. Because the data field in *GenericPointer* is a raw-pointer to the class *AgassizBase*, it can point to an object of any class derived from *AgassizBase*.

To allow the above pointer manipulating mechanism to fully control the pointers used in IR, all IR classes must observe the following rules: (1) Agassiz-pointer classes are used to replace C++ raw-pointer types; (2) The class *GenericPointer* is used to replace raw-pointer type *"void *"*; (3) All other classes are derived from the super class *AgassizBase*.

4.2 Discussion

The above reference count approach allows us to effectively detect dangling pointers and memory leakage. However, it also adds some overhead to the system. First, the reference count field and its manipulation add some memory and run-time overhead. Second, calling a member function in our IR may incur a longer call-chain comparing to an approach without such an error detecting mechanism. Third, such an approach instills a stricter programming style which requires some extra programming effort. However, we believe such extra effort have been more than paid off by less debugging time caused by the pointer problems. We now use an example to illustrate the particular programming style needed under this approach.

In general, classes in our real-IR can be divided into two categories: content classes and pointer classes. A content class is a derived class of the class *AgassizBase*. It provides holders for a program entity and is not visible to IR users. Each content class has a corresponding pointer class. The pointer class for a content class *A* is a derived class of the template class *Pointer<A>*. This pointer class defines an interface to access content class A and is visible to IR users. Figure 3 compares an implementation of the class *Symbol* using agassiz pointers with an implementation using regular C++ pointers. As can be seen from the figure, to access the name attribute of a symbol, our approach requires two function calls while the regular approach requires only one. Furthermore, maintaining the consistency between class SymbolContent and class Symbol requires extra programming effort. This is because the class *Symbol* has a similar member function set as in the class *SymbolContent*. A member function in the class *SymbolContent* provides the implementation while its corresponding member function in the class *Symbol* provides an interface to access that implementation. One way to reduce the programming effort is to implement a utility that generates the correponding pointer class for each content class defined in our IR. However, we not yet found it to be a problem since it usually needs to be done only once for each class.

Using agassiz-pointers	Using C++ raw-pointers
class SymbolContent : public AgassizBase{	class Symbol {
private: String mesgName;	private: String mesgName;
protected: String mfsgName()	public: String mfsgName()
{return mesgName;}	{return mesgName;}
};	};
class Symbol : public Pointer<SymbolContent> {	
public: String mfsgName()	
{return mpoPointer->	
mfsgName();}	Symbol *eoSymbol;
};	eoSymbol->mfsgName();
Symbol eoSymbol;	
eoSymbol.mfsgName();	

Figure 3. Comparing the agassiz-pointer approach with the regular C++ pointer approach

4.3 Utility Functions

Many high-level utility functions are implemented through member functions in the IR classes. They provide programmers with a powerful and easy-to-use environment, and help to enforce consistency among various data structures. These utility functions can be divided into four categories:

(1) Component inquiry. These utility functions provide a compositional view of each class, regardless of how each component is implemented in the class. For instance, the *IfStmt* class has member functions to support the retrieval of the *if-condition, then-part* and *else-part* of an *if* statement.

(2) Data structure traversal. We use a set of classes to implement the traversal of data structure collections. The class *IterBase* is a common super class for these classes. It defines a common interface for all traversals, including initializing and resetting a traversal, getting the current node, and moving to the next node.

(3) Program transformation. Program components may be added, deleted, duplicated or moved, during program optimization and transformation. Utilities to support these transformations are built in the IR classes. These utilities enforce the consistency of the IR during transformations. For example, a member function *mfoCopy* is built in the class *Procedure* for procedure cloning. It duplicates the body and the local symbol tables of the procedure. Our IR also allows users to tag the newly modified IR components and undo the modification later according to the specific tag. It allows users to coordinate the program analyses and transformations among different compiler phases for more efficient output code. For example, induction variable substitution may generate a lot of unnecessary integer operations which could be a major overhead for a small loop if the loop is determined to be not parallelizable later.

The ability to undo induction variable substitution creates much more efficient output code.

(4) Debugging assistance. A member function *mfvBrowse* provides a well formated text output of a class components while another member function *mfvUnparse* prints out the C or Fortran source code of the class. These functions can help programmers to keep track of the content of a data structure without knowing its implementation detail. At the program level, these functions can dump the IR of the entire program to a text file or produce a source program.

4.4 Evaluating IR Design

It is not easy to evaluate the design of an IR quantitatively, especially if we want to take its functionality, user support and programmability into consideration. Nevertheless, we present here two quantitative measures to evaluate our IR design. One metric is the time required to generate the IR for a program, including the parsing time and the cleanup time. Another metric is the IR size for a program. Because we take an object-oriented approach using a pointer-error detection mechanism, we want to make sure that such an approach does not substantially increase the size and the time to generate the IR. Also, our cleanup phase may duplicate code segments to *normalize* control-flow, we need to make sure that such normalization does not substantially increase the real-IR size.

We compare our Agassiz Compiler with SUIF-1 on some C and Frotran programs from the SPEC95 benchmark suite. Both compilers are compiled by GCC optimization option –O2. The collected data are shown in Table 1. These data were collected on a 200 MHZ Intel Pentium Pro machine with 128MB main memory running Linux 2.0.30. The time shown in the table is in seconds while the size is in Kbytes.

As can be seen from Table 1, the Agassiz IR generation is generally faster than the SUIF IR generation. For all of the programs except the program 145.fppp, the time used in creating SUIF IR (in the second column) is as much as 3 ~ 10 times the time used in creating Agassiz real-IR (in the fourth column). It may be due to two main reasons. First, the interface between SUIF passes are files. A significant portion of the SUIF IR generation time is system time dedicated to I/O. Thus, the SUIF IR generation time could be substantially reduced by modifying its passes so that they communicate via internal data structures, as has been done in current SUIF-2. Second, the Agassiz IR generation time includes the time of the cleanup phase. This cleanup phase not only normalizes the program constructs as SUIF does, but also normalizes the program control flow structures which the SUIF does not perform. Because a program with normalized control flow generally allows more efficient algorithms to be used in later phases, the cleanup time will be amortized by the later analyses. For these reasons, we also show the user portion of the SUIF IR generation time (the third column), and further divide the user portion of the time in the Agassiz IR generation into *parsing time* (the fifth column) and *cleanup time* (the sixth column). As indicated Table 1, the Agassiz parsing time is smaller than the user portion of the SUIF IR generation time for all programs. However, if we compare the user portion of the IR generation time, the Agassiz compiler is slower than SUIF in eight out of 14 programs.

Table 1. Comparing Agassiz with SUIF-1 in speed and IR sizes (The SUIF-1 IR was generated by executing command "scc –v -suif-link -.sln file-names").

Programs	Time (sec.)					IR Sizes (KB)		
	SUIF		Agassiz			SUIF	Agassiz	
	Tot. = User + Sys.	User	Tot. = User + Sys.	User = Parsing + Cleanup		IR	Before Cleanup (raw-IR)	After Cleanup (real-IR)
				Parsing	Cleanup			
099.go	303.33	41.35	103.10	15.39	86.57	15,448	21,096	38,884
124. m88ksim	863.03	99.29	104.24	40.14	62.00	11,224	57,832	68,096
129. compress	41.77	6.97	4.43	2.65	1.71	940	2,692	3,108
130.li	136.21	21.26	26.08	8.16	17.52	3,980	12,244	15,672
132.ijpeg	396.19	101.04	100.34	27.87	71.19	11,284	35,168	49,096
147.vortex	968.65	431.12	223.55	70.61	150.36	28,796	75,044	89,372
101.tomcatv	5.26	1.44	1.01	0.15	0.8	392	136	344
102.swim	12.98	1.87	1.96	0.46	1.5	468	296	712
103.su2cor	71.36	5.56	22.92	2.8	20.05	2,040	1,576	6,640
104.hydro2d	56.70	10.69	10.41	2.78	7.53	1,676	1,520	3,432
107.mgrid	18.41	6.26	4.07	0.73	3.32	784	464	1,368
125.turb3d	54.99	8.94	9.36	2.24	7.07	2,116	1,200	2,804
145.fppp	97.18	22.82	207.36	4.28	199.02	3,008	2,068	25,096
146.wave5	254.48	29.32	54.43	12.02	41.10	5,596	6,348	16,588

Table 1 also shows that the Agassiz real-IR is usually larger than the SUIF IR, ranging from approximately 1 ~ 8 times larger. Two main reasons account for the larger sizes. First, our pointer-error detection mechanism incurs storage overhead in the data structures. Second, the cleanup phase may increase the IR size by duplicating codes to normalize control flow structures. We are looking into the IR size issue and hope to come up with strategies to reduce the size overhead further.

5. Analyses and Optimizations

In this section, we outline the analysis and optimization techniques currently implemented in the Agassiz compiler. These techniques are primarily for multithreaded code generation and back-end optimization. We also discuss how the IR supports these analyses and optimizations.

5.1 The Hierarchical Interprocedural Data Flow Analysis

The interprocedural data flow analysis in our compiler provides *factored use-def* (FUD) chains [16] for all data structures in a program. To collect precise FUD chains, alias analysis is indenspensible. Unlike other approaches which separate the alias analysis from the traditional scalar data flow analysis, we use a hierarchical approach to integrate them into a common unified framework.

We first classify the data structures in a program into two categories according to the possible maximum level of dereference to the data structures [1]:

- Recursive data structures. It is assumed to have an unlimited dereference level to a recursive data structure. In the definition of *"struct S { struct S *next; ...} p;"*, the variable *p* is a recursive data structure. An expression *"p.next->next->next"* represents a two-level dereference to *p*; A dereference with more levels can be constructed by appending more "->next" to the expression.
- Non-recursive data structures. The maximum dereference level to a non-recursive data structure is a constant value. We call this constant value the *pointer level* of the data structure. For example, a variable s in the definition *"struct { char *c; int v;} *s;"* has a pointer level of two because there can be up to two levels of dereference from the variable (*s->c). On the other hand, a variable *i* defined by *"int i"* is a variable with a zero pointer level and, thus, cannot be dereferenced.

Using the above classification, we can then separate the pointer analysis into two subproblems: (1) analysis for recursive data structures, and (2) analysis for non-recursive data structures. We further divide the analysis for non-recursive data structures into several subproblems. Each subproblem analyzes the data structures of a certain pointer level, and annotates the points-to targets of the data structures to their dereference expressions. Finally, we solve these subproblems by analyzing the data structures with the highest pointer level, and then use the result to analyze the data structures of the next lower pointer level until we reach the pointer level of zero. This subproblem ordering is based on the observation that (1) a dereference from a data structure p with a pointer level n results in an access to a data structure q pointed to by p; (2) without type-casting, the pointer level of q is less than n.

This hierarchical data flow analysis algorithm handles the pointer-induced aliasing in C and the parameter-induced aliasing in Fortran in a uniform way. Because reference parameters of a subroutine can be handled as pointers, we set the pointer level of the reference parameters to one. The analysis for pointer level one for a Fortran program propagates the actual parameters to the use of their corresponding formal parameters. This makes the use of actual parameters in the subroutines explicit, and hides the reference parameters to the analysis of pointer level zero.

Our data flow analysis algorithm is interprocedural and context-sensitive. We tag interprocedural data flow values with their call-chains, which are the call-graph paths along which the values are passed into the procedure. We parameterize the maximum length of the call-chains to control the context-sensitivity. This allows us to study its impact on the efficiency and the precision of the alias analysis. A more complete description of our data flow analysis algorithm is available in [17].

Our IR supports the hierarchical data flow analysis in several ways. Our study of eight SPEC95 CINT programs shows that an average of 38.73% pointer variables have

---

[1] In our discussion, if a field of a structure is dereferenced, we say the whole structure is also dereferenced.

initializers defining their initial values [9]. Ignoring these initial values causes unknown points-to values when they are used before explicit assignments assign new values to them, thus reducing the precision of the analysis. For this reason, variable initial values are not neglectable in the data flow analysis. The IR supports the initializer handling with two utilities One is the member function *mfoInitializerToAssignStmts* defined in the class *Variable*. It generates a list of assignment statements, each assigns an initial value to an element of the variable. Another member function *mfoInitializersToAssignStmts* is provided in the class *CompoundStmt*. It generates a list of assignment statements to model the effect of the initializers for all variables defined in the scope introduced by the *CompoundStmt*. Especially, when the *CompoundStmt* is the body of a *"main"* procedure, the assignments also include the initializers for all global variables. These utilities relieve the users from the language-specific detail for initializers.

Besides the initializer support, the IR also provides a good base for the hierarchical data flow analysis. First, it facilitates the grouping of data structures by their pointer levels. Second, not encoding the source language operators makes it straight forward to locate dereference expressions by searching operators "*", "->", and "[]". Finally, the compositional representation of the high-level program constructs make it easy to insert Φ-functions for those constructs, and to use the syntax-directed data flow equations to evaluate the fix-point data flow values.

5.2 Front-End Optimizations

The front-end optimization phase comes after the data flow analysis phase. It improves the effectiveness of the IR and the preciseness of the FUD chains. It also exposes more information for later analyses and optimizations. We first identify the optimizations that are important to later analyses and to multithreaded code generation. These include traditional optimizations such as constant folding, constant propagation, copy propagation, control-flow dead code (or unreachable branch) elimination, data flow dead code (or unused code) elimination, loop invariant code motion and induction variable substitution. They also include two other optimizations: (1) indirection removal; and (2) non-zero-iteration loop identification. Indirection removal is an optimization that replaces a pointer dereference expression with the definite points-to targets of the pointer. This optimization can reduces the number of indirect accesses caused by pointer dereferences, thus reducing the number of memory accesses in the program. Recognizing a *while-loop* has non-zero-iteration can transfer the loop to *do-while-loop*. It can also refine the data flow information by eliminating the bypassing edge from the loop-entry node to the loop-exit node in the control-flow graph.

The above optimizations often interact with each other. For instance, control-flow dead code elimination can refine the FUD chains and the points-to information, thus exposing more opportunity for other optimizations such as copy propagation and dereference expression simplification. In general, there are two approaches to implement such a group of optimizations. A *separated approach* implements each optimization independently. Each optimization conducts its own specific data flow analysis, which may be simpler than an integrated data flow analysis that serves all optimizations. This approach also provides the flexibility to allow individual optimizations to be reordered and/or repeated for a better result. An *integrated approach*, on the other hand, performs one unified data flow analysis for all optimizations. Each optimization incrementally updates the data flow information to reflect the refinement of the information as well as to ensure the correctness of the code transformation. Those optimizations are interleaved at the statement level during the data flow graph traversal and communicate each other via incremental data flow information updates. Integrating the optimizations has the advantage of avoiding duplicated data flow analyses. Furthermore, because an integrated approach allows more quick interactions among different optimizations, it may achieve a better result than that of a separated approach given the same number of iterations [5].

We use an integrated approach in our front-end optimizations using an extended version of FUD chains. FUD is a well-defined and compact representation of the use-definition chains [16]. The main difficulty in the FUD chain generation is the placement of Φ-functions, for which some efficient algorithms are available [7]. Some researchers have already noticed that Φ-functions can incorporate control-flow information, thus support incremental update during control-flow dead-code elimination [11,16]. We extend the definition of Φ-function to support its refinement with more accurate alias information.

5.3 Multithreaded Code Generation

Generating efficient code for concurrent multithreaded architectures is one of the main goals in the design of Agassiz compiler. Such architectures can exploit loop-level parallelism and provide hardware support for run-time data dependence checking, and thread execution and synchronization. The multithreaded code is generated in two steps. First, we estimate the *benefit* of parallelization for each loop nest, and select the most profitable loop nests for parallelization. Second, we generate multithreaded code, currently targeted for the superthreaded architecture, to execute the selected loop nests in parallel. In this section, we describe the dependence graph and the algorithm for selecting the appropriate loop nests for parallelization. We also briefly describe how to generate multithreaded code.

Dependence Graph. In general, a dependence graph is a graph that depicts the execution order of its nodes. In our dependence graph, a node can be either a statement or an address calculation for a write operation. We include the address calculation for write operations in our dependence graph because this information is very important in facilitating run-time dependence check between threads in the superthreaded architecture. Edges in our dependence graph depicts control dependence, data dependence and reference dependence between the nodes in the graph. The control dependence edges are added to the graph according to the program control-flow while the data dependence edges are determined by the data dependence test. We also add a reference dependence edge from a node which calculates the address for a write operation to the statement that actually contains the write operation.

In order to *parallelize* C programs, our data dependence test needs to be more comprehensive than a traditional data dependence test. First, our data dependence test needs to handle *while-loops* that may not have an explicit loop index variable. We perform induction variable analysis in the optimization phase and pass the identified index variable to the data dependence test via annotation. Second, our data dependence test needs to handle pointer dereferences. It uses the points-to information provided by the data flow analysis to determine the potential targets of a pointer dereference. Finally, in addition to the traditional data dependence attributes, such as type, distance and direction, our dependence test also returns a reason describing why the test returns a *TRUE* dependence. For example, a *TURE* dependence may be assumed by the test because the points-to information is not precise enough or the subscript expression is non-linear. These reasons can be used in our heuristic algorithms to facilitate possible data speculation.

Selecting Loops for Parallelization. The hardware and the software overhead incurred in parallelizing a loop may overshadow any performance gain from executing the loop in parallel. Most multithreaded architectures allow only one parallel loop level in a nested loop structure as in multiprocessors. Hence, we need to prudently select the appropriate loop level for parallelization.

We first estimate the parallelism of each loop using the loop-level dependence graph. Edges for the dependencies that can be enforced by the hardware are ignored. For example, edges for loop-carried anti-dependencies and output-dependencies can be ignored because the hardware provided in the superthreaded architecture can enforce these dependencies. We also ignore the edges for the speculated dependencies, which are unlikely to happen at run-time. The loop-carried control dependencies, for instance, can be speculated because jumping out of a loop only occurs in the last iteration of the loop. Another example is to speculate on the data dependences which may occur with a low probability (perhaps from profiling information), e.g., data dependences from pointer variables. The largest strongly connected component of the modified dependence graph is then used to approximate the minimum starting delay of the next loop iteration.

The next step is to select the appropriate loops for each nested loop structure for the parallelization. We estimate two execution times for each loop. *Parallel-execution-time* is the time to execute the loop if we parallelize the current loop level and sequentially execute its inner loops. In estimating the *parallel-execution-time*, we apply an algorithm similar to the one described in [6] with the minimum starting delay calculated in the first step and an estimated number of iterations. Profiling feedback can provide more accurate information for the number of iterations of each loop to improve this estimation. *Sequential-execution-time*, on the other hand, is the time to execute the loop if we sequentially execute the current loop level and parallelize one of its inner loops. The final execution time for the loop is the minimum between its parallel-execution-time and its sequential-execution-time. , We choose an appropriate loop level for parallelization by calculating:

$$shortest\text{-}time(loop\text{-}A) = min(parallel\text{-}execution\text{-}time, work\text{-}load\ when\ all\ its\ nested\ loops\ are\ executed\ with\ their\ shortest\text{-}time)$$

Loops are selected for parallelization so that the smallest *shortest-time* is achieved for the outer loop of each nested loop structure.

Code Generation. To generate parallel code for the superthreaded architecture, we first reorder the statements in a loop into three stages. The first stage computes the basic sequential part of the loop iteration, such as updating the induction variables or loop terminating conditions in a While-loop. The second stage calculates the necessary addresses for dynamic dependence checking, while the third stage performs the main computation in an iteration. We then insert primitives for run-time dependence check and synchronization in the loop. Easy-to-use utility functions are provided in IR to insert these primitives.

An effective and efficient algorithm to generate parallel code will maximize the overlap between loop iterations while enforced all dependencies. However, the algorithm to find an optimal parallization is known to be *NP-hard*. We need to use heuristics to obtain a reasonable solution with an acceptable performance. The discussion on the design of such algorithms is beyond the scope of this paper.

6. Related Work

There exists several infrastructures for research on parallelizing and optimizing compilers. Among these compilers, SUIF [15], Polaris [2] and McCAT [8] are interesting comparisions with our Agassiz compiler. SUIF is a parallelizing and optimizing compiler for both C and Fortran programs, consisting of a kernel and a toolkit. Unlike our Agassiz compiler which uses separated high-level and low-level IR, the SUIF kernel defines a mixed-level program representation, including both high-level program constructs and low-level machine operations. The SUIF toolkit provides utilities to support research on parallelization of numeric and non-numeric programs, interprocedural analysis, dependence analysis, and MIPS instruction generation.

Polaris is a parallelizing Fortran compiler. It implements optimization techniques, such as automatic detecting of parallelism and distributing of data, that are necessary to transform a given sequential Fortran program into a form that runs efficiently on a target machine. The kernel of Polaris defines a high-level IR which is very similar to our real-IR. However, the implementation of the Polaris IR employs a more sophisticated memory error detecting mechanism, which not only counts the number of pointers pointing to an object but also enforces an explicit ownership on the objects.

McCAT is a compiler/architecture testbed which provides a unified approach to the development and performance analysis of compilation techniques and high-performance architectural features. The core of McCAT is a C compiler providing both a high-level and a low-level IR, and equipped with many analyses and transformations at both IR levels. Similar to our compiler, McCAT also has a phase to convert a program with *goto* statements into an equivalent program without *goto* statements. However, McCAT does not provide any IR representation for *goto* statements. This makes it difficult to represent a program with unrestricted *goto* statements which cannot be converted to an equivalent program without goto statements. Our Agassiz compiler, on the other hand, can represent unrestricted goto statements and mark a program segment with unrestricted *goto* statements and *goto* targets as unstructured program segment. This information can be used to simply later analyses.

7. Conclusions and Current Status

In this paper, we present the overall design of the Agassiz compiler. The Agassiz compiler is an integrated compiler targeting the concurrent multithreaded architectures (such as Multiscalar [12] and Superthreaded processors [13]). It has a loop-level parallelizing compiler as its front-end and an instruction-level optimizing compiler as its back-end to support such architectures. In this paper, we focus on the IR design of the Agassiz compiler, and describe how we support the front-end analyses, various optimization techniques, and source-to-source translation for the parallelization of both C and Fortran programs.

The compiler is currently being developed jointly at the University of Minnesota and at the Fudan University in Shanghai, PRC. A few SPEC95 benchmark programs (mostly C programs) have been successfully run all the way through from the front-end parallelizing compiler to the modified gcc back-end compiler, and simulated on our execution-driven simulator for superthreaded architectures. We are currently evaluating the effectiveness of various analysis and parallelization techniques, and working on ways to improve the back-end compiler to generate more efficient superthreaded code.

Acknowledgments

This work was supported in part by the National Science Foundation under grant nos. MIP-9610379 and CDA-9502979; by the U.S. Army Intelligence Center and Fort Huachuca under contract DABT63-95-C-0127 and ARPA order no. D346, and a gift from the Intel Corporation.

We would like to thank Dan Laney, Youfeng Wu and the anonymous referees for their comments which resulted in numberless improvements and clarifications of the paper.

References

1. The Agassiz Compiler. http://www.cs.umn.edu/Research/Agassiz/
2. W. Blume, R. Eigenmann, K. Faigin, J. Grout, J. Hoeflinger, D. Padua, P. Petersen, W. Pottenger, L. Rauchwerger, P. Tu, and S. Weatherford. *Polaris: Improving the effectiveness of Parallelizing Compilers*. Languages and Compilers for Parallel Computing. Lecture Notes in Computer Science 892. K. Pingali, U. Banerjee, D. Gelernter, A. Nicolau, and D. Padua (Eds.) pages 141-154. Springer-Verlag, 1994.
3. Doug Burger and Todd M. Austin. *The SimpleScalar Tool Set.* University of Wisconsin-Madison Computer Sciences Department Technical Report #1342, 1997.
4. S. Cho, J.-Y. Tsai, Y. Song, B. Zheng, S. J. Schwinn, X. Wang, Q. Zhao, Z. Li, D. J. Lilja, and P.-C. Yew. *High-Level Information - An Approach for Integrating Front-End and Back-End Compilers.* In Proceedings of the International Conference on Parallel Processing, pages 345-355, Auguest 1998.
5. Cliff Click and Keith D. Cooper. *Combing Analyses Combing Optimizations.* In ACM Transactions on Programming Languages and Systems, Vol.17, No.2, pages 181-196, March 1995.
6. Ron Cytron. *Limited Processor Scheduling of Doacross Loops.* In Proceedings of the International Conference on Parallel Processing, pages 226-234, Auguest, 1987.
7. Ron Cytron, Jeanne Ferrante, Barry K. Rosen, and Mark N. Wegman. *Efficiently Computing Static Single Assignment Form and The Control Dependence Graph.* In ACM Transactions on Programming Languages and Systems, pages 451-490, Vol 13, No 4, October,1991.
8. L. Hendren, C. Donawa, M. Emami, G. Gao, Justiani, and B. Sridharan. *Designing the McCAT Compiler Based on a Family of Structured Intermediate Representations.* In Proceedings of the 5th International Workshop on Languages and Compilers for Parallel Computing, August 1992.

9. Bo Huang. *Context-Sensitive Interprocedural Pointer Analysis*. PhD Thesis, Computer Science Department, Fudan University, P.R.China, in preparation.
10. Richard Jones and Rafael Lins. *Garbage Collection*. John Wiley & Sons Ltd, 1996.
11. Richard C. Johnson. *Efficient Program Analysis Using Dependence Flow Graphs*. Ph.D. Thesis, Computer science, University of Cornell University, 1994.
12. G. S. Sohi, S. Breach, and T. N. Vijaykumar. *Multiscalar Processors*. In Proceeding of the 22th International Symposium on Computer Architecture (ISCA-22), 1995.
13. J.-Y. Tsai and P.-C. Yew. *The Superthreaded Architecture: Thread Pipelining with Run-Time Data Dependence Checking and Control Speculation*. In Proceedings of the Int'l Conf. on Parallel Architectures and Compilation Techniques, October 1996.
14. J.-Y. Tsai. *Integrating Compilation Technology and Processor Architecture for Cost-Effective Concurrent*. Ph.D. Thesis, Computer Science, University of Illinois at Urbana-Champaign, April 1998.
15. Robert P. Wilson, Robert S. French, Christopher S. Wilson, Saman P. Amarasinghe, Jennifer M. Anderson, Steve W. K. Tjiang, Shih-Wei Liao, Chau-Wen Tseng, Mary W. Hall, Monica S. Lam, and John L. Hennessy. *SUIF: An Infrastructure for Research on Parallelizing and Optimizing Compilers*. In SUIF document, http://suif.stanford.edu/suif/suif1/.
16. Michael R. Wolfe. *High-Performance Compilers for Parallel Computing*. Addison-Wesley, Redwood City, CA, 1996.
17. Bixia Zheng and Pen-Chung Yew. *A Hierarchical Approach to Context-Sensitive Interprocedural Alias Analysis*. Technical Report 99-018, Comuper Science Department, University of Minnesota, April 1999.

The Scc Compiler: SWARing at MMX and 3DNow!

Randall J. Fisher and Henry G. Dietz

School of Electrical and Computer Engineering
Purdue University, West Lafayette, IN 47907-1285
{rfisher, hankd}@ecn.purdue.edu

Abstract. Last year, we discussed the issues surrounding the development of languages and compilers for a general, portable, high-level SIMD Within A Register (SWAR) execution model. In a first effort to provide such a language and a framework for further research on this form of parallel processing, we proposed the vector-based language SWARC, and an experimental module compiler for this language, called Scc, which targeted IA32+MMX-based architectures.

Since that time, we have worked to expand the types of targets that Scc supports and to include optimizations based on both vector processing and enhanced hardware support for SWAR. This paper provides a more formal description of the SWARC language, describes the organization of the current version of the Scc compiler, and discusses the implementation of optimizations within this framework.

1 Introduction

In the SWAR processing model, a wide data path within a processor is treated as multiple, thinner, SIMD-parallel data paths. Each register word is effectively partitioned into *fields* that can be operated on in parallel. In this paper, we refer to one word of fields as a *fragment*, and a multi-fragment object as a *vector*.

Current compiler support for the SWAR model falls into four major categories: compiler "intrinsics", classes or types representing a fragment, semi-automatic vectorization of loops, and languages which provide first-class vector objects. The first two categories are typically limited to giving the programmer low-level access to the SWAR instructions of the target. The third provides an abstract model which hides the use of these instructions by employing well-known techniques to parallelize loops in existing C code. The fourth category provides an abstract model in which the semantics of the language indicate which operations can be automatically parallelized. We will briefly discuss these support methods as they apply to the MMX and 3DNow! families of SWAR extensions.

Compiler intrinsics are preprocessor macros which provide a function-call-like interface to the target's SWAR instructions. Generally, these are easy to implement and simply hide inlined assembly code which is used to execute a single SWAR instruction. Intel's C/C++ compiler [6,7], MetroWerks CodeWarrior [10], Sybase's Watcom C/C++ [14], and the lcc-win32 project

L. Carter and J. Ferrante (Eds.): LCPC'99, LNCS 1863, pp. 399–414, 2000.
© Springer-Verlag Berlin Heidelberg 2000

(www.remcomp.com/lcc-win32) all provide some level of support for using MMX and/or 3DNow! instructions via intrinsics.

New class or type definitions which represent a fragment provide a first-class feel to these objects and the operations on them. To do this, class definitions provide overloaded operators, while non-class definitions typically require a modification to the language. Often, these models are built on top of a set of intrinsics, and support only the partitionings and operations directly associated with the targeted hardware. Several compilers employ this technique. The Intel compiler includes class libraries for MMX. Free Pascal [2] includes predefined array types for MMX and 3DNow!, and extends Pascal to allow some first-class operations on these types. Oxford Micro Devices' compiler for its A236 Parallel Video DSP chip [13] provides predefined struct types for MMX, but requires modifications to the C language.

Under strict conditions, and with hints from the programmer, some compilers are able to vectorize simple data-parallel loops. This support is in the early stages and is limited in the data types and operations that can occur in the body of the loop. We expect the development of this style of parallelism to follow that of Fortran loop manipulation. The Intel and MetroWerks compilers provide limited vectorization for MMX. The MetroWerks' compiler also supports 3DNow!.

In languages which provide first-class vector objects, both the precision of the data and the number of elements in the vector may be virtualized beyond the limits of the target's SWAR extensions. A full set of operations on these vectors is provided, rather than a subset based on the SWAR instructions available on the target. To the best of our knowledge, it is still true that only the SWARC language provides this type of model.

We have chosen this last approach because we believe it offers the best opportunity for performance gains over a large range of applications and target architectures. Using the SWARC module language and related compilers, users can write portable SIMD functions that will be compiled into efficient SWAR-based modules and interface code that allows these modules to be used within ordinary C programs.

The level of hardware support for SWAR is inconsistent across architecture families. In our previous work [4], we discussed the reasons for this and the basic coding techniques needed to support a high-level language, such as SWARC, on any type of SWAR target including 32-bit integer instruction sets that have no explicit support for SWAR.

This paper will focus on our work since LCPC 98. Section 2 contains a brief explanation of the SWARC language. Section 3 provides an overview of the organization of Scc, the first implementation of an experimental SWARC compiler. In section 4, we consider the implementation of compiler optimizations which we introduced last year within the Scc framework. In section 5, we discuss some preliminary performance numbers. A brief summary, and pointers to the support code that we have developed, are given in section 6.

2   The SWARC Language

The SWARC language is intended to simplify the writing of portable SWAR code modules that can be easily combined with C code to form a complete application. It does this by allowing the programmer to specify both object precision and SIMD-style SWAR parallelism in a vector-based language which is similar to C. While a complete definition of the SWARC syntax is beyond the scope of this paper, we will briefly describe the most important extensions beyond C's semantics.

The key concept in SWAR is the use of operations on word-sized values to perform SIMD-parallel operations on fields within a word. Because the language should be portable, and the supported field sizes and alignments depend on the target machine, the programmer's specification should only provide *minimal constraints* on the data layout selected by the compiler. Also, as a module language, SWARC code should integrate well with ordinary C code and data structures. While SWARC is based on C, these issues lead to adjustments in the type system, operators, and general structure of the language.

2.1   The SWARC Type System

A SWARC data type declaration specifies a first-class array type whose elements are either ordinary C-layout objects or SWAR-layout integer or floating-point fields with a *specified minimum precision*. The syntax for declaring a SWARC object is similar to the bit-field specification used in C **struct** declarations, and takes the general form: *type:prec[width]*.

The base C type *type* may be any of the C types **char**, **short**, **int**, or **float**. The modifiers **signed**, **unsigned**, and **const**, and the storage classes **extern**, **register**, and **static** can be applied to this base, and have the same meanings as in C. Also, many SWAR targets support operations on natural data types which require *saturation arithmetic*, in which results that do not fit in the range of the data size are set to the nearest storable value. Therefore, SWARC allows either **modular** or **saturation** to be specified as an attribute of the type.

The precision specifier : indicates that the object should have a SWAR layout, and that the minimum precision required for the data may be specified with an optional integer precision *prec*. Omitting the precision specifier indicates that the object should have a C, rather than a SWARC, layout. For example, the SWARC declaration **char c;** is equivalent to the C declaration **char c;**. Using the precision specifier without an integer precision is equivalent to specifying a SWAR-layout with the native precision for the equivalent C-layout type, e.g., **float:** is equivalent to **float:32**. Note that while the compiler may store data with a higher precision than specified, saturation is always to the declared precision of the data.

The optional [*width*] specifier indicates the C-layout array dimension or number of SWARC-layout vector elements. **char:7[14] d;** declares d to be a vector with 14 visible elements, each of which is an integer field with *at least* 7 bits precision. If the [*width*] is omitted, it is taken to be one.

These type extensions require several modifications to the C type coercion rules. Scalar objects are promoted to the dimension of the other type. If neither object is a scalar, and the dimensions are mismatched, a warning is generated and the wider object is truncated to the width of the other. Expressions which mix C- and SWAR- layout objects, result in the SWAR-layout even if this requires the precision to be reduced. Otherwise, an expression with mixed precision yields a result with the higher precision. Also, where mixed, **modular** expressions are cast to **saturated** expressions.

2.2   Control Constructs and Statements in the SWARC Language

Control flow constructs in SWARC are a superset of those in C, and operate similarly to those in MPL [9]. From the SWARC programmer's point of view, conditionally executed statements must be applied only to those vector elements for which the condition is true. Because SWAR instructions are applied across all the elements in a fragment, a conditionally executed instruction must be applied under an *enable mask* which limits its effects to the elements which are enabled for the operation. SWARC control constructs must be modified to properly use enable masking and to hide the underlying operations from the programmer. The SWARC constructs include:

- *if/else* statements, which operate as do C **if** statements when the conditional expression has a width of one. Otherwise, the **if** body is executed iff the condition is true for some enabled element of the conditional vector. In this case, the body is executed under enable masking. Likewise, the **else** body is executed, under masking, when the condition is false for some enabled element of the conditional vector.
- *where/elsewhere* statements, which operate as do SWARC **if** statements, except that the **where** and **elsewhere** bodies are always executed. These bodies are masked to limit their effects to the correct set of elements.
- *everywhere* statements, which enable all elements of the vector for the following statement.
- *while* statements, which operate as do C **while** statements if the conditional expression has a width of one. Otherwise, the **while** body is executed as long as the condition is true for at least one enabled element in the vector. An element is disabled when the condition becomes false for that element, and stays that way until the loop is exited. Thus, the set of enabled elements is monotonically non-increasing with each iteration. Once all the elements become disabled, the loop exits, and the enable mask is restored to its condition before entering the loop.
- *for* and *do* statements, which are related to the SWARC **while** in the same way that the C **for** and **do** statements are related to the C **while**.
- *continue* and *break* statements, which operate as in C except that an optional expression indicates how many nesting levels to continue or break from.
- *return* statements, which operate as in C except that no expression is allowed to be returned from a SWARC function (i.e., functions return void).

- function calls, which operate as in C except that arguments are passed by address, not by value. The call is executed as the body of an implied **everywhere** to ensure compatibility with ordinary C code.
- A special block statement, which encloses ordinary C code can be inserted wherever a statement can appear or as a top-level declaration. These blocks are enclosed by a ${ $} pair, and are emitted into the output code.

2.3 The SWARC Operators

The semantics of the standard C operators have been modified to work in a consistent and intelligent way with SWAR data:

- Logical and arithmetic operators operate within each field of vector data.
- The trinary operator applies enable masking to its alternatives.
  Logical and comparison operators return 0 in every false field and -1 (all 1 bits) in every true field. This modification simplifies the implementation of enable masking. The short-circuit evaluation of the binary and trinary logical operators is optional in SWARC.
- The assignment operators work as in C, but are extended as in C* [15,5] to perform associative reductions when storing a vector value into an array or when the operator is used as a unary prefix.

New operators also have been added to facilitate operations common to SIMD processing within the SWAR environment:

- The minimum (?<), maximum (?>), and average (+/) operators have been added and can be used as binary or assignment operators.
- The operators ||= and &&= have been added to perform the SIMD ANY and ALL operations for assignments and reductions.
- The **typeof**, **widthof**, and **precisionof** operators return, respectively, the declared type, dimension, and precision of their expression arguments.
- The vector element shift ([<<n] and [>>n]) and rotate ([<<%n] and [>> %n]) operators have been added to ease the implementation of inter-element communication and similar algorithms.

2.4 An Example SWARC Function

An example of code that can be written in SWARC is the Linpack benchmark DAXPY loop. While the language does not preclude double-precision data, current SWAR hardware does not support it. Therefore, we will perform a SAXPY (Single-precision AXPY) instead. A C version of the original loop looks like this:

```
for (i=0; i<4; i++) dy[i] = dy[i] + da*dx[i];
```

In SWARC, the same code is written as a vector expression. Here, we show the code wrapped in a function body which can be in-lined or copied directly into the SWARC source:

```
void swar_saxpy(float:[4] x, float:[4] y, float a) {y+=(a*x);}
```

In the next section, we will discuss the organization of the experimental SWARC compiler, Scc, and follow this example as it is compiled to C code.

3   The Organization of the Scc Compiler

The Scc compiler consists of the front end, a back end, and a set of utilities which are used throughout the compiler. The purpose of the front end is to determine what type of processing must be performed on each source file, parse SWARC source code, and convert the SWARC source into a type-coerced, intermediate representation (IR) tree representing the vector operations. The back end has the task of converting the intermediate vector tree form into lists of tuples representing operations on word-sized data *fragments*, and generating C code to implement the operations described by these tuples based on the capabilities of the target architecture.

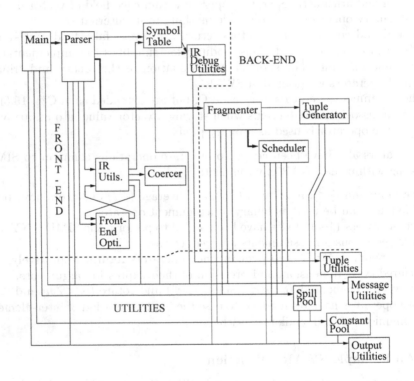

Fig. 1. Organization of the Scc Compiler

Figure 1 is a diagram of the compiler showing the functional units as blocks and the calls between them as arrows. An arrow from unit A to unit B indicates that some function in unit A calls a function in unit B. The primary flow of data through the compiler follows the heavy line from the main function, through the parser, the fragmenter, and finally the scheduler. The dashed lines roughly indicate the separation between the front end, back end, and the utilities.

3.1   The Front End

The front end is comprised of six major functional units.

- The main function handles command-line options and determines how each source file is to be handled. SWARC sources are preprocessed if necessary, then passed to the SWARC parser to be translated into C code and written to the output C file. Ordinary C sources are emitted verbatim to the output C file, and C header code is written to the C header output file, for handling by the C compiler. All other code is passed to the C compiler for linking.
- The SWARC parser generates top-level declarations and prototypes for the C output, and drives the remainder of the front end. It was built using PCCTS (the Purdue Compiler Construction Tool Set, see the network newsgroup comp.compilers.tools.pccts). As each function body is parsed, an IR tree is built to represent it. This tree contains nodes representing scalar and vector operations, and may be optimized by the front end optimizer before being passed to the back end for code generation.
- The symbol table stores information on SWARC identifiers.
- The coercer performs type checking and coercion on the IR tree.
- The IR utilities are used by the parser and coercer to generate and restructure pieces of the IR tree. This tree has a child-sibling structure in which each operation is stored in a parent node. Its child is at the top of a tree representing the operation's first operand, and each of the child's siblings are at the top of a tree representing one of the remaining operands. These can be leaves representing a constant or identifier, or trees representing complex expressions. Parent nodes are also used to represent code blocks and control constructs.
- The front end optimizer reconfigures the IR tree for a function by performing several optimizations. These include scalar and vector constant folding, removal of unreachable or unnecessary code, and aggressive vector-level algebraic simplification. These will be discussed in section 4.

An Example Intermediate Representation Tree. Figure 2 is a representation of the IR tree that the front end generates for our SAXPY example. The notation "4x32f" indicates an entity or operation which has four fields containing 32-bit floating point values. We see that a 4x32f add is performed on the 4x32f value loaded from memory location y and the product of the scalar (1x32f) a, casted to a 4x32f, and the 4x32f x. The 4x32f result is then stored in memory location y.

3.2   The Back End

The major functional units of the back end include: the fragmenter, which divides vector data into word-sized fragments and drives the other parts of the back end, the tuple generator, which generates a tuple tree for each fragment, and the scheduler, which schedules the tuples and generates output code. These units require more explanation than those of the front end, and will be described in the following subsections.

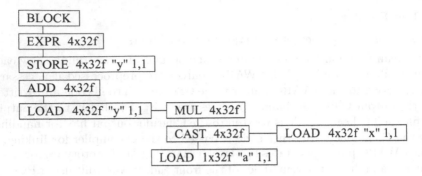

Fig. 2. IR tree for SWAR SAXPY

The Fragmenter. The primary task of the fragmenter is to convert the IR tree into lists of tuple DAGs, which more closely represent the operations in the output language. SWARC data is generally in the form of vectors which contain more elements than can be stored in a single CPU register. Vector operations are encoded in the IR tree as single tree nodes, but need to be converted into a series of equivalent operations on the fragments of the vector arguments. These operations are stored as trees of tuples in the master tuple list, with their roots listed in an array created for each vector operation. Once the lists for the operations in a basic block have been generated, the fragmenter passes the them to the scheduler to be converted into C output code.

Thus, what we call fragmenting is closely related to strip mining and serves a similar purpose. The primary difference is that fragmenting does not generate loops, nor does it generate the associated indexing or end-of-vector tests. It simply generates fragment-based operations that have the minimum possible overhead and maximum flexibility in scheduling. While we have found no previous references to fragmenting, it seems to be too obvious to be new. Future versions of Scc may use strip mining in combination with fragmenting for long vectors, where excessive code size might limit performance.

In figure 3, we see how an 8-element vector addition is fragmented into four word-sized parallel additions. In the top half of the figure, a single vector addition is conceptually applied to two vectors, A and B, each of which has eight 32-bit (8x32) data elements. Assuming that the target's registers have a width of 64 bits, the fragmenter can only pack two 32-bit fields into each fragment as a 2x32 SWAR entity. The lower half of the figure shows how the vector is fragmented, with each pair of elements assigned to a single fragment. The corresponding fragments of the two vectors are then added with a single hardware operation yielding a total of four additions for the vector operation.

The Tuple Generator Functions. Each tuple generator function is responsible for constructing a tuple tree to perform an operation on one fragment of a vector. The trees generated are stored in the master tuple list, with each node

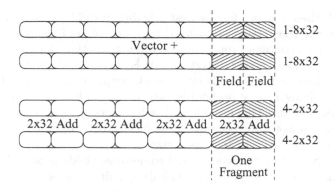

Fig. 3. Fragmentation of a Vector Addition

representing data or one of the sub-operations to be performed in the execution of the operation. These trees also have the child-sibling structure described earlier.

In previous work, we have shown that the available operations vary widely across SWAR target architectures and often support only certain data precisions. These variations must be accounted for during the construction of the tuple DAGs in the fragmentation phase. This may be done either through the promotion of data to supported field sizes or through the emulation in software of unsupported operations using techniques which we have developed [4]. Scc employs both of these methods during tuple generation.

Common subexpression elimination is performed in these functions when possible. Reduction in strength optimizations can also be performed in these functions; however, care must be taken because these optimizations depend on the availability of an instruction with the correct data type and field size. Finally, several fragment-level optimizations can be applied during tuple generation to lessen enable masking and spacer manipulation overhead, or to exploit the special situations created by the use of fragmentation, spacer bits, and enable masks. These optimizations will be discussed in section 4.

The Scheduler/Register Allocator. Once a tuple tree list for a basic block has been generated, the fragmenter calls the scheduler to generate output code for the list. The combined scheduler/allocator then performs a modified exhaustive search of the possible schedules for the tuple list based on schedule permutation [12]. A detailed model of the target pipeline is used to estimate the cost of each schedule. At first, the scheduler attempts to schedule the block without allowing any register spills. If this is not possible, it tries again allowing one pseudo-register, then two, etc., until it is able to schedule the block, or until a predetermined maximum is reached.

In each of these iterations, the scheduler first builds an initial tuple ordering by back-tracing the stores, then attempts to find an optimal schedule by improving upon it. It starts by placing certain restrictions on the memory access modes allowed, then searches for the best schedule possible. If no schedule can be found, then the restrictions are relaxed by a degree, and the scheduler tries again. This process continues until the scheduler finds that it cannot schedule the block without using more registers than it is currently allowed.

Once a schedule for the basic block is found, output code is generated for it. This schedule is known to be optimal for the target architecture based on the pipeline cost estimation. This estimate takes into account emulation overhead, multiple pipeline usage, target-specific instruction costs, operand source differences, and costs related to register renaming.

Unfortunately, our current cost model sometimes yields poor estimates because it assumes that memory accesses will always hit in the second-level cache. Many will hit in the first-level cache, thereby returning sooner than the model predicts. Similarly, our model is incorrect when an L2 cache miss occurs. We hope to improve the cache analysis in future versions and a better model should be easy to integrate in our scheduler.

3.3   Example of C Output from Scc

Returning to our SAXPY example, the generated C code for the SWAR version of the loop targeting an AMD K6-2 (with four elements to keep it brief) is:

```
void swar_saxpy(p64_t *x, p64_t *y, float *a)
{
        register p64_t *_cpool = &(mmx_cpool[0]);
        {
                movq_m2r(*(((p64_t *) a) + 0), mm0);
                pand_m2r(*(_cpool + 2), mm0);
                movq_r2r(mm0, mm1);
                psllq_i2r(32, mm0);
                por_r2r(mm0, mm1);
                movq_r2r(mm1, mm2);
                pfmul_m2r(*(((p64_t *) x) + 1), mm1);
                pfmul_m2r(*(((p64_t *) x) + 0), mm2);
                pfadd_m2r(*(((p64_t *) y) + 1), mm1);
                pfadd_m2r(*(((p64_t *) y) + 0), mm2);
                movq_r2m(mm1, *(((p64_t *) y) + 1));
                movq_r2m(mm2, *(((p64_t *) y) + 0));
        }
_return: femms();
}
p64_t mmx_cpool[] = {
        /*   0 */        0x0000000000000000LL,
        /*   1 */        0xffffffffffffffffLL,
        /*   2 */        0x00000000ffffffffLL,
        /*   3 */        0xffffffff00000000LL
};
```

The first five statements of the inner block load the 32-bit float value **a** into both fields of a 64-bit register. The sixth copies this value for use with another fragment. The remaining instructions perform the SAXPY on the two fragments of the vector data in **x** and **y**. Note that the above code is not optimally scheduled due the aforementioned errors in the current cost estimation model.

4 Implementation of Compiler Optimizations for SWAR

At LCPC 98, we introduced and discussed several static compiler optimizations that apply to SWAR programming. These were based on tracking data, spacer, and mask values, and aggressively simplifying code dealing with spacers and masks. While some of these techniques can only be applied for particular targets, data types, or field sizes, others apply to all targets. Some optimizations can be implemented at both the vector and fragment levels.

In this section, we discuss how these optimizations have been, or will be, implemented in the Scc experimental compiler. We will briefly reintroduce these optimizations here, but refer you to [4] for a more detailed discussion. Three such optimizations are: promotion of field sizes, SWAR bitwise value tracking, and enable masking optimization.

4.1 Promotion of Field Sizes

In SWARC, the programmer may specify the minimum precision required for a value. This allows the compiler to avoid inefficient field sizes, and to exploit the target's specialized hardware. When used, promotion saves the cost of emulating unsupported operations. However, not all unsupported operations are inefficient, and in some cases, the parallelism gained outweighs the related overhead. This depends not only on the size of the target's registers, but on the set of supported field sizes and the set of supported instructions.

One of our goals is to determine when promotion is beneficial, and when emulation is better. For example, whenever the floor of the register size divided by the field size is equal for both field sizes, there would be no parallelism loss if the larger is used. In this case, it may still be better to emulate the smaller size if the extra bits can be used by an optimization such as spacer value tracking [4].

Currently, the Scc compiler targets only IA32 architectures with 64-bit enhancements including MMX [6], 3DNow! [1], and Extended MMX [3]. These systems support precisions of 8-, 16-, 32-, and 64-bits directly, and Scc emulates most operations on 1-, 2-, and 4-bit fields efficiently. Data of other precisions is promoted in the back end during fragmentation to a supported or emulated size.

4.2 Vector Algebraic Simplification and Bitwise Value Tracking

Last year, we introduced the topic of bitwise value tracking as it related to the optimization of compiler-inserted masking operations. These are primarily composed of bitwise AND, OR, and shift operations, using constant-valued masks and shift counts. We now generalize this idea to apply to a larger set of operations and types of data. A masking example still suffices to convey the idea. Consider the following C code in which the low byte of a 16-bit word is moved into the high byte with masking:

```
x = (( (x & 0x00ff) << 8 ) & 0xff00);
```

Simple constant folding will not improve the above code because no single operation has two constant operands. However, by aggressively applying the algebraic properties of the operations involved, we can restructure the code so that constant folding can be applied. Distributing the shift over the inner expression, then performing constant folding, yields:

```
x = (( (x << 8) & (0x00ff << 8) ) & 0xff00);
x = (( (x << 8) & 0xff00 ) & 0xff00);
```

From here, we see that the AND operations can be folded because they are associative and each has a constant operand. In this particular example, they also happen to have the same value, although this is not true generally. The code is finally converted to the equivalent, but simpler, form:

```
x = ((x << 8) & 0xff00);
```

Note that unless we are able to fold the operations at each step, we will be simply replacing one set of operations with an equal number of different operations which are probably equally expensive. We have identified a strict set of conditions which must be met to make this optimization worthwhile:

- The top-level operation *op1* must have one operand which evaluates to a constant value, and another which is a tree rooted at an operation *op2*.
- *op2* must have one operand which evaluates to a constant, and a second which is a tree rooted at an operation *op3*, over which *op2* is distributive.
- *op3* must have one operand which evaluates to a constant, and be associative with *op1*. Note that *op1* and *op3* may differ. For example, in 1-bit fields, additions and exclusive-ORs are associative.
- Other restrictions may be imposed due to the exact form of the expression tree and the asymmetry of any of the operation's properties. For example, *op1* or *op3* may be required to be commutative so that operands may be reordered and associative combining of operations applied.

After ensuring that the above conditions are met, the algorithm to perform this optimization on an expression tree has four basic steps:

- Distribute *op2* over *op3*.
- Reorder the tree if necessary, depending on the commutative properties of *op1* and *op3*.
- Combine *op1* and *op3*.
- Perform constant folding on the tree.

After this last step, *op1* has been eliminated from the tree. This process can then be continued up the expression tree in the attempt to remove more operations. In Scc, this optimization can be applied at the vector level to algebraically simplify vector operations, and again at the fragment level to optimize masking and spacer operations on the tuple trees for each fragment.

4.3 Enable Masking Optimizations

The individual fields of a SWAR register cannot be disabled. Thus, undesired field computations must be arithmetically nulled, thereby incurring a significant cost. This cost can be avoided on a per fragment basis if the compiler can prove statically that one of two conditions hold. First, if all fields of the fragment are enabled, no masking is done, and the corresponding fragment of the result is directly computed. Second, if all fields of the fragment are disabled, no masking is done, and the corresponding fragment of the result is copied from the original value. Otherwise, the masking may still be avoided if the compiler can generate code that allows all fields to be active and later corrects the *inactive* field values.

In Scc, conditional statements, such as `if`s, generate multiple tuple lists for each word-sized fragment of the vector: one for evaluating the conditional value, one for the body, and one for each possible alternative such as an `else` clause. Because of this, Scc makes it easy to apply the above algorithm. During the fragmentation phase, when the conditional code is being generated, the compiler performs an analysis which reveals fragments fitting either of the two above cases. These fragments are noted and enable masking operations are skipped during the generation of code for the fragment's body and alternatives.

5 Performance Evaluation

At the time of this writing, we have relatively few direct comparisons of performance — it is only recently that vectorized support has been added to the Intel C/C++ and MetroWerks Code Warrior compilers. Prior to these additions, Scc was the *only compiler* providing support for multi-word objects using the MMX and 3DNow! instruction set extensions. Prototype versions of the compiler have been available on the WWW since August 1998, and hundreds of uses of the WWW-interfaced version have been recorded. The most common comments are very positive, with a few very negative comments about Scc's early inability to handle very long vectors or to generate good error messages. In addition, we have data for two benchmarks, one integer MMX and one floating point 3DNow!

5.1 The Integer Benchmark — Subpixel Rendering

The pixels of color LCD (Liquid Crystal Display) panels are not square dots capable of displaying any color; rather, each pixel actually consists of three separate subpixels, one each for red, green, and blue. Generally, the subpixels are arranged as rectangular stripes that are 1/3 as wide as they are tall. Using this fact and rendering at 3 times the horizontal resolution, image quality can be dramatically improved.

The problem is that treating the subpixels like full pixels yields severe color fringing. To remedy this, we use a 5-point software filter that applies 1/9, 2/9, 3/9, 2/9, 1/9 weightings. Unfortunately, the filter is relatively expensive, partly because the weightings are awkward, but also because the memory reference pattern for subpixels has a stride of three bytes.

We constructed an optimized serial C version of this code for use with the PAPERS video wall library. We also assigned this problem to 16 individual students as part of a SWARC project in the "Programming Parallel Machines" course (Spring 1999 in Purdue's School of Electrical and Computer Engineering). The result was that at least a few of the students achieved more than 5x speedup over the optimized C code using Scc-generated MMX code. This was a surprisingly good result; in fact, even though some students wrote their own MMX code by hand, the fastest version used *unedited* Scc-generated code.

5.2   The Float Benchmark — Linpack

The Top 500 Supercomputers list (http://www.top500.org/) uses a version of Linpack to rank the floating point speeds of a wide range of machines. An updated version of the standard C source which corrects for problems with the timers on PC-compatible systems is available via ftp from:

ftp://ftp.nosc.mil/pub/aburto/linpackc/linpackc.c.

This achieved 54 MFLOPS using 32-bit fields on a K6-2 400MHz test platform.

Rewriting just a few lines of code in SWARC (a 100-element chunk of the core DAXPY, DDOT, and DSCAL loops) and using Scc to generate 3DNow! code, the performance went to something around 80-100 MFLOPS. However, that performance was significantly hindered by our scheduler's overly-conservative estimations of load cost; by simply hand-tweaking the 3DNow! code schedule, we achieved more than 220 MFLOPS. Because memory bandwidth, etc., are also important factors, it is difficult to say how much closer to the machine's theoretical peak 1.6 GFLOPS could be achieved; all the above performance numbers were obtained using the standard version of Linpack, which is not cache-friendly. The performance we obtained is impressive by any standard — especially because our reference platform is a $2,000 laptop!

6   Conclusion

The SWARC language was developed to provide a portable, virtualized, high-level language for SWAR-based parallel processing. This language has been successfully targeted to IA32+MMX-based architectures via the experimental Scc module compiler. This compiler provides a framework for further research on SWAR processing such as emulation of unsupported operations and field sizes, optimization of vector and fragment operations, and instruction scheduling for SWAR-capable targets. In this paper, we have briefly described the SWARC language and the operation of the Scc compiler as it converts vector SWARC source code to scheduled, fragment-based C code modules.

We are currently expanding the targets of the Scc module compiler from MMX-based processors to generic 32-bit integer processors and processors enhanced with 128-bit extensions such as Intel's SSE [6] and Motorola's Alti-Vec [11]. At this writing, however, only basic libraries for using MMX, Extended MMX, and SSE with Gnu C have been released. These libraries, and a web interface to a recent version of the Scc compiler, can be accessed at:

http://shay.ecn.purdue.edu/šwar/Index.html.

References

1. Advanced Micro Devices, Inc., *AMD-K6 Processor Multimedia Extensions*, Advanced Micro Devices, Inc., Sunnyvale, California, March 1997.
2. Michael Van Canneyt and Florian Klampfl, *Free Pascal supplied units: Reference Guide*, http://rs1.szif.hu/m̃arton/fpc/units, December 1998.
3. Cyrix Corporation, *Multimedia Instruction Set Extensions for a Sixth-Generation x86 Processor*, Cyrix Corporation, ftp://ftp.cyrix.com/developr/hc-mmx4.pdf, August 1996.
4. Randall J. Fisher and Henry G. Dietz, Compiling For SIMD Within A Register, *11th International Workshop on Languages and Compilers for Parallel Computing*, Chapel Hill, North Carolina, August 1998.
5. P. J. Hatcher, A. J. Lapadula, R. R. Jones, M. J. Quinn, and R. J. Anderson, A Production Quality C* Compiler for Hypercube Multicomputers, *Third ACM SIGPLAN Symposium on Principles and Practices of Parallel Programming*, Williamsburg, Virginia, April 1991, pp. 73-82.
6. Intel Corporation, *Intel Architecture Software Developer's Manual: Vol. 1 Basic Architecture*, Intel Corporation,
   http://developer.intel.com/design/pentiumII/manuals/24319002.PDF,   May 1999.
7. Joe Wolf, *Coding Techniques for the Streaming SIMD Extensions With the Intel C/C++ Compiler*, Intel Corporation,
   http://developer.intel.com/vtune/newsletr/methods.htm, July 1999.
8. Joe Wolf, *Advanced Optimizations With the Intel C/C++ Compiler*, Intel Corporation, http://developer.intel.com/vtune/newsletr/opts.htm, July 1999.
9. MasPar Computer Corporation, *MasPar Programming Language (ANSI C compatible MPL) Reference Manual, Software Version 2.2*, Document Number 9302-0001, Sunnyvale, California, November 1991.
10. MetroWerks, Inc., *MetroWerks Desktop Products - CodeWarrior for Windows, Profession Edition*, MetroWerks, Inc.,
    http://www.metrowerks.com/desktop/windows/.
11. Motorola, Inc., *AltiVec Technology Programming Environments Manual, Preliminary Rev. 0.2*, Motorola, Inc.,
    http://www.motcom/SPS/PowerPC/teksupport/teklibrary/manuals/altivec_pem.pdf, May 1998.
12. A. Nisar and H. G. Dietz, Optimal Code Scheduling for Multiple Pipeline Processors, *1990 International Conference on Parallel Processing, vol. II*, Saint Charles, Illinois, pp. 61-64, August 1990.

13. Oxford Micro Devices, Inc., *New Method for Programming Intel Multimedia Extensions (MMX)*, Oxford Micro Devices, Inc.,
    http://oxfordmicrodevices.com/pr040396.html.
14. Sybase, Inc., *Watcom C/C++ 11.0 Datasheet*, Sybase, Inc.,
    http://www.sybase.com:80/products/languages/cdatash.html.
15. Thinking Machines Corporation, *C* Programming Guide*, Thinking Machines Corporation, Cambridge, Massachusetts, November 1990.

Loop Shifting for Loop Compaction

Alain Darte and Guillaume Huard

LIP, ENS-Lyon, 46, Allée d'Italie, 69007 Lyon, France.
`Firstname.Lastname@ens-lyon.fr`

Abstract. The idea of decomposed software pipelining is to decouple the software pipelining problem into a cyclic scheduling problem **without** resource constraints and an **acyclic** scheduling problem with resource constraints. In terms of loop transformation and code motion, the technique can be formulated as a combination of loop shifting and loop compaction. Loop shifting amounts to move statements between iterations thereby changing some loop independent dependences into loop carried dependences and vice versa. Then, loop compaction schedules the body of the loop considering only loop independent dependences, but taking into account the details of the target architecture. In this paper, we show how loop shifting can be optimized so as to minimize both the length of the critical path and the number of dependences for loop compaction. Both problems (and the combination) are polynomially solvable with fast graph algorithms, the first one by using an algorithm due to Leiserson and Saxe, the second one by designing a variant of minimum-cost flow algorithms.

1 Introduction

Modern computers now exploit parallelism at the instruction level in the microprocessor itself. A "sequential" microprocessor is not anymore a simple unit that processes instructions following a unique stream. The processor may have multiple independent functional units, some pipelined and possibly some other non-pipelined. To take advantage of these "parallel" functionalities in the processor, it is not sufficient to exploit instruction-level parallelism only inside basic blocks. To feed the functional units, it may be necessary to consider, for the schedule, instructions from more than one basic block. Finding ways to extract more instruction-level parallelism (ILP) has led to a large amount of research from both a hardware and a software perspective (see for example [13, Chap. 4] for an overview). A hardware solution to this problem is to provide support for speculative execution on control as it is done on superscalar architectures and/or support for predicated execution as for example in the IA-64 architecture [9]. A software solution is to schedule statements across conditional branches whose behavior is fairly predictable. Loop unrolling and trace scheduling have this effect. This is also what the **software pipelining** technique does for loop branches: loops are scheduled so that each iteration in the software-pipelined code is made from instructions that belong to different iterations of the original loop.

L. Carter and J. Ferrante (Eds.): LCPC'99, LNCS 1863, pp. 415–431, 2000.

Software pipelining is a NP-hard problem when resources are limited. For this reason, a huge number of heuristic algorithms has been proposed, following various strategies. A comprehensive survey is available in the paper by Allan et al. [2]. They classify these algorithms roughly in three different categories: modulo scheduling [16,24] and its variations ([23,14,18] to quote but a few), kernel recognition algorithms such as [1,21], and "move-then-schedule" algorithms [15, 19,5]. Briefly speaking, the ideas of these different types of algorithms are the following. **Modulo scheduling** algorithms look for a solution with a cyclic allocation of resources: every λ clock cycles, the resource usage will repeat. The algorithm thus looks for a schedule compatible with an allocation modulo λ, for a given λ (called the initiation interval): the value λ is incremented until a solution is found. **Kernel recognition** algorithms simulate loop unrolling and scheduling until a "pattern" appears, that means a point where the schedule would be cyclic. This pattern will form the kernel of the software-pipelined code. **Move-then-schedule** algorithms use an iterative scheme that alternatively schedules the body of the loop (loop compaction) and moves instructions across the back-edge of the loop as long as this improves the schedule.

The goal of this paper is to explore more deeply the concept of move-then-schedule algorithms, in particular to see how moving instructions can help for loop compaction. As explained by B. Rau in [22], *"although such code motion can yield improvements in the schedule, it is not always clear which operations should be moved around the back edge, in which direction and how many times to get the best results. [...] How close it gets, in practice, to the optimal has not been studied, and, in fact, for this approach, even the notion of "optimal" has not been defined"*. Following the ideas developed in **decomposed software pipelining** [10,27,4], we show how we can find directly in one preprocessing step a "good" [1] loop shifting (i.e. how to move statements across iterations) so that the loop compaction is more likely to be improved. The general idea of this two-step heuristic is the same as for decomposed software pipelining: we decouple the software pipelining problem into a cyclic scheduling problem **without** resource constraints (finding the loop shifting) and an **acyclic** scheduling problem with resource constraints (the loop compaction).

The rest of the paper is organized as follows. In Section 2, we recall the software pipelining problem and well-known results such as problem complexity, lower bounds for the initiation interval, etc. In Section 3, we explain why combining loop shifting with loop compaction can give better performance than loop compaction alone. A first optimization is to shift statements so as to minimize the critical path for loop compaction as it was done in [4] using an algorithm due to Leiserson and Saxe. A second optimization is to minimize the number of constraints for loop compaction. This optimization is the main contribution of the paper and is presented with full details in Section 4. Section 5 discusses some limitations of our technique and how we think we could overcome them in the future.

---

[1] We put "good" in quotation marks because the technique remains of course a heuristic. Loop compaction itself is NP-complete in the case of resource constraints ...

2 The Software Pipelining Problem

As mentioned in Section 1, our goal is to determine, in the context of move-then-schedule software pipelining algorithms, how to move statements so as to make loop compaction more efficient. We thus need to be able to discuss about "optimality" and about performances relative to an "optimum". For that, we need a model for the loops we are considering and a model for the architecture we are targeting that are both simple enough so that optimality can be discussed. These simplified models are presented in Section 2.1. To summarize, from a theoretical point of view, we assume a simple loop (i.e. with no conditional branches [2]), with constant dependence distances, and a finite number of non pipelined homogeneous functional units.

Despite this simplified model, our algorithm can still be used in practice for more sophisticated resource models (even if the theoretical guarantee that we give is no longer true). Indeed, the loop shifting technique that we develop is the first phase of the process and does not depend on the architecture model but only on dependence constraints. It just shifts statements so that the critical path and the number of constraints for loop compaction are minimized. Resource constraints are taken into account only in the second phase of the algorithm, when compacting the loop, and a specific and aggressive instruction scheduler can be used for this task. Handling conditional branches however has not been considered yet, although move-then-schedule algorithms usually have this capability [19,27]. We will thus explore in the future how this feature can be integrated in our shifting technique. We could also rely on predicated execution as modulo scheduling algorithms do.

2.1 Problem Formulation

We consider the problem of scheduling a loop with a possibly very large number of iterations. The loop is represented by a finite, vertex-weighted, edge-weighted directed multigraph $G = (V, E, d, w)$. The vertices V model the **statements** of the loop body: each $v \in V$ represents a set of **operations** $\{(v, k) \mid k \in \mathbb{N}\}$, one for each iteration of the loop. Each statement v has a delay (or latency) $d(v) \in \mathbb{N}^*$. The directed edges E model dependence constraints: each edge $e = (u, v) \in E$ has a weight $w(e) \in \mathbb{N}$, the **dependence distance**, that expresses the fact that the operation (u, k) (the instance of statement u at iteration k) must be completed before the execution of the operation $(v, k + w(e))$ (the instance of statement v at iteration $k + w(e)$).

In terms of loops, an edge e corresponds to a **loop independent dependence** if $w(e) = 0$ and to a **loop carried dependence** otherwise. A loop independent dependence is always directed from a statement u to a statement v that is textually after in the loop body. Thus, if G corresponds to a loop, it has no circuit C of zero weight $(w(C) \neq 0)$.

---

[2] Optimality for arbitrary loops is in general not easy to discuss as shown in [25].

The goal is to determine a schedule for all operations (v, k), i.e. a function $\sigma : V \times \mathbb{N} \to \mathbb{N}$ that respects the **dependence constraints**:

$$\forall e = (u, v) \in E, \ \forall k \geq 0, \ \sigma(u, k) + d(u) \leq \sigma(v, k + w(e))$$

and the **resource constraints**: if p non pipelined homogeneous resources are available, no more than p operations should be being processed at any clock cycle. The performance of a schedule σ is measured by its **average cycle time** λ:

$$\lambda = \liminf_{N \to \infty} \frac{\max\{\sigma(v, k) + d(v) \mid v \in V, \ 0 \leq k < N\}}{N}.$$

Among all schedules, schedules that exhibit a cyclic pattern are particularly interesting. A **cyclic schedule** σ is a schedule such that $\sigma(v, k) = c_v + \lambda k$, for some $c_v \in \mathbb{N}$ and $\lambda \in \mathbb{N}$. The schedule σ has **period** λ: the same pattern of computations occurs every λ units of time. Within each period, one and only one instance of each statement is initiated: λ is, for this reason, called the **initiation interval** in the literature. It is also equal to the average cycle time of the schedule.

2.2   Lower Bounds and Complexity Results

The average cycle time of any schedule (cyclic or not) is limited both by the resource and the dependence constraints. We denote by λ_∞ (resp. λ_p) the minimal average cycle time achievable by a schedule (cyclic or not) with infinitely many resources (resp. p resources). Of course, $\lambda_p \geq \lambda_\infty$. For a circuit C, we denote by $\rho(C)$ the duration to distance ratio $\rho(C) = \frac{d(C)}{w(C)}$ and we let $\rho_{max} = \max\{\rho(C) \mid C \text{ circuit of } G\}$ ($\rho_{max} = 0$ if G is acyclic). We have the following well-known lower bounds:

$$\lambda_\infty \geq \rho_{max} \ \text{(due to dependences) and} \ \lambda_p \geq \frac{\sum_{v \in V} d(v)}{p} \ \text{(due to resources)}.$$

Without resource constraints, the scheduling problem is polynomially solvable. Indeed, $\lambda_\infty = \rho_{max}$ and there is an optimal **cyclic** schedule (possibly with a fractional initiation interval if λ_∞ is not integral). Such a schedule can be found efficiently with standard minimum ratio polynomials algorithms [11, pp. 636-641]. With resource constraints however, the decision problem associated to the problem of determining a schedule with minimal average cycle time is NP-hard. It is open whether it belongs to NP or not. When restricting to cyclic schedules, the problem is NP-complete (see [12] for an overview on this problem).

3   Loop Shifting and Loop Compaction

3.1   Performances of Loop Compaction Alone

Loop compaction consists in scheduling the body of the loop without trying to mix up iterations. The general principle is the following. We consider the directed graph $A(G)$ that captures the dependences lying within the loop body, in other words the loop independent dependences. These correspond to edges e such that $w(e) = 0$. The graph $A(G)$ is acyclic since G has no circuit C such that $w(C) = 0$. $A(G)$ can thus be scheduled using techniques for directed acyclic graphs, for example list scheduling. Then, the new pattern built for the loop body is repeated to define a cyclic schedule for the whole loop. Resource constraints and dependence constraints are respected inside the body by the list scheduling, while resource constraints and dependence constraints between different iterations are respected by the fact that the patterns do not overlap.

Because of dependence constraints, loop compaction is limited by critical paths, i.e. paths P of maximal delay $d(P)$. We denote by $\Phi(G)$ the maximal delay of a path in $A(G)$. Whatever the schedule chosen for loop compaction, the cyclic schedule σ satisfies $\lambda_\sigma \geq \Phi(G)$. Furthermore, if a list scheduling is used, Coffman's technique [6] shows that there is a path P in $A(G)$ such that $p\lambda_\sigma \leq \sum_{v \in V} d(v) + (p-1)d(P)$. How is this related to optimal initiation intervals λ_∞ and λ_p? We know that $\sum_{v \in V} d(v) \leq p\lambda_p$, thus:

$$\lambda_\sigma \leq \lambda_p + \frac{p-1}{p}\Phi(G) \tag{1}$$

For the acyclic scheduling problem, $\Phi(G)$ is a lower bound for the makespan of any schedule. Thus, list scheduling is a heuristic with a worst-case performance ratio $2 - 1/p$. Here unfortunately, $\Phi(G)$ has - *a priori* - nothing to do with the minimal average cycle time λ_p. This is the reason why loop compaction alone can be arbitrarily bad.

Our goal is now to mix up iterations (through loop shifting, see the following section) so that the resulting acyclic graph $A(G)$ – the subgraph of loop independent dependences – is more likely to be optimized by loop compaction.

3.2 Loop Shifting

Loop shifting consists in the following transformation. We define for each statement v a shift $r(v)$ that means that we delay operation (v, k) by $r(v)$ iterations. In other words, instead of considering that the vertex $v \in V$ in the graph G represents all the operations of the form (v, k), we consider that it represents all the operations of the form $(v, k - r(v))$. The new dependence distance $w_r(e)$ for an edge $e = (u, v) \in E$ is now $w_r(e) = w(e) + r(v) - r(u)$ since the dependence is from $(u, k - r(u))$ to $(v, k - r(u) + w(e)) = (v, k - r(v) + w_r(e))$. This defines a transformed graph $G_r = (V, E, d, w_r)$. Note that the shift does not change the weight of circuits: for all circuits C, $w(C) = w_r(C)$.

Now, if $w_r(e) \neq 0$, the two operations in dependence are computed in different iterations in the transformed code: if $w_r(e) > 0$, the two operations are computed in the original order and the dependence is now a loop carried dependence. If $w_r(e) = 0$, both operations are computed in the same iteration, and we place the statement corresponding to u textually before the statement corresponding to v so as to preserve the dependence as a loop independent dependence. This reordering is always possible since the transformed graph $G_r = (V, E, d, w_r)$ has no zero-weight circuit (G and G_r have the same circuit weights). If $w_r(e) < 0$, the loop shifting is not legal.

In the context of synchronous VLSI circuits [17], such a function $r : V \to \mathbb{Z}$ satisfying $w(e) + r(v) - r(u) \geq 0$ for all edges $e = (u, v)$ is called a *legal retiming* and what we called $\Phi(G)$ is called the **clock period** of the circuit. This link between loop shifting and circuit retiming is not new. It has been used in several algorithms on loop transformations (see for example [5,3,4,8]), including software pipelining.

3.3   Selecting Loop Shifting for Loop Compaction

How can we select a "good" shifting for loop compaction ? Let us first consider the strategies followed by the different move-then-schedule algorithms. Enhanced software pipelining as well as its extensions [19], circular software pipelining [15], and rotation software pipelining [5] use similar approaches: they do loop compaction, then they shift backwards (or forwards) the vertices that appear at the beginning (resp. end) of the loop body schedule. In other words, candidates for backwards shifting (i.e. $r(v) = -1$) are the sources of $A(G)$ and candidates for forwards shifting (i.e. $r(v) = 1$) are the sinks of $A(G)$. This "rotation" is performed as long as there are some benefits for the schedule, but no guarantee is given for such a technique. In decomposed software pipelining, t he algorithm is not an iterative process that uses loop shifting and loop compaction alternately. Loop shifting is chosen once, following a mathematically well-defined objective, and then the loop is scheduled. Two intuitive objectives may be to shift statements so as to minimize:

- the maximal delay $\Phi(G)$ of a path in $A(G)$ since it is tightly linked to the guaranteed bound for the list scheduling. As shown in Section 3.1, it is a lower bound for the performances of loop compaction.
- the number of edges in the acyclic graph $A(G)$, so as to reduce the number of dependence constraints for loop compaction. Intuitively, the fewer constraints, the more freedom for exploiting resources.

Until now, all effort has been put into the first objective. In [10] and [27], the loop is first software-pipelined assuming unlimited resources. The cyclic schedule obtained corresponds to a particular retiming r which is then used for compacting the loop. It can be shown that, with this technique, the maximal critical path in $A(G_r)$ is less than $\lceil \lambda_\infty \rceil + d_{\max} - 1$. In [4], the shift is chosen so that the critical path for loop compaction is minimal, using the retiming algorithm due to Leiserson and Saxe [17] for clock-period minimization. The derived retiming r is such that $\Phi(G_r) = \Phi_{\text{opt}}$ the minimum achievable clock period for G. It can also be shown that $\Phi_{\text{opt}} \leq \lceil \lambda_\infty \rceil + d_{\max} - 1$.

Both techniques lead to similar guaranteed performances for non pipelined resources. Indeed, the performances of loop compaction (see Equation 1) now become:

$$\lambda_\sigma \leq (2 - \frac{1}{p}) \lceil \lambda_p \rceil + \frac{p-1}{p}(d_{\max} - 1) \qquad (2)$$

Unlike for loop compaction alone, the critical path in $A(G_r)$ is now related to λ_p. The performances are not arbitrarily bad as for loop compaction alone.

Both techniques however are limited by the fact that they optimize the retiming only in the critical parts of the graph (for an example of this situation, see Section 4.1). For this reason, they cannot address the second objective, trying to retime the graph so that as few dependences as possible are loop independent. In [4], an integer linear programming formulation is proposed to solve this problem. We show in the next section that a pure graph-theoretic approach is possible, as Calland et al. suspected.

4   Minimizing the Number of Dependence Constraints for Loop Compaction

We now deal with the problem of finding a loop shifting such that the number of dependence constraints for loop compaction is minimized. We first consider the particular case where all dependence constraints can be removed (Section 4.1): we give an algorithm that either finds such a retiming or proves that no such retiming exists. Section 4.2 is the heart of the paper: we give an algorithm that minimizes by retiming the number of zero-weight edges of a graph. Then, in Section 4.3, we run a complete example to illustrate our technique. Finally, in Section 4.4, we extend this algorithm to minimize the number of zero-weight edges without increasing the clock period over a given constant (that can be for instance the minimal clock period). This allows us to combine both objectives proposed in Section 3.3: applying loop shifting so as to minimize both the number of constraints and the critical path for loop compaction.

4.1   A Particular Case: The Fully Parallel Loop Body

We first give an example that illustrates why minimizing the number of constraints for loop compaction may be useful. This example is also a case where all constraints can be removed.

Example 1

```
s=1
do i=1,n
    s=s*(a(i)+b(i))
enddo
```

The dependence graph of this example is represented in Figure 1(a) with edge weights indicated next to them: we assume an execution time of two cycles for the loads, one cycle for the addition, and three cycles for the multiplication (indicated by 'd=' on the figure). Because of the multiplication, the minimal clock period cannot be less than 3. Figure 1(b) depicts the retimed graph with a clock period of 3 and the retiming values (next to the nodes) found if we run

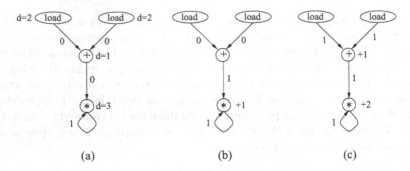

Fig. 1. (a) The dependence graph of Example 1, (b) After clock period minimization, (c) After loop-carried dependence minimization.

Leiserson and Saxe algorithm. Figure 1(c) represents the graph obtained when minimizing the number of zero-weight edges still with a clock period of 3. We assume some limits on the resources for our schedule: we are given one load/store unit and one ALU.

As we can see on Figure 2(a), the simple compaction without shift gives a very bad result (with initiation interval 8) since the constraints impose a sequential execution of the operations. After clock period minimization (Figure 2(b)), the multiplication has no longer to be executed after the addition and a significant improvement is found, but we are still limited by the single load/store resource associated with the two loop independent dependences which constrain the addition to wait for the serial execution of the two loads (the initiation interval is 5). Finally with the minimization of the loop-carried dependences (Figure 2(c)), there are no more constraints for loop compaction (except resource constraints) and we get an optimal result with initiation interval equal to 4. This can not be improved because of the two loads and the single load/store resource. In this example, resources can be kept busy all the time.

Example 1 was an easy case to solve because it was possible to remove all constraints for loop compaction. After retiming, the loop body was fully parallel. In this case, the compaction phase is reduced to the problem of scheduling tasks without precedence constraints, which is, though NP-complete, easier: guaranteed heuristics with a better performance ratio than list scheduling exist. More formally, we say that the body of a loop is **fully parallel** when:

$$\forall e \in E, \ w(e) \geq 1$$

When is it possible to shift the loop such that all dependences become loop carried? Let $l(C)$ be the length (number of edges) of a circuit C in the graph G, we have the following property:

Proposition 1. *Shifting a loop with dependence graph G into a loop with fully parallel body is possible if and only if $w(C) \geq l(C)$ for all circuits C of G.*

Proof. A complete proof can be found in [7].   □

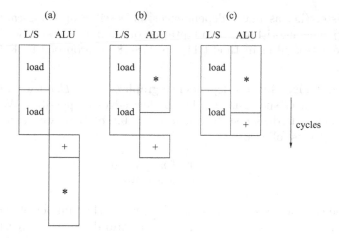

Fig. 2. (a) The loop compaction for Example 1, (b) After clock period minimization, (c) After loop-carried dependence minimization.

From Proposition 1, we can deduce an algorithm that finds a retiming of G such that the loop body is fully parallel, or answers that no such retiming exists.

Algorithm 1 (*Fully Parallel Body*)

- define $G' = (V \cup \{s\}, E', w')$ from $G = (V, E, w)$ by adding a new source s to G, setting $E' = E \cup \{(s, u) \mid u \in V\}$, $\forall e \in E$, $w'(e) = w(e) - 1$ and $\forall e \in E' \backslash E$, $w'(e) = 0$.
- apply the Bellman-Ford algorithm on G' to find the shortest path from s to any vertex in V. Two cases can occur:
  - the Bellman-Ford algorithm finds a circuit of negative weight, in this case return FALSE.
  - the Bellman-Ford algorithm finds some values $\pi(u)$ for each vertex u of G', in this case set $r = -\pi$ and return TRUE.

The complexity of this algorithm is dominated by the complexity of the Bellman-Ford algorithm, which is $O(|V||E|)$. We can also notice that if the graph is an acyclic directed graph it can always be retimed so that the loop has a fully parallel body since it does not contain any circuit (and consequently, there is no circuit of negative weight in G'). In this case, the algorithm can be simplified into a simple graph traversal instead of the complete Bellman-Ford algorithm, leading to a $O(|V| + |E|)$ complexity.

4.2   Zero-Weight Edges Minimization (General Case)

Since we cannot always make the loop body fully parallel, we must find another solution to minimize the constraints for loop compaction. We give here a pure graph algorithm to find a retiming for which as few edges as possible are edges with no register (i.e. as many dependences as possible are loop-carried after loop shifting). The algorithm is an adaptation of a minimal cost flow algorithm, known as the out-of-kilter method ([11, pp. 178-185]), proposed by Fulkerson.

Problem Analysis. Given a dependence graph $G = (V, E, w)$ we are looking for a retiming r of G such that G_r has as few edges as possible. We want to count the number of edges e such that $w_r(e) = 0$. For that, we define the cost $v_r(e)$ of an edge e as follows:

$$v_r(e) = \begin{cases} 1 & \text{if } w_r(e) = 0 \\ 0 & \text{otherwise} \end{cases}$$

We define the cost of the retiming r as $\sum_{e \in E} v_r(e)$, the number of zero-weight edges in the retimed graph. We say that r is **optimal** when $\sum_{e \in E} v_r(e)$ is minimal, i.e. when r minimizes the number of zero-weight edges of G. We will use **flows** in G defined as functions $f : E \to \mathbb{Z}$ such that:

$$\forall v \in V, \quad \sum_{e=(.,v) \in E} f(e) = \sum_{e=(v,.) \in E} f(e)$$

A nonnegative flow is a flow such that $\forall e \in E$, $f(e) \geq 0$, such a flow corresponds to a union of circuits (a multi-circuit) [11, p. 163].

For a given legal retiming r and a given nonnegative flow f, we define for each edge $e \in E$ its **kilter index** $ki(e)$ by:

$$ki(e) = \begin{cases} v_r(e) & \text{if } f(e) = 0 \\ v_r(e) - 1 + f(e)w_r(e) & \text{otherwise} \end{cases}$$

It is easy to check that the kilter index is always nonnegative since $v_r(e) = 1$ if and only if $w_r(e) = 0$, and since the flow is nonnegative. The following proposition gives us a condition of optimality of any retiming r related to this kilter index.

Proposition 2. *Let r be a legal retiming. If there is a flow f such that $\forall e \in E$, $ki(e) = 0$, then r is optimal.*

Proof. A complete proof can be found in [7].   □

Proposition 2 alone does not show how to get an optimal retiming. It remains to show that we can find a retiming and a flow such that all kilter indices are zero. We now study when this happens.

Characterization of Edges. Let us represent the flow and retimed weight of an edge e by the pair $(f(e), w_r(e))$: we get the diagram of Figure 3, called the kilter diagram. Values $f(e)$ and $w_r(e)$ for which $ki(e) = 0$ correspond to the black angled line. Below and above this line, $ki(e) > 0$. We call conformable an edge for which $ki(e) = 0$ and non conformable an edge for which $ki(e) > 0$. As it can

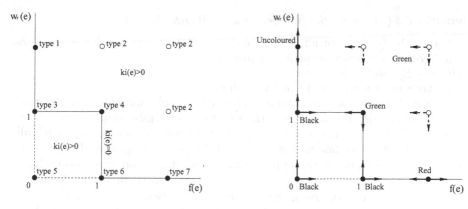

Fig. 3. Kilter diagram, types and colors of edges.

be seen on the figure, we assign a type to each couple $(f(e), w_r(e))$ depending on its position relatively to the line for which $ki(e) = 0$ (this translates into simple conditions on $f(e)$ and $w_r(e)$).

If every edge is conformable, that is if $ki(e) = 0$ for each edge e, then the optimal is reached. Furthermore, we can notice that for each conformable edge e, it is possible to modify by one unit, either $w_r(e)$ or $f(e)$, while keeping it conformable, and for each non conformable edge, it is possible to decrease strictly its kilter index by changing either $w_r(e)$ or $f(e)$ by one unit. We are going to exploit these possibilities in order to converge towards an optimal solution, by successive modifications of the retiming or of the flow.

Algorithm. The algorithm starts from a feasible initial solution and makes it evolve towards an optimal solution. The null retiming and the null flow are respectively a legal retiming and a feasible flow: for them we have $ki(e) = v_r(e)$ for each edge $e \in E$, which means a kilter index equal to 1 for a zero-weight edge and 0 for any other edge. Notice that for this solution any edge is of type 1, 3 or 5. Only the edges of type 5 are non conformable. The problem is then to make the kilter index of type 5 edges decrease without increasing the kilter index of any other edge. To achieve that, we assign to each type of edge a color (see Figure 3) that expresses the degree of freedom it allows:

black for the edges of type 3, 5 and 6: $f(e)$ and $w_r(e)$ can only increase.
green for the edges of type 2 and 4: $f(e)$ and $w_r(e)$ can only decrease.
red for the edges of type 7: $f(e)$ can increase or decrease but $w_r(e)$ should be kept constant.
uncolored for the edges of type 1: $f(e)$ cannot be changed while $w_r(e)$ can increase or decrease.

We can now use the painting lemma (due to Minty, 1966, see [11, pp. 163-165]) as in a standard out-of-kilter algorithm, and give our algorithm. A complete proof of the algorithm can be found in [7].

Algorithm 2 (*Minimize the Number of Zero-Weight Edges*)

1. start with $r(v) = 0$ for all vertices $v \in V$ and $f(e) = 0$ for all edges $e \in E$ and color the edges as explained above.
2. if $\forall e \in E$, $ki(e) = 0$
   a) then return: r is an optimal retiming.
   b) else choose a non conformable edge e_0 (it is black) and apply the painting lemma. One and only one of the two following cases occurs:
      i. there is a cycle containing e_0, without any uncolored edge, with all black edges oriented in the same direction as e_0, and all green edges oriented in the opposite direction. Then add one (respectively subtract one) to the flow of any edge oriented in the cycle in the direction of e_0 (resp. in the opposite direction).
      ii. there is a cocycle containing e_0, without any red edge, with all black edges oriented in the same direction as e_0, and all green edges oriented in the opposite direction. This cocycle determines a partition of the vertices into two sets. Add one to the retiming of any vertex that belongs to the same set as the terminal vertex of e_0.
   c) update the color of edges and go back to Step 2.

Complexity. Looking for the cycle or the cocycle in the painting lemma can be done by a marking procedure with complexity $O(|E|)$ (see [11, pp. 164-165]). As, at each step, at least one non conformable edge becomes conformable, the total number of steps is less than or equal to the number of zero-weight edges in the initial graph, which is itself less than the total number of edges in the graph. Thus, the complexity of Algorithm 2 is $O(|E|^2)$.

4.3 Applying the Algorithm

We now run a complete example for which minimizing the number of zero-weight edges gives some benefit. The example is a toy example that computes the floating point number a_n given by the recursion:

$$a_n = (a_{n-1})^2 + (a_{n-2})^4 + (a_{n-3})^8$$

The straight calculation of the powers is expensive and can be improved. A possibility is to make the calculation as follows (after initialization of first terms):

Example 2

```
do i = 3, n
  b(n) = a(n-1)*a(n-1)
  c(n) = b(n-1)*b(n-1)
  d(n) = c(n-1)*c(n-1)
  t(n) = b(n) + c(n)
  a(n) = t(n) + d(n)
enddo
```

Assume, for the sake of illustration, that the time to multiply is twice the time to add. The dependence graph is depicted on Figure 4: the clock period is already minimal (equal to $\lambda_\infty = 4$ due to the circuit of length 3). The corresponding loop compaction is given, assuming two multipurpose units. The resources impose the execution of the 3 multiplications in at least 4 cycles, and because of the loop independent dependences, the second addition has to wait for the last multiplication before starting, so we get a pattern which is 5 cycles long.

Fig. 4. Dependence graph and the associated schedule for two resources.

The different steps of the algorithm are the following (see also Figure 5). Step 1: we choose, for example, (d, a) as a non conformable edge, we find the circuit (a, b, c, d, a) and we change the flow accordingly. Step 2: we choose (t, a) as a non conformable edge, we find the cocycle defined by the sets $\{a\}$ and $V \setminus \{a\}$, and we change the retiming accordingly. Step 3: we choose (c, t) as a non conformable edge, we find the circuit (t, a, d, c, t) and we change the flow accordingly. Step 4: we choose (b, t) as a non conformable edge, we find the cocycle defined by the two sets $\{t\}$ and $V \setminus \{t\}$, and we change the retiming accordingly. Step 5: all edges are now conformable, the retiming is optimal: $r(t) = r(a) = 1$ and all other values equal 0.

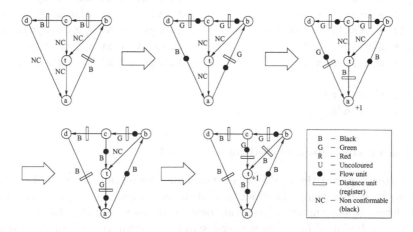

Fig. 5. The different steps of the zero-weight edge minimization.

Note that, at each step, we have to choose a non conformable edge: choosing a different one than ours can result in a different number of steps and possibly a different solution, but the result will still be optimal. Note also that, on this example, the clock period remains unchanged by the minimization, there is no need to use the technique that will be presented in Section 4.4. After the minimization (Figure 6), there remain two (instead of four) loop independent dependences that form a single path. We just have to fill the second resource with the remaining tasks. This results in a 4 cycles pattern which is (here) optimal because of the resource constraints.

Fig. 6. Dependence graph and schedule for two resources after transformation.

The resulting shifted code is given below. Since the different retiming values are 1 and 0, an extra prelude and postlude have been added compared to the original code:

```
b(3) = a(2)*a(2)
c(3) = b(2)*b(2)
d(3) = c(2)*c(2)
do i=4,n
   c(n) = b(n-1)*b(n-1)      (computed at clock cycle 0)
   t(n-1) = b(n-1) + c(n-1)  (computed at clock cycle 0)
   a(n-1) = t(n-1) + d(n-1)  (computed at clock cycle 1)
   b(n) = a(n-1)*a(n-1)      (computed at clock cycle 2)
   d(n) = c(n-1)*c(n-1)      (computed at clock cycle 2)
enddo
t(n) = b(n) + c(n)
a(n) = t(n) + d(n)
```

4.4   Taking the Clock Period into Account

We now discuss about the problem of minimizing the number of edges with null weight without increasing the clock period of our graph over a given constant Φ. Full details about the transformation described below and the changes in the algorithm can be found in [7]. As we can see in [17], we can transform the original graph G in a way such that any legal retiming r of the transformed graph is a legal retiming of G and $\Phi(G_r) \leq \Phi$. More precisely this transformation consists in adding new edges to G with a weight chosen sufficiently low to ensure that any critical path between the head and tail of these new edges has to contain at least one register. But these new edges are only constraints on the retiming and are not to be taken into account in the cost of the retiming. Therefore we need to change our definition of the kilter index for these constraining edges. Finally once the new kilter index and the colors of the new edges are defined properly, our algorithm can apply without changes. The complexity of the overall procedure is now $O(|E||V|^2)$ since the algorithm still performs in at most $|E|$ steps, but can be complete with the new edges added.

5   Conclusions, Limitations and Future Work

As any heuristic, the "shift-then-compact" algorithm that we proposed can fall into traps, even if we rely on an optimal (exponential) algorithm for loop compaction. In other words, for a given problem instance, the shift that we select may not be the best one for loop compaction. Nevertheless, the separation between two phases, a cyclic problem without resource constraints and an acyclic problem with resource constraints, allows us to convert worst case performance results for the acyclic scheduling problem into worst case performance results for the software pipelining problem (see Equation 2). This important idea, due to Gasperoni and Schwiegelshohn [10], is one of the interests of decomposed software pipelining. No other method (including modulo-scheduling) has this property: how close they get to the optimal has not been proved.

This separation into two phases has several other advantages. The first advantage that we already mentioned is that we do not need to take the resource model into account until the loop compaction phase. We can thus design or use very aggressive (even exponential) loop compaction algorithms for specific architectures. A second advantage is that it is fairly easy to control how statements move simply by incorporating additional edges. This is how we enforced the critical path for loop compaction to be smaller than a given constant. This constant could be Φ_{opt}, but choosing a larger value can give more freedom for the second objective, the minimization of loop independent edges. As long as this value is less than $\lambda_p + d_{\max} - 1$, Equation 2 still holds. Another advantage (that we still need to explore) is that the first phase (the loop shifting) can maybe be used alone as a precompilation step, even for architectures that are dynamically scheduled: minimizing the number of dependences inside the loop body for example will reduce the number of mispredictions for data speculation [20].

Despite the advantages mentioned above, our technique has still one important weakness, which comes from the fact that we never try to overlap the patterns obtained by loop compaction. In practice of course, instead of waiting for the completion of a pattern before initiating the following one (by choosing the initiation interval equal to the makespan of loop compaction) , we could choose a smaller initiation interval as long as resource constraints and dependence constraints are satisfied. For each resource p, we can define end(p) the last clock cycle for which p is used in the acyclic schedule σ_a. Then, given σ_a, we can choose as initial interval the smallest λ that satisfies all dependences $\{\forall e = (u, v) \in E, \sigma_a(v) \geq \sigma_a(u) + d(u) - \lambda w(e)\}$ and larger than $\text{end}(p) + 1$ for all resources p.

While this overlapping approach may work well in practice, it does not improve in general the worst case performance bound of Equation 2. We still have to find improvements in this direction, especially when dealing with pipelined resources. We point out that Gasperoni and Schwiegelshohn approach [10] does not have this weakness (at least for the worst case performance bound): by considering the shifting and the schedule for infinite resources as a whole, they can use a loop compaction algorithm with "release dates" (tasks are not scheduled as soon as possible) that ensures a "good" overlapping. In the resulting worst case performance bound, d_{max} can be replaced by 1 for the case of pipelined resources. The problem however is that it seems difficult to incorporate other objectives (such as the zero-weight edge minimization described in this paper) in Gasperoni and Schwiegelshohn approach since there is no real separation between the shifting and the scheduling problems. Nevertheless, this loop compaction with release dates looks promising and we plan to explore it.

Currently, our algorithm has been implemented at the source level using the source-to-source transformation library, Nestor [26], mainly to check the correctness of our strategies. But we found difficult to completely control what compiler back-ends do. In particular, lot of work remains to be done to better understand the link between loop shifting and low-level optimizations such as register allocation, register renaming, strength reduction, and even the way the code is translated! Just consider Example 2 where we write instead $t(n) = c(n) + d(n)$ and $a(n) = t(n) + b(n)$. This simple modification reduces λ_∞ and Φ_{opt} to 3! Minimizing the number of zero-weight edges still lead to the best solution for loop compaction (with a clock period equal to 4), except if we simultaneously want to keep the clock period less than 3. Both programs are equivalent, but the software pipelining problem changes. How can we control this? This leads to the more general question: at which level should software pipelining be performed?

References

1. Alexander Aiken and Alexandru Nicolau. Perfect pipelining; a new loop optimization technique. In *1988 European Symposium on Programming*, volume 300 of *Lecture Notes in Computer Science*, pages 221–235. Springer Verlag, 1988.
2. Vicki H. Allan, Reese B. Jones, Randall M. Lee, and Stephen J. Allan. Software pipelining. *ACM Computing Surveys*, 27(3):367–432, September 1995.
3. Tsing-Fa Lee Allen, C.-H Wu Wei-Jeng Chen, Wei-Kai Cheng, and Youn-Long Lin. On the relationship between sequential logic retiming and loop folding. In *Proceedings of the SASIMI'93*, pages 384–393, Nara, Japan, October 1993.
4. P.Y. Calland, A. Darte, and Y. Robert. Circuit retiming applied to decomposed software pipelining. *IEEE Transactions on Parallel and Distributed Systems*, 9(1):24–35, January 1998.
5. L.-F. Chao, A. LaPaugh, and E. Sha. Rotation scheduling: a loop pipelining algorithm. In *30th ACM/IEEE design automation conference*, pages 566–572, 1993.

6. E. G. Coffman. *Computer and job-shop scheduling theory.* John Wiley, 1976.
7. Alain Darte and Guillaume Huard. Loop shifting for loop compaction. Technical Report RR1999-29, LIP, ENS-Lyon, France, May 1999.
8. Alain Darte, Georges-André Silber, and Frédéric Vivien. Combining retiming and scheduling techniques for loop parallelization and loop tiling. *Parallel Processing Letters*, 7(4):379–392, 1997.
9. Carole Dulong. The IA-64 architecture at work. *Computer*, 31(7):24–32, July 1998.
10. F. Gasperoni and U. Schwiegelshohn. Generating close to optimum loop schedules on parallel processors. *Parallel Processing Letters*, 4(4):391–403, 1994.
11. M. Gondran and M. Minoux. *Graphs and Algorithms.* John Wiley, 1984.
12. C. Hanen and A. Munier. Cyclic scheduling on parallel processors: an overview. In P. Chrétienne, E. G. Coffman, J. K. Lenstra, and Z. Liu, editors, *Scheduling Theory and its Applications.* John Wiley & Sons Ltd, 1995.
13. John L. Hennessy and David A. Patterson. *Computer architecture: a quantitative approach (2nd edition).* Morgan-Kaufmann, 1996.
14. R. A. Huff. Lifetime-sensitive modulo scheduling. In *Conference on programming language design and implementation (PLDI'93)*, pages 258–267. ACM, 1993.
15. Suneel Jain. Circular scheduling. In *Conference on programming language design and implementation (PLDI'91)*, pages 219–228. ACM, 1991.
16. Monica S. Lam. Software pipelining; an effective scheduling technique for VLIW machines. In *SIGPLAN'88 Conference on Programming Language, Design and Implementation*, pages 318–328, Atlanta, GA, 1988. ACM Press.
17. C.E. Leiserson and J.B. Saxe. Retiming synchronous circuitry. *Algorithmica*, 6(1):5–35, 1991.
18. J. Llosa, A. González, E. Ayguadé, and M. Valero. Swing modulo scheduling: a lifetime-sensitive approach. In *Conference on Parallel Architectures and Compilation Techniques (PACT'96)*, Boston, MA, 1996. IEEE Computer Society Press.
19. Soo-Mook Moon and Kemal Ebcioğlu. An efficient resource-constrained global scheduling technique for superscalar and VLIW processors. In *25th annual international symposium on Microarchitecture*, pages 55–71, 1992.
20. Andreas I. Moshovos, Scott E. Breach, T.N. Vijaykumar, and Gurindar S. Sohi. Dynamic speculation and synchronization of data dependences. In *24th International Symposium on Computer Architecture (ISCA'97)*, pages 181–193, Jun 1997.
21. M. Rajagopalan and V. H. Allan. Specification of software pipelining using petri nets. *International Journal of Parallel Programming*, 22(3):273–301, 1994.
22. B. R. Rau. Iterative modulo scheduling: an algorithm for software pipelining. In *27th annual international symposium on Microarchitecture*, pages 63–74, 1994.
23. B. R. Rau. Iterative modulo scheduling. *International Journal of Parallel Programming*, 24(1):3–64, 1996.
24. B. R. Rau and C. D. Glaeser. Some scheduling techniques and an easily schedulable horizontal architecture for high performance scientific computing. In *Proceedings of the Fourteenth Annual Workshop of Microprogramming*, pages 183–198, October 1981.
25. U. Schwiegelshohn, F. Gasperoni, and K. Ebcioğlu. On optimal parallelization of arbitrary loops. *Journal of Parallel and Distributed Computing*, 11:130–134, 1991.
26. Georges-André Silber and Alain Darte. The Nestor library: A tool for implementing Fortran source to source transformations. In *High Performance Computing and Networking (HPCN'99)*, volume 1593 of *Lecture Notes in Computer Science*, pages 653–662. Springer Verlag, April 1999.
27. J. Wang, C. Eisenbeis, M. Jourdan, and B. Su. Decomposed software pipelining. *International Journal of Parallel Programming*, 22(3):351–373, 1994.

Speculative Predication
Across Arbitrary Interprocedural Control Flow

H.G. Dietz

Department of Electrical Engineering
University of Kentucky
Lexington, KY 40506-0046
hankd@engr.uky.edu

Abstract. The next generation of microprocessors, particularly IA64, will incorporate hardware mechanisms for instruction-level predication in support of speculative parallel execution. However, the compiler technology proposed in support of this speculation is incapable of speculating across loops or procedural boundaries (function call and return). In this paper, we describe compiler technology that can support instruction-level speculation across arbitrary control flow and procedural boundaries.
Our approach is based on the concept of converting a conventional control flow graph into a **meta state** graph in which each meta state represents a set of original states speculatively executed together.

1 Introduction

Speculative execution refers to the concept of executing code before we know if the code will need to be executed. Because this generally has the effect of exposing more instruction-level parallelism, an appropriate architecture might achieve significant speedups — despite the fact that some operations performed speculatively were unnecessary.

However, speculatively executing unnecessary instructions is not always harmless. Speculatively executing some operations, such as stores, could cause the program to produce incorrect results. **Predicates** are simply a way for the compiler to mark speculative instructions so that hardware can directly nullify the operation if the speculated condition proves to be false. In this sense, the word "predicate" is a misnomer; the predicate need not be evaluated before the instruction is issued, but more accurately serves as a **guard** to prevent the instruction from causing potentially harmful effects unless and until the condition is satisfied.

1.1 Then and Now...

Neither the concept of speculative execution nor predication is new. The basic concept of VLIW (Very Long Instruction Word) computers is that compiler technology [Ell85] can be used to move operations from likely future control

L. Carter and J. Ferrante (Eds.): LCPC'99, LNCS 1863, pp. 432–446, 2000.

flow paths up into parallel execution slots within instructions in a dominating block of code; pure hardware speculation is used in most modern microprocessors (e.g., Intel's Pentium III). The concept of explicit predicates or guards appears in the CSP and Occam languages and the SIMD (Single Instruction, Multiple Data) concept of **enable masking**. However, it is only now that mainstream microprocessors are on the verge of combining both speculation and predication.

For example, Intel's IA64 EPIC (Explicitly Parallel Instruction Computer) instruction set will make extensive use of these features [AuC98]. Speculation is explicitly supported in a variety of ways, with the potential for large instruction-level parallelism widths. There is also a generous set of predicate registers, any of which can be used to guard any instruction, and there are instructions to simplify construction of complex predicates. In summary, compiler technology for predicated speculation is about to become very important.

Unfortunately, compiler techniques for predicated speculation [AuH97] thus far have been somewhat ad hoc. They focus on converting sequences of possibly-nested if statements into predicates and use of logic minimization techniques to simplify predicate construction.

1.2   Meta State Conversion

In contrast, the approach taken in this paper is to **directly transform a program's conventional state machine description into an equivalent machine description using speculative predicated meta states**. Each meta state consists of a set of guarded original states that can be executed together, and the control flow arcs between meta states behave just like the arcs in the original state machine. We call this process **meta state conversion (MSC)**. Aside from the benefits of having a more formal model for speculative predication, because arbitrary state machines can be given as input, this approach offers the ability to speculate across *arbitrary* control flow and even interprocedural boundaries.

Of course, even this approach is not 100% new. In 1993, we proposed a different type of MSC compilation technique for transforming arbitrary MIMD (Multiple Instruction, Multiple Data) code into pure SIMD (Single Instruction, Multiple Data) code [DiK93]. That technique converted sets of MIMD processing element states that might be executing at the same time on different processors into single, aggregate, meta states representing the complete behavior of the system. Once a program was converted into a single finite automaton based on meta states, that automaton was implemented as pure SIMD code using enable masking to control which processing elements execute which portions of each meta state.

In fact, the way that MSC works for speculative execution is mostly a degenerate case of how it works for MIMD-to-SIMD conversion. In effect, speculation allows a processor simultaneously to be in its current state and one or more potential future states. This is roughly equivalent to generating a SIMD program representing MIMD execution of identical per-processor programs such that some

MIMD processing elements logically began execution earlier than others, which also would cause current and future states to coexist.

The good news is that speculative MSC is easier than MIMD-to-SIMD MSC. For example, if there are N processors each of which can be in any of S states, then it is possible that there may be as many as $S!/(S-N)!$ states in the SIMD meta-state automaton. Without some means to ensure that the state space is kept manageable, the technique is not practical. In that MSC is closely related to NFA to DFA conversion, as used in building lexical analyzers, this potential state space explosion is not surprising. However, for speculative MSC, $N = 1$; the result is that the number of meta states is never more than the number of original states!

This seems strange, since each speculative meta state may contain any of the 2^S possible combinations of original states. However, for speculative MSC, each meta state must begin with precisely *one non-speculative state*, the *core* state, that uniquely identifies it. There are only S potential core states, thus, there cannot be more than S meta states. The speculative MSC algorithm presented in section 3 of the current work confirms this analysis.

1.3   Outline of This Paper

In order to perform a state machine transformation, it is first necessary to express the program as a conventional state machine. The following section describes how this is done for arbitrary programs and gives two examples. Section 3 presents the complete algorithm for speculative MSC, including examples and discussion of how the algorithm can be tuned to be more effective for specific types of target machines. Given a speculative meta state machine, Section 4 briefly overviews the issues involved in generating efficient code for the program. In closing, Section 5 summarizes the contributions of this paper and directions for future work.

2   Construction of the Original State Machine

The conventional state machine version of an original program is created by converting the code into a control flow graph in which each node, or original state, represents a basic block [CoS70]. We assume that these basic blocks are made maximal by a combination of simple local optimizations, removal of empty nodes, and code straightening [CoS70]. However, in order to represent *arbitrary* global and interprocedural control flow, a few tricks are needed.

One might expect that supporting arbitrary global control flow would be a problem, but it is not. In practice, it is most common that each state will have zero, one, or two exit arcs. Zero exit arcs mark termination of the program — for example, a block ending with `exit(0)` in a unix C program. Tw o arcs most often correspond to the `then` and `else` clauses of an if statement or to the exit and continuation of a loop. However, constructs like C's `switch` or Fortran's computed-goto can yield more than two exit arcs. For speculative MSC, there is no algorithmic restriction on the number of control flow exit arcs a state may have. Of course, state machines representing loops, even irreducible ones, also are perfectly valid.

```
if (A) {
    do { B } while (C);
} else {
    do { D } while (E);
}
    F
```

Listing 1: Simple Example

Listing 1 gives C code for a simple example taken from the MIMD-to-SIMD MSC paper [DiK93]. MSC is primarily a transformation of control flow. Thus, in this example, the specific operations within A, B, C, D, E,or F are not important. It is sufficient to assume that A, C, and E are such that static analysis cannot provide information that would eliminate any of the constructs, e.g., none of these expressions yields a compile-time constant.

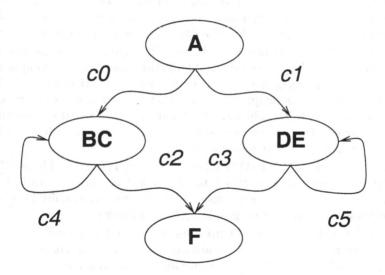

Fig. 1. State Graph for Simple Example

The result of mechanically converting this code is Figure 1. Each arc is labeled with the condition under which it is taken. Thus, $c0$ corresponds to A being true, $c1$ corresponds to A being false, $c2$ corresponds to C being false, etc.

Throughout this paper, we will identify predicates by the condition labels from which they are derived. For example, the predicate 5. would correspond to condition $c5$ being used as a guard, and $c5$ is really E is true, so an instruction guarded by predicate 5. would have effect only if E is true. Since we are tracking blocks of instructions rather than instructions, we would say that, for example, **5.DE** represents all the instructions in node **DE** (i.e., the code from **D** followed by that from **E**) being executed under guard of the predicate 5. Since speculation can pass through multiple nodes, this would be denoted by using multiple predicates; for example, speculatively executing a second iteration of **DE** at the very start of the program would yield the predicated representation **1.5.DE**.

The tricks are needed to handle interprocedural control flow. In the case of non-recursive function calls, it might suffice to use the traditional solution of in-line expanding the function code (i.e., inserting a copy of the original state graph for the function body). However, to be fully general, our approach should not result in a state graph larger than the sum of the graphs for the component functions, and the approach must be able to handle **recursion**. Our tricks accomplish both goals by simply splicing together separate state graphs — essentially using the fact that `call` and `return` are really just "funny looking `gotos`."

A `call` to a function is, literally, a `goto` accompanied by some stack activity. Because the stack activity is nothing more than manipulation of some data (even if part of that data looks like a return address), the instructions that implement this activity merely become part of the caller's basic block. Thus, `call` becomes an unconditional `goto`; literally, a single exit arc from the caller to the first block in the called function. The fact that the `call` may be recursive is irrelevant.

Much like `call`, a `return` also is fundamentally a `goto` accompanied by some stack activity that can be placed within a block. However, there is a complication: the target of the `return` is not known in the same sense that we know it for a `goto`. The trick here is simply to realize that a `return` can only `goto` one of the sites from which it could have been called. Thus, `return` is essentially a somewhat odd-looking `switch` statement — a multiway branch — which is perfectly acceptable in a state machine.

A simple example of this `call/return` processing is given in Listings 2 and 3 and Figure 2. Listing 2 shows two C functions, `main()` and `g()`. In Listing 3, the `goto`-converted version is given; notice that recursion essentially looks like a loop. The resulting original state graph is given in Figure 2.

For completeness, notice that Figure 2 has every arc labeled with a condition despite the fact that many of these conditions are actually the constant *true*. In particular, conditions *c0*, *c1*, *c4*, and *c5* are all the constant true.

There is one additional complication that can arise in constructing the original graph: some states may need to be given the attribute that they are inherently non-speculative. For example, many operating system calls, especially those involving I/O, have this property. These operations are simply encoded as separate states that are marked as non-speculative, with the result that these states will be represented verbatim as meta states in the converted graph. Note that marking operations with the non-speculative attribute requires that they be isolated from any other operations that were in the same basic block, which may require cracking basic blocks into multiple states.

```
main(...)                          main:
{                                    A
  A                                    goto g;
  g(...);                          x:
  B                                    B
  g(...);                              goto g;
  C                                y:
}                                      C
                                       exit(...);
g(...)
{                                  g:
  D                                    D
  if (E) {                             if (E) {
    F                                    F
    g(...);                              goto g;
    G                                z:
  }                                      G
  H                                    }
  return;                            H
}                                      switch (...) {
                                       Case x: goto x;
                                       case y: goto y;
                                       case z: goto z;
                                       }
```

Listings 2 and 3: Recursive Function Example and goto-Conversion

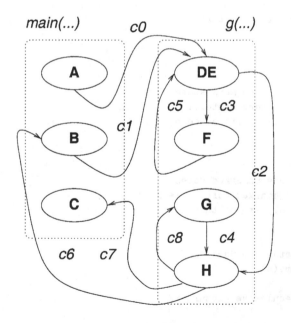

Fig. 2. State Graph for Recursive Function Example

3 Speculative Meta State Conversion

The speculative MSC algorithm is a surprisingly straightforward transformation
of the state graph. In large part, this is because the potential state space explosion seen in both MIMD-to-SIMD MSC [DiK93] and NFA-to-DFA conversion
simply cannot occur when performing speculative MSC. Still, there are a few new
problems that the speculative MSC algorithm must address and a multitude of
new performance-tuning issues.

Like most state-space conversions, our algorithm begins with the start state.
Clearly, the start state of the original program is also the non-speculative **core**
of the start meta state for the transformed program. In speculative execution,
potential future states from the original program graph can be executed simultaneously with the start state, so our next step is a "closure," which we will view
as the recursive application of "reaching," to add predicated original states into
the new start meta state. As this meta state is constructed, if we choose not to
merge a particular reachable state into this meta state, that state is instead added to a work list of meta states remaining to be processed, and an appropriate
arc is added to the meta state graph. This same procedure is then applied to
process each meta state until the work list has been emptied. This process is as
straightforward as it sounds.

The following C-based pseudo code gives the base algorithm for speculative
predicated meta-state conversion:

```
meta_state_convert(state start)
{
 state s;
 metastate m;

 /* Make a node for the meta state
 that will be the start state...
 it has the original start as core
 */
 make_core(start);

 /* While there are unmarked cores */
 while ((s = get_umarked_core()) != Ø) {
  /* We are taking care of this core */
  mark_core(s);

  /* Create a metastate name */
  make_state_name(s);

  /* Compute speculative closure */
  m = {true.s};
  m = reach(s, m, true, s, maxdepth);

  /* Optimize predicates in m using
```

```
logic minimization, etc.
*/
m = optimize_predicates(m);

/* Insert meta state contents */
make_state_contents(s, m);
 }
}
```

Of course, the real work is done in the `reach()` algorithm, which is applied recursively to speculatively merge states. Wisely choosing which states to merge into each meta state is a very difficult problem. In the general case, each original state may have any number of exit arcs. If there are k successor states for the start state, there are 2^k different ways in which the successors could be merged for speculative execution. Of course, each of the successor states may have one or more successors as well, and these states also may be merged for speculative execution. Thus, we see an explosion not in the number of meta states constructed, but in the potential complexity within each meta state.

How extensive should speculative merging be? Although it might seem that the entire program could be merged into the speculative start state, such merging generally is not possible because cycles in the graph would yield infinitely large meta states. The reason is that program loops require a (speculative) *copy of each instruction for each iteration*, so `while` loops that have unbounded iteration effectively would be unwound infinitely. In any case, only a relatively small, machine-dependent, degree of speculation is profitable, so the merging of successor states should be kept appropriate for the target architecture.

For our initial `reach()` algorithm, we suggest three very simple rules for limiting speculation:

1. Set a maximum depth, called `maxdepth` in `meta_state_convert()`, beyond which speculation is not considered. If `maxdepth` = 0, no speculation is done. If `maxdepth` = 1, only speculation across single original state transitions will be allowed. Setting `maxdepth` = ∞ essentially disables this constraint.
2. Because potentially infinite loop expansion would otherwise be difficult to avoid, having multiple copies of an original state within a meta state is disallowed. This has the side benefit of significantly simplifying bookkeeping for code generation.
3. A state that was created with the non-speculative attribute is always a meta state unto itself, never speculatively executed.

Using these three rules, the `reach()` algorithm is:

```
metastate
reach(state core,    /* core original state */
metastate m,         /* meta state */
pred p,              /* predicate to s */
state s,             /* reach is from s */
```

```
int depth)          /* depth from core */
{
  /* Next level of successors */
  foreach (s → x on condition c) {
    /* Is this end of speculation? */
    if (nonspeculative(s) ||
        nonspeculative(x) ||
        (depth < 1) ||
        ({q.x} ∈ m)) {
      /* At an edge of the meta state
         because depth reached or
         state is already included;
         add another meta state core,
         doing nothing if it exists
      */
      make_core(x);

      /* Add meta state exit arcs */
      make_exit_arc(core, p & c, x);
    } else {
      /* Keep speculating on successors */
      m = m ∪ {(p & c).x};
      m = reach(core, m, p & c, x, depth - 1);
    }
  }
  return(m);
}
```

To better understand how the algorithm works, it is useful to return to our examples. Using maxdepth = ∞, the simple example given in Figure 1 becomes the meta state graph shown in Figure 3.

At first glance, it might be somewhat disturbing that **1.3.F** is not also absorbed into the start meta state of Figure 3, instead yielding a separate meta state for **F**. This occurs because **0.2.F** was merged into that state first, thus, the existence of another copy of **F** in the meta state blocked the speculation of **1.3.F** by rule 2. The **1.3.F** speculation does not need to be blocked in the sense that **0.2.F** and **1.3.F** are not involved in detection of a loop, but the ability to optimize **F**'s code based on knowing it came through the **0.2.** path might yield optimizations that would not have been possible if both the **0.2.** and **1.3.** paths were merged to describe a single copy of **F**'s code. In summary, the result may look strange, but we will have to wait for speculative predicated hardware before we can know if performance is damaged.

It is interesting to note that this graph is quite different from that generated using MIMD-to-SIMD MSC [DiK93] on the same input. That graph is given in Figure 4. Notice the increase in the number of meta states: the original graph had 4 states and so does the speculative meta state graph, but the SIMD meta state graph has 8. The concepts may be similar, but the behavior of the two MSC algorithms is clearly very different.

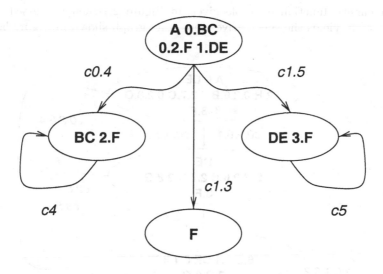

Fig. 3. Speculative Meta-State Graph for Simple Example

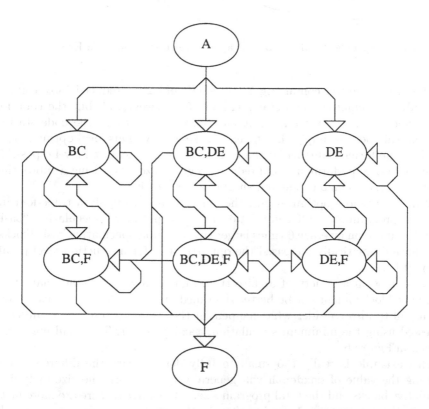

Fig. 4. SIMD Meta State Graph for Simple Example

The recursive function example given in Figure 2, when processed using maxdepth $= \infty$, yields the speculative meta state graph shown in Figure 5.

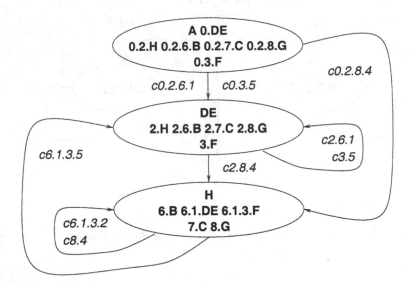

Fig. 5. Speculative Meta-State Graph for Recursive Function Example

The original graph containing 7 states (Figure 2) is reduced into a graph with only 3 speculative meta states (Figure 5). However, all but the code for **A** is *replicated in every meta state*. Of course, just because the code started out identical does not imply that it remains so after various local optimizations have been performed; further, if the code is truly identical, it may be possible to improve cache performance and reduce program size by creating a subroutine wrapper for the common code and sharing access to that.

Still, if we ignore optimizations, the basic result is roughly a three-fold increase in program size. Of course, we also have produced speculative "basic blocks" that are on av erage 6 times larger than the non-speculative basic blocks, so we have dramatically increased the opportunities for instruction level parallelism (ILP).

Depending on a variety of architectural and compiler back-end characteristics, huge blocks might not be better than medium size blocks. For this reason, it is useful to also consider what happens if the recursive function example is processed using the minimum speculation, maxdepth $= 1$. The resulting graph is given in Figure 6.

This example is really too small to fully demonstrate the difference, but reducing the value of maxdepth will generally reduce both the size of typical speculative blocks and the total program size. Interestingly, there are more meta states in the maxdepth $= 1$ version than in the maxdepth $= \infty$ version; we do not know for certain if this is a quirk of the example, but suspect that it is not.

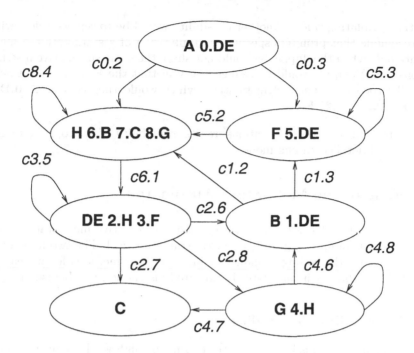

Fig. 6. Minimally Speculative Graph for Recursive Function Example

In effect, using deeper speculation allowed some cores to be omitted because they were always speculated correctly before that core state would have been reached, no matter which paths were taken. We expect this general property to hold for most program state graphs.

In summary, the algorithm as we have presented it offers just one tunable parameter, maxdepth, and even use of this is somewhat unclear. Howev er, many variations are possible:

- Make individual speculation decisions based on the estimated improvement (cost in terms of time or space) in that particular speculation. E.g., do not speculatively execute block **A** with block **B** unless parallel execution of these two blocks is possible and would be expected to yield speedup over not speculating.
- While performing speculative MSC, if a state is encountered that can be divided into a portion worth speculating and a portion not worth speculating, that state can be split into two states and speculation applied only to the profitable portion. The MIMD-to-SIMD MSC algorithm used a similar technique to split states where execution time imbalances existed [DiK93].
- Rule 2 for speculative state merging can be augmented by a technique that requires more bookkeeping, but better handles speculation involving loops. For example, by unrolling a loop by a factor of two, we would obtain different states for the loop body such that two iterations could be speculated

without violating rule 2. Another possibility would be to replace rule 2 with a technique that prohibits speculative duplication of a state within a meta state *only* when the duplicates could not share the same speculative instructions; i.e., Figure 3 would be changed only in that the **F** meta state would be absorbed into the start meta state, which would then contain **A 0.BC 1.DF** (**0.2** *or* **1.3**).**F**.

Experimentation with these variations awaits availability of appropriate target hardware and detailed timing models.

4   Coding of the Meta-State Automaton

Given a program that has been converted into a speculative meta state graph, most aspects of coding the graph are fairly straightforward. The two most interesting issues are the coding of multiway branches and methods for increasing the probability that each speculatively-executed instruction will be useful.

4.1   Multiway Branch Encoding

Although multiway branches are relatively rare in high-level language source code, the state machine conversion process often converts **return** instructions into multiway branches. Additional multiway branches can be the direct result of the speculative meta state conversion process itself; for example, state **G 4.H** in Figure 6 essentially inherited one exit arc from original state **G** and two more from **H**.

For conventional machines, the most effective way to code a multiway branch is generally to create a customized hash function that can be used to index a jump table [Die92]. Oddly, predication offers a simpler way that essentially **converts switch statements into return statements**.A **return** is really an indirect **goto** in which the designated storage cell (e.g., a particular register) holds the destination address. Thus, we can implement arbitrary multiway branches by simply applying the appropriate predicates to instructions that place the target value in that storage cell.

For example, consider meta state **G 4.H** in Figure 6. To implement the 3-way branch, code like that shown in Listing 4 should suffice.

```
(4.6).load addr_register, location_of( B 1.DE)
(4.7).load addr_register, location_of( C)
(4.8).load addr_register, location_of( G 4.H)
        goto *(addr_register)
```

Listing 4: Predicated Multiway Branching

4.2   Common Subexpression Induction

The true limit on performance improvement by speculative predication is not how much can be grouped together for parallel execution, but how much *useful* work can be executed in parallel. Speculating with greater depth may increase the number of instructions available for parallel execution, but it also tends to lower the probability that those instructions will be useful, i.e., that they are on the control flow path that the code actually takes.

Because the examples in this paper all describe basic blocks as the fundamental unit of code, it is easy to forget that instructions, not blocks, are the predicated units of execution. The fact that two blocks differ does not imply that they contain wholly different instructions.

Often approximated by SIMD hand coders [NiT90][WiH91], Common Subexpression Induction (CSI) [Die92a] is a compilation technique that, given a set of guarded blocks of code, attempts to rewrite the code to maximize the set of common subexpressions (instruction sequences) that can be shared by multiple, originally disjoint, guards. Although CSI was originally developed as a SIMD optimization designed to allow a larger fraction of the SIMD processing elements to be enabled for each instruction, the exact same technique applied to predicated speculative execution yields an increase in the probability that the the operations being performed are useful.

The SIMD CSI algorithm can be summarized as follows. First, a guarded DAG is constructed, then this DAG is improved using inter-thread CSE. The improved DAG is then used to compute information for pruning the search: earliest and latest, operation classes, and theoretical lower bound on execution time. Next, this information is used to create a linear schedule (SIMD execution sequence), which is improved using a cheap approximate search and then used as the initial schedule for the permutation-in-range search that is the core of the CSI optimization.

Although the SIMD CSI algorithm is usable for speculative predication, we can significantly simplify the algorithm. For SIMD machines, masking (predication) is a "modal" operation; thus, the cost of an instruction sequence is a function of the number of times that masks are changed, which depends on the precise (sequential) instruction order. For speculative predication, only the creation of the guards has cost, so the CSI algorithm need not search all linear instruction orders to determine the best coding. We are currently developing this new predicated variant of CSI.

5   Conclusions

The evolution of a new breed of microprocessors, predicated speculative execution engines, appears to demand a whole new breed of compiler transformations. However, just as neither hardware for predication nor speculation is truly new, the required compiler technology also can be most effectively fashioned from the techniques developed before. The approach detailed in this paper is quite new, and embodies several new algorithms, but is clearly derived from compiler technology developed for MIMD-to-SIMD conversion in 1992-1993.

In this paper, we hav e demonstrated a simple, fully general, way for a compiler to manage predicated speculative execution spanning arbitrary control flow and procedural boundaries. We anticipate further adaptation and improvement of compiler techniques which were originally developed for SIMD architectures.

References

[AuC98]   David I. August, Daniel A. Connors, Scott A. Mahlke, John W. Sias, Kevin M. Crozier, Ben-Chung Cheng, Patrick R. Eaton, Qudus B. Olaniran, and Wen-mei W. Hwu, "Integrated Predicated and Speculative Execution in the IMPACT EPIC Architecture," *Proceedings of the 25th International Symposium on Computer Architecture*, July 1998.

[AuH97]   David I. August, Wen-mei W. Hwu, and Scott A. Mahlke, "A Framework for Balancing Control Flow and Predication," *Proceedings of the 30th International Symposium on Microarchitecture*, December 1997.

[CoS70]   J. Cocke and J.T. Schwartz, *Programming Languages and Their Compilers*, Courant Institute of Mathematical Sciences, New York University, April 1970.

[Die92]   H.G. Dietz, "Coding Multiway Branches Using Customized Hash Functions," Technical Report TR-EE 92-31, School of Electrical Engineering, Purdue University, July 1992.

[Die92a]   H.G. Dietz, "Common Subexpression Induction," Proceedings of the 1992 *International Conference on Parallel Processing*, Saint Charles, Illinois, August 1992, vol. II, pp. 174-182.

[DiK93]   H. G. Dietz and G. Krishnamurthy, "Meta-State Conversion,"*Proceedings of the 1993 International Conference on Parallel Processing*, vol. II, pp. 47-56, Saint Charles, Illinois, August 1993.

[Ell85]   Ellis, J.R., *Bulldog: A Compiler for VLIW Architectures*. MIT Press, Cambridge, MA, 1985.

[NiT90]   M. Nilsson and H. Tanaka, "MIMD Execution by SIMD Computers," Journal of Information Processing, Information Processing Society of Japan, vol. 13, no. 1, 1990, pp. 58-61.

[WiH91]   P.A. Wilsey, D.A. Hensgen, C.E. Slusher, N.B. Abu-Ghazaleh, and D.Y. Hollinden, "Exploiting SIMD Computers for Mutant Program Execution," Technical Report No. TR 133-11-91, Department of Electrical and Computer Engineering, University of Cincinnati, Cincinnati, Ohio, November 1991.

Porting an Ocean Code to MPI Using TSF*

F. Bodin, Y. Mével, S. Chauveau, and E. Rohou

IRISA, Campus Universitaire de Beaulieu, 35042 Rennes, France

1 Introduction

TSF [1] is an extensible program transformation tool. TSF provides a scripting language to implement simple interactive code transformations for Fortran 77/90 and can be used as a platform for building tools. TSF scripts are interpreted and are loaded dynamically from a script "database".

To illustrate how TSF can be used in the process of code parallelization we describe its use for the porting of an ocean code, ADJOIN-MICOM, to parallel computers. The code is about 20000 lines and contains 600 loop nests that access to 150 2D and 3D arrays. To understand the "size" of the parallelization tasks, spending one hour to transform each loop nest would correspond to 3.75 months of continuous work (40 hours a week)! Automating the needed code rewriting, in comparison, has represented less than a week of work. Applying the transformations can be done in a matter of hours. However, the reader should be aware that we are only addressing, in this paper, the rewriting process. Analyzing, running, debugging and optimizing the code still represents months of work.

2 TSF

The TSF is an extension of FORESYS [3], a Fortran re-engineering system. TSF is not very different, for what it allows to do, to tools such as Sage++, MT1 or Polaris. It provides functions to analyze and to modify syntax abstract trees which complexity is hidden by some "object" abstraction. However, TSF differs greatly in the manner the program is presented to the user. TSF is centered around a scripting language that provides interactive and simple access to the Fortran programs. The scripts are dynamically loaded, compiled, on the fly, to lisp and interpreted. They are interactive and user oriented, contrary to tools such as Sage++ that are batch and compiler writer oriented. The TSF script mechanism allows the user to write its own program transformations as well as to access to analysis (such as data dependence, interprocedural analysis of parameter passing, etc.) that are usually internal to restructuring tools.

* The work described in this paper was partially supported by the European Union ESPRIT project 23502, 'FITS'.

L. Carter and J. Ferrante (Eds.): LCPC'99, LNCS 1863, pp. 447–450, 2000.

The TSF scripting language is in spirit very close to the Matlab language but instead of dealing with matrices it deals with Fortran statements. And similarly to Matlab that provides access to complex operators, TSF scripts via function called "built-in" give access to various program transformations (such as loop blocking, etc.) and analysis (such as data dependencies, etc.). The following script illustrates the style of programming the scripting language proposes:

```
SCRIPT AccessAnalysis ()                   //beginning of the script
  expArray := $csel                        //Fortran selection in expArray
  IF (expArray.VARIANT == "vardim") THEN   //check if the selection is
                                           //an array access
    externalTool := "../AnalyzeArrayAccess"//analysis program path
    STARTTOOL(externalTool)                //start the analyzer
    reachedIndex := expArray.REACHABLEINDEX//get surrounding index
                                           //variables
    SEND(reachedIndex)                     //send enclosing loop indexes
                                           //to the analysis program
    nbdim := expArray.DIMENSION            //number of array dimensions
    WHILE (nbdim != 0)                     //for all dimensions
      dim := expArray.DIMENSION(nbdim)     //get the access expression
      SEND (dim.LINEARFORM(reachedIndex))  //send the array access
                                           //expression in linear form
      nbdim := nbdim - 1                   //next dimension
    ENDWHILE
    RECV(comment)                          //receive the analysis result
    INSERTCOMMENT($csel,comment)           //insert it as a comment
    CLOSETOOL(externalTool)                //stop the analysis program
  ENDIF                                    //
ENDSCRIPT                                  //end of the script
```

If the user selects an array access expression and then activates the previous script, the program "AnalyzeArrayAccess" receives the loop nest index variables and the array accesses in linear form. The result of the analysis is inserted in the code as Fortran comments for instance.

3 Parallelizing ADJOIN-MICOM

ADJOIN-MICOM, developed at EPSHOM in Toulouse, France, is a linear version of the non-linear shallow Atlantic ocean model, MICOM. The parallelization of MICOM has been performed for shared memory and distributed memory architectures [2]. The parallelization is based on distributing the first two dimensions of all the arrays on the processors. The communications are implemented using fake zones. These fake zones are also used for limiting data exchanges via redundant computations. The same parallelization scheme has been applied for ADJOIN-MICOM and we reused the MPI based run-time library that was developed for the former MICOM code.

Figure 1 gives an example of the structure of the loop nests and the resulting transformation. All loops have a similar structure that can be exploited by the tools. Loops J scans the North-South direction of the Atlantic ocean. To avoid the computation of the model on ground coordinates, ocean segments are stored in integer arrays ISU(J), IFU(J,L), ILU(J,L), which respectively contains the number of segments, the starting coordinate and the final coordinate in the West-East direction. The loop in K is the depth and is not subject to parallelization. Rewriting the code for parallel execution is straightforward and is decomposed in the following tasks, each one corresponding to a script:

1. Check if loops are parallel: The task of checking if the loops are parallel could not be performed using a standard data dependency analysis such as the one provided by FORESYS. The loop bounds are not known and iterate on three levels while this is really a 2 dimensional iteration space. Furthermore, indirect accesses to the code exist as shown Figure 1. In this figure, in array access VISCA(I,JAU(I,J)) the array JAU(I,J) may contain J, J+1 or J-1. So using that fact, it is easy to check if the loops are parallel or not. The TSF script that checks if the loops are parallel, simply looks, for each array, if there is different accesses, one being a write.

2. Change array declarations and convert the loop bounds to implement the owner computes rules: These transformations are really straightforward except for one thing. If the loop bounds in the original code were II1 or JJ1 that implies that the extreme bound of the grid is to be avoided. As a consequence the loop structure has to be changed in such manner that a guard can be inserted.

3. Insert communications: Inserting the communication routines is one of the most error prone tasks. In the non optimized version of the code (the one we are producing) before each loop the fake zones must be updated if there are referenced (via a runtime function called **update8**).The difficulties solved using the script mechanism are twofold:

   a) some of the loops contains tenths of array accesses. It is very easy to forget some arrays.

   b) The insertion of the communication routines needs the declaration of the arrays to be known. These declarations are in different include files. Making no error here, is difficult and it takes time to find the declaration of an array.

4. Insert debug instrumentation: Debugging the parallel code is achieved by comparing the content of arrays in the sequential and parallel codes after each loop nest. After each loop nest a call to a **debug** routine is inserted for each modified array in the loop. The **debug** routine computes a checksum of the array. Inserting calls to the debug routine has to be done twice and consistently for the parallel and the sequential version of the code.

The main difficulty here is related to the volume, not the complexity of the transformations. However, these transformations cannot be achieved by an automatic parallelizer.

```
DO 80 K = 1, KK !DEPTH                          DO 80 K = 1,KK
  KNM = K + KK*(NM-1)                              KNM = K + KK*(NM-1)
  DO 68 J = 1, JJ1 !NORTH-SOUTH                    CALL UPDATE8(VISCA,-NBDY+1,IDM+NBDY,1-NBDY,JJ+NBDY,1,1)
    JA = J - 1                                     CALL UPDATE8(DPUA,-NBDY+1,IDM+NBDY,1-NBDY,JJ+NBDY,1,2*KDM)
    DO 68 L = 1,ISU(J)                             CALL UPDATE8(DPU,-NBDY+1,IDM+NBDY,1-NBDY,JJ+NBDY,1,2*KDM)
      DO 68 I = IFU(J,L),ILU(J,L) !WEST-EAST       DO J = 1-MARGIN,JJ+MARGIN
        VISCA(I,JAU(I,J)) = VISCA(I,JAU(I,J)) - AUX1A(I,J)    IF ((J+JSTART-1) .LE. (J_MAX-1)) THEN
        DPUA(I,JA,KN) =                                 JA = J - 1
&           DPUA(I,JA,KN) + AUX2A(I,J)*AMAXS(DPU(I,JA,KM),ONEMM)   DO 68 L = 1,ISU(J)
68  CONTINUE                                             DO I = MAX(1-MARGIN,IFU(J,L)),MIN(II+MARGIN,ILU(J,L))
    DO 60 J = 1, JJ                                         VISCA(I,JAU(I,J)) = VISCA(I,JAU(I,J)) - AUX1A(I,J)
      DO 60 L = 1, ISU(J)                                  DPUA(I,JA,KM) =
        DO 60 I = IFU(J,L),ILU(J,L)                &           DPUA(I,JA,KM) + AUX2A(I,J)*AMAXS(DPU(I,JA,KM),ONEMM)
          PU(I,J,K+1) = PU(I,J,K)+DPU(I,J,KNM)             END DO
60  CONTINUE                                     68    CONTINUE
    DO 70 L = 1, ISV(J)                              END IF
      DO 70 I = IFV(J,L), ILV(J,L)               END DO
        PV(I,J,K+1) = PV(I,J,K)+DPV(I,J,KNM)     IDD = '.INAUX001'
70  CONTINUE                                     CALL DEBUG(VISCA,1,1,0,'./VISCA.D3'//IDD)
50  CONTINUE                                     CALL DEBUG(DPUA,1,KDM+1,0,'./DPUA.D3'//IDD)
80 CONTINUE                                      DO 50 J = 1-MARGIN,JJ+MARGIN
                                                   DO 60 L = 1,ISU(J)
                                                     DO 60 I = MAX(1-MARGIN,IFU(J,L)),
                                                &           MIN(II+MARGIN,ILU(J,L))
                                                       PU(I,J,K+1) = PU(I,J,K)+DPU(I,J,KNM)
                                                60  CONTINUE
                                                   DO 70 L = 1,ISV(J)
                                                     DO 70 I = MAX(1-MARGIN,IFV(J,L)),
                                                &           MIN(II+MARGIN,ILV(J,L))
                                                       PV(I,J,K+1) = PV(I,J,K)+DPV(I,J,KNM)
                                                70  CONTINUE
                                                   IDD = '.INAUX002'
                                                50  CONTINUE
                                                   CALL DEBUG(PV,1,KDM+1,0,'./PV.D3'//IDD)
                                                   CALL DEBUG(PU,1,KDM+1,0,'./PU.D3'//IDD)
                                                80 CONTINUE
```

Fig. 1. ADJOIN-MICOM: loop example before and after parallelization.

4 Conclusions and Future Work

TSF is proposed as an additional tool to other development and automatic parallelization tools. While no complex code transformation was used to port the application it still requires a lot of functionality to allow the user to easily developed its own program transformations without having to deal with low-level details such as graphical interface, compilation and abstract syntax trees. We believe TSF offers a good tradeoff between simplicity and transformation power.

Acknowledgments. We would like to thank Rémy Baraille and Nicolas Filatoff from the EPSHOM for the ADJOIN-MICOM code and the fruitful interactions.

References

1. F. Bodin, Y. Mevel, and R. Quiniou, *A user level program transformation tool*, Proc, Int. Conference on Supercomputing, 1998
2. A. Sawdey, M. O'Keefe and R. Bleck. *The Design, Implementation and Performance of a Parallel Ocean Circulation Model.* In G. Hoffmann and N. Kreitz (Ed.): Proc. 6th ECMWF Workshop on the Use of Parallel Processors in Meteorology: Coming of Age, 523–550, 1995
3. Simulog SA, *FORESYS, FORtran Engineering SYStem, Reference Manual Version 1.5*, Simulog, Guyancourt, France, 1996

A Geometric Semantics for Program Representation in the Polytope Model

Brian J. d'Auriol*

Dept. of Computer Science, The Univ. of Texas at El Paso, El Paso, Texas 79968-0518

Abstract. A new *geometric* framework for parallel program representation is proposed to address the difficulties of parallel programming. The focus of this work is the expression of collections of computations and the inter-, intra-relationships thereof. Both linguistic and non-linguistic carried geometric semantics are presented and characterized. A formal review of the basic Polytope Model is given.

1 Introduction

A new *geometric* framework for parallel program representation is proposed to address the difficulties of parallel programming. The focus of this work is the expression of collections of computations and the inter-, intra-relationships thereof. Such collections are encapsulated by polytopes, wherein particular computations are mapped to selected internal integer points. Spatial relationships can be quantified by the dimension of the polytope and by the spatial orientation of the contained computations. Temporal, hierarchal or other relationships can also be represented by superimposing dependency graphs over the geometric object(s). The notion of such collections of program fragments is central to human perception of program design, for example, the separation of program fragments into modules, objects, functions, etc. The software development process is thus completed by (a) specifying one or more groupings by describing polytopes and (b) constructing relationships between particular computations and between polytopes. A complete program may be represented by hierarchies of polytopes.

Geometric representation of programs has been established by advances in parallelizing compiler research, in particular, the Polytope Model [1,2,3]. The typical benefit is the analysis of the parallelism and inhibiting factors and subsequent possible optimizations. This work extends the Polytope Model by presenting the semantics of geometric representation of program with the focus that the *human initially expresses the solution to a given problem geometrically.*

Semantically, the geometric specification has either (a) *linguistic carried semantics*, that is, an induced semantics due to some initial linguistic formulation of the program or (b) *non-linguistic carried semantics*, that is, has no such predefinition of semantics.

This paper is organized as follows. Section 2 presents a succinct and formal review of the Polytope Model. Section 3 presents non-linguistic carried semantics. Finally, conclusions are given in Section 4.

* Partially supported by University of Akron, Grant No. FRG 1391

L. Carter and J. Ferrante (Eds.): LCPC'99, LNCS 1863, pp. 451–454, 2000.

2   Linguistic Carried Semantics

The following p-nested loop-nest structure, denoted by $\mathcal{L}$, is considered in this paper and is consistent with the literature, for example [2].

for $I_1 = f_{1_l}(l_1)$ to $f_{1_u}(u_1)$ step s_1
   for $I_2 = f_{2_l}(i_1, l_2)$ to $f_{2_u}(i_1, u_2)$ step s_2
       $\vdots$

       for $I_p = f_{p_l}(i_1, i_2, \ldots, i_{p-1}, l_p)$ to $f_{p_u}(i_1, i_2, \ldots, i_{p-1}, u_p)$ step s_p
         $\hat{S} = (S_1, S_2, \ldots)$

where each $I_j, j \in \mathbf{Z}, 1 \leq j \leq p$, is a loop-index variable with corresponding integer i_j values given by f_{l_j}, f_{u_j} and $s_j, s_j \neq 0$, f denotes a parameterized affine integer function, u, l are integer bounds and $\hat{S}$ is an ordered list of program statements, S_k. The usual semantics of $\mathcal{L}$ applies.

Let $\overrightarrow{p_1 p_2}$ denote a vector from point p_1 to p_2. Some definitions, axioms and lemmas are summarized below (proofs are ommited but may be found in [4]).

Definition: The domain of an $i_j, 1 \leq j \leq p$ induced by $\mathcal{L}$ is given by: $\mathrm{dom}(i_j) = \{f_{j_l}, f_{j_l} + s_j, f_{j_l} + 2s_j, \ldots, f_{j_l} + ks_j, \ldots\}$ for $f_{j_l} + ks_j \leq f_{j_u}$. **Definition:** Each $i_j, 1 \leq j \leq p$ induced by $\mathcal{L}$ defines a set $\mathcal{S}_j$ of parallel vectors $\overrightarrow{0(k)}, k \in \mathrm{dom}(i_j)$ differing only in their length.

Lemma 1. *The set $\mathcal{S}_j$ induced by $\mathcal{L}$ is finite and enumerable if and only if either (a) $f_{j_l} \leq f_{j_u}$ for $s_j > 0$ or (b) $f_{j_l} \geq f_{j_u}$ for $s_j < 0$ holds.*

Axiom 1 *A coordinate reference system defined by the basis vector, $\mathbf{B}_j = \overrightarrow{0(b_1, b_2, \ldots, b_n)}, b_k \in \{0, 1\}, \sum_n (b_k) = 1$ for each i_j induced by $\mathcal{L}$ exists.*

Axiom 2 *The set of basis vectors, $\mathbf{B}_j, 1 \leq j \leq p$ induced by $\mathcal{L}$ form an orthogonal basis set in $\mathbf{R}^p$ with origin $\mathbf{O}$.*

Consider the case where some $S_k \in \hat{S}$ is another for loop nest. Let S_k induce an object in $\mathbf{R}^q$ (Axiom 2). If $k = 1$ then S_k can be said to *extend* the space of $\mathcal{L}$, thus, $\hat{S} - \{S_1\}$ exists in $\mathbf{R}^{p+q}$. If however, $k > 1$, then, $S_l, 1 \leq l \leq k$ exists in $\mathbf{R}^p$ and $S_l, l > k$ exists in $\mathbf{R}^{p+q}$. Consequently, there exists a set of subspaces such that $\mathbf{R}^p$ is composed of a restricted set of $\mathbf{R}^k, 1 \leq k \leq p$ subspaces. These results are summarized in the following lemma.

Lemma 2. *Given $\mathcal{L}$ and some $S_k, k \geq 1$, if S_k is itself a for loop nest, then S_k exists in $\mathbf{R}^p$ and is said to extend the space by q dimensions where q is the number of loops in S_k.*

Lemma 3. *Given $\mathcal{L}$, $\exists$ a polytope, P in $\mathbf{R}^p$ that contains all $\mathrm{dom}(i_j), 1 \leq j \leq p$.*

Lemma 3 summarizes the primary basis of the Polytope Model and various presentations of it can be found (e.g. [3]). It is included here for completeness. **Definition:** An active polytope is defined as: $\hat{P} = (P, < v_j, \hat{S} > \cup < v_{j'}, \mathrm{NULL} >, \mathrm{scan}(P))$ where NULL denotes a null statement and $\mathrm{scan}(P)$ denotes a total order of all points in P.

Lemma 4. *Given some $\mathcal{L}$, there is an equivalent $\hat{P}$; also, given some $\hat{P}$, there is an equivalent $\mathcal{L}$.*

3 Non-linguistic Carried Semantics

Distinctly, an *initial* program specification in the geometric domain is considered. Here, there is no inherent initial semantics. Some basic definitions follow. **Definition:** The domain of an i_j, $1 \le j \le p$ is a specified set of values $V_j = \{v_1, v_2, \ldots, v_k\}$ such that the vector $\overrightarrow{0, v}, \forall v \in V$ is perpendicular to $\mathbf{B}_j$. The domain is written: $\mathrm{dom}(i_j) = \{v_1, v_2, \ldots, v_k\} = i_j\{v_1, v_2, \ldots, v_k\}$. **Definition:** A valid computation point, f, is defined to be an element from the set of all points in $\mathbf{R}^k$ for some fixed $k, 1 \le k \le p$ such that $f \in \hat{F} = \{(v_1, v_2, \ldots, v_k)|v_j \in i_j, 1 \le j \le k, 1 \le k \le p\}$ and that there exists an instance $< f, \hat{\mathsf{S}} >$. **Definition:** The set of all valid computation points is denoted by $F \subseteq \hat{F}$. Note that f may exist in some subspace $\mathbf{R}^k, 1 \le k \le p$, hence, there exists associations of $\hat{\mathsf{S}}$ to valid computation points in multiple but different subspaces. Here, subspace is restricted to that defined by orthogonal combinations of one or more basis vectors (or by any multiple of such vectors). For example, in $\mathbf{R}^3$, there is one $\mathbf{R}^3$, three $\mathbf{R}^2$ (corresponding to each plane) and three $\mathbf{R}^1$ (corresponding to each axis) subspaces. The maximum number of such subspaces is denoted by $\hat{p}$. Feautrier in [5] describes subspaces in the context of a 'data space' (which is different). Further discussion of subspaces appear in [6,4].

Lemma 5. *Given some F in $\mathbf{R}^k$ for some fixed $k, 1 \le k \le p$, all $f \in F$ can be contained in a convex polytope P in $\mathbf{R}^k$.*

Proof. The proof requires showing that all $F_k, 1 \le k \le p$ are contained in respective p bounded polyhedrons [7][Chapter 7]. For the case of F_p, select two values, x_j, y_j from $V_j, 1 \le j \le p$ such that x_j is the minimum and y_j is the maximum of V_j. Let two respective half-spaces, H_{x_j}, H_{y_j} be defined by x_j and y_j such that the intersection of H_{x_j}, H_{y_j} with $\mathbf{B}_j$ is orthogonal. The intersections of such half-spaces $H_{x_j}, H_{y_j}, 1 \le j \le p$ defines a polyhedron [7][Chapter 7]. Note that the intersection of the $2p$ half-spaces are orthogonal to each basis vector, exactly, one minimum and one maximum for each such basis vector. Thus the polyhedron is bounded in $\mathbf{R}^p$. The cases for $F_k, 1 \le k \le p-1$ are similar. $\square$

A result from Lemma 5 is the classification of computation points into valid and non-valid, both of which are contained in the polytope. Moreover, such computation points can be *bound* to more than one domain set. In the following, *static bindings* are used for specifying a restriction on the set of valid computation points whereas *dynamic bindings* are used to describe the enclosing polytope.

A mathematical representation for polytopes specified by non-linguistic carried semantics, that is, allowing for both types of bindings, is subsequently presented. In the following, let I denote the vector $I = [i_1, i_2, \ldots, i_p]$ of all $\hat{p}$ possible domain sets in $\mathbf{R}^k, 1 \le k \le p$ (note although p domain sets are specified, k combinations of these domain sets are allowed). Let G be a $p \times \hat{p}$ *domain specification* matrix, such that $g_{i,j} \in G$ is a function that enumerates a domain set. Thus, G provides for (a) the definition of the specific domain sets for each $i \in I$ in a specific subspace, and (b) the partial specification of the (enclosing) polytopes.

Let $\uplus$ denote the association of a set of values (as given by some $g \in G$) to some $i \in I$: $i \uplus g$. Essentially, this operator allows for locality in set definitions, thus for example, $i_1 \uplus g_1$ and $i_1 \uplus g_2$ specify two valid (local) bindings for i_1 (the scope of the binding is contextually implied). Let the matrix operator, $\odot$ denote a *vector-matrix dot-product* such that: $I \odot G = [i_1 \uplus g_{1,1} + i_2 \uplus g_{2,1} + \ldots + i_p \uplus g_{p,1}, i_1 \uplus g_{1,2} + i_2 \uplus g_{2,2} + \ldots + i_p \uplus g_{p,2}, \cdots, i_1 \uplus g_{1,\hat{p}} + i_2 \uplus g_{2,\hat{p}} + \ldots + i_p \uplus g_{p,\hat{p}}]$. Hence, $I \odot G = [i_1\{x|x \in g_{1,1}\} + i_2\{x|x \in g_{2,1}\} + \ldots + i_p\{x|x \in g_{p,1}\}, i_1\{x|x \in g_{1,2}\} + i_2\{x|x \in g_{2,2}\} + \ldots + i_p\{x|x \in g_{p,2}\}, \cdots, i_1\{x|x \in g_{1,\hat{p}}\} + i_2\{x|x \in g_{2,\hat{p}}\} + \ldots + i_p\{x|x \in g_{p,\hat{p}}\}]$ The complete bounds for the polytope(s) are given by the following system:

$$L \leq I \odot G \leq U \tag{1}$$

where L and U are lower and upper, respectively, constant p length vectors.

4   Conclusion

This paper proposes geometric specification as a new method of parallel program specification. The focus of geometrical specification is the construction of spatially/temporally ordered groups of computations. The grouping of computations can be abstracted by enclosing the computations by polytopes. Two types of geometrical semantics, linguistic carried and non-linguistic carried semantics, have been presented. A formal review of the basic Polytope Model is given; such a succinct but formal presentation of the Polytope Model has not been identified in the literature. Mathematical representation based on multiple domain bindings for the non-linguistic carried case has also been presented.

References

1. C. Lengauer, "Loop parallelization in the polytope model," *CONCUR'93*, 1993, E. Best, (ed.), Lecture Notes in Computer Science 715, Springer-Verlag, pp. 398–416, 1993.
2. P. Feautrier, "Automatic parallelization in the polytope model," in *The Data Parallel Programming Model*, G. Perrin and A. Darte, (eds.), Lecture Notes in Computer Science 1132, pp. 79–103, Springer-Verlag, 1996.
3. U. Banerjee, *Dependence Analysis*. 101 Philip Drive, Assinippi Park, Norwell, MA, USA, 02061: Kluwer Academic Publishers, 1997.
4. B. J. d'Auriol, S. Saladin, and S. Humes, "Linguistic and non-linguistic semantics in the polytope model," Tech. Rep. TR99-01, Akron, Ohio, 44325-4002, January 1999.
5. P. Feautrier, "Dataflow analysis of array and scalar reverences," *International Journal of Parallel Programming*, Vol. 20, pp. 23–53, Feb. 1991.
6. B. J. d'Auriol, "Expressing parallel programs using geometric representation: Case studies," *Proc. of the IASTED International Conference Parallel and Distributed Computing and Systems (PDCS'99)*, Cambridge, MA, USA, Nov., 3-6, 1999, Nov. 1999. in press.
7. A. Schrijver, *Theory of Linear and Integer Programming*. Wiley-Interscience Series in Discrete mathematics and Optimization, New York: Johm Wiley & Sons, 1986. Reprinted 1998.

Compiler and Run-Time Support for Improving Locality in Scientific Codes

(Extended Abstract)

Hwansoo Han, Gabriel Rivera, and Chau-Wen Tseng

Department of Computer Science, University of Maryland, College Park, MD 20742

1   Introduction

Modern microprocessors provide high performance by exploiting data locality with carefully designed multi-level caches. However, advanced scientific computations have features such as adaptive irregular memory accesses and large data sets that make utilizing caches effectively difficult. Traditional program transformations are frequently inapplicable or insufficient. Exploiting locality for these applications requires compile-time analyses and run-time systems to perform data layout and computation transformations. Run-time systems are needed because many programs are not analyzable statically, but compiler support is still crucial both for inserting interfaces to the run-time system and for directly applying program transformations where possible. Cooperation between the compiler and run-time will be critical for advanced scientific codes. We investigate software support for improving locality for advanced scientific applications on both sequential and parallel machines. We examine issues for both irregular adaptive and dense-matrix codes.

2   Irregular Adaptive Codes

Irregular adaptive codes are scientific applications with irregular and changing memory access patterns, where poor spatial and temporal locality can cause high cache miss rates. Unlike applications with regular memory access patterns, irregular applications are hard to optimize at compile time, since their access patterns are unknown until run time. They consist of lists of nodes and edges, computing values for each edge based on its nodes. Locality is improved by rearranging nodes and edges so that related nodes are placed nearby and accessed closely in time, increasing the probability they remain in cache. An inspector/executor paradigm can be used to optimize these irregular applications. The compiler inserts calls to an *inspector*, which analyzes memory access patterns and transforms data layout and computation order at run time. The transformed code, or *executor*, then performs the computation more efficiently. The overhead of the inspector is amortized in scientific applications performing computations for multiple time steps, since the inspector does not need to be re-executed each time.

L. Carter and J. Ferrante (Eds.): LCPC'99, LNCS 1863, pp. 455–458, 2000.
© Springer-Verlag Berlin Heidelberg 2000

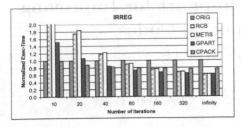
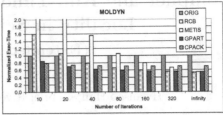

Fig. 1. Normalized Execution Time for Optimizations (ORIG = 1.0)

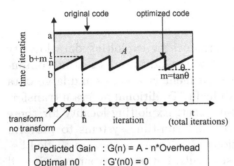
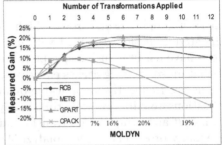

Fig. 2. Optimization for Adaptive Codes

We are investigating the effectiveness of a number of algorithms for improving locality. Simple sorting algorithms (CPACK) based on original memory access patterns reduce cache misses with low preprocessing overhead [2]. More sophisticated partitioning schemes based on geometric coordinate information (RCB) or multi-level graph refinement (METIS) yield greater locality, but with much higher overhead [1,4]. We develop a graph partitioning algorithm (GPART) based on hierarchical graph clustering, which randomly combines nodes until partitions approach the L1 cache size, then lays out nodes based on partitions [3]. It achieves performance close to RCB and METIS with lower overhead. Figure 1 shows normalized execution times for 2 irregular kernels Irreg and Moldyn as the total number of iterations varies. Performance is improved by 30–50% for long-running applications. Complications arise for *adaptive* computations, where the access pattern changes. Benefits of locality transformations are reduced in proportion to the disruption, but reapplying transformations after every change is too expensive. By considering different overheads and benefits of each locality transformation, we developed a cost model to select the type and frequency of transformations [3]. Our model needs to run a few time steps to measure the benefit of transformations and the percentage of access pattern changes. After that, it chooses an algorithm and frequency of application for the best performance. The first graph in Figure 2 illustrates how to choose optimal number of

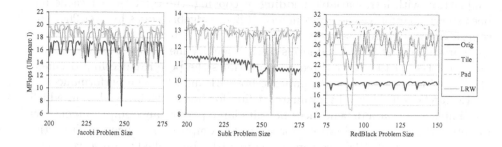

Fig. 3. Uniprocessor Performance of Tiled 3d Codes

transformations applied (n_0). The second graph in Figure 2 shows preliminary verification of the model, comparing experimentally measured gain (curves) with predicted gain (vertical bars) by our cost model.

3   Dense-Matrix Codes

Dense-matrix codes have simple, consistent memory access patterns. Locality is generally excellent, but reuse is lost for certain pathological (but common) problem sizes due to ping-pong or severe conflict misses. For instance, when unit stride accesses A(i,j) and B(i,j) map to the same cache set, spatial reuse across inner loop iterations is lost. Also, stencil codes exhibit group-temporal reuse across outer loop iterations between references typically of the form A(i,j), A(i,j+1). Often variables are laid out so that conflict misses prevent this reuse.

In earlier work, simple compiler padding techniques are shown to be effective in eliminating both forms of conflict misses [6,7]. Generally only a few cache lines of inter-variable padding are needed to avoid ping-pong conflict misses. Larger pads (though still smaller than the L1 cache) are used to preserve group-temporal reuse. Existing inter-variable padding algorithms which solve this problem (and can improve performance of some SPEC95 benchmarks by up to 15%) target only the L1 cache.

We extend these techniques to avoid conflicts in additional levels of cache. Ping-pong conflict misses are avoided simply by using the largest cache line size when testing conflicts. When padding cannot preserve all group-temporal reuse on the L1 cache, we obtain reuse on the L2 cache by spacing out variables on this cache using inter-variable pads which are multiples of the L1 cache size. Such pad sizes will simultaneously preserve the best L1 layout while improving L2 reuse. Experiments show these enhanced techniques can avoid conflict misses and reduce miss rates, but actual performance improvements are not significant for current processor architectures. Overall, we find most locality optimizations do not need to explicitly target multi-level caches.

Tiling is a well-known locality optimization which reorganizes the iteration space into small tiles or blocks. In linear algebra codes, such as matrix multiplication, we execute the tiles repeatedly, improving data locality. When applied in conjunction with intra-variable padding or copying, tiling for the L1 cache has been shown to improve the performance of linear algebra codes by over 200% on some architectures. A possible modification to tiling is to select tile sizes in order to improve reuse at additional levels of the memory hierarchy. However, results indicate L1-sized tiles offer three or more times the performance improvement of L2-sized tiles, since they can improve both L1 and L2 cache performance.

Researchers have usually evaluated tiling for linear algebra codes, in which the simplicity of data dependences permits large performance improvements by targeting the L1 cache. However, for scientific computations such as 3D partial differential equation (PDE) solvers, tiling may also be applied to preserve group-temporal reuse where inter-variable padding fails due to capacity constraints. Figure 3 compares the performance of three tiling approaches with ORIG, the untiled version, as we vary the problem sizes of three 3D scientific codes. As in the case of linear algebra codes [8], we find combining intra-variable padding with tile size selection (PAD) to be more effective than tile size selection alone (LRW) [5] or selecting tile sizes irrespective of array dimensions (TILE). These results show an improvement of about 23% for Jacobi and Subk and 61% for RedBlack SOR as a result of tiling with padding.

4 Conclusion

Preliminary experimental results on representative program kernels show significant performance improvements are possible. However, much work remains to automate compile-time transformations and make run-time systems efficient for more realistic scientific applications. The goal is worth pursuing because it holds the promise of making high-performance computing more accessible for scientists and engineers.

References

1. M. Berger and S. Bokhari. A partitioning strategy for non-uniform problems on multiprocessors. *IEEE Transactions on Computers*, 37(12):570–580, 1987.
2. C. Ding and K. Kennedy. Improving cache performance of dynamic applications with computation and data layout transformations. In *Proceedings of the SIGPLAN PLDI*, Atlanta, May 1999.
3. H. Han and C.-W. Tseng. Improving locality for adaptive irregular scientific codes. Technical Report CS-TR-4039, Dept. of Computer Science, University of Maryland, College Park, September 1999.
4. G. Karypis and V. Kumar. A fast and high quality multilevel scheme for partitioning irregular graphs. In *Proceedings of the 24th ICPP*, Oconomowoc, August 1995.
5. M. Lam, E. Rothberg, and M. E. Wolf. The cache performance and optimizations of blocked algorithms. In *Proceedings of the ASPLOS-IV*, SantaClara, April 1991.
6. G. Rivera and C.-W. Tseng. Data transformations for eliminating conflict misses. In *Proceedings of the SIGPLAN PLDI*, Montreal, June 1998.
7. G. Rivera and C.-W. Tseng. Eliminating conflict misses for high performance architectures. In *Proceedings of the ICS*, Melbourne, July 1998.
8. G. Rivera and C.-W. Tseng. A comparison of compiler tiling algorithms. In *Proceedings of the 8th Conference on Compiler Construction*, Amsterdam, March 1999.

Code Restructuring for Improving Real Time Response through Code Speed, Size Trade-offs on Limited Memory Embedded DSPs

Vipin Jain[1], Siddharth Rele[1], Santosh Pande[1], and J. Ramanujam[2]

[1] Compiler Research Laboratory, PO Box 210030, Department of Electrical & Computer Engineering and Computer Science, University of Cincinnati, Cincinnati, OH 45221-0030.
[2] Department of Electrical and Computer Engineering, Louisiana State University, Baton Rouge, LA 70803

1 Introduction

Embedded systems are constrained by limited on-chip memory and by real time performance requirements. The traditional approach to solve these problems has been to write the embedded code in assembly language, which can no longer be followed due to the increasing complexity of the embedded systems. Programming in high-level language simplifies the software development cycle , incurring a code size and a performance penalty. Traditional compiler optimizations have focussed on improving code speed rather than code density or code size. We present optimizations that improve code density and performance.

1.1 Motivating Example

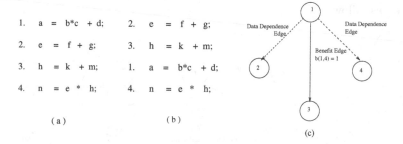

```
1.   a = b*c + d;        2.   e = f + g;

2.   e = f + g;         3.   h = k + m;

3.   h = k + m;         1.   a = b*c + d;

4.   n = e * h;         4.   n = e * h;


        (a)                     (b)
```

Fig. 1. Sample C Code and its Data Dependence Graph

Consider the code in Figure 1(a) to be targeted towards TI TMS320C2X, which is a DSP commonly used in embedded systems. For the code shown, it is not possible to exploit IIP generating complex instructions, but if the statement 1 is moved before statement 4, then a complex instruction MPYA which will carry out the addition in statement 1 and multiplication in statement 4 in parallel, can be generated. For generating MPYA, the product must be computed in P

L. Carter and J. Ferrante (Eds.): LCPC'99, LNCS 1863, pp. 459–463, 2000.

register before its accumulation. Figure 1(b) shows the re-organized loop body after performing code restructuring transformation thus exposing an opportunity to exploit IIP.

2   Code Restructuring Framework

The problem of finding an appropriate code sequence in a basic block which generates the best code (i.e., a sequence that leads to the most compact code) can be reduced to a similar problem of finding a maximum weighted path cover for a given directed acyclic graph (DAG) $G(V, E_b, E_d)$ where V is the set of nodes and E_b is a set of directed benefit edges and E_d is a set of directed dependence edges. Each statement in a basic block corresponds to a node n where $n \in V$. A directed benefit edge $eb(n, m)$ exists between two nodes n and m if some benefit $b(e_b)$ is gained due to scheduling the node m (statement) after the node n (statement). The benefit is determined by an empirical cost-benefit function $f(n, m)$ that maps an ordered pair of two statements corresponding to nodes n and m to a benefit $b(e_b)$. This benefit intuitively represents the amount of parallelism possible by scheduling the two statements one after the other and the possibility of utilizing a suitable complex instruction to exploit the parallelism. Of course the data flow constraints of computation and datapath constraints of DSP instructions must permit such a complex instruction generation. A directed dependence edge $ed(n, m)$ exists from node n to node m if node m is data-dependent on node n and has to be scheduled after node n in any legal sequence of nodes. Thus, the problem can be formulated in graph-theoretic form as follows.

Problem statement: Given a graph $G(V, E_b, E_d)$, find a maximum weighted path cover which also satisfies the partial order in the graph G represented by the set of data dependence edges E_d obeying data flow constraints of computation and data path concurrency of underlying DSP instruction, where the path cover is defined as follows.

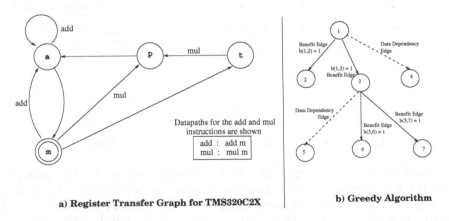

a) Register Transfer Graph for TMS320C2X   b) Greedy Algorithm

Fig. 2. Register Transfer Graph and Greedy Algorithm Example

Definition 1. *A path cover of a weighted graph $G(V, E_b, E_d)$ is a subgraph $C(V, E', E'')$ of $G(V, E_b, E_d)$ such that*
1. *For every node v in C, $deg(v) \leq 2$.*
2. *There are no cycles in C.*

This problem has been well studied and is NP-hard. We do a greedy heuristic. The basic idea is to start with the root node of the data dependence graph and keep on building the sub-graph by adding an edge $e_b(n, m)$ which has the maximum possible benefit $b(e_b)$ such that the data dependency is not violated in the resulting schedule of nodes. The algorithm is linear in sum of the number of benefit and dependence edges in the graph. This algorithm is not optimal, but such cases are rare due to sparse opportunities for IIP available in the DSP.

2.1 Benefit Algorithm

We use the following algorithm to estimate the amount of intra instruction parallelism possible between two successive statements.

Step 1: Obtain a partial functional description of the target Instruction Set Architecture(ISA).

Step 2: Obtain a Register Transfer Graph(RTG) for the target architecture that shows all the data paths traversed when the instructions contained in the Instruction Set Architecture are executed.Figure 2(a) shows the RTG for TMS320C25 ISA.

Step 3: Form Ordered pairs by analyzing the ISA and RTG to obtain all the parallel data paths, where the instructions forming the pair use different data paths , indicating that a complex instruction can be generated leading to the exploitation of the IIP. As seen from the RTG in Figure 2(a), the MPY instruction follows data paths t to p and m to p, while the ADD instruction follows the data paths a to a and m to a. These paths are independent of each other and hence these instructions can be overlapped to generate a complex instruction MPYA. Other such kind of pairs are found and stored in a set for further comparisons.

Step 4: Analyze the expression trees of the two statements and obtain the data paths for them.

Step 5: If the data paths needed for execution belong to the set of the parallel data path pairs present in the RTG, then the benefit of executing the two statements successively is one (since IIP can be exploited by generating complex instructions for them), else it is zero.

3 Implementation and Results

We have implemented this heuristic in the SPAM compiler targeted to generate code for the TMS320C25 DSP and tested on a number of benchmarks and found that the performance of the generated code–measured in dynamic instruction cycle counts–improves by as much as 7% with an average of 3%. The results are tabulated in table 1. The average code size reduction over code compiled

Table 1. Results

Benchmarks	No Code Restructuring		Code Restructuring		% Improvement	
	CLK Cycles	Code Size	CLK Cycles	Code Size	CLK Cycles	Code Size
Perfect-I	400	80	375	75	1.3	6.3
IIR Biquad	356	178	346	173	0.6	2.8
Perfect-II	576	72	536	67	6.9	1.5
Higbie	8100	162	7900	158	1.3	1.9
Whetstone	13440	128	12810	122	1.6	3.9
DSPstone	496	62	488	61	1.6	1.6

without exploiting parallelism is 2.9%. We also studied the effect of loop unrolling which allows IIP to be exploited across iterations. Loop unrolling can be used for some form of register allocation optimizations leading to a reduction in the number of load/spills; thus further reduction in the code size could take place. An improvement of 3 to 4% in dynamic instruction count can be obtained by unrolling some loops 5 to 6 times. This shows that there is a good amount of IIP across iterations. There are other advantages of loop un-rolling such as eliminating spill code over loop body boundaries as shown by [1].

4 Related Work

Landskov et al. [2] have discussed various techniques for local microcode compaction. The problem addressed by our work is machine specific, which considers data paths traversed and suitably rearrange them such that parallelism between data paths can be exploited by suitably generating a complex instruction. The motivation is to decrease code size and increase code efficiency. However this demands intimate knowledge of register transfer paths traversed by the instructions and can be done as machine specific optimization for which the generic techniques of microcode compaction are not effective. Liao et al. [3] formulate the problem of instruction selection in code generation for embedded DSP processors as directed acyclic graph (DAG) covering. The authors give a binate covering formulation for optimal code generation on a one-register machine. The authors have shown that optimal instruction selection in the case of accumulator-based architectures requires a partial scheduling of nodes in the DAG. In addition to the selection of complex instructions the authors have also tried to minimize the reloads and spill. Their method detects opportunities for combining neighboring simple instructions. However, limited opportunities exist if restricted to combining neighboring simple instructions. One could expose far more opportunities for combining such instructions through code restructuring transformation obeying data dependencies, which is the focus of this work. In this work, we show that upto 7% of improvement in performance could be obtained coupled with around 2.9% code size reduction.

References

1. David J. Kolson, Alexandru Nicolau, Nikil Dutt, and Ken Kennedy. Optimal register assignment to loops for embedded code generation. In *ACM Transactions on Design Automation of Electronic Systems*, pages 251–279, April 1996.
2. D. Landskov, S. Davidson, B.D. Shriver, and P.W. Mallett. Local microcode compaction techniques. In *ACM Computing Surveys*, pages 261–294, September 1980.
3. Stan Liao, Srinivas Devadas, Kurt Keutzer, and Steve Tjiang. Instruction selection using binate covering for code size optimization. In *International Conference on Computer-Aided Design*, 1995.

Compiling for Speculative Architectures*

Seon Wook Kim and Rudolf Eigenmann

School of Electrical and Computer Engineering
Purdue University, West Lafayette, Indiana

Abstract. The traditional target machine of a parallelizing compiler can execute code sections either serially or in parallel. In contrast, targeting the generated code to a speculative parallel processor allows the compiler to recognize parallelism to the best of its abilities and leave other optimization decisions up to the processor's runtime detection mechanisms. In this paper we show that simple improvements of the compiler's speculative task selection method can already lead to significant (up to 55%) improvement in speedup over that of a simple code generator for a Multiscalar architecture. For an even more improved software / hardware cooperation we propose an interface that allows the compiler to inform the processor about fully parallel, serial, and speculative code sections as well as attributes of program variables. We have evaluated the degrees of parallelism that such a co-design can realistically exploit.

1 Introduction

Parallelizing compilers have made significant progress over the past ten years. While they could exploit parallel machines effectively in only two out of twelve scientific/engineering programs in 1990 [1], today they are successful in half of these programs [2,3]. Still, there remains a tremendous potential to be exploited. For example, today's compilers are still limited in exploiting parallelism in most C programs. Speculative architectures [4,5,6,7,8] can potentially overcome these limitations.

This paper makes two contributions towards our goal of developing advanced compiler technology that exploits speculative processors. First, starting from a simple code generator for Multiscalar architectures [4], we have improved the methods for selecting speculative tasks (i.e., code sections that will be executed speculatively in parallel) [9]. Second, we propose an improved software/hardware interface that allows the compiler to inform the processor about code sections that are provably parallel or serial and those that are worth parallelizing speculatively at runtime. We have identified these code sections in several programs and have evaluated the degree of parallelism that can be exploited.

---

* This work was supported in part by NSF grants #9703180-CCR and #9872516-EIA. This work is not necessarily representative of the positions or policies of the U. S. Government.

L. Carter and J. Ferrante (Eds.): LCPC'99, LNCS 1863, pp. 464–467, 2000.

Table 1. Simulation results on the Multiscalar architecture. The table shows the improvements of three Perfect Benchmarks due to our enhanced task selection techniques. We measured IPC (instructions per cycle), speedup (the ratio of execution time on one processor to that on four processors), and load imbalance. Each processor has a two-way superscalar architecture. For comparison, the table shows the real speedups obtained by the automatically parallelized programs on a 4-processor Sun UltraSPARC server.

| | | Multiscalar | | | | | |
| | | Original | | | Improved | | |
Benchmarks	Sun	IPC	Speedup	Load imbalance	IPC	Speedup	Load imbalance
TRFD	2.42	2.28	1.42	38.4%	3.27	1.97	9.5%
BDNA	2.22	1.55	1.48	49.0%	1.62	1.55	5.7%
ARC2D	4.07	1.69	1.49	38.7%	2.42	2.13	6.6%

2 Informed Task Selection

As a starting point of our project we have measured the performance of a number of programs on a Multiscalar architecture simulator. We expected to see good parallel efficiency on numerical programs, such as the Perfect Benchmarks. However we have found that, on a machine with 4 processing units (PU) both the speedup relative to a 1-PU architecture and the number of instructions issued per machine cycle (IPC) are limited. In fact, the speedup is much less that the one measured for the compiler-parallelized programs executed on a 4-processor Sun UltraSPARC server. Table 1 shows these measurements.

We have found that one reason for the limited performance is the simple task selection scheme applied in the compiler: Each basic block is dispatched to the next PU for parallel execution. However, each loop iteration consists of at least two basic blocks - the actual loop body and a small block containing the branch code to the next iteration and loop end. It is obvious that these two basic blocks are not only intrinsically sequential but also very different in length, leading to load imbalance. Combining the two basic blocks requires knowledge of the program's loop structure. We have modified the compiler (a modified version of GCC) so that it performs this transformation. It results in improvements of up to 55% in speedup, as shown in Table 1.

Additional improvements can be made if the compiler considers data dependence information. For example, loop iterations which the compiler can prove as dependent can be combined into a single task. The compiler/architecture interface, described in the next section, will enable this and other optimizations.

3 Compiler / Hardware Co-design

Our goal is a scenario where the compiler detects parallelism to the maximum of its abilities and leaves the rest up to the speculative hardware. More specifically, the parallelizing compiler will detect and mark parallel loops, which will then be executed by the processor in fully-parallel mode. Fully parallel execution will not

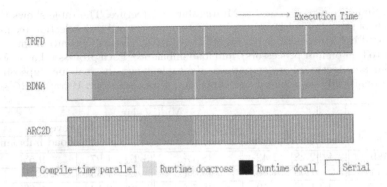

Fig. 1. Maximum parallelism that can be exploited in the programs TRFD, BDNA and ARC2D. Compile-time parallel sections can be exploited without speculative hardware support. Runtime Doall regions can be detected as fully parallel by the hardware. Doacross sections are partially parallel regions, also detectable at runtime.

involve any speculative data tracking mechanism, saving overhead and obviating the need to reserve speculative data space. Data space is saved because, in speculative operation, all written data would have to be buffered until the task is no longer speculative. This can severely restrict the size of allowable speculative tasks. Further overhead can be saved by marking serial (i.e, dependent) code sections. The code generator will create a single task from such code sections, avoiding task squashes as a result of dependence violations at runtime. Only code sections that are neither parallel nor serial will become speculative tasks. To enable this operation our basic compiler/architecture interface will

- define (the boundaries of) serial, parallel and speculative tasks,
- define variable attributes as shared dependent, shared independent, speculative, private, or reduction operation. Speculative variables are those whose accesses cannot be disambiguated at compile time. Private variables are those that the compiler can prove to be written before read within a task. Reduction variables are only used as results of reduction operations.

Note that this interface requires a minimal extension of the Multiscalar architecture: speculation can be suspended, such that the machine behaves like a multiprocessor. This mode will be employed during the execution of fully parallel tasks.

We have evaluated performance opportunities of this scenario. The bars in Figure 1 show sections in the execution of TRFD, BDNA and ARC2D that can be detected as parallel at compile time (using the Polaris parallelizer) and at runtime, respectively. Runtime parallelism is split into sections that are fully parallel (doall) and sections that need synchronization (doacross). We have performed this analysis using the Max/P tool [10]. The figure shows that there are both significant regions of compile-time and runtime parallelism. Developing efficient mechanisms to exploit this potential is the object of our ongoing work.

4   Conclusion

We have presented a new compiler/architecture model for speculative processors. Parallel tasks that can be detected at compile time are run in non-speculative, multiprocessor mode. Program sections that may have dependences are parallelized speculatively by the architecture. From the architecture's point of view, non-speculative parallel execution can save significant overhead and can increase the parallel task size. We are currently completing the integration of the Polaris parallelizing compiler with a GCC-based code generator, which will provide the proposed architecture interface. The code generator will use high-level information from the optimizing preprocessor to generate the information required in the interface and to improve the quality of the generated code. In an initial study to improve the selection of speculative parallel tasks we have already achieved performance gains of up to 55% in speedup.

References

1. William Blume and Rudolf Eigenmann. Performance Analysis of Parallelizing Compilers on the Perfect Benchmarks Programs. *IEEE Transactions on Parallel and Distributed Systems*, 3(6):643–656, November 1992.
2. M. W. Hall, J. M. Anderson, S. P. Amarasinghe, B. R. Murphy, S.-W. Liao, E. Bugnion, and M. S. Lam. Maximizing multiprocessor performance with the SUIF compiler. *IEEE Computer*, pages 84–89, December 1996.
3. W. Blume, R. Doallo, R. Eigenmann, J. Grout, J. Hoeflinger, T. Lawrence, J. Lee, D. Padua, Y. Paek, B. Pottenger, L. Rauchwerger, and P. Tu. Parallel programming with Polaris. *IEEE Computer*, pages 78–82, December 1996.
4. Gurindar S. Sohi, Scott E. Breach, and T. N. Vijaykumar. Multiscalar processors. *The 22th International Symposium on Computer Architecture (ISCA-22)*, pages 414–425, June 1995.
5. Lance Hammond, Mark Willey, and Kunle Olukotun. Data speculation support for a chip multiprocessors. *Proceedings of the Eighth ACM Conference on Architectural Support for Programming Languages and Operating Systems (ASPLOS'98)*, October 1998.
6. J. Gregory Steffan and Todd C. Mowry. The potential for thread-level data speculation to facilitate automatic parallelization. In *Proceedings of the Fourth International Symposium on High-Performance Computer Architecture (HPCA-4)*, pages 2–13, February 1998.
7. J.-Y. Tsai, Z. Jiang, Z. Li, D.J. Lilja, X. Wang, P.-C. Yew, B. Zheng, and S. Schwinn. Superthreading: Integrating compilation technology and processor architecture for cost-effective concurrent multithreading. *Journal of Information Science and Engineering*, March 1998.
8. Ye Zhang, Lawrence Rauchwerger, and Josep Torrellas. Hardware for speculative parallelization in high-end multiprocessors. *The Third PetaFlop Workshop (TPF-3)*, February 1999.
9. T. N. Vijaykumar and Gurindar S. Sohi. Task selection for a multiscalar processor. *The 31st International Symposium on Microarchitecture (MICRO-31)*, December 1998.
10. Seon Wook Kim. MaxP: Maximum parallelism detection tool in loop-based programs. Technical Report ECE-HPCLab-99206, HPCLAB, Purdue University, School of Electrical and Computer Engineering, 1999.

Symbolic Analysis
in the PROMIS Compiler*

Nicholas Stavrakos[1], Steven Carroll[1], Hideki Saito[1],
Constantine Polychronopoulos[1], and Alex Nicolau[2]

[1] Center for Supercomputing Research and Development,
University of Illinois at Urbana-Champaign,
{stavrako, scarroll, saito, cdp}@csrd.uiuc.edu
[2] Department of Information and Computer Science,
University of California at Irvine,
nicolau@ics.uci.edu

1 Introduction

PROMIS is a multilingual, parallelizing, and optimizing compiler which is being developed at the Univ. of Illinois with its optimizing ILP backend developed at Univ. of California at Irvine[4]. In PROMIS, symbolic analysis is performed through an abstract interpretation[2] of the input program. Abstract interpretation is a technique for approximating the execution of the program by mapping symbolic (closed form) values computed at compile time to the actual values computed at runtime. This paper describes the symbolic analysis framework in the PROMIS compiler, and its application to Java program optimizations.

2 Symbolic Analysis Framework

2.1 Basics

The conditional operator $\tau(e)$ returns 1 if e evaluates to *true* and 0 otherwise. With this operator, control sensitive information can be encoded into the expressions of the IR. Fig. 1(b) illustrates how the τ operator is used to merge two different versions X_1 and X_2 of the variable X into a new version X_3. X_3 evaluates to X_1 if the branch condition C_1 is *true* and X_2 otherwise. The operators π and δ are used for loops. $\pi(L)$ returns 1 for the first iteration of the loop L and 0 for all subsequent iterations. Conversely, $\delta(L)$ returns 0 for the first iteration and 1 for all remaining iterations (Fig. 1(d)).

The symbolic interpreter performs SSA conversion and the computation and simplification of symbolic expressions. The values of versioned variables are saved in *symbolic environments*. An environment is propagated to each statement. Each statement is interpreted and its side effects are computed. These effects

---

* This work is supported in part by DARPA/NSA grant MDA904-96-C-1472, and in part by a grant from Intel Corporation.

L. Carter and J. Ferrante (Eds.): LCPC'99, LNCS 1863, pp. 468–471, 2000.

are applied to the incoming environment of a statement resulting in new versions for the affected variables.

Each control flow path through the program has its own symbolic environment. This provides each control flow path with only the versions that it would see during execution of the routine. It also maintains the conditions that must be met in order for control to flow down that path. These conditions are used in the optimization of the program (e.g., removal of redundant exception checks in Java).

Furthermore, the symbolic environment also maintains the most recently defined version of a particular variable. Thus, when the symbolic environment is saved after the interpretation of the routine has been completed, it can identify the live versions at the end of the routine. At control confluence points, two or more environments must be merged together to preserve the single live version requirement mentioned above. This environment merging is quick and straightforward. First, the common predecessor in the control flow graph is identified. Then, any versions that have been added after this common predecessor are merged into new versions. Due to space limitations, interpretation of loops is beyond the scope of this paper.

```
IF(C₁) THEN              IF(C₁) THEN
    X = ...                  X₁ = ...
ELSE                     ELSE
    X = ...                  X₂ = ...
ENDIF                    ENDIF
... = X                  X₃ = X₁τ(C₁) + X₂τ(!C₁)
                         ... = X₃
```

$$IF(C_1)\ THEN\qquad\qquad IF(C_1)\ THEN$$

(a) Input   (b) Versioned/Interpreted

```
    J = 0                    J₁ = 0
20  DO I=1,n             20  DO I = 1,n
        J = J + 1                J₃ = J₁*π(20) + J₂*δ(20)
    END DO                       J₂ = J₃ + 1
                             END DO
```

(c) Input   (d) Versioned/Interpreted

Fig. 1. Conditional Algebra Operators τ, π, and δ

2.2   Intra- and Interprocedural Symbolic Analysis

Symbolic analysis is applied in two phases: intraprocedural and interprocedural. Since there are no dependencies between interpretation of different routines intraprocedurally, phase one is applied in parallel to all the routines in the program.

During intraprocedural interpretation each routine is converted into SSA form. The program is analyzed and optimized with the intraprocedural information it can gather from the routine. Two special properties of the intraprocedural SSA construction are exploited in the later interprocedural phase. First, uses of incoming global and parameter variables are assigned version 0. Second, symbolic indirect variable (SIV) stubs are created to represent references to global/parameter variables via pointer dereferences.

All optimizations (e.g. constant propagation, induction variable elimination [3], etc.) are applied to the routine during intraprocedural symbolic analysis. The result of the analysis is a routine that is optimized with local information only. All global references are parameterized, allowing the interprocedural phase to easily pass information across call sites. The resulting routine is optimized for all possible values and aliases of the parameterized global/parameter references.

Next, interprocedural symbolic analysis is performed on the program. Interprocedural symbolic analysis comes in two flavors: forward and backward.

Forward interprocedural analysis is applied when a function call is encountered during the interpretation of another function. The callee function is not reinterpreted; rather the saved symbolic environment is queried to determine its side effects given the caller's symbolic environment. The two environments are linked together by associating parameters and global variables in the caller to the corresponding variables in the callee. Also, SIV stubs in the callee are associated with the appropriate objects in the caller. This linking of symbolic environments at the call site allows for context sensitive analysis of the function call.

Backward interprocedural symbolic analysis occurs when the interpretation of a function requires information from the call sites of that function. To correctly interpret the function, PROMIS gathers all possible values, from all the call sites of a variable and propagates this information to the requesting optimization pass. The specific optimization technique determines whether it can use this information or whether it should simply give up due to complexity concerns.

3   Symbolic Analysis for Java

Java's exception model is a major performance problem. Many redundant exception checks are introduced into the code during bytecode to native code translation. Figure 2 shows the original Java source code along with its translated native code. The ELSE clause is only executed if the previous checks were all false (i.e. ArrayRef != NULL). Using this control sensitive information, (maintained in the symbolic environments) PROMIS can easily eliminate the two redundant exception checks in the native code, thus allowing further optimizations.

4   Summary

This paper described the symbolic analysis framework of the PROMIS compiler. The framework is a critical part of the compiler. It is not only capable of analyzing and optimizing code, but also of supplying information to other parts of the compiler. This ability to propagate control sensitive values both intraprocedurally and interprocedurally allow the integration of many classical analysis and optimization techniques into our framework. Interested readers can refer to our technical reports[1,6,5].

```
            Tmp1 = ArrayRef[Index]
            Tmp2 = ArrayRef[Index+1]

                      ⇓

IF (ArrayRef == Null) THEN
    throw NullPointerException
ELSE IF ((Index < 0) || (Index > Size)) THEN
    throw ArrayOutOfBoundsException
ELSE
    Tmp1 = ArrayRef[Index] // ⟸ useful statement
    IF (ArrayRef == Null) THEN // ⟸ redundant test
        throw NullPointerException
    ELSE IF ((Index+1 < 0) || // ⟸ redundant test
            (Index+1 > Size)) THEN
        throw ArrayOutOfBoundsException
    ELSE
        Tmp2 = ArrayRef[Index+1] // ⟸ useful statement
    ENDIF
ENDIF
```

Fig. 2. Translation of Array Element Reference in Java

Acknowledgements. The authors are grateful to their PROMIS Project associates Prof. N. Dutt, P. Grun, A. Halambi, and N. Savoiu of University of California at Irvine and J. Brokish, P. Kalogiannis, W. Ko, C. Koopmans, and K. Marukawa of CSRD for their contribution to PROMIS.

References

1. S. Carroll. Optimizing java for native execution. Master's thesis, Univ. of Illinois, 1999. (in preparation).
2. P. Cousot and R. Cousot. Abstract interpretation: A unified lattice model for static analysis of programs by construction or approximation of fixpoints. In *Proceedings of the ACM SIGPLAN Symposium on Principles of Programming Languages (POPL)*, pages 238–252, January 1977.
3. M. Haghighat. *Symbolic Analysis for Parallelizing Compilers.* Kluwer Academic Publishers, 1995.
4. H. Saito, N. Stavrakos, S. Carroll, C. Polychronopoulos, and A. Nicolau. The design of the PROMIS compiler. In *Proceedings of the International Conference on Compiler Construction (CC)*, March 1999.
5. N. Stavrakos. *Symbolic Analysis: A Unified Framework for Analyzing and Optimizing Programs.* PhD thesis, Univ. of Illinois, 2000. (in preparation).
6. N. Stavrakos, S. Carroll, H. Saito, C. Polychronopoulos, and A. Nicolau. Symbolic analysis in the PROMIS compiler. Technical Report 1564, Center for Supercomputing Research and Development, Univ. of Illinois, May 1999.

Data I/O Minimization for Loops on Limited Onchip Memory Processors*

Lei Wang and Santosh Pande**

Compiler Research Lab, PO Box 210030,
Department of Electrical & Computer Engineering and Computer Science
University of Cincinnati, Cincinnati, OH- 45219
E-mail: {leiwang, santosh}@ececs.uc.edu

1 Introduction

Due to significant advances in VLSI technology, 'mega-processors' made with
a large number of transistors has become a reality. These processors typically
provide multiple functional units which allow exploitation of parallelism. In order to cater to the data demands associated with parallelism, the processors
provide a limited amount of on-chip memory. The amount of memory provided
is quite limited due to higher area and power requirements associated with it.
Even though limited, such on-chip memory is a very valuable resource in memory hierarchy. An important use of on-chip memory is to hold the instructions
from short loops along with the associated data for very fast computation. Such
schemes are very attractive on embedded processors where, due to the presence
of dedicated hard-ware on-chip (such as very fast multipliers-shifters etc.) and
extremely fast accesses to on-chip data, the computation time of such loops is
extremely small meeting almost all real-time demands. Biggest bottleneck to performance in these cases are off-chip accesses and thus, compilers must carefully
analyze references to identify good candidates for *promotion* to on-chip memory.
In our earlier work [6], we formulated this problem in terms of 0/1 knapsack
and proposed a heuristic solution that gives us good promotion candidates. Our
analysis was limited to a single loop nest. When we attempted extending this
framework to multiple loop nests (intra-procedurally), we realized that not only
it is important to identify good candidates for promotion but a careful restructuring of loops must be undertaken *before performing promotion* since data i/o
of loading and storing values to on-chip memory poses a significant bottleneck.

2 Our Approach

Our analysis begins by undertaking intraprocedural loop fusion assuming unlimited memory. We first calculate the amount of data re-use between the statements
after carrying out loop fusion. We then calculate the *closeness factor* of every pair

---

* Supported in part by NSF through grant no. #EIA 9871345
** Corresponding author

L. Carter and J. Ferrante (Eds.): LCPC'99, LNCS 1863, pp. 472–476, 2000.

of statements. Closeness factor between two statements quantifies the amount of data reuse per unit memory required. We decorate the program dependence graph (PDG) with this information by inserting undirected edges between the nodes of the PDG that represent statements. We then group the statements greedily under a given loop nest i.e. statements which have higher closeness factor are grouped together over those which have lesser. At every step, when we group statements, we examine if we must include some other statement(s) so as to preserve the dependences. Sometimes we may not be able to include statements due to dependence and memory capacity constraints. In such cases, we adjust the dependence groups to eliminate *useless* re-use edges. Finally, we iterate to expand the group of statements and when we exceed the capacity of the on-chip memory we halt. We carry out the above steps of grouping and adjusting the dependence groups until there are no more re-use edges. After finding out all possible groupings and then grouping the statements having more CF, we block the groups so as to fit the available memory size.

2.1   Block Size v/s Data I/O

Block size is another major feature to decide when to stop bringing more statements (data elements) into one group. The trade off is that due to more statements (array elements) being brought into the same group, the re-uses will be introduced, but it is possible the existing data reuse utilization may be reduced due to reduction in block size.

Example:
```
for i=1 to 50
    c[i]=a[i-1]+b[i+2]+d[i-1];    //S1
    r[i]=d[i+7]+e[i]+f[i]+g[i];   //S2
    k[i]=a[i+4]+b[i-3];           //S3
```

If we group statement S1 and S3 together only, and on chip memory is big enough all the data elements, then all the data for the inner loop in the following example will be stored in the onchip memory. The total data I/O saved (in the inner loop) of one block will be 26 (13 for a[]s, 13 for b[]s). Total I/O saved is 70.

Output Loops:
```
for i'=1 to 50 step 18            //L1
    for i=i' to min(i'+17, 50)
        c[i]=a[i-1]+b[i+2]+d[i-1];   //S1
        k[i]=a[i+4]+b[i-3];          //S3

for i=1 to 50                     //L2
    r[i]=d[i+7]+e[i]+f[i]+g[i];   //S2
```

Obviously, between S2 and S1, there is data reuse (d[]). Once we bring in S2 into the group, the loop will be:

```
for i'=1 to 50 step 10          //L1
  for i=i' to min(i'+9, 50)
    c[i]=a[i-1]+b[i+2]+d[i-1]; //S1
    r[i]=d[i+7]+e[i]+f[i]+g[i];//S2
    k[i]=a[i+4]+b[i-3];         //S3
```

If we group all three, S1, S2 and S3 together, the total I/O saved per block will be 12 (5 for a[], 5 for b[], 2 for d[]). Total I/O saved is 12 * 5 = 60. Thus, one can see that the grouping of statements should stop at S1 and S3 and should not include S2. This is one why we stop bringing more statements into the group, though they have reusable data. In the above example its is easy to calculate that the total reuse in the first grouping is 90 and we need 260 data elements to be stored on the onchip memory. It is evident that the statements s2 has no reuse with respect to a[] and b[]. If we decide to utilize the reuse of d[], then the total reuse becomes 148 in the second grouping shown. But, for this we have to store 460 elements on the onchip memory due to the arrays r[],e[],g[] and f[] which contribute nothing to the reuse. The Closeness Factor for the first group will be $90/260 = .35$ while in the second case it will be $148/460 = .32$. Since, we always chose the grouping with higher CF, this example depicts how increase in CF results in less I/O. In essence, what we want to check is that, after we bring a new statement, whether the total data I/O is reduced or not. As shown above, CF serves as correct measure of data i/o and thus, we focus on increasing CF.

3   Results

Table 1. I/O comparison for benchmarks 1 and 2

Code	Original I/O	Optimized I/O	Saved I/O	% I/O Reduction
Benchmark 1	$18*10^6$	$11.25*10^6$	$6.75*10^6$	37.5
Benchmark 2	27692	22532	5160	18.63

Due to limited space available, we are presenting results for two of the benchmarks, used for testing.

Benchmark 1: This code shows a matrix multiplication loop, which isused frequently in DSP applications.

Benchmark 2: The second benchmark is for convolution.

A lot of reuse opportunites are provided by these codes, making our optimization important. The results have been summarised in table 1.

4   Related Work and Conclusion

We now contrast our work with existing work related to solving data locality and data re-use problems on memory hierarchy. Two important directions of work are: Tiling or iteration space blocking [7] and data-centric approaches such as data shackling [3]. In tiling or data blocking (which is a control centric transformation), a loop nest is tiled to maximize temporal locality [5,4]. In data centric transformations, all the iterations that touch a data shackle are executed together giving better control to the compiler to directly focus on data than resorting to side effect of control centric transformation [3].

Our work differs from these in that we focus on data i/o as against issues of locality. This is important since in our problem, we are faced with a small amount of memory that results in excessive load/stores of short arrays between on-chip and off-chip memories. Thus, in order to minimize data i/o, we must not only concentrate on re-use of fetched values (as is typically the goal in the most memory hierarchy oriented optimizations described above) but also carefully analyze the flow and use of generated values and transitive closure of their uses and values which they generate in turn. CF serves as a measure of this.

Some approaches have focused on loop distribution for locality. [2] show that the fusion problem for maximizing data locality is NP-hard. They present a greedy and max-flow/min-cut algorithm to maximize re-use leaving parallelism intact. The edge weights used are: 1 - flow and input dependence edges, 0 - output and anti-dependence, t - fusion preventing edges. [1] independently developed max-flow/min cut algorithm. They also proposed concept of fusible clusters. Due to very limited amount of on-chip memory, we are not only interested in maximizing the amount of re-use, but also the amount of re-use per unit of memory occupied, called the Closeness Factor(CF). Using total re-use as a measure may in fact incur higher amount of data I/O. This is the difference between our work and [2] [1].

4.1 Conclusion

We have proposed a framework on how to get a better performance by analyzing the flow of values and their re-use to effectively reduce data i/o for limited on-chip memory processors. A new concept of Closeness Factor has been developed which is the measure of data reuse between statements per unit memory requirement. The loop restructuring algorithm proposed by us helps to effectively utilize the on-chip memory while preserving the data dependences between the statements in the loop. Good performance enhancements for DSP codes are obtained using our framework.

References

1. G. Gao, R. Olsen, V. Sarkar, and R. Thekkath. Collective loop fusion for array contraction. In *Languages and Compilers for Parallel Computing (LCPC)*, 1992.
2. K. Kennedy and K. McKinley. Maximizing loop parallelism and improving data locality via loop fusion and distribution. In *Languages and Compilers for Parallel Computing (LCPC)*, 1993.
3. I. Kodukula, N. Ahmed, and K. Pingali. Data centric multi-level blocking. In *ACM Programming Language Design and Implementation(PLDI)*, pages 346–357, 1997.

4. N. Mitchell, K. Hogstedt, L. Carter, and J. Ferrante. Quantifying the multi-level nature of tiling interactions. In *International Journal of Parallel Programming*, volume 26:6, pages 641–670, 1998.

5. R. Schreiber and J. Dongarra. Automatic blocking of nested loops. In *Technical report, RIACS, NASA Ames Research Center, and Oak Ridge National Laboratory*, May 1990.

6. A. Sundaram and S. Pande. An efficient data partitioning method for limited memory embedded systems. In *ACM SIGPLAN Workshop on Languages, Compilers and Tools for Embedded Systems(LCTES)(in conjunction with PLDI '98), Montreal, Canada, Springer–Verlag*, pages 205–218, 1998.

7. M. Wolfe. Iteration space tiling for memory hierarchies. In *Third SIAM Conference on Parallel Processing for Scientific Computing*, December 1987.

Benchmark 1	Benchmark 2
```do I = 1 .. N do J = 1 .. N do K = 1 .. N C[I,J]=C[I,J]+A[I,K]*B[K,J] //S1 do I = 1 .. N do J = 1 .. N do K = 1 .. N D[K,J]=D[I,J]*C[I,K] - B[K,J] //S2```	```for i=1 to N c[i]=a[i]-b[i]; //S1 r[i]=d[i-9]/e[i]; //S2 k[i]=a[i+1]*b[i-1]+p[i]-q[i]; //S3 for i=1 to N n[i]=d[i]*c[i]+e[i]; //S4 f[i]=o[i]+d[i]/e[i]; //S5 g[i]=r[i]/m[i+1]; //S6 h[i]=n[i]*m[i+1]+e[5+i]-c[i+10];//S7```

Time Skewing for Parallel Computers

David Wonnacott

Haverford College, Haverford, PA 19041, USA
davew@cs.haverford.edu
http://www.haverford.edu/cmsc/davew/index.html

1   Introduction

Time skewing [Won99a] is a compile-time optimization that can achieve *scalable locality* for a class of iterative stencil calculations, given a sufficient number of time steps and sufficient cache memory. That is, the cache hit rate can be made to grow with the problem size, and we can eliminate (for large problems) idle time due to high *machine balance* (the ratio of processor speed to memory bandwidth [CCK88,McC95]). Scalable locality lets us apply processors with increasing machine balance to increasingly large problems, just as scalable parallelism lets us apply higher levels of parallelism to larger problems. The cache required for time skewing grows with the machine balance, but not with the problem size.

The full class of calculations for which time skewing can be used is defined in [Won99a]. For this abstract, we simply note that we work with code in which each value can be expressed as a function of values from the previous time step (such as the three point stencil calculation in Figure 1), and allow procedures with imperfectly nested loops (such as Figure 1 and the TOMCATV program of the SPEC95 benchmark set).

```
for (int t = 0; t<T; t++)
  for (int i = 0; i<=N-1; i++)
    old[i] = cur[i]
  for (int i = 1; i<=N-2; i++)
    cur[i] = 0.25 * (old[i-1] + old[i]+old[i] + old[i+1]);
```

Fig. 1. Three Point Stencil

This abstract gives an overview of our generalization of time skewing for multiprocessor architectures. This transformation lets us eliminate processor idle time caused by any combination of inadequate main memory bandwidth, limited network bandwidth, and high network latency, given a sufficiently large problem and sufficient cache. As in the uniprocessor case, the cache requirement grows with the machine balance, not the problem size.

L. Carter and J. Ferrante (Eds.): LCPC'99, LNCS 1863, pp. 477–480, 2000.

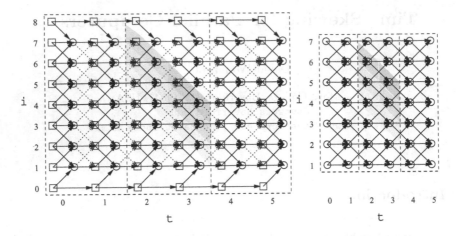

Fig. 2. Time-Skewed Iteration Spaces for Figure 1, N=9, T=6

2 Uniprocessor Time Skewing

Our exposition of the uniprocessor time skewing algorithm will follow its application to the code in Figure 1. We begin by producing a graph that describes the flow of values among the iterations of the program statements. Figure 2 shows the graphs we generate for the original code (left) or after an optional copy propagation that simplifies some later steps (right). The squares correspond to the copy statement, and circles to the computation; solid arrows indicate data flow, and dashed arrows other dependences.

We first identify (interprocedurally) the most frequently executed region(s) of the code. We measure the *compute balance* (floating point calculations per live floating point value) of the surrounding loops, until we find a scope at which the compute balance grows with the size of the input. We say that such code exhibits *scalable compute balance*. This is often true of the time step loop.

We then group the iterations of these loops into tiles (shown with dashed lines in Figure 2), ensuring that compute balance grows with tile size. Thus, we can achieve arbitrarily high cache hit rate by increasing tile size, if we prevent memory traffic for temporaries within a tile and cache interference. We accomplish this by executing the iterations within a tile using a skewed wavefront (the shaded region), creating an array to hold the values for a few wavefronts, and transforming the mapping of values to memory so that all temporaries are stored in this array. Our implementation makes extensive use of the Omega Library.

We can derive the tile size, and thus the cache requirement, from machine parameters: We set the tile size τ to ensure each tile has more processing than memory time, or $\frac{ON\tau}{C} \geq \frac{2DN}{B}$ (where C is CPU speed, B is main memory bandwidth, and each iteration does O floating point operations and writes D bytes of floating point data). To run our example code with $C = 300$ and $B = 40$, we set $\tau = 30$, requiring 720 bytes of cache.

3   Multiprocessor Time Skewing

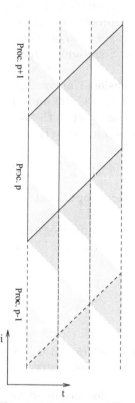

Fig. 3. Multiproc. Tiling

Although there are dependences among the tiles shown in Figure 2, we could achieve some level of concurrency by distributing these tiles across multiple processors and inserting posts and waits to ensure that the dependences are preserved.

However, we can do much better by using the tiling shown in Figure 3, and hiding communication cost with an idea presented by Rosser in [Ros98, Chapter 7.1]. We divide each tile into three regions, executed in the following order: the "send slice" (light gray) contains iterations that must be executed to produce results that are needed by the processor below; the iterations in the center are not involved in communication; and the "receive slice" (dark gray) contains iterations that cannot be executed until data are received from the processor above.

Let $\sigma = \frac{N}{P-1}$ (the "height" of the blocks of the i loop). Each tile loads $D(\sigma + 2\tau)$ bytes along its left and top edges, stores the same number of bytes at the right and bottom edges. Thus, memory traffic will take no more time than computation if $\frac{O\tau\sigma}{C} \geq \frac{2D(2\tau+\sigma)}{B}$. Each tile sends (and receives) $2D\tau$ bytes. If the transfer of one block of data of this size takes less time than the execution of the center region of the tile, then the entire communication cost will be hidden. This will be the case if $L + \frac{2D\tau}{B_N} \leq \frac{O}{C}(\sigma\tau - \tau^2)$, where B_N is the network bandwidth (in Mbytes/sec) and L is the network latency (in microseconds).

We can minimize the cache requirement (as in the uniprocessor case, $3D\tau$) by minimizing τ, which can be made almost as small as $\frac{2DC}{OB}$ (though σ becomes very large as τ approaches this limit). Alternatively, we can reduce σ (and gain more parallelism for a given problem size) by increasing τ and using more cache.

Continuing the hypothetical example from the previous section, assume $L = 1000$ and $B_N = 10$. Our constraints are (a) to match compute balance to machine balance, $160\tau\sigma \geq 4800\tau + 4800\sigma$, and (b) to hide communication time, $40\tau\sigma \geq 40\tau^2 + 4800\tau + 3000000$. We can reduce our cache to approximately what was needed in the uniprocessor code by making τ close to 30. If we set $\tau = 30$, constraint (b) would require $\sigma > 2650$, but we could not satisfy constraint (a) (though we would be very close to the proper compute balance, given $\sigma > 2650$). The values $\tau = 31, \sigma = 2571$ satisfy both constraints, as do $\tau = 60, \sigma = 1430$ (which uses 1440 bytes of cache) and $\tau = 682, \sigma = 912$ (which uses 16K bytes of cache). Thus, if our hypothetical machine has 16K of L1 cache, we can eliminate idle time due to both memory access and communication when $N > 912P$.

4   Further Details

The details of applying time skewing to more complex codes, and a detailed comparison with related work, are outside the scope of this abstract. See [Won99a] for details of uniprocessor time skewing, and [Won99b] for multiprocessors. These reports discuss related work at length. Most work on tiling, other than ours and that of Song and Li [SL99], requires perfectly nested loops; Song and Li have not discussed optimization for multiprocessors.

Our algorithm for applying time skewing to multidimensional arrays has undergone significant revision since the version discussed at LCPC '99 and in [Won99b]. The new algorithm, and a detailed comparison of our work with that of Högstedt, Carter, and Ferrante [HCF99], will be included in an article that is currently in preparation.

Other information about scalable locality and time skewing can be found on the time skewing web page:

http://www.haverford.edu/cmsc/davew/cache-opt/cache-opt.html

Acknowledgements. We would like to thank Larry Carter, Karin Högstedt, Michelle Mills Strout, and the other reviewers and participants at LCPC '99 for their thoughts about this work.

This work is supported by NSF grant CCR-9808694.

References

[CCK88]   D. Callahan, J. Cocke, and K. Kennedy. Estimating interlock and improving balance for pipelined machines. *Journal of Parallel and Distributed Computing*, 5(4):334–358, August 1988.

[HCF99]   Karin Högstedt, Larry Carter, and Jeanne Ferrante. Selecting tile shape for minimal execution time. In *roceedings of the eleventh annual ACM symposium on Parallel algorithms and architectures*, pages 201–211, June 1999.

[McC95]   John D. McCalpin. Memory bandwidth and machine balance in current high performance computers. *IEEE Technical Committee on Computer Architecture Newsletter*, Dec 1995.

[Ros98]   Evan J. Rosser. *Fine-Grained Analysis of Array Computations*. PhD thesis, Dept. of Computer Science, The University of Maryland, September 1998.

[SL99]   Yonghong Song and Zhiyuan Li. New tiling techniques to improve cache temporal locality. In *ACM SIGPLAN '99 Conference on Programming Language Design and Implementation*, pages 215–228, May 1999.

[Won99a]   David Wonnacott. Achieving Scalable Locality With Time Skewing. In preparation. Includes material from Rutgers University CS Technical Reports 379 and 378. A preprint is available as http://www.haverford.edu/cmsc/davew/cache-opt/tskew.ps.

[Won99b]   David Wonnacott. Time skewing for parallel computers. Technical Report DCS-TR-388, Dept. of Computer Science, Rutgers U., February 1999.

Run-Time Parallelization Optimization Techniques *

Hao Yu and Lawrence Rauchwerger **

Department of Computer Science
Texas A&M University
College Station, TX 77843-3112
{h0y8494,rwerger}@cs.tamu.edu

Abstract. In this paper we first present several compiler techniques to reduce the overhead of run-time parallelization. We show how to use static control flow information to reduce the number of memory references that need to be traced at run-time. Then we introduce several methods designed specifically for the parallelization of sparse applications. We detail some heuristics on how to speculate on the type and data structures used by the original code and thus reduce the memory requirements for tracing the sparse access patterns without performing any additional work. Optimization techniques for the sparse reduction parallelization and speculative loop distribution conclude the paper.

1 Run-Time Parallelization Requires Compiler Analysis

Current parallelizing compilers cannot identify a significant fraction of parallelizable loops because they have complex or statically insufficiently defined access patterns. To fill this gap we advocate a novel framework for their identification: speculatively execute the loop as a `doall`, and apply a fully parallel data dependence test to determine if it had any cross–processor dependences; if the test fails, then the loop is re–executed serially. While this method is inherently scalable its practical success depends on the fraction of ideal speedup that can be obtained on modest to moderately large parallel machines. Maximizing the resulting parallelism can be obtained only through a minimization of the run-time overhead of the method, which in turn depends on its level of integration within a restructuring compiler. This technique (the LRPD test) and related issues have been presented in detail in [3,4] and thus will not be presented here.

We describe a compiler technique that reduces the number of memory references that have to be collected at run-time by using static control flow information. With this technique we can remove the shadowing of many references

* A full version of this paper is available as Technical Report TR99-025, Dept. of Computer Science, Texas A&M University
** Research supported in part by NSF CAREER Award CCR-9734471, NSF Grant ACI-9872126, DOE ASCI ASAP Level 2 Grant B347886 and a Hewlett-Packard Equipment Grant

that are redundant for the purpose of testing valid parallelization. Moreover we group 'similar' or 'related' references and represent them with a single shadow element, thus reducing the memory and post-execution analysis overhead of our run-time techniques. We introduce a method that speculates on the actual data structures and access patterns of the original sparse code and compacts the dynamically collected information into a much smaller space. We further sketch an adaptive optimization method for parallelizing reductions in irregular and sparse codes. Other parallelism enabling loop transformations, e.g., loop distribution, requiring precise data dependence analysis are applied speculatively and tested at run-time without additional overhead.

The presented techniques have been implemented in the Polaris compiler [1] and employed in the automatic parallelization of some representative cases of irregular codes: SPICE 2G6 and P3M.

2   Redundant Marking Elimination

Same-Address Type Based Aggregation. While in previous implementations we have traced every reference to the arrays under test we have found that such an approach incorporates significant redundancy. We only need to detect attributes of the reference pattern that will insure correct parallelization of loops. For this purpose memory references can be classified, similar to [2] as: Read only (RO), Write-first (WF), Read-first-write (RW) and Not referenced (NO). NO or RO references can never introduce data dependences. WF references can always be privatized. RW accesses must occur in only one iteration (or processor) otherwise they will cause flow-dependences and invalidate the speculative parallelization. The overall goal of the algorithm is to mark only the necessary and sufficient sites to unambiguously establish the type of reference: WF,RO,RW or NO by using the dominance (on the control graph) relationship.

Based on the control flow graph of the loop we can aggregate the marking of read and/or write references (**to the same address**) into one of the categories listed above and replace them with a single marking instruction. The algorithm relies on a DFS traversal of the control dependence graph (CDG) and the recursive combination of the elementary constructs (elementary CDG's). The final output of the algorithm is a loop with fewer marks than the number of memory references under test. If predicates of references are loop invariant then the access pattern can be fully analyzed before loop execution in an inspector phase. This inspector can be equivalent to a LRPD test (or simpler run-time check) of a generalized address descriptor.

Grouping of Related References. Two memory addresses are **related** if they can be expressed as a function of the same base pointer. For example, when subscripts are of the form $ptr + affine\ function$, then all addresses starting at the pointer ptr are related. Intuitively, two related references of the same type can be aggregated for the purpose of marking if they are executed under the same control flow conditions, or more aggressively, if the predicates guarding of one reference imply the other reference.

A *marking group* is a set of subscript expressions of references to an array under test that satisfies the following conditions: (a) the addresses are derived from the same base pointer, (b) for every path from the entry of the considered block to its exit all *related* array references are of the same type, i.e., have the same attribute (WF, RO, RW, NO). The *grouping algorithm* tries to find a minimum number of disjoint sets of references of maximum cardinality (subscript expressions) to the array under test. Once these groups are found, they can be marked as a single abstract reference. The net result is a reduced number of marking instructions (because we mark several individual references at once) and a reduced size (dimension) of the shadow structure that needs to be allocated because several distinct references are mapped into a single marking point. Similarly, a **Global Reference Aggregation** can be achieved when groups of references formed with different base pointers occur under the same conditions.

3   Some Specific Techniques for Sparse Codes

The essential difficulty in sparse codes is that the dimension of the array tested may be orders of magnitude larger than the number of distinct elements referenced by the parallelized loop. Therefore the use of shadow arrays will cause the allocation of too much memory and generate useless work during the phases of the test making it not scalable with data size and/or number of processors.

Shadow Structures for Sparse Codes. Many sparse codes use linked structure traversals when processing their data. The referenced pointers can take any value (in the address space) and give the overall 'impression' of being very sparse and random. We use a compile time heuristic to determine the type of data structure and access pattern employed by the program and then, speculatively, use a conformable shadow data structure. Correct speculation results in minimal overhead, otherwise the parallelization becomes more expensive.

We have identified several situations where such a technique is beneficial, the most notable one being the use of linked lists in a loop. We classify the accesses of the base-pointers used by such a loop as (a) monotonic with constant stride, (b) monotonic with variable stride and (c) random. For each of these possible reference patterns we have adopted a specialized representation: (i) monotonic constant strides are recorded as a triplet [offset,stride,count], (ii) monotonic references with variable stride are recorded in an array and a tuple for their overall range [min,max], (iii) random addresses use hash tables (for large number of references) or simple lists to be sorted later and a tuple for their range.

The run-time marking routines are adaptive: They will verify the class of the access pattern and use the simplest possible form of representation. Ideally all references can be stored as a triplet, dramatically reducing the space requirements. In the worst case, the shadow structures will be proportional to the number of marked references. The reference **type** (WF, RO, RW, NO) will be recorded in a **bit vector** possibly as long as the number recorded references.

After loop execution the analysis of the recorded references will detect collisions using increasingly more complex algorithms: (1) Check for overlap of address ranges traversed by the base pointers (linked lists) using range information. (2) If there is overlap then check (analytically) triplets for collisions; Check collision of monotonic stride lists by merging them into one array (3) Sort random accesses stored in lists (if they exist) and merge into other the previous arrays. (4) Merge hash tables (if they exist) into the previous arrays.

3.1 Sparse Reduction Parallelization through Selective Privatization

Usually reductions are parallelized by accumulating in private arrays conformable to their shared counterpart and then, after loop execution, merged in parallel on their shared data. Such an approach is not beneficial if reductions are sparse because the final update (merge) would require much more work than necessary, since only a fraction of the private arrays is actually modified during the loop execution. Moreover, if the contention to the reduction elements is low, then privatization through *replication* across *all* processors is also sub-optimal.

We developed a hybrid method that first compacts the reduction references on every processor through the use of private conformable (across processors) hash tables and then uses the collected cross-processor collision information to selectively privatize only those reduction elements that cause contention across processors. Furthermore, this information can be reused during subsequent instantiations of the loop without the need to hash the reference pattern.

3.2 Speculative Loop Distribution

Loops with statically unavailable access patterns cannot be safely transformed because the required data dependence analysis is not possible. We adopt a speculative approach in which we assume that certain pointers are not aliased and prove the transformation correct at run-time. For example, we apply the distribution of a linked list traversal out of a loop assuming that it is not modified by the remainder of the loop. This condition is then verified at run-time together with the rest parallelization conditions (which subsume it) without additional overhead. This method has been applied in the parallelization of loops in SPICE.

References

1. W. Blume *et. al.* Advanced Program Restructuring for High-Performance Computers with Polaris. *IEEE Computer*, 29(12):78–82, December 1996.
2. J. Hoeflinger. *Interprocedural Parallelization Using Memory Classification Analysis.* PhD thesis, University of Illinois, August, 1998.
3. L. Rauchwerger. Run–time parallelization: A framework for parallel computation. TR. UIUCDCS-R-95-1926, Dept of Comp. Science, University of Illinois, Sept. 1995.
4. L. Rauchwerger and D. Padua. The LRPD Test: Speculative Run-Time Parallelization of Loops with Privatization and Reduction Parallelization. *IEEE Trans. on Parallel and Distributed Systems*, 10(2), 1999.
5. J. Wu, *et. al.* Runtime compilation methods for multicomputers. In Dr. H.D. Schwetman, editor, *Proc. of the 1991 Int. Conf. on Parallel Processing*, pages 26–30. CRC Press, Inc., 1991. Vol. II - Software.

Thresholding for Work Distribution of Recursive, Multithreaded Functions *

Gary M. Zoppetti, Gagan Agrawal, and Lori L. Pollock

Department of Computer and Information Sciences
University of Delaware, Newark DE 19716
{zoppetti, agrawal, pollock}@cis.udel.edu

1   Introduction

Work distribution, i.e., assigning tasks to different processors, is an important task in compiling for parallel architectures. In this paper, we focus on addressing the work distribution problem in the context of a fork-join parallel language and a multithreaded architecture.

Multithreaded parallel architectures (MTAs) have been designed to achieve good parallel efficiency on irregular applications. MTAs mask communication or synchronization costs by switching to a different thread whenever a high latency operation is encountered. Our work specifically targets the EARTH (*Efficient Architecture for Running THreads*) model [2]. A distinct advantage of this design is that it can be built from off-the-shelf components. Considerable effort has been expended in developing language and compiler support for the EARTH model. EARTH-C is a parallel dialect of C designed to support high-level programming on MTAs. The EARTH-C compiler was developed by extending the McCAT compiler infrastructure [1,3]. The EARTH-C language primarily targets a fork-join model of parallelism where parallel computations do not interfere with each other.

The EARTH-C language allows the programmer to specify a function to be *basic* or *remote*. Basic functions are executed on the same processor as the caller. Remote functions can be executed by another processor. Since spawning functions on a separate processor has considerable runtime overhead, it is desirable to declare functions to be basic as long as sufficient parallelism exists to keep all processors busy. The current EARTH-C compiler does not perform automatic analysis for deciding whether a function should be considered basic or remote; instead, this is the responsibility of the programmer. In experiences with a number of applications, this decision can be an important factor in achieving good performance [1]. This decision becomes particularly important for recursive functions. Initial recursive calls of large granularity should be spawned to other processors, whereas later recursive calls of small granularity should be executed locally.

---

* This research was supported by NSF Grant CCR-9808522. Author Agrawal was also supported in part by NSF CAREER award ACI-9733520

L. Carter and J. Ferrante (Eds.): LCPC'99, LNCS 1863, pp. 485–489, 2000.

In this paper, we present an automatic analysis for analyzing recursive functions and deciding at which level they should be executed locally. Our analysis is based on a performance estimation model we have developed. We present initial experimental results to demonstrate the performance gains from this transformation.

2   Problem Definition and Solution

Work distribution in the context of the EARTH model and the EARTH-C language is shared by the programmer and the runtime system. A function can be declared by the programmer as basic or remote.

A basic function may access only local memory, and they are not processed by the thread generator (they are treated as a single thread). Since they are always executed on the same processor as the caller, basic functions avoid remote spawning costs. However, parallelism is sacrificed at the expense of reduced overhead because basic functions execute sequentially on the same processor as the caller.

By default, each function is considered remote. When a remote function is called, it is executed on a processor determined by either the programmer or the runtime load balancer. If the programmer does not specify a processor, the remote function invocation is encapsulated within a *token* and placed in the local *token buffer*. Subsequently, the load balancer may decide to "steal" this token and transfer it to another processor for execution. Remote functions enable parallel execution, but incur a spawning cost which may involve the load balancer. Furthermore, since remote functions are partitioned into multiple threads, thread switching overheads are involved.

It is desirable to use basic functions when task granularity is small and the overhead for spawning a remote function is dominant. Alternatively, if task granularity dominates overhead, it *may be* desirable to spawn a remote function to reap the gains of parallel execution.

Let us now consider remote, recursive functions. It is assumed that the initial granularity will be large. Clearly it is undesirable for a remote, recursive function to continue spawning remote instances until the base case is reached. The recursive calls near the bottom of the invocation tree will likely be of small granularity and much expense will be paid in overheads. Instead, it will be advantageous to execute the top levels of the invocation tree in parallel, spawning other remote instances (on other processors), until a point is reached where the overhead expended for remote execution should be avoided and put toward directly solving the problem. This corresponds to invoking a basic version of the remote function when task granularity becomes sufficiently small. The point at which we invoke the basic version is called the *threshold* and the process of determining this value and using it to invoke a portion of the call tree sequentially is called *thresholding*.

A recursive function that computes the nth Fibonacci number will be used to demonstrate thresholding. Program 1 illustrates a remote function r_fib that uses thresholding to compute, in conjunction with b_fib, the nth Fibonacci number. Note that b_fib will be invoked when *threshold* is reached. Because the return type of r_fib is not prefixed with basic, the function is remote. {^ and ^} in r_fib are used to denote a parallel statement sequence.

Program 1 Computing the nth Fibonacci number: a *remote, recursive, thresholded* function (left) that invokes the *basic* function (right) when *threshold* is reached.

```
int r_fib (int n) {                     basic int b_fib (int n) {
  int r1, r2;                             int r1, r2;

  if (n <= threshold)                     if (n <= 1)
    return (b_fib (n));                     return (1);
  {^ r1 = r_fib (n - 1);                  r1 = b_fib (n - 1);
     r2 = r_fib (n - 2); ^}              r2 = b_fib (n - 2);
  return (r1 + r2);                       return (r1 + r2);
}                                       }
```

We now provide empirical data that demonstrate the benefits of thresholding. The results given in this section have been obtained by experimentally determining the optimal *threshold* value and creating the thresholded, remote function and the basic function by hand.

Two benchmarks were used to test the effectiveness of thresholding: Fibonacci and N-Queens. The N-Queens function calculates the number of different ways N queens can be placed on an NxN chessboard such that no two queens can attack each other. Table 1 shows the number of processors used, the time without thresholding (T_{nt}), the time with thresholding (T_t), and the speedup due to thresholding ($Speedup_t$).

Fibonacci was run with an input of $N = 30$. For N-Queens, the input was $N = 12$. A *threshold* value of N would result in the program being executed sequentially, i.e., a basic function would immediately be invoked and no parallelism would be exploited. T_{nt} corresponds to a *threshold* value of 0, i.e., all recursive calls were spawned and a basic version of the function was never executed. To find T_t, *threshold* was varied until the least execution time was found.

For each benchmark, *threshold* was at least $N-3$. This created enough remote function instances to utilize each processor yet kept overhead to a minimum.

3   Overview of the Solution

We have developed an algorithm that takes as inputs the following for each function: a control flow graph, a control dependence graph, intraprocedural ud-chains, and a dominance tree. The algorithm attempts to locate a unique base case, the conditional statement testing for the unique base case, and the set of recursive calls. Using information gleaned from the above statements, an effort is made to form and solve a recurrence relation. We use a static performance estimator to assess the cost of the recursive function excluding recursive calls. This cost is used in forming the recurrence relation.

The solution to the recurrence relation is used in the performance model to determine *threshold*. The crux of our model is the following: if executing a function f sequentially at the ith level in the invocation tree is cheaper than spawning recursive invocations which will execute sequentially at the $(i + 1)^{st}$ level, then thresholding at the ith level will be cheaper than thresholding at any value $j > i$.

Table 1. Thresholding Times and Speedups

Benchmark	Procs	T_{nt} (sec.)	T_t	$Speedup_t$[1]
Fibonacci	1	35.63	0.14	259.30
	2	25.77	0.11	235.47
	4	13.91	0.09	155.35
	8	14.11	0.09	157.55
N-Queens	1	52.74	7.77	6.78
	2	35.93	4.07	8.82
	4	19.67	2.09	9.40
	8	19.79	1.93	10.24

4   Summary

We have provided execution times for two benchmarks to demonstrate the speed-ups possible using thresholding for work distribution of recursive, multithreaded functions. Besides yielding better performance, thresholding enables larger problems to be solved since the proliferation of threads is held in check. Through development of a performance estimation model and static analysis of multithreaded programs, we are able to automatically identify recursive, multithreaded functions which are good candidates for thresholding; estimate the level of thresholding to be performed; and automatically perform the code transformation.

Acknowledgments. We would like to thank Laurie Hendren and the ACAPS group at McGill University for providing us with a copy of the McCAT EARTH-C compiler. Additionally, we thank Guang Gao, Xinan Tang, and the rest of the CAPSL group at Delaware for answering our questions and giving us computing time on the EARTH-modeled multithreaded architecture *earthquake*.

---

[1] This value represents the speedup due to thresholding for a given number of processors, and should not be confused with conventional speedup.

References

1. Laurie J. Hendren, Xinan Tang, Yingchun Zhu, and Guang R. Gao. Compiling C for the EARTH multithreaded architecture. *International Journal of Parallel Programming*, 1997.
2. Herbert H. J. Hum, Olivier Maquelin, Kevin B. Theobald, Xinmin Tian, Xinan Tang, Guang R. Gao, et al. A design study of the EARTH multiprocessor. In *Proceedings of the IFIP WG 10.3 Working Conference on Parallel Architectures and Compilation Techniques*, June 1995.
3. Xinan Tang, Rakesh Ghiya, Laurie J. Hendren, and Guang R. Gao. Heap analysis and optimizations for threaded programs. In *Proceedings of the 1997 Conference on Parallel Architectures and Compilation Techniques*, November 1997.

An Empirical Study of Function Pointers Using SPEC Benchmarks

Ben-Chung Cheng[1] and Wen-mei W. Hwu[2]

[1] Department of Computer Science
[2] Department of Electrical and Computer Engineering and
The Coordinated Science Laboratory
University of Illinois at Urbana-Champaign
Urbana, IL 61801, USA

Abstract. Since the C language imposes little restriction on the use of function pointers, the task of call graph construction for C programs is far more difficult than that found in *Fortran* programs. From the experience of implementing a call graph extractor in the IMPACT compiler, we found the call graph construction problem has evolved into an interprocedural pointer analysis problem. In this paper, we report several interesting function pointer usage patterns found in the SPECint92 and SPECint95 benchmarks. They can be considered as critical issues in the design of a complete call graph extractor.

1 Introduction

A fundamental requirement for performing interprocedural optimizations is a complete call graph, which represents the invocation of functions for a program. If the programming language supports function variables, which defers the actual callee determination until run-time, the construction of a complete call graph requires extra compile-time analysis. Although a call graph is required for interprocedural data-flow analysis, call graph construction itself requires incremental interprocedural data-flow analysis, since function variables may be defined interprocedurally. The final call graph is resolved iteratively where existing function variables receive new function names propagated from already exploited functions in the partial call graph [1,2]. In this paper, we examine several interesting code constructs we experienced from SPEC benchmark suites while implementing a call graph extractor which is an integral part in the interprocedural pointer analysis framework of the IMPACT compiler [3]. A complete version of this paper can be found in [4].

2 Code Examples of SPEC Benchmarks

We found function pointers used in the SPECint92 and SPECint95 benchmarks can be roughly classified into four categories, as *simple variables*, *formal parameters*, *entries in statically initialized arrays*, and *fields in anonymous objects*. Due

L. Carter and J. Ferrante (Eds.): LCPC'99, LNCS 1863, pp. 490–493, 2000.

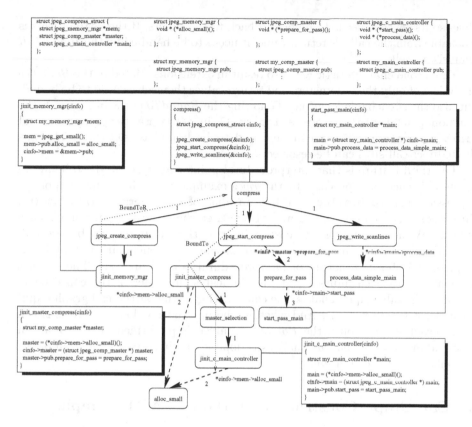

Fig. 1. Partial call graph of *ijpeg.*

to space constraints, we will focus on the fourth case by using a code fragment extracted from benchmark *132.ijpeg* with the following characteristics.

The first characteristic is dynamically allocated function pointers. Once a heap-object is allocated by the callee and attached to a formal parameter, not only values from the caller will be bound to the callee, values will need to be bound from the callee to the caller as well. Consider the call graph path marked with *BoundToR* in Figure 1 where *BoundToR* stands for the reversed version of the original *BoundTo* analysis proposed by Hall and Kennedy [2]. In function `compress`, the address of variable `cinfo` is passed as a formal parameter to all subsequent callees [1]. In function `jinit_memory_mgr`, it allocates an object of type `my_memory_mgr`, which is a superset of struct `jpeg_memory_mgr`. Then it initializes the function pointer field `alloc_small` through two levels of indirections for dynamic memory allocation as to invoke `alloc_small`. When function `jinit_memory_mgr` returns, the location of `cinfo->mem->alloc_small` is still

---

[1] The type of cinfo in compress is "struct jpeg_compress_struct" but is "struct jpeg_compress_struct *" in all other functions.

alive, so its content needs to be bound back to the callers. If the heap objects is reachable from the callee's return value, it needs to be handled by the *BoundToR* analysis as well.

The second characteristic will also result in extensions related to the *BoundTo* analysis: not only the parameters and return values themselves need to be bound, but also their reachable locations. Following the *BoundTo* paths in Figure 1, the function pointer `cinfo->mem->alloc_small` in `jinit_master_compress` and `jinit_c_main_controller` can be found to be bound to `alloc_small`, thus the indirect call sites can be resolved.

The third feature is that interprocedural pointer analysis needs to be aware of the existence of type cast. In the *ijpeg* example listed in Figure 1, pointer expression `mem->pub.alloc_small` is an alias of `cinfo->mem->alloc_small`, since the structs pointed by `mem` and `cinfo->mem` share the same initial sequence of fields. Without handling type cast, pointers of these forms cannot be resolved.

One final feature we want to discuss in the *ijpeg* benchmark is that it exemplifies the iterative nature of interprocedural pointer analysis. The number associated with each indirect call edge indicates the order of the callee being added to the call graph. That is, the construction of the partial call graph requires at least four iterations. And whether the optimal number of iterations can be achieved depends on if the *BoundTo* analysis is performed in the top-down traversal and the *BoundToR* analysis is done in the bottom-up traversal of the currently resolved call graph.

3   Call Graph Construction in the IMPACT Compiler

We constructed the complete call graphs of all SPECint92 and SPECint95 benchmarks using the IMPACT compiler. More details of the interprocedural pointer analysis algorithm can be found in [3]. Table 3 lists the resolution of function pointers excluding those found in dead functions. In this table, number n at cell *(a, b)* other than the dead-function columns represents that in benchmark *a*, n function pointers are resolved to have *b* callees. The ideal case is to resolve a function pointer into one callee, since the indirect call site can be converted into a direct one, so that the overhead associated with indirect function calls can be eliminated. As the table shows, benchmark *ijpeg* would benefit most from the call-site conversion: 381 out of 427 indirect call sites can be transformed into direct ones. If the resolved callee number is small, the indirect callee can be converted into a series of `if-then-else` statements or a `switch` statement predicated by the function pointer's content. This transformation trades the indirect call overhead with branch penalties. When the resolved number of direct callees is large, call-site transformation is not feasible. However, a more accurate estimate of the indirect call site's side-effects can be obtained since only a subset of the functions in the whole program can be reached. Table 3 also shows that some benchmarks have unresolved call sites. We verified these function pointers by tracing the program and using the system debugger. We found these pointers are indeed uninitialized and not exercised with multiple profile inputs.

Table 1. Resolution of function pointers.

Benchmark	Simple			Parameter					Global					Heap					Dead functions	
	0	1	2	0	1	2	3	≥4	0	1	2	3	≥4	0	1	2	3	≥4	Total	Dead
li	0	0	0	0	0	0	0	1	0	0	0	0	3	0	0	0	0	0	357	1
sc	0	0	0	0	0	0	0	1	1	0	0	0	0	0	0	0	0	0	179	8
eqntott	0	0	0	0	2	0	9	0	0	0	0	0	0	0	0	0	0	0	62	2
espresso	0	0	0	0	2	3	0	10	0	0	0	0	0	0	0	0	0	0	361	46
m88ksim	0	0	0	0	0	0	0	0	0	0	0	0	3	0	0	0	0	0	252	13
perl	0	0	0	0	0	0	0	0	0	0	0	0	0	3	0	0	0	0	276	13
ijpeg	0	0	0	0	0	0	0	0	0	0	0	0	0	4	381	16	11	15	477	179
vortex	0	0	0	0	1	0	1	0	0	0	0	0	0	1	1	2	0	2	923	295
ccl	0	0	15	0	0	0	0	19	0	0	0	0	32	0	3	0	0	0	1452	51
gcc	4	11	16	0	3	0	0	14	1	1	0	0	73	0	9	0	0	0	2019	187

Removing dead functions can speedup the compilation process and reduce the resultant code size. Dead functions can be inherent in the program or resulted because of function inlining. The rightmost portion in Table 3 shows the number of dead functions found in each benchmark, where the total number of functions is also listed for easy comparison. It indicates that some SPEC benchmarks contain a significant number of dead functions.

4   Conclusions

We presented a case study from the *132.ijpeg* benchmark to illustrate why the call graph construction problem needs the full strength of interprocedural pointer analysis. The statistics of resolved indirect call sites indicate that substantial code transformations can be enabled by the resolved call graph for some SPEC benchmarks, including indirect/direct call-site conversion, function inlining, and dead code removal. Future research area includes the study of real programs written in object-oriented languages like *C++* or *Java*. In such cases the call graph construction is even more difficult because of object inheritance and function overloading. Another possible research area is the study of how to formally validate the correctness of a statically constructed call graph.

References

1. A. Lakhotia, "Constructing call multigraphs using dependence graphs," in *Conference Record of the 20th Annual ACM Symposium on Principles of Programming Languages*, January 1993.
2. M. W. Hall and K. Kennedy, "Efficient call graph analysis," *ACM Letters on Programming Languages and Systems*, vol. 1, pp. 227–242, September 1992.
3. B. C. Cheng and W. W. Hwu, "A practical interprocedural pointer analysis framework," Tech. Rep. IMPACT-99-01, Center for Reliable and High-Performance Computing, University of Illinois, Urbana, IL, 1999.
4. B. Cheng and W. W. Hwu, "An empirical study of function pointers using spec benchmarks," Tech. Rep. IMPACT-99-02, Center for Reliable and High-Performance Computing, University of Illinois, Urbana, IL, May 1999.

Data Driven Graph: A Parallel Program Model for Scheduling

V. D. Tran, L. Hluchy, and G. T. Nguyen

Institute of Informatics, Slovak Academy of Sciences
upsyviet@savba.sk

Abstract. In this paper, we present a new powerful method for parallel program representation called Data Driven Graph (DDG). DDG takes all advantages of classical Directed Acyclic Graph (DAG) and adds much more: simple definition, flexibility and ability to represent loops and dynamically created tasks. With DDG, scheduling becomes an efficient tool for increasing performance of parallel systems. DDG is not only a parallel program model, it also initiates a new parallel programming style, allows programmers to write a parallel program with minimal difficulty. We also present our parallel program development tool with support for DDG and scheduling.

1 Introduction

Advances in hardware and software technologies have led to increased interest in the use of large-scale parallel and distributed systems for database, real-time, and other large applications. One of the biggest issues in such systems is the development of effective techniques for the distribution of tasks of a parallel program on multiple processors. The efficiency of execution of the parallel program critically depends on the strategies used to schedule and distribute the tasks among processing elements.

2 Parallel Program Models

Most of static scheduling algorithms use a directed acyclic graph (DAG) to represent the precedence relationships and the data dependencies of tasks of a parallel program [1],[2],[3]. Each node of the graph represents a task and each edge represents the precedence relationship and communication between the tasks. DAG model is simple but it can represent only programs with static behavior and without loops. It cannot represent programs with loops or dynamically created tasks.

2.1 Data Driven Graph Model

For a flexible model, which contains all advantages of the existing models and can represent also loops and dynamical behavior, we propose new approach to representation of parallel program called Data Driven Graph (DDG). The main ideas of DDG are following:

L. Carter and J. Ferrante (Eds.): LCPC'99, LNCS 1863, pp. 494–497, 2000.

– Each task is defined by its input and output data. The set of input and output data creates a task interface, which hides all implementation details of the task. No relationship among tasks is explicitly defined. The tasks with the same output data are called producers of the data. Similarly the tasks with the same input data are called consumers of the data.
– A scheduler manages all tasks and data of the parallel program. It determines the relationship among tasks according to their interfaces, i.e. their input and output data. For backward compatibility with existing program models, the scheduler creates a graph by connecting producers and consumer of the same data.
– The behavior of the parallel program is defined by its data. A data on a processor is ready when it is produced by a task and is sent to the processor. When all input data of a task are ready, the scheduler will execute the task.

2.2 DDG Versus DAG

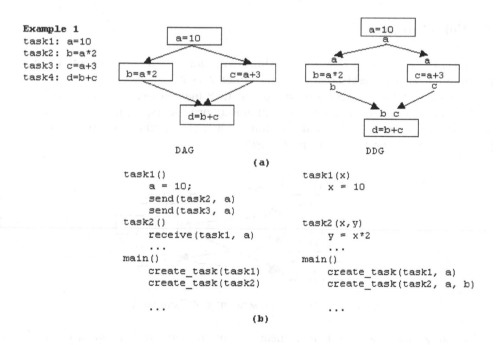

Fig. 1. Similarities and differences between DAG and DDG

Fig. 1 shows the similarities and differences between DAG and DDG. For the simplicity, each task is represented by one command line. At the first sight of the graphs (Fig. 1a), there is no difference except that DDG gives more information about communication. Because most of existing scheduling algorithms is based on DAG, the compatibility with DAG is very important for DDG. Despite that DDG uses a different method from DAG for definition, existing scheduling algorithms can be applied for DDG as for DAG.

The largest advantage of DDG is the style of source codes (Fig. 1b). The source code of DDG is very similar to the source code of a normal sequential program. The task implementation does not contain any communication routines, which are typical of parallel programs. If the task creation create_task(task1, a) is replaced by function calling task1(a), the source code of DDG is actually the source code of a sequential program. It means that transforming a sequential program to a parallel program in DDG is done with minimal difficulty. Programmers can write a parallel program in the style of the sequential program, which they are used to, then replace function calling by task creation. For DAG, the situation is different. Each task contains communication routines and has to know which tasks it communicates with and where the tasks are. That requires major modification in the source code when transforming a sequential to a parallel program. Programmers have to learn to use new communication libraries such as PVM, MPI or new parallel programming languages.

3   Scheduling

In Section 2, we assume that the scheduler will manage all communication. In this section, we will describe how the scheduler does it.

Scheduler in DDG consists of two parts: task management modules, which synchronize data, control communication among processors, supply proper data for tasks and execute tasks; and scheduling algorithms, which assign tasks to processors and determine priorities of tasks.

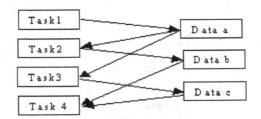

Fig. 2. Data structure in scheduler of Example 1

Scheduler has one task management module on each individual processor. The task management module maintains a structure of tasks and data on the processor such as in Fig. 2. When a task is created, the task management connects it with its input and output data. When a task finishes, its output data is ready. The task management will check all consumers of the data. If a consumer is already assigned to another processor and the processor does not contain the data, the task management module will send a copy the data to the module on the processor. Each task management module has also a queue of task waiting for execution. If a consumer has all its input data ready, it will be assigned to the waiting queue. When a processor is idle, the task management module will choose the task with the highest priority from the waiting queue and execute it. The task management is a part of DDG API.

4   Conclusion

This paper has presented the new program model DDG, which has many advantages over classical DAG, ITG models. The definition of DDG is simple, flexible, tasks in DDG are independent, easy to write, and parallel programs in DDG are clear, easy to modify, maintain and upgrade. DDG model is also compatible with classical DAG model, so existing scheduling algorithms can be applied for DDG. DDG API initiates a new parallel programming style, allows programmers to write flexible, effective parallel program with minimal difficulty. DDG is not only a parallel program model, it also opens a new space for research and development in parallel programming, for example automatic parallelization a sequential program by a parallel compiler based on DDG.

Acknowledgements. We thank the Slovak Scientific Grant Agency which supported our work under Research Project No.2/4102/99.

References

1. S. Ha, E. A. Lee: Compile-Time Scheduling of Dynamic Constructs in Dataflow Program Graph, IEEE Trans. Parallel and Distributed Systems, vol. 46, no. 7, pp. 768-778, 1997.
2. Y. Kwok, I. Ahmad: Dynamic Critical-Path Scheduling: An Effective Technique for Allocating Task Graphs to Multiprocessors, IEEE Trans. Parallel and Distributed Systems, vol. 7, no. 5, pp. 506-521, 1996.
3. E. Maehle, F. Markus: Fault-Tolerant Dynamic Task Scheduling Based on Dataflow Graphs, Proc. IPPS'97, Workshop on Fault-Tolerant and Distributed Systems, Switzerland 1997.

Author Index

Lecture Notes in Computer Science

For information about Vols. 1–1777
please contact your bookseller or Springer-Verlag